Donated by
William Jerome

The Science of Being as Being

Studies in Philosophy and the
History of Philosophy

General Editor: Jude P. Dougherty

Volume 55

The Science of Being as Being

Metaphysical Investigations

Edited by Gregory T. Doolan

The Catholic University of America Press
Washington, DC

Library of Congress Cataloging-in-Publication Data

The science of being as being : metaphysical investigations /
edited by Gregory T. Doolan.

p. cm. — (Studies in philosophy and the history of
philosophy ; v. 55)

A collection of papers in honor of John F. Wippel.

Includes bibliographical references and index.

ISBN 978-0-8132-1886-1 (cloth : alk. paper)

1. Metaphysics.   2. Scholasticism.   I. Doolan, Gregory T.
II. Wippel, John F.   III. Title.   IV. Series.

BD125.S35 2012

110—dc23

2011028631

For John F. Wippel
magister, scholaris, amicus

There is a science that investigates being as being and the attributes that belong to this in virtue of its own nature. Now this is not the same as any of the so-called special sciences; for none of these others treats universally of being as being.

Aristotle, Metaphysics IV, 1, 1003a20–25

Contents

The Science of Being as Being

Gregory T. Doolan

Introduction

The essays in this volume originated from papers presented as part of the fall 2008 School of Philosophy lecture series at the Catholic University of America. The series was entitled "Metaphysical Themes—in Honor of John F. Wippel." As with the series, this volume is intended to honor Wippel on the occasion of his seventy-fifth year. Thus, the essays herein reveal the contributors' profound respect for Wippel. Moreover, these essays reveal the significant influence he has had on scholarship in the areas of metaphysics and medieval philosophy. As is befitting the honoree, all of these contributions to the volume are of the first water, offering the reader but a sampling of the work of a much greater community of scholars who both respect and are influenced by John F. Wippel.

In organizing the contributions to this volume, I thought it only fitting to arrange them in an order following the insights of that master whom Wippel knows so well: Thomas Aquinas. Part 1 of the volume concerns the subject matter of metaphysics. According to Aquinas, every science studies a subject matter as well as the principles and causes of that subject matter. Indeed, the ultimate goal of any science is to acquire knowledge of these causes. Still, scientific inquiry does not begin with an examination of such causes; instead, he tells us, it must begin by first identifying the subject matter itself.[1] This is what the essays in part 1 attempt to do.

Thus, in chapter 1 Robert Sokolowski offers reflections on the phrase originated by Aristotle: "the science of being as being." Looking first

---

1. See, e.g., Thomas Aquinas, *In Physicam* I, lect. 1; *In Metaphysicam*, Prologus.

at how this phrase is used by Aristotle, Thomas Aquinas, and Wippel, Sokolowski then examines the more general question of how it is used throughout the history of philosophy. As he explains, the use of this phrase time and again is more than a mere repetition; rather, it is a recapitulation.

The remaining chapters of part 1 present this recapitulation with reference to three historical periods: antiquity, the middle ages, and the present day. In chapter 2 Dominic O'Meara addresses the transformation of metaphysics in late antiquity, considering the development of the science of being as being precisely insofar as it is understood to be a science. O'Meara argues it is during this last period of Greek philosophy not only that metaphysics is made into a science, but also that the limits of this science are brought out.

In chapter 3 Jan A. Aertsen addresses the recapitulation of the phrase "the science of being as being" during the medieval period, asking why metaphysics in the Middle Ages is called "First Philosophy." As he shows, during this period the Aristotelian conception of First Philosophy is transformed, giving a new foundation to the primacy of the *philosophia prima*.

Part 1 concludes with the recapitulation presented within a contemporary context. In chapter 4, Andreas Speer argues that despite the clear differences between present-day metaphysical and post-metaphysical discourses, there is nevertheless a common ground shared by the two: both camps tend to neglect the *history* of metaphysics. As he notes, their shared view is that this history has no argumentative status and that, consequently, it does not belong to metaphysics. In contrast to this contemporary attitude, Speer seeks to return to the origins of metaphysical discourse for a better understanding of present issues.

Having addressed in part 1 the general question regarding the subject matter of metaphysics, the volume continues in part 2 by examining more particular questions, namely the sort of philosophical difficulties that Aristotle termed *aporiae*. Following Aristotle, Aquinas concurs that one must begin the search for truth by identifying such difficulties. The philosopher who does not do so is like someone on a journey who does not know where he is going. Not only would the philosopher be lost on his journey toward the truth, but he would not even realize his destination should he arrive at it, since the goal on this intellectual journey is the solution to philosophical difficulties.[2] It is in recognition of this methodology adopted by Aristotle and Aquinas that part 2 of this volume contains essays addressing metaphysical *aporiae*.

This section begins with my own contribution as chapter 5, acting as a transition from part 1. The *aporia* I examine touches upon the subject matter of metaphysics for Thomas Aquinas. Since he holds that substance is the primary mode of being, he identifies metaphysics as concerned with studying this genus and, hence, with studying all substances inasmuch as they are substances. Nevertheless, he also holds that material and immaterial substances share no common natural genus, a position that seems to call into question the possibility of a single science of substance qua substance. As I attempt to show, the solution to this *aporia* is found in a distinction Thomas draws between a natural and a metaphysical genus, with the latter possessing an analogical character.

In chapter 6, Jorge J. E. Gracia considers an *aporia* regarding the individuation of races. Viewed from one perspective, a race has characteristics of a universal since it seems to be common to many individual human beings; viewed from another perspective, however, a race seems to be simply a collection of individual humans and, as such, is itself an individual as an instance of a collection. Gracia looks to the tradition of scholastic philosophy to discern whether races are truly individual and, if so, how they are individuated.

In chapter 7, James Ross considers the topic of merely metaphysical possibility. The question he raises is whether there are alien possibilities, in other words whether there are possible things or states of affairs other than those that ever actually exist or lie within the capacities of finite things. Ross argues against the modal ontologies developed in the twentieth century by metaphysicians and philosophers of nature; he contends that conceivability cannot ensure real possibility. Instead, Ross concludes that metaphysical possibility depends upon the existence of a free divine creator.

This reference to the creator in the concluding chapter of part 2 reminds us that for Thomas Aquinas, metaphysics can be called by another name: theology. For, having identified the subject matter of this science and examined various *aporiae* concerning it, the metaphysician ulti-

2. Aristotle, *Metaphysics* III, 1, 995a 24–995b4; Thomas Aquinas, *In Metaphysicam* III, lect. 1.

mately seeks the first principle of this subject matter: God as the cause of being as being. It is because metaphysics studies God in this respect that it can be called "theology." Nevertheless, Thomas is careful to draw a distinction between what he terms "philosophical theology" (*theologia philosophica*) and "theology of sacred scripture" (*theologia sacrae Scripturae*).[3] It is with this distinction in mind that I have located the remaining essays in part 3 of this volume since each concerns, in some respect, the relationship between these two theologies. This relationship is first addressed in chapter 8, where Stephen F. Brown considers how the role of metaphysics in revealed theology is viewed by another medieval thinker, Godfrey of Fontaines.

The contributor of chapter 9 is none other than John F. Wippel himself. The reader will likely be surprised at first to see an essay by Wippel included here since this volume—as with the lecture series from which it is derived—is meant to honor him. The reader will be less surprised, however, upon recognizing this paper as an example of Wippel's academic generosity: for when one of the guest speakers in that series took ill, he volunteered to fill the spot so that the series could continue uninterrupted. And so, Wippel's work is included here not as honoring himself but, rather, as a reminder of why he so rightly deserves to be honored.

In his essay, Wippel examines Thomas Aquinas's views regarding the so-called preambles of faith: those doctrines concerning both God and creatures that faith presupposes but that can also be proven philosophically. Wippel's analysis touches upon the relationship of metaphysics to revealed theology, but the paper remains a distinctly philosophical one. In it he not only examines Thomas's general philosophical approach toward the preambles, but also attempts to determine how many truths Aquinas includes under the general heading of "preambles of faith." In chapter 10, Brian J. Shanley examines one of these preambles in more detail for us: divine providence. Looking at each of Thomas's major considerations on this topic, Shanley shows that according to Aquinas, God's providence can indeed be philosophically demonstrated, yet in such a way that a deeper doctrine of providence must remain a matter of faith.

In chapter 11 Eleonore Stump considers biblical stories that portray God as personally present to human beings, and she asks both what it is

---

3. *Super Boetium De Trinitate*, q. 5, a. 4 co.

for God to be present as well as what it is for human persons to have God present to them. As she notes, some philosophers and theologians reject the doctrines of divine eternity and simplicity as implying a disconnection between God and human beings. Stump argues to the contrary by looking at what personal presence entails and shows that the doctrine of divine simplicity does not entail the agnosticism frequently associated with it. According to Stump, there is a kind of knowledge of God that is compatible with the doctrine of simplicity—a kind of knowledge that is sufficient for God's being personally present to human beings as is described in biblical stories. In support of this position, she turns to the thought of Thomas Aquinas.

For Christians, one of the "Last Things" is resurrection. It is only fitting, therefore, that this topic be addressed in the last chapter of this volume. In chapter 12 Marilyn McCord Adams offers a metaphysical consideration of this Christian doctrine, asking the question, "Why bodies as well as souls in the life to come?" As she notes, the answer is clear from the perspective of dogmatic theology, for the doctrine of the resurrection is proclaimed by the New Testament and declared by the Nicene and Apostles' creeds. Nevertheless, philosophical theology seeks understanding in the form of theoretical coherence. And from this perspective, she argues, it seems that the body is unnecessary after death, noting that medieval accounts of the life to come do not seem to give bodies anything to do. How, then, do medieval philosophical theologians reconcile this Christian doctrine with their metaphysics? Adams attempts to answer this question by examining three such authors on this topic: Bonaventure, Thomas Aquinas, and Duns Scotus.

My brief introduction to this volume will, I hope, reveal that each of the essays contained in it is a fitting contribution to the whole, which, in turn, is itself a fitting tribute to a man who has done much for the study of metaphysical themes.

I would like to thank all of these contributors for their original pieces, as well as my research assistants, Taylor Fayle and David Sailer, for their tireless efforts in assisting me with editing this volume. My thanks also go to the Franklin J. Matchette Foundation, the Thomas and Dorothy Leavey Foundation, and the George Dougherty Foundation for providing funding that made possible the 2008 lecture series. In doing so, they made this volume possible as well. I am grateful to the late Kurt

Pritzl, O.P., who, as dean of the School of Philosophy at the Catholic University of America, arranged the lecture series. I am also grateful to Jude P. Dougherty, dean emeritus and general editor of the series in which this volume appears. Finally, I would like to express my gratitude to both the former director of the Catholic University of America Press, David J. McGonagle, and the current director, Trevor C. Lipscombe, along with all of the editors and staff at CUA Press for all of their help with this publication.

Part One

The Subject Matter of Metaphysics

Robert Sokolowski

---

1 ⧓ The Science of Being as Being in Aristotle, Aquinas, and Wippel

As my contribution to this collection of papers in honor of John F. Wippel, I would like to discuss a topic that he explores in his own writings, the science of metaphysics, one of whose classical names is "the science of being as being." The phrase itself originates in Aristotle, who begins book 4 of his *Metaphysics* with the blunt statement, "There is a particular science [*estin epistēmē tis*] that theorizes being as being [*to on hēi on*] and that which belongs to it as such."[1] Thomas Aquinas uses the same phrase to speak about the subject of metaphysics, and in Latin it is expressed *ens inquantum est ens.*[2] Aquinas's way of using the term is not just a repetition of Aristotle but reflects the influence of such thinkers as Augustine, Boethius, and Avicenna. Wippel in turn comments on the usage made by all these thinkers, and he uses the term himself. Finally, other contributors to this book also use the phrase, and in doing so they reflect Wippel's commentary and usage.

This sequence of uses by different authors is an example of what Thomas Prufer called "recapitulation."[3] The words and thoughts of one person come to life in the speech and the minds of others, and each time they come to life they are not just repeated but recapitulated—ordered

1. Aristotle, *Metaphysics* IV, 1, 1003a21–22, ed. W. D. Ross (Oxford: Clarendon, 1958). Translations from Aristotle are my own.

2. See, e.g., *In duodecim libros Metaphysicorum Aristotelis expositio* IV, lect. 1, ed. M.-R. Cathala and Raymond M. Spiazzi (Turin-Rome: Marietti, 1950), 151:534.

3. Thomas Prufer, *Recapitulations: Essays in Philosophy* (Washington, D.C.: The Catholic University of America Press, 1993).

anew into *capitula,* or chapters, into new headings or bullet points. They are re-syntaxed, we might say, and to re-syntax something is to rethink it. The rearrangement will inevitably reflect the thoughts and interests of the time in which it occurs, but it will not be governed by them unless the writer is a slave to his time, in which case he would be not a recapitulator but only a mouthpiece.[4]

There is nothing strange or exotic about the procedure of recapitulation; we do it all the time in regard to all sorts of things. None of us can start from scratch, neither in our philosophy nor in our other ways of thinking; Aristotle himself was recapitulating Plato and the Presocratics. Whenever we think, we reprocess what others have thought, and we even recapitulate continually what we ourselves are thinking. When we compose something, we almost always redraft what we have written earlier, and the right formulation will usually occur to us not when we are looking for it but on the next morning, after we have intellectually and imaginatively digested the document that we put together on the day before. Writing is like a conversation we have with ourselves over time, between our present and our past selves. All human thinking is rethinking—filling in details, rounding things out, and making adjustments, sometimes large but usually small.

Such rethinking, moreover, is not just a matter of reconfiguring signs and symbols in a hermetically closed system; it is a response to the way things are, but it is a response we make with the help of others, those whom we recapitulate and those with whom we converse. These other people help us to see *things* and to understand what they are; we do not just repeat what other people have said, and we do not just live in meanings and in opinions.[5] This is the spirit in which I would like to explore here the science of being as being. I do not want to just tell you what Aristotle and others have said, but to express why it is interesting and important and possible for us to use the phrase "being as being." I would like to

4. For examples of successful pictorial recapitulations of Christian mysteries, consider the works of the early Flemish painters, such as Jan van Eyck, Dirk Bouts, and Hans Memling. Their images use contemporary landscapes, cityscapes, clothing, furniture, and utensils, as well as contemporary faces and gestures, but they do not dissolve the mystery into the world of the artists. To the contrary, they enable the mystery to appear in a pictorial syntax appropriate to that world.

5. Of course, if we are unwilling or unable to let things truly appear, then we may indeed be simply reshuffling words, images, and opinions.

show that something valuable is going on and that something significant is being disclosed when we try to become engaged in this science.

This chapter consists of six parts. The first tries to define Aristotle's science of being as being and contrasts it with sciences that examine only a part of being. The second turns to Aquinas and Wippel's comments on him. It examines how we are said to discover the *esse* of things through the act of judgment, and how the judgment of separation expresses the transcendence of *esse* to both material and finite being. In the third part I question an ambiguity I find in this transcendence: are "separate substances" (angels) included within the subject of metaphysics, or are they included among its principles? The fourth section tries to respond to this difficulty by exploring three themes: material forms, separate forms, and *esse subsistens.* The fifth section contrasts Aquinas's doctrine on *esse commune* and his understanding of *esse subsistens.* The sixth and final section brings out the religious dimension of Thomistic metaphysics.

THE PHRASE "BEING AS BEING"

What does it mean to think about and understand being as being? Let us turn first to Aristotle's development of this topic. He introduces this science abruptly in book 4 of the *Metaphysics,* at the start of the first chapter. He then immediately draws a distinction. He contrasts this science, the science of being as being, with other theoretic sciences that "cut off" a "part" of being and consider what belongs to that part. The Greek word for part is *meros,* and the word for cutting off is *apotemnō,* to sever, cut off, lop off, slice off. This is a graphic term, and it permits us to call the part a segment of being. As examples of such partial inquiries, Aristotle mentions the mathematical sciences. The science of being as being is thus distinguished from sciences that lop off a part of being and study that. The phrase "being as being" continues to be used throughout chapter 2. It occurs sometimes in variant forms, such as the plural "beings as beings" and "the one as one."[6]

That is what Aristotle does in book 4. He presents another introduction and definition of this science two books later in the *Metaphysics,* in book 6, chapter 1. There he says that we are seeking the principles and

6. On the plural see *Metaphysics* IV, 2, 1003b15–16 and on the "one as one" see 1004b5.

causes of beings as beings (in the plural), and he again contrasts such an inquiry with sciences that examine a kind—and here he calls the part a *genos*—of being. As an example of such a partial science he first mentions physics, which examines things that have within themselves their own principle of motion and rest. Such motion and rest imply that this kind of being involves matter. After discussing physics for a while, Aristotle briefly mentions mathematics as another example of a partial science. He then goes on to ask whether there is a kind of being that is separate—separate from matter and motion—and he says that if there is such a kind of being, a theological science will explore it.

Many questions arise in these two chapters of the *Metaphysics*, the initial chapters of books 4 and 6, but I want to concentrate on just one issue. I want to concentrate on the contrast that Aristotle draws between sciences of a segment or a kind of being and the science of being as such. Aristotle does not just say flatly and simply that he is going to treat being as being. He does not just say there is this unusual science and we are going to pursue it. Rather, as he sets out on this project, he distinguishes this venture from an inquiry into a part or kind of being. The contrast is important, and it should not be overlooked. We do not just have the science of being as being by itself; we have it in contrast with sciences of a part. What does this mean?

Consider what happens when we inquire into a kind of being, as we do in physics or mathematics, or, to broaden the contrast, when we engage in biology, which studies living things; or economics, which studies commodities and exchanges; or astronomy, which studies celestial bodies. In such partial sciences, we study being as mobile, being as quantitative, being as living, being as economic, or being as celestial. An intellectual motion—we could call it a confinement—takes place at the origin of such inquiry. Being is there as the background or the matrix, and we narrow our focus down to one of its kinds. We work with being as . . . quantified; or with being as . . . living. We try, for example, to work out mathematical relationships or the properties and principles of living things. As we do so, however, being itself always remains there behind us. Being stays at our back. Permit me to paraphrase Andrew Marvell. We focus on a given field, but "At our back we always hear / Being's winged chariot circling near."[7]

---

7. Andrew Marvell, "To His Coy Mistress," in *The Poems and Letters of Andrew Marvell*, 3rd ed., ed. H. M. Margoliouth, vol. 1, *Poems*, revised by Pierre Lagouis with E. E. Duncan-

Being, that from which this part has been cut, is always at our back, and moreover it is not just at our back and all around us, but also always at work in its own silent and surreptitious way in what we are focusing on. Being is in the part as well as in the whole. We overlook it and take it for granted or as given, but it is there. A science of the part is, therefore, essentially a forgetful science. It forgets where it came from. It is oblivious of its own origins and principles and of many of its ingredients. It is an ungrateful offspring, accepting its inheritance and spending it, but remaining unmindful of where it came from.

So what do we do about this? How can we become more grateful and more reverent toward our origins? Following our teacher Aristotle, let us give our progenitors the respect that is due to them. We set out to engage in the science that discusses being as . . . being. This Aristotelian phrase is very dynamic but also very strange. We start off with being, just as we do in all the partial sciences, and we *start* to narrow it down. We take being *as* . . . (as what?) . . . as being! We start narrowing it down, but then—surprise!—we stop narrowing it, and we turn around and go back to our starting point. We recover our origins. We go back to the beginning. Moreover, we go back not just to any beginning but to the first one of all, to the underived beginning, behind which there is nothing to investigate or even to think of. This is the ultimate brick wall behind which there is nothing else. We do watch our back. We go back to *the* beginning from which all parts and kinds are sorted out.

We could not make this move without contrasting it against the partial sciences. If we tried to perform it just by itself, we would not be able to define it. We would not find any friction or any grip through which we could clarify what we are doing. We could not have made the strategic distinction that we need. There is a science of being as being only because there are partial sciences in which being is at work. We need these partial sciences so that we can get behind them and achieve a science of being as being. We have first to become oblivious to being if we are going to remember it. The partial sciences whet our appetite for the theoretic life and put us on the road to first philosophy, but the road does not lead to yet one more partial science. It leads to this strange science of being as being.

Let us look more closely at this maneuver of confinement. I want to

---

Jones (Oxford: Clarendon Press, 1971), 27–28: "But at my back I always hear / Time's winged chariot hurrying near."

introduce a metaphor to make it stand out more clearly. We start with the most general context "being," and we initiate a restriction, we say "being as . . ." But then, suddenly, like good open-field runners, we "reverse field" and go back to what we started from. When we do this, we annul the "as" of confinement. Instead of concentrating on "being as mobile" or "being as numerable" or "being as alive," we begin to focus on "being as . . . BEING!" We bounce back. We are thrown back on what we normally and always leave behind and presuppose. The "as" annihilates itself, but unless it did so—unless it led us to expect a confinement and then disappointed us—there would be no turn of our minds to this new subject. We go back to what everyone else leaves behind. Philosophy is here defined against the other sciences, which are not even aware of the confinement at work in their establishment.

I use the metaphor of "reversing field" to describe the move made into first philosophy. In football, this would mean that instead of running toward the opponent's goal line, we turn around and start running toward our own. Most people watching the game would ask, "What's going on? What on earth is he doing? He's running toward his own end zone!" The other team would not even try to stop us. Even our cheerleaders would stop cheering us on. But that is the way we are, and that is philosophy. We want to get back to our beginnings, to the principles that are at work in everything. Philosophy is not for everybody, even though everyone draws on being in whatever he says, thinks, and does—even though everyone in fact attempts (if only in a confused way) something like a study of being as being whenever he ventures an opinion about the whole of things.[8]

And although the partial scientist explicitly considers only his partial field, many of the dimensions of being "shine through" or are "at work" in his partial science. Being shows up in many ways: for example, in his use of the word "is," in his assumption and use of the principle of non-contradiction, and in the very idea of definition or intelligibility or distinction. It also shows up in the partial scientist's syntax and predication, and in his use of postpredicaments such as "same" and "other," "prior" and "posterior." These are all things that the science of being as being

---

8. When people inquire into metaphysics, they expect at first to be informed about new and astonishing things, but in fact what they learn will be very old and very familiar, even if hitherto unnoticed.

does deal with; they are all proper to being as such, but they are also ingredients in the partial sciences. Incidentally, one of the more curious things that Aristotle says the science of being as being treats is whether Socrates and Socrates seated are the same.[9] The question may sound trivial, but it raises the issues of identity and accidental being. Only this science, furthermore, can come to terms with the nature of sophistry and dialectics.[10] The science of being as being is also the science of truth; at the beginning of book 2 of the *Metaphysics* Aristotle refers to it as "the investigation concerning truth [*hē peri tēs alētheias theōria*]," and later, in books 5 and 6, he speaks about the true as one of the meanings of being.[11] This science would, therefore, also deal with the distinction between our opinions of things and the way things really are. I would claim that this science would also examine the way things can exist in the mind, in pictures, and in words.

The partial scientist cannot handle these things in his partial science—as a biologist or botanist or physicist—but he nevertheless cannot help using them. We cannot give a psychological or a biological explanation of the principle of noncontradiction, for example, or of the intelligibility of things; we can clarify such things only in the science of being as being.[12] For that matter, we cannot give a psychological clarification of psychology, or a biological explanation of biology, and it is philosophically amusing when such scientists try to do this. What would it mean to give a biological explanation of the science of biology? It would have to show that the science is a product of bodily, organic processes, and that it is carried on in order to sustain bodily life. All partial sciences are partial; they do not watch their backs. The things that come from behind us are what the first philosopher works on, namely, the things that permeate the partial sciences but cannot be treated by them.

I should mention some other features of the science of being as being, or philosophy. It is eminently realistic and concrete, because it deals with what is, with things or beings as such. Furthermore, it does not just speak about things over against us; it also speaks about ourselves as the

9. Aristotle, *Metaphysics* IV, 2, 1004b1–2. This chapter gives a long list of the features of being that the science examines.

10. Ibid., 1004b17–26.

11. *Metaphysics* II, 1, 993a30; V, 7, 1017a31–35; VI, 2, 1026a34–35.

12. Trying to handle the issue of being as a psychological question would be what is known as psychologism.

ones to whom being appears, and in doing so it again does not carry out an enterprise, for example, in psychology, sociology, anthropology, economics, history, or biology. First philosophy clarifies what we are as agents of truth. We are a special kind of entity because being is an issue for us and because we are an issue for ourselves. The science of being as being is called in Latin the science of *ens qua ens,* but it is also the science of *mens qua mens.* It turns to "intellect as intellect" in contrast with intellect as psychological or sociological or biological. I would also suggest that Aristotle's maneuver into first philosophy is similar to the transcendental reduction of Husserl, which also is a procedure leading away from unselfconscious partial science into first philosophy. By getting to "mind as mind" Husserl also gets to being as being. And while we have been concentrating on special sciences as the contrast for first philosophy, we might also have thought about areas outside of science, such as ethical conduct, politics, and poetics as foils for the turn to being as being. These things also arise from the matrix of being, as partial domains within it.

METAPHYSICS AND JUDGMENT

So far we have been working under the aegis of Aristotle. We turn now to a theme from Thomas Aquinas, one that has been extensively developed by Wippel, namely, the judgment of separation (*separatio*) as the establishment of the field for the science of being as being. As Wippel and others have argued, the most important place where Aquinas examines this issue is in his commentary on the *De Trinitate* of Boethius, where Thomas discusses the division and method of the sciences.[13] Aquinas's treatment of the topic is prompted by a claim made by Boethius about the division of sciences, but it can also be seen as a condensation and recapitulation of Aristotle's discussion in *Metaphysics* books 4 and 6. Aquinas introduces a number of new ideas in his analysis.

Aquinas, following Aristotle, distinguishes two kinds of intellectual

---

13. See Thomas Aquinas, *Super Boetium De Trinitate* (hereafter *In De Trin.*), q. 5, a. 3 co., Opera omnia, iussu Leonis XIII edita cura et studio Fratrum Praedicatorum 50 (Rome, 1992), 147:119–149:274. For Wippel's treatment of the theme of *separatio* in Aquinas, see his *Metaphysical Themes in Thomas Aquinas* (Washington, D.C.: The Catholic University of America Press, 1984), 69–104; id., *Metaphysical Thought of Thomas Aquinas: From Finite to Uncreated Being* (Washington, D.C.: The Catholic University of America Press, 2000), 44–62.

operations: the first act of the intellect, simple apprehension, in which we express an intelligibility and come to know what a thing is; and the second act, the act of judging, the act of composing and dividing, which looks to (*respicit*) the existence of the thing in question. Thus, by the first act we understand *what* ostriches or unicorns are, but through the second act, the judgment, we deal with whether ostriches or unicorns really are and how they are. As Wippel writes, "Thomas's point is this: if it is through the intellect's first operation that we discover quiddities or understand what things are, it is only through its second operation that we discover their existence (*esse*)."[14]

Judgments in turn can be of two kinds. First, there are judgments of existence, such as "There are ostriches," "The ostrich lives," or, negatively, "There are no unicorns," "The unicorn is not." Second, there are judgments of attribution, such as "The ostrich runs around" or "The ostrich does not fly." Both kinds of judgments deal with the existence of what they refer to, whether it is the simple or the qualified (attributed) mode of existing. It is real ostriches that run around and real ostriches that do not fly.

But the initial discovery of the existence of something, such as ostriches or, more exotically, electrons and neutrons, is still far from the entrance into the study of being as being. Judgment gives us a direct, naive awareness of the reality of particular kinds of things. It does involve reason; it is more than the elementary awareness of reality that we have in sensory experience, where we could be said to encounter the resistance of things but not yet their existence. When we judge we move into reason—I would say we move into syntax—and we register the actuality of things, their existence. We have an initial contact with being. We have not yet, however, turned toward being as being.

Let us stay with this initial sense of being for a moment and try to concretize it by offering two more examples. Suppose we are out for a walk and it starts to rain and we say, "It is starting to rain and we are far from home." We register not only *raining,* but that it *is* raining. The thing is presented to us as really being. The hard fact is given to us, and it can be presented through either a judgment of existence or a judgment of attribution. We bump into the reality of this particular being, and we

---

14. Wippel, *Metaphysical Thought,* 3.

do so through the act of judgment. But now let us take a more dramatic example. Consider the kind of awareness that Joseph Stalin had when he finally realized, or judged, that Hitler was indeed invading the Soviet Union. Stalin had been in denial about the threat, and he refused to believe warnings that people sent him. He took no precautions, and he was shocked and awed when Operation Barbarossa actually began to be— when it came into existence—on June 22, 1941. Stalin might well have judged, for himself and for others, "This *is* an invasion; it's really happening; this is not a drill." Thus, as Wippel writes, "Here, . . . owing to its cooperation with the common sense [power], the intellect will be in a position to judge that the object one is perceiving (and which is acting on the external senses) actually exists. . . . One will now make an initial judgment of existence regarding the particular thing one is perceiving."[15]

The actuality in question, of course, is that of a particular kind of thing. We are dealing not with sheer existence but with the existence of something definite. In this example it is an invasion, in the other example a rainstorm. It is true that Stalin did not directly perceive the invasion, but he did perceive its effects—for example, we might suppose, in the reports he received and the somewhat jittery behavior of his subordinates. So here we have an awareness of the reality or existence of things, registered and presented to us by the act of judging.

But as rational human beings we need not stay with a particular judgment regarding a particular occurrence. We can go beyond any such particular judgments and get a comprehensive idea of "reality" or "that which is." We might express this awareness by a more generalized aphorism, such as "Those are the facts" or "Things are what they are" or, in the memorable words of Walter Cronkite, "That's the way it is." We have reached a sense of the world as real. But even this more global sense of being is not yet the entrance into first philosophy. It is still not the metaphysical understanding of being as being. This generalized notion is what Wippel calls the primitive or premetaphysical notion of being.[16] It

15. Ibid., 38. My examples are of individual entities, but we could also deal with the existence of "kinds" of things. A person might ask, for example, whether there really is such a thing as benevolent friendship (or is everything ultimately a matter of surreptitious self-interest?), or whether there really is such a thing as malice (or is everything ultimately a matter of misunderstanding and fear?).

16. Ibid., 39.

is a generalized sense of what is. To allude to what we said earlier in this chapter, we could say that at this point we have not yet reversed field; we are still moving forward in our cognition, even if we are doing so in a more global way. We have a sense of "being," but not of being as such, or being as being.

What happens next, and what establishes the science of being as being, is that another judgment comes into play, one different from the judgments of existence and attribution that give us the reality of things. The new judgment is specifically a negative judgment, what Aquinas terms a judgment of separation (*separatio*). In what we have described so far, the being we have encountered has been material and mobile. Thus, the rain that is falling, or the tanks crossing the Russian border and the Stukas bombing the railroad stations, are all material and mobile, and, so far as we know, this kind of thing is all that there is. Reality, as we have experienced and conceived it so far, involves matter and motion, and if we were to stop at this point to analyze what we have before us, we would be involved in physics as the highest and most comprehensive science, and its principles and causes would be the highest we could seek. We would be studying being as material and mobile.

But as we reflect further and think more carefully about what we have encountered, we come to see that being need not be constricted to matter and motion. In our experiencing and in our physics we have developed and used such notions as substance, actuality and potentiality, identity and difference, and even being and truth. We could not have had a physics or any thoughtful experience without the involvement of these forms. But we realize that although these dimensions of things occur in the material and mobile being we experience, they could also occur outside of matter and motion. They do not need to be constricted to material and mobile being. We come to see that they enjoy what Wippel calls negative or neutral immateriality.[17] These dimensions *are* found in material and mobile beings, but they also can go beyond such beings; they can also be found in things that are separate from matter and motion. We express this transcendence in the judgment of separation, in which we assert that being and all that belongs to it as such need not be material and mobile—although it obviously can be material and mobile, and in some

17. Ibid., 60.

instances actually is so. We can, therefore, think about the things we experience not just as material but also simply as being.

And we can go still further and see that being need not be limited to any particular kind of being. As Wippel puts it, "That by reason of which something is recognized as being need not be identified with or restricted to that by which it is recognized as being of a given kind."[18] Being taken as being includes material things, but it can also encompass immaterial things, and it cannot be limited to any particular kind of being. In this way, we attain being as being, which Thomas also calls *ens commune*, or being in general. This is the subject of metaphysics, and we set out to determine its principles and causes.

What will this science do? What sort of explanations will it provide? As I have indicated earlier, it will develop such themes as the principle of noncontradiction and other metaphysical and logical principles, as well as the notions of substance and form, essence and existence, the potential and the actual, truth and falsity, predication and syntax, and identity and difference.[19] This science would explore how things are in the world, how they are in the mind, and how they can exist in speech and in images. Such themes cannot be handled in biology or chemistry or physics, and not even in psychology or sociology, even though they occur in all such sciences. Furthermore, one of the things this science will do is to show that its subject, *ens commune*, cannot account for itself, and that it needs a cause of its existence. The science reasons to God as the uncaused, universal cause of the being of things, and it explores how we can speak about the God who is so much beyond anything we can directly experience. God is not included within the subject matter of metaphysics; he is considered in this science not as part of its subject but as the cause or principle of its subject, which is *ens commune*. Such knowledge of God as the cause of beings is the goal or the end of first philosophy.

---

18. Wippel, *Metaphysical Themes*, 103.

19. Thomists emphasize the role of judgment in the discovery of being, but I would like to expand the domain of judgment to cover all of syntax. The paradigmatic form of judgment is predication and the judgment of existence, but other forms of syntax serve as appendages to judgment. They amplify it, but they also share in its articulative and assertive force. All syntactic articulation is implicitly assertion. On the role of syntax in truth and being, see Robert Sokolowski, *The Phenomenology of the Human Person* (New York: Cambridge University Press, 2008), 31–96.

A QUESTION

Wippel's treatment of this topic is comprehensive and subtle, but in reading it I find a problem, which you may have discerned in my exposition of this topic. My question is, what does the judgment of separation separate our target from? Does it separate the notion of being from matter and motion, or does it separate it from any limited kind of being at all? These two strands are found in his argument, and it seems to me that it would be desirable to distinguish them more explicitly than he does in some passages.

Perhaps I could make my question more obvious and more vivid by saying that it deals with the status of immaterial substances, which Aquinas in his commentary on Boethius's *De Trinitate* calls the "separate substances" as well as "angels."[20] Such beings are positively immaterial, but they are finite and created. My question is, do such separate intelligences fall under *ens commune,* the subject of metaphysics, or not? Are angels part of the subject of metaphysics, or are they among the principles and causes of the subject of metaphysics?

Let me summarize the problem I wish to raise. I find the following two lines of argument interwoven in Wippel's treatment of this topic.

1. In some passages he says that the judgment of separation moves us beyond material and hence mobile things. The judgment of separation shows that notions such as being, substance, and truth need not be limited to material things but can also be applied to immaterial and divine things. These positively immaterial beings will come into metaphysics as the causes and principles of its subject, *ens commune.* They will not be included in the subject of metaphysics. Thus, Wippel says "Being as being is the subject of metaphysics; things separate from matter and motion in the positive sense—divine things—are studied by metaphysics only as principles of its subject."[21] He also writes, "Divine things, such as God and separate substances, are . . . regarded as causes of being in general (*ens commune*)."[22] In this approach, it seems to me, angels would not

20. For Thomas's references in this work to these beings as "separate substances," see q. 1, aa. 1, 3; q. 5, a. 1; q. 6, a. 1, 3,4. For his references to them as "angels," see the q. 1, a. 2; q. 4, a. 2; q. 5, aa. 1, 4.
21. Wippel, *Metaphysical Themes,* 31.   22. Ibid.

fall within *ens commune* but would be among its causes and principles. In this formulation, *ens commune* encompasses just material and mobile being. I would see this as an Aristotelian way of approaching first philosophy.

2. But at other times Wippel says that the judgment of separation moves us beyond limited beings of any kind (and not just beyond material and mobile beings). It moves us beyond any *kind* of being, including spiritual beings, and in this approach angels *would* fall under *ens commune*. For example, he writes that the judgment of separation is "a negative judgment in that it denies that that by reason of which something is described as being is to be identified with that by reason of which it is a being of a given kind, for instance, material and changing being, or quantified being, or, for that matter, spiritual being."[23] Metaphysics, he says "treat[s] of being in general . . . or without restriction, precisely insofar as it is being rather than insofar as it is being of a given kind."[24] In this viewpoint, *ens commune,* the subject of metaphysics, would encompass both material being and separate substances—in one passage Wippel refers to "being in general and that which falls thereunder, that is, created being"[25]—and only God, not created separate substances, would remain outside it. God would be considered in metaphysics as the cause and principle of *ens commune*. I would see this as a Thomistic way of describing first philosophy.

There seem to be two lines of argument here: the one that leads us to transcend material being and the one that leads us to transcend finite being of any kind, and some passages of Wippel's writings seem to oscillate between the two. The two lines of argument are, of course, related. The second reinforces the first. If in our judgment of separation we have gone beyond the limitations inherent to any kind of being, we will obviously have also gone beyond the limitations of material being, which is a kind of being. However, if we establish only the first transcendence— if we show only the possible immateriality of being as being—we have

23. Ibid., 79.
24. Ibid., 79n31.
25. Ibid., 31. See also 81 and 103. On 103–4 mobile being is shifted into changing being (and hence possibly immaterial). See also *Metaphysical Thought,* 44, 48–49, 53–54, 60–61. On 49 Wippel writes, "One judges that being, in order to be realized as such, need not be material, or changing, or quantified, or living, or for that matter, spiritual."

not yet determined that being can transcend all finite kinds of being. We have not yet determined that it can transcend angelic beings, or separate forms.

I think, however, that the two lines of argument can be reconciled. Going beyond material and mobile being can be seen as a step toward the fuller transcending of finite being. Trying to go beyond being in matter and motion would prompt us to go one step further and ask whether being as such can transcend all finite kinds as well. Material and mobile beings are obviously divided into multiple kinds of things, multiple species whose individual instances come and go. This highly perceptible sense of kinds could be a step toward kinds as such, even to the kinds that are found within immaterial being, where, according to Aquinas, every individual is a kind unto itself and therefore able to exhaust the perfections of what it is.

PROPOSAL FOR A RESPONSE

Let us explore the elements found in these two approaches.[26] This section will not be *about* the science of being as being; it will be an exercise in the science itself, an attempt to clarify the way of being of forms, both material and separate, as well as the meaning of the act of *esse*.

Material Forms

Consider first the forms of material things. Consider something like being patriotic or patriotism. Only human beings in their embodiment can be patriotic, because the attribute involves belonging to some native community and having a patrimony, something inherited through the sharing of life. We can talk in different ways in regard to this attribute. We can say, "Johnson is patriotic," and we can also say, "Johnson is a patriot." In both cases, we refer to the individual human beings who embody the form. But we can also shift our focus and talk about patriotism as such, and when we do so we disregard, we positively abstract from, any particular instances of this form (we do not just leave them indeterminate). We can distill the form of patriotism, and we can talk about the

---

26. I have found the following article by John Tomarchio helpful for the material in this section: "Aquinas's Concept of Infinity," *Journal of the History of Philosophy* 40 (2002): 163–87.

form itself. We can say a lot of things about it, for example, that patriotism involves a native community.

Such an isolated form can never exist by itself. Patriotism can exist in a real way only as instantiated in Johnson, Smith, and Jones, but it can be talked about by itself, and what we say about it is true of the form itself and of all the things that instantiate the form. What we say is not true simply about our concept of the form or our idea of the form. We are talking about a kind of being or a way of being, and not just about an idea. We would do well to avoid talking about the *concept* of patriotism; it is much better to talk about "being patriotic" and about "what it is to be patriotic," or about patriotism itself.

The form of patriotism does not subsist. It does not stand on its own. It is embodied and individualized in people, and it really exists only in that way. But the form of patriotism cannot be exhausted by its instances, not even by all of them. Each patriot has his own patriotism, and each has it in a limited manner. No human being can embody all the potentials of the form of patriotism. Some people embody it more than others; we could say that Alexander Hamilton was more patriotic than Aaron Burr, and a character in a movie might be a purified paradigm of patriotism, such as the man played by Mel Gibson in the film *The Patriot*. This is what a work of art does; it sublimates the form of things, but not even the fictional, artistic paradigm can be sheer patriotism, the very form. The form exists as distributed and confined, but in itself, considered absolutely, it contains everything that patriotism can be, and not even all the patriots together can exhaust it. These features are true of all the forms that are essentially material, that is, all the forms that need to determine material beings to be actual.

For another example, consider the form of being musical. We can say that Elvis is musical and that Elvis is a musician, but we can also talk about the form of musicality or about music as such. In this case also, no musician, not even Elvis or Mozart, can exhaust the virtualities of music, even though musicality as such does not subsist or stand itself by itself, even though it needs Elvis and Mozart to be actualized. Material forms exist only in their embodiments, but they are not exhausted by any of them, nor by all of them.

I have one more point to make about material forms. They can really exist, as I have said, only in their embodiments, but in addition they can exist in the mind or the intellect. They can take on a cognitive existence correlated with their real existence. Patriotism can exist in the minds of those who think about it, but in a different manner from the way it exists in those who embody it. In this regard, the phenomenon of a picture or a dramatization of the form is especially interesting, because it express-es not only real patriotism but the patriotism as it is conceived by those who depict it. The being of the depicted or dramatized patriotism is in-termediate between the real and the cognitive existence. And still more interesting is the way the form of patriotism exists in the name that sig-nifies it, in the word *patriotism.* The form exists in the word as its sense or meaning. The word is different from a picture, because it captures the form of patriotism in its intellectualized purity (whereas an image cap-tures patriotism in only one version), but the name still signifies real pa-triotism and, indirectly at least, real patriots. The exploration of the way of being of material forms—in things, in the mind, in images, and in words—is part of the task of the science of being as being.

Separate Forms

So much for material forms. Let us move now to separate, immaterial form. Suppose there is an angel whose form is something like loyalty, "The Loyalty Angel." His loyalty would not be like ours, because his form could not be embodied in us, but let us say it is something like what we call loyalty. He is loyal in the way that only an angel can be, and he does not need to perform loyal acts in order to become loyal, the way we must do in order to appropriate our loyalty, nor does he grow or mature or ripen in regard to what he is. That angel would be the separate and per-fected form of that characteristic, as Raphael is the archangel of healing, Michael the warrior archangel, and Gabriel the announcer. The Loyalty Angel would not be the form in which the patriots Johnson, Smith, and Jones participate in. He would be the pure angel of celestial loyalty: he would be fully actual in his substance from the beginning, and he would exhaust the perfection of his kind of loyalty.

Or let us consider "The Musical Angel," the intensified and unified form of the muses, the pure form of Polyhymnia or Euterpe. The Loy-alty Angel and The Musical Angel, the separate form of loyalty and the separate form of harmony, do not participate in a form; each *is* a form. Notice, also, that nothing else participates in them. They are not like the forms of patriotism or human music. They are not that in which patriots and musicians participate. They are subsistent beings; they do stand on their own. Each of them, furthermore, exhausts the potentialities of what he is. Each is fully charged and fully activated. An angel might on occasion come down and "touch" a human patriot or musician; he might affect the imagination of a human being and help him acquire an intelligible species; but he would not share his own angelic form with the human being.[27] Angels exist in another way, and let us also remember that there are myriads of angels, each with its own specific excellence fully achieved.

So now we have encountered embodied forms (such as patriotism) and separate forms (such as angels). I would say that the Aristotelian strain in the judgment of separation stops at this point. It transcends material and mobile being and leads to separate form, even to a first separate form, but it does not go any further. This is the outer rim of Aristotle's world. It is true that Aristotle talks about being as well as about form, but his understanding of being comes to its completion in the separate form that is the capstone of the cosmos. As Thomas Prufer writes, for Aristotle, "Minded soul contemplating form which is form of . . . and form in . . . frees that form toward the more primary way of being: being form only, being form alone."[28] The Prime Mover of Aristotle is like a super angel for Aquinas. It is the highest and best thing that can be.

Esse commune

We now turn to the Thomistic line of argument in regard to the judgment of separation. This approach introduces a new dimension and focuses on the question of being even more sharply than Aristotle's approach does. If Thomas were to discuss The Loyalty Angel and The Musical Angel, for example, he would admit that such beings exhaust the potential of *what* they are—they exhaust their own form; they *are* all that they could be. But he would also point out that they still are not altogether simple. They might be "necessary angels" (to use the elegant term of Wallace Stevens),

---

27. Aquinas says that higher angels can endow lower angels with intelligible species, but angels cannot instill intelligible species into a human intellect, because our minds take in such species only through phantasms. See *Summa theologiae* (hereafter *ST*) I, q. 111, aa. 1–3, and q. 106, a. 1.

28. Prufer, "Aristotelian Themes," in *Recapitulations,* 7. The ellipses are in the original text.

but they still depend on something beyond themselves for what they are and for the fact that they are.[29] Why are they not purely simple and radically necessary? *Because it does not follow from what they are that they have to be.* They do not exist simply on their own, and they could be conceived not to be. They are necessary and sempiternal beings, but there is a sense in which they still need to be explained. They depend on something different from them for their being. They are necessary, but still *ab alio.*[30]

Because of this dependence, both angels and material beings have something in common existentially despite their great difference in kind. They can both be grouped together and included under one notion, the notion of being. They all *are* and they can be called beings, and the Thomistic name for all of them, for them and whatever else there is, is *ens commune,* being in general, or being as being. Just as Johnson and Smith are patriots, and Elvis and Mozart are musicians, so all of them, Johnson, Smith, Elvis, Mozart, as well as The Loyalty Angel and The Musical Angel and everything else besides, are beings. They are all included within *ens commune,* and *ens commune* is the subject of metaphysics, the science of being as being.

But what makes them to be *beings?* Is there another form that makes them to be beings, as there is a form of patriotism that lets Johnson be patriotic? Is there a form for actual existence? Do angels have one form that makes them what they are and another form that makes them to actually be? Do *we* have a form that makes us human and another form that makes us to be? No, we do not want to say that, neither for angels nor for ourselves, because here we are stretching beyond form: we are no longer dealing with a kind of being. The act of being is not a kind of being. Rather than speak of a form of actuality, we should talk about *esse* or the act of *esse.* As patriotism is to Johnson the patriot, so *esse* is to

29. Wallace Stevens, *The Necessary Angel: Essays on Reality and the Imagination* (New York: Vintage Books, 1965). Also, "Angel Surrounded by Paysans": "Yet I am the necessary angel of earth, / Since, in my sight, you see the earth again, / Cleared of its stiff and stubborn, man-locked set, / And, in my hearing, you hear its tragic drone." See *The Collected Poems of Wallace Stevens* (New York: Knopf, 2008), 496–97.

30. Wippel's comments on the *De Ente et Essentia* of Aquinas show that separate forms play a strategic role in the discovery of the distinction between essence and existence, and hence in the transition to *esse subsistens.* See his essay, "Essence and Existence in the *De Ente,* Chapter 4," in *Metaphysical Themes,* 107–32.

The Loyalty Angel, The Musical Angel, and to Johnson, Smith, and Jones, both in themselves and in their ways of being patriotic, as well as Elvis and Mozart and their ways of being musical.

The act of being is the capstone here, and all (finite) entities share in it. Each entity enjoys its own act of existing. But we can broaden the range of our speech and move beyond particular acts of being; we can also speak in a more general manner about the act of existing. When the act of *esse* is considered in a universal and abstract way, it is called *esse commune* by Aquinas. *Esse commune* is, as Wippel says, the act of being when it is "viewed in general."[31] We can intellectually distill *esse commune* from particular existents (the procedure is somewhat analogous to the distillation of patriotism from patriots).

Esse commune is far richer than the share of existence found in any particular entity. According to Wippel, Aquinas implies "that any finite substance simply has or participates in *esse commune* without exhausting it."[32] Each entity has its own principle of being, its own act of existence, and hence it limits *esse commune* to itself, to its kind and its individuality, but no entity or entities, not even the material world and everything in it, nor an angel and all the angels combined, nor even the material and angelic world together, could empty out the virtualities of *esse,* the potential of existence, even of finite existence. The world around us is a marvelous place and a source of wonder. It is a wonderful world, as Louis Armstrong assures us. Think of our privileged planet and the multitudes of kinds that it allows to proliferate, not only in biological forms but in the characters and actions of men: so many essences and so much diversity of being right here at home, and in addition there are the galaxies and black holes of the cosmos, the fields and particles, and the various energies of things. But even with all this diversity, *esse commune* could give rise to still more kinds and particulars than the world we marvel at. There might have been unlimited other things and their stories, perhaps even other universes. Everything that is only *participates* in *esse commune;* it does not exhaust it.

I would like to make one more point about *esse commune.* It does

31. Wippel, *The Metaphysical Thought of Thomas Aquinas,* 120.

32. Ibid., 121. See also 123, where Wippel says that *esse commune* "signifies this act principle considered universally and in its fullness of perfection rather than as received in any given participant."

not subsist or stand on its own. It exists in only two ways: as participated by various things and as conceived by us. In this respect it is more like material forms, more like patriotism, than like separate forms or angels, because material forms also exist only in their instances and in our minds (and their existence in our depictions and our words reflects their existence in our minds). Because *esse commune* does exist as conceived by us, it ought to be grateful to us, and especially to people like Louis Armstrong, who sings about it, and Thomas Aquinas, who theorizes it. It owes something to us. We are the custodians of being or, as Heidegger says, the shepherds of being. We furnish it, with all its virtuality, with something of a home in our minds and our words.[33] We are special in the cosmos, because within it we alone, it would seem, can marvel at *esse commune* and let it exist intellectually.

ESSE SUBSISTENS: BEYOND BEING AND ESSE COMMUNE

So now we have come to *ens commune* (which includes embodied forms and separate forms) and the *esse commune* in which entities participate. All this takes us pretty far. How far does it take us? Can there be anything beyond this, or have we here come up against the ultimate brick wall? Do *ens commune* and *esse commune* provide the widest and ultimate context, that beyond which nothing can be thought? No, not yet, not in Thomistic metaphysics. Why not? Because in each of its instances *ens commune* still involves a distinction between *what* it is and *that* it is, and between its essence and its *esse*. *Ens commune* cannot account for its own actuality; it only participates in *esse*. It does not and cannot depend on itself. What it is does not explain why it is. As rich and varied as *ens commune* is, it still receives its being from elsewhere, from something beyond *ens commune*, and this reception could depend on one source only, on the being whose essence entails existence. This source could be nothing but *esse* subsisting in itself and of itself, which of course is God as Creator.[34]

---

33. There can be depictions of patriotism, in dramas, movies, and paintings, but could there be an image of *esse commune*? Probably not (why not?), but we do signify it with words.

34. On the difference between *esse commune* and *esse subsistens,* see Wippel, "Platonism and Aristotelianism in Aquinas," in his *Metaphysical Themes in Thomas Aquinas II* (Washington, D.C.: The Catholic University of America Press, 2007), 285–86: "Thomas speaks of par-

There could be only one such subsistent existence, only one that could stand on its own in this way. It is individuated not through being any *kind* of being, not even by fulfilling any specific form, as angels do, nor by being made concrete by this particular mass of matter, as embodied forms are individuated. *Esse subsistens* is individuated simply by being sheer, undifferentiated *esse*. All beings that share in existence depend specifically on this "being" or principle that exists in the most independent way. It "stands on its own"—it subsists—in a way that is more radical than the way in which pure forms (such as angels) can stand alone. *Esse subsistens* is infinitely different from any *forma subsistens*.[35]

The totality of things, *ens commune*, might not have been; its essences do not entail existence, not even as a whole. *Esse subsistens*, in stark contrast, could be all that there is. It has, however, chosen not to be alone. It, or he, has chosen to create beings that participate in its existence. The Scottish philosopher David Braine writes that this being, the divine existence, is "transcendent in nature; yet not distant, but immediate to each thing, . . . [with] an intimacy to each thing which none can share."[36] Neither Polyhymnia nor Euterpe, neither The Loyalty Angel nor The Musical Angel, could be so intimate to the things that are in this world, because God is subsistent *esse* and not simply subsistent form, and all things, created and preserved, are continually given their being by him. The Musical Angel touching Mozart is as nothing compared with God letting something, anything, be.

Saint Augustine, toward the end of the *Confessions*, expresses this sheer *esse* of God (its being beyond any kind of being), as well as the dependence of every kind of being on it. Through the Holy Spirit, he says, we see that "whatever is in any particular manner is good [*bonum est, quidquid aliquo modo est*]." Why is it good? "Because it is from him who is not in any particular manner, but [just] is—is [*ab illo enim est, qui non*

---

ticipating in *esse commune*, i.e., in the act of being viewed universally rather than as realized in any one particular being. Speaking this way carries with it a certain risk, since some might conclude that Thomas is therefore identifying *esse commune* and *esse subsistens*. Thomas explicitly rejects any such identification. . . . *Esse commune* is not something that exists apart from actually existing entities except in the order of thought. If God were to be identified with *esse commune*, God would exist only in the intellect."

35. Aquinas uses the term *forma subsistens* to signify angels in *ST* I, q. 50, a. 2 ad 3, and q. 50, a. 5 co.

36. David Braine, *The Reality of Time and the Existence of God* (Oxford: Clarendon Press, 1988), 1.

aliquo modo est, sed est est]."[37] By repeating the word *est* in this striking way, Augustine says that God simply *is;* he exists not in any particular mode nor as any particular kind. The *est* of God is not like that of any other; it is reduplicated: *est* and nothing else. The second *est* prevents us from adding any thing or any mode to the first.[38] Augustine makes this assertion not in a metaphysical treatise but in the *Confessions,* which is a prayer addressing God. It is true that these phrases themselves are grammatically in the third person; they comprise an incipient metaphysical discourse, which perhaps needs to be stated in the third person. But to speak about God as sheer *esse* is not incompatible with Christian prayer; to the contrary, it clarifies the setting for prayer. The repetition of the verb—*sed est est*—is still in ordinary language and it is a rhetorical trope, but it is on the verge of metaphysics. One *est,* an ordinary one, would not have been sufficient.

To return to the vocabulary of Thomas Aquinas, the actuality of God as sheer *esse* is different from *esse commune,* the virtuality of finite existence, which does not stand alone and which needs to be modified in order to be real. *Esse commune* needs things in order to be realized, but God could be all that there is, with no lessening of goodness and perfection. God is not a separate form, nor is he the ground of being in the sense of *esse commune.* He is *esse subsistens,* and he could be without the world. The being of all other things, moreover, depends not on an inevitable emanation from God, but on his deliberate choice to create.

Esse subsistens, in its sheer simplicity and perfection, is beyond our experience and understanding. Our minds and our words are proportioned to material things and the forms that make them what they are. We are at home with enmattered intelligibilities. We can, nevertheless, devise a name for *esse subsistens* (we have just done so), and we formulate this name by using the word *to be* and contrasting *esse subsistens* against both separate forms and *esse commune.* We define the name by making a judgment of separation. We give a meaning to the name by making dis-

---

37. Augustine, *Confessionum Libri XIII,* bk. 13, c. 31, ed. Lucas Verheijen, O.S.A., CCSL 27 (Turnhout: Brepols, 1986), 270. My translation. I am grateful to Kevin White for this reference and for other assistance in this paper.

38. One can read the text as simply repeating the word *est,* or one can read the second *est* as a predicate, as saying "he is 'he is.'" This is the interpretation given by James J. O'Donnell in his *Augustine: Confessions* (Oxford: Clarendon, 1992), ad loc. O'Donnell says that Augustine's phrase is related to the *ego sum qui sum* of Exodus 3:14, where it is in the first person singular.

tinctions; we need these distinctions to be able to signify what the name refers to.[39] The world we experience and bring to speech points toward a primary mover and ultimately toward a cause of existence (which is the truth of the primary mover), but our minds, words, and images cannot capture the intelligibility of what is so indicated. As Thomas Prufer writes, "The world implies God, but it does not manifest him as he is in himself."[40] Our words need God's own Word if we are to do more than gesture toward such undifferentiated perfection of being; and yet, we do use our own words to indicate it as being beyond our knowing.

METAPHYSICS AND RELIGION

Let us recall the various forms and excellences that we have distinguished. First, there are embodied forms, such as ostriches and patriotism. They need individual bodily substances to exist, but they can also exist in our minds and in dramas, pictures, and words. Such forms are never fully exhausted, not even by splendid instances or by poetic creations. They are only participated. Second, there are separate forms, or angels. Each of them exists as a limited kind of being, but it exists as fully actualized in its form. Other things do not participate in it. Third, there is *esse commune*, which is not a form but the virtuality of finite existing. It is participated by all finite things, whether embodied or separate. It could have given rise to many other beings that would have been different from those that actually exist. Fourth, there is *esse per se subsistens*, the divine and creative cause of all things. It does exist or subsist, and it is unique in its absolute and simple perfection of being. It alone could have been all that there is. Its essence entails existence. To the extent that things exist and share in existence, they participate in this perfect, simple, and unlimited *esse*.

Thomistic philosophical exploration comes to its final context when it reaches the pure existence of God as the first and final cause of the *esse*

39. Wippel alludes to the need for such contrasts when he writes, "In the order of discovery one may move from one's discovery of individual beings as participating in *esse commune* to the caused character of such beings, and then on to the existence of their unparticipated source (*esse subsistens*)." *The Metaphysical Thought of Thomas Aquinas*, 117. See also 121 and 131.

40. Thomas Prufer, "A Protreptic: What Is Philosophy?," in *Studies in Philosophy and the History of Philosophy*, vol. 2, ed. John K. Ryan (Washington, D.C.: The Catholic University of America Press, 1963), 3–4.

of things. At this point Thomistic metaphysics has moved from its subject, being as being, and has come to rest in its goal or end, the cause of its subject. Before concluding my discussion, however, I wish to make a slight digression, from metaphysics to religious worship. In our philosophy of being, we have distinguished three different kinds of ultimate and transcendent principles: separate forms, as examined by Aristotle; *esse commune,* as the virtuality of existence for things in general; and *esse subsistens,* the being of God the Creator. But things that are ultimate are more than an object of philosophical curiosity. Each of these ultimates is also an object of human reverence or religious worship. We reach them in our metaphysics, but we also depend on them in a definitive way. We recognize and perhaps even sense that dependency, and we express it in religious veneration.

Thus, the separate forms can be seen as the gods, good or bad, that are worshiped in pagan religion. John Henry Newman, for example, says, "Jupiter and Neptune, as represented in classical mythology, are evil spirits, and nothing can make them otherwise."[41] *Esse commune,* with its virtuality of being, can be the object of philosophical and poetic piety, such as that expressed by Heidegger, who speaks about being as eventful and as sending us our destiny at different moments in history. *Esse commune* could be considered as the "Es" in Heidegger's phrase, "Es gibt . . ."[42] And of course *esse subsistens* is what Christians worship as Creator and Redeemer. To be devoted to God as creative *esse,* in his transcendence and yet his metaphysical proximity to all creatures, is a very different thing from honoring and fearing separate forms (the powers that be), and different also from finding poetic and philosophical satisfaction in things. Once we see that God can be like this, and once we believe that he is this way, we find that we are "no longer at ease here, in

41. John Henry Cardinal Newman, *An Essay in Aid of a Grammar of Assent* (Notre Dame: University of Notre Dame Press, 1979), 326. What shall we say about religions in which animals or celestial bodies are worshiped? Do they really worship such bodily things, or do they not rather confuse the embodied and the separate forms?

42. See Martin Heidegger, "Zeit und Sein," in *Zur Sache des Denkens,* Gesamtausgabe, Abteilung I, Band 14 (Frankfurt am Main: Klostermann, 2007), 5–30. Heidegger says he wishes to bring "das Es und sein Geben" into view (9), and that "Sein gehört als die Gabe dieses Es gibt in das Geben" (10). He says that the "Es" needs to be thought "aus der Art des Gebens her . . . , das zu ihm gehört" (24). These phrases are not ordinary predications but indicators of a unique source and manifestation. Predication takes place within the logical space opened by the "Es" and its "Geben."

the old dispensation, / with an alien people clutching their gods."[43] This religious aspect of metaphysics should not be overlooked. We do not just cognize what is ultimate; we also revere it. In fact we usually conceive it first in worship and only later in philosophy.

By reaching the ultimate actuality of subsistent *esse,* we gain a new perspective on all the other dimensions of beings. For example, we can distinguish, with Aquinas, between the *esse subsistens* of God and the *esse commune* of created things, and we can compare their respective potentialities and activities. We can also look back on the forms of things, and speak about form from the perspective of *esse* as existential act, as *esse commune,* and as *esse subsistens.* The ancient doctrine of *eidos* can be viewed in a new light. We get a new and more intense appreciation of what it means to be "first" in the order of being. We can draw parallels and analogies where they are appropriate and think more carefully about the nature of things, about what it is for things to be and what it is for us to understand them. Even accidental being takes on a new dimension. Both *esse* and form become validated through the metaphysics we have inherited. The Thomistic perspective brings out features that may not be as sharply delineated in Aristotle's science of being as being.

As we explore the themes of being and form, however, we enter into contemporary controversy. Form and being deserve special attention in our modern and postmodern world since the rejection of form is one of the founding principles of modernity and one of the self-evident premises of postmodernity. In the premodern understanding, which Aristotle and Thomas share and which we should try to recover and recapitulate, material things were defined by their formal cause, and separate forms (whether called "separate substances" or "angels") were a reinforcement and completion of embodied forms. Things were definable and intelligible because they were determined by form, and they had their being through their form. But one of the major resolutions of modern philosophy was to eliminate form, both the embodied and the separate. Modern philosophy resolved to remove forms—from the face of the earth, from the vault of the sky, and also from the human intellect, that part of the soul that Aristotle was willing to call the place of forms, the *topos eidōn.*[44] By remov-

43. T. S. Eliot, "Journey of the Magi," in *The Complete Poems and Plays: 1909–1950* (New York: Harcourt, 1952), 69.

44. Aristotle, *De Anima* III, 4, 429a27–28, ed. by Sir David Ross (Oxford: Clarendon, 1961).

ing form, modernity has also extinguished the question of being as being, and it has reduced human thinking to the brain and the body, the product of evolution and natural process. It has diluted both being and intellect. The work of John F. Wippel and other Thomist metaphysicians, therefore, is not just historical. It also serves to revive the question of being and to make room for the human difference. It helps restore us to our proper place in the order of things.

Dominic O'Meara

2 ∽ The Transformation of Metaphysics in Late Antiquity

The theme of my chapter is the development of metaphysics understood as a philosophical discipline or science. Perhaps as humans we have always had some interest in metaphysical questions—questions about the ultimate constitution of reality, about the reasons for the existence of things and of ourselves. But as regards the treatment of such questions within the framework provided by a conception of rational scientific knowledge: this is a development that we can trace back to Greek philosophy. I would like to propose that the last period of Greek philosophy—from about the third to the sixth centuries AD—made new and interesting contributions to metaphysics as a philosophical discipline, indeed made metaphysics into a metaphysical science, while also bringing out the limits of such a science.

This thesis may seem at first somewhat exaggerated. After all, one might object, Greek philosophical metaphysics was founded much earlier, by Plato and by Aristotle—perhaps even before them, by Parmenides. However, it is only in a very special way that we can say that Parmenides provides us with a metaphysical science, and the great metaphysical works of Plato and Aristotle, in particular Plato's *Republic* and Aristotle's *Metaphysics,* present what are more in the way of sketches of what a metaphysical science *might* be like, pointing to its subject matter, its methods, and some central propositions. These texts provide program-

It is a pleasure to be able to offer these pages to John Wippel as a small token of my appreciation of the man and the metaphysician. I am grateful for the helpful questions posed when this paper was given as a lecture in Washington at the Catholic University of America and as part of a seminar directed by Eugene Afonasin in Novosibirsk.

matic projects and preliminary explorations rather than a worked-out metaphysical science comprising a unified system of theorems. I would like to suggest that, as far as we know, such a system is first to be found in the philosophical schools of late antiquity. The late Professor Gérard Verbeke gave a lecture in 1978 in the Machette lecture series on this topic, and I have myself worked on it over the years. I would like to bring together this research and that done by others, so as to sketch here the overall picture that, it seems to me, is beginning to emerge.[1]

This chapter has four parts. In part 1, I introduce the way in which the great Aristotelian commentator of the early third century, Alexander of Aphrodisias, in interpreting Aristotle's metaphysical treatise, sought to find in it a metaphysical science. In part 2, I attempt to show how the Neoplatonist philosopher of the early fifth century Syrianus not only adopted Alexander's reading of Aristotle, but also was inspired by it in finding this same metaphysical science already in Plato. As a Platonist, however, Syrianus was acutely aware of the problem of transcendence: if the first principles of reality transcend human knowledge, then how could there be a science of them? I will describe how Syrianus dealt with this problem. Then in part 3, I will show how all of this resulted in a masterpiece of metaphysics, the *Elements of Theology*, written by Syrianus's pupil Proclus. Finally, in part 4, I will refer to what is perhaps the last great metaphysical work of Greek philosophy, the *Treatise on First Principles*. This work—written by Proclus's ultimate successor as the last head of the Platonist school of Athens in the early sixth century, Damascius—is one in which the limits of metaphysical science are explored with extraordinary subtlety and insistence.

TURNING ARISTOTLE'S *METAPHYSICS* INTO METAPHYSICAL SCIENCE

Let us then begin with Alexander of Aphrodisias. We can take it that the commentary Alexander wrote on Aristotle's metaphysical treatise was

1. Gérard Verbeke, "Aristotle's Metaphysics Viewed by the Ancient Greek Commentators," in *Studies in Aristotle*, ed. Dominic O'Meara (Washington, D.C.: Catholic University of America Press, 1981), 107–27; Dominic O'Meara, "Le problème de la métaphysique dans l'Antiquité tardive," *Freiburger Zeitschrift für Philosophie und Theologie* 23 (1986): 3–22; Klaus Kremer, *Der Metaphysikbegriff in den Aristoteles-Kommentaren der Ammonius-Schule* (Münster: Aschendorff, 1961). I will refer to more recent studies in what follows.

connected with his work in Athens as a professor of Aristotelian philosophy. Indeed all the philosophers we will be considering in this paper were teachers, and their works were connected with their teaching. The significance of this fact becomes clearer if we consider that these teachers saw themselves as representatives of the philosophy they taught—Alexander representing Aristotelian philosophy; Syrianus, Proclus, and Damascius representing Platonic philosophy. They were representatives in the sense that they thought of the work of the philosopher they taught, be it Plato or Aristotle, as containing the best, the true, philosophy. Thus Alexander, for example, felt that to find philosophical truth we could do no better than to read Aristotle's work.[2]

A consequence of this approach was the canonization, so to speak, of the works of Plato or of Aristotle, both in the sense that they were given great authority and in the sense that their works were organized so as to constitute a unified systematic body of knowledge. In the case of Alexander, this approach was facilitated by the fact that Aristotle's works, when published some two centuries before, had already been given some sort of systematic order, being arranged in groups dealing with logic, physics, metaphysics, ethics, and politics. In teaching this corpus of texts, Alexander did not hesitate to assume its systematic unity, with consequences, as we will now see, both for how he saw metaphysics as a science and for what he thought metaphysics was about.

Alexander's commentary on Aristotle's *Metaphysics,* as it has come down to us in Greek, covers only the first five books of Aristotle's treatise.[3] In these books, Aristotle speaks of a supreme science that he calls wisdom and that would deal with the first principles or causes of all things. He also speaks of a universal science of being, of being as being, of substance, of a science called first philosophy, of a science that concerns the axioms that ground all demonstrations (in particular the principle of noncontradiction), and of a science of divine substance, which he calls theology. Alexander, in explaining these books of Aristotle's treatise, takes it that Aristotle has a unified conception and is speaking

2. Alexander of Aphrodisias, *De anima,* ed. Ivo Bruns (Berlin: George Reimer, 1887), 2:4–9.

3. Alexander, *In Aristotelis metaphysica commentaria,* ed. Michael Hayduck (Berlin: George Reimer, 1881). The commentary on book 1 is translated by William Dooley (London: Duckworth, 1989), on books 2 and 3 by William Dooley and Arthur Madigan (London: Duckworth, 1992), and on book 4 by Arthur Madigan (London: Duckworth, 1993).

throughout of one and the same science. Thus wisdom *is* first philosophy, which *is* theology.[4] Not only do these different designations refer to one science, but the various objects they deal with must also be unified, as we will see shortly.

Taking it thus that Aristotle is speaking of one and only one science—let us call it "metaphysics" for convenience—Alexander makes another important move in supposing also that this science is to be conceived along the lines of a demonstrative science as such science is formalized in Aristotle's *Posterior Analytics*. This is a very significant step.[5] Whereas today we often read Aristotle's treatise as exploratory, dialectical, aporetic, and a work in progress, Alexander by contrast expects to find in it a science structured with the full rigor of what is stipulated for demonstrative science in Aristotle's *Posterior Analytics*. According to Alexander, therefore, metaphysics as a demonstrative science uses axioms, has a subject matter (a *hupokeimenon genos*); starting from definitions, it elaborates demonstrative syllogisms proving the essential properties of its object.[6]

Alexander identifies the axioms of metaphysics as those discussed by Aristotle in book 4—in particular the principle of noncontradiction—and takes it that these foundational axioms are the concern of metaphysics since they have to do with all being, and metaphysics deals with all being.[7] The subject matter, the *hupokeimenon genos,* of metaphysics is thus all being, or being as being. However, the genus of being at issue is not a genus of the type that subsumes coordinate species. Rather it is a kind of genus constituted by beings that are beings as relating to a central kind of being—as coming from it and relating to it—the relation of *aph'henos, pros hen.* Thus beings form the genus of being as relating to a central type of being, that of substance.[8]

This relation is both definitional and existential: the senses of being other than substance logically presuppose that of substance; and other beings, that is, beings in categories other than substance, derive their

---

4. Alexander, *In Aristotelis metaphysica commentaria,* ed. Hayduck, 15:32–33; 18:10–11; 171:5–11.

5. It has been brought out by Maddalena Bonelli, *Alessandro di Afrodisia e la metafisica come scienza dimostrativa* (Naples: Bibliopolis, 2001). In the following I refer to Bonelli's study, in which the relevant passages of Alexander's commentary are fully and carefully discussed.

6. Ibid., ch. 2.   7. Ibid., 249–50.

8. Ibid., 122.

existence (*huparxis*) from substance.[9] There is, furthermore, a hierarchy of substances such that higher primary substances are the causes of the existence of lower secondary substances. And primary substances are being in its primary and most intense form. This primary substance is Aristotelian divine substance, the transcendent Intellect of book 12.[10] (Unfortunately, it is not clear how divine substance, in Alexander's view, is the cause of the existence of the lower members of the genus of being, of lower substances, and of being in the other categories). Finally, Alexander identifies the essential properties demonstrated by metaphysics as those of which Aristotle speaks in book 4: unity/multiplicity, sameness/difference, the equal/the unequal.

From what has been said above, it would seem to be the case that Alexander takes a distinctive and very influential position on a central problem concerning the subject matter of metaphysics, on which Aristotle himself seems unclear, namely, whether metaphysics is a universal science dealing with being as being, a sort of general ontology; or whether it is a specialized science dealing with divine being, divine substance, a philosophical theology. Alexander's position would be that being is not a genus in the ordinary sense, subsuming species, but rather constitutes a series of prior and posterior terms in which the primary term is the cause of being for the terms that follow it and is that to which they refer.[11] And this primary term is divine substance, cause of the being of all other members of the genus of being. Thus the science of divine substance *is* the science of all being insofar as it is the science of being in its primary form, which is the cause of all secondary sorts of being.[12]

Yet Maddalena Bonelli—in her excellent book in which she brings out so well the way in which Alexander uses Aristotle's *Posterior Analytics* to formalize Aristotelian metaphysics—suggests that Alexander leaves the issue open, sometimes distinguishing the universal science of being from theology, sometimes identifying the two.[13] Still, I do not see how Alexander, who thinks of the genus of being as a series of prior and posterior terms, could hold that there could be a science of being in gen-

---

9. Ibid., 116–17, 120–21.

10. Alexander, *In Aristotelis metaphysica commentaria*, ed. Hayduck, 138:17–23; 147:3–148:10).

11. Ibid., 249:28–33.

12. Ibid., 251:24–38 and the references given in note 10.

13. Bonelli, *Alessandro di Afrodisia*, ch. 5, esp. 232–33.

eral subsuming specialized sciences of species of being. For being is not, for Alexander, a genus that subsumes species, and so the corresponding sciences will not be a universal science subsuming specialized sciences. On this point I find myself in agreement with Verbeke's interpretation as he presented it already in 1978.[14]

PLATONIZING ARISTOTELIAN METAPHYSICAL SCIENCE

Let us change schools and visit the Platonists of late antiquity. Here Plato's dialogues form the authoritative canon. Yet Aristotle is by no means absent from the curriculum. If we frequent, a little later, in the mid third century, Plotinus's school in Rome, we will find him reading and using Aristotle's *Metaphysics* and Alexander of Aphrodisias's commentaries.[15] Aristotle was also discussed by Plotinus's pupil Porphyry and by Porphyry's pupil Iamblichus. Iamblichus, who headed a philosophical school in Syria in the early fourth century, seems to have inspired the elaborate curriculum that would be followed in the Platonist schools of Athens and of Alexandria in the fifth and sixth centuries.

This curriculum consisted of two cycles. The first cycle, described as the "minor mysteries," was based on a reading of texts by Aristotle; it was followed by the second cycle, the "major mysteries," which involved study of selected dialogues of Plato.[16] We have a description of this curriculum as the young Proclus experienced it in Athens in 432 under the direction of the head of the Athenian school at the time, Syrianus.[17] In the first cycle, Proclus read Aristotle's works in logic, ethics, politics, physics, and metaphysics. Then Proclus moved on to the second cycle, to the study of Platonic dialogues arranged according to the same series of sciences.

We should note here two aspects of this curriculum. (1) The series of sciences is regarded as an ascending scale of philosophical knowledge, starting from practical knowledge and ending with the highest theoretical knowledge, metaphysics. This highest knowledge constituted the

14. Verbeke, "Aristotle's Metaphysics," 121. See Alexander, *In Aristotelis metaphysica commentaria*, ed. Hayduck, 250:20–33; 266:5–14.

15. Porphyry, *Vita Plotini*, ch. 14:5–7 and 13.

16. On this curriculum cf. Leendert Gerrit Westerink, Jean Trouillard, and Alain-Philippe Segonds, *Prolégomènes à la philosophie de Platon* (Paris: Les Belles Lettres, 1990), 43–76.

17. Marinus, *Vita Procli*, ch. 13.

goal of the curriculum and of philosophy itself, as bringing the human soul nearer to divine life. (2) The first Aristotelian cycle, in ascending the scale of knowledge, remained preliminary, preparatory, and imperfect with regard to the second, Platonic cycle. What this means, as regards Aristotle's metaphysical treatise, is that it constituted the highest level of knowledge, as corresponding to the summit reached in the first cycle. Yet it was merely preparatory and imperfect in comparison with the Platonic dialogue regarded as representing metaphysics at the summit of the second, Platonic cycle, Plato's *Parmenides*. There were thus good reasons for Platonists of the fifth and sixth centuries to take an interest in Aristotle's metaphysical treatise. Yet this treatise, considered as containing the highest theoretical knowledge, was seen as an imperfect foreshadowing of Plato's *Parmenides*.

As luck would have it, we can still read Syrianus's commentary on Aristotle's *Metaphysics,* and so we can have an impression of the way in which he presented it to his young pupil Proclus.[18] On closer inspection, however, we notice that Syrianus's commentary is not really a commentary at all, in the ordinary sense. Syrianus comments on books 3, 4, 13, and 14 of Aristotle's treatise and explains his purpose as follows.[19] In books 13 and 14 Aristotle is essentially concerned with criticizing Platonic and Pythagorean metaphysics. It is Syrianus's purpose to refute these criticisms so that the pupil will not end up having contempt for Platonic/Pythagorean metaphysics. In book 3 Aristotle presents and argues for conflicting positions on various metaphysical issues; Syrianus wishes to show which positions are correct and which are incorrect, the correct ones being those of the Platonist. And finally, in book 4, Aristotle presents a general account of metaphysics that Syrianus on the whole accepts: he will therefore content himself with a paraphrase of the text, referring the pupil to Alexander of Aphrodisias's commentary for detailed explanation of particular passages. Thus, for commentary on Aristotle's work, the pupil is referred to Alexander.[20] But since the pupil is to be led

18. Syrianus, *In metaphysica commentaria,* ed. Wilhelm Kroll (Berlin: Reimer 1902); an English translation has been published by John Dillon and Dominic O'Meara (London: Duckworth, 2006 and 2008).

19. On what follows, see my introduction to the translation of Syrianus's commentary on 3–4 (London: Duckworth, 2008), 3–5, where references are collected.

20. A useful philological study of Syrianus's use of Alexander's commentary can be found

in the direction of Platonic metaphysics, he will need Syrianus's work as an antidote to the criticisms of Platonism that come up in Aristotle and in Alexander's texts.

The implications of this use of Aristotle and Alexander in Syrianus's teaching are considerable. We may think that Aristotle and Alexander are simply being instrumentalized, made subservient to Platonist interests. But what in fact happens, as we can see in Syrianus's commentary, is that Syrianus takes over Alexander's interpretation of Aristotelian metaphysical science and uses it to interpret Plato. Thus Syrianus thinks that the highest science of which Plato speaks in the *Republic*—the knowledge of Forms and of the Form of the Good that Plato calls "dialectic"—is the same as Aristotelian wisdom, first philosophy, or theology.[21] And hence he assumes that Alexander's formalization of Aristotelian metaphysics applies to Platonic metaphysics, or dialectic. As a consequence, in Syrianus Platonic metaphysics is a demonstrative science of the type stipulated in Aristotle's *Posterior Analytics*. It is definitory and demonstrative. To these methods Syrianus adds the Platonic methods of analysis and division.[22]

Metaphysics, furthermore, deals with universal axioms, in particular with the principle of noncontradiction.[23] It concerns an underlying genus, that of being as being. But this genus is of a special type: it constitutes a series of prior and posterior beings such that primary being (divine substance) is the highest form of being and is the cause of the existence of derivative kinds of being.[24] Divine being, for Syrianus, corresponds to the transcendent Platonic Forms, which are the thought of a divine Intellect responsible for the making of the world, a divine Intellect that recalls Aristotle's divine intellect. Insofar as metaphysics deals with divine being, it is *also* a science of all being.[25]

Finally, for Syrianus, metaphysics demonstrates the essential properties of being, which include both those mentioned by Aristotle and the

in Concetta Luna, *Trois études sur la tradition des commentaires anciens à la Métaphysique d'Aristote* (Leiden: Brill, 2001).

21. Syrianus, *In metaphysica commentaria*, ed. Kroll, 55:27–33.

22. Ibid., 3:30; 4:26–29; 12:10–12.

23. See my study, "Le Fondement du principe de non-contradiction chez Syrianus," in *Syrianus et la métaphysique de l'Antiquité tardive*, ed. Angela Longo (Naples: Bibliopolis, 2009).

24. Syrianus, *In metaphysica commentaria*, ed. Kroll, 57:23–24; 61:19–24.

25. Ibid., 57:29–30.

major kinds mentioned in Plato's *Sophist*, in particular rest and motion.[26] In a very curious way, then, Alexander's formalization of Aristotelian metaphysics, in entering the curriculum of Syrianus's school, showed the way to formalizing a new Platonic metaphysical science, which Syrianus supposed to be imperfectly present in Aristotle's metaphysical treatise and fully developed in Plato's *Parmenides*.

However, although the fit between Alexander's formalization of metaphysical science, as a science of divine substance, and Plato's dialectic, as a science of the transcendent Forms, seemed so good, Syrianus was aware of a major difficulty that Theophrastus had already formulated in connection with Aristotle's metaphysics: how is knowledge of transcendent divine being possible?[27] This difficulty is made more intense for Syrianus by a conflict in his thought. On the one hand, there is his Platonist conviction that divine Intellect and its object of thought (the Forms) transcend the limits of human discursive reasoning;[28] on the other hand, there is his adoption of Alexander's formalization of metaphysics, which makes of it an eminently discursive science. The fundamental question then is this: how can there be a human science of realities that transcend the level of objects knowable by human science?

The solution to this difficulty that we can find in Syrianus's commentary on Aristotle's *Metaphysics* can be summarized as follows.[29] According to Plato's *Timaeus*, the divine Intellect (or demiurge) that makes the world also makes souls, both world-soul and individual souls, composing them from certain formal principles, in particular from mathematical laws.[30] If then the human soul does mathematics, it discovers in its very nature an innate knowledge of mathematical laws, which it articulates in mathematical demonstrations. And these mathematical laws correspond to the laws of the universe, since they are also what are followed in the divine Intellect's ordering of the world.[31] The items of innate knowledge in human soul (named "substantial *logoi*" by Syrianus)[32] include mathemati-

---

26. Ibid., 5:16–33.

27. Theophrastus, *Metaphysics*, ed. André Laks and Glenn Most (Paris: Les Belles Lettres, 2002), 4 (4b); 25 (9b).

28. Syrianus, *In metaphysica commentaria*, ed. Kroll, 4:34–37; 100:28–29; 147:14–15.

29. See my article cited above, n. 1.

30. Syrianus, *In metaphysica commentaria*, ed. Kroll, 4:5–11.

31. Ibid., 27:31–37; 88:24–27.

32. Ibid., 91:29–34; 161:30–34.

cal laws and are themselves images both of their creator—the divine Intellect—and its object of thought—the transcendent Forms.

Thus human soul has access, through its innate knowledge, to images of divine Intellect and the Forms. Consequently, in developing scientific knowledge, such as pure mathematics, the human soul is projecting images of transcendent divine being. Thus there can be scientific, discursive knowledge of divine being in the sense that there can be scientific articulation of innate concepts that image this being.[33] Consequently, metaphysics, as an eminently discursive, scientific form of knowledge, does not directly think transcendent being, which escapes discursive knowledge; rather, it works with innate knowledge in the soul, namely with concepts that can be articulated and that express, as images, this transcendent being. In this way there can be science of what is beyond science.[34]

We will not, however, find in Syrianus's commentary on Aristotle's *Metaphysics* an exposé of this Platonized Aristotelian metaphysical science. For, as we have seen, Syrianus is concerned mostly with refuting Aristotelian criticisms of Platonism. Syrianus presupposes a canon of Pythagorean and Platonic texts in which he assumes this metaphysical science is to be found. But he does not himself give an exposé of this science. To judge from the curriculum he followed, we would imagine that the best place to find this science would be Plato's *Parmenides*. However, we do not have access to a commentary by Syrianus on the *Parmenides*.

UNFOLDING METAPHYSICAL SCIENCE

But we can turn to the work of Syrianus's last and most important pupil, who had studied Aristotle's *Metaphysics* with him, namely, Proclus. We

33. I have attempted to examine in what sense concepts "image" transcendent being in "Intentional Objects in Later Neoplatonism," in *Ancient and Medieval Theories of Intentionality*, ed. Dominik Perler (Leiden: Brill, 2001), 115–25.

34. One might wonder whether Syrianus himself developed his conception of metaphysical science as the discursive articulation of innate concepts imaging transcendent being, or whether he inherited this conception—for example, from Iamblichus. In the absence of adequate information about Iamblichus, it is difficult to be sure about this. However, the theory of mathematical science that seems to play an important role in this context appears to go back to Iamblichus (cf. Anne Sheppard, "*Phantasia* and Mathematical Projection in Iamblichus," *Syllecta Classica* 8 [1997]: 113–20; Dominic O'Meara, *Pythagoras Revived. Mathematics and Philosophy in Late Antiquity* [Oxford: Clarendon Press, 1989], 133–34). It is thus not unlikely that Syrianus's conception of metaphysics also goes back to Iamblichus.

still have access to a commentary by Proclus on Plato's *Parmenides*. And we also have an enormous work of his having the title *Platonic Theology*. But I would like to suggest that to find a presentation of metaphysical science elaborated along the lines suggested by Syrianus's adaptation of Alexander's formalization of Aristotle, we should turn to Proclus's *Elements of Theology*.[35] This work had considerable success in medieval philosophy: there are medieval Arabic, Latin, and Georgian versions of it. And it is often the first work of Proclus to be read today. I would like to show now that it presents us with metaphysical science as it was conceived by Syrianus. But first perhaps a few preliminary words are needed about Proclus's book.

The title of the book refers to "theology"—theology understood here in its Aristotelian sense, as indicating the science of divine substance. Indeed Syrianus refers to Aristotle's metaphysical work as a "theological treatise."[36] The word "elements" in the title of Proclus's text suggests that it is a manual for the use of students, evoking also more specifically Euclid's *Elements*. The Euclidean echo has led some scholars to describe Proclus's book as being a metaphysics demonstrated *more geometrico*. But in fact a quick glance shows that the work does not have a Euclidean form:[37] it does not open with a list of definitions, common notions, and axioms, as does Euclid's *Elements*. Instead, it consists of a chain of demonstrations proving conclusions, each of which is also placed at the head of its corresponding demonstration. If the work has a mathematical or geometrical air to it, this may be because mathematical science is a fundamental inspiration to the concepts of scientific knowledge developed by Aristotle and by Syrianus. Finally—and this is really exceptional— no ancient authority is cited in the text; there is no appeal to quotations taken from Plato and Aristotle. However, in his edition, E. R. Dodds has shown that there is an implicit presence of Plato's *Parmenides* in the text, of which we will see an example shortly.

Looking now more closely at Proclus's *Elements of Theology*, I would

35. Proclus, *Elements of Theology*, ed. with English translation by E. R. Dodds (Oxford: Clarendon Press, 1963); Proclus's commentary on the *Parmenides* was recently published in a new edition by Carlos Steel (*Procli in Platonis Parmenidem commentaria* [Oxford: Oxford University Press, 2007–2009]) and has been translated by Glenn R. Morrow and John M. Dillon (*Proclus' Commentary on Plato's "Parmenides"* [Princeton, N.J.: Princeton University Press, 1987]).

36. Syrianus, *In metaphysica commentaria*, ed. Kroll, 80:17.

37. See my discussion in *Pythagoras Revived*, 196–98.

like to show that this text is indeed an exposé of metaphysical science as Syrianus conceived it. To do this I need to show that it exhibits certain features. It should articulate innate concepts concerning transcendent realities; it should use axioms; it should develop demonstrations; it should have to do both with divine realities as the causes of being and with being in general; and it should deal with essential properties of being.

It is not hard to see that some of these features do in fact characterize Proclus's text. We are indeed dealing in it with the realm of the divine, which, for the Platonist, goes from the first cause of all things—the One—through Intellect, and down to soul.[38] In dealing with these divine realities, Proclus is also speaking of the causes of being. And a number of the propositions that are formulated are of a generality that covers all being (for example proposition 1: "All multiplicity in some way participates unity"). Certain essential properties of being are examined, in particular unity and multiplicity. We can also see that conclusions are established on the bases of rigorous demonstrative arguments, and that the conclusions of some arguments are then used as premises in arguments establishing further conclusions, the whole making an impressive demonstrative chain that mirrors the constitutive chain of being.

We can also detect the use of axioms in the demonstrations. For example, the demonstration of proposition 1, which consists in the refutation of its negation (*modus tollens*), rests ultimately on two axioms to which Proclus appeals at the end of the demonstration: that the whole is greater than the part, and that nothing comes from nothing.[39] But is this demonstrative science, as presented in Proclus's *Elements of Theology,* a scientific articulation, not of transcendent beings, but of our innate concepts about these beings, as this is required by Syrianus's explanation of the possibility of metaphysical science as he conceives it? This feature of Syrianus's conception of metaphysical science is perhaps less obviously present in Proclus's book, but I would like to suggest that it is indeed there.

For this purpose, however, we need to refer first to a passage in another work by Proclus, his *Platonic Theology.* There, in book 2, chapter 12, we find the following passage:

38. Proclus, *Théologie platonicienne,* I, 26, ed. Henri Dominique Saffrey and Leendert Gerrit Westerink (Paris: Les Belles Lettres, 1968–97), 1.114:23–116:3.
39. Proclus, *Elements of Theology,* prop. 1, ed. Dodds, 2:11–13).

What then would be the very first concept [*noêma*] of the science [i.e., "theology"] which proceeds from [divine] Intellect and reveals itself? What other concept would we say it is but that which is the most simple and most knowable of the concepts in this science? For this concept is also what is most especially like the knowledge in Intellect. What is it then? "The One," Parmenides says, "if it is one, would not be many." For the many necessarily participate the One, but the One does not participate the One, but is the One itself.[40]

Proclus here asks what the absolutely primary concept (*noêma*) of theology is, and finds it in a proposition he takes from Plato's *Parmenides:* "That the one, if it is one, would not be many" (137c4–5). This quotation comes from the first hypothesis of the second part of the *Parmenides,* which Platonists in late antiquity read as referring to the highest metaphysical principle—the cause of all being, the One. We note that the concept is expressed as a proposition and that, according to Proclus, it is the first concept of theology.

If we come back now to Proclus's *Elements of Theology,* we find in proposition 1 that all multiplicity is unified in some way, and in proposition 4 that all that which is unified (i.e., all multiplicity) is other than the One as one. In other words, proposition 4 turns out to be equivalent to the first concept of theology as specified in Proclus's *Platonic Theology.* We can see in this way that the conclusions of the demonstrations in the *Elements of Theology,* which appear as propositions at the head of their respective demonstrations, are in fact concepts—concepts that are expressed as propositions about beings. Proposition 4, which distinguishes all unified multiplicities from what is one in itself, is introduced on the basis of the preceding three propositions. This fourth one marks an important stage in the argument since it separates out unified multiplicities from that which unifies them and which itself, ultimately, cannot be a unified multiplicity but must be a one in itself. We thus reach the claim that all reality, as unified multiplicity, depends in its being on a prior cause of its unity—a cause that is not a unified entity, but a pure transcendent One. Proclus can then develop a series of arguments that concern the way in which the various levels of beings derive from a very first principle, the transcendent One.

I conclude that in Proclus's *Elements of Theology* we have an exposé

40. Proclus, *Théologie platonicienne,* II, 22, ed. Saffrey and Westerink, 2.66:4–9.

of metaphysical science as this science was conceived by Syrianus and inspired by Alexander of Aphrodisias's reading of Aristotle. This metaphysical science is not a direct knowledge of transcendent being, but a discursive articulation of innate concepts that yield propositions about transcendent being.[41] One can also sense that the philosopher might wish to use this discursive knowledge to go beyond it to reach, in a mode of knowledge beyond that of scientific discursivity, divine being itself.

In this connection it might be appropriate to recall the suggestion in Plato's *Parmenides* (135d–136a) that the second part of the dialogue is intended as an exercise for the young, inexperienced Socrates. Proclus takes up this idea in his commentary on the *Parmenides,* and Syrianus describes the conflicting arguments of book 3 of Aristotle's *Metaphysics* as exercises. As a manual, Proclus's *Elements of Theology* can also, I believe, be considered an exercise in metaphysical thinking.[42] It is not the last word in metaphysical knowledge, but a stage leading ultimately, we can suppose, to a grasp of divine being transcending discursivity.

TRANSCENDING METAPHYSICAL SCIENCE

The last part of this paper concerns the last head of the Platonist school of Athens, Damascius, who, less than half a century after Proclus's death, was obliged by the emperor Justinian's anti-pagan policies to leave Athens in the early 530s and exile himself with other philosophers in Persia. As regards our present concerns, we can still consult two works of Damascius: a commentary on Plato's *Parmenides* and a *Treatise on First Principles* whose full title is *Puzzles and Solutions Concerning the First Principles.*[43]

This latter work is very remarkable. It proposes, with reference to the

41. See also Proclus, *Procli in Platonis Parmenidem commentaria,* ed. Steel, 895:24–896:17; 981:20–982:30; 986:7–29.

42. Cf. Dominic O'Meara, "La Science métaphysique (ou théologie) de Proclus comme exercice spirituel," in *Proclus et la Théologie Platonicienne,* ed. Alain-Philippe Segonds and Carlos Steel (Paris: Les Belles Lettres, 2000), 279–90; for Syrianus see my introduction (8) to the English translation of Syrianus's commentary on 3–4.

43. The latter work is published under the title *Traité des premiers principes* (hereafter *Puzzles*) with a French translation by Leendert G. Westerink and Joseph Combès (Paris: Les Belles Lettres, 1986–91). Damascius's commentary on the *Parmenides* has also been edited and translated by Westerink and Combès as *Commentaire du Parménide de Platon* (Paris: Les Belles Lettres, 1997–2003).

first principles or causes of reality, that is, the subject matter of metaphysics, an elaborate panorama of difficulties and contradictions in the various claims we make about such principles. It may seem, on reading this book, that anything that is said about such first principles is subject to contradiction and that nothing firm remains. In contrast to the clear and straight path traced by Proclus's *Elements of Theology* through metaphysical questions, Damascius's work appears as a sea of uncertainty, conflicting positions, confusion, doldrums, with no clear direction and no horizon.[44] This impression given by Damascius's work has led some scholars to find in it an expression of despair regarding the declining and darkening world of the pagan intellectual, who could find little room to breathe in Justinian's Christianized empire.

More philosophically, we can notice that the conflicting arguments developed by Damascius (one argument overturning another) recall the conflicting arguments orchestrated by the philosophical skeptic who finds himself obliged in consequence to suspend judgment. Is this where Damascius is going? Metaphysics, pushed hard enough in its contradictions, destroys itself and becomes skepticism? Or, to use an image Damascius himself exploits, are we, in metaphysics, walking in the void?[45] Is not purely theoretical, conceptual rumination, devoid of any empirical grounding, destined to come to nothing? However, none of these judgments concerning the meaning of Damascius's approach correspond to the way in which Damascius himself understands his enterprise.[46] I would like to show this after having given first an example of the aporetic, conflicting arguments presented in this extraordinary book.

At the beginning of his book, Damascius discusses the very first metaphysical principle, the One, in terms of the concepts of part and whole—concepts exploited already in what was supposed to be the corresponding part of Plato's *Parmenides*. Damascius argues that the One is (1) part of a whole and (2) not part of a whole. Let us take first claim

44. Damascius's treatise has been discussed, for example, by Alessandro Linguiti, *L'Ultimo Platonismo greco. Principi e conoscenza* (Florence: Olschki, 1990), and by Sara Rappe, *Reading Neoplatonism: Non-discursive Thinking in the Texts of Plotinus, Proclus and Damascius* (Cambridge: Cambridge University Press, 2000), ch. 9. Cf. Valerio Napoli, *Epekeina tou henos. Il principio totalmente ineffabille tra dialettica ed esegesi in Damascio* (Catania, Italy: CUECM, 2008).

45. For example, Damascius, *Puzzles*, ed. Westerink-Combès, 8:1.

46. This point has been argued in detail by Carole Tresson, "L'Aporie ou l'expérience métaphysique de la dualité dans le Peri Archôn de Damascius" (PhD diss., University of Fribourg, 2009).

(1) that the One is part of a whole. The concept of the "whole" can be defined in various ways. For example, by "whole" we may mean that which lacks nothing. Or "whole" may mean the order of causes and effects. Or "whole" may mean all of that which can be thought.[47] On any of these accounts of the whole, it is clear that the One is part of a whole. Now let us take the contradictory claim, (2) that the One is not part of a whole. Damascius shows this by arguing that if the whole is a series of causes and effects, these causes and effects are coordinated as a series. But if the very first principle, the One, is the cause of everything, then it will be the cause of the coordinated series as a whole and, therefore, cannot be a member of the series. So it is not part of the whole.[48] Damascius then, shortly after, goes on to argue that the One is one, and not one. It is one as the primary degree of unity in the series of things that are unified multiplicities, and it is not one as not being a member of the series.[49]

But how does Damascius himself understand these contradictions through which he brings his reader? What does he think is going on in these difficulties? A number of times, Damascius refers to the Socratic image of the pains associated with giving birth, the labor pains of a soul trying to give birth to the knowledge within it.[50] So too do we suffer in trying to bring out in our thinking the One within us. In trying to articulate in our thought (in our concepts and reasonings) and in our discourse what cannot be so known and said, we lose it in what comes from it. And yet we want to find it, to return to it. Projecting the unknowable onto the level of the knowable, we both distance ourselves from the unknowable and, yet, are seeking a way to return to it.

The labor pains from which we suffer are the difficulties, the puzzles, the contradictions that arise as we reason from our concepts about the unknowable.[51] And at the same time they are the way in which we can

47. Damascius, *Puzzles*, ed. Westerink-Combès, 1:9–2:6.
48. Ibid., 2:9–18.
49. Ibid., 4:1–12.
50. See, for example, ibid., 86, 10–16, and Tresson, "L'Aporie ou l'expérience métaphysique de la dualité dans le Peri Archôn de Damascius," ch. 7.
51. Damascius indicates fairly frequently that his critical analysis concerns the *concepts* (*ennoia, epinoia*) we use in thinking about the transcendent. See, for example, *Puzzles*, ed. Westerink-Combès, 2:5 and 19; 4:14; 6:9; 7:18–21. He thus works in the context of the conception of metaphysical science we have found in Syrianus. I believe that the anonymous commentary on the *Parmenides*, which has been attributed by Pierre Hadot to Porphyry, presupposes the theory of metaphysics as the discursive articulation of concepts (see *Commentarium*

think discursively about the unknowable. What Damascius is offering us then is an exercise[52] in discursive reasoning about metaphysical principles that reveals the limits, the inadequacy of such reasoning in relation to the transcendent, while being the means to discover this transcendent within and beyond our thinking about it.[53]

Damascius thus shows the limits of metaphysical science and, in pushing it to its limits, shows how it can impel the reasoning soul beyond itself toward the transcendent. Far from being a work of despair—a confession of the ultimate failure of Greek metaphysics—Damascius's work is the crowning achievement of the development of metaphysical science, a development that started with Alexander of Aphrodisias and continued with Syrianus and Proclus.

In adapting Alexander's formalization of Aristotelian metaphysical science to Platonism, Syrianus knew that such a science was a means toward, not the equivalent of, knowledge of the transcendent. Proclus knew it too, even if his *Elements of Theology,* in presenting metaphysical science with such systematic beauty, could give the impression of being a definitive statement. And, lest we have any illusions about the adequacy of our metaphysical science, Damascius could cure us of these, opening our minds to what lay behind, or above, our own metaphysical efforts.

---

in Platonis "Parmenidem," ed. Alessandro Linguiti [Florence: Olschki, 1995], I, 25–30; II, 1–4, 13, 20; IV, 17; VI, 23–26; IX, 11–20) that we find in Syrianus and Damascius and, thus, that it should be dated rather later, to the fourth or fifth century. But this suggestion requires a separate investigation.

52. Damascius, *Puzzles,* ed. Westerink-Combès, 82:10.

53. Ibid., 8:12–20. For indications of how the critique of metaphysical concepts can become a means for going beyond them, see Carole Tresson and Alain Metry, "Damaskios' New Conception of Metaphysics," in *History of Platonism: Plato Redivivus,* ed. Robert Berchman and John Finamore (New Orleans: University Press of the South, 2005), 222–26.

Jan A. Aertsen

3 ✑ Why Is Metaphysics Called "First Philosophy" in the Middle Ages?

The idea of a "First Philosophy" presupposes a plurality of philosophies, among which an order exists. The discipline that claims the title *philosophia prima* pretends to precede all other philosophical disciplines, but in what sense is it "prior" and for what reason? Is it the first in rank because of the ontological dignity of its object, or is it prior to the other sciences for epistemic reasons?

In one of his essays, John F. Wippel calls attention to the interesting fact that Thomas Aquinas, in his accounts of metaphysics, identifies this science with "First Philosophy," but gives different reasons for this naming. In his commentary on the *De Trinitate* of Boethius, he states that metaphysics is called First Philosophy because "all the other sciences, deriving their principles from it, come after it." In the prologue of his commentary on Aristotle's *Metaphysics,* he maintains that this science is called First Philosophy, "insofar as it considers the first causes of things," which are identified as God and the intellectual substances.[1]

The variety of motives for this naming is striking; the fact is not unique to Aquinas but reflects a more general tendency, namely a distancing from the Aristotelian theological model. In my contribution, I want to show that medieval philosophy transformed the Aristotelian conception of First Philosophy and gave a new foundation to the primacy of the *philosophia prima*.

---

1. Thomas Aquinas, *Super Boetium De Trinitate* (hereafter *In De Trin.*), q. 5, a. 1 co., *Editio Leonina* 50.138:165–67: "Dicitur etiam philosophia prima, in quantum alie omnes scientie ab ea

ARISTOTLE AND THE IDEA OF A FIRST PHILOSOPHY

The idea of a First Philosophy and its presupposition, the plurality of philosophies, are Aristotle's legacy. The idea is introduced in the sixth book of the *Metaphysics* in the context of a comprehensive division of the philosophical disciplines. Aristotle wants to make plausible that besides physics and mathematics a third theoretical science is necessary. If there is something, he argues, that is eternal, immovable, and immaterial, the knowledge of it clearly belongs to a theoretical science—not, however, to physics or to mathematics, for those disciplines do not deal with such things—but to a science prior to both. This "first science" Aristotle calls "theology" since it is obvious that if the divine is present anywhere, it is present in what is immovable and immaterial; and the subject matter of the most dignified science must be the most dignified genus (*honorabilissimum genus*).[2]

This characterization of First Philosophy remains in the sixth book merely hypothetical ("*If* there is something immovable"); only in book 12 is it shown that there actually exists an unmovable, divine substance. In Aristotle's works the title "First Philosophy" marks his theological determination of metaphysics; this discipline is called "first" because it is the first in dignity, since it deals with the first and highest being.[3] It is to this idea that Aquinas is referring in his second explanation of the title "First Philosophy."

The medieval transformation of the idea of a First Philosophy is determined by two moments of tension in Aristotle's account. He himself advances a "doubt" as a kind of appendix to the theological determination of First Philosophy in book 6: one could wonder (*dubitabit*) whether

---

sua principia accipientes eam consequuntur." *In duodecim libros Metaphysicorum Aristotelis expositio*, Proemium, ed. M.-R. Cathala and R. Spiazzi (Turin: Marietti, 1950), 2: "Dicitur autem *prima philosophia*, inquantum primas rerum causas considerat." Cf. the chapter entitled "'First Philosophy' according to Thomas Aquinas" in John F. Wippel's *Metaphysical Themes in Thomas Aquinas* (Washington, D.C.: The Catholic University of America Press, 1984), 55–67.

2. Aristotle, *Metaphysics* VI, 1, 1026a 19–22. *Metaphysica. Lib. I–XIV. Recensio et Translatio Guillelmi de Moerbeka*, in *Aristoteles latinus*, ed. Gudrun Vuillemin-Diem (Leiden: Brill, 1995), 25.3.2.127: "Quare tres erunt philosophie theorice: mathematica, phisica, theologia. Non enim immanifestum quia si alicubi divinum existit, in tali natura existit; et honorabilissimam scientiam oportet circa honorabilissimum genus esse."

3. Cf. Augustin Mansion, "Philosophie première, philosophie seconde et métaphysique chez Aristote," *Revue philosophique de Louvain* 56 (1958): 165–221.

First Philosophy is universal, or whether it deals with some genus and one single nature.[4] Why this uncertainty urges itself, Aristotle does not say, but the dilemma of universality and particularity is a first coordinate in the medieval transformation of First Philosophy.

The beginning of his answer does not contain anything really new. If there is no other substance than those that are formed by nature, physics will be the first science; but if there is an immovable substance, the study of it must be prior and must be "first philosophy"—accordingly, Aristotle later designates (VII, 11, 1037a14–16) physics as "second philosophy." But he then adds that this science is "universal in this way, because it is first" (*universalis, quia prima*), and it belongs to it, "to consider being as being."[5]

Aristotle's additional remark relates "firstness" to universality and reacts to an unspoken problem in his division of philosophy into physics, mathematics, and theology. As *particular* disciplines, they cannot consider the principles and objects common to them, but rather they presuppose a first, architectonic philosophy with a *universal* pretension. For that reason Aristotle, at the end of his reply to the uncertainty noted above, refers back to the ontological conception of First Philosophy that he presents in the fourth book of the *Metaphysics*: the task of this science is the consideration of being as being.

The relationship between (ontological) universality and (theological) particularity remains unclear in Aristotle's understanding of metaphysics. Is the investigation of being in general the precondition for the consideration of divine being or, rather, its effect? Is First Philosophy distinguished from physics insofar as it deals with immovable being or insofar as it is a universal science? The great medieval commentators on the *Metaphysics*, like Albert the Great, Thomas Aquinas, and Duns Scotus, made an original contribution to the ongoing debate on the nature of this discipline by raising the question as to the "proper subject" of metaphysics. They applied to First Philosophy the notion from the *Posterior*

---

4. *Metaphysics* VI, 1, 1026a 22–25 (ed. Aristoteles latinus 3.2.127): "Dubitabit enim utique aliquis utrum prima philosophia sit universalis aut circa aliquod genus et naturam unam."

5. Ibid., 1026a 28–32 (ed. Aristoteles latinus 3.2.127): "Si quidem igitur non est aliqua altera substantia preter natura consistentes, phisica utique erit prima scientia. Sed si est aliqua substantia immobile, hec prior et philosophia prima, et universalis sic quia prima; et de ente in quantum ens huius utique erit speculari."

Analytics of the "subject of a science" as constituting the science's unity and its distinction from other sciences.

Another moment of tension in the Aristotelian tradition of First Philosophy is caused by the post-Aristotelian designation of this science by the name "metaphysics." This identification seems to question its status of being first, because the name "meta-physics," which was never conceived as a purely extrinsic denomination, was intended to express the ultimate character of this philosophy in the order of sciences. This designation corresponds with an important Aristotelian distinction in the dynamics of human knowledge.[6]

In several places in his writings, Aristotle distinguishes between what is prior and more knowable "in relation to us" (*quoad nos*) versus what is prior and more knowable "by nature" or "absolutely" (*simpliciter*).[7] What is prior and posterior in the order of human knowledge is inversely proportional to what is prior and posterior in the order of being. Material, natural things are prior in relation to us because human knowledge starts with sense perception; what is immaterial is posterior in relation to us, although it is ontologically prior to material being.

The Arab philosopher Avicenna explicitly applies this distinction to the name "metaphysics." The name signifies "that which is after nature" (*post naturam*)—meaning by "nature" the totality of material things—but Avicenna emphasizes that this "posteriority" is only relative to us since what we first observe is natural being. The name, however, that this discipline deserves if it is considered in itself, is the science of "what is before nature" (*ante naturam*), because the things investigated in this science are prior to nature on account of their essence and universality.[8]

---

6. Hans Reiner, "Die Entstehung und ursprüngliche Bedeutung des Namens Metaphysik," *Zeitschrift für philosophische Forschung* 8 (1954): 210–37.

7. The two main texts are *Posterior Analytics* I, 2, 71b 33–72a6 and *Physics* I, 1, 184a16ff.

8. Avicenna, *Liber de philosophia prima sive scientia divina* I, c. 3, in *Avicenna Latinus: Liber de philosophia prima sive scientia divina I–IV*, ed. Simone Van Riet (Louvain: Peeters and Leiden: E. J. Brill, 1977), 24–25: "Nomen vero huius scientiae est quod ipsa est de eo quod est post naturam. . . . Iam autem dictum est quod natura est corporis naturalis quod habet naturam. . . . Quod vero dicitur post naturam, hoc posteritas est in respectu quantum ad nos: primum enim quod de eo quod est et scimus eius dispositiones est hoc quod praesentatur nobis de hoc esse naturali. Unde quod meretur vocari haec scientia, considerata in se, hoc est ut dicatur quod est scientia de eo quod est ante naturam: ea enim de quibus inquiritur in hac scientia per essentiam et per scientiam sunt ante naturam." Olga Lizzini, "Utility and Gratuitousness of Metaphysics: Avicenna, *Ilāhiyyāt* I, 3," *Quaestio* 5 (2005): 307–44.

First Philosophy is "metaphysics," because it is last in the order of human knowledge; it is first, because it really is "antephysics." The epistemological differentiation of what is first appears to be the second coordinate in the medieval transformation of the idea of a First Philosophy.

AVICENNA AND THE DOCTRINE OF THAT WHICH IS FIRST KNOWN

Directive of this transformation are two innovative doctrines of Avicenna in his work *De philosophia prima sive scientia divina,* which is not a commentary on Aristotle's *Metaphysics* but, rather, an independent and systematic account.[9]

The text from Avicenna's *Metaphysics* that is probably most frequently cited in the Middle Ages is his exposition of the primary notions of the intellect (in the first treatise). These notions, he states, are "impressed immediately in the soul by a first impression (*prima impressio*) and are not acquired from other and better known notions."[10] Why, we might ask, is it necessary to accept such notions? Avicenna's argument rests on an analogy between two orders of knowledge: the order of demonstrable propositions and that of concepts. Just as in the order of demonstration a reduction must take place to first principles, known through themselves (*per se*), so, too, in the conceptual order such a reduction must occur. In his argument the first member of the analogy is meant to elucidate the other member, because the order of demonstration is the better known; it takes for granted Aristotle's analysis of scientific knowledge in his *Posterior Analytics.*

Scientia is grounded knowledge, knowledge on the basis of demonstration; consequently, science is always derived knowledge insofar as the conclusion is inferred from something prior. This structure, however, raises the problem of the ultimate foundation of science, for an ongoing "resolution" or "reduction" to something prior would lead to an infinite regress. Aristotle recognizes that an infinite regress is impossible; the re-

---

9. Amos Bertolacci, *The Reception of Aristotle's* Metaphysics *in Avicenna's* Kitāb al-Sifā': *A Milestone of Western Metaphysical Thought,* Islamic Philosophy, Theology, and Science. Texts and Studies 63 (Leiden: E. J. Brill, 2006).

10. Avicenna, *Liber de philosophia prima* I, c. 5 (ed. Van Riet 31–32): "Dicemus igitur quod res et ens et necesse talia sunt quod statim imprimuntur in anima prima impressione, quae non acquiritur ex aliis notioribus se."

duction must stop and end in a first principle that is not derived from something else, but is immediately known.[11]

Avicenna's originality consists in the transfer of the finite structure of demonstrative knowledge (*scientia*) to the order of concepts as well. For the Arab philosopher, it is a logical complement of the Aristotelian analysis that the impossibility of an infinite regress and the reduction to a first likewise holds for the order of concepts: there must be primary notions that are not acquired from something prior, but are conceived *per se*. Such are notions that are common to all things (*communia omnibus rebus*) and, thus, are not reducible to something more general—notions such as "thing" (*res*), "being" (*ens*), and "one" (*unum*).[12]

Avicenna's doctrine of the primary notions realizes the philosophical ideal of a systematic beginning of human thought—the search for a first that is the condition of all further knowledge. This aspect may explain the strong impact of this doctrine on Latin philosophy. Medieval authors incorporated it in their accounts of the *transcendentia,* the notions that transcend the Aristotelian categories because of their commonness; an essential mark of the transcendentals is their cognitive priority. Thomas Aquinas (in *De veritate* q. 1, a. 1) and Henry of Ghent (in the *Summa* a. 34, q. 3) start their expositions with the Avicennian analogy between the two orders of intellectual knowledge and the reduction to a first that is known *per se* and, therefore, is *notissimum*. Henry of Ghent concludes that *secundum Avicennam* and *secundum rei veritatem*, there are primary notions without which nothing is known or understood.[13]

Avicenna starts his *Metaphysics* (tr. I, ch. 1) with a critical inquiry into the "subject" of this science. "It is certain that every science possesses its proper subject (*subiectum proprium*)," but in the case of First Phi-

---

11. Aristotle, *Post. Anal.* I, c. 3.

12. Avicenna, *Liber de philosophia prima* I, c. 5 (ed. Van Riet 33): "Quae autem promptiora sunt ad imaginandum per seipsa, sunt ea quae communia sunt omnibus rebus, sicut res et ens et unum, et cetera."

13. Henry of Ghent uses the expression *"secundum Avicennam et secundum rei veritatem"* in the *Summa quaestionum ordinarium* (hereafter *Summa*), a. 22, q. 5 (ed. Paris 1520, fol. 134vD) and a. 25, q. 3 (156rS). Cf. ibid., a. 24, q. 7 (ed. Paris 1520, fol. 144rH): "Nihil enim talium cognoscitur in creatura aut intelligitur ut tale nisi prius cognoscendo ei intelligendo ipsum sub intentione entis et unius et caeterarum primarum intentionum, ut quod sit ens aut unum, quae necessario prima impressione saltem prioritate naturae concipiuntur de quolibet antequam concipitur aliquid eorum quia album aut quia homo." See Jan A. Aertsen, "What Is First and Most Fundamental? The Beginnings of Transcendental Philosophy," in *Was ist Philosophie im Mittelalter?,* ed. Jan A. Aertsen and Andreas Speer (Berlin: Walter De Gruyter, 1998), 305–21.

losophy it is not evident what this subject is.[14] The Arab philosopher was the first to apply logically the notion *subiectum* (*scientiae*) from the Aristotelian theory of science to this discipline and to raise the question as to the subject of metaphysics, which would become the "basic question" for medieval commentators.

Avicenna argues that the proper subject of this science is not God but being-as-being. He dismisses the theological understanding of metaphysics that had prevailed among the commentators in late antiquity, who interpreted First Philosophy as the science of that which is "beyond [*epekeina*] the physical" or "above [*hyper*] nature."[15] Avicenna upholds an ontological conception; the distinctive feature of this science is its "commonness." In the determination of First Philosophy, the focus moves from particularity toward universality.

Avicenna did not explicitly link the new conception of metaphysics with his doctrine of the primary notions of the intellect, but the connection of both teachings determined the medieval transformation of First Philosophy. Its first coordinate is the rejection of the theological interpretation in favor of a universalistic ontology—converged with the epistemological coordinate of what is first known, especially because medieval authors modified Avicenna's doctrine of the first concepts in a certain respect.

Whereas the Arabic philosopher names a plurality of such notions, most medieval thinkers attribute a priority to "being" (*ens*): it is the *primum intelligibile*. Thomas Aquinas, for instance, asserts: "That which the intellect first conceives, as best known, and into which it resolves all its conceptions, is 'being,' as Avicenna says at the beginning of his *Metaphysics*."[16] Although Thomas supports this claim by a reference to Avicenna, in fact he modifies his exposition. Henry of Ghent identifies that which is first known as *ens inquantum ens,* the traditional expression for

14. Avicenna, *Liber de philosophia prima* I, c. 1 (ed. Van Riet 4): "Constat autem quod omnis scientia habet subiectum suum proprium. Inquiramus ergo quid sit subiectum huius scientiae."

15. Klaus Kremer, *Der Metaphysikbegriff in den Aristoteles-Kommentaren der Ammonius-Schule,* Beiträge zur Geschichte der Philosophie und Theologie des Mittelalters, Band 39, Heft 1 (Münster: Aschendorff, 1961). Cf. Carlos Steel, "Theology as First Philosophy. The Neoplatonic Concept of Metaphysics," *Quaestio* 5 (2005): 3–21.

16. Thomas Aquinas, *Quaestiones disputatae de veritate,* q. 1, a. 1, *Editio Leonina* 22/1.5:100–104: "Illud autem quod primo intellectus concipit quasi notissimum et in quod conceptiones omnes resolvit est ens, ut Avicenna dicit in principio suae Metaphysicae."

the subject matter of metaphysics. He refers to Avicenna for this phrase, but although the latter adopts the Aristotelian formula, the Arab philosopher does not employ it in his exposition of the primary notions. The identification of the first concept of the intellect with the proper "subject" of metaphysics is Henry's innovation.[17]

ALBERT THE GREAT: FIRST PHILOSOPHY AND THE PRIMACY OF BEING

One conception of metaphysics that is particularly illuminating regarding the effort to redefine First Philosophy is found in the writings of Albert the Great, who played a central role in the thirteenth-century reception of Aristotle—he composed commentaries on the entire *corpus aristotelicum*. In the first treatise of his Commentary on the *Metaphysics* (ca. 1264), he makes what he calls a "digression" in order to explain what the "proper subject" (*proprium subiectum*) of this science is.

A preliminary account is necessary, Albert states, because of the diversity of opinions among philosophers. He lists three different positions on this issue. Some philosophers claimed that the first causes are the proper subject of metaphysics, because science is knowledge of the causes and First Philosophy traces reality back to first or ultimate causes. Others held that God and the divine things are the subject. A third group of philosophers maintained that it is "being" (*ens*).[18] Employing the manner of a disputation, Albert advances arguments pro and contra the three views and decides the discussion on the basis of the formal features of a "subject of science."

---

17. Henry of Ghent, *Summa (Quaestiones ordinariae), art. XXXI–XXXIV. Opera omnia,* vol. 27, ed. R. Macken (Leuven: University Press, 1991), 190, a. 34, q. 3: "Et est iste 'conceptus entis in quantum ens est,' secundum Avicennam in I° *Metaphysicae.*" On Henry's identification, see Martin Pickavé, "Heinrich von Gent über das Subjekt der Metaphysik als Ersterkanntes," *Documenti e Studi sulla tradizione filosofica medievale* 12 (2001): 493–522, esp. 512.

18. Albert the Great, *Metaphysica* I, tract. 1, c. 2, ed. Bernhard Geyer, *Editio Coloniensis,* 16/1 (Münster: Aschendorff, 1960), 3:27–4:26: "Et est digressio declarans, quid sit huius scientiae proprium subiectum; et est in eo disputatio de tribus opinionibus philosophorum, quae sunt de subiecto. . . . Nonnulli enim fuerunt, qui posuerunt causam in eo quod causa est prima in unoquoque genere causarum, esse subiectum huius scientiae, ratione ista utentes, quod ista scientia considerat de causis ultimis, ad quae resolvuntur omnes causae. . . . Ideo fuerunt alii qui dixerunt deum et divina subiectum esse scientiae istius. . . . Amplius, tam hi quam primo inducti philosophi ratiocinantur ens non posse subiectum huius scientiae."

Subiectum of a science is the common predicate to which the parts of the science are reduced and upon which the properties demonstrated in the science are consequent. Neither the first causes nor the divine things, however, are the common predicate of what is considered in metaphysics. Moreover, God is what is sought (*quaesitum*) in First Philosophy and, therefore, cannot be the subject, since a feature of a subject of science is that its existence is presupposed in the science involved; consequently no selfsame thing is both *subiectum* and *quaesitum* in a science—Albert even adopts the terminology of the *Avicenna latinus*.[19]

From the exclusion of the other positions it follows that only being as being (*ens inquantum ens*) can be the proper subject. But Albert also provides an interesting positive reason for this stand. This science is called "First" philosophy since it deals with something that is first. The question is, thus, why and in what sense "being" is the first and not, as one would expect, God or the first causes. Albert's argument for the primacy of being is ontological: *ens* is the first foundation (*primum fundamentum*) of all things and is itself not founded in something prior.[20] His conclusion that First Philosophy is the science of "being" is typical of the outcome of the medieval discussion on the subject of metaphysics.

Albert summarizes the result of his disputation with a striking phrase: metaphysical knowledge is concerned with the *prima* and *transcendentia*.[21] He was the first medieval thinker to connect this science with the doctrine of the transcendentals. Since metaphysics studies what is most honorable, most certain, and prior to all, namely "being" in its totality (*per totum*), it can be called *philosophia prima*.[22]

Metaphysics is First Philosophy because it is the science of being, the

---

19. Albert, *Metaphysica* I, tract. 1, c. 2 (ed. Colon. 16/1.3:62–80) and ibid. (4.38–50), in particular: "Quod autem erronea sit haec opinio, constat per hoc quod nihil idem quaesitum est et subiectum in scientia aliqua; deus autem et divina separata quaeruntur in scientia ista; subiecta igitur esse non possunt." Cf. Avicenna, *Liber de philosophia prima* I, c. 1 (ed. Van Riet 4): "Dico igitur impossibile esse ut ipse Deus sit subiectum huius scientiae, quoniam subiectum omnis scientiae est res quae conceditur esse, et ipsa scientia non inquirit nisi dispositiones illius subiecti. . . . Sed non potest concedi quod Deus sit in hac scientia ut subiectum, immo est quaesitum in ea."

20. Albert, *Metaphysica* I, tract. 1, c. 2 (ed. Colon., 16/1.4:57–68): "Cum enim sit prima ista inter omnes scientia, oportet quod ipsa sit de primo, hoc autem est ens . . . , oportet, quod omnium principia per istam scientiam stabiliantur per hoc quod ipsa est de ente, quod est primum omnium fundamentum in nullo penitus ante se fundatum."

21. Ibid. (ed. Colon. 16/1.5:12–15).

22. Ibid. (ed. Colon. 16/1.5:52–58).

primum fundamentum of things. Albert presents still another reason for its primacy that is typical of his conception. In his commentary on book 4 of Aristotle's *Metaphysics,* he again discusses the question as to the "subject" of First Philosophy, and he interprets this notion in a more ontological sense than Avicenna did: *subiectum* is that which is presupposed in all subsequent things and underlies all of them. Only "being," therefore, can be the subject of metaphysics because being has absolutely nothing prior to it, whereas all else presupposes being. Being is through "creation" (*creatio*). In support of this view Albert quotes the famous fourth proposition from the *Liber De causis*—a book that he regards as the completion of Aristotle's *Metaphysics:* "The first of created things is *esse* and there is no other created thing before it."[23]

Characteristic of Albert's position is that it conceives "being as being"—the subject of metaphysics—as created. The reason that metaphysics deserves the name "First Philosophy" is that this discipline is concerned with the *primum creatum.* The contrast to Aristotle is strong: whereas the Greek philosopher relates the primacy to the "most dignified genus" of things, the divine, Albert interprets the firstness in the horizon of creation. The idea of creation is for him a philosophical perspective, not a strictly Christian *theologoumenon.* The fact that the *Liber De causis,* the work of a non-Christian author, speaks of "creation" confirms this conviction. Albert observes in his commentary on *De causis* that all ancient philosophers have assumed that being is not only caused but created, that is, "produced from nothing."[24]

But is "being" really a first when it is called the *primum creatum?* Albert himself raises the objection that what is first does not have anything before it, but created being presupposes something, namely, the First Cause. In his reply, he points out that the firstness of being has to be understood in the sense that it does not presuppose anything of itself (*nihil*

---

23. Ibid., IV, tract. 1, c. 2 (ed. Colon. 16/1.163:20–34): "[Ens] dicitur subiectum sicut id quod praesupponitur in omnibus sequentibus et omnibus substat eis. . . . Sic enim omnia sequentia enti demonstrantur inesse, ut entia per informationem esse habentia insunt enti per creationem solam esse habenti, eo quod nihil penitus ante se habeat, reliqua autem ad minus sibi praesupponunt ipsum ens. Sic enim intelligitur, quod in libro *De causis* dicitur, quod 'prima rerum creatarum est esse, et non est ante ipsum creatum aliud.' Omnia autem alia sunt per informationem, ut bonum et omnia alia."

24. Albert the Great, *De causis et processu universitatis a prima causa* II, tract. 1, c. 17, ed. Winfried Fauser, *Editio Coloniensis,* 17/2 (Münster: Aschendorff, 1993), 80:73–74.

sui), that is, with respect to its essential and intrinsic determinations. To be sure, created being presupposes the Creator and is therefore not the first *simpliciter*. But the Creator does not belong to the being of things. Being is the first in the reduction (*resolutio*) of things to their essential principles (*essentialia*).[25]

AQUINAS AND SCOTUS: THE FIRST OBJECT OF THE INTELLECT AND FIRST PHILOSOPHY

The idea of First Philosophy acquires in the Middle Ages a new *epistemological* foundation: Metaphysics is First Philosophy, not because it treats of the first and supreme being, but because it deals with what is first conceived by the intellect. The new foundation was realized in two steps: first by the interpretation of what is first known (*primum cognitum*) as the *primum obiectum* of the intellect, and second by the identification of the first "object" of the intellect with the proper "subject" of metaphysics.

The first step was made by Aquinas in his criticism of the position of Franciscan thinkers (Gilbert of Tournai, Bonaventure) who reject the Aristotelian inversion of the cognitive order and the order of being. According to Aristotle, what is prior known to us is ontologically posterior, but for these Franciscan thinkers there is a complete parallelism between the two orders: human intellectual knowledge has an "absolute" beginning, since what is first known is the first being.[26] Thomas Aquinas criticizes this position in his commentary on Boethius's *De Trinitate*.

In question 1, article 3, he examines whether God is what is first known by the mind. In his reply, Thomas distinguishes between two different senses of the phrase "first known." If the phrase is taken according to the order of the different powers of the soul (*ordo potentiarum*), then the singular or sensible (*singulare vel sensibile*) is what is first known, since all knowledge of the intellect is derived from the senses.

25. Ibid. (ed. Colon. 17/2.81:79–88): "Cum enim dicitur, quod primum nihil supponit ante se, intelligitur, quod nihil sui supponit ante se, hoc est, de essentiantibus et intrinsece constituentibus ipsum. Et sic esse primum est, quod nihil ante se supponit. Quia tamen est processus sive effluxus a primo, necesse est, quod supponat ante se creatorem. Sed ille nihil sui est. Primum enim principium non ingreditur essentialiter constitutionem rei alicuius. Propter quod resolutio entium non devenit usque ad primum principium, quando in essentialia fit resolutio."

26. On this position, see Wouter Goris, *Absolute Beginners: Der mittelalterliche Beitrag zu einem Ausgang vom Unbedingten* (Leiden: Brill, 2007).

But if it is taken according to the order of the objects of one and the same power (*ordo obiectorum*), then what is first knowable to each power is its "proper object" (*proprium obiectum*).[27]

As regards the intellect, its objects are forms abstracted from sensible representations, or phantasms. Among them there exists an order, since forms that are more universal are first known by the intellect. From this Thomas draws the conclusion that what is first known by the intellect (i.e., its proper object) is not what is absolutely (*simpliciter*) first, namely God; rather, it is what is first in the domain of things abstracted by the intellect, like "being" and "one" (*ens et unum*).[28]

What is innovative in Aquinas's discussion is his interpretation of what is first known in terms of the "proper object" of the intellect. The term *obiectum* is a medieval "invention," appearing for the first time as a philosophical expression in early-thirteenth-century treatises on the soul and its powers; its correlate is *potentia* as *habitus*.[29] The effect of the "turn to the object" is that the Avicennian primary notions, whose original background is the theory of science in the *Posterior Analytics,* are now referred to the Aristotelian psychology of knowledge in *De anima.*

The "objectifying" tendency is manifest in Aquinas's account in the *Summa theologiae.* He argues there that what is first conceived by the intellect is "being" (*ens*), because something is knowable insofar as it is in

---

27. Thomas Aquinas, *In De Trin.,* q. 1, a. 3 (ed. Leon. 50.87:112–22): "Et ideo dicendum est quod primo cognitum homini potest accipi dupliciter: aut secundum ordinem diversarum potentiarum aut secundum ordinem obiectorum in una potentia. Primo quidem modo, cum cognitio intellectus nostri tota derivetur a sensu, illud quod est cognoscibile a sensu, est prius notum quam illud, quod est cognoscibile ab intellectu, scilicet singulare vel sensibile intelligibili. Alio modo, scilicet secundum alium modum cuilibet potentiae est cognoscibile primo suum proprium obiectum."

28. Ibid. (ed. Leon. 50.87–88:112–46). Note in particular: "Intellectus autem agens non facit intelligibilia formas separatas quae sunt ex se ipsis intelligibiles, sed formas quas abstrahit a phantasmatibus, et ideo huiusmodi sunt, quae primo intellectus noster intelligit. Et inter hec illa sunt priora, que primo intellectui abstraenti occurrunt; hec autem sunt que plura compreendunt . . . ; et ideo magis uniuersalia sunt primo nota intellectui. . . . Unde patet quod deus et aliae substantiae separatae nullo modo possunt esse prima intellecta, sed intelliguntur ex aliis." Ibid., ad 3 (88:174–79): "Quamvis illa que sunt prima in genere eorum que intellectus abstrait a phantasmatibus sint primo cognita a nobis, ut ens et unum, non tamen oportet quod illa quae sunt prima simpliciter, quae non continentur in ratione proprii objecti, sicut ista."

29. Lawrence Dewan, "'Obiectum.' Notes on the Invention of a Word," *Archives d'Histoire Doctrinale et Littéraires du Moyen Âge* 48 (1981): 37–96. Cf. Theo Kobusch, "Objekt," in *Historisches Wörterbuch der Philosophie,* vol. 6, ed. Johann Ritter and Karlfried Gründer (Basel: Schwabe, 1984), 1026–52.

act. Consequently, "being" is the *proprium obiectum* of the intellect and the *primum intelligibile*, just as sound is the *primum audibile*.[30] Sound is the formal aspect by which something is audible and capable of becoming an object for the sense of hearing. A similar relation exists between being and intellect. Being is the condition of the intelligibility of things and is the proper object of the intellect.

Scotus's thought represents a new stage in the medieval debate on the first object of the intellect because he presents a further differentiation of this object. He distinguishes three orders of intelligibility to which three primacies (*primitates*) correspond: a first in the order of origin (*ordo originis*) of knowledge, a first in the order of perfection (*ordo perfectionis*), and a first in the order of adequation (*ordo adaequationis*).[31] The last concept is new to the medieval discussion; it means the object of any power, or faculty, is commensurate to it in such a way that the object is proportioned to all possible objects of that power. The question as to the first "adequate object" of the intellect thus concerns the scope of human reason—its possibilities and boundaries.

In his examination of this question, Scotus ascribes to Aquinas the view that the "quiddity of a material thing" (*quidditas rei materialis*) is the adequate object of the human intellect. The *Doctor subtilis* regards this position as completely false and emphasizes the fatal consequences of Aquinas's conception for the possibility of metaphysics.[32] This science is possible only if the intellect conceives something under a more general aspect than Thomas holds, namely under the aspect of being in general (*ens in communi*). Otherwise metaphysics would not be a *scientia transcendens* any more than physics is. According to Scotus, the first object of our intellect could not be anything that is more particular than "being-

30. Thomas Aquinas, *Summa theologiae* I, q. 5, a. 2, *Editio Leonina* 4.58: "Illud ergo est prius secundum rationem, quod prius cadit in conceptione intellectus. Primo autem in conceptione intellectus cadit ens: quia secundum hoc unumquodque cognoscibile est quod est actu. . . . Unde ens est proprium objectum intellectus: et sic est primum intelligibile, sicut sonus est primum audibile."

31. Duns Scotus, *Ordinatio* I, d. 3, p. 1, q. 1–2, n. 69, *Editio Vaticana* 3.48.

32. Ibid., q. 3, nn. 110–12 (ed. Vaticana 3.69–70). For a more complete analysis of the controversy and the question whether Scotus's criticism is justified, see Jan A. Aertsen, "Aquinas and the Human Desire for Knowledge," *American Catholic Philosophical Quarterly* 79 (2005): 411–30.

as-being" (*ens inquantum ens*) since being in itself would, then, in no way be understood by us.[33]

It is noteworthy that Scotus here uses the expression *scientia tran-scendens,* an expression he employs in the prologue of his *Questions on the Metaphysics* to explain the name "meta-physics." "It is from '*meta,*' which means '*trans,*' and '*ycos,*' which means '*scientia.*' It is, as it were, the 'transcending science' (*scientia transcendens*) because it is concerned with the *transcendentia.*"[34] In the passage just before this explanation, Scotus had introduced the term *transcendentia* as another name for the *communissima,* such as being qua being and its properties.

Scotus's criticism of Aquinas indicates a necessary correlation between the *subiectum* of metaphysics and the first adequate *obiectum* of the intellect: both are "transcendental." For this reason the science of metaphysics precedes the other disciplines out of inner necessity; metaphysics is First Philosophy because its first object is being in general.[35] Aquinas's first explanation of the title "First Philosophy" agrees with this idea: "the other sciences, deriving their principles from it [metaphysics], comes after it."[36]

FRANCIS OF MARCHIA: THE PRIMACY OF *RES* AND THE SPLITTING UP OF METAPHYSICS

A fundamental presupposition in the medieval transformation of the idea of First Philosophy attributed to metaphysics is the priority of "be-

33. Duns Scotus, *Ordinatio* I, d. 3, p. 1, q. 3, n. 117 (ed. Vaticana 3.72–73); ibid., n. 118 (ed. Vaticana, 73): "Praeterea, tertio, et redit quasi in idem cum secundo: quidquid per se cognosci-tur a potentia cognitiva, vel est eius obiectum primum, vel continetur sub eius obiecto primo; ens ut ens est communius sensibili, per se intelligitur a nobis, alias metaphysica non esset magis scientia transcendens quam physica; igitur non potest aliquid esse primum obiectum intel-lectus nostri quod sit particularius ente, quia tunc ens in se nullo modo intelligeretur a nobis."

34. Duns Scotus, *Quaestiones in Metaphysicam* I, prologus, n. 18, ed. Girard Etzkorn et al. (St. Bonaventure, N.Y.: Franciscan Institute, 1997), 9: "Et hanc scientiam vocamus metaphysi-cam, quae dicitur a 'meta,' quod est 'trans,' et 'ycos' 'scientia,' quasi transcendens scientia, quia est de transcendentibus."

35. Cf. ibid. II, q. 2–3, n. 93 (ed. St. Bonaventure 227–28), where Scotus presents this con-sideration as another argument against Aquinas's view: "Avicenna vult I *Metaph.* (c. 5), quod 'ens et res faciunt primam impressionem in animam'; quod videtur, quia primus habitus poten-tiae habet pro obiecto obiectum primum potentiae primi habitus, ut metaphysicae obiectum primum est ens in quantum ens."

36. See n. 1 above.

ing" to other concepts: *ens* is what is first conceived by the intellect and is the *primum cognitum*. This primacy of being was eventually challenged by a Franciscan master at the University of Paris in the early fourteenth century, Francis of Marchia (ca. 1290–after 1344). In his *Questions on the Metaphysics*, the first *quaestio* he raises is "Whether *res secundum quod res* is the subject of metaphysics or something else?"[37] Francis replaces the traditional phrase *ens inquantum ens* by the transcendental notion *res* ("thing"), a determination that had no precedent in Aristotle's *Metaphysics*, but one that belongs to Avicenna's primary notions.

Marchia's reply claims that "being" does not meet an essential condition of the subject of metaphysics, namely its conceptual primacy. "Being" is a property of "thing" and is thus posterior to "thing." Francis appeals to the authority of Avicenna, who had described the extensional identity of "being" and "thing" in the following terms: "The concept of *ens* is always concomitant with *res*, because the thing has being either in the singulars or in the estimation or in the intellect. If it were not so, it would not be a thing." Now the term "concomitant" suggests a conceptual priority of "thing," since it implies a relation of "posterior" and "prior"; that which "accompanies" "thing" is later than that which is "accompanied." Thus, "being" is not the first concept and consequently cannot be the subject of metaphysics.[38]

Francis also questions the firstness of metaphysics as such by pointing to the paradoxical place of this discipline in the order of the sciences: it is both the first and the last science—here the other coordinate in the medieval process of transformation becomes apparent. On the one hand, metaphysics is the first discipline, for it is argued that the prior and bet-

---

37. Francis of Marchia, *Quaestiones in Metaphysicam* I, q. 1, ed. Albert Zimmermann, in *Ontologie oder Metaphysik? Die Diskussion über den Gegenstand der Metaphysik im 13. und 14. Jahrhundert, Texte und Untersuchungen*, 2nd ed. (Leuven: Peeters, 1998), 84–98; analysis of the question is presented on 348ff. Cf. Sabine Folger-Fonfara, *Das "Super"-Transzendentale und die Spaltung der Metaphysik: Der Entwurf des Franciscus von Marchia*, Studien und Texte zur Geistesgeschichte des Mittelalters 96 (Leiden: Brill, 2008).

38. Francis of Marchia, *Quaestiones in Metaphysicam* I, q. 1 (ed. Zimmermann 86): "Ex quo patet secundum intentionem Avicennae, quod intentio entis concomitatur intentionem rei. Sed intentio posterior concomitatur intentionem prioris . . . Ergo intentio entis, cum non sit prima intentio, non erit primum subiectum metaphysicae." Cf. Avicenna, *Liber de philosophia prima* I, c. 5 (ed. Van Riet 36): "Nec separabitur a comitantia intelligendi ens cum illa ullo modo, quoniam intellectus de ente semper comitabitur illam, quia illa habet esse vel in singularibus vel in aestimatione vel intellectu. Si autem non esset ita, tunc non esset res."

ter known to us the subject of a science is, the prior that science is in the order of learning—and "being" and "thing" are the first conceptions of the intellect, as Avicenna teaches. But on the other hand, metaphysics is, again according to Avicenna, the last science, the completion of human thought. Viewed from this final perspective, *res* or *ens* does not seem to be the first subject of this discipline, for in that case it would not be the last science.[39]

Marchia's reply is surprising, because he accepts the idea entertained in the objection that metaphysics is the first and the last science—not, however, in the sense of a tension *within* one and the same science, but as indicating two distinct metaphysical sciences. He draws the remarkable conclusion that metaphysics is twofold (*duplex metaphysica*): a general (*communis*) and a particular (*particularis*) metaphysics. The subject of general metaphysics is the thing as thing (*res secundum quod res*), not contracted to a thing of a determinate genus, but common to all things of the first intention. By contrast, the subject of particular metaphysics is "immaterial thing" (*res separata a materia*).[40] Both sciences can be called "metaphysics," since both "transcend the bounds of physics" (*metas physice transcendens*), however, each in a different way: general metaphysics because it deals with what is common to things, particular metaphysics because its subject matter is the immaterial.[41]

39. Francis of Marchia, *Quaestiones in Metaphysicam* I, q. 1 (ed. Zimmermann 84–85): "Item: Quanto subiectum alicuius scientiae est prius et nobilius [*corrige*: notius] quoad nos, tanto illa scientia erit prior ordine doctrinae, cum intellectus noster procedat a notioribus nobis ad ignotiora, I Physicorum. Sed ens et res sunt priora et notiora nobis omnibus suis inferioribus, secundum Avicennam I Metaphysicae. . . . Ergo scientia de re et de ente est prior ordine doctrinae omnibus scientiis suorum inferiorum. Metaphysica autem est ultima vel paenultima secundum Avicennam I Metaphysicae et Philosophum IV Ethicorum. Ergo primum obiectum metaphysicae non est res nec ens."

40. Ibid. (ed. Zimmermann 88–89): "Quarta conclusio: Quod duplex est metaphysica, quaedam communis, et quaedam propria sive particularis. . . . Secundum hoc dico, quod subiectum metaphysicae communis primum est res secundum quod res est, non contracta ad aliquam rem determinati generis . . . , sed est res simpliciter communis ad rem primae intentionis. Subiectum vero metaphysicae particularis est res separata a materia secundum rationem et secundum rem." Francis also deals with this distinction at three other places in his work: the *prooemium* of his *Metaphysics* commentary, ed. R. L. Friedman, *Documenti e Studi sulla tradizione filosofica medievale* 16 [2005]: 502–13); *Quaestiones in Metaphysicam* VI, q. 16 (ed. Zimmermann, 98–100); and *In Sent.*, prologus q. 2, in *Quodlibet cum quaestionibus selectis ex commentario in librum Sententiarum*, ed. Nazzareno Mariani, Spicilegium Bonaventurianum 29 (Grottaferrata: Collegium S. Bonaventura, 1997), 370–74.

41. Francis of Marchia, *Quaestiones in Metaphysicam* I, q. 1 (ed. Zimmermann 89): "Et utraque potest vocari metaphysica, licet diversimode, quia utraque transcendit metas physicae,

According to Marchia, the title "First Philosophy" belongs to the discipline that is first in the order of intellectual knowledge and is therefore attributed by him to general metaphysics, dissociated from the consideration of God in particular metaphysics. In the prologue of his *Metaphysics* commentary, he presents a comprehensive division of the sciences, in which *metaphysics communis* precedes all particular sciences, and *metaphysica specialis* is the last of them; it comes after physics, mathematics, and politics, and is the ultimate end (*finis*) of human knowledge.[42]

Marchia's claim of a *duplex metaphysica* is a turning point in the history of metaphysics. He considers the science to be no longer a discipline that is both universal (ontology) and particular (theology), both the first and the last science. His claim anticipates the process of splitting up metaphysics into a *metaphysica generalis* and a *metaphysica specialis* in German philosophy of the seventeenth century. The end point of this development was the work *Philosophia prima sive Ontologia*, published by Christian Wolff in 1730. He employed the new term "ontology" for the part of philosophy that deals with being in general (*ens in genere*). Wolff separates this science from (particular) metaphysics and identifies it with "First Philosophy," because it teaches "the first principles and the first notions, used in thought (*in ratiocinando*)."[43] The primacy of First Philosophy is related to the first concepts—and that was, as we have seen, a medieval "invention."

---

quia utraque est de entibus abstractis, sed una positive, alia privative." *In Sent.*, prologus q. 2 (ed. Mariani 371): "Dico hic quod metaphisica hoc idem est quod metas physice transcendens, et sic duplex est metaphisica: quaedam est metaphisica communis que procedit ex principiis communibus entis . . . ; quedam est metaphisica particularis que considerat de ente separato secundum rem."

42. Ibid., prooemium (ed. Friedman 512): "Sed metaphysica communis praecedit ordine doctrinae omnes scientias particulares. Metaphysica autem particularis sequitur ordine doctrinae omnes scientias particulares." (513): "Post politicam vero, per quam homo disponitur ad intelligendum entia simpliciter separata, sequitur quaedam metaphysica specialis, quae est de entibus separatis . . . . Et ista est finis omnium scientiarum humanorum, ad quam omnes scientiae humanae ordinantur."

43. Christian Wolff, *Philosophia prima sive Ontologia*, prol., § 1, *Gesammelte Werke*, vol. 2, Lateinische Schriften, Bd. 3, ed. Jean Ecole (Hildesheim: Georg Olms Verlagsbuchhandlung, 1962), 1: "Dicimus autem haec philosophiae pars *Ontologia*, quia de ente in genere agit, nomen suum sortita ab objecto, circa quod versatur. *Philosophia prima* eadem appellari suevit, quia prima principia notiones primas tradit, quae in ratiocinando usum habent." Cf. Elisabeth Rompe, "Die Trennung von Ontologie und Metaphysik. Der Ablösungsprozeß und seine Motivierung bei Benedictus Pererius und anderen Denkern des 16. und 17. Jahrhunderts" (PhD diss., University of Bonn, 1968), and Ernst Vollrath, "Die Gliederung der Metaphysik in eine Metaphysica generalis und eine Metaphysica specialis," *Zeitschrift für philosophische Forschung* 16 (1962): 258–83.

Andreas Speer

4   The Fragile Convergence
Structures of Metaphysical Thinking

METAPHYSICAL THINKING AFTER THE END
OF METAPHYSICS

The present state of metaphysics is ambivalent. On the one hand, speaking of a "postmetaphysical" age has become a jargon of "philosophical correctness" that is very often not even conscious of the origin of its mental state, which looks upon the opportunities of occidental metaphysics as exhausted. Heidegger puts it this way[1] and, at the same time, narrates the history of metaphysics as a story of complete decline, as the attempt to render the eventful openness of being tangible as being and to make it accessible to thinking, finally doomed to fail[2]—a thinking that, moreover, apparently is not afraid of the divine's point of view to (re)construct reality as a mostly homogenous relation of order. The initially latent ontotheological condition of metaphysics and its qualification as an ideal counterworld discourse have contributed to the opinion mentioned in the beginning, that this form of metaphysics has lost its meaning finally and that we have entered a postmetaphysical age.

Why then should we answer a question that now at best is of histori-

1. Martin Heidegger, *Nietzsche II,* 6th rev. ed. (Stuttgart: Günther Neske, 1998), 60–68, 177–80.

2. Notably Heidegger's introduction to *Sein und Zeit,* or the preface of the lecture *Die Grundbegriffe der Metaphysik: Welt, Endlichkeit, Einsamkeit,* ed. F.-W. von Herrmann, Gesamtausgabe 29/30, 2nd ed. (Frankfurt am Main: V. Klostermann, 1992), esp. ch. 3 of the preface, 37–87. See also Costantino Esposito and Pasquale Porro, eds., *Quaestio* 1: *Heidegger e i medievali* (Turnhout: Brepols, 2001).

cal interest? Does metaphysical thinking not rather belong in the archive of philosophical ideas, useful at best as reservoir for some philosophical models of reasoning? Indeed, at least the prevalent basic intuitions of continental philosophical discourse of highlighting the difference in contrast to synthesis as well as the inevitability of decentering and perspectivism in theoretical and practical respects seem to run counter to metaphysical thinking in a contradictory way, inasmuch as the latter is based on the principle of convergence and the possibility of a homogenous perception of reality that goes along with a comprehensive foundation of thinking.

And exactly these questions concerning the foundation of knowledge, its relation to reality, and the structural conditions of a coherent perception of reality have led to a new and constantly growing interest in the once suspiciously studied discipline in the analytical Anglo-Saxon philosophical discourse—if you just think about the critical attitude of the founding fathers of analytical philosophy concerning metaphysics. A glance at the many "Introductions and Companions to Metaphysics," which, not accidentally, remind readers of the famous *Cursus metaphysici* of the late Scholastics and the early modern times, to the contrary, shows an astonishing naturalness in identifying and discussing present metaphysical questions. There, the historical context of the problems classified as metaphysical is mostly left aside or reduced to some arbitrary historical marks that do not exceed the pure labeling of the argument through assigning a name. The fact that a concept's or a problem's history itself has an argumentative status is of no importance for such reconstructions of metaphysical issues. Moreover, the treated topics seem to have an immediate actuality as if they can be found in a likewise present form and have to be answered. At least, these present debates show how vivid the metaphysical discourse is, free of any postmetaphysical fatigue.

Against all assumed contrariness of the sketched ideal types of present metaphysical and postmetaphysical discourses, a surprising common ground appears. Both discourses take no notice, or just selective notice, of the history of metaphysics, which seems to have no argumentative status and, consequently, does not belong to metaphysics, or at best does so accidentally. From that, the at least partial blindness concerning the genealogy of metaphysical problems and dogmatics intrinsic to both attitudes can be explained. This is valid factually, considering the origin and the character of metaphysical problems, and historically, concerning those authority narratives of new beginnings and breakings with traditions that are brought forward with the gesture of irreversibility or regaining of lost original authenticity, to the point of the historical "showdown" of the claimed break off of the metaphysical method of reasoning because of a supposed hopelessness.

But how to escape this ambivalence? In this chapter, with recourse to the history of metaphysics, I want to try to regain the original of the metaphysical discourse and thus to free it from the mentioned reductions. In this connection it is necessary to lay open metaphysical thinking in its origin. This way the factual origin will emerge clearly, especially in returning to the historical origin. Thereby, I am focusing on the metaphysical thinking in the first place rather than on the history of the discipline of metaphysics. Thus, the aim of such an archaeology is not the exploration of the past, but the better understanding of our present issues.

THE STRUCTURAL PRINCIPLE OF
METAPHYSICAL THINKING

Almost unnoticed we have already entered that discourse that is at issue here. For metaphysical thinking aims at a critical self-assurance and the definition of its own limitations, rather than at establishing an ideal counterworld, as a commonly cultivated prejudice wants us to believe. Its factual and historical origin is to be found in the former, and this chapter shall particularly treat these fragile starting conditions of metaphysical thinking. Thus, it is necessary to first return to the historically reconstructable beginnings of metaphysics to look, at the same time, for that other beginning, which is always in question when thinking wants to critically assure itself of its basic principles and conditions.

Precisely, that is Aristotle and the lecture, which—for librarian or other reasons—is handed down with the title of "Metaphysics" since the first century before Christ.[3] Aristotle himself used a different de-

3. See Hans Reiner, "Die Entstehung und ursprüngliche Bedeutung des Namens Metaphysik," *Zeitschrift für philosophische Forschung* 8 (1954): 210–37; id., "Die Entstehung der Lehre vom bibliothekarischen Ursprung des Namens Metaphysik," *Zeitschrift für philosophische For-*

scription: "First Philosophy" (ἡ πρώτη φιλοσοφία)[4] or "First Science" (ἡ πρώτη ἐπιστήμη)[5]—in the doubled sense of the word, for the master from Stagyra equalized those who were searching for (ζήτησις) and (those who were) on their way (μέθοδος) to that excellent knowledge (ἐπιστήμη)[6] he defined as the knowledge of the first causes and principles (τὰ πρῶτα αἴτια καὶ τὰς ἀρχὰς)[7] with the first philosophers (πρῶτοι φιλοσοφήσαντες), who had been looking for the causes out of which all being is composed, out of which it emerges as the first, and to which it returns as the last.[8] Considering the knowledge's genetic reconstruction, references to the evidence of everyday experience, such as that of the craftsman or the doctor, correspond to this recourse to the concrete historical initial situation, to which we also, to a great extent, owe our knowledge of the so-called Presocratics.

In that way, the train of thought in the beginning of the *Metaphysics* is a peculiar mixture of experience- and reason-based argumentation. For Alexander of Aphrodisias, one of the eldest in a long line of commentators, starting with the general everyday practice is indicated for the modality in which Aristotle usually begins his analyses to finally reach general ideas or general terms (κοιναὶ ἔννοιαι).[9] Starting with the fleeting perception limited to a singular impression (αἴσθησις), memory (μνήμη) offers the opportunity to store those impressions and, thus, to provide the basis for experience (ἐμπειρία), which is always related to a multiplicity of kindred and similar impressions. These allow us a better orientation in comparable situations, but without the ability to extract a general rule. By contrast, to identify the regular is an art (τεχνή) that finally leads to knowledge (ἐπιστήμη) in a literal sense, which thereby exceeds artistry, because it always considers the principle of the respectively identified regularity also.

---

schung 8 (1954): 77–99; further Pierre Aubenque, *Le problème de l'être chez Aristotle*, 2nd ed. (Paris: Presses universitaires de France, 1994), 28–44.

4. Aristotle, *Metaphysics* VI, 1, 1026a24.   5. Ibid., XI, 4, 1061b30ff.

6. Ibid., I, 2, 983a21–23.   7. Ibid., 1, 982b28ff.

8. Ibid., 3, 983b7–9: "τῶν δὴ πρώτων φιλοσοφησάντων οἳ πλεῖστοι τὰς ἐν ὕλης εἴδει μόνας ᾠήθησαν ἀρχὰς εἶναι πάντων· ἐξ οὗ γάρ ἔστιν ἅπαντα τὰ ὄντα, καὶ ἐξ οὗ γίγνεται πρώτου καὶ εἴς ὃ φθείρεται τελευταῖον."

9. Alexander of Aphrodisias, *Commentarius Alexandri Aphrodisiensis in libros metaphysicos Aristotelis* (hereafter *Comm. In lib. Met. Aristotelis*), I, 2, 982a6, ed. Hermann Bonitz (Berlin: G. Reimer, 1847), 9:22; cf. id., *On Aristotle's Metaphysics 1*, trans. W. E. Dooley (Ithaca, N.Y.: Cornell University Press, 1989), 27:20ff. Concerning the conceptual origin, see also Dooley's commentary, ibid., 20 n. 33.

We already behold the *structural principle* of our brief reconstruction of the genesis of knowledge from perception to memory, of experience and art to knowledge according to Aristotle's specification in *Metaphysics* I, 1: it is a matter of connecting simple units of information and data and of mastering complexities. This happens through assigning single elements to a sequence and, finally, through the introduction of a criterion, which functions as the condition according to which the elements of the respective sequence can be "caught" inside the limitations given by that criterion. It is about convergence rather than about homogeneity.

CONVERGENCE: THE EPISTEMIC STRUCTURAL MOMENT

The conceptual historical origin of the terminus I use to label the facts in hand can probably be found in Augustine and Isidor of Seville. Both use the term *convergere* to describe the uniform inclination of all points on a circumference to its center.[10] By contrast, in modern mathematical analysis, convergence is defined as the character of a sequence or a series that possesses a limit. This limit, which is in some respects already part of the definition of a convergent sequence, is approached by a sequence that does not necessarily have to reach that limit in the end. But without such a limit a sequence is divergent.[11]

The present meaning of convergence seems to me to match the basic intuition of the Aristotelian train of thought in the beginning of his lecture on metaphysics pretty closely: the Aristotelian genesis of knowledge namely presupposes an assumed limit concerning the respective epistemic field, which points to the target of the operation of cognition within its thereby already given bounds. It is especially these conditions of the mathematical concept of convergence that shall be examined in what follows.

10. Augustine, *De ordine,* lib. I, cap. 2, lin. 8: "ut enim in circulo quantumuis amplo unum est medium, quo cuncta conuergunt"; Isidor of Seville, *Etymologiarum siue Originum libri XX,* lib. 3, cap. 12, par. 1: "Quarum prima circulus est figura plana, quae uocatur circumducta; cuius in medio punctus est, quo cuncta conuergunt, quod centrum geometriae uocant, Latini punctum circuli nuncupant." Ibid., lib. 19, cap. 19., par. 10: "Punctus autem in medio circini centrum a Graecis dicitur; in cuius medium cuncta conuergunt."

11. One example would be $\sqrt{2}$ or π as a non-algebraic number. In mathematical language this convergence condition can be formulated as follows: For every $\varepsilon \gg 0$ one N exists, so that: $a_n \varepsilon\,]a <\min> \varepsilon, a+\varepsilon[$ for every $n \leq N$. Consequently, the sequence (a_n) converges against a exactly, if in every however small ε-environment of a almost all elements of the sequence are situated. Here, "almost all" means "all but at most a finite number of exceptions."

The farther our view should reach in the described operation of cognition, the more comprehensive the epistemic fields should be, the more general rules have to be found, the more we have to learn about the causes and how these are connected to each other, as Aristotle tried to show: for example in the form of conclusions. To gain access to more complex conclusions and extensive epistemic fields we need more general principles, which allow a linking of known and greater connections in the first place. For knowledge characterizes itself by the fact that we can always give the reasons on which our connection, our judgment, is based.

In this context, Aristotle himself talks about a knowledge about "certain principles and causes" (περί τινας αἴτίας καὶ ἀρχάς ἐπιστήμη), to which he assigns an architectural function with regard to the genesis of knowledge.[12] This knowledge he calls wisdom, but not in an emphatic manner. Moreover, he extracts this concept following from the original meaning of σοφία as efficiency based on competence and knowledge—like the efficient carpenter in Homer or the meteorologist in Pindar.[13] Still, Aristotle continues, somebody is called wise not because he acts due to his skills, but because of the possession of the concept and the knowledge of the causes. From this consideration it follows that all forms of experience-, action-, and knowledge-like world orientation are referred to each other according to the insight into the rules and causes "architecturally," whereas the primacy befits the theoretical sciences rather than the generative.[14] Therefore an Egyptian priest caste, exempted for a life of leisure, was required to find those most excellent sciences "which do not aim at giving pleasure or at the necessities of life."[15]

For Aristotle, this is definitely no myth, but part of a heuristic related to experience, which starts from the opinion we have of the wise (περὶ τοῦ σοφοῦ) when it comes to identifying those causes and principles, since the knowledge of them is called wisdom (σοφία).[16] Furthermore, the specific feature of this way of accessing is underlined by Thom-

---

12. Aristotle, *Metaphysics* I, 1, 982a2.
13. See Homer, *Ilias* XV, 411sq.; Pindar, *Nem.* 7, 17; about this Hans Leisegang, "Sophia," in *Realencyclopädie der Classischen Altertumswissenschaft* 2/5 (Stuttgart: Metzler, 1927), coll. 1010–39, and Andreas Speer, "Weisheit," in *Historisches Wörterbuch der Philosophie*, vol. 12 (Basel: Schwabe, 2004), coll. 371–97, esp. coll. 371ff.
14. Aristotle, *Metaphysics* I, 1, 981a30–b2; ibid., 2, 982b7–9.
15. Ibid., I, 1, 981b20–25.
16. Ibid., 2, 982a6–b4.

as Aquinas, who ascertains about this passage in his commentary on the *Metaphysics* that the definition of wisdom complies with what people usually thought about wise men.[17] For the wise know all, as far as possible, without having a knowledge about all things in detail. Then, we consider somebody wise who is capable of comprehending what is difficult and of understanding what is not easy to understand for men, somebody who is more exact and able to teach in any science, especially in relation to those sciences that are chosen for the sake of themselves and, furthermore, only for the sake of knowledge, wherein their excellence can be found in particular compared to the "applied" sciences.[18]

From this heuristic Aristotle deduces the attributes of that science in which the dynamics of knowledge seems to converge with the claim to know everything. In comparison to the other epistemic fields, it has an exceptional position inasmuch as no other, greater criterion can be found in the search for convergence criteria. Moreover, this first science is the highest point of reference for the highest degree perceivable, "for by reason of these, and from these, all other things come to be known, and not these by means of the things subordinate to them."[19] The convergence criteria of the sought first science are universality, exactness, and knowledge about the first principles and causes.[20] Yet, such knowledge is most difficult to gain since it is farthest away from perception; it is more exact because it needs less qualifications; it enables to teach at most inasmuch as it enables us to tell the cause of everything, and particularly therein forms the precondition to recognize, more than any other knowledge, for what sake anything needs to be done. Still it is knowledge that is not in search of a purpose and understanding for its own sake—not in the sense of a *l'art pour l'art* but as reflection upon those conditions and principles, "for by reason of these, and from these, all other things come to be known."[21]

---

17. Thomas Aquinas, *In duodecim libros Metaphysicorum Aristotelis expositio* (hereafter *In Meta.*), ed. M.-R. Cathala and Raymond M. Spiazzi (Turin: Marietti, 1950), I, lect. 2, n. 36: "Postquam Philosophus ostendit quod sapientia sit quaedam scientia circa causas existens, hic vult ostendere *circa quales causas et circa qualia principia sit.* [. . .] Primo *colligit definitionem sapientiae* ex his quae homines de homine sapiente et sapientia opinantur."

18. Aristotle, *Metaphysics* I, 2, 982ª6–19; see Thomas Aquinas, *In I Meta.*, lect. 2 (ed. Marietti nn. 36–44).

19. Aristotle, *Metaphysics* I, 2, 982b2–4: "διὰ γὰρ ταῦτα καὶ ἐκ τούτων τἆλλα γνωρίζεται, ἀλλ' οὐ ταῦτα διὰ τῶν ὑποκειμένων."

20. Ibid., 2, 982a17–32.

21. Ibid., 1, 982b1–3: "τοιαύτη δ' ἐστὶν ἡ μάλιστ' ἐπιστημοῦ· μάλιστα δ' ἐπιστητὰ τὰ πρῶτα καὶ τὰ αἴτια· διὰ γὰρ ταῦτα καί ἐκ τούτων τἆλλα γνωρίζεται."

Aristotle, too, uses a mathematical problem to make sure in retrospect that the followed path of the genesis of knowledge, namely "the acquisition of it, must in a sense end in something which is the opposite of our original inquiries,"[22] which starts with wondering about the functioning of supposedly self-moving artifacts such as marionettes, about the phenomenon of solstice, or—and this is Aristotle's example—about the problem of the incommensurability of the diagonal in a square, one of the greatest paradigms in the history of Greek mathematics. The search (ζήτησις) should start with the opposite, which means with the better end, namely with a better understanding of the respective issue. Suchlike knowledge consists in knowledge of the causes of the functioning of marionettes and the apprehension of the impossibility of measuring the diagonal in a square with the smallest entity, namely a natural number, comparably. Consequently, in the end there is no exceeding of a limit, but instead a better understanding of the reason and the limit of our perception and our knowledge, "for there is nothing," Aristotle continues, "which would surprise a geometer so much as if the diagonal turned out to be commensurable."[23] In this observation we find a first constitutive structural moment of metaphysical thinking that, starting from aisthesis, lifts off to the conditions of understanding. I call it the *epistemic structural moment.*

Here, thinking does not only take account of the conditions of understanding of the particular skillfulness or form of knowledge; this look is rather directed at the conditions of understanding as such. Yet, the further the analysis proceeds, the plainer it becomes that the context of discovery already presupposes a certain context of reasoning; both are inversely interrelated with each other. For the search for those conditions under which we can know something shows that what is perceived first is not the first in the order of reasons, but rather is what is always inferred from the limit conditions of the particular principle, however without this principle being able to be perceived in the way that these two orders—"for us" (πρὸς ἡμᾶς) and "in itself" (καθ᾽ αὐτὸ)—would coincide.

22. Ibid., 2 983a11ff.: "δεῖ μέντοι πως καταστῆναι τὴν κτῆσιν αὐτῆς εἰς τοὐναντίον ἡμῖν τῶν ἐξ ἀρχῆς ζητήσεων."

23. Ibid., 983a12–20. Concerning the problem of irrationality in geometry see Walter Burkert, *Weisheit und Wissenschaft: Studien zu Pythagoras, Philolaos und Platon* (Nürnberg: H. Carl, 1962), esp. 424–40 regarding the explanations of geometric achievements of the Pythagoreans and the mathematical secret.

For this reason the possibility to reverse the direction of investigation, in order to evolve this science deductively, has lapsed.[24]

In the aftermath, this methodical self-restriction of metaphysical thinking did not remain unquestioned; rather, it has sometimes been criticized vehemently. Do we not have to claim for a higher degree of apodeictical obligation, for example according to the type of mathematics? As it is known, the *mos geometricus* as a model of strict knowledge axiomatics has not lost its fascination even today.[25]

However, for Aristotle—as above all Pierre Aubenque has emphasized—the first science as a result remains a "sought-after science" (ἡ ἐπιστήμη ζητουμένη); such is the by no means rhetorical name of the science Aristotle presents at first. This gesture of searching (ζήτησις) determines the aim (σκοπός), the method (μέθοδος), and the character or nature (φύσις) of philosophizing from the spirit of metaphysical thinking.[26]

DIVINE KNOWLEDGE: THE ANTHROPOLOGICAL STRUCTURAL MOMENT

Then, on the other hand, which purpose could the search for such a knowledge serve? Why should all our effort aim for such a search? The motivation to set out for this, for nature (φύσις), and the aim (τέλος) of

24. Cf. Pierre Aubenque, "Aristoteles und das Problem der Metaphysik," *Zeitschrift für Philosophische Forschung* 15/3 (1961): 321–33, esp. 328–32; further in detail id., *Le problème de l'être chez Aristote*, 45–66.

25. In this context we may be reminded of Descartes, who justified his claim for a reformation of the sciences with reference to the *mos geometricus* and who gave reason to this recourse by criticizing the insufficient scholastic method and its Aristotelian concept of science. Yet, also prior to the so-called Aristotle reception of the twelfth and thirteenth centuries we find—starting with the order of the theoretical sciences from *Metaphysics* VI, 1 handed down in Boethius (*De Trinitate* 2), against the background of the reception of Euclid in the twelfth century—impressive attempts of an axiomatic-theorematic groundwork of sciences in the so-called School of Chartres.

Cf. Andreas Speer, "Das 'Erwachen der Metaphysik.' Anmerkungen zu einem Paradigma für das Verständnis des 12. Jahrhunderts," in *Metaphysics in the Twelfth Century: On the Relationship among Philosophy, Science and Theology*, ed. Matthias Lutz-Bachmann, Alexander Fidora, and Andreas Niederberger, Textes et Études du Moyen Âge 19 (Turnhout: Brepols, 2004), 17–40, esp. 33–39; see also Mechthild Dreyer, "Regularmethode und Axiomatik. Wissenschaftliche Methodik im Horizont der *artes*-Tradition des 12. Jahrhunderts," in *"Scientia" und "ars" im Hoch- und Spätmittelalter*, ed. Ingrid Craemer-Ruegenberg and Andreas Speer, Miscellanea Mediaevalia 22 (Berlin: Walter de Gruyter, 1994), 147–55.

26. Aristotle, *Metaphysics* I, 2, 983a20–23. Cf. Aubenque, "Aristoteles und das Problem der Metaphysik," 322–25.

this first science resulted—according to Aristotle—from the difficulties man consistently gets into when he wonders and arrives at the conclusion that he basically does not know anything.[27] Yet the only sort of person who searches for this kind of insight is someone who possesses not only almost every necessity but also what serves for the lightening and organization of spare time. The sort of knowledge that man does not search for a purpose is free, as the respective science is the only one free—as we call the man free, "who exists for his own sake and not for another's."[28]

Already commentators from late antiquity like Alexander of Aphrodisias pointed to the anthropological implications and revealed the references, especially to the tenth book of the *Nicomachean Ethics*.[29] There, Aristotle combines the problem of perfect felicity with the most complete activity of reason, such as the wise possesses. Because εὐδαιμονία must always be sought in an activity corresponding to a certain virtue. Günther Patzig has accurately spoken of minimal metaphysics, which has resolved to expressing as perfectly as possible the differentiating characteristic and the task deduced therefrom.[30] From this teleology derives the claim that thinking and acting have to occur according to the insights of reason. Yet, this primacy of the theoretical form of life stands with a reservation, because the aim expressed therein points beyond the limits of the humanly possible: because human life is finite, and because the noblest activity, wherein felicity is, does not last the whole period of life. Moreover, life, in which these conditions are fulfilled, is higher than that of what is human as human. And this insight of Aristotle absolutely corresponds with our experience. In this way, man could not live inasmuch as he is man, but only inasmuch as he contains something divine within him.[31]

As "divine," Aristotle defines the hierarchically highest of sciences also in his lecture on metaphysics, and this in two respects: on the one hand, if God possessed it in the highest degree, on the other hand, with regard to the other sciences, for they are directed toward divine things.[32]

---

27. Aristotle, *Metaphysics* I, 2, 982b11–21.

28. Ibid., 982b23–28.

29. Alexander of Aphrodisias, *Comm. In lib. Met. Aristotelis* I, 2, 982b (ed. Bonitz 15:6–23); cf. Alexander of Aphrodisias, *On Aristotle's Metaphysics 1*, 37:6–23.

30. Günther Patzig, *Ethik ohne Metaphysik* (Göttingen: Vandenhoeck & Ruprecht, 1971), 40ff.

31. Aristotle, *Nicomachean Ethics* X, 7, 1177b24–31.

32. Aristotle, *Metaphysics* I, 2, 983a6–10.

This is not about gaining a divine point of view, because it is impossible for man to pass the natural limits of cognition. "Divine," according to Alexander of Aphrodisias, here at first means "free from necessity," and at the same time means the knowledge about the first causes and principles, which is the highest knowledge.[33] For Alexander, Aristotle's exhortation articulated in the tenth book of his *Nicomachean Ethics*—namely, that humans, although mortal, should not limit their striving to something human, as men, and to something mortal, as mortals, but that we should "make ourselves immortal, and strain every nerve to live in accordance with the best thing in us" as far as possible—can be explained in this respect. Because this divine in us, to the little extent it may be, is precisely the far pleasantest, or, in other words, is our true self.[34]

Here, Alexander of Aphrodisias has a sharp eye on the epistemic quality of the definition of an anthropological limit that reaches far beyond a mere protreptic. It turns out to be another constitutive structural moment of metaphysical thinking because it reconnects the dynamics of cognition—unfolded in the introductory passage of the *Metaphysics*— which finds itself under the circumstances of assumed convergence, with the conditions of the finite human's possibilities of cognition. Therewith, the search for a last point of convergence in the dynamics of cognition gains an unconcealed practical veneer in the request for a life according to both the most complete and the specific activity of reason.[35] To me, this practical accent seems to be characteristic of the *anthropological structural moment* of metaphysical thinking. Obviously, it is not senseless for man to question about a last point of convergence of all knowledge, although it seems inaccessible by oneself at first. To the contrary, it is rather necessary if he wants to comprehend his life in a greater context.

33. Alexander of Aphrodisias, *Comm. In lib. Met. Aristotelis*, I, 2, 982b (ed. Bonitz 15:17–18): "τὸ δὲ θεῖον πάσης χρείας ἐλεύθερον"; cf. Alexander of Aphrodisias, *On Aristotle's Metaphysics 1*, 37:19–20.

34. Alexander of Aphrodisias, *Comm. In lib. Met. Aristotelis*, I, 2, 982b (ed. Bonitz 15:18–20); cf. Alexander of Aphrodisias, *On Aristotle's Metaphysics 1*, 37:20–24; cf. Aristotle, *Nicomachean Ethics* X, 7, 1177b31–34; ibid., 1178a2–3: "δόξειε δ' ἂν καὶ εἶναι ἕκαστος τοῦτο, εἴπερ τὸ κύριον καὶ ἄμεινον."

35. Thomas Aquinas has systematically unfolded the implications of this central Aristotelian theory in his doctrine on the *finis ultimus* in the *Summa theologiae* I-II, qq. 1–5. Further, see my essay "Das Glück des Menschen" in *Thomas von Aquin: Die* Summa theologiae—*Werkinterpretationen*, ed. Andreas Speer (Berlin: Walter de Gruyter, 2005), 141–67.

ARCHAEOLOGY: THE HISTORICAL STRUCTURAL MOMENT

This insufficiency must be an explanation for the fact that Aristotle, when he answers the question of the nature of the sought science, at first refers to "those who have before us approached the investigation of being and philosophized about truth."[36] For they had also spoken of certain principles and causes that would be useful for his own inquiry, whether another type of cause had been found or the already existing been mentioned.[37] Thus, Aristotle firstly finds his answer in a recourse to theories mainly of the Ionic philosophers of nature, whom he came across and partly depicted and discussed in detail, in order to show how all of his predecessors "were again forced by the truth itself, as we said, to inquire into the next kind of principle"[38] if the hitherto answer turned out to be insufficient. In that sense, absolute exceptions like those that are dealt with in metaphysics are also included in historical processes of development—as R. G. Collingwood tried to show—because those fundamental convictions that the metaphysician tries to grasp and classify are not mere answers to questions, but rather requirements for questions. They themselves cannot be understood without those questions, which need to be answered historically and to which they give answers. In his philosophical autobiography Collingwood writes that as an archaeologist he realized the meaning of the "questioning activity" for cognition.[39] Consequently—for Aristotle also formulated his hermeneutic directive this way—one "should be grateful, not only to those with whose views we may agree, but also to those who have expressed more superficial views; for these also contributed something [to truth], by developing before us the powers of thought."[40]

As Aristotle's detailed elaboration of his predecessors shows, he takes seriously this conclusion, which points to another structural moment of

36. Aristotle, *Metaphysics* I, 3, 983b1–3: "ὅμως δὲ παραλάβωμεν καὶ τοὺς πρότερον ἡμῶν εἴς ἐπίσκεψιν τῶν ὄντων ἐλθόντας καὶ φιλοσοφήσαντες περὶ τῆς ἀληθείας."

37. Ibid., 983b3–6.

38. Ibid., 984b9–11: "πάλιν ὑπ' αὐτῆς τῆς ἀληθείας, ὥσπερ εἴπομεν, ἀναγκαζόμενοι τὴν ἐχομένην ἐζήτησαν ἀρχήν."

39. R. G. Collingwood, *An Autobiography* (London: Oxford University Press, 1939), 35.

40. Aristotle, *Metaphysics* III, 1, 993b11–14: "οὐ μόνον δὲ χάριν ἔχειν δίκαιον τούτοις ὧν ἄν τις κοινώσαιτο ταῖς δόξαις, ἀλλὰ καὶ τοῖς ἐπιπολαιοτέρως ἀποφηναμένοις· καὶ γὰρ οὗτοι συνεβάλοντο τι· τὴν γά ἕξιν προήσκησαν ἡμῶν."

metaphysical thinking. Therefore, the *historical structural moment* is by no means of an external nature, but belongs to the core of the search for the first science.[41] With reference to *Metaphysics* III, for example, this search is aporetic at first. Yet, to me that seems to be characteristic of metaphysical thinking, which is—as we have seen—the expression for the obvious necessity of a final point in the genesis of knowledge, which constitutes the sequence of knowledge as such in its function as limit and without which—as Averroes insistently underlined in his commentary of metaphysics—all knowledge would be destroyed.[42]

Yet, in continuing that search, metaphysical thinking at the same time finds itself confronted with the fact that a knowledge *habitus* on the basis of wisdom, corresponding with the criteria explicated in the beginning, is absolutely impossible for humans. Therefore, Pierre Aubenque spoke about a "productive failure" of the Aristotelian metaphysics project. Thus, he saw the specific productivity of metaphysics precisely in the fact that a programmatic project of a first philosophy, which due to the primacy of its principle and the universality of its object (against the background of the other sciences) is capable of examining the total reality in a highest possible unity. Moreover, precisely in this search for unity, it finds its possible answer at least for man, as against its inspectioned property.[43] For as Plato noted in his *Symposium* (204 A), it is only humans who philosophize; neither animals do so—because they are not in possession of the necessary requirement, which is reason—nor the gods—since they already know everything.

THE BASIC LAW OF CONVERGENCE

According to the just explicated structural organization of convergence, this inquiry presupposes a principle "which every one must have who

41. Consequently, Aristotle's recourse to his historical predecessors in *Metaphysics* I, 3–10, is not just a mere return to the different basic types of causality and, correspondingly, to different forms of principles. This would be a shortened reading. Cf. Michael Frede, "Aristotle's Account of the Origins of Philosophy," *Rhizai: Journal for Ancient Philosophy and Science* 1 (2004): 9–44.

42. Averroes, *In II Metaph.*, comm. 8–11 (ed. Ven. 1562–74, repr. Frankfurt a. M. 1962), 32vM–33vM; his starting point is the conclusion of Aristotle in *Metaphysics* III, 2, 994a1ff., that there must be a principle and that the causes of existing neither can proceed in a continuous sequence nor, by its nature, can continue infinitely.

43. Aubenque, "Aristotles und das Problem der Metaphysik," 332ff.

understands anything that is."[44] Albeit Aristotle concerning the unity and the character of the searched science: whether it should be defined as ontology (IV, 1 and 4; VI, 1), as substance metaphysics (VII, 1; XII, 1), or as theology (VI, 1; XI, 7); whether it remains differentiated and thus inspires those debates, which have formed the metaphysical discourse for centuries even until the present, Aristotle leaves no doubt about the necessity of a first principle and its character.

He defines this principle, which could not possibly be a hypothesis (ὑπόθεσις), as the generally known principle of noncontradiction, according to which the same cannot be both said and not said about one and the same thing in the same respect at the same time.[45] This principle functions as the very basic law of convergence in every human activity of reason: the principle is its limit in constitutive and determining respects and thus describes the possibility and the limitation of developing epistemic fields. In a way, this ἀνυπόθετον of thinking is always assumed. Therefore, it cannot directly be proved correct—this attempt would necessarily lead into an infinite regress. Yet, a negative demonstration of the impossibility of the claim might be possible "if our opponent will only say something." Aristotle, in a moment of elenchic polemic, continues to say that anybody who wants to deny this rule is like a plant and should better not speak.[46]

Instead, if we discerningly refer to reality, we obviously have always discerned something, even though our intellect resembles a nocturnal bird rather than an eagle; thus to those things that are by their nature the most evident of all, the intellect is as the night owl to the blaze of day.[47] On the other hand, nobody will miss the door concerning the examination of truth, however difficult it is to adequately meet truth. For this ex-

44. Aristotle, *Metaphysics* IV, 3, 1005b15ff.; see the following note.

45. Ibid.: "ἦν γὰρ ἀναγκαῖον ἔχειν τὸν ὁτιοῦν ξυνιέντα τῶν ὄντων, τοῦτο οὐχ ὑπόθεσις."

46. Ibid., 4, 1006a9–18. Not least with reference to Aristotle himself, especially to the *Posterior Analytics* I, 3, 72b5–73a20, it is pointed to the alleged circularity of the method of reasoning. A noteworthy attempt to overcome this circular dilemma of reasoning productively by a further transcendental foundation of the principle of noncontradiction can be found in Thomas Aquinas's commentary on the *Metaphysics*. See my essay "The Epistemic Circle: Thomas Aquinas on the Foundation of Knowledge" in *Platonic Ideas and Concept Formation in Ancient and Medieval Thought*, ed. Gerd van Riel and Caroline Macé, Ancient and Medieval Philosophy, series 1, vol. 32 (Leuven: Leuven University Press, 2004), 119–32.

47. Aristotle, *Metaphysics* II, 1, 993b9–11. Concerning this motif, see the detailed analysis of Carlos Steel, *Der Adler und die Nachteule, Thomas und Albert über die Möglichkeit der Metaphysik*, Lectio Albertina 4 (Münster: Aschendorff, 2001).

amination requires the knowledge of the causes.[48] These striking images and proverbs from the beginning of the second book of *Metaphysics,* which have become the starting point for many interpretations themselves, stand for that everyday evidence Aristotle consistently directs our attention toward for a good reason.

In his commentary on the *Metaphysics,* Thomas Aquinas picks up the proverb (*exemplum vulgaris proverbi*) of the door, and through it lets us take a look inside the house, which still is very difficult to explore and in regard to which one can easily be deceived. On the other hand, the issue of that door itself is different; for it is open to everybody and directly meets the eye—nobody will be deceived by it. Also that which enables someone to recognize everything else is well-known to everybody, and no one can misunderstand it. These are by nature the first known self-evident principles: that nothing can be affirmed and denied at the same time; that the whole is greater than its parts; and so on. Concordantly, for Thomas these form the door to any other cognition.[49] Every activity of reason is based on this simple assumption of truth from which we always have to grasp something.

THE CONVERGENCE MODEL

At this point I want to pause for a moment to try to take interim (provisional) stock of our hitherto reconstruction of metaphysical thinking. In questioning the historical starting point, this reconstruction has, at the same time, started to look for the cause of those questions that can be assigned to the first science sought after, moreover, a science that originally inspired the search in an historical and fundamental sense. The question of convergence, and thus the question of its conditions under which knowledge can be created, stood in its center.

In the convergence model, they can be reconstructed through the assumption of a limit that defines the aim and, at the same time, the borders of the operation of cognition with reference to the respective epis-

48. Aristotle, *Metaphysics* II, 1, 993a30–b5.

49. Thomas Aquinas, *In II Meta.,* lect. 1 (ed. Marietti no. 277): "Interiora enim domus difficile est scire, et circa ea facile est hominem decipi: sed sicut circa ipsum introitum domus qui omnibus patet et primo occurrit, nullus decipitur, ita enim est in consideratione veritatis: nam ea, per quae intratur in cognitionem aliorum, nota sunt omnibus, et nullus circa ea decipitur: huiusmodi autem sunt prima principia naturaliter nota, ut non esse simul affirmare et negare, et quod omne totum est maius pars et similia."

temic field. Yet, it could be shown that the constant approximation to the given epistemic limit within the restricted field was bound to the definition of another, namely to the *anthropological limit,* which narrows the possibility of reaching the defined epistemic limit; factually it is even excluded—although this possibility has been challenging for metaphysical thinking in the past and present, again and again. Therein lies its character, which aims at the conditions of the general possibility of constituting epistemic fields. Under the conditions of cognition of human reason, the definitions of limits seem to be the very truth which we can never grasp totally but from which we always need to grasp something. Thus, *epistemic convergence* is fragile in its core. Consequently, the unity of the epistemic field of metaphysics is in question, too—a question to which Aristotle accepted several alternative answers, obviously not without intention, even though in his *Posterior Analytics* he explicitly underlines the criterion of unity for every science.[50]

Hence, if we define the epistemic field of the first philosophy according to the criteria from *Metaphysics* I, 2—namely universality, exactness, priority considering the principles, autarchy, and ordering primacy in Thomas Aquinas's words as "universal truth of being" (*universalis veritas entium*)—this can be possible only under the perspective of the relation of man to the truth that is to be identified.[51] From the limitation of our reason (*propter defectum intellectus nostri*)[52] Thomas deduces the necessity that men should support each other at recognizing truth, since nobody is capable of that all by himself.[53] Therefore, we find a historical succession of those who went in on this search.[54]

50. Aristotle, *Posterior Analytics* I, 28, 87a37ff. Here, Aristotle especially emphasizes the unity of the subject area that is claimed in respect of the species concept. In addition to the concept of γένος, above all the concept of ὑποκείμενον becomes more important in this connection—as in *Metaphysics* III, 2, 997a18–22. See Albert Zimmermann, *Ontologie oder Metaphysik? Die Diskussion über den Gegenstand der Metaphysik im 13. und 14. Jahrhundert. Texte und Untersuchungen,* 2nd rev. ed. (Leuven: Peeters, 1998), 130–34. As Zimmermann shows in his large-scale study, the question of the characteristic science subject, the *proprium subiectum,* is of central importance in the debates on the understanding of metaphysics in the thirteenth and fourteenth centuries.

51. Thomas Aquinas, *In II Meta.,* lect. 1 (ed. Marietti n. 273): "Sed philosophia prima considerat universalem veritatem entium. Et ideo ad hunc philosophum pertinet considerare, quomodo se habeat homo ad veritatem cognoscendam."

52. Ibid. (ed. Marietti n. 282): "Unde manifestum est, quod difficultas accidit in cognitione veritatis, maxime propter defectum intellectus nostri."

53. Ibid. (ed. Marietti n. 287): "Ostendit quomodo se homines adinvicem iuvant ad considerandum veritatem. Adiuvantur enim unus ab altero ad considerationem veritatis dupliciter."

54. Ibid. (ed. Marietti n. 288): "Est autem iustum ut his, quibus adiuti sumus in tanto bono,

We have introduced this necessity as the *historical convergence condition,* which arises from the necessity of choosing one access to a problem in a given situation without certainty that this choice allows a complete answer to the question. It seems trivial that such an access must be available at all at a given time. Yet, it is not if we think about the fact that Thomas's answer to the inquired questions would not have been possible without the reception of Aristotle beforehand, which is more than a mere translation of a number of ancient texts and some Greek and Arabic commentaries.[55] If we can detect some narrowings of philosophical problems and the given solutions in the present, it is to a great extent due to the fact that alternatives of thinking, like those tradition offers, are not available to a satisfactory degree any more. To the contrary, philosophical departures have been bound closely to the rediscovery and reacquisition of lost and forgotten traditions.

We have been following such a line of tradition also. Aristotle and his commentators represent a central metaphysical discourse. Yet not in an exclusive sense, since we could have chosen another point of departure. In all of that, our reading of Aristotle did not have the end in itself, but was in service for the problem at issue and found itself in a special proximity to the depicted reconstruction of metaphysical thinking, which orientates itself through the convergence model in the area of conflict of its epistemic, anthropological, and historical structural moments. Finally, this choice represents a metaphysical intuition, which consists of a preference concerning the place of philosophical reflections, which always refer back to their point of origin in the concrete everyday experience, namely to the lived convergence experiences in everyday understanding and acting—like in a marketplace where we constantly find weighing, counting, and measuring.

---

scilicet cognitione veritatis, gratias agamus [. . .], non solum his, quos quis existimat veritatem invenisse, quorum opinionibus aliquis communicat sequendo eas; sed etiam illis, qui superficialiter locuti sunt ad veritatem investigandam, licet eorum opiniones non sequamur; quia isti etiam aliquid conferunt nobis. Praestiterunt enim nobis quoddam exercitium circa inquisitionem veritatis."

55. An expression of the complexity of Aristotle's reception in the Middle Ages is conveyed in *Allgemeinen Zeitschrift für Philosophie* (*AZP*) through the three-part overview of Rüdiger Arnzen, Guy Guldentops, Andreas Speer, Michele Trizio, and David Wirmer, "Philosophische Kommentare im Mittelalter—Zugänge und Orientierungen. First part: I. Einführung—II. Sprachkreise" (*AZP* 32.3 [2007], 157–77); "Second part: III. Platonica—IV.1&2 Aristotelica arabica et byzantina" (*AZP* 32.2 [2007], 259–90); "Third part: IV.3: Aristotelica latina—V. Hebraica—VI. Ausblick" (*AZP* 33.1 [2008], 31–57).

CONVERGENCE BEYOND THE LIMITS OF REASON

Nicholas of Cusa takes such an everyday situation—which might be situated at the Roman Campo dei Fiori in the summer of 1450—as a starting point for his search for wisdom. For him, this search also originates in a natural desire (*appetitus nostrae naturae inditus*) that finds expression in a striving for knowledge.[56] We would primarily know of that because of experience itself rather than from books. For cognition of wisdom is immediate; it can be found on the streets and in front of the doors—as is said not only in the biblical literature on wisdom. It can be found vestigially in measuring, counting, and weighing.[57] There, Cusanus stands with a sharp eye in the middle of the Roman marketplace, where exactly this happens: a well-regulated exchange of thoughts and items between humans who obviously seem to understand each other immediately. From these observations Cusanus finds the basic principle of his further considerations: the simple is by nature prior to the composed; consequently, the composed cannot measure the simple—for the composed is related to unity, not vice versa. Thus, the simple forms the underlying measurement. Yet, as Nicholas's Socratic protagonist says, that for, through, and wherein all that is countable, weighable, and measureable can be counted, weighed, and measured, could not be reached through the means of numbers, weight, or a measure.[58] We recognize our model of convergence.

The search for wisdom lets us recognize those convergences that enable us to understand the world; still, at the same time we realize the limitations of our speculative, discursive, and concept-forming rationality. This operation of thought is no exclusive skill possessed only by the especially instructed, such as the philosophers. As a structuring principle it is present at every act of cognition. While our reasonable concepts structure

---

56. Nicholas of Cusa, *De venatione sapientiae*, prol., n. 1 (Op. omn. XII, 4,18sq.): "Sollicitamur appetitu naturae nostrae indito ad non solum scientiam, sed sapientiam seu sapidam scientiam habendum." The mentioned scenery forms the background story of another dialogue on wisdom, namely the *Idiota de sapientia*.

57. Ibid., *Idiota de sapientia* I, nn. 5–7 (Op. omn. V, 8–13); cf. *De venatione sapientiae*, 11,21.

58. Ibid., n. 6 (Op. omn. V, 11sq.): "Sicut enim simplex prius est natura composito, ita compositum natura posterius; unde compositum non potest mensurare simplex, sed e converso. Ex quo habes, quomodo illud, per quod, ex quo et in quo omne numerabile numeratur, non est numero attingibile, et id, per quod, ex quo et in quo omne ponderabile ponderatur, non est pondere attingibile. Similiter et id, per quod, ex quo et in quo omne mensurabile mensuratur, non est mensura attingibile."

the data of the senses, our intellectual concepts lead to the first conditions of our cognitions. This insight is achieved by the mind (*mens*) itself, when it analyzingly turns to the conditions of cognition.

For Cusanus, the dynamics arises from that, due to which the intellect starts to search for a principle affirmed per se, what can neither be denied nor transcended again. "I must grasp something that is most certain—something presupposed and undoubted by all pursuers [of wisdom]," as Cusanus formulates his central idea when analyzing the reasons for wisdom, "since what is unknown cannot be known through that which is even more unknown."[59] Every pursuer would sooner or later stop if he knew that there was nothing to be pursued. This also accounts for the pursuer of wisdom. Because everybody who searches is looking for something. If he did not look for something, he would not be searching. Therefore, the impulse (*motus*) immanent to all researchers does not lead to nothing.[60] Even more: all questions and operations of the human mind presuppose a final, absolute unity that cannot be doubted, since it is "most precise—including that mind accomplishes all things in and through this oneness."[61] Further: "Therefore, that which is presupposed in every doubting must," according to Cusanus, "necessarily, be most certain. Therefore, because absolute oneness is the being of all beings, the quiddity of all quiddities, the cause of all causes, the goal of all goals, it cannot be called into doubt. But subsequent to absolute oneness there is a plurality of doubts."[62] Also the lack of preciseness (*praecisio*) in connecting and adapting (*adaptio congrua*) the known and the unknown—expression for the limitedness of human reason (*ratio*)—must not lead to the conclusion that our desire for knowledge

59. Ibid., *De venatione sapientiae*, c. 2, n. 6 (Op. omn. XII, 9,9–11): "Cum ignotum per ignotius non possit sciri, capere me oportet aliquid certissimum, ab omnibus venatoribus indubitatum et praepositum, et in luce illius ignotum quaerere."

60. Ibid., *De apice theoriae*, n. 2 (Op. omn. XII, 118,14–20): "Quicumque quaerit, quid quaerit. Si enim nec aliquid seu quid quaereret, utique non quaereret. [. . .] Nam motus, qui omnibus studiosis adest, non est frustra."

61. Ibid., *De coniecturis* I, c. 5, n. 19 (Op. omn. III, 24sq.,1–6): "Contemplare igitur mentis tuae unitatem per hanc absolutionem ab omni pluralitate, et videbis non esse eius vitam corruptibilem in sua unitate absoluta, in qua est omnia. Huius autem absolutae unitatis praecisissima est certitudo, etiam ut mens omnia in ipsa atque per ipsam agat. Omnis mens inquisitiva atque investigativa non nisi in eius lumine inquirit."

62. Ibid. (Op. omn. III, 25,8–14): "Id igitur, quod in omni dubio supponitur, certissimum esse necesse est. Unitas igitur absoluta, quia est entitas omnium entium, quiditas omnium quiditatum, causa omnium causarum, finis omnium finium, in dubium trahi nequit. Sed post ipsum dubiorum est pluralitas."

was pointless.[63] For Cusanus, especially the negativity that can be found in the awareness of the impropriety and limitedness bears the moment of a "sprout affirmation" (*praegnans affirmatio*).[64]

Cusanus represents what Collingwood calls a new "question context." The Aristotelian metaphysical discourse appears to be sterile for Nicholas, unlike for the late medieval school. For them the problem regarding the *proprium subiectum* of the first and noblest science—that is, on the peculiar object of metaphysics in contrast to a theology based on revelation—led to debates that became more and more complex and even confusing.[65] This problem seems less a question in his mind than the Aristotelian understanding of science, which is satisfied by primarily claiming satisfactory convergence conditions for the particular sciences, including the first science. However, the architecture of knowledge and the dynamics of the intellectual synthesis that, according to Nicholas, does not pause for anything but its own unity, is underestimated.[66]

On the other hand, is such a last point of convergence reachable for a reason, which moves toward the conditions of its constitution and limits? For Cusanus, too, the outmost point of convergence lies beyond the radius of the powers of comprehension of the human mind in the case of the latter pushing forward its inquiries according to reason, that is, the discursive, finite *ratio*.[67] Still, the limits of the *via rationis* are not the

63. Ibid., *De docta ignorantia* I, c. 1, n. 4 (ed. min., Heft 15a, 8): "Praecisio vero combinationum in rebus corporalibus ac adaptatio congrua noti ad ignotum humanum rationem supergreditur. [. . .] Si igitur hoc ita est [. . .] profecto cum appetitus in nobis frustra non sit, desideramus scire nos ignorare."

64. See Marc-Aeilko Aris, "'Praegnans affirmatio.' Gotteserkenntnis als Ästhetik des Nichtsichtbaren bei Nikolaus von Kues," *Theologische Quartalsschrift* 181 (2001): 97–111, es. 105.

65. See e.g. Hervaeus's *Defensa* and the prologue of the commentary on the *Sentences* by Prosper of Reggio Emilia. See Engelbert Krebs, *Theologie und Wissenschaft nach der Lehre der Hochscholastik an der Hand der bisher ungedruckten "Defensa doctrinae D. Thomae" des Hervaeus Natalis*, Beiträge zur Geschichte der Philosophie des Mittelalters 11.3-4 (Münster: Aschendorff, 1912). See also Andreas Speer, "*Sapientia nostra.* Zum Verhältnis von philosophischer und theologischer Weisheit in den Pariser Debatten am Ende des 13. Jahrhunderts," in *Nach der Verurteilung von 1277: Philosophie und Theologie an der Universität von Paris im letzten Viertel des 13. Jahrhunderts. Studien und Texte*, ed. Jan A. Aertsen, Kent Emery Jr., and Andreas Speer, Miscellanea Mediaevalia 28 (Berlin: Walter de Gruyter, 2000), 248–75; Stephen F. Brown, "*Duo Candelabra Parisiensia*: Prosper of Reggio in Emilia's Portrait of the Enduring Presence of Henry of Ghent and Godfrey of Fontaines Regarding the Nature of Theological Study," in *Nach der Verurteilung von 1277*, 320–56.

66. See n. 63 above.

67. Nicholas of Cusa, *De coniecturis* II, c. 3, n. 87 (Op. omn. III, 84,3f.): "Mens humana, rationis medio investigans, infinitum ab omni apprehensionis suae circulo eiciens."

limits of the intellect (*intellectus*), which is able to observe the infinity of the absolute quantity in a noncomprehending manner above all discursive ability—comprehending according to reason (*ratio*).[68] The Aristotelian regress prohibition does not include this concept of infinity before all quantity, for this infinity that "exists in and of itself" cannot be transcended: as an absolute presupposition (*absoluta praesupposito*) it is prior to all logical and reasonable consideration (*logica et rationales consideratio*) of things and to all classification according to species and category in such a way that "all these different modes—as many might be conceived—are very easily reconciled and harmonized when the mind elevates itself unto infinity."[69]

METAPHYSICS AS SCIENCE

But is the mind really capable of doing this? Is it not true for all attempts to find a new language trying to overcome the restrictions formulated in the principle of noncontradiction, what Immanuel Kant so insistently described in the beginning of the preface of the first printing of the *Kritik der reinen Vernunft,* his *Critique of Pure Reason*? Namely: in the attempt to ascend higher and higher to conditions farther away, reason ultimately takes refuge in those principles "which transcend the region of experience," and therefore falls into "confusion and contradictions."[70] The battlefield, according to Kant, of the endless quarrels arising therefrom is called metaphysics. This used to be called the queen of all sciences and, for him, she deserved that honorable name due to the high importance of her object. Yet, "now, it is the fashion of the time to heap contempt

---

68. Ibid., *De docta ignorantia* I, c. 4, n. 12 (Ed. min., Heft 15a, 18): "Supra omnem igitur rationis discursum incomprehensibiliter absolutam maximitatem videmus infinitam esse, cui nihil opponitur, cum qua minimum coincidit."

69. Ibid., *Idiota de mente* c. 2, n. 67 (Op. omn. V, 103,1–3): "Hae omnes et quotquot cogitari possent modorum differentiae facillime resolvuntur et concorduntur, quando mens se ad infinitatem elevat." For a consideration of this problem in detail, see my essay "Verstandesmetaphysik. Bonaventura und Nicolaus Cusanus über die (Un-)Möglichkeit des Wissens des Unendlichen" in *Die Logik des Transzendentalen. Festschrift für Jan A. Aertsen zum 65. Geburtstag,* ed. Jan A. Aertsen and Martin Pickavé, Miscellanea Mediaevalia 30 (Berlin: Walter de Gruyter, 2003), 525–53; see also Hans Gerhard Senger, "Die Sprache der Metaphysik," in *Ludus sapientiae: Studien zum Werk und zur Wirkungsgeschichte des Nikolaus Cusanus* (Leiden: Brill, 2002), 63–87.

70. Immanuel Kant, *Kritik der reinen Vernunft* (KrV), A VII/VIII.

and scorn upon her."[71] Different from present metaphysical critics, Kant himself tries hard to form the basis of "any future metaphysics that will be able to come forward as science"—thus the programmatic title of the *Prolegomena*. For he is convinced of the necessity of such a critical foundation of reason.

Like Aristotle, Kant presupposes a history to his efforts. In contrast to the former, he is less merciful to his predecessors: between the despotism of dogmatism and the anarchy of skepticism and indifferentism, he finds metaphysics—as opposed to logic, mathematics, and natural sciences, which all have already followed the secure path of the sciences— fallen so far behind that its procedure resembles a mere groping around under mere concepts, which is the worst of all. What has emphatically been praised as a complete restart of metaphysics and been given the nimbus of the special against the background of the philosophical debates of the past, basically just leads back to the starting point of our inquiry for the origin of metaphysical thinking. Of course, Kant glances at the Aristotelian etiology when he declares the starting conditions of reason (human reason to be more precise) as the starting conditions and conditions of the limit of metaphysical thinking, as Aristotle did within the fields of theoretical philosophy.

Particularly therein Kant is by no means as exclusive as a look right into those traditions we have primarily observed so far shows. Especially the great debates of the thirteenth and fourteenth centuries on basic problems of the theories of cognition and science, on radius and limits of reason, and on the objects of metaphysics and its classification into general and particular metaphysics are an excellent expression of that critical self-assuring in which we have seen the proprium of metaphysical thinking.[72]

INTERNAL CONVERGENCE AND TRANSCENDENTAL SCIENCE

Finally, I would like to give voice to one participant of that debate. It is the voice of a thinker who might have recognized, thought through, and

---

71. *KrV*, A VIII. On the background of the prefaces see the commentary of Eckart Förster, "Die Vorreden," in *Immanuel Kant: Kritik der reinen Vernunft*, ed. Georg Mohr and Marcus Willaschek, Klassiker Auslegen 17/18 (Berlin: Akademie Verlag, 1998), 37–55, esp. 37–40.

72. An image of this debate is sketched by the magisterial study by Albert Zimmermann,

defended the consequences of the Aristotelian starting conditions of metaphysical thinking like no other: it is Thomas Aquinas, who has provoked many contemporaries in this, as the following debates will show.[73] The prologues of the respective commentaries on Aristotle are of special interest since they not only offer a mostly complex methodological classification of the text to be commented on in the way of an *accessus,* but also express the specific interest of the commentator and his personal motifs.

This becomes obvious especially in the prologue of his commentary on the *Metaphysics.* It stands out again how hard Thomas founds the epistemologic ordering-relations in man's natural desire for knowledge, which he, like Aristotle, equates with the desire for felicity and, moreover, to which he gives reason threefold, from the order of cognition according to the affirmation of cognition, from the comparison between reason and sensation, and finally from the cognition of the intellect.[74] Three fields of metaphysical thinking derive from that which corresponds to the three Aristotelian models of the sought-after first science: first philosophy, metaphysics, and theology—namely, inasmuch as these consider the analysis of the highest cause, the most universal principle, and that which is separated from any materiality and thus has the most recognizable as its object.

Ontologie oder Metaphysik?; cf. Wouter Goris, *The Scattered Field. History of Metaphysics in the Postmetaphysical Era* (Leuven: Peeters, 2004). Also see Sabine Folger-Fonfara, *Das "Super"- Transzendentale und die Spaltung der Metaphysik: der Entwurf des Franziskus von Marchia,* Studien und Texte zur Geistesgeschichte des Mittelalters 96 (Leiden-Boston: Brill, 2008), 89–125.

73. A good overview of the debates following Thomas Aquinas can still be found in Martin Grabmann, *Die theologische Erkenntnis- und Einleitungslehre des hl. Thomas von Aquin auf Grund seiner Schrift "In Boethium de trinitate": im Zusammenhang der Scholastik des 13. und beginnenden 14. Jahrhunderts dargestellt* (Freiburg/Schweiz: Paulusverlag, 1948). See also further: Josef Koch, *Durandus de S. Porciano O.P. Forschungen zum Streit um Thomas von Aquin zu Beginn des 14. Jahrhunderts,* Beiträge zur Geschichte der Philosophie des Mittelalters 26 (Münster: Aschendorff, 1927); id., *Kleine Schriften,* 2 vols., Storia e Letteratura 128 (Rome: Edizioni di storia e letteratura,1973); see also Maarten J. F. M. Hoenen, "Being and Thinking in the 'Correctorium fratris Thomae' and the 'Correctorium corruptorii Quare.' Schools of Thought and Philosophical Methodology," in *Nach der Verurteilung von 1277: Philosophie und Theologie an der Universität von Paris im letzten Viertel des 13. Jahrhunderts. Studien und Texte,* ed. Jan A. Aertsen, Kent Emery Jr., and Andreas Speer, Miscellanea Mediaevalia 28 (Berlin: Walter de Gruyter, 2000), 417–35.

74. Thomas Aquinas, *In Meta.,* prooemium and I, lect. 1 (ed. Marietti nn. 1–4). On this see Jan A. Aertsen, "Thomas von Aquin: Alle Menschen verlangen von Natur nach Wissen," in *Philosophen des Mittelalters: eine Einführung,* ed. Theo Kobusch (Darmstadt: Primus, 2000), 186–201.

Exceeding Aristotle, Thomas tries not only to formally assign these fields to just one science, but also to relate these different views coherently according to the Aristotelian differentiation between subject (*subjectum*), cause (*causa*), and quality (*passio*) of a science with reference to the inherent ordering claim. Ultimately, it is about the internal convergence of metaphysical thinking. For Thomas, this is rooted in the observation of universal being (*ens commune*), namely being as such (*ens inquantum ens*) as the actual subject (*subjectum*) of metaphysics, of which all conclusions of this science can be predicated.[75]

At the same time, this subject of metaphysics corresponds to the intentional openness of human reason, which possesses the intuitive access to the complete reality of being through its primary concepts and the principle of noncontradiction grasped therewith. Yet, the limitations of a reason bound to the conditions of materiality become obvious in reference to its aim. Here, an insurmountable restriction opens up that runs counter to the proportionedness between recognizing and recognized, and which stands in the way of the actual unity necessary for perfect convergence.[76]

Thus, human reason's direct access to the field of reality is denied; for human reason is bound to imagination, through which alone knowledge about reality may be achieved, since that field of reality exists separated from those conditions of materiality. Thus knowledge about the high-

75. Thomas Aquinas, *In Meta.*, prooemium (ed. Marietti): "Secundum igitur tria praedicta, ex quibus perfectio huius scientiae attenditur, sortitur tria nomina. Dicitur enim scientia divina sive theologia, inquantum praedictas substantias considerat. Metaphysica, inquantum considerat ens et ea quae consequuntur ipsum. Haec enim transphysica inveniuntur in via resolutionis, sicut magis communia post minus communia. Dicitur autem prima philosophia, inquantum primas rerum causas considerat. Sic igitur patet quid sit subiectum huius scientiae, et qualiter se habeat ad alias scientias, et quo nomine nominetur." Cf. Zimmermann, *Ontologie oder Metaphysik?*, 200–228; Jan A. Aertsen, "Was heißt Metaphysik bei Thomas von Aquin?," in *"Scientia" und "ars" im Hoch- und Spätmittelalter*, ed. Ingrid Craemer-Ruegenberg and Andreas Speer, Miscellanea Mediaevalia 22 (Berlin-New York: Walter de Gruyter, 1994), 217–39; John F. Wippel, *The Metaphysical Thought of Thomas Aquinas* (Washington, D.C.: The Catholic University of America Press, 2000), 11–22, 44–62.

76. Thomas Aquinas, *In Meta.*, prooemium (ed. Marietti): "Intelligibilia enim et intellectum oportet proportionata esse et unius generis, cum intellectus et intelligibile in actu sint unum." In *Summa theologiae* I, q. 84, a. 7, co. Thomas defines the *obiectum proprium* of the human intellect as "quidditas sive natura in materia corporali existens." The resulting consequences for the cognition of the immaterial determines the possibility of metaphysics; cf. *Summa theologiae* I, q. 88, a. 2. See Speer, "The Epistemic Circle," 127–30; Goris, "Anthropologie und Erkenntnislehre," 125–40, esp. 134–37.

est cause consequently is not the excellent subject, but the superb aim of the first science[77]—in the sense of our convergence principle, which truly knows about the necessity of a limit condition, but thereby has not defined it completely; it does not even have to reach it. For Thomas, this restriction with regard to the possibility of recognizing the principle of all being, the divine being, accounts only for metaphysics—which he consequently binds to the epistemic conditions of human reason and, moreover, in its core conceived it as a transcendental science but not as a science of the transcendent.

This restriction of metaphysics does not account for humans' desire of knowledge as such, for this cannot be in vain.[78] Still, this desire for knowledge points beyond metaphysics to another theology that is based on the extension of the sources of cognition; thus, it also points beyond the limitations of natural reason.[79]

FRAGILE CONVERGENCE

The convergence of metaphysical thinking turns out to be far more fragile than it may seem from the point of view of later debates, which very often just fall for the static structures of a disciplinary discourse, which denies the anthropological and historical conditions of convergence. Yet, absolute knowledge cannot be the aim of the first philosophy, because that is impossible for human cognition. Nevertheless, a philosophy that departs from that kind of premise necessarily is self-restricting, in both theoretical and practical respects. It is aware of the fact that it is not truth in the perfect sense, but—as all human knowledge—is finite wisdom.[80]

---

77. For detailed information, see Zimmermann, *Ontologie oder Metaphysik?* 207–22, and in an exemplary way Thomas Aquinas, *Super Boetium De Trinitate* (hereafter *In De Trin.*), q. 5, aa. 1 & 4.

78. Thomas Aquinas, *In I Meta.*, lect. 1 (ed. Marietti n. 4): "Hoc autem proponit Aristoteles ut ostendat, quod quaerere scientiam non propter aliud utilem, qualis est haec scientia, non esse vanum, cum naturale desiderium vanum esse non possit." Thomas also refers to this argument of Aristotle in the discussion of the realization of a human's desire for felicity; cf. *Summa contra Gentiles* (hereafter *SCG*) III, c. 48: "Impossibile est naturale desiderium esse inane: 'natura nihil facit frustra' [*De caelo* II, 11]. Esset autem inane desiderium naturae si nunquam posset impleri. Est igitur implebile desiderium naturale hominis. Non autem in hac vita."

79. *In De Trin.*, q. 2, a. 2; ibid., q. 5, a. 4. Cf. SCG I, c. 4. See also Aertsen, "Thomas von Aquin," 195–200.

80. For more information see my inaugural lecture from Würzburg, "Endliche Weisheit.

In this way philosophy differentiates itself from other sciences and, at the same time, exceeds them.

This option for a *metafisica povera*, for which metaphysics finds itself within the limitations of finite discursive reason, does not exclude that we may continue to question; the history of metaphysics shows that. No less a person than Immanuel Kant himself in this respect speaks almost programmatically—to be understood literally, for this is the introductory sentence of the first preface of his *Critique of Pure Reason*—about a special fate of human reason: "[it] is called upon to consider questions, which it cannot decline, as they are presented by its own nature, but which it cannot answer, as they transcend every faculty of the mind."[81]

Still, to me it seems that we firstly have to secure this field of metaphysical thinking before we set out to enter other fields. That means to always assure oneself of the respective convergence conditions carefully. These not only are of an epistemic nature, but also include anthropological and historical convergence conditions—not just in passing—as we could see. For arguments have contexts, and a philosophy that wants to be more than an abstract discourse presupposes the interest of those who philosophize, who as humans themselves live in a concrete historical situation and raise such questions.

Consequently, all attempts to declare one of these convergence conditions as absolute are doomed to fail. These are rather related to each other and are mutually dependent. This arrangement of dependence causes that fragility which consequently redirects metaphysical thinking to its origin, which then has to be reassured again. Thus, it becomes a critical discourse of foundation. Therein lies the core activity of metaphysical thinking.

Eine Annäherung an die Philosophie," *Recherches de Théologie et Philosophie médiévales* 49, no. 1 (2002): 3–32.

81. *KrV,* A VII: "Die menschliche Vernunft hat das besondere Schicksal in einer Gattung ihrer Erkenntnisse: daß sie durch Fragen belästigt wird, die sie nicht abweisen kann; denn sie sind ihr durch die Natur der Vernunft selbst aufgegeben, die sie aber auch nicht beantworten kann, denn sie übersteigen alles Vermögen der menschlichen Vernunft."

Part Two

Metaphysical *Aporiae*

Gregory T. Doolan

5 ∽ Aquinas on *Substance* as a Metaphysical Genus

The topic that I wish to address in this chapter is influenced in no small part by the writings of John F. Wippel. It touches upon a theme that Wippel has examined in detail, namely Thomas Aquinas's treatment of the subject matter of metaphysics. Following Aristotle, Thomas identifies this subject matter as being qua being, or as he terms it, *ens commune:* being in general.[1] He observes, furthermore, that this science could also

1. See Thomas Aquinas, *Super Boetium De Trinitate* (hereafter *In De Trin.*) q. 5, a. 4 co., *Editio Leonina* 50.154:143–206; id., *In duodecim libros Metaphysicorum Aristotelis expositio* (hereafter *In Meta.*), Proemium, ed. M.-R. Cathala and Raymond M. Spiazzi (Turin: Marietti, 1950), 1. Regarding Thomas's position on the subject matter of metaphysics, see John F. Wippel, *Metaphysical Themes in Thomas Aquinas* (Washington, D.C.: The Catholic University of America Press, 1984), 55–67; id., *The Metaphysical Thought of Thomas Aquinas* (Washington, D.C.: The Catholic University of America Press, 2000), 3–22; Ralph McInerny, *Praeambula Fidei: Thomism and the God of the Philosophers* (Washington, D.C.: The Catholic University of America Press, 2006), 210–18; Lawrence Dewan, O.P., "What Does It Mean to Study Being 'as Being,'" in *Form and Being: Studies in Thomistic Metaphysics* (Washington, D.C.: The Catholic University of America Press, 2006), 13–34; Albert Zimmermann, *Ontologie oder Metaphysik? Die Diskussion über den Gegenstand der Metaphysik im 13. und 14. Jahrhundert*, 2nd rev. ed. (Leuven: Peeters, 1998), 200–223.

For Aristotle's identification of being qua being as the subject matter of this science, see *Metaphysics* IV, 1, 1003a20–32. After reiterating this view in VI, 1, 1025b1–18, however, he proceeds to show that it belongs to this science to study what is separable and immovable and, hence, divine. For this reason he refers to this science as "theology" and also calls it "first philosophy," noting that it deals with the highest genus. As Aristotle himself observes, this leads to the question whether first philosophy is indeed universal, or whether it studies only one type of being, what he terms "separate substance" (1025b1–1026a32). In short, the question arises whether Aristotle is identifying two distinct sciences or a single, unified science. For discussion of this problem and how it was addressed by Aristotle's various interpreters, see ch. 2 in this book by Dominic O'Meara and ch. 3 by Jan A. Aertsen.

be called the science of substance (*scientia substantiae*).[2] Here, again, he follows Aristotle, who in book 4 of the *Metaphysics* presents being as *pros hen* equivocal and substance as the primary entity.[3] Or, to put it in Thomas's terms, being is analogical and substance is the primary kind of being. For this reason, he explains, even though metaphysics studies all beings insofar as they are beings (including accidents), it primarily and principally studies substance.[4]

To be more precise, Thomas says that metaphysics studies substance *inasmuch as it is substance* (*substantia inquantum est substantia*). He adds this qualification because this science is not alone in studying substances: the special, or particular, sciences study them as well. But Thomas adds that these other sciences study only *such* substances—in other words particular kinds of substances, such as *lion* or *ox*.[5] By contrast, metaphysics studies all substances according to the common *ratio* of substance.[6] Thus, it studies both material and immaterial substances.[7] Indeed, Thomas notes that if we follow the Porphyrian tree laid out in the *Isagoge*, materiality and immateriality are the first differences that divide the genus *substance*. If, then, for Thomas metaphysics principally studies substance, it would seem that it is this genus that it principally studies—a genus that includes all substances.[8]

2. *In III Meta.*, lect. 5 (ed. Marietti 110:391); ibid., lect. 6 (ed. Marietti 111:394); *In I De caelo*, lect. 20, nn. 198–99, *Editio Leonina* 3.81–83.

3. See *Metaphysics* IV, 2, 1003a32–b23. Regarding Aristotle's treatment of both of these points, see Joseph Owens, *The Doctrine of Being in the Aristotelian Metaphysics*, 3rd ed. (Toronto: Pontifical Institute of Mediaeval Studies, 1978), 264–79.

4. *In IV Meta.*, lect. 1 (ed. Marietti 152–53:546). Commenting on Aristotle's *Metaphysics* he goes so far as to note that for this reason substance can, in a sense, be taken as the subject matter of this science. See *In V Meta.*, lect. 7 (ed. Marietti 229.842): "Subiectum autem huius scientiae potest accipi, vel sicut communiter in tota scientia considerandum, cuiusmodi est ens et unum: vel sicut id de quo est principalis intentio, ut substantia."

5. *In IV Meta.*, lect. 1 (ed. Marietti, 153:547).

6. *In III Meta.*, lect. 6 (ed. Marietti 112:398).

7. *In VII Meta.*, lect. 11 (ed. Marietti 369:1526). Thomas explains in this text, however, that metaphysics studies these two kinds of substances in different respects. In this science (which he here calls "First Philosophy"), immaterial substances are examined inasmuch as they are both substances and *such* substances, which is to say immaterial ones. By contrast, First Philosophy does not examine sensible substances inasmuch as they are *such* substances, but only inasmuch as they are substances, or also beings, or insofar as they lead the metaphysician to an understanding of immaterial substances.

8. *Scriptum super libros Sententiarum magistri Petri Lombardi Episcopi Parisiensis* (hereafter *In Sent.*) II, d. 3, q. 1, a. 5, s.c. 2, eds. Pierre Mandonnet (Vol. 1–2) and M. F. Moos (Vol. 3–4) (Paris: Lethielleux, 1929–47), 2.99. Cf. Porphyry, *Isagoge* I, c. 3.

A closer examination of Thomas's writings, however, reveals that the matter is in fact more complex than I have stated it. Although the Porphyrian tree indeed presents a logical unity in its consideration of the genus *substance,* Thomas's metaphysical thought holds that this logical unity glosses over what is in fact an ontological diversity.[9] For he argues in a number of places that even though material and (created) immaterial substances belong to the same genus logically considered, as regards their real natures these beings share no common genus at all.

In support of this conclusion, Thomas cites Aristotle's observation in book 10 of the *Metaphysics* that the corruptible and incorruptible do not belong to the same genus.[10] According to Thomas, the reason is that these two sorts of beings differ in their degrees of actuality. As he puts it in terms of his metaphysics of *esse,* material and immaterial substances have diverse modes of existing (*diversi modi essendi*); for that reason, they share no common natural genus, whether proximate or remote.[11] For the same reason, he concludes that terrestrial and celestial bodies also do not share any common natural genus. Given the physics of his day, Thomas holds that celestial bodies, unlike terrestrial ones, are incorruptible. Hence, he tells us that even though the logician treats both sorts of bodies as sharing the common genus *body* and also *substance,* the metaphysician does not.[12]

Thomas's conclusion that these three types of beings share no common natural genus seems to call into question the possibility of a science of substance qua substance. For if there is not a single, real genus that includes all substances, we might ask how metaphysics can be said to study all substances according to the common *ratio* of substance. To those familiar with Thomas's metaphysics, a solution to this *aporia* will likely come to mind: the nature of substance must be analogical. As I will argue, this is indeed Thomas's position. But it is a position that itself

9. Bernard Montagnes, *The Doctrine of the Analogy of Being according to Thomas Aquinas,* trans. Edward M. Macierwoski (Milwaukee, Wisc.: Marquette University Press, 2004), 86–87.

10. *Metaphysics* X, 10, 1058b26–1059a15.

11. *In Sent.* II, d. 3, q. 1, a. 1, ad 2 (ed. Mandonnet, 2.88); *In De Trin.,* q. 4, a. 2 co.; ibid., q. 6, a. 3 co. (ed. Leon. 50.123–25); *Summa theologiae* (hereafter *ST*) I, q. 88, a. 2 ad 4, *Editio Leonina* 5.367; *De spiritualibus creaturis* (hereafter *De spir. creat.*), a. 2, ad 16, *Editio Leonina* 24/2.32.

12. *In De Trin.,* q. 4, a. 2 co. (ed. Leon. 50. 123–25); ibid., q. 6, a. 3 co. (ed. Leon 50.167–68); *Quaestiones disputatae de potentia* (hereafter *De pot.*), q. 7, a. 7, ad s.c. 1, in *Quaestiones disputatae,* ed. P. Bazzi, M. Calcaterra, T. S. Centi, E. Odetto, P. M. Pession (Turin and Rome: Marietti, 1965), 2.205.

raises still more difficulties. For example, the question arises how substance can be analogical if, as Aristotle claims, it does not admit of more
and less?[13] Again, if substance is analogical, what does Thomas consider
the primary instance to be? Is it a creature? If so, which one and why? Is
it God? If so, how is this possible given Thomas's position that God is not
contained in any genus, including the genus *substance*?

In addressing these and other difficulties, my chapter will consist of
four main parts and a conclusion. In the first, I will examine in more detail the distinction Thomas draws between a logical genus and a natural
one. In the second part, I will attempt to clarify what he means by "substance" through looking at his definition of the term. Having done this, I
will show in the third part that we can find in Thomas's writings a third
sense of genus, namely, what he terms a "metaphysical genus" that is analogical, and I will argue that it is according to this sense that he speaks of
a science of substance. In the fourth part, I will consider how, according
to Thomas, this metaphysical genus stands in relation to God. The fifth
and final part of my chapter will consist of concluding thoughts.

THOMAS'S DISTINCTION BETWEEN A LOGICAL AND
A NATURAL GENUS

In a number of works, Thomas considers the characteristics of genus and
difference, noting that they are found differently in material substances than in immaterial ones. If we consider a material substance, he explains, its genus is taken from a material principle, whereas its difference
is taken from a formal one. Thus, in man the genus *animal* is taken from
man's sensitive nature, whereas the difference *rational* is taken from
man's intellective nature. With that said, Thomas is careful to note that
even though genus and difference are related to each other proportion-
ately as matter to form, they are not identical with the very matter and
form of material substances. Although a human being is composed of
soul and body, when we say that "*man* is a rational animal," we do not
mean that *man* is composed of *rational* and *animal*.

In Thomas's view this fact becomes clear when we consider the signification of these terms. The genus *animal* is not predicated of a human

13. Aristotle, *Categories*, 5, 2b22–28.

being such that it signifies simply his matter, which is only a part of him. Rather, it signifies the whole of the thing in that species: for example, the whole man. Similarly, when the difference *rational* is predicated of a human being, it does not signify simply the soul of that human being, which is only a part of him. Rather, again, it signifies the whole human being. With that said, Thomas notes that genus and difference signify the whole in different ways. Since the genus designates what is material in the thing, it expresses the whole only in an indeterminate way. By contrast, the difference expresses the whole in a determinate way because it designates the thing by a determinate form.[14]

As regards immaterial substances, however, Thomas notes that genus and difference are taken in another way since these beings are not composed of matter and form. Rather, they are what he terms "simple quiddities" (*simplices quiditates*), or pure forms. Hence, their genus and difference cannot be taken from different parts of their essence but must be taken from the whole of it, although in different respects. As he explains, immaterial substances are like one another in their immateriality, but they differ from each other in their grade of perfection according to the degree to which they approach pure act and fall short of it due to their potentiality. Consequently, the genus of these beings is taken from their immateriality and from the characteristics that follow from it (such as their intellectuality), whereas their differences follow from their grade of perfection, which, Thomas adds, is unknown to us.[15] Indeed, he notes that even the genus of immaterial substances is, properly speaking, unknown to us. To the extent that we can know it, we know it by way of negation, as when we know that such beings are *im*-material, *in*-corporeal, *without* shape, and so forth.[16]

Moreover, as I have noted, Thomas holds that these immaterial substances cannot in reality belong to the same genus as material ones. Again, he bases this position on Aristotle's observation that the corruptible and incorruptible must differ generically. In his commentary on the

---

14. *De ente et essentia* (hereafter *De ente*), c. 2, *Editio Leonina* 43.372:164–373:242; ibid., c. 5 (ed. Leon. 43.379:85–104); *Summa contra Gentiles* (hereafter *SCG*) II, c. 95, *Editio Leonina* 13.568–69; *In VII Meta.*, lect. 12 (ed. Marietti 373:1546–374:1550); *In Sent.* II, d. 3, q. 1, a. 5 co. (ed. Mandonnet, 2. 99–100).

15. *De ente*, c. 5 (ed. Leon. 43.379:98–115); *SCG* II, c. 95 (ed. Leon. 13.568–69); *In Sent.* II, d. 3, q. 1, a. 5 co. (ed. Mandonnet, 2. 99–100).

16. *In De Trin.*, q. 6, a. 3 co. (ed. Leon. 50.167–68).

Metaphysics, Thomas explains why this is the case. Corruptibility and incorruptibility are contraries since the former entails a potential to go out of existence whereas the latter entails the lack of such potential. As contraries, they must differ from each other formally. This observation might lead us to conclude that the corruptible and incorruptible differ simply in terms of species. If that were the case, the two could belong to the same genus; but in fact we are told the difference between them is more fundamental: the corruptible and incorruptible must be generically diverse. According to Thomas, Aristotle reaches this conclusion because matter and potency pertain to genus, whereas form and act pertain to species. Hence, contraries that pertain to form and act result in a difference in species, whereas contraries that pertain to potency result in a diversity in genera. It is for this reason that the corruptible and incorruptible cannot belong to the same genus.[17]

Still, Thomas adds that nothing prevents them from belonging to the same genus "logically speaking" since they are able to share a single, common notion (*una communa ratio*) such as "substance," "quality," and so forth.[18] If we wonder why this is the case, he provides an answer in his commentary on Boethius's *De Trinitate.* In q. 4, a. 2, he tells us again that the genus of a material substance is taken from its matter. Nevertheless, he reminds us that a genus does not signify simply the matter of the substance but the whole substance because the genus has in itself both matter and form. Therefore, when the natural philosopher considers the genus of a material substance, he does so with respect to both parts of it (we might add that the same is true of the metaphysician). By contrast, when the logician considers a genus, he does so only with respect to what is formal in it. According to Thomas, it is for this reason that the logician's definitions are called "formal definitions." In short, the logician prescinds from considering the material aspect of a genus and, consequently, prescinds from considering the genus's potency or lack thereof. Thus, as a further consequence, neither does he consider its corruptibil-

---

17. *In X Meta.,* lect. 12 (ed. Marietti 504:2136–505:214545). Thomas adds, furthermore, that because the corruptible has the potential not to exist whereas the incorruptible does not have this potential, the corruptible and incorruptible divide Being (*ens*) essentially (*per se*). Since Being is not a genus, he notes that it should be of no surprise that the corruptible and incorruptible do not belong to the same natural genus. Cf. *In V Meta.,* lect. 22 (ed. Marietti 288:1119–289:1127); *In De Trin.,* q. 4, a. 2 co. (ed. Leon. 50.123–25).

18. *In X Meta.,* lect. 12 (ed. Marietti 505:2142).

ity or incorruptibility. Thomas concludes that it is precisely because logic prescinds from such considerations that things which do not belong to a common natural genus (such as the corruptible and incorruptible) can nevertheless belong to a common logical one.

Continuing on in the same article, he explains that we find this distinction between a logical and natural genus whenever we consider the similitude of things to the First Act (viz., God)—a similitude that occurs in different ways for those things that have matter (viz., terrestrial bodies), those that have a different kind of matter (viz., celestial bodies), and those that have no matter at all:

> It is clear that a stone in matter, which exists according to a potency for existence [*esse*], attains [a likeness] to this [First Act because] it subsists; similarly, the sun attains to it according to a potency to place, but not to existence; and an angel does so lacking all matter. Hence, the logician, finding in all of these things something material from which he has taken the genus, places all of them in the single genus *substance*. But the natural philosopher and the metaphysician, who consider *all* the principles of a thing, not finding any agreement in matter, say that they differ in genus.[19]

In this passage, Thomas presents a hierarchy of beings in terms of their degrees of actuality—a hierarchy that the metaphysician recognizes consists of diverse natural genera.[20] Still, the metaphysician refers to all of

---

19. *In De Trin.*, q. 4, a. 2 (ed. Leon. 50.124:167–83): "[C]ontingit enim quandoque quod illud de similitudine primi actus <quod> consequitur res aliqua in materia tali, aliud consequatur sine materia, et aliud in alia materia omnino diversa; sicut patet quod lapis in materia, quae est secundum potentiam ad esse pertingit ad hoc quod subsistat, ad quod idem pertingit sol secundum materiam ad ubi et non ad esse, et angelus omni materia carens. Vnde logicus, inveniens in omnibus his illud materiae ex quo genus sumebat, ponit omnia in uno genere substantiae; naturalis vero et metaphysicus, qui considerant omnia principia rei, non invenientes convenientiam in materia, dicunt genere differre, secundum hoc quod dicitur in X Metaphysice, quod corruptibile et incorruptibile differunt genere et quod illa conveniunt genere quorum materia est una et generatio ad invicem." All Latin translations are my own.

20. This is not to claim that all differences between genera are founded on degrees of actuality. Moreover, as Thomas notes elsewhere, this hierarchy is found not only between the material and the immaterial, but even among the immaterial as well. Considering the nature of angels, he explains that because they do not have matter to diversify their essences, each angel must differ from another according to its grade of being. Thus, Thomas famously argues that each angel is unique in its species (see e.g. *ST* I, q. 50, a. 4). This conclusion may lead us to wonder whether he considers angels to be unique in their genera as well. He offers something of an answer to this question in his *Quaestiones disputatae de anima* (a. 7, ad 17), where he notes that as far as the metaphysician is concerned, genus and difference are not found *at*

the beings in this hierarchy as "substances," indicating that he recognizes some commonality among them. To understand why that is, I will turn now to consider Thomas's definition of the term "substance."

THOMAS'S DEFINITION OF "SUBSTANCE"

In his efforts to define the term "substance," Thomas is keenly aware that we are presented with a difficulty from the outset: it is impossible to offer a proper definition in terms of genus and difference. The reason is that the genus *substance* is a most general genus (*genus generalissimum*), so there is nothing prior to it in terms of which to define it.[21] Still, he notes in his *Commentary on the Sentences* that we can offer what he refers to as a quasi definition (*quasi definitio*) of "substance"—in other words a working definition of it.[22] As with much of Thomas's philosophical thought, his views of substance are influenced by Aristotle. Nevertheless, there are some significant differences between the two philosophers on this topic. For both of these reasons, I will first consider what Aristotle has to say about substance before examining Thomas's definition.

In chapter 5 of his *Categories,* Aristotle notes the following: "Substance, in the truest and primary and most definite sense of the word, is that which is neither predicable of a subject nor present in a subject."[23] To illustrate the sorts of things that he is referring to, he offers the example of an individual man or an individual horse. Let us consider the examples of Socrates and Seabiscuit (assuming both individuals were alive today). Although many things are predicable of these two subjects, such as height and weight and color, the subjects themselves are not predicable of other subjects: we cannot meaningfully and truthfully say, for example, "This man Socrates is that horse Seabiscuit." Or, again, "This horse Seabiscuit is that man Socrates." Moreover, neither are these sub-

---

all in spiritual substances since such beings are pure forms (*formae tantum*) and simple species (*species simplices*).

21. On this point, see *De pot.,* q. 7, a. 3, ad 4 (ed. Marietti 2.194).

22. *In Sent.* IV, d. 12, q. 1, a. 1, ql. 1, ad 2 (ed. Moos 4.499).

23. Aristotle, *Categories,* trans. E. M. Edghill, in *The Works of Aristotle,* vol. 1, ed. W. D. Ross (Oxford: Clarendon Press, 1928), 5.2a11–13. For a recent overview of Aristotle's *Categories* and the debates surrounding this work, see Paul Studtmann, *The Foundations of Aristotle's Categorial Scheme* (Milwaukee, Wisc.: Marquette University Press, 2008). See also Joseph Owens, "Aristotle on Categories," *Review of Metaphysics* 14 (1960): 73–90.

jects present *in* subjects, in contrast to the accidental traits that *are* present in *them.*

Aristotle refers to this sense of "substance" as "first" or "primary" substance. He then tells us that there is another sense of the term, namely as species that include primary substances, and as genera that include species. To illustrate what he means, he notes that an individual man is included in the species *man,* and that that species in turn is included in the genus *animal.* Aristotle refers to this second sense of substance, logically enough, as "second" or "secondary" substance. And he tells us that unlike primary substance, secondary substance *is* predicable of others: namely of primary substances. For example, *man* is predicable of Socrates. Moreover, some secondary substances are predicable of other secondary substances, namely genera of the species they contain. Thus, the genus *animal* is predicable of the species *man.*[24]

Aristotle then concludes that primary substances are most properly called "substances" because all else is predicated of them. And he notes that species are more properly called substances than are genera—not only because they are more closely related to primary substances but also because genera are predicated of species. With that said, Aristotle adds that no species is more truly substance than another. The same is the case with primary substances: an individual man is not more truly a substance than is an individual ox. In short, substance does not admit of degrees since it is predicated of its member univocally.[25] From this consideration of substance in the *Categories,* we may conclude that for Aristotle, although the genus *substance* contains subaltern genera and species, most properly speaking what it contains are individuals, namely, the sorts of things that are neither predicable of a subject nor present in a subject.

Aristotle provides a more detailed analysis of substance in book 7 of his *Metaphysics*—this time with an eye to the metaphysical significance of the term. In chapter 3 of that book, he tells us that the term "substance" is used in several senses, referring to at least four objects: essence, universal, genus, and subject. Returning to his definition from the *Categories,* he explains that a subject is that of which everything else is predi-

---

24. Aristotle, *Categories,* 5.2a36.
25. Ibid., 5.2b26–38.

cated but is not itself predicated of anything else. He then identifies the different senses of "substance" as subject.[26] But before examining these various senses in more detail, Aristotle notes the following: "Thus, by means of an outline, we have said what 'substance' is, namely, that which is not [predicated] of a subject, but that of which other things [are predicated]. However, this is not all that should be said; for this is not enough. Indeed, this much is obvious."[27]

In his commentary on the *Metaphysics,* Thomas explains why Aristotle makes the point of noting that he has only outlined what "substance" is. It is because it might seem to someone that having identified these four senses, Aristotle has provided a sufficient understanding of the matter. Thomas then interprets Aristotle's statement further, explaining that the outline to which he is referring is his definition of "substance." Going beyond the literal sense of the text, Thomas next notes that this definition states what "substance" is only in a universal way (*in universali*). The implication is that the definition is somehow lacking. As Thomas proceeds to explain,

We need to know "substance" and other things not only by a universal and logical definition; for this is not sufficient for knowing the nature of a thing since the very thing that is designated by such a definition is evident. Indeed, such a definition does not treat the principles of the thing, upon which depends knowledge of the thing. Rather it treats some common condition of the thing by which such a definition (*notificatio*) is given.[28]

26. Namely, as form, matter, or composite. Of these three, Aristotle identifies form as the primary sense of substance (1029a1–7). In his commentary on this text, Thomas notes that this division of "substance" taken as "subject" is based on analogous predication, and he notes that Aristotle identifies the primary sense as form since it is prior to both matter and the composite. See *In VII Meta.,* lect. 2 (ed. Marietti 321:1276).

When he considers these three senses of "substance" again in his commentary on Aristotle's *De Anima,* however, it is clear that Thomas himself considers the composite to be the primary sense. See *Sentencia libri De anima* II, lect. 1, *Editio Leonina* 45/1.69:96–117.

27. Aristotle, *Metaphysics* VII, 2, (1029a7–9): "Nunc quidem igitur typo, dictum est quid sit substantia, quia quod non de subiecto, sed de quo alia. Oportet autem non solum ita. Non enim sufficiens. Ipsum enim hoc manifestum" (ed. Marietti 320:570). I am quoting here the Latin Aristotle included in the Marietti edition since this text is based upon the Moerbeke translation upon which Thomas is commenting, as discussed below.

28. *In VII Meta.,* lect. 2 (ed. Marietti 322:1280): "Et quia posset alicui videri, quod ex quo Philosophus ponit omnes modos, quibus dicitur substantia, quod hoc sufficeret ad sciendum quid est substantia; ideo subiungit dicens, quod nunc dictum est quid sit substantia 'solum typo', idest dictum est solum in universali, quod substantia est illud, quod non dicitur de subiecto, sed de quo dicuntur alia; sed oportet non solum ita cognoscere substantiam et alias res, scilicet per definitionem universalem et logicam: hoc enim non est sufficiens ad cognoscen-

As Thomas notes further on in his *Metaphysics* commentary, Aristotle's definition of "substance" is not a metaphysical definition but, rather, a logical one.[29] It does not provide us with knowledge of substance as an ontological reality because it says nothing about the principles that constitute substance.

How then does the metaphysician define "substance"? Thomas touches upon this topic in the *De veritate*. In the very first article of that work he considers what truth is, and in the course of this examination, he cites Avicenna's observation that the first concept of the intellect to which all other concepts resolve is being (*ens*). All of our other concepts add to the concept of being—not, however, by adding to it something from outside of itself, in the way that a difference adds something to a genus or an accident adds to a subject; for every nature whatsoever is essentially a being. As an example of how being is added to, Thomas gives substance, noting that "The name 'substance' expresses a certain special mode of existing (*modus essendi*): namely, as *being in itself* (*ens per se*)."[30]

The formulation *ens per se* is one that Thomas employs throughout his writings to refer to substance.[31] Nevertheless, in those texts where he

dum naturam rei, quia hoc ipsum quod assignatur pro definitione tali, est manifestum. Non enim huiusmodi definitione tanguntur principia rei, ex quibus cognitio rei dependet; sed tangitur aliqua communis conditio rei per quam talis notificatio datur."

29. *In VII Meta.*, lect. 13 (ed. Marietti 379:1575–76). Still, implicit in Thomas's account is a recognition of a connection between the logical and metaphysical views of substance. As Étienne Gilson notes, "Since, however, the notion of substance is one of the Aristotelian categories, it is impossible to discuss it, even from the point of view of the metaphysician, without bearing in mind what logic says about it. Far from being indifferent to actual reality, the logic of Aristotle starts from the primary substance, which is the only actually existing reality." Étienne Gilson, "Quasi Definitio Substantiae," in *St. Thomas Aquinas 1274–1974: Commemorative Studies*, vol. 1, ed. Armand Maurer (Toronto: Pontifical Institute of Medieval Studies, 1974), 114–15.

30. *Quaestiones disputatae de veritate* (hereafter *De ver.*), q. 1, a. 1 co., *Editio Leonina* 22/1.5:100–23: "substantia enim non addit super ens aliquam differentiam quae designet aliquam naturam superadditam enti sed nomine substantiae exprimitur specialis quidam modus essendi, scilicet per se ens, et ita est in aliis generibus."

In translating *ens per se* as "being in itself" as opposed to the more literal "being *through* itself" I follow Wippel, who notes the following advantages to this translation: "(1) because when applied to substance this is surely what Thomas means by so describing substance, i.e., as that which exists in itself (and not in something else), or as that which exists in its own right; (2) because to translate it as being *through* itself might possibly lead to the mistaken interpretation that Thomas regards substances (finite) as beings which do not depend on something else for their existence, i.e., as uncaused" (Wippel, *Metaphysical Thought*, 229 n. 112).

31. See, e.g., *ST* I, q. 52, a. 1 co. (ed. Leon 5.20); ibid., II-II, q. 23, a. 3, ad 3; *De pot.*, q. 5, a. 10 co. (ed. Marietti 2.155–56); *Quaestiones disputatae de virtutibus*, q. 2, a. 1, ad 22; *In IV Meta.*, lect. 1 (ed. Marietti 159:539). On this topic, see Wippel, *Metaphysical Thought*, 228–29.

explicitly considers the definition of "substance," he tells us that this formulation is problematic. On this point, it is not Aristotle who influences Thomas's metaphysical thought, but rather Avicenna. For Thomas himself notes in a number of places that, according to Avicenna, *ens per se* cannot be the definition of "substance."[32] This observation prompted Étienne Gilson to search for the origin of the statement in Avicenna's writings. As Gilson has shown, however, it is impossible to find the explicit statement anywhere in his works. Nevertheless, the spirit of it can be found in Avicenna's metaphysical writings, and it is these writings that influence Thomas's views about substance.[33]

As a general rule, Thomas's *ex professo* considerations of the definition of "substance" occur in texts where he wishes to show that God is not contained in any genus, even the genus *substance*. Citing Avicenna time and again, he notes that *ens per se* cannot be its definition. To show why he reaches this conclusion, I will focus on just one of these texts, namely, *Summa contra Gentiles* I, c. 25. There, after offering several arguments to prove that God is not contained in any genus, Thomas acknowledges that it might seem to someone that God is at least contained in the genus *substance*. According to this line of reasoning, even if we grant that the name itself, "substance," cannot properly belong to God since he does not substand (*substat*) accidents, someone might still argue that God belongs in this genus because what is *signified* by the name belongs to him. For, the argument goes, a substance is a being in itself (*ens per se*), and certainly God is such a being since he does not exist in another.[34]

Nevertheless, Thomas explains that this line of reasoning is problematic because *ens per se* is not an appropriate definition of "substance." The problem arises because, as I have already noted, the genus *substance* is a *summum genus,* and as such it cannot properly be defined in terms of genus and difference. Indeed, if we consider the formulation "being in itself," neither "being" nor "in itself" can function as a genus. Thomas reminds us that being does not have the nature (*ratio*) of a genus.[35] And he

---

32. For references to Avicenna on this point, see *In Sent.* I, d. 8, q. 4, a. 2, ad 2 (ed. Mandonnet, 1.222–23); *In Sent.* IV, d. 12, q. 1, a. 1, ql. 1, ad 2 (ed. Moos, 4.499); *De pot.,* q. 7, a. 3, ad 4 (ed. Marietti 2.194).

33. Gilson, "Quasi Definitio Substantiae," 111–12; Cf. Wippel, *Metaphysical Thought,* 229–30.

34. *SCG* I, c. 25 (ed. Leon. 13.76–77).

35. This is a point that he already made earlier in the same chapter in his efforts to prove that God is not in a genus.

contends that the phrase "in itself" seems to convey nothing but a pure negation, for the reason something is called a "being *in itself*" is really due to the fact that it does *not* exist in another. Consequently, the phrase "in itself" cannot constitute the nature (*ratio*) of a genus since it does not tell us what the thing is but rather what it is not.

Having thus shown why he thinks *ens per se* cannot be the definition of *substance,* Thomas tells us the following:

The nature [*ratio*] of substance, therefore, must be understood in this way: that a substance is "a thing to which it belongs to exist *not* in a subject." Now, the name "thing" is designated from the quiddity, just as the name "being" [*ens*] is designated from the act of existing [*esse*]. Thus, in the nature of substance is understood "that which has a quiddity to which it belongs to exist *not* in another."[36]

According to Thomas, for something to have a quiddity or essence in this way is for it to have an essence that is distinct from its *esse.* In the formulation *ens per se,* the significance of this real distinction between these two principles is lost. And, Thomas concludes, it is because these two principles are not really distinct in God that God cannot belong to any genus, even the genus *substance.*

Thomas offers similar variations of this definition of "substance" in other works where he wishes to prove that God is not included in any genus.[37] Considering these various texts, Wippel has observed that we can draw the following conclusions regarding Thomas's account of substance. The first is that for Thomas "being in itself" (*ens per se*) is not an appropriate definition of substance. The second conclusion is that he considers a more appropriate definition to be "a thing to whose quiddity it belongs to exist *not* in another." The third conclusion is that even this definition in Thomas's view is not truly a definition in the strict sense but, rather, only a quasi definition.[38]

---

36. *SCG* I, c. 25 (ed. Leon. 13.76–77): "Oportet igitur quod ratio substantiae intelligatur hoc modo, quod substantia sit res cui conveniat esse non in subiecto; nomen autem rei a quidditate imponitur, sicut nomen entis ab esse; et sic in ratione substantiae intelligitur quod habeat quidditatem cui conveniat esse non in alio. Hoc autem Deo non convenit: nam non habet quidditatem nisi suum esse."

37. See *In Sent.* IV, d. 12, q. 1, a. 1, ql. 1, ad 2 (ed. Moos 4.499); *De pot.,* q. 7, a. 3, ad 4 (ed. Marietti 194). Thomas offers a somewhat different version in *ST* I, q. 3, a. 5, ad 1 (ed. Leon. 4.44): "Sed significat essentiam cui competit sic esse, idest per se esse: quod tamen esse non est ipsa eius essentia." However, he returns to his prior formulations in *ST* III, q. 77, a. 1, ad 2.

38. Wippel, *Metaphysical Thought,* 230–34.

If we wonder why the genus *substance* must entail this real distinction between essence and *esse,* Thomas explains elsewhere that it is a characteristic of every genus that the essence of its members is other than their *esse.* For all things that are directly in a given genus must agree in quidditative content. If their essences were not distinct from their *esse,* then one thing within the genus would not differ from another. Rather, all would be one being, which is absurd. Thus, he concludes that everything directly in the genus *substance* must be composed at the very least of essence and *esse.*[39] It is the distinction between these two principles within a being that enables it to be ordered within one of the categories of being (*ordinabilis in praedicamento*).[40]

Although Thomas refers to his definition of "substance" as merely a quasi definition, it is worth noting that it does not suffer from the limitations that he finds with Aristotle's definition. Whereas Thomas considers that definition of "substance" to be merely a logical one since it does not treat the principles of a thing, his Avicennian inspired definition does treat of such principles, namely of essence and *esse.* For Thomas, then, this quasi definition of "substance" is a metaphysical one. With that said, he thinks that the real distinction between essence and *esse* to which the definition refers also has bearing in the logical order. Thomas makes this point clear in a text from the *Prima Pars* of the *Summa theologiae.* In question 88, article 2, he considers whether we can know immaterial substances through a knowledge of natural things. Responding to the Fourth Objection, he shows why such knowledge is impossible, and he does so by highlighting the distinction between the logical genus *substance* and the natural one:

Immaterial created substances do not in fact agree in natural genus with material substances since there is not in them the same nature [*ratio*] of potency and matter. Nevertheless, they do agree with them in a logical genus, since even immaterial substances are in the genus *substance,* for their quiddity is not their *esse.* But God does not agree with material things either according to a natural genus or according to a logical genus, since God is not in any way in a genus.[41]

39. *De ver.,* q. 27, a. 1, ad 8 (ed. Leon. 22/3.792:221–31).

40. *De ente,* c. 5 (ed. Leon. 43.379:72–74).

41. *ST* I, q. 88, a. 2, ad 4 (ed. Leon. 5.367): "Substantiae immateriales creatae in genere quidem naturali non conveniunt cum substantiis materialibus, quia non est in eis eadem ratio potentiae et materiae: conveniunt tamen cum eis in genere logico, quia etiam substantiae imma-

This passage brings us back to our initial *aporia* regarding metaphysics as the science of substance. For it seems that it is not enough that immaterial and material substances share a common logical genus for there to be a single science that is the science of substance. Indeed, as I have mentioned, Thomas tells us that the metaphysician is concerned not with logical considerations but with real ones. If there is no real common genus that includes all substances, then it seems that there cannot be a single science of substance *as* substance. With that said, Thomas clearly sees some real commonality between all those created things that he calls substances, namely, that there is in them a real distinction between essence and *esse*. Moreover, he explains in the *Summa contra gentiles* that since potency and act divide *ens commune,* whatever follows potency and act is common both to material substances and to created immaterial ones—such as to receive and to be received, to perfect and to be perfected.[42]

A solution to our *aporia* is suggested by a text in Thomas's *Disputed Questions on Spiritual Creatures.* In article 1, he considers whether created spiritual substances are composed of matter and form. The tenth objection argues that they must be because they are included in a genus and everything that is in a genus has matter. In response, Thomas notes that

The form of a genus for which matter belongs to its essence [*ratio*] cannot exist outside of the intellect except in matter, as is the case with the form of *plant* or *metal.* But this genus *substance* is not the sort for which matter belongs to its essence. Otherwise it would not be a metaphysical genus but a natural one. Hence, the form of this genus does not depend upon matter according to its own existence [*esse*], but it can also be found without matter.[43]

In this text, Thomas introduces a third sense of genus that we have not yet considered, what he refers to as a "metaphysical genus." A metaphysi-

teriales sunt in praedicamento substantiae, cum earum quidditas non sit earum esse. Sed Deus non convenit cum rebus materialibus neque secundum genus naturale, neque secundum genus logicum: quia Deus nullo modo est in genere, ut supra dictum est. Unde per similitudines rerum materialium aliquid affirmative potest cognosci de angelis secundum rationem communem, licet non secundum rationem speciei; de Deo autem nullo modo." Emphasis added in translation.

42. *SCG* II, c. 54 (ed. Leon. 13.392).

43. *De spir. creat.,* a. 1, ad 10 (ed. Leon. 24/2.17–18:574–81): "Ad decimum dicendum quod forma generis de cuius ratione est materia non potest esse extra intellectum nisi <in> materia, ut forma plantae aut metalli; sed hoc genus 'substantiae' non est tale de cuius ratione sit materia, alioquin non esset metaphysicum, sed naturale; unde forma huius generis non dependet a materia secundum suum esse, sed potest inveniri etiam extra materiam."

cal genus, he tells us, differs from a natural one because it does not depend upon matter according to its existence, or *esse*. Does it differ from a logical genus? That Thomas does not say. We may presume, however, that it does so differ given his designation of this genus as "metaphysical" and also given his discussion of it in terms of *esse*. In short, he does not present it as a mere logical intention.

But what exactly *is* a metaphysical genus? Unfortunately, Thomas does not tell us anything more than what I have quoted; moreover, to the best of my knowledge, this text presents the only occasion where he explicitly refers to a genus in this way. Still, from looking at Thomas's other metaphysical considerations, we can get a sense of what he means. And, as I will argue, it is according to this sense of genus that Thomas considers metaphysics to be the science of substance.

SUBSTANCE AS A METAPHYSICAL GENUS

We can begin to get a sense of what Thomas means by a metaphysical genus if we consider again that last line in the text quoted above from *On Spiritual Creatures:* he tells us that the form of the metaphysical genus *substance* does not depend upon matter according to its own existence (*esse*), but it can also be found without matter. The implication is that even though some substances are in matter, matter is not essential to substance taken as a metaphysical genus. Thomas's words here are reminiscent of observations in his earlier commentary on Boethius's *De Trinitate* (ca. 1257–1259).[44]

In question 5 of that work, Thomas considers the division and methods of the sciences, identifying the sorts of objects that are studied in metaphysics, in both articles 1 and 4. Unlike the objects studied by the natural philosopher, which depend upon matter both for their existence (*esse*) and for their being understood, the objects studied by the metaphysician do not depend upon matter in either respect. Thomas identifies two classes of such objects. On the one hand, there are those that never exist in matter, such as God and the angels. In the words of Wip-

---

44. Dating of Thomas's texts in this chapter follows Jean-Pierre Torrell's *Saint Thomas Aquinas,* vol. 1, *The Person and His Works,* rev. ed., trans. Robert Royal (Washington, D.C.: The Catholic University of America Press, 2005). Torrell dates *In De Trin.* to 1257–58, or at the beginning of 1259 (345), and he dates *De spir. creat.* to 1266–69 (336).

pel, we may refer to these objects as "positively immaterial." On the other hand, there are those objects that are sometimes found in matter and sometimes not. Following Wippel again, we may refer to such objects as "negatively" or "neutrally immaterial."[45] As examples of such objects, Thomas offers substance, quality, being (*ens*), potency, act, and one and many.[46] He provides clarification about this second class of objects in article 4 when responding to the fifth objection.

That objection begins by noting that the subject matter of metaphysics is being (*ens*) and principally the sort of being that is substance, as is clear from book 4 of Aristotle's *Metaphysics*. Since some substances are material, it is argued that being and substance do not abstract from matter. Thomas responds by noting that being and substance are not separate from matter as though to be *without* matter were an essential characteristic for them in the same way that for the species *ass,* to be without reason is an essential characteristic. Rather, being and substance are separate from matter in another sense, namely because to be *in* matter is not of their essence, even though they are sometimes found under that condition. Thus, he suggests, a better comparison is with the genus *animal,* which abstracts from the difference *rational* even though some animals are rational.[47] I take Thomas's point here to be that it would be incorrect to refer to the genus *animal* as *irrational;* rather, it would be better to say that the genus is *non-rational.* Similarly, because both being and substance can be found in matter, they are not properly speaking *immaterial* but rather *non-material,* for they are metaphysically open to both materiality and immateriality.

From the foregoing, I conclude that when Thomas refers to substance as a metaphysical genus, he is considering the genus in this respect, namely as non-material—or in Wippel's terms as negatively or neutrally immaterial. As Thomas explains in a number of texts, the genus *substance* is separate from matter in this way because the essential characteristic (*ratio*) of substance is that it subsists in itself—a characteristic that in no way depends upon having a body. For bodily nature in some

---

45. Wippel, *Metaphysical Themes,* 30, 72–73; ibid., *Metaphysical Thought,* 8–9, 52–53.

46. This list appears in article 1, at the end of which he adds, "and so forth." In article 4, he offers a similar list, but lists only being (*ens*), substance, potency, and act. See *In De Trin.,* q. 5, a. 1 co. (ed. Leon. 50.138:154–67); ibid., a. 4 co. (ed. Leon. 50.154:182–98).

47. *In De Trin.,* q. 5, a. 4, ad 5 (ed. Leon. 50.156:305–13).

way is related to the accident of dimensions, which do not cause subsistence. Indeed, dimensions fall within the category of quantity and, as such, depend upon substance as their intelligible matter. Thus, quantity cannot exist without substance, but substance can exist without quantity; more precisely, substance can exist without dimensions and, hence, without matter.[48] According to Thomas, we arrive at this metaphysical understanding of substance not by an act of abstraction, but rather by what he terms *separatio:* a negative judgment. As Wippel has shown at great length, it is only when we make the judgment that substance does not depend upon quantity that we recognize its nature as negatively or neutrally immaterial—or, to put it in the terms of our consideration here, that we recognize substance as a metaphysical genus.[49]

What of Thomas's claim, then, that the three grades of substance—terrestrial, celestial, and immaterial—do not share a common genus? When he makes this claim, it is always in the context of discussing natural genera. When, however, he presents substance as a metaphysical genus, he sees no problem finding commonality among these grades of beings. I would argue that this is because what Thomas has termed a "metaphysical genus" is not only negatively immaterial but also analogical in character. To speak of a genus in this manner may sound contradictory. Thomas himself tells us that a genus is predicated univocally of its species and not according to priority and posteriority, which is the mark of the analogous.[50] Indeed, he cites the analogical nature of being

48. *De spir. creat.,* a. 5 co. (ed. Leon. 24/2.58–62). Cf. *In De Trin.,* q. 5, a. 3; *SCG* II, c. 91. In the text from *De spir. creat.,* Thomas employs this line of reasoning to prove that there must exist created immaterial substances for the genus *substance* to be complete.

49. *In De Trin.,* q. 5, a. 3. Wippel, *Metaphysical Themes,* 69–104; id. *Metaphysical Thought,* 44–62. As Lawrence Dewan explains, "Substance, along with 'a being,' belongs to the domain of what all naturally know. Metaphysical reflection can only serve to render that knowledge less subject to impediments, freer from the influence of our various lesser habitual cognitive stances" (Dewan, "Importance of Substance," in *Form and Being: Studies in Thomistic Metaphysics* [Washington, D.C.: The Catholic University of America Press, 2006], 110).

50. See, e.g., *De principiis naturae* (hereafter *De prin. nat.*), c. 6; *Expositio Libri Peryermenias* (hereafter *In De interp.*), lect. 8, n. 5. Thomas is not here rejecting the possibility of a hierarchy within a genus in terms of any sort of priority and posteriority: within every genus there can and must be priority and posteriority based upon the *differentiae* that constitute the species within the genus. Hence, his position is that there is a "first" within any genus. See, e.g., *ST* I-II, q. 61, a. 1, ad 1; *Super Librum De causis* (hereafter *In Lib. de caus.*), prop. 4; *In I De interp.,* lect. 8, nn. 5–6; *Sententia super Physicam* V, lect. 3.

Regarding the hierarchies of species within genera, Thomas frequently cites Aristotle's observation that the species of things are like numbers. On this point, see Rudi A. te Velde, *Participation and Substantiality in Thomas Aquinas* (New York: E. J. Brill, 1995), 227–30.

(*ens*) as one reason why being is not a genus.[51] However, despite this position, on a number of occasions Thomas in fact alludes to being as a genus and even at times calls it such explicitly. For example, in the introduction to his commentary on the *Metaphysics,* we find him observing that the subject matter of this science is being in general (*ens commune*), which he says is the *genus* for which separate substances are the common and universal causes.[52]

Why would Thomas call being a genus here when he is so careful to point out elsewhere (indeed, even later within that very work) that it is not a genus? An explanation is suggested in his commentary on the *Sentences,* where he tells us that the term "genus" can be taken in two ways. Taken properly, it is predicated of several things that share the same essence. Taken more broadly, however, it is said of any community that embraces and contains many things.[53] Thus, he notes elsewhere that we can call things "genera" that in fact transcend genera—like being (*ens*) and one.[54] In short, Thomas sometimes uses the very term "genus" in an extended, or metaphorical, way to speak of analogical communities since they are like genera in point of being common, or universal. With this reading in mind, I take him to be employing this broader sense of the word "genus" when he uses the term "metaphysical genus" to refer to the genus *substance.*

Thus, I would argue, Thomas's position that the corruptible and incorruptible do not share a common genus must be read as referring to a common *natural* genus. As he himself notes in the *De potentia,* Aristotle's observation is intended to exclude only a univocal community among things, not an analogical one.[55] Thus, the various natural genera that are called by the name "substance" are not unrelated classes; rather,

51. See, e.g., *De principiis naturae,* c. 6; *In I De interp.,* lect. 8, n. 5; *In I Meta.,* lect. 9 (ed. Marietti 41–42:139).

52. *In Meta.,* proemium (ed. Marietti 1–2). Cf. *De ente,* c. 6 (ed. Leon. 43.380:54–8); *SCG* I, c. 28; *ST* I, q. 2, a. 3, *quarta via; Quaestiones disputatae de malo* (hereafter *De malo*), q. 1, a. 1, ad 11.

53. *In Sent.* II, d. 34, a. 1, a. 2, ad 1 (ed. Mandonnet 2.876–77).

54. *De malo,* q. 1, a. 1, ad 11, *Editio Leonina* 23.7:379–92.

55. *De pot.,* q. 7, a. 7, ad s.c. 1 (ed. Marietti 586). For Aquinas, in any real analogical community, the higher members cause the lower. This is no less true in the case of substance. As he explains his commentary on Boethius's *De Trinitate,* q. 5, a. 4 co. (ed. Leon. 50.153:126–31): "principia accidentium reducuntur in principia substantiae, et principia substantiarum corruptibilium reducuntur in substantias incorruptibiles; et sic quodam gradu et ordine in quaedam principia omnia entia reducuntur."

as we have seen, they constitute a hierarchy. And, Thomas tells us, it belongs to metaphysics to study the order among these substances.[56]

In his work *On Separate Substances,* he presents this order in terms of the degrees to which substances participate *esse* more or less perfectly. Examining the three classes of substance mentioned above in part 1 (terrestrial, celestial, and immaterial), he explains that immaterial substances participate in *esse* most perfectly and terrestrial substances do so the least.[57] In short, for Thomas, some substances are more truly substances than are others. Is he, then, contradicting Aristotle's observation in the *Categories* that *substance* does not admit of more and less? Not if we recall Thomas's position that Aristotle's consideration of substance in that work is a logical consideration. Logically considered, substance cannot admit of degrees, but metaphysically considered this is a possibility.[58]

If, however, the metaphysical genus *substance* is analogical, not only is it found according to priority and posteriority in its members, but it must also have a prime analogate: something in which the common characteristic (*ratio*) is found perfectly.[59] Indeed, Thomas holds that in any genus there must be something first that is most perfect and by which everything else in the genus is measured.[60] What is it that is first

56. *In III Meta.,* lect. 6 (ed. Marietti 112:398). As he explains in *In I Sent.,* d. 19, q. 5, a. 2, ad 1 (ed. Mandonnet 1.492), some things that the logician treats as univocal according to the logical order are in fact analogical according to the order of reality. As an example, he offers the term "body" as it is predicated of both terrestrial and celestial bodies. I would contend that Thomas holds the same view regarding the term "substance" when predicated of terrestrial bodies, celestial bodies, and angels. For discussion about the passage from *In I Sent.,* see, e.g., Ralph McInerny, *The Logic of Analogy: An Interpretation of St. Thomas* (The Hague: Nijhoff, 1961), 96–124; id., *Aquinas and Analogy* (Washington, D.C.: The Catholic University of America Press, 1996), 6–14; Montagnes, *Doctrine of Analogy,* 44, 60 n. 100; Wippel, *Metaphysical Thought,* 548–50.

57. *De substantiis separatis,* c. 8, *Editio Leonina* 40.54:109–55:163. As Montagnes notes, when Thomas considers the degrees of substance, he always opts to follow this Aristotelian tripartite hierarchy of substantiality (terrestrial body, celestial body, immaterial substance) rather than the Neoplatonic tripartite hierarchy of *esse, vivere, intelligere* (*Doctrine of Analogy,* 109–11 n. 78).

58. Commenting on Aristotle's observation from the *Categories* regarding substance, Thomas focuses on its metaphysical significance, noting that it should not be taken to mean that one species of substance cannot be more perfect than another. Rather, it means that one and the same *individual* does not participate in its species to a greater or lesser degree at one time rather than another. Furthermore, it also means that among individuals of the same species of substance, one cannot participate in that species more than another. See *ST* I, q. 93, a. 3, ad 3. Cf., *ST* I-II, q. 52, a. 1 co.

59. See, e.g., *De malo,* q. 7, a. 1, ad 1.

60. See, e.g., *In Sent.* I, d. 8, q. 4, a. 2, obj. 3 & ad 3 (ed. Mandonnet 1.221, 223); *SCG* I, c. 28; *ST*

in the genus *substance* that acts as this measure? It would seem that the likely answer is God. But this answer is problematic for several reasons. To begin with, we have seen Thomas conclude that God is not contained in any genus, whether logical or natural. One might reply that the metaphysical genus we are considering differs from these other sorts of genera—but then there is still the problem of definition. As we have seen, Thomas's metaphysical definition of substance is phrased in such a way as to exclude God, in whom essence and *esse* are identical.[61]

To resolve these difficulties, I will now turn to the fourth section of my chapter.

GOD'S RELATION TO THE METAPHYSICAL GENUS *SUBSTANCE*

Despite Thomas's insistence that God is not contained in any genus, it is clear from his writings that he does consider God to be, in some sense, a substance. Indeed, he commonly refers to God by this name. For example, Thomas tells us that although metaphysics considers being in general (*ens commune*) as its "genus," it also considers the separate substances, namely as the common and universal causes of that "genus." What are these substances? Thomas identifies them as God and the Intelligences.[62] Elsewhere, he refers to God as the "first simple substance" (*substantia prima simplex*).[63] Does this means that he considers God to be first in the

---

I, q. 2, a. 3, *quarta via; In Lib. de caus.*, prop. 16. From these texts, it is clear that he holds the same position regarding both natural (univocal) genera and metaphysical (analogical) genera, namely that in every genus there is a first that is the measure of everything else contained in the genus.

Thomas gets this axiom from *Metaphysics* II, 1, 993b25–31. Regarding his use of both this text and the axiom he sees within it, see Vincent de Couesnongle, "La causalité du maximum. L'utilisation par S. Thomas d'un passage d'Aristote," *Revue des sciences philosophiques et théologiques* 38 (1954): 433–44, 658–80; id. "La causalité du maximum. Pourquoi Saint Thomas a-t-il mal cité Aristote?" *Revue des sciences philosophiques et théologiques* 38 (1954): 658–80.

61. It might seem, therefore, that the first in this genus is instead the highest *class* of substances, namely immaterial substance. But since such substances also exist according to degrees, then perhaps it is instead the highest one of these. Even that answer, however, appears problematic since such a substance would be not an absolute measure but only a contingent one given the fact that God happened to make it the highest. As Thomas tells us, the world is best as God has intended it, but he could always make it better. One way to do this would simply be to make a more noble angel. Regarding Thomas's views on this world as the best see *De pot.* q. 1, a. 5, ad 14–15; ibid., q. 3, a. 6, ad 26; ibid., q. 3, a. 16, ad 17; ibid., q. 5, a. 1, ad 14.

62. *In Meta.*, proemium (ed. Marietti 1–2).

63. See, e.g., *De ente*, c. 1 (ed. Leon. 43.370:63).

genus *substance* as well? In a number of texts, his answer to this question is "yes."

According to Thomas, God does belong in a sense to the genus *substance*—but not as contained in it the way a species or individual is contained. For if he were contained in the genus, he would be comprehended under it as participating in its nature; but God participates nothing. Rather, Thomas explains, God is in the genus *substance* by reduction (*per reductionem*) as its principle or cause, in the way that *point* is in the genus *continuous quantity; unity* in the genus *number;* or *white* in the genus *color.*[64] And he reminds us that the first in a genus is the measure of all that is in the genus. As he explains, the term "measure" is most properly spoken of regarding the genus *quantity.* For it is by means of a measure that the quantity of a thing is made known, and a measure is whatever is simplest or first in the genus—either absolutely (as numbers are measured by unity), or from our perspective (as continuous quantities are measured: cloth by the palm, roads by the furlong).[65]

From this original sense of measure, he explains,

the name "measure" was transferred to all genera, so that whatever is first, most simple, and perfect in the genus is called the measure of everything else in the genus. For that reason, every single thing is understood to have more or less of the truth of the genus as it approaches to or recedes from the first. Such is the case with *white* in the genus *color.* Thus, also, in the genus *substance* that which has *esse* most perfectly and most simply is called the measure of all substances, which is God. Hence, it is not necessary that he be in the genus *substance* as contained but only as the principle, having in himself every perfection of the genus, as unity does in the genus *number.*[66]

64. See *In Sent.* I, d. 8, q. 4, a. 2, ad 3 (ed. Mandonnet 1.222–23); *In De Trin.*, q. 1, a. 2, ad 4; *De pot.*, q. 7, a. 3, ad 7; *De pot.*, q. 7, a. 7, ad 4; ibid., q. 9, a. 3, ad 3.

65. *In Sent.* I, d. 8, q. 4, a. 2, ad 3 (ed. Mandonnet 1.223).

66. Ibid. (ed. Mandonnet 1.223): "Exinde transumptum est nomen mensurae ad omnia genera, ut illud quod est primum in quolibet genere et simplicissimum et perfectissimum dicatur mensura omnium quae sunt in genere illo; eo quod unumquodque cognoscitur habere de veritate generis plus et minus, secundum quod magis accedit ad ipsum vel recedit, ut album in genere colorum. Ita etiam in genere substantiae illud quod habet esse perfectissimum et simplicissimum, dicitur mensura omnium substantiarum, sicut Deus. Unde non oportet quod sit in genere substantiae sicut contentum, sed solum sicut principium, habens in se omnem perfectionem generis sicut unitas in numeris, sed diversimode; quia unitate non mensurantur nisi numeri; sed Deus est mensura non tantum substantialium perfectionum, sed omnium quae sunt in omnibus generibus, sicut sapientiae, virtutis et hujusmodi. Et ideo quamvis unitas contineatur in uno genere determinato sicut principium, non tamen Deus."

Still, Thomas is careful to add that even though we may draw this comparison between God in the genus *substance* and unity in the genus *number,* there is a significant difference between these two first principles. Whereas unity is the measure only of *number,* God is the measure not only of substantial perfections but of all perfections found in any genus, such as wisdom, power, and so forth. Thus, unlike unity, which is contained in the one determinate genus *number,* God is not contained in the genus *substance.*[67]

As helpful as this clarification is regarding God's relation to the various genera of beings,[68] it in turn requires further clarification. Thomas's initial point about God as the principle of the genus *substance* at first appears to resolve our question regarding the primary instance of substance, but his subsequent claim that God is in fact present in all genera seems to call that resolution into question. For God is the cause of the genus *quality,* but Thomas does not think that we can thus properly call him "a quality," much less the primary instance of *quality.* God is not an accident, even though he is the first principle of all accidents.[69] We might be tempted to conclude that, similarly, God is not properly speaking a substance but is called such only as the principle of the genus *substance.* Nevertheless, Thomas does not reach such a conclusion. For he notes in the *De potentia* that God is present in the genera of accidents in a different way than he is present in the genus *substance.* Accidents are called beings only in relation to substance, which is the primary kind of being. Consequently, accidents are not measured by a first thing that is itself an

---

67. Ibid. Because of this difference between these created principles and God, in one of his later writings on this topic, Thomas is unwilling to speak of God as included in a genus even as a principle. In *ST* I, q. 3, a. 5, which addresses whether God is in a genus, Thomas concludes his response by noting that "Quod autem Deus non sit in genere per reductionem ut principium, manifestum est ex eo quod principium quod reducitur in aliquod genus, non se extendit ultra genus illud: sicut punctum non est principium nisi quantitatis continuae, et unitas quantitatis discretae. Deus autem est principium totius esse, ut infra ostendetur. Unde non continetur in aliquo genere sicut principium" (ed. Leon. 4.44). Cf. *ST* I, q. 4, a. 3, ad 2.

Still, even if this change in language reflects a change in view, two things should be kept in mind: first, Thomas does not hesitate in the *Summa theologiae* to refer to God as a substance; second, as regards his treatment of what I have termed a "metaphysical genus," Thomas clearly presents God as first in the genus *substance* (*ST* I, q. 2, a. 3, *quarta via*).

68. Or, more precisely, their relation to him.

69. Regarding Thomas's position that God is not an accident, see e.g. *In Sent.* I, d. 8, q. 4, a. 2, ad 1 (ed. Mandonnet 1.222); *SCG* I, c. 14; ibid., c. 25; ibid., IV, c. 10. With that said, the names of some accidents, such as wisdom, can be predicated of God essentially. See *ST* I, q. 13, aa. 1–3; *De pot.* q. 7, a. 4; ibid., a. 7, esp. ad s.c. 2.

accident but rather, Thomas tells us, they are measured by a first thing that is a substance, namely God.[70]

From this text we find indication that for Thomas, God is not called a substance simply because he is the cause of substances. Indeed, we need to be careful when reading Thomas on this point not to attribute to him the error that he attributes to Moses Maimonides. As he recounts in the *Summa theologiae,* Maimonides held that it is impossible for us to predicate any affirmative names of God essentially (*per substantialiter*) because we cannot know God's essence. According to him, we can name God only by way of either negation or causality. According to the former way, we do not name *what* God is but rather what he is *not;* according to the latter, we name him in terms of his causality, in actual fact naming the relation of his effects to him—not God himself. Thus, Thomas explains that for Maimonides, to say that "God is good" is not to saying anything about his essence. Rather it is to say that "God is not evil" or that "God is the cause of goodness."[71]

Among the reasons that Thomas gives for rejecting this view is that it does not account for why some names are more fitting of God than others. If the statement "God is good" simply were to mean that God is the cause of good things, we might just as well say that "God is a body" since he is the cause of bodies. But that is absurd given that God, unlike a body, does not possess the potentiality of matter. In contrast to Maimonides, therefore, Thomas insists that some names, like "good," are indeed predicated essentially of God. For God is universally perfect, and as such he prepossesses all creaturely perfections in a simple way. Creatures thus represent God, but not as something of the same species or genus. Instead, they represent him as things that fall short of an excelling principle. Thus, it does not follow that God is good because he *causes* goodness; rather, Thomas tells us, the converse follows: God causes goodness because he *is* good.[72] Similarly, we could say that for Thomas, God is not called a substance because he causes substances, but rather he causes substances because he *is* substance.

With that said, it should be noted that Thomas does not think all affir-

---

70. *De pot.,* q. 7, a. 4, ad 7 (ed. Marietti 196). Thomas is responding here to the objection that because God is first in all the genera, not only is substance found in him but accidents as well.

71. *ST* I, q. 13, a. 2 co. (ed. Leon. 4.141). Cf. *De pot.,* q. 7, a. 5 co. (ed. Marietti 198–99).

72. *ST* I, q. 13, a. 2 co. (ed. Leon. 4.141). Cf. *De pot.,* q. 7, a. 5 co. (ed. Marietti 198–99).

mative names can be predicated of God essentially.[73] When we consider
the names that signify the perfections that proceed to creatures from God,
some signify them in such a way that the imperfect mode by which the
creature participates in the divine perfection is included in the very signification of the name. This is the case with names like "stone" and "man"
and any name that denotes the species of a created thing. Such names can
be said of God only metaphorically. By contrast, others express the divine
perfections in an absolute way, so that the imperfect mode of the creature's participation is not included in the signification of the name. These
are the sorts of affirmative names that can be predicated of God literally
(*proprie*) and essentially. As examples, Thomas offers the names "being"
(*ens*), "good," and "living." And following from this line of reasoning, I
would argue that we could add to this list the name "substance."[74]

Considering further the names of these absolute perfections, Thomas follows Pseudo-Dionysius in noting that they can be said of God in
three ways: affirmatively, negatively, and eminently. As an example, he
offers the name "wisdom." Because God is the cause of wisdom in creatures, there is a likeness between that wisdom and God, so that we may
say, "God is wise." God's wisdom, however, is not that of creatures. Thus,
Thomas notes that this name can be denied of God, so that we may say,
"God is *not* wise." Still, wisdom is not denied of him as though he lacks
it; rather, he possesses it in an eminent way. Hence we may say "God is
super-wise," by which we mean that God is Wisdom Itself.[75]

According to Thomas, we must follow this approach in naming God
because even the names of absolute perfections entail imperfection in
some respect: not as regards what he refers to as the "thing that is signified" (*res significata*) but, rather, as regards the "mode of signification"
(*modus significandi*). Thomas explains that the human intellect acquires
its knowledge through the senses; consequently, when we express names
such as "wise" and "good," we do so according to the mode by which the
intellect conceives them. Since our knowledge begins with sensation, it is

73. For an overview of Thomas's doctrine of naming God, see Gregory P. Rocca, *Speaking
the Incomprehensible God* (Washington, D.C.: The Catholic University of America Press, 2004).

74. *ST* I, q. 13, a. 3, ad 1 (ed. Leon. 4.143); *SCG* I, c. 30 (ed. Leon. 13.92).

75. *De pot.*, q. 7, a. 5, ad 2 (ed. Marietti 199). Regarding the Dionysian influence on Thomas's doctrine of naming God, see Fran O'Rourke, *Pseudo-Dionysius and the Metaphysics of
Aquinas* (New York: E. J. Brill, 1992), esp. 31–61. See also Cornelio Fabro, *Participation et Causalité* (Paris and Louvain: Publications Universitaires, 1961), esp. 531.

never able to transcend the mode that it finds in sensible things, which is a mode of composition and concretion. Hence, in every term that we use, there is always imperfection regarding the mode of signification. Thomas explains that this is why Dionysius says that names of absolute perfections can be both affirmed and denied of God: they are affirmed regarding the thing that is signified (namely, the perfection), but denied regarding the mode of signification (namely, of composition and concretion found in creatures).[76]

Following this Dionysian approach as well as Thomas's metaphysics of substance, then, we could say that "God is a substance," "God is not a substance," "God is supersubstantial." Thomas himself observes that we do not negate or deny the name "substance" of God as though he were not properly a substance. We deny this name of God because it does not belong to him according to the mode of signification, but instead does so according to a more excellent mode. It is for this reason, Thomas notes, that Dionysius speaks of God as above all substance.[77] But what, exactly, is the mode of signification that is denied of God when we do call him a substance? Thomas offers an answer to this question in the *De potentia* when he considers whether there is power in God. As he explains:

> Our intellect struggles to express God as something most perfect. For it cannot arrive at him except from the likeness of [his] effects, and it does not find in creatures anything that is most perfect that entirely lacks imperfection. Therefore, from the diverse perfections discovered in creatures, it struggles to describe him, although something falls short with each of these perfections. Still, it is for this reason that anything of imperfection that is attached to any of these perfections is removed from God. For example, "*esse*" signifies something complete and simple, but it does not signify "something subsisting"; "substance" signifies "something subsisting" but which is the subject of others. Thus, we attribute "substance" and "*esse*" to God—but "substance" by reason of subsistence, not by reason of substanding; and "*esse*" by reason of simplicity and completion, not by reason of inherence, by which it inheres in another.[78]

76. *In Sent.* I, d. 8, q. 1, a. 1 ad 3 (ed. Mandonnet 1.195–96); ibid., q. 4, a. 1, ad 2 (ed. Mandonnet 1.219–20); *SCG* I, c. 30 (ed. Leon. 13.92); *ST* I, q. 13, a. 3, ad 1 (ed. Leon. 4.143).

77. *ST* I, q. 13, a. 3, ad 2 (ed. Leon. 4.143).

78. *De pot.*, q. 1, a. 1 co. (ed. Marietti 9): "Sed et sciendum, quod intellectus noster Deum exprimere nititur sicut aliquid perfectissimum. Et quia in ipsum devenire non potest nisi ex effectuum similitudine; neque in creaturis invenit aliquid summe perfectum quod omnino im-

After this discussion, Thomas proceeds to explain how power is present in God, but it is his consideration of substance that concerns us here. According to Thomas, when we predicate "substance" of God, the mode of signification that is denied of him is the characteristic of substanding: standing under accidents. As he explains elsewhere, *esse* is common to all genera, but both subsisting and substanding are proper only to the first category, namely the category *substance*.[79] The sense we get from Thomas is that substanding is characteristic of substance taken only as a logical or natural genus, not as an absolute perfection. Because the sort of substances we know exist according to the manner of concretion and composition, when we use this term "substance," its mode of signification does indeed include the notion of "substanding." But the *thing* that is signified (the *res significata*) is "subsisting."[80] According to Thomas, the term "subsisting" (*subsistere*) names a determinate mode of existing (*modus essendi*), namely as a being in itself (*ens per se*).[81] With this *res significata* in mind, Thomas explains that the term "substance" can be said of God as signifying "existing in itself" (*existere per se*).[82]

We might ask why Thomas employs this language of *ens per se* when, as we have seen, he has rejected it as a definition of "substance." Here, it should be remembered that in those texts where Thomas does reject this definition, his concern is to show that God is not contained in any genus, whether logical or natural. Thus, in those texts, he is considering substance as found in the predicamental order of finite being. Considered as such, substance is "a thing to whose quiddity it belongs to exist *not* in

---

perfectione careat: ideo ex diversis perfectionibus in creaturis repertis, ipsum nititur designare, quamvis cuilibet illarum perfectionum aliquid desit; ita tamen quod quidquid alicui istarum perfectionum imperfectionis adiungitur, totum a Deo amoveatur. Verbi gratia esse significat aliquid completum et simplex sed non subsistens; substantia autem aliquid subsistens significat sed alii subiectum. Ponimus ergo in Deo substantiam et esse, sed substantiam ratione subsistentiae non ratione substandi; esse vero ratione simplicitatis et complementi, non ratione inhaerentiae, qua alteri inhaeret. Et similiter attribuimus Deo operationem ratione ultimi complementi, non ratione eius in quod operatio transit. Potentiam vero attribuimus ratione eius quod permanet et quod est principium eius, non ratione eius quod per operationem completur."

79. *In Sent.* I, d. 23, q. 1, a. 1 (ed. Mandonnet 1.552–58).

80. *De spir. creat.*, a. 5 co. (ed. Leon. 24/2.58–62).

81. See *In Sent.* I, d. 23, q. 1, a. 1 (ed. Mandonnet 1.552–58), where Thomas distinguishes between *esse*, *subsistere*, and *substare* in the course of distinguishing between *essentia*, *subsistentia*, and *substantia*.

82. *ST* I, q. 29, a. 3, ad 4 (ed. Leon 4.332).

another," and thus it entails a composition of essence and *esse*. If, however, the *ratio* or essential characteristic of substance is subsistence, as Thomas tells us it is, then his quasi definition of substance presents simply one *mode* of subsistence.[83] It is a subsistence according to the mode of concretion and composition found in created beings. Thomas, however, identifies another mode of subsistence, namely, as it is found in God in an eminent way according to his simplicity. Thus, God is the primary instance of substance, but not primary according to Thomas's Avicennian inspired definition. For what that definition defines is precisely a secondary mode of subsisting.[84]

If God's mode of subsistence is the primary one, the question might arise why Thomas defines substance as he does. For, as he himself notes, with analogical naming, the prime analogate is always placed into the definition of the others of the same name. For example, "healthy" as said of an animal is included in the definition of "healthy" as said of medicine, for medicine is called "healthy" insofar as it is the cause of an animal's health.[85] Given this observation, it might seem that God, as the primary instance of substance, ought to enter into the definition of other substances.[86] For Thomas, however, God's effects are not named from God; rather, it is the other way around. As he explains, sometimes what is first in reality is not what is first to us. If we consider again the example of the analogous term "healthy," Thomas explains that because of medicine's healing power, its "healthiness" is in fact naturally prior to the health of the animal, for a cause is always prior to its effect. Nevertheless, because we know this power through its effect, we name it from the effect. In this way, something is taken as prior according to the order of our understanding that is not prior according to the order of reality.[87]

---

83. See *De spir. creat.*, a. 5 (ed. Leon. 24/2.61:206–11): "Est autem de ratione substantiae quod per se subsistat, quod nullo modo dependet a corporis ratione, cum ratio corporis quaedam accidentia, scilicet dimensiones, aliquo modo respiciat, a quibus non causatur subsistere."

84. *In Sent.* I, d. 8, q. 4, a. 2, ad 1 (ed. Mandonnet 1.222). Focusing on the notion of "substance" as what substands accidents, Thomas notes that since God exists *per se* without substanding any accidents, he is the sort of substance that is properly called a "subsistence." In other words, God is Subsistence Itself. See *De pot.* q. 9, a. 1, ad 4 (ed. Marietti 226).

85. *ST* I, q. 13, a. 6 co. (ed. Leon. 4.150).

86. Montagnes raises this question, *mutatis mutandi* regarding God and the definition of "being" (*ens*) (*Doctrine of Analogy*, 45–46).

87. *ST* I, q. 13, a. 6 co. (ed. Leon. 4.250). Regarding Thomas's doctrine of analogy and the

I would contend that we find the same situation regarding the *ratio* of substance: God is the primary instance of substance in reality—prior to the substances that are his effects; nevertheless, our knowledge of substance is through his effects, and so created substance is prior to us. For this reason, in Thomas's terms, we "impose" (*imponimus*) by priority the name "substance" on created substances. This is reflected in the very etymology of the word, for as he notes, the name "substance" is imposed from "substanding" (*substare*), which God does not do.[88] Nevertheless, when we negate this mode of signification from the name "substance," we are left with the thing signified (*res significata*), namely "substance" taken as the absolute perfection of subsistence. And this belongs primarily to God who, Thomas tells us, is *Esse Per Se Subsistens:* the Act of Being Subsisting through Itself.[89] In this respect, God is first in the metaphysical genus *substance.*

CONCLUSION

From these considerations, I believe that we can draw the follow conclusions regarding Thomas's view of metaphysics as the science of substance. For Thomas, the subject matter of metaphysics is being in general (*ens commune*), but substance is the primary focus of the science because substance is the primary instance of being. He presents substance as a genus, indeed one of the highest genera identified in Aristotle's *Categories.* Thomas cautions us, however, that the treatment of substance in that work is a logical one. A logical consideration of this genus presents it as including all the various (finite) beings we call "substances." A metaphysical consideration, however, reveals that in reality, corruptible and incorruptible substances cannot belong to the same genus.

Hence, if we follow Thomas's strict sense of "genus" as referring to a univocal community, there is not a single, real genus *substance* that includes all substances. If, however, we follow his broad sense of "genus" as

---

distinction between what our understanding takes as prior and what is prior in reality, see Montagnes, *Analogy of Being,* 45–46; McInerny, *Aquinas and Analogy,* 160–61.

88. *In Sent.* I, d. 8, q. 4, a. 2, s.c. 2 (ed. Mandonnet 1.221).

89. See, e.g., *In Sent.* I, d. 23, a. 2 co.; *ST* I, q. 4, a. 2 co.; ibid., q. 44, a. 1 co.; *De ver.,* q. 21, a. 5, ad 1; *De pot.,* q. 7, a. 2, ad 5; ibid. q. 9, a. 1, ad 4; *Quodlibet 7,* q. 1, a. 1, ad 1; *De sub. sep.* c. 8. Regarding Thomas's doctrine of analogy and the distinction between the imposition of a name and what it signifies, see *ST* I, q. 13, a. 6. Cf. *De malo,* q. 1, a. 5, ad 19.

referring to an analogical community, then we can find in his writings the notion of what he refers to, on at least one occasion, as a "metaphysical genus." According to this sense, there is for Thomas a single, real genus *substance* that does include all substances. As I have argued, it is this genus that he is referring to when he speaks of metaphysics as the "science of substance."

It is because this metaphysical genus is analogical that it is able to contain all substances: both the material and the immaterial, the corruptible and the incorruptible. To be more precise, it contains all *finite* substances, for God is not contained in this analogical genus as though sharing a common formality with created substances. Rather, Thomas tells us that God is included in it as its principle, since he *is* in an eminent way what other substances *have* by participation, namely subsistence in the act of existing (*esse*).

Here, I would argue, we can draw a parallel with Thomas's account of being in general (*ens commune*). Presenting it as a metaphysical genus, he explains on more than one occasion that the subject matter of metaphysics is being in general, not God. Neither, for Thomas, is God included *under* being in general as though he were contained by it, sharing a common formality with finite beings.[90] Rather, he presents God as the principle of this metaphysical genus. Similarly, when he tells us that the metaphysician is primarily concerned with studying substance *as* substance, Thomas is referring to finite substance, the class of beings described in his quasi definition: things to whose quiddity it belongs to exist *not* in another. Dependent on the First Substance for their existence, this class of beings subsist in themselves but not *through* themselves. For Thomas, it is this class of beings that is the metaphysical genus *substance,* and it is this genus that metaphysics studies insofar as it is called the science of *substance.*

---

90. Indeed, for Thomas being in general is synonymous with finite, or created, being. See, e.g., *De ver.*, q. 10, a. 11, ad 10. See also *In librum beati Dionysii De divinis nominibus expositio* V, lect. 2, ed. Ceslaus Pera (Turin: Marietti, 1950), 244:655–245:660. There, Thomas shows that God transcends *esse commune*. Since *esse commune* is equal in scope to *ens commune*, his arguments in this text also imply that God transcends *ens commune*.

Jorge J. E. Gracia

6 ∽ A Scholastic Perspective on the Individuation of Races

Does it make sense to speak of a Scholastic perspective and solution to the problem of the individuation of races when the word "race" did not become common in European languages until the sixteenth century, when its etymology and provenance are in dispute, and when the very notion of peoples as races is traced by some to the age in which Europeans began encountering peoples from places other than Europe and the Mediterranean basin? Sixteenth-century Scholastics confronted issues that had to do with peoples from the newly "discovered" territories in the Americas in particular. Francisco de Vitoria, Francisco Suárez, and Bartolomé de Las Casas had much to say about so-called Indians and the nations and peoples of the Americas. And the talk of people as "Black" or "White" was not unusual at the time. (I put the names of races and racial designations in quotation marks to indicate that I am using common terminology, but that I should not be taken as necessarily endorsing it.) But prima facie it appears anachronistic to talk about the philosophical thought of anyone before the sixteenth century in connection with race.

To this reservation must be added that in the Aristotelian context within which most Scholastic authors worked in the Middle Ages and the Counter-Reformation, the question of individuation was usually posed in terms of substances, such as a human being or an animal, or the features (properties and accidents) of substances, such as the color of their eyes or their weight. But a race does not seem to be either a substance or a feature of a substance, so what could Scholastics have to contribute to the discussion of the individuation of races?

Three considerations might help put aside these initial reservations. First, in our discipline there is a well-established practice of examining the philosophical views of historical figures in the context of problems they did not address. We need think only of Scholastics themselves as good examples. Certainly Aristotle did not have anything to say about the Trinity, but Scholastics used his thinking to elucidate this Christian doctrine. Second, some Scholastics dealt with the individuation of such entities as aggregates and collections that are not unlike races in some respects, and this practice should help tie the discussion of race to Scholastic thought without doing violence to it. Third, the thrust of the analysis presented here is philosophical, not historical—it is not intended to establish the proper interpretation of the views of historical figures concerning the individuation of races, but to probe and evaluate various possible positions with the aim of moving toward a satisfactory view.

Because the notion of race is quite contested, I begin, in the first part, by proposing a conception of it that I have defended elsewhere. This conception of race should serve as an anchor for the discussion, even if it makes some of the conclusions I reach dependent on the viability of this conception. Then I turn to the question of the individuality of races in the second part, and follow it with a discussion of various conceptions of individuality in the third part. Finally, I take up the individuation and discernibility of races in the fourth and fifth parts respectively.

RACE

Let me present the following understanding of a race, which I have defended elsewhere:

A race is a sub-group of individual human beings who satisfy the following two conditions: (1) each member of the group is linked by descent to another member of the group who is in turn also linked by descent to at least some third member of the group; and (2) each member of the group has one or more physical features that are (i) genetically transmittable, (ii) generally associated with the group, and (iii) perceptually perspicuous.[1]

The two key conditions presented in this formula are metaphysical in that they describe what race is through a general categorization of it. In order

1. Jorge J. E. Gracia, *Surviving Race, Ethnicity, and Nationality: A Challenge for the Twentieth Century* (Lanham, Md.: Rowman and Littlefield, 2005), 85.

for something to be a race, the members of the race have to be linked by descent and have one or more physical features that are genetically transmittable, generally associated with the race, and perceptually perspicuous. But these conditions can also function epistemically, since knowing that a particular human being satisfies them with respect to a particular race entails that one has identified that person as a member of that race.

No single one of these conditions, taken by itself, is sufficient for racial membership unless one were to adopt the notorious One-Drop Rule, but this view is inconsistent and, therefore, unacceptable.[2] The One-Drop Rule is inconsistent as a racial marker because it functions effectively only when applied to some races but not others: a "White" person with one drop of "Black" blood is "Black," but a "Black" person with one drop of "White" blood is still "Black." This means that being related by descent to a member of some race, who is in turn related by descent to at least some other member of that race, is not sufficient for someone to be a member of the race, for the person in question may not share in any of the features generally associated with it. This implication is the reason why we say that people can change races. I would argue that, strictly speaking, there is no such racial change. There is only the recognition that the persons in question do not satisfy the conditions sufficient for belonging to a particular race, although they meet the conditions of belonging to another race. The change is one of labeling, that is, of what we call the persons, rather than a change of being, that is, of what the persons are.[3]

Likewise, having features associated with a certain race does not automatically make a person a member of the race or serve effectively to identify the person as such. Indians, from India, are frequently as dark as "Blacks," but they are not generally regarded as being "Black" and they do not consider themselves to be so. Italians from Southern Italy are also frequently as dark and have some features that satisfy the non-descent conditions of membership in the "Black" race. Yet, because they do not satisfy the descent condition, they are not thought to be "Black."

To be a member of a race one has to be linked by descent to someone who is a member of the race and who, in turn, is linked by descent to still another member of the race. For A to be "Black," she has to be linked by birth to B, who is both "Black" and linked by descent to C, who is also

2. For the One Drop Rule, see Scott L. Malcomson, *One Drop of Blood: The American Misadventure of Race* (New York: Farrar, Straus, and Giroux, 2000).

3. For further elucidation, see Gracia, *Surviving Race, Ethnicity, and Nationality,* 91–92.

"Black." In addition, *A* must share in a pool of physical features that are genetically transmittable, generally considered to be racial indicators, and perceptually perspicuous, such as skin color, hair texture, and nose shape. For *A* to be "Black," she must be dark skinned, or have curly hair, and so on. It is not required that *A* have all the features generally associated with the race imputed to her, but she must have some. If she has some of them and is related by descent to other members of the race, then *A* is considered to be a member of the race.

But we may ask, although races are composed of individual persons, are races themselves individual? Prima facie it appears that groups are individual insofar as they are composed of individual members. After all, if grains of sand are physical and have weight, then a pile composed of grains of sand would also have to be physical and have weight. Yet, this implication does not always hold. Indeed, there is a well-known fallacy in logic, known as the fallacy of composition, which consists in assuming that wholes have the same characteristics as their parts, or that composites have the same characteristics as their components. In the case of the pile of grains of sand, it would be a mistake to conclude that because each grain has the characteristic of weighing one gram, the pile of sand also weighs one gram or that because the components of a pile of sand are grains of sand, the whole pile is also a grain of sand. And the reverse does not necessarily hold either, for the fallacy of division applies in this case. The characteristics of a whole may not apply to its components. If a pile of sand weighs one kilogram, the grains of which it is composed do not each weigh one kilogram.

From this conclusion it should be clear that the individuality of the members of a racial group does not entail the individuality of the group, and vice versa. In principle, the fact that the group of "Blacks" is composed of individuals does not entail that the group itself is individual. And indeed, it may sound odd to some to say that it is individual. Why? Because we generally tend to think of individuality in various ways, some of which do not apply to such things as groups. Suppose, for example, that we are thinking of an individual as a kind of Aristotelian substance, which is a frequent way of thinking about it. In this case, it certainly would be very odd to say that the group of "Blacks" is individual, in that this claim would entail that "Blacks" constitute an individual substance of the sort a cat or a dog is.

A proper understanding of the presumptive individuality of racial groups requires that we look into this matter more deliberately. First, we need to understand individuality. Second, we need to establish whether racial groups are indeed individual and explain the relation of the individual members that compose the groups in question—Mary, Juan, and Mobutu—to the groups to which they belong. And third, we need to understand the conditions under which kinds become individual (a metaphysical issue), if indeed they do, as well as the conditions under which we become aware of them as individual or recognize them as such (epistemological issues). The metaphysical issue is the problem of individuation, whereas the epistemic issue of individual discernibility breaks down into the problem of identification and the problem of reidentification. Let us begin with individuality.

INDIVIDUALITY

To say that individuality is the character of being individual and that an individual is something that has this character seems trivial. What it means exactly, however, has been contested throughout the history of philosophy. Individuality has been inadvertently confused with, or purposefully interpreted as, personhood, substantiality, uniqueness, persistence through time, spatial continuity, indivisibility, incommunicability, and impredicability.[4]

The identification of individuality with personhood has the unwelcome result that only persons could be viewed as individual: only entities such as Juan or Carolyn are individual, and this sheet of paper on

4. I have presented a philosophical discussion of the most important of these in Jorge J. E. Gracia, *Individuality: An Essay on the Foundations of Metaphysics* (Albany: State University of New York Press, 1988), ch. 1. For the discussion of historical views, their authors, and pertinent bibliography, see id., *Suarez on Individuation* (Milwaukee, Wisc.: Marquette University Press, 1982 and 2000); id., *Introduction to the Problem of Individuation in the Early Middle Ages*, 2nd rev. ed. (Munich: Philosophia Verlag, 1988); and id., ed., *Individuation in Scholasticism: The Later Middle Ages and the Counter-Reformation* (Albany: State University of New York Press, 1994). Also id. and Kenneth Barber, eds., *Individuation and Identity in Early Modern Philosophy* (Albany: State University of New York Press, 1994). John Wippel has contributed substantially to this discussion. See, for example, *The Metaphysical Thought of Godfrey of Fontaines* (Washington, D.C.: The Catholic University of America Press, 1981); "Godfrey of Fontaines, Peter of Auvergne, and John Baconthorpe," in *Individuation in Scholasticism*, 221–56; and *The Metaphysical Thought of Thomas Aquinas: From Finite Being to Uncreated Being* (Washington, D.C.: The Catholic University of America Press, 2000).

which this is written, my cat Peanut, or a cell are not. When individuality is conceived as substantiality, it turns out that only substances are individual. If we assume that a substance is what Aristotle had in mind in *Categories*—that is, what is neither predicable of nor part of a subject—then only things such as this man or this cat are individual, but not this pile of bricks or the color of this paper on which I am writing. When individuality is taken as uniqueness, every individual turns out to be a single member of a kind. If this is so, then the only individuals would be beings such as God and the last dodo bird, because only they belong to kinds that have only one member. Human beings, for example, cannot be unique qua human, but only qua Peter, Yi, or François.

If, however, individuality is understood as persistence through time, nontemporal and instantaneous entities would be excluded. God, as conceived in the Judeo-Christian tradition, could not be individual under these conditions. But what would justify such restriction? Something very similar can be said concerning spatial continuity. To be spatially continuous would disqualify any discontinuous entities from being individual. But again, this does not make sense, for even those entities such as a cat, which appear to have gross continuity, include spaces between the atoms that make them up. Regarding individuality as indivisibility would necessitate that only simples be individual. But simples in what sense? Simple beings in the sense in which Jewish and Christian theologians conceive God to be? Or simples in the sense of primitive concepts, such as "one," whose analysis is either impossible or circular? In either case, the class of individuals would be quite restricted. Finally, some hold individuality to be the same as impredicability: to be individual is not to be predicable. But if predicability applies only to words, as I think it is wise to hold, then only those words that are not predicable would be individual. The same applies if we think of concepts rather than words. Things and their properties then would not be individual, a conclusion that is contrary to some of our most basic intuitions and ordinary usage.

This is not the place to develop a proper view of individuality, or even to give an adequate account of the views I have just presented and the arguments for and against them. Suffice it to say that the controversy is complex and much has been written on it, and that the Middle Ages contributed substantially to it, anticipating many of the views that would later become standard.

Rather than attempt to broker among various conceptions of individuality available in the history of philosophy, which would be impossible within the present circumstances, for present purposes I adopt a view I have defended elsewhere.[5] In accordance with it, an individual is best conceived as a non-instantiable instance of an instantiable. This view is sufficiently broad to apply to persons and non-persons, substances and non-substances, and entities that are unique or not, persist through time or not, and are simple or complex. Moreover, it allows us to distinguish clearly between individuals and non-individuals. The latter—also called universals—are instantiable. Let me give some examples of both: "this cat," "that woman," "that leaf," and "the white color on this surface" are individual, but "cat," "woman," "leaf," and "white color on a surface" are not. Something is individual when—although an instance of an instantiable—it cannot itself be instantiated, that is, when there can be no instances of it. My cat "Peanut" is an individual because she is an instance of "cat" but there cannot be instances of her; "Peanut" is not instantiable into "this Peanut" and "that Peanut." On the other hand, "cat" is not an individual insofar as it can be instantiated; there can be instances of "cat," as in fact the existence of Peanut clearly shows. And "mammal" is not individual because, although it is an instance of "animal," it is itself instantiable into "cat" and "human." Now let us explore how this notion of individuality applies to individual humans and individual groups, for these are the concepts pertinent to races.

INDIVIDUAL HUMANS AND INDIVIDUAL RACES

The notion of "human" has been one of the most contested in the history of philosophy, but for our purposes we need not settle on a comprehensive view of it. It is enough to point out some of the conditions that every human must satisfy. Two of these seem to be widely accepted and will do for present purposes: humans must have certain kinds of bodies and minds.[6] The kind of body they have is described in anatomy and biology; the kind of mind is described in psychology. By accepting the conditions that humans have both bodies and minds, I do not intend to

5. Gracia, *Individuality*, 43–56.
6. Some think of these as conditions of persons. See P. F. Strawson, *Individuals* (London: Methuen, 1959).

imply that minds are immaterial and that bodies are not, or that they are two distinct kinds of realities. My task here is not to settle the notorious mind-body problem, and, therefore, I refrain from staking out a position in this area, since doing so is not essential for my task and would involve complexities for which I have no space here.

For my limited purposes, it is enough to say that an individual human is a non-instantiable instance of the instantiable kind "human." The notion of an individual human seems uncontroversial, for surely such beings as Aristotle and Socrates are not universal, that is, they are not instantiable. Aristotle and Socrates do not function like "human" or "cat." Of course, sometimes we speak of someone other than Aristotle as being "an Aristotle." We say things such as "He is an Aristotle" or "He is a real Aristotle." But in these cases, we do not mean that the person in question is an instance of Aristotle; rather, we mean that the person is like Aristotle, or has the same characteristics Aristotle had, or something along those lines.

Contrary to the fairly uncontroversial notion of an individual human, the notion of an individual group of humans appears controversial. The reason may be in part that groups of this sort appear to have some features that characterize both individuals and universals. This fact makes one wonder whether such groups are actually one or the other, and not both, *or* whether there is something wrong with their classification in any of these ways.

Perhaps it would be useful to refer to other entities that pose similar problems to help us understand that this problem is not parochial to groups of humans. One of the most notorious is "works of art." Consider Carlos Estévez's painting *Numerical Thoughts*.[7] Is this work of art universal or individual? On the one hand, it appears to be universal insofar as it functions as an instantiable of which instances are possible: a copy can be made by a student of Estévez's work; a reproduction of the painting can appear on the website mentioned in note 7; the reproduction can appear in a catalogue of one of Estévez's exhibitions; the reproduction can be printed in a copy of a book that I own; and so on. Yet, Estévez's painting was produced at a certain time and place and in fact exists cur-

7. An image of this painting can be seen in the website "Cuban Art outside Cuba": http://www.philosophy.buffalo.edu/capenchair/CAOC/index.html.

rently at my Toronto apartment, where it hangs in my studio. All of these considerations seem to suggest the painting's individuality.

There are many theories about how to deal with the universality and individuality of works of art, but again my business here is not with this particular problem.[8] I mention this issue to bring attention to the fact that groups of humans are not idiosyncratic in posing difficulties when one attempts to classify them as individual or universal.

Another kind of entity that also poses problems and whose situation is closer to the case that concerns us is a homogeneous group. Consider a pile of sand composed of one million grains. Each of the grains of sand that compose the pile is individual because each of them is a non-instantiable instance of the universal "grain of sand"; there can be no instances of "this grain," only of "grain of sand." But is the pile of sand itself individual?

One response is that it is not, and a reason that may be given for this answer is that the pile is divisible. But, of course, this answer relies on a conception of individuality as indivisibility, which I am not using here. Individuality, as used here, does not consist in indivisibility, but rather in non-instantiability. So, we need to rephrase the question: Is a pile of sand instantiable or non-instantiable? That is, is it like "cat" or like "this cat"? If it is like "cat," it is universal; and if it is like "this cat," it is individual. Put in these terms, the answer appears obvious: it is not like "cat," for there cannot be instances of "this pile of sand"; there can only be instances of "pile of sand." To divide the pile of sand is not to instantiate it insofar as the results would be either grains of sand or smaller piles of sand. Obviously, grains of sand are not instances of the pile or even of "pile of sand," but of "grain of sand." And the smaller piles of sand in which the pile could be divided would not themselves be instances of the original pile of sand, but merely parts of it. These parts in turn are instances of the universal "pile of sand" as long as such parts are not individual grains.

The fallacy of composition mentioned earlier prevents us from saying that features of members of groups are also and necessarily features

---

8. For more on this topic, see: Nicholas Wolterstorff, "Toward an Ontology of Art Works," *Nous* 9 (1975): 115–42; Joseph Margolis, "The Ontological Peculiarity of Works of Art," *Journal of Aesthetics and Art Criticism* 36 (1977): 45–50; Stephen Davies, *The Philosophy of Art* (Malden, Mass.: Blackwell, 2006); id., *Philosophical Perspectives on Art* (Oxford: Oxford University Press, 2007); and Gracia, *Individuality*, 101–4.

of the group considered as a whole. The weight of each grain of sand in a pile of sand is certainly not the same as the weight of the pile. But one thing is clear: if all the members of a group have a feature in common, the group as a whole cannot have a feature that is incompatible with such a feature. In a pile of sand, if each grain weighs something, it is impossible for the whole pile to weigh nothing, because weighing something and weighing nothing are incompatible; the pile, just as the grains of which it is composed, must weigh something.

A similar argument can be used to establish that if the members of a pile of sand are individual, the pile itself cannot be universal. Moreover, because individual and universal are mutually exclusive and exhaustive notions within a certain domain, if the pile of sand is not universal, it must be individual within that domain. This conclusion can be applied to human groups as well. If such human groups as races are composed of individual members, then the groups themselves must also be individual. "Blacks" and "Whites," considered as groups of persons, are therefore individual.

At first, this conclusion may appear counterintuitive, but it is so in part because "individual" is allowed to carry the connotation of substance or person. Obviously, the group of "Whites" is neither a substance nor a person. A person is someone like Mary or Pedro, and a group of persons is nothing like this. And a substance, in the Aristotelian sense we are using here, is something like a cat or Mary, whereas a group of persons is nothing like this. The kind of unity that ties the parts of a human is different from the kind that ties a race, but this unity is not what counts for individuality.

Nor is the individuality of a group undermined, because the members of the group are neither continuous with, nor adjacent to, each other, for individuality does not have to do with spatial continuity. The members of a group can be spread out over a vast territory and have between them members of other groups. On a beach, there can be members of the groups of pink-colored pebbles, white-colored pebbles, and black-colored pebbles, scattered all over the beach and intermingled. But this does not by any means entail that the group of pink-colored pebbles on the beach, for example, is not individual and thus that it is instantiable. This group, like the other groups of colored pebbles, is individual in the same way its members are. The same can be said about races. "Blacks" and "Whites" may live together in the same territory and intermingle in it, but each of the groups is individual. Keep in mind that some groups of people can share some, or even all, of their members in context. For example, ethnic groups such as Hispanics and Mexicans may coincide in membership in a particular place, as the group of "Whites" and the group of Poles do so in certain places. But this does not entail that to be a Hispanic is to be a Mexican, or that to be "White" is to be a Pole. Co-extension in context does not entail co-intension.

In spite of what has been said, however, there are some aspects of racial groups that appear to suggest a dimension of universality in them: members of these groups seem to be instances of the group kind. This or that "Black" appears to be an instance of "Black." So, are "Black" and "White" universals after all?

The answer is affirmative, but note that the universals in question are not the groups, but rather the relational features of belonging to the groups. A race can be conceived in two ways, as a group or as a relation among the members of a group.[9] To sort this out we need to distinguish further between universals and individuals as follows (elliptical or tacit understandings are placed within parentheses and examples are placed within square brackets):

Universals
>   race
>   this race (kind) [e.g., "Black"], that race (kind) [e.g., "White"]

Individuals
>   this (instance of) race [e.g., "Black"], that (instance of) race
>   [e.g., "White"]
>   this (instance of this) race (kind) [e.g., this "Black"], that
>   (instance of this) race (kind) [e.g., that "White"]

Part of the confusion between the individuality and universality of races arises because the same linguistic expression can be used to refer to both individuals and universals. For example, expressions such as "this race" can be used to mean different things: "this race kind," "this instance of race," and "this instance of this race kind." If we keep these uses in mind,

---

9. For further elaboration of this point, see Gracia, *Surviving Race, Ethnicity, and Nationality,* 85 ff.

however, some of the difficulties regarding the individuality and universality of racial groups disappear. This suggestion makes possible for us to turn to their individuation.

INDIVIDUATION OF HUMANS AND OF RACES

If both humans and races are individual, we are entitled to ask about the conditions of their individuation. By *individuation* I mean the process whereby they become individual, not the process by which knowing subjects become aware of them as individual. The former is a metaphysical matter, whereas the latter is epistemic. In order to distinguish these processes, I refer to the first as *the question* or *problem of individuation,* and to the second as *the question* or *problem of the discernibility of individuals.* The latter can be further divided into the *question* or *problem of identification of individuals* and *the question* or *problem of the reidentification of individuals.*

Note that the non-instantiability of humans or, for that matter, of races is not what is at stake in this investigation in that this is precisely what requires an account. Rather, our concern is with the conditions necessary and sufficient for a human or a race to be individual, that is, a non-instantiable instance. For example: what accounts for the non-instantiability of Peter or the "White" race? In the pertinent philosophical literature, this is usually called *the principle of individuation.*

Philosophers have been proposing theories of individuation for the better part of the history of the discipline, and Scholastics were pioneers in this regard. But no theory has been deemed so far to be immune from serious objections. These theories roughly fall into three large divisions: feature theories, relational theories, and sui generis theories. According to the first, the conditions of individuality are to be found in one or more features unique to an individual.[10] Boethius was the first explicitly to formulate this theory at the dawn of the Middle Ages. He argued that it is the accidental features of a substance that account for its numerical difference.[11]

---

10. I discuss these and other theories of individuation, with pertinent bibliographical references, in Gracia, *Individuality,* ch. 4.

11. Boethius, *De Trinitate,* I, 1.24–26, in *The Theological Tractates,* ed. H. F. Stewart and E. K. Rand (Cambridge, Mass.: Harvard University Press, 1918; reprint, 1968), 6.

But by numerical difference he seems to have in mind uniqueness, and uniqueness has nothing to do with non-instantiability, so his proposal cannot account for individuality conceived as non-instantiability. Consider justice, for example. Justice is a unique virtue, and yet it is not individual. So, having justice, or being just, cannot account for the individuation of the human being who has the feature of justice or who is just. Either the feature or features purported to individuate are themselves instantiable or they are not. If they are, then it is not possible to argue cogently that one or more of them can effectively constitute the necessary and sufficient conditions of the non-instantiability of that of which they are features. A bunch of instantiables cannot yield but something instantiable, even if more complex, as Peter Abelard eloquently argued.[12] Put animal and rational together and you get rational animal, but rational and animal taken together are not less instantiable than rational and animal considered separately. This shows that a bundle of universals cannot account for individuality, even if it can explain uniqueness, that is, difference from everything else, when it is not found elsewhere.

Relational theories argue that relations constitute the necessary and sufficient conditions of individuality. The strongest and most favored of these views argues that spatio-temporal relations account for individuality. Mary's spatio-temporal location is a necessary and sufficient condition of her individuality. To be here and now, or there and then, is both required and enough for something to be individual. In the Middle Ages, again Boethius provided the first impetus for this view when he argued that if accidents failed to establish numerical difference, place would do it insofar as it could not be shared.[13] Place, however, was understood differently by different authors in the Middle Ages, so even those who argued for place as the principle of individuation often held different views. For example, Aquinas held that place could be used to distinguish among numerically different material individuals, but that it does not account for their numerical difference.[14]

But this view also runs into difficulties. Spatio-temporal location is an

---

12. Peter Abelard, *Glossae secundum magistrum Petrum Abaelardum super Porphyrium* (hereafter *Glossae super Porphyrium*), ed. B. Geyer, in *Beiträge zur Geschichte der Philosophie des Mittelalters*, Band XXI, Heft 1–3 (Münster: Aschendorff, 1919–27), 12.

13. Boethius, *De Trinitate*, I, 1.27–31, p. 6.

14. Thomas Aquinas, *Expositio super librum Boethii De Trinitate* (hereafter *In De Trin.*), q. 4, a. 4, ed. B. Decker (Leiden: E. J. Brill, 1959), 155.

external relation, and external relations appear to be just too adventitious to constitute necessary and sufficient conditions of non-instantiability. How could a relation of X to Y be a necessary and sufficient condition of X's non-instantiability when the latter appears to be an internal feature of X? Does not the individuality of X in this view become dependent on Y, when we know that X can exist and persist independently of Y? Is not spatio-temporal location a function of what something is, rather than the reverse? Indeed, does not the very relation in question presuppose individuality insofar as it presupposes individual relata?[15]

The failure of feature and relational theories to account for individuality has led some philosophers to argue that these conditions are supplied by something *sui generis* to every individual. This has been called by different names in the history of philosophy, two of which are well known: *haecceitas* (thisness) and bare particular. Duns Scotus is behind the first and Gustav Bergmann behind the second.[16]

But this position also has serious problems. The most obvious is that it is not informative. To say that the necessary and sufficient conditions of individuality are sui generis to the individual is not saying more than that the condition of being individual is being individual or, alternatively, that there must be a condition of being individual even though we cannot tell what it is. This is disingenuous.[17]

As an alternative to these and other inadequate theories, I have elsewhere proposed that the principle of individuation is existence, whether actual or possible.[18] This means that if anything exists, either in the realm of actuality or in the realm of possibility, it is individual, and if anything is an individual, then it exists either in the realm of actuality or in the realm of possibility.

There are at least three antecedents of this view in the Middle Ages. The earliest appears to be Avicenna, to whom some Scholastics attributed the view that existence is the principle of individuation.[19] Aquinas

---

15. Cf. Abelard, *Glossae super Porphyrium*, 13, 64.

16. Duns Scotus, *Opus oxoniense* II, d. 3, q. 6, *Editio Vaticana* 17.273–93; Gustav Bergmann, "Individuals," *Philosophical Studies* 9 (1958): 78–85.

17. Suárez makes the point in *Disputationes metaphysicae V: De unitate individuali ejusque principio*, s. 2, par. 6, *Editio Vivès* 25.149–50.

18. I defend this position in Gracia, *Individuality*, ch. 4.

19. For discussions of this position, see Duns Scotus, *Opus oxoniense*, Bk. II, d. 3 (ed. Vaticana 17.229–355), and Suárez, *Disputationes metaphysicae* V, 5 (ed. Vivès 25.177–80).

has also been interpreted as an antecedent of this view. According to this interpretation, the act of existence *(esse)* that Thomas distinguishes from essence, functions as the principle of individuation.[20] And one could argue that Suárez is also an antecedent, although strictly speaking, according to him individual substances are individuated by their essences as they exist.[21]

In short, according to this view, for Mary to be individual, it is required that her existence be either actual or possible. I exist in the realm of actuality, but my younger brother does not. This difference separates us. That he exists in the realm of possibility means that he could exist or could have existed in actuality, although he does not. In some cases at particular times, a possible individual could still come to exist in reality, if conditions are propitious. This is the case of my male children. But in others it could not—the case of my younger brother (both of my parents are dead).

The existential theory takes for granted certain accompanying conditions. One of these is that the entities in question instantiate a universal—in the cases pertinent to our discussion, a human or a race. After all, when speaking of individuation, we are speaking of the individuation of a universal, and this means that the universal is assumed. This condition is built into the very notion of individual as a non-instantiable instance of an instantiable. Another condition is that the universal not involve a contradiction. Such things as square circles cannot exist and, therefore, cannot be individual because the universal square-circle includes incompatible properties that manifest themselves in a contradictory concept and make it impossible for it to be instantiated.

This theory of individuation amounts to the view that only individuals exist: the world, both actual and possible, is composed of non-instantiables. Does this make sense? Just consider our experience. Where are the instantiables in it? Where is red, human, and cat? Our experience is always of this or that instance of red, this or that instance of cat, and this

20. See Jorge J. E. Gracia, "Suárez's Criticism of the Thomistic Principle of Individuation," *Atti del Congresso di S. Tommaso d'Aquino nel suo VII Centenario* (1977): 563–68, and Joseph Owens, "Thomas Aquinas," in *Individuation in Scholasticism: The Later Middle Ages and the Counter-Reformation, 1150–1650*, ed. Jorge J. E. Gracia (Albany: State University of New York Press, 1994), 173–94.

21. Suárez, *Disputationes metaphysicae* V, s. 5, and s. 6, par. 1 (ed. Vivès 25.177–80).

or that instance of human. Universals are not part of what we see, touch, taste, hear, or smell; they are only part of what we think about the things we experience. Moreover, the annihilation of what some philosophers regard as universals in the world, such as the color of my eyes (brown), does not affect the color of someone else's eyes who has the same color as mine, so this must mean that the color of my eyes is an instance of brown rather than brown itself. In short, instantiables are the universals of whose instances we have experience.

The only necessary and sufficient condition of the individuality of humans, apart from a cogent humanity, is their existence, and the same should be true of groups of humans such as a race. The individuation both of humans and of groups composed of humans is existence. "Blacks" and "Whites" are individual groups because they exist. Of course, the groups do not exist as Aristotelian substances do. These groups are nothing but the aggregates of members and their relations. Ultimately, what exists are their individual members, who stand in certain relations to each other. The "Black" race is nothing but the group of "Blacks" who stand to each other in relations of descent and similarity with respect to some of the features contained in a particular set associated with "Blacks." The existence of the group reduces to the existence of the members, and one could say that the principle of individuation of the group is in fact the principle of individuation of the members, or that the members individuate the group.

This is the reverse of what occurs when one considers the individuation of the components and features of Aristotelian substances. The black color of Pedro's eyes is individuated by an existing Pedro, for the existence of the color of his eyes depends on Pedro's existence. If no Pedro, then no black color of Pedro's eyes; although no black color of Pedro's eyes does not entail no Pedro since Pedro can exist without eyes. In Aristotelian substances, the individuation of features is accounted for in terms of the substances that they characterize, whereas in groups of substances the situation is reversed: the individuation of the group is accounted for in terms of the individuality of its members.

This account of the individuation of groups should not be very surprising insofar as groups, like the features of substances, depend on the substances that compose the groups. Aristotelian substances have ontological priority both over the features and the parts that compose them and over the groups into which they can be gathered. This fact lends support to a point about groups made earlier: unlike Aristotelian substances, groups are aggregates resulting from relations among their members, and those relations vary.

Given the deficiencies of relational and spatio-temporal views of individuation, one may ask why they have been so popular in the history of philosophy. The reason is that they appear to function well as theories of discernibility, and it is common to treat the problem of individuation as if it concerned discernibility. Let me turn to discernibility, then.

DISCERNIBILITY OF INDIVIDUAL HUMANS AND INDIVIDUAL RACES

Individuation and the conditions of individuality might be described as metaphysical insofar as they concern the way things are. But often they are interpreted epistemically to mean awareness of individuality and the conditions of such awareness. Understood thus, the conditions apply to how a knower may effectively discern individuals, which in our case refers to humans and races. It is important to keep the metaphysical and epistemological issues separate, for the conditions of individuation and those of individual discernibility need not be the same, and in fact it seldom makes sense for them to be the same. In the Middle Ages, Aquinas in particular understood the importance of the distinction between individuation and individual discernibility. This is evident when he argues that place can be the reason we distinguish numerically different substances, but it is not what accounts for that difference; for that we need matter under dimensions.[22]

As mentioned earlier, the problem of discernibility can be divided into two further problems: identification and reidentification. The first has to do with discerning individual humans and races at particular times. We could also call this *synchronic discernibility of individuals* (whether of persons or groups). The second has to do with discerning individuals at

---

22. Although Aquinas consistently identifies the principle of individuation of material beings as matter under dimensions, sometimes he says these are indeterminate dimensions, whereas other times he says they must be determinate. We find this shift even within a single work: see *In De Trin.* q. 4, a. 4; q. 5, a. 2 (ed. Decker 155). Wippel discusses these varying accounts in his *Metaphysical Thought of Aquinas,* 360–71.

two (or more times), and this could be called the *diachronic discernibility of individuals*. Nonetheless, I use "identification" and "reidentification" because, although these terms are less descriptively accurate, they are less cumbersome.

Identification

How do we become aware of individual humans and races? Or, to put it in philosophically standard vocabulary: what are the necessary and sufficient conditions of the identification of humans and races?

As in the case of individuation, many theories have been offered for individual identification. Most popular among these are bundle, relational, and unique feature views. The bundle view argues that we identify individuals through the bundle of features that characterize them and that is unique to them. Consider two cards: one is 2×4 and white, the other 5×8 and yellow. The claim is that I can identify the first because it is 2×4, a card, and white, and I can identify the second because it is 5×8, a card, and yellow. This claim, of course, makes sense prima facie, except that there would be a problem if the two cards shared all their discernible features, such as when we have two cards that are both 2×4 and white. What could we use to become aware of them as two individuals under these conditions? This problem was raised by Boethius, as we saw earlier, although his formulation of the problem lacked a sharp distinction between the epistemological problem of identification and the metaphysical one of individuation.[23] There is also a difficulty in that the features belonging to the bundles are universal and therefore cannot by themselves cause us to know the cards as individual, that is, as non-instantiable; depending on circumstances, they only allow us to distinguish one card from another. Indeed, how do I know that the bundles of features characterize individuals? How can I know that "2×4 white card" actually characterizes this and not that?

These considerations lead some to think in terms of relations as constituting the principle of individuation rather than of bundles of features.

---

23. I explore Boethius's formulation in detail and compare his view with that of other authors from the early part of the Middle Ages in Jorge J. E. Gracia, "Metaphysical, Epistemological, and Linguistic Approaches to Universals: Porphyry, Boethius, and Abailard," in *Medieval Masters: Essays in Memory of Msgr. E. A. Synan*, ed. R. E. Houser (Houston: University of Saint Thomas, 1999), 1–24.

The cards are discerned as individual because one is located here now, whereas the other is located there now.[24] This account makes sense, but it is not quite right insofar as "here" and "now" are relational terms that, without a point of reference, can be applied to the same individuals. What determines that one card is here and the other is there? Clearly a point of reference, for the spatial—and the same could be said for the temporal—locations are at play. This point of reference is the subject, the judging I. The "here," "there," and "now," are relational terms that, like "left of" and "right of," are used to express a relation between the things in question and a subject. There is a spatio-temporal grid that I, for example, use to locate and identify the individual cards, but a grid without a point of reference is as ineffective to discern individuals as universal features are. It works because I function as its point of reference. One card is in a certain place and at a certain time in relation to me, and so is the other card.

Still, there remains the problem noted before, that relations by themselves are universal and therefore cannot help us to know individuals qua individuals, that is, qua non-instantiable instances. Indeed, relations between individuals presuppose individuality rather than establish it.[25] Through a spatio-temporal grid, I succeed in discerning two bundles of universals, but how do I know that these two bundles are actually individual, that is, non-instantiable? The only way to do this is to assume, as my view concerning individuation proposes, that for bundles of features to characterize something, that something must already be individual and must be assumed to have some level of existence. This is the only way I can infer that the two cards are indeed two individual cards. Nothing in the situation itself, or the empirical data I have available, can do this.

Apart from the bundle and relational views of individual discernibility, there is another that we need to consider because it seems to work. Let us go back to our example of the two cards that we need to be aware of as individuals and stipulate that they have at least one discernible feature that is not common to both—say, the color. Surely this feature appears to be sufficient to tell each card apart from everything else that surrounds it in my field of vision, as long as there are no other cards present

24. This fact is perhaps what is behind Aquinas's view of place as principle of individual discernment. See the text from *In De Trin.* mentioned above in nn. 14 and 22.
25. Max Black, "The Identity of Indiscernibles," in *Universals and Particulars: Readings in Ontology,* ed. Michael Loux (Notre Dame, Ind.: University of Notre Dame Press, 1976), 250–62.

of the same color as the one I need to discern. The color is not enough in cases where there are other cards of the same color present in my field of vision, but it is enough in this case. And it is a case in which context plays a decisive role in the identification of individuals. But although this is enough to distinguish the cards, it does not account for their non-instantiability. In this case also, we need to assume that their existence entails their individuality. So, it turns out that the feature view of individuation is ineffective, unless it is combined with the existential view. Moreover, the feature view turns out to be ultimately relational, even if those who uphold it do not always understand it to be so.

From this discussion we can conclude that only relational views of identification are effective. Second, individual identification can take place based on anything that serves to distinguish one thing from others within a particular field of sense experience. And third, relational views are ineffective without the existential assumption provided by the existential view of individuation.

Now let us turn to individual humans and races and apply to them what we have established. In the case of humans, each is discerned by a subject as an individual in terms of features or relations that are unique within an observer's field of sense experience, provided that the subject assumes that existence involves non-instantiability. I perceive Juana as an individual in that she exists in my field of perception and I perceive her either as having unique features in that field—a certain color of hair, a certain stature, and so on—or as being in a unique spatio-temporal location—there now, for instance. This account seems quite uncontroversial. But what do we make of groups?

The problem that arises with groups is that they are composed of many individuals, most of whom are not, and cannot be, part of the field of a subject's sense experience. Thus, even if they had uniquely distinguishing features or spatio-temporal locations, and even if I assumed that their existence entailed their non-instantiability, I would not be aware of them or of their existence. Think, for example, of all "Whites" who lived and died before 1942, the year of my birth. They are surely members of the racial group "Whites," but I have not, nor could I have, a sense experience of them, or know of their existence except secondhand. So, how can I identify them as individuals, that is, as non-instantiable?

Two cases need to be considered here: first, one in which I am acquainted with all the members of the group; second, one in which I am acquainted with only some members of the group. In the first case, I discern the individual group composed of individuals that are part of my field of sense experience through my awareness of the individuality of every member of the group and the relations holding among them. In short, identification in this case requires that I both discern the members of the group and be aware that they are members of it. Consider the case of a nuclear family composed of Pedro, Mary, and their daughter Lolita. The identification of this nuclear family can be reduced to the identification of the members of the family, Pedro, Mary, and Lolita, and the knowledge that Pedro and Mary are married and Lolita is their daughter.

In the second case, I do not have access to every member of the family in my field of sense experience. As a result three conditions are necessary for the discernibility of the individual group: (1) I need to be able to discern at least one member of the group as individual; (2) I need to have credible reports of the existence of other persons; and (3) I need to know that both the individual human(s) I directly identify and those about whom I have reports are in fact members of the group. When I see only Pedro, in order for me to identify the individual nuclear family composed of Pedro, Mary, and Lolita, I need to identify Pedro and know that he is married to a woman called Mary and has a child with her called Lolita. Mary and Lolita are identified by me as individual members of the group because of their relation to Pedro and on the basis of credible descriptions of them. This procedure makes it possible for me to discern this nuclear family as individual.

The same requirements apply, mutatis mutandis, to other human groups, such as races. I do not need to know all "Blacks" to identify the individual "Black" race, but I do need to know at least one "Black" and the relations that tie him to some other "Blacks" about whom I have credible reports, even if I do not directly experience them.

But a problem remains: race membership seems to vary from place to place. Consider, for example, that to be "Black" in Cuba is something very different from being "Black" in the United States. In Cuba, to be "Black" entails an unmixed appearance. A mixed-looking person is not usually considered "Black" but mulatto. In the United States, according to the One Drop Rule, to be "Black" requires only that one have a "Black" ancestor, even if one looks "White." But in Cuba, persons of mixed "Black" and "White" ancestry who look "White" pass for "White," whereas those who appear "Black" are considered "Black." Clearly the criteria of racial classification used in the United States and Cuba are different. In Cuba, racial membership is established primarily according to physical appearance, whereas the American One Drop Rule emphasizes ancestry. Race is thought of very differently in the United States and in Cuba. And if we did some serious investigation about views of race in other countries of Latin America and other parts of the world, we would probably find substantive differences in the views those societies have as well.

It seems to be clear, then, that even if there is general agreement that some people are members of a particular race, there are always cases of people whose membership is in doubt. And if this is the case, we might ask how we can speak of the individual discernibility of the group in question. If we cannot establish that race R_1 is composed of persons A, B, and C, but only that it is composed of persons A and B, and that C is a member of the race only under certain conditions, how can we speak of the discernibility of R_1?

The answer to this difficulty is that, although the individuation of a group is contingent on the identity of the group, the lack of certainty concerning exact membership does not prevent us from being aware of some properties of the group that apply to the members as we know them. For example, the identity of the group, "most students of those present in this classroom," depends on the number of students present in the classroom, but this fact does not prevent us from holding truthfully that the students have weight and volume. That the number of the group "most students of those present in this classroom" depends on the number of students is clear when we consider different possible class sizes. If the number of students in the classroom is three, it is clear that the group of most students present is two. If the number of students is twenty, however, then we know "most" could be fifteen, sixteen, seventeen, and eighteen for sure, but not clearly eleven, since a majority does not seem to be the same as "most." Yet, it is true that in both cases we know that the group is composed of entities that have weight and volume. To repeat, then, indetermination in the exact number of members of a group does not preclude that the members be individual and discernible as such.

Reidentification

The question concerning the reidentification of individual humans and individual races asks what makes us discern them as the same at different times. For example, how do I know that Santiago is the same individual in 1985 and 1999, or that the group of "Whites" is the same individual group in 1669 and 1966?

Obviously, I need to know several things: (1) the individual human or group at t_1, (2) the individual human or group at t_2, and (3) that the first human or group is the same as the second. So I need to identify two individual humans or groups at two (or more) pertinent times and then determine the identity between the two. Now, we have already seen how identification takes place, so we need not repeat how it does. We can assume that we have satisfied conditions (1) and (2). But on what basis can we satisfy (3)?

Concerning individual humans, there is only one way I see for this to work. If existence is a sufficient condition of individuality, and if we can establish that there is no interruption in existence for an individual human between t_1 and t_2, then we can conclude that we have the same individual at those times. And how do I know that there is no interruption in existence? Through the relations I have with the things in question, such as, for example, direct sense perception. I can know, for example, that student X in my Monday class is the same individual student at the beginning of the class (at 1 PM) and at the end of the class (at 3 PM) because I have been observing him continuously. Direct empirical evidence is not, of course, the only evidence I can count on. Other kinds may also be used. Credible reports is another, for example. Note, however, that in no case will there be an apodictic kind of certainty; only degrees of probability would be involved. We need not forget Hume.

The case of race is different, however, for two reasons: first, membership is not always clear, and second, membership changes. The answer to the first difficulty was given already in the case of identification. The answer to the second is that this procedure applies to the case of all groups of entities some of whose members exist at some times and not at others. This requires considering possible, potential, and actual entities at different times. So let us look briefly at the notions of possibility, potentiality, and actuality to see what they involve.

"Possible" and "impossible" may be understood in terms of contradiction. Strictly speaking, contradiction is a property of concepts, propositions, or language, but it may be applied derivatively to other things such as a square circle. So, the possible is what is not contradictory, and the impossible what is contradictory.

Within possibility, one may distinguish between the "merely possible," such as the son I had when I was twenty-two (I did not have one), and the "actualized possible," which includes my maternal great-grandfather. The difference between the merely possible and the actualized possible is that the merely possible is never actual, whereas the actualized possible is actual at some time or at all times. This leads us to the distinction between "actual" and "non-actual."

One may speak of "actual" with respect to temporal and nontemporal entities. With respect to nontemporal entities, I take "actual" in the sense of existing at all times or, to put it differently, that there is no time at which the entity or entities in question do not exist. Thus, such entities as God, for example, if actual and nontemporal, cannot be said not to exist at any time, even if such entities are not supposed to exist in time.

With respect to temporal entities, one may speak of "actual" in two senses: to be actual in the sense of existing at a particular time and at no other time, and to be actual in the sense of existing at some time, whether in the past, the present, or the future. In the first sense, Napoleon was actual between 1769 and 1821, but was not actual before 1769 or after 1821. In the second sense, Napoleon is actual because he did exist between 1769 and 1821, even if he did not exist at other times. Likewise, if it turns out that I will have a grandchild named Ignatius, Ignatius is actual.

What has been said about "actual" helps explain the distinction between the actualized possible and the merely possible. The actualized possible is actual at some time or at all times, whereas the merely possible is never actual, whether in the past, the present, or the future.

The notion of "potential" lies somewhere between the notions of "actual" and "possible." It shares with the notion of "possible" the fact that it is not contradictory. But the potential is not merely noncontradictory, it is that which has some probability of becoming actual. My nonexisting uncle, Alexander, is possible in the sense of not being contradictory, but he is not potential, because under current circumstances he could never become actual. Potentiality involves not just noncontradiction, but some probability of actualization. One might explain this by saying that there are at least five conditions for X to be potentially Y at t_1:

1. X is not Y at t_1
2. X is actual at t_1
3. Y is not actual at t_1
4. Under certain circumstances, X becomes Y at t_2.

Consider an example. Baby X is potentially adult Y at t_1, if and only if: baby X is not adult Y at t_1; baby X is actual at t_1 (i.e., baby X exists at t_1); adult Y is not actual at t_1 (i.e., adult Y does not exist at t_1); and under certain circumstances, baby X becomes adult Y at t_2.

We may regard a race, then, as including all members that are actual, in addition to those that are potential and possible, using the senses of these terms presented.

INDIVIDUATION OF RACES

In conclusion, I have proposed a view of individuality as non-instantiability and have distinguished it from other conceptions, including uniqueness. I have argued that races are individual and that they are individuated by virtue of the individuality of their members and the relations that hold among them. Moreover, I have distinguished between individuation and the discernibility of individuals, both at particular times (synchronic identification) and at two (or more) different times (diachronic reidentification). And I have provided an account of how this discernibility, whether as identification or reidentification, takes place. Ultimately, the point of reference of an individual observer is required. But in all three cases—individuation, identification, and reidentification—an existential assumption is required for a satisfactory account. As it should be clear, this view relies on a tradition that goes back to the Middle Ages and flourished in the schools.

James Ross

---

7 ∞ Merely Metaphysical Possibility

The question here is whether there are alien possibilities, that is, possible things or states of affairs other than those that ever actually exist or lie within the capacities of finite things.[1] To answer that, I give reasons why conceivability cannot ensure real possibility, and why there are not *in re* any mere possibilities, and why recent modal ontologies developed in the twentieth century[2] and widely employed by metaphysicians and philosophers of nature are mistaken.[3]

---

1. I began the topic in my *Thought and World* (Notre Dame, Ind.: University of Notre Dame Press, 2008), 32–36 where I say, "what merely might have been, as far as it is real and determinate, is accounted for by the abilities and dispositions of actual things and is otherwise empty, though there are also conventional, notional, definitional, and merely syntactical cases as well; (iv) there is no world of mere *possibilia* and *a fortiori*, no real domain of worlds; (v) metaphysics is not grounded in prior logic or in a domain of explanatorily prior and self-accounting logical possibilities. Explanation winds down to what exists and stops there." However, I did not give a sketch of how to regard and how to employ the formal modal logic generally or how to classify modalities (see the fourth section, below).

2. The basic propositional modal systems (but not the strictly formal quantified models) and their use syllogistically were known to Pseudo-Scotus and others. See Charlene Senape McDermott, "Notes on the Assertoric and Modal Propositional Logic of the Pseudo-Scotus," *Journal of the History of Philosophy* 10 (1963): 273–306; Paul Thom, *Medieval Modal Systems: Problems and Concepts*, Ashgate Studies in Medieval Philosophy (Aldershot, UK: Ashgate, 2003); and also Simo Knuuttila, "Medieval Theories of Modality," in *The Stanford Encyclopedia of Philosophy* (hereafter *SEP*) http://plato.stanford.edu/entries/modality-medieval, with its fine bibliography that also cites his own more extensive treatments.

3. My interest in real modalities started while at the Catholic University of America as a student in 1953 with Duns Scotus's modal argument in his *De Primo Principio*. From this argument I later adapted ideas (especially that one cannot establish real possibility from conception alone), in my *Philosophical Theology* (Indianapolis: Bobbs-Merrill, 1968) and in several papers and lately in *Thought and World*, cited above.

Appropriately, this topic is related to the views John F. Wippel explored historically in his 1981 *Review of Metaphysics* paper, "The Reality of Non-existing Possibles according to Thomas Aquinas, Henry of Ghent and Godfrey of Fontaines,"[4] as well as to the ideas of Duns Scotus,[5] and so, generally fits into a familiar line of interest and importance for metaphysics. However, this is not a history essay, but a metaphysical one.

The opening question, as I said, is whether there could have been things of entirely other sorts than any of the things that ever exist contingently or even lie within the power of finite things—even beyond what we can conceive, alien possibilities.[6]

This chapter consists of five parts in which I support the following: (1) There are no real ranges of mere possibilia or domains of merely possible worlds. (2) Predication is not just class inclusion, as first order logic represents it, but is a different linguistic and judgmental act altogether[7]—one simulated only imperfectly with extensional logic, and in fact one only intelligent beings are capable of because it requires abstractive judgmental ability.[8] (3) We cannot reliably infer from conceptual consis-

---

4. John F. Wippel, "The Reality of Non-Existing Possibles according to Thomas Aquinas, Henry of Ghent and Godfrey of Fontaines," *The Review of Metaphysics* 34 (1981) 729–59.

5. See Calvin Normore, "Scotus' Modal Theory," in *The Cambridge Companion to Duns Scotus,* ed. Thomas Williams (Cambridge: Cambridge University Press, 2003), 129–60.

6. See Christopher Menzel, "Actualism," in *SEP,* http://plato.stanford.edu/entries/actualism, "Imagine a race of beings—call them 'Aliens'— . . . different enough, in fact, that no actually existing thing could have been an Alien, any more than a given gorilla could have been a fruitfly." David Lewis earlier introduced the phrase "alien possibilities" to refer to possibilities uncaptured by "recombination of actual things," in *On the Plurality of Worlds* (Oxford: Blackwell Publishing, 1986), 92.

7. For reasons similar to those Henry Veatch urged years ago, I, too, say predication is not merely location of an object within a range of things bearing a name—that can be done by machine—but involves abstraction that only humans can perform, to separate by thought the repeatable structures of things from their particularity (see Veatch's *Intentional Logic,* New Haven, Conn.: Yale University Press, 1952). The relation of predicate to argument (e.g., (x)(Hx implies Rx) (all humans are rational)) as notated with first-order quantification does not express real predication (e.g., that every human is constitutively rational), but only that everything called "a human" is one of the things called "a rational thing." It is like Ockham's fourteenth-century deflation of the notion of predication into coincidence of names.

8. While such extensionality is acceptable for simple quantified logic that does not depend on meaning relationships, it is not the same as genuine predication that does so depend, and undercuts understanding the Barcan formula and its converse, other than as *de dicto* and as a purely formal, extensional transformations, but not as *de re* true because they have false cases. For instance, the first-order notation neither expresses essentiality nor does it distinguish accidentals from *propria;* and it implies that for anything that is essential to something, there is

tency to real possibility (or from mere verbal inconsistency to real impossibility either). (4) There are omissions and defects in all the recent "possible worlds" metaphysics. (5) There is another way—at least one—that I sketch, of retaining and utilizing the formal modal systems to order and audit our metaphysical, scientific and ordinary reasoning.[9] In it, the natural modalities are attributed on account of the potentialities and repugnancies of things—as formulated more and more generally by the natural sciences, and perhaps ground out in fundamental physical forces or structures not yet well understood[10]—while the metaphysically intrinsic modalities of necessity and contingency are reductively grounded in *esse a se* and *ab alio* (as Avicenna and Aquinas thought), and the logical modalities (that are basically forms of consistency and inconsistency) are attributed to things by *extrinsic denomination* on account of the logical properties of propositions *about* them.

An important but not novel outcome is that for anything to be possible beyond the remote capacities of whatever finitely exists, there has to exist a free divine creator able to have elected otherwise than, and beyond, the order and capacities of nature (as, for instance, are divine incarnation and human bodily resurrection).[11] Yet the two claims—that fi-

---

something that has that feature in every possible world—which is not what is coherently meant by essentiality—and, moreover, that all possible individuals exist and none exist contingently (see reference to Williamson in n. 58 below).

9. Logics, when *applied* in metaphysics and philosophy of nature, operate as insurance schemes to license and audit thought-transformations so as to protect against reasoning from true premises to false conclusions and against misconstruals of the formal relations among propositions. We need different logics for different purposes (just as we need marine, house, life, and health insurance). Such formulations are also used as shorthand to keep the relationships of ideas clear—though one has to be aware that natural language semantic relations (and natural, as opposed to formal, implications) often alter the shorthand implicitly (see James Ross, "Contextual Adaptation," *American Philosophical Quarterly* 46 (2009): 19–30.).

10. Structures or forces that *are* what they do. See my *Thought and World*, ch. 7, "Real Natures."

11. So though personal resurrection from the dead is logically possible (consistently conceivable as far as our conceptions go, though they clearly do not include all the *de re* conditions for it) and metaphysically possible (given almighty divine power), it is not naturally possible because not within the ability of anything in the order of nature, and in fact is opposed to it. In fact, apart from faith in the resurrection of Jesus, the *de re* possibility may not be accessible, because the overflow conditions would not be determinate. Furthermore, the cosmos may include things we have not experienced yet, say extragalactic clouds that are intelligent (Sir Fred Hoyle, *Frontiers of Astronomy* [New York: Harper and Row, 1954]), or rational animals with right-handed amino acids—things imagined and conceptually consistent as far as their descriptions go—that may still not be naturally possible, as Newtonian absolute space was not.

nite possibility is not exhausted by the capacities in nature and that there is a free divine creator—are epistemically entangled enough so that neither provides a cognitively independent premise to establish the other.

The chief philosophical interest of this essay, I think, is that conceivability cannot assure real possibility; that there are overflow *de re* constitutive conditions for things; that modern modal metaphysics is full of anomalies; and that we can employ the formal logic in the ways I describe,[12] and not particularly in the conclusion that alien possibility requires a free divine creator, which theists already accept and nontheists ignore.[13]

QUICK WORKING DISTINCTIONS

(1) *Natural possibility*—what is within the remote or proximate capacity of nature. (2) *Logical possibility*,[14] namely consistency—absence of entailed contradiction—either in (2a) purely formal syntactic systems and (2b) semantic systems—with explicit definitions and ranges of reference (e.g., in math, the numbers), or more broadly (2c) in adapted formal structures with empirical conceptions (e.g., our talk about counterfactuals *de re* and about what cannot happen). And (3) *metaphysical* or real possibility that includes *natural*, supernatural,[15] and, if there were any,

---

12. Some naturalists argue for a reductive analysis of modalities into the quantum states of matter (that have "branching" [potential] outcomes) so that nothing but the micro-order of nature determines and grounds real possibility (see James Ladyman and Don Ross, et al., *Every Thing Must Go* [Oxford: Oxford University Press, 2007], and Alastair Wilson, "Modal Metaphysics and the Everett Interpretation," *Pittsburgh Philosophy of Science Archive* (2006), http://philsci-archive.pitt.edu/archive/00002635).

13. Because nontheists think a self-subsistent free creator whose essence we cannot know is not an explanatory advance (the god of the gaps objections). Still, neither do they offer nor do they have an explanation for the reality of their possible worlds. They seem to think consistency is enough for such multitudes, but not for a deity.

14. Think of purely logical possibility as revolving around the notions of consistency, and involving two loci: (a) purely formal structures of uninterpreted systems and (b), less strictly, the formal transformation within a conceptually interpreted body of propositions such as geometry or arithmetic (with less strict analogues for propositions expressed in ordinary languages, special disciplines, and crafts). We can subdivide logical possibility into syntactical and semantic consistency, where consistency is absence of a contradiction (and if a proposed formal system contains a contradiction, that contradiction is derivable in a finite number of steps, as Church's theorem assures).

15. So, the supernatural, even if it happens in accord with nature but not by nature, falls within the realm of the metaphysically possible but not the naturally possible. And that can be

alien possibilities, as well as necessity to be or be so really,[16] Metaphysical, that is ontological, *impossibility,* including natural impossibility, has no *de re* extension at all (but is attributed to intentional objects such as round squares, velocities exceeding light, and star-sized tomatoes).

Notice that consistency (formal and conceptual, pure or applied) is always relative to a notional, conceptual base: that is, relative either to a system of formal definitions and transformations, or to a vocabulary, or, restricted more narrowly, to the principles, say, of physics or biology, or of civil law, or to practices of ordinary discourse about physical or spiritual things.[17] Thus, entirely relative cosmic space was inconsistent for Newton's physics, but the opposite, absolute space, was inconsistent for Einstein's special relativity; necessity known a posteriori, that is through experience, was inconsistent for David Hume and for Kant, but it was consistent for Aristotle, Aquinas, and Saul Kripke; "humans who survive death" was inconsistent for Lucretius, but consistent for Plato. Even the principle that some well-formed propositions are neither true nor false is inconsistent in classical logic but is consistent in intuitionist logic and is supposed by many contrary-to-fact suppositions (for instance, "Had I lived in 1066, I would have been a child of a Norman invader"—yes? no? Nothing determines it).[18] Consistency is context bound, not free-floating.

There are no propositions that are referentially about contingent nonexistent (and nonpotential) things or kinds; that is because where there are no names, there are no truths; truth *de re*[19] goes only as far as refer-

---

either something that is not *eo ipso* contrary to nature (like inspiration or grace) or something contrary to nature, like resurrection.

16. Thus, to speak of what is consistent for God is to speak denominatively from our language-based notions; it is not to speak intrinsically and nonrelatively, because God does not have a plurality of concepts except by extrinsic denomination (from the vantage of creatures), for there is only the Logos. See Thomas Aquinas, *Summa theologiae* (hereafter *ST*) I, q. 14; see also Wippel, cited above, n. 4.

17. Since all consistency/inconsistency is formality-relative and/or conceptual system-relative, there is no absolute and antecedent measure of consistency for alien things, and thus there is no measure of absolute divine power in the way the medieval masters analyzed it (by consistency of conception). Descartes almost had it right that God could do what seems absolutely impossible to us: although he did not explain it well or use plausible examples, Descartes did have the idea that what seems contradictory to us may be so only relatively to our conceptual system; instead, intuitionist logic or non-Euclidean geometries would have done well as examples of how God might have made things differently.

18. Ross, *Thought and World*, 45–65.

19. There can be truth merely *de dicto* from mere convention. So the proposition "witches have brooms" can be a conventional truth, but not about anything real.

ence does.[20] So, although whatever is naturally possible is metaphysically possible, whether such a thing is also conceptually consistent may depend on the resources of some language to express it. Transfinite arithmetic was not possible till the forms of expression were invented; so too, for alternative geometries and for twelve-tone composition. Thus, something may be really possible, even naturally possible (i.e., within the abilities of natural things), but still not at a given time conceivable for us. Such was the case with spaceship navigation until a few generations ago; and for most of humankind, such is the case with nanotechnology now.

CONSISTENT CONCEIVABILITY DOES NOT ENSURE REAL POSSIBILITY

We need to cut any automatic connection we might be tempted to make between consistent conceivability and real possibility for the following three reasons.[21]

(1) The first reason is that consistent conceivability by us, even in principle (but outside contexts like mathematics and logic), does not ensure real possibility because conceptions cannot determine the overflow *de re* conditions for finite things. Yet such conditions are made part of the truth-conditions for what we say by our *references* to things perceived (e.g., by our naming or indicating such things). It is not enough for something to be among the truth-conditions—among what in fact has to be so, for what we say to be so—to make such conditions into parts of the *meanings* of our words, not even into belief-elements of the meanings (as "herbivorous" is part of what is meant by "deer"); that depends on linguistic

20. Ross, *Thought and World*, 48–53.

21. The view that consistent conceivability *does* ensure real possibility is a very old mistake of philosophers; even Thomas Aquinas seems to have believed it (see e.g., *ST* I, q. 25). And Duns Scotus, who appeared to be proving the possibility of a first efficient cause a posteriori in *De Primo Principio* (having realized that concepts alone do not do it), fell back into it by reasoning that since it was not contradictory to deny there is an infinite regress of essentially ordered efficient causes, it is possible that there is a first uncaused cause (that is, since the infinite regress option does not have an inconsistent denial, its opposite—that there is a first efficient cause in the order of essentially ordered causes—is really possible, when all that might have followed is that the opposite is consistent). That approach is just the application of the "consistency implies real possibility" principle in another place. And of course, philosophers took that rule as obvious right up until rather recently (long after my saying it was false, in *Philosophical Theology*, 1968; I think Thomas Reid, in his *An Inquiry into the Human Mind on the Principles of Common Sense* of 1764, also recognized it to be false in criticizing Descartes' *Meditation* VI).

practice. The merely *de re* conditions are the conditions that overflow the linguistic meanings of the words (like the chemical constitutions of gasoline), but that, if unsatisfied, would leave what we say untrue.[22] And often the overflow *de re* conditions are not known of at all, and some are merely accidental (like the engine design of a car we think is across the street). For instance, the micro-conditions for table sugar (sucrose, i.e., $C_{12}.H_{22}.O_{11}$) are not presented in the meanings of the ordinary word, but unless those conditions are satisfied (with approximations), there is not any table sugar.

For millennia such chemical constitutions (and other constitutions, e.g., atomic) were unknown, but opaquely relied upon by chefs who used sugar. Those constitutions were in practice inconceivable, and yet they were *de re* conditions for the recipes. Whether supersonic air flight was possible did not depend on meanings but on whether we could make planes fly faster than 753 miles per hour at sea level (1050+ feet per second); the same holds for whether it is possible to dissolve gold in Kool-Aid. Concepts are not enough; overflow *de re* conditions count.

For example, a new unified theory of electromagnetism and gravity may not go far enough to ensure the natural or even metaphysical possibility of such a unification because the overflow *de re* conditions picked up by the referring components may conflict, as with "star-sized tomatoes," and "phlogiston." Or its conditions may be in nature vacuous, as the claim "there is silicon-based life" or "there is life without six-atom molecules" may be. Such a conflict or vacuity may either lie in the overflow but now knowable conditions (like those for phlogiston, ether, and caloric) or lie within the hidden and inaccessible conditions, say those for "superstring" theory, just as the molecular formula(s) for life is hidden now.

So "consistent as far as it goes" does not go far enough to make possibility be independent of the existence of the objects involved. And of course, "it's imaginable" is an even worse guide to real possibility, such as cars and chipmunks that talk.[23] The conditions for a supposition may be

---

22. It is a contingent matter of usage, one of convenience mainly, which *de re* conditions become parts of word meaning, that is, become belief-elements of meaning. "Water" includes "H_2O" for some people (I mean a real reference to a hydrogen-oxygen compound); for others it is an empty co-name; and for others it is not included at all. But it is an overflow *de re* condition: there is no water without chemical composition, H_2O (understood for a family of such compounds that count as water). See Ross, *Thought and World,* 55–65.

23. Further, given that our words retain their present meanings and references, it is suppositionally inconsistent (and thus impossible) that we should be brains in a vat (or otherwise deceived *ab initio*) while our beliefs stay the same as they are now, because the beliefs have to be

indeterminate, as with "cure for cancer" or "transplanted brains," leaving the supposed thing without any sufficient constitutive condition. Or the conditions may be in natural conflict; we can think of stars that move forever, as Aristotle did: but there cannot be any.[24]

(2) A second reason why merely logical consistency cannot assure real possibility is that *there are no logical relations in nature,* only simulations (approximations) of them. (I think that accords well with medieval thinkers who regarded logical relations as relations of reason only, not as real relations.) Thus, real, *de re* necessity and impossibility are not logical relations or conditions at all. (I state this reason briefly here, offering fuller explanations elsewhere.)[25]

Logical relations cannot be real relations because logical and mathematical relations are pure functions, that is, like addition: for example, $2 + 2 = 4$, they are complete in each single case, but exactly the same in every one of an infinity of distinct cases ($n + n = 2n$), differing only in input values (such as $10 + 10$ vs. $5 + 6$) and in the resultant outputs. Simple examples of pure functions are doubling, multiplication, conjunction, and *modus ponens* in logic (if p then q, p therefore q). But there are no actual infinites. So, no matter how precisely we intend a physical process to be doubling or adding or conjoining, there are always other, incompatible functions (operations) that would yield exactly the same outputs on the same inputs *for our run of cases*—no matter how far we finitely repeat and carry out the operations. (A pocket calculator never strictly adds; it just simulates addition, usually faster and more reliably that we can actually add.)

No matter how far we run a line of physical cases for any pure function, there are incompatible functions it realizes just as well. So, a given sequence of real events could be the output of one of those incompatible functions instead of the one hypothesized—if it could be a case of any at

referentially about what they are *now* about (say, trees and water with all their overflow *de re* conditions) even to be mistaken, but by supposition, cannot be, if we encounter none of the objects we do encounter. For there would be no place to pick up the overflow *de re* truth-conditions that depend on our acquaintance with the objects.

24. Some people have asked about inventions. Insofar as the *de re* conditions of an invention are known from the behavior of other existing things and of the components, possibility is determinable from conception; but, as space travel and even skyscraper buildings make clear, the unknown *de re* conditions can defeat conception, just as previously unknown lamination of beams under stress defeated the builders of the West Gate Bridge in Australia, which collapsed in a high wind.

25. See Ross, *Thought and World*, 31–32, 54–55, 137–46, and ch. 6 for more on real sameness.

all, which I say it is *not*.[26] So logical consistency cannot be the same as, or even assure, real possibility.[27] Thus there are no purely logical relations among material things, and logical *identity* ($x = x$) is not a real relation (as Aquinas also noted, e.g., in *De Potentia*, q. 7, a. 11, ad 3–5).[28]

(3) A third reason why conceivability is not a reliable guide to real possibility is that the principle "whatever is possible is necessarily possible"—if applied to natural things and if understood without restriction—conflicts with the principle that possibilities involving contingent things have no content absent the existence of such things or of natural things capable of causing such things. It also conflicts with the idea that all such things and their properties exist contingently. That is because "if there are no names, there is no truth *de re*,"[29] and "if there are no things, there are no (genuine) names."[30]

26. See the addition/quaddition examples of Saul Kripke, *Wittgenstein on Rules and Private Language* (Cambridge, Mass.: Harvard University Press, 1982), 9ff.

27. Put another way, logical, mathematical, and other formal relations are pure functions and, thus, not realizable by anything that could in the same determinate state be a case of an equally most particular incompatible pure function; but that is always the case with a physical process (see Ross, *Thought and World*, ch. 6). Thus, no physical process can be or realize (as opposed to simulate) a logical relation. That is not just a limit of knowing; it is a limit of physical being. So, logical consistency cannot assure real possibility. Of course, that does not mean that one state of affairs cannot imply another by extrinsic denomination from the properties of the propositions about them. So we attributively say things like "That can't happen without that other." And we also say that sort of thing on account of the natural capacities and limitations of things, namely, on account of what nature always does, or won't ever do.

28. On this point, see Jeffrey Brower, "Medieval Theories of Relation," *SEP,* http://plato.stanford.edu/entries/relation-medieval.

29. We can say, "Before there were humans, it was, nevertheless, true that humans are animals." But what "was before" is denominated (extrinsically, i.e., relationally characterized) by reference to "what came to be," the real humans. Likewise, how could it have been true no matter what that "humans cannot breathe ammonia" when 5 billion years ago there was no such thing as being a human or even animate life at all? (Of course, that does not mean the opposite was true, either.) There was no such proposition or even such a determinate natural kind. The supposed situation is constructed denominatively by humans from what eventually came to be.

Such a judgment is vantaged—that is, referentially anchored—in what really sometime exists (billions of years later, in this case). Had "the later" not come to be, there would have been no proposition, no state of affairs, and no situation of "its not having been or its not having been true." Similarly, had you and I never existed, there would have been no truth or fact that "you and I (by name) never existed." That is because the kind (as nature or essence) is the characteristic capacity of the cases, taken one by one, the way "human" is to Socrates. So, "no cases, no natures." The nature of a thing is the operative and constitutive capacity of the thing—nature is essence exhibited in characteristic operation (see Thomas Aquinas, *De Ente et Essentia*, c. 1); the nature makes the thing to be that sort of thing—the way "Three Blind Mice" makes a particular singing or playing to be that (sort of) song (an abstract particular).

30. Naming (referring) is a success notion; purported names are only names by piggy-

In a word, consistent conceivability of a supposedly real thing does not entail its real possibility, or even provide more than an initial prospect for it. For all real things have *de re* conditions that overflow our conceptions. It is just such conditions for alien possibilities—that is, for supposed merely metaphysical possibilities—that are in principle inaccessible to us. The underlying idea is that reality overflows our truth about it.[31]

So, if we did not believe that there is a free divine creator who might have elected otherwise and beyond the natural order of things,[32] we might, and probably should, regard alien possibilities as an empty hypothesis, just the way most traditional monistic, materialist, and idealist metaphysical systems from Plotinus through Spinoza regard what exists as exhaustive and exclusive of anything else. My conclusion from the foregoing is that consistent conceivability does not entail real possibility.

MODERN MODAL METAPHYSICS

Next, I criticize modern modal metaphysics that is based on the Kripke models for Quantified Modal Logic, for four reasons: (1) for supposing there really are extensional domains (ranges) of possible worlds;[33] (2) for supposing that everything merely possible somehow exists (either as possibilia, or as relatively actual, as does David Lewis); (3) for not explaining what possibility is and how it could be prior to actual being—(a) as some suppose, by treating the actual world as a subdomain of the possible but without an explanatory relation to it, or (b) as others suppose, by treating the possible as a subdomain of the actual, also, without any explanation of what actualization or instantiation is or how it comes about;[34]

---

back on those who believed there were such things (or by error or convention), e.g., Aphrodite, Zeus, and Santa Claus.

31. Ross, *Thought and World,* 19. "It takes a lakeful of reality to make a drop of truth."

32. The only way to show that something finite and totally beyond the capacities of nature is possible is to show that a free almighty creator exists whose power extends to whatever would not both be and not be (in the same respect) together (*simul*) (Thomas Aquinas, *ST* I, q. 25, a. 3 co., *Editio Leonina* 4.293–94: "quod implicat in se esse et non esse simul").

33. I have criticized that idea from various vantages in *Thought and World;* "God: Creator of Kinds and Possibilities," in *Rationality, Religious Belief, and Moral Commitment,* ed. Robert Audi and William J. Wainwright (Ithaca, N.Y.: Cornell University Press, 1986), 351–84; "The Crash of Modal Metaphysics," *Review of Metaphysics* 43 (1989): 251–79; and "Aquinas' Exemplarism, Aquinas' Voluntarism," *American Catholic Philosophical Quarterly* 64 (1990): 171–98.

34. See Menzel, "Actualism," cited above, for an exploration of such options. But note, instantiation and exemplification are not *explanatory* relations.

and (4) for implicitly relying upon the principle that consistent conceivability implies possibility, a principle that I hope to have shown false in the second part of this paper.[35]

Metaphysicians such as Alvin Plantinga, Robert Adams, David Lewis, and many others[36] tried to answer "what makes claims of real possibility, necessity, and impossibility true or false?" by offering *ontological interpretations* of purely formal "possible worlds" logic. They all postulate that there are other possible worlds, with innumerable worlds having nothing contingent in common with the actual world. And they explain what such worlds are and what they contain, variously, according to their metaphysics (by what they call their "intuitions").[37] But they do not offer a reductive or other kind of explanation of what possibility is (apart from "naturalist" exceptions referred to above in n. 12), despite Hilary Putnam's pointing out, along with many others, that "it is of course evident that one cannot explain the notion of possibility itself in terms of possible worlds."[38]

35. See Wilson, "Modal Metaphysics," cited in n. 12 above, for a general sketch of the strategies used for interpreting the formal systems, and for his proposed outline of a strictly naturalistic (Everett) interpretation in terms of quantum probability states. His exploration displays that the formal modal systems have no metaphysical meaning except as one is imposed by an interpretation (an "applied semantics"). That makes vivid the question of whether the standard quantified formal systems have any *true* interpretation at all (noting the oppositions among Plantinga, Stalnaker, Lewis, and various naturalists). I, of course, say, "no, there is no true, non-denominative, *de re* interpretation" of quantified modal logic; see the fourth part of this paper, below. For a glimpse of some other aspects under discussion, see Tamar Szabó Gendler and John Hawthorne, eds., *Conceivabilty and Possibility* (Oxford: Clarendon Press, 2002) (particularly the editors' "Introduction" and the papers by David Chalmers and Kit Fine). Also see Chalmers's website: consc.net/master.html for his articles on modality, particularly his "Materialism and the Metaphysics of Modality," printed in *Philosophy and Phenomenological Research* 59:473–93 (which contrasts his anti-materialist views with those of several of his critics), and his "Conceivability and Possibility" also published in Gendler and Hawthorne, cited above, 145–200.

36. See James Garson, "Modal Logic," *SEP,* http://plato.stanford.edu/entries/logic-modal, for explanation of the systems and bibliography, as well as the earlier Michael J. Loux, "Introduction," in his *The Possible and the Actual: Readings in the Metaphysics of Modality,* ed. Michael J. Loux (Ithaca, N.Y.: Cornell University Press, 1979), and Daniel Nolan's more recent article, "Modal Fictionalism," in *SEP,* http://plato.stanford.edu/entries/fictionalism-modal, including the later supplement to it, explaining an outcome by Rosen no more believable than Lewis's original realism.

37. Taken without proof according to a deplorable habit among philosophers of using unrefined beliefs, called "intuitions," as if they were self-evident or obvious (to them) and, thus, without need for justification.

38. Hilary Putnam, *Realism and Reason, Philosophical Papers,* vol. 3 (Cambridge: Cam-

I reason that the implicit, unexamined assumption throughout was some version of the principle "whatever is consistent is possible," because the metaphysics was developed to fit and apply the formal systems in which possibility is a kind of formal consistency, and no additional criterion of possibility is offered. It is the applied form of *that,* that I challenge above.

The originating insight of the formal logicians such as Kripke had been to treat necessity, possibility, and impossibility as logical quantifiers, namely, as "all," "some," and "none" applied to *worlds* (considered as total consistent arrays of propositions or states of affairs), the way we usually apply such quantifiers to individuals, properties, and relations. Following that approach, the statement, "it is necessarily true that .p ." means "it is true in every possible world that p".[39] And the statement, "it is possible that p.." means "it is true in some world or other that p". Thus, the statement, "it is necessarily true that all men are mortal" comes to saying, "it is true in every possible world that every thing that is (called) a human is one of the things that is (called) a mortal." And to say, "it is possible that some men are carpenters" comes to saying "it is true in some possible world(s) that some of the things called 'men' are some of the things called 'carpenters.'" That idea supposed that a "world" (of states of affairs, say) is composed of (perhaps infinite) individuals and their properties and relations.

Thus, in the formal models of quantified modal logic, possible worlds are the different arrays of all consistent permutations of truth and falsity (or one and zero) for all propositions (or states of affairs), like a giant

---

bridge University Press, 1983), 67. Possibility cannot be explained by more possibility. It has to ground out in something. That is why some naturalists (see Wilson, cited above, n. 12) claim that real possibility, necessity, and impossibility ground out in the branching probabilities of quantum mechanics. There are no real subjects of mere possibility, no items that can be made to be actual or actualized like bulbs being turned on in a marquee of possibilities. There is no real change, no real transition from possibility to actuality, despite talk as if there is. And the supposed relations variously called "instantiation" and "exemplification" between individuals and their properties are ontologically empty and not explanatory at all. Lewis called them "inert." They are mere extensions of talk in first-order logic about the relation of individual variables (symbols) to predicate variables (symbols), without further rationale made into an ontological primitive (or vacuity).

39. That would mean a necessary proposition with an individual subject, such as "Socrates is necessarily an animal," would entail that Socrates exists no matter what (i.e., in every possible world). That is one reason I say the converse Barcan formula cannot formulate essential predication.

graph where each proposition ("Socrates is bald," "Plato hates dogs," etc.) is a column head. On such a graph, the worlds are the different lines of t's and f's across under the column heads, with each whole line being a different consistent assignment of "true" or "false" (or one and zero) to *every* proposition (with the necessities getting "true" in every row, and the impossibilities getting "false" in every row)—like a big truth table (analogous to Carnap's "state-descriptions"). Thus, each line is a world. Both the columns headed by propositions and the rows of truth-value permutations are infinite in number.

♾

Once rigorously symbolized, such models were used to construct formal proofs of consistency of the various sets of axioms (like "p implies possibly p" and "possibly p implies necessarily possibly p"), in other words, proofs that no contradiction could be derived from the axioms by any permitted transformation. And, for some axiom systems, there were formal proofs of completeness—that is, proofs that every proposition that is true in the system is finitely provable (i.e., that there are no true sentences in the system that cannot in principle be finitely derived from the axioms by permitted transformations—in contrast to arithmetic, say, which is incomplete). The formal models were also used to compare different axiomatic systems and precisely determine their differences.

The metaphysicians then took over such formal structures by supplying metaphysical readings, interpretations, for the characteristic features, as explained below.

A historical comment: The notion of "possible worlds" as "other arrangements of contingent things there might have been" has an antecedent, for instance, in Augustine's idea of other created world-histories there might have been, had God willed it. It also has an antecedent in Duns Scotus's idea of divine election from among maximal nonrepugnant combinations of *notae* (with qualifications, as Calvin Normore explains it).[40] And the notion occurs by the same name, "possible worlds," in Leibniz's idea that God might have made entirely other arrangements of all finite things. But the first recent usage of the idea by the formal logicians was for constructed *uninterpreted* models for logical structures without any content at all, to allow the formal proofs and comparisons I mentioned above. It was entirely independent of metaphysics.

40. Normore, "Scotus' Modal Theory," 129–60, esp. 154–55.

The disputing metaphysicians provided what Alvin Plantinga aptly called "applied semantics" for the logic. They assigned metaphysical meanings, metaphysical values, to the variables of the formal systems in order to express their ontological claims—namely, in order to tell us what real possible worlds and their contents are, and how they relate to what is actually so. Those metaphysicians assigned such meanings the way applied mathematicians assign empirical values to pure calculus to make commercial calculations, assign different values to the same calculus to make hydraulic calculations, and so on.[41] For instance, for Plantinga the possible worlds consist of all properties, relations, and individual essences that are exemplifiable by individuals, with the actual world being one actualized selection—one instantiation or exemplification, from among all possibilities—with all the rest uninstantiated. His interpretation has a distinctly Platonist texture because it supposes that abstract objects such as worlds, properties, and individual essences (whether exemplified or not) really exist and would exist even if all the particular objects did not, or were different.

Other philosophers used the same formal logic but interpreted it differently by assigning different values (meanings) to its variables. For example, David Lewis, a nominalist, reads the predicates (like "being humans") as collections (sets) of physical individuals. He said that possible worlds are large physical objects (sets of physical objects), just like this universe (the cosmos), but are not physically accessible from one another—like unreachable galaxies. For Lewis, all items *in* any world (objects such as you and me) are actual relatively to one another, and they are merely possible relatively to anything in any other world. Thus, all worlds are equally real, and an object, say, you, could not literally have been, or acted, otherwise; but you do have counterparts in other worlds, who *do* act otherwise (in the other world). So, the brothers we might have had are in fact brothers that our counterparts *do* have in some other world, and prizes we might have won are in fact prizes our counterparts do win in other worlds. And all the objects of all the worlds are equally real things. (How that might explain what really might have happened to me or *you* is never made persuasive; it seems to be just an imperialistic replacement of what we mean, instead.)

41. For instance, in the case of commercial calculation, to figure out the monetary break-even point in cost-price-volume analysis.

The modal ontologists, whether realists like Plantinga or nominalists like Lewis (though perhaps not the modal fictionalists, like Rosen and Rescher)[42] are committed to the existence of infinities of possible worlds, and of possible individuals (or individual essences), and of possible states of affairs (or propositions or facts). And they do not think of propositions, states of affairs, and so on, as merely thought-constructs, but rather as realities. Further, they all share commitment that the possibilities that exist are all that can exist in the sense that those possibilities are all that there are. They do not provide any additional explanation for why that should be so, beyond the background idea, I think, that consistency is equivalent to possibility.

These metaphysicians pretty much converged on interpreting an axiom system known as S-5 that contains the following characteristic axioms: (1) whatever is necessary is necessarily necessary; (2) whatever is possible is necessarily possible.[43] And although they did not independently (of the modal applications) justify their differing interpretative ontologies, in the ensuing debates they do talk about which interpretations of the logic work better and which face fewer anomalies than others both in resolving problems and in fitting with our general discourse. Thus, in practice, they employ an "inference to best explanation" justification (say, of possibilism over actualism, or of realism over fictionalism). Lewis, instead, straightforwardly bypassed ordinary discourse, saying he was proposing a new way of describing the world—a way that need only be justified by its success at (materialist/physicalist) explanation and that need not fit either what one believed or how one talked beforehand. Nevertheless, implicitly they all acknowledge that the applied logic (the metaphysically interpreted modal logic) has to be justified (though they differ in what counts for that); yet they are open to abandoning neither the merely extensional notion of predication nor the idea of literal domains of worlds—ideas that cause them to *imagine extensions*, ranges, of merely possible worlds, individuals, and properties.

The result is that the modal ontologists say, with variations, that the objects in possible worlds are all there is (and in a broad sense, all there

---

42. See Nolan, "Modal Fictionalism."

43. Though, as I have remarked, if the natures of finite things are divinely created along with the things, then what is possible is not necessarily possible (see Ross, "The Crash of Modal Metaphysics" and "Aquinas' Exemplarism, Aquinas' Voluntarism").

can be because they are all the possibilities there are).[44] But none of the contemporary modal metaphysicians offers to explain the being, reality, or origin of possible worlds (although most are also quick to dismiss the idea of one divine self-subsistent being as lacking justification). And none explains how the term "exists" applied to worlds could, by any stretch, mean the same thing as it does when I say that you or I exist[45] (although they resolutely believe it is univocal because it is "existential generalization").[46] None even attempts to explain, additionally, what possibility *de re* is.[47] Nor do they inquire whether one needs different interpretations of the systems for different sorts of discourse, as I think we do.[48] For in nature we might say that whatever is naturally possible is necessarily possible, relatively to the order of nature, but we might deny that is so in metaphysics generally.[49]

So, the bottom line is that "possible worlds" ontology was constructed from the writers' conflicting "intuitions" used to interpret (assign ontological values to) the extensional, quantified formal logic of possibility

44. So, some of these ontologists end up giving the impression that one and the same thing—your possible brother (or his individual essence)—might have become or been made actual or instantiated: an absurdity, if taken literally. By contrast, a smaller group think that existence and actuality are the same and that it is only actual things that could have been otherwise (actualists). And one outlier, Lewis, exotically contrives for everything (consistent) both to be possible in relation to everything in other worlds and to be actual relatively to everything in its own world, as well as for all the worlds to be equally real. See Lewis, *On the Plurality of Worlds*.

45. With the exception again of Lewis, who employs the term "exists" as univocal existential generalization, and, as applied to worlds it means what he means when he says, "I exist." Of course, most of the modal ontologists mean by "exist" nothing more than "is existentially quantified over" (in effect "referred to," modeled on things pointed at, and, loosely, enumerated: "this one," "that one," "those," etc.).

46. None seem to grasp that once you take existential generalization out of a pure formal context it gets captured by the new semantic context and altered (in sense) and in its contextual implications, as I explain in "Contextual Adaptation."

47. Lewis thought that "to exist" is to be an item within the domain of a physically consistent world or to be a world; similarly, naturalistic proposals, like the Everettian probabilistic reductions to quantum states, and the naturalism of Ladyman and Ross, *Everything Must Go*, aim at similar univocity.

48. Kit Fine does too, but in a different way; see his "The Varieties of Necessity," in *Conceivabilty and Possibility*, ed. Tamar Szabó Gendler and John Hawthorne (Oxford: Clarendon Press, 2002), 253–82.

49. My hypothesis (see the fourth part above) is that natural possibility, necessity, and impossibility are *entia rationis* (by logical construction) with a perfect and reductive foundation in the real potentialities of things that are described not only in the special sciences that have restricted domains, such as biology, but more generally in basic physics.

and necessity, but offered without an independent rationale for taking any such interpretation, that is, any assignment of ontological values and ranges of objects, to be true at all. That is why I said in an earlier paper "the satanic notation whispered the ontology."[50] But that is still the fashion now, and it will hold the ground until philosophers lose interest in it—as they do when contrivance becomes too complicated.

Nevertheless, the propositional modal systems such as S-4 and S-5[51] (which have nearly the same modal principles used by Scotus and the Pseudo-Scotus)[52] can be employed to audit, make articulate, and even provide formal shorthand for our modal predication. In using them, however, we need to keep clear that we are describing real situations by extrinsic denomination from the formal and idealized properties of propositions *about* them, and that in treating quantification extensionally we are not replicating predication, and are using the systems instrumentally, without commitment to infinite domains, ranges of propositions, or states of affairs, and or to infinities of things and properties. Propositions are thought-entities consequent on the emergence of humans. They are not antecedent to the cosmos or to humans.[53] States of affairs, facts, and so on are obtuse abstractions, *entia rationis,* that we make for efficient generalization about the world. Thus, the real world is not nondenominatively composed of states of affairs, and our thoughts are not composed of propositions. A modal ontology that supposes such constitution of reality is a fantasy.

---

50. Ross, "The Crash of Modal Metaphysics."

51. The key axiom of S-5 is the following: Possibly p implies Necessarily Possibly p [$\Diamond p \to \Box \Diamond p$]. Or in another formulation: Possibly Necessarily p implies Necessarily p [$\Diamond \Box p \to \Box p$].

Now I think that that interpreted axiom does not hold if the natures of finite things come to be with the things, which I think a creation doctrine implies; still, a Neoplatonic tradition of divine ideas, which I think Plantinga shares, holds that the natures are eternally determined by the divine ideas. It comes down to whether finite things are possible because God chooses to make or think them, as against possibility being somehow given by the divine understanding prior to the divine will—something at issue in an old debate about the relationship of divine will to divine understanding.

52. See McDermott, "Notes on the Assertoric and Modal Propositional Logic of Pseudo-Scotus," 273–306.

53. It is an error to say that divine thought is propositional unless one speaks by extrinsic denomination vantaged, anchored, in what we say to describe our own thoughts. For, as I have argued elsewhere, "if there are no things, there are no names for them," *Thought and World,* 50–60. The real natures of things are created with the things (as Wippel remarks in "The Reality of Nonexisting Possibles," the section on Aquinas), just as we humans can make some entirely new natures, such as acrylic paint, transponders, and lasers. The real kind does not preexist the objects.

THE REAL STATUS OF MODALITIES *DE RE*

For present purposes we can distinguish three kinds of modalities: logical, ontological, and natural. (1) *Logical modalities* (necessity, possibility, and impossibility) are formalized in propositional logic and then extended to universal, existentially general, and singular propositions; usually they fit the axioms of S-4 or the stronger axioms of S-5. In practice they are extrinsically attributed to real things on account of the logical properties of propositions about them (something, say, my being a bird, is said to be impossible because the proposition, "that human is a bird," is inconsistent, for instance—with the cautions of the second part, above).[54] Those are the modalities, I say, that modal metaphysicians mistake for real, intrinsic modalities of things and states of affairs. (2) *Ontological modalities* are the entitative, intrinsic modalities, necessity and contingency, necessity being the entitative modality of the divine, contingency the entitative modality of everything else that really exists[55] (perhaps along with certain other intrinsic transcendental modes as well that are not part of the current discussion).[56] (3) *Natural modalities* are the modalities of necessity and possibility within the order of nature, and of impossibility attributed to certain intentional objects on the basis of the

54. For those unfamiliar with the notion of extrinsic denomination or attribution: an extrinsic denomination is a characterization of a thing from its relation to something else (e.g., my former colleague, my neighbor, my caretaker, etc.). So to say something is necessary or impossible, especially logically, is to say something rooted in propositions *about* it. But to say about the impossible, that it *is* impossible, is not in the relevant sense to say anything about anything.

55. There is a puzzle about aseity. We do not have any real cases where we know *both* what something is and that it exists because of *what* it is. We do not know the essence of any *per se* thing (the essence of God, for instance). Some might propose the natural numbers as cases, but they are intentional objects only and exist because of the structure of the abstract system, not on account of item-by-item essences. For instance, there is a natural number 11 because it is the successor of 10 by one; and we can see that denying it exists is contradictory because it is axiomatic that every natural number has a successor by one, not because of *what* it is (eleven) but because of the succession axiom.

So, is "a thing that exists on account of what it is," a mere construction, perhaps to answer the question, "what is there beyond what exists that might not have existed to explain the existence of the contingent at all"? Don't we too have to reason from possibility (that is, the consistency of there being something that exists on account of itself) to its real existence?

56. Perhaps, like Scotus's disjunctive transcendentals, e.g., finite/infinite. See Allan Wolter, O.F.M., *The Transcendentals and Their Function in the Metaphysics of Duns Scotus* (St. Bonaventure, N.Y.: Franciscan Institute, 1946). See also Gyula Klima, "Buridan's Logic and the Ontology of Modes," available on his website, http://www.fordham.edu/gsas/phil/klima/MODI.HTM

former. They are reductively grounded in the actuality and the potentialities (both active and receptive) of existing natural things. The more general expression, "metaphysically possibile," or broadly "really possible," includes both what is within the capacity of nature and what is within the capacity of the divine, though the latter, beyond what is actual, is mostly cognitively indeterminate for us. Other writers, of course, want to include within the "metaphysically possible" whatever is consistent in itself; but I have objected to that above because possibility (outside merely formal systems) cannot be measured as mere consistency.

The formal logic (though independently constructed) is not explanatorily prior to one's metaphysics. It is without content until interpreted. For instance, bifurcation of truth and falsity (that is presupposed by the modal systems) is not adequate for the analysis of all counterfactuals—see *Thought and World*, chs. 2 and 3); and which modal system to use, say S-4 or S-5 $\{\Diamond p \supset (\Box \Diamond p)$ and $\Box p \supset (\Box \Box p)\}$[57] depends on whether one thinks whatever is possible is necessarily possible (S-5) or holds the logically weaker idea that real possibilities come to be with the (creation of) things, for which S-4—which does not require that whatever is possible is necessarily possible—may fit better.

The mere existence of different consistent systems of formal modal logic requires one to select a system suitable for one's ontology, not the reverse.[58] Furthermore, metaphysics does not use all the resources of any of the formal logical systems because they have endless theorems with no co-

57. I take this axiom to conflict with divine creation of all finite kinds; but it does accord with certain readings of divine exemplarism of all finite kinds (see Gregory T. Doolan, *Aquinas on the Divine Ideas as Exemplar Causes* (Washington, D.C.: The Catholic University of America Press, 2008).

58. "Modal Logic," *Wikipedia*, http://en.wikipedia.org/wiki/Modal_logic#Axiomatic_ Systems, lists axioms for eleven systems. Furthermore, I do not think an exceptionless bifurcation between truth and falsity is suitable for a full-scale analysis of counterfactuals (see Ross, *Thought and World*, ch. 3). And the Barcan formula, and its converse, commit one to the proposition that it is not contingent which individuals there are (in conflict with creation). See Timothy Williamson, "for together they are tantamount to the claim that it is non-contingent what individuals there are" ("Laudatio: Professor Ruth Barcan Marcus," in *Themes from Barcan Marcus*, ed. M. Frauchiger and W. K. Essler, Lauener Library of Analytical Philosophy 3 [Frankfurt: Ebikon, forthcoming]).

Furthermore because in Quantified Modal Logic predication is mere extensional inclusion (one thing within the *range* of another), the metaphysician adapters have to devise (make up) extensions—*domains* (worlds, individuals, properties, etc.)—for the expressions when that is exactly what one does not want for *de re* modality because it is not *true*.

herent empirical content (for instance multiple iterated modal operators beyond the first few), just as ordinary statements have innumerable (e.g., disjunctive) formal implications that lack additional empirical content.

Certain defective intentional objects involve contradiction, and certain imagined, intended, or expected situations and things are *called* impossible by extrinsic attribution because there cannot consistently be any *such* thing. Yet there *are* not really any things, sorts, or situations that cannot be. There are no impossible *things, not even thoughts*. So, impossibility is not a metaphysical or natural modality of any real thing or situation.

My proposal is that (a) natural modalities are *entia rationis* with a perfect (indeed, a reductive) foundation in the real potentialities (both active and passive propensities and repugnancies of things, that is, in what nature will and will not do). For reasoning about such real potentialities a suitably interpreted system of Quantified Modal Logic can be employed as a transformational syntax (inference license). (b) A modal logic can also be employed for the intrinsic ontological modes of contingency and necessity fully founded in act-potency generally (as if we were using a common calculus for a different subject matter). (c) We can also use a logical modal system by extrinsic denomination to attribute modal relations (e.g., co-possibility or incompatibility and the like) to real things and situations on account of the formal features of propositions *about* them; and by further extension we can attribute modalities to intentional and imaginary objects and to situations that way as well. But there are no real domains at all of mere possibilities, necessities, and impossibilities.

Moreover, as I said in the third part, the direct extensional interpretation of the quantified modal logic that the modal metaphysicians have been employing has no true *de re* application because there are no such domains of things or even of such real *abstracta*. So, modern modal metaphysics rests on serious mistakes, especially on taking merely invented extensions, worlds, individual essences, and properties to be real.

CONCLUSION

There are no domains, extensions, of mere *possibilia* at all, and nothing alien is possible without a free divine creator (since by definition alien things are not within the capacity of any finite existent). There are not even *propositions* for such things because (1) "if there are no things, there are no names for them"; (2) "if there are no things, then there are no real natures," because natures are intrinsic capacities (essences) exhibited by things in their operations; and, more broadly, (3) "if there are no things, there are no *de re* truths about them at all."[59] Furthermore, real things have (at least some) cognitively inaccessible overflow *de re* conditions; that is, some conditions are absolutely inaccessible to humans, as is the essence of God, and others are relatively inaccessible to humans, as were the chemical compositions of water for millennia and as the constitutive difference between living and nonliving matter is still hidden now, and as is the fundamental physical constitution of things, still.

Finally, because there are no propositions that are determinately and referentially about things that never exist, and because contingent things do have overflow *de re* conditions, our conceptions for such things are always incomplete; so, consistent conceivability cannot ensure real possibility.

59. Further argumentation for such claims can be found in Ross, *Thought and World*.

Part Three

The Two Theologies

Stephen F. Brown

8 ∾ The Role of Metaphysics in the Theology of Godfrey of Fontaines

In this chapter I will focus on Godfrey of Fontaines' *Quodlibet IV,* q. 10 (1287), *Quodlibet VIII,* q. 7 (1292/1293), and *Quodlibet IX,* q. 20 (1293/1294), disputed in Paris.[1] However, I begin far from Paris and Godfrey—with Richard Fishacre, the Dominican who lectured in the 1240s at Oxford. He initiated the reading of the *Sentences* at Oxford and did so in the morning hours that had been reserved for the study of the Scriptures themselves. He informs us that the way the Scriptures themselves are studied is according to the moral or tropological interpretation of the Bible: presenting the ultimate goal of Christian living as the enjoyment of eternal life and indicating the ways the Scriptures tell us how we must now live if we are to attain that goal. The difficult doctrinal questions concerning the Trinity, the Incarnation, and the other chief truths of Christian belief were reserved for the afternoon period of disputation. Fishacre wanted to move the doctrinal questions to the morning hours. He argued that disputations were in fact also the study of Scripture—the difficult doctrinal questions of Scripture that had been codified, as it were, in the *Sentences* of Peter Lombard and that should not be separated from the study of

---

1. These *Quodlibeta* are edited in the series *Les Philosophes Belges.* See *Les quatre premiers Quodlibets de Godefroid de Fontaines,* ed. by Maurice De Wulf and Auguste Pelzer, Les Philosophes Belges 2 (Louvain: Institut supérieur de philosophie de l'Université, 1904); *Le huitième Quodlibet de Godefroid de Fontaines,* ed. by Jean Hoffmans, Les Philosophes Belges 4 (Louvain: Institut supérieur de philosophie de l'Université, 1924); *Le neuvième Quodlibet de Godefroid de Fontaines,* ed. by Jean Hoffmans, Les Philosophes Belges 4 (Louvain: Institut supérieur de philosophie de l'Université, 1928).

Scripture.[2] Robert Grosseteste, the bishop of Lincoln, with jurisdiction over Oxford, opposed this innovation. Grosseteste needed to be persuaded by papal intervention to allow Fishacre to carry out his project.[3]

Fishacre, perhaps in deference to Bishop Grosseteste, compromised his method a bit when he read the *Sentences*. When he begins his lectures on the *Sentences*, he says: "Since you have already read the Scriptures (that is, tropologically), we now will study the difficult doctrinal questions." He does this; but he does more. For example, he discusses with doctrinal precision God's simplicity: What is it? How is it compatible with the Trinitarian character of God? and so on. But then he asks: How can we be simple? How can we avoid duplicity? What are the many ways of being duplicitous? In short, he adds a sermon to the doctrinal study. In technical language, along with doing *disputatio* (the difficult doctrinal questions), he adds *praedicatio*—giving Lombard a moral focus or tropological reading.[4]

The next Oxford commentator on Lombard's *Sentences* was the Franciscan Richard Rufus of Cornwall. He did not miss Fishacre's addition of the tropological dimension in his *Sentences* commentary. He notes that *magistri,* or masters, have four *officia* or responsibilities: *iubilatio* (cel-

2. Richard Fishacre, *Commentarium in libros Sententiarum*, prologus, ed. R. James Long, "The Science of Theology according to Richard Fishacre: Edition of the Prologue to his *Commentary on the Sentences*," *Mediaeval Studies* 34 (1972): 96–97: "Divisio autem huius scientiae sic est, quia in natura media duo sunt: scilicet virtus motiva et apprehensiva, quae dicuntur aliis nominibus affectus et aspectus. Natura autem suprema est bonitas summa et summa veritas. Ideo haec scientia quae est de uno ex duobus, habet partes duas: una est de unitate affectus cum summa bonitate, et alia est de unitate aspectus cum summa veritate. . . . Una ergo pars est de sanctis moribus, alia de quaestionibus circa fidem difficilibus. . . . Utraque fateor harum partium in sacro Scripturae sacrae canone—sed indistincte—continetur. Verumtamen tantum altera pars, scilicet de moribus instruendis, a magistris modernis cum leguntur sancti libri docetur. Alia tamquam difficilior disputationi reservatur. Haec autem pars difficilior de canone sacrarum Scripturarum excerpta in isto libro qui Sententiarum dicitur ponitur. Unde non differt hic legere et disputare. . . . Quia ergo in praecedentibus de moribus instruendis audistis, ratio ordinis et consummationis exigeret ut et secunda pars, quae est de quaestionibus circa fidem difficilibus, nunc convenienter legeretur." (The English translations here and below are my own.)

For a general introduction to the life and writings of Richard Fishacre, see R. James Long and Maura O'Carroll, *The Life and Works of Richard Fishacre OP.,* Veröffenlichungen der Kommission für die Herasugabe ungedruckter Texte aux der mittelalterlichen Geisteswelt 21 (München: Verlag der Bayerischen Akademie der Wissenschaften, 1999).

3. James McEvoy, *Robert Grosseteste* (New York: Oxford University Press, 2000), 160–71.

4. R. James Long, "The Moral and Spiritual Theology of Richard Fishacre; Edition of Trinity Coll. MS O.1.30," *Archivum Fratrum Praedicatorum* 40 (1990): 5–143, esp. 15–20.

ebration), *lectio, praedicatio,* and *disputatio.* The duties of a master are not a "choose-what-you-will" list for Rufus. When you arrive for *iubilatio,* you celebrate the Eucharist or chant office; you do not dispute difficult doctrinal questions. When you are carrying out the office of *disputatio,* you do not preach. *Disputatio* is not *praedicatio.* Rufus himself might even prefer to be preaching, but when his present duty is to dispute difficult doctrinal questions, that is, to read the *Sentences,* he submits to this obligation to dispute, that is, to read the *Sentences.*[5]

Rufus seems to have won the debate concerning the role of the unadulterated character of the *disputatio;* this is quite likely why Roger Bacon picks on him in his fierce criticism of the dominance given to Lombard's *Sentences* in the study of theology. Rufus had won at least in the sense that *Sentences* commentaries thereafter were not a time for sermons: they were disputations. As a corollary to what I have just said, we must remember that *disputatio* is one of four offices of a master. Disputing doctrinal questions is not the totality of his duties. I imagine that this should be kept in mind when we see the efforts of some scholars today who seem to want to rescue Thomas Aquinas from a disputational prison or isolation chamber where he has often been placed by modern scholars. Trying to bring a focus on Aquinas as a broader theologian, they have more recently focused on his sermons or scriptural commentaries or the religious practices of his Dominican community. It is important to see a bigger picture when there is one and we have the sources to restore it. But it is also important to do *disputatio* when you have been assigned to do *disputatio.*

5. Richard Rufus of Cornwall, *Commentarium in libros Sententiarum,* prologus (cod. Oxon., Balliol 62, f. 6va): "Dividitur autem hic universus labor in quattuor partes, quasi quattuor quadrantes, scilicet in iubilationem, lectionem, praedicationem, quaestionem. Primo quadrante in ecclesiastico officio Deum laudamus. Secundo, originalem litteram Sacrae Scripturae vomere ingenii exponendo, quasi exarando, referamus. Tertio, rudes et quasi informes moribus informamus. Quarto, nodosa enodamus, difficilia explanamus, ambigua certificamus, obscura, prout possibile est, elucidamus. De hoc ultimo quadrante solo intenditur in praesenti negotio. . . . Quibusdam placet hic quaedam generalia de ipsa theologia dubitare, et hoc gratia huius summae Magistri. Quod non videtur mihi necessarium, cum haec summa non sit ipsa theologia nec aliqua pars eius; est enim Divina Scriptura in se integra, perfecta absque hac et omni alia summa. Sed sunt tales summae elucidationes aliquae aliquorum quae in illa obscure dicta sunt, propter nos utiles et adhibitae. Quia tamen mos est, aliqua et nos tangamus." For a general introduction to the life and writings of Richard Rufus, see Peter Raedts, *Richard Rufus of Cornwall and the Tradition of Oxford Theology* (New York: Oxford University Press, 1987).

So, when you have announced a subject such as "The role of metaphysics in the theology of Godfrey of Fontaines," you have committed yourself to do *disputatio*—or at least to report on the *disputationes* of Godfrey related to theology. My introductory digression is just a suggestion that "the role of metaphysics" is just one aspect of Godfrey's theology.

Question 10 of Godfrey's *Quodlibet IV* (1287) introduces us to Godfrey's view of theology. In this context, and it is a disputational context, he means by theology a deductive habit that begins with the knowledge that God and the blessed have and that is revealed in the Scriptures. From the articles of the Creed that provide the central beliefs of Christian revelation, a theologian deduces further things from these articles of the faith in the way that conclusions are deduced from principles. The model he provides for theology of this kind is that of a subalternated science, which borrows its principles from a subalternating science. Historically it is a position attributed to Thomas Aquinas's portrait of theology as a subalternated science. But given that Godfrey is disputing in 1287, it could be aimed at some of Thomas's followers.[6]

The substance of Godfrey's argument is centered on this question: "Is theology science?" His response is couched in the following terms: science properly depends on two qualities, certitude and evidence. Without both you do not have science. In Godfrey's words:

I answer that we say that since science is a sure habit possessing both the certitude of evidence and the certitude of conviction, whereas faith is a sure habit having only the certitude of conviction, not the certitude of evidence, then since the certitude of a conclusion derives from the certitude of the principles, the kind of certitude a conclusion possesses will correspond to the kind of certitude the principles have. When the certitude of the principles is the certitude of both evidence and conviction, the conclusion also will have the double certitude. Since then believed principles do not have the certitude of evidence which is the main characteristic of a scientific conclusion, then from such principles there can be no certain scientific, <i.e. evident>, knowledge of the conclusion.[7]

6. For an indication of the three different interpretations given to the position of St. Thomas shortly after his lifetime, see Aegidius Magrini, O.F.M., *Ioannis Duns Scoti Doctrina de scientifica theologiae natura* (Rome: Pontificium Athenaeum Antonianum, 1952), 20–38.

7. Godfrey of Fontaines, *Quodlibet IV*, q. 10 (ed. PB 2.261): "Respondeo dicendum quod cum scientia sit habitus certus certitudine evidentiae et adhaesionis, fides autem sit habitus certus certitudine adhaesionis non evidentiae, opinio autem est habitus nec certus certitudine evidentiae nec adhaesionis, certitudo autem conclusionis est ex certitudine principiorum, se-

Godfrey continues:

To say, therefore, that the principles of theology . . . are only believed and not known <by evidence>, and thus possessing only the certitude of conviction, still produce scientific certitude in the conclusions drawn from them is to say that the conclusions may be better known than the principles, namely, that the conclusions have the twofold certitude of evidence and conviction, while the principles only have the latter one. This is really to hold contradictory things. Furthermore, for those dealing with such a study to proclaim such fictions concerning theology itself is to detract both from sacred theology and its teachers.[8]

Is theology, then, as disputational possible? Are its masters reduced to these *officia: iubilatio, lectio,* and *praedicatio?* Godfrey answers: "No." He does not abandon the ship of *disputatio;* he adjusts:

When theology is posited as science, it is necessary that its principles or starting premises become in some way evident and known or understood. In fact, evidence has to be of a kind that respects the excellence of its subject matter and the weakness of the human knower. Thus, to one instructed in theology, it is much more evident than to the simple layman that Christ, God and man, has risen, and how this is possible and not impossible. Furthermore, it is more evident to a theologian than to a layman that we will rise. Therefore, even though such things are not as evident as are the principles of other sciences because of their lack of proportion to our intellect, still they are known by a kind of evidence that is sufficient. And it is true that this kind of knowledge does not completely take away faith, since it does not provide a perfect knowledge of an object of faith in itself. For, it is established, according to Aristotle, that what we are able to know from probable arguments concerning immaterial beings is in some way knowledge in contrast to the ignorance of laymen. The same is the

---

cundum modum certitudinis principiorum etiam est modus ceritudinis conclusionum. Cum ergo principia habent certitudinem evidentiae et adhaesionis, conclusio ex illis elicita etiam huiusmodi certitudinem habet. Cum ergo principia credita vel opinata non habeant certitudinem evidentiae quae est de ratione conclusionis scitae, ideo ex principiis creditis vel opinatis non acquiritur certa scientia de conclusione."

For a general introduction to Godfrey's portrait of theology, see Paul Tihon, S.J., *Foi et théologie selon Godefroid de Fontaines* (Paris-Bruges: Desclée–De Brouwer, 1966).

8. Godfrey of Fontaines, *Quodlibet IV,* q. 10 (ed. PB 2.262): "Dicere ergo quod principia theologiae . . . sunt solum credita et non scita vel intellecta et sic solum certitudinem adhaesionis habentia, et tamen efficiunt certitudinem scientiae in conclusionibus ex ipsis elicitis, est dicere quod conclusiones sint notiores principiis, scilicet duplicem certitudinem habentes, cum principia non habeant nisi unam. Et hoc est dicere contradictoria et multum derogare sacrae theologiae et doctoribus ipsius, tales fictiones de ipsa theologiae attractantibus ipsam propalare."

case here with theology. . . . For, simple people have a different kind of knowledge than those instructed in theology; and the knowledge that the blessed have is different than the knowledge of the other two groups. The knowledge the simple have in no way is called science. The knowledge those instructed in theology have is what is called science of the faith or the science that does not take away faith, and is therefore an imperfect form of knowledge. The third kind of knowledge, that of the blessed, is altogether perfect science and it totally takes away faith. Concerning the kind of knowledge we have in theology, Augustine, in Book XIV of his *De Trinitate,* says: "Many of the faithful are not strong in this science, even though they are strong in the faith itself. For it is one thing to know what a man must believe in order to gain the blessed life; it is another thing to know how that which is believed may help the pious and be defended against the impious."[9]

Up to this point Godfrey has rejected deductive theology as a discipline claiming the title of science properly so-called, since it cannot deliver the perfect evidence that causes assent to its principles, the articles of the faith. He has accepted, however, science in a sense accommodated to the lofty realities theology deals with and accommodated to our limited knowledge of them here *in via.* What he endorses is the theology that shortly after him will be called declarative theology—whose origin is assigned to book 14 of the *De Trinitate* of Augustine. It is the theology that helps the pious and defends against the impious.

9. Ibid. (ed. PB 2.264): "Et ideo cum theologia ponatur esse scientia, oportet quod principia eius fiant aliquo modo evidentia et nota sive intellecta, et hoc quidem evidentia quae convenit excellentiae talis materiae respectu infirmitatis talis scientis. Unde instructo in theologia multo evidentius fit quod Christus Deus et homo resurrexit, sive quomodo hoc possibile sit et non impossibile, quam simplici laico. Et ideo etiam theologo est evidentius quod nos resurgemus quam laico. Licet ergo non sint ita evidentia propter improportionem eius sicut princpia aliarum scientiarum, sunt tamen tali evidentia nota quae sufficit. Et verum est quod hoc etiam fidem simpliciter non evacuat, quia non facit omnino perfectam notitiam rei in se ipsa et cetera. Constat enim secundum Philosophum, illud quod de immaterialibus scire possimus ex probabilibus est aliquo modo scire respectu ignorantiae laicorum. Ita etiam in proposito. Fideles participantes scientiam beatorum quasi subalternantis sive magis proprie principalis; in quantum adiuvantur et illustrantur aliquo lumine supernaturali imperfecto respectu luminis gloriae, et adiuti sensui et memoria sive notitia quam ex sensibus et naturali ingenio habere possunt, habent scientiam respectu ignorantiae laicorum. Aliam ergo notitiam habent simplices de his quae fidei sunt, aliam instructi in theologia, et aliam beati. Prima nullo modo dicitur scientia; secunda dicitur scientia fidei sive fidem non evacuans et ideo imperfecta; tertia dicitur visio et est scientia omnino perfecta fidem omnino evacuans et cetera. De hoc Augustinus, decimo quarto *de Trinitate:* hac scientia non pollent fideles (<in>fideles *ed.*) plurimi quamvis polleant ipsa fide; aliud enim est scire quid homo credere debeat propter adipiscendam vitam beatam, aliud scire quemadmodum hoc ipsum et piis opituletur et contra impios defendatur."

Various problems can be encountered by pious believers. We might attempt to describe them as follows. First, some believers have difficulties because the terms related to discussions of the articles of the Creed are not understood. Secondly, some believers, when they encounter reasons supporting the opposite of Christian beliefs, become confused, and this prevents them from reconciling these reasons with their beliefs. Thirdly, some Christians lack examples, helps, or analogies that could bring some support to what they believe. Fourthly, pious Christians might have difficulties because probable reasons are not available to support Christian beliefs; in other words: even though one can believe something to be true by the power of the will, still if probable reasons are not available, then faith might be viewed as not having intellectual support. Although the technical name "declarative theology" appears after the *Quodlibeta* that we are considering, its practice is founded on Augustine's exhortation at the beginning of book 14 of the *De Trinitate:* "Do not seek after all kinds of knowledge; rather pursue the kind of knowledge by which our most wholesome faith which leads to eternal life, is begotten, nourished, defended and strengthened."[10]

One of the great early-fourteenth-century defenders of declarative theology, the Franciscan Peter Aureoli, claimed that Aquinas as well as almost all masters of theology were practitioners of this type of theology: "For sure, this doctor in his *Summa,* and generally all doctors of theology, formulate questions concerning the articles of the faith, and then go on to give solutions to these questions, and they provide clarifications concerning them, and they add arguments supporting them, as when they ask . . . whether in God there is a trinity of persons or whether the incarnation is possible."[11] Aquinas, in reality, not only does declarative theology. He indicates throughout his works why it is necessary to do so. We might begin with his Commentary on Boethius's *De Trinitate,* where he examines how a theologian deals with the principles or starting points of theology, the articles of the faith. His answer is as follows:

---

10. Augustine, *De Trinitate* XIV, c. 1, n. 3 (PL 42.1037).

11. Peter Aureoli, *Scriptum super Primum Sententiarum,* ed. Eligius M. Buytaert (St. Bonaventure, N.Y.: Franciscan Institute, 1952), prooem., sect. 1, 139: "Sed certum est quod iste Doctor, in *Summa* sua, et universaliter omnes doctores theologi, formant quaestiones de articulis fidei, et ad eas dissolvendum, declarandum et concludendum procedunt, ut cum quaeritur: Utrum Deus sit tantum unus, vel Utrum in Deo sit trinitas personarum; vel Utrum Incarnatio sit possibilis, et huiusmodi."

"Now, in divine science the articles of the faith are like principles and not like conclusions. They are defended against those who attack them, as the Philosopher (*Metaphy. IV*, 4–6, 1005b 35–1011b 22) argues against those who deny principles. Moreover, they are clarified by certain analogies, just as principles that are naturally known are made evident by induction but not proved by demonstrative reasoning."[12]

Aquinas, then, also has an approach to theology where he is defensive of the principles, or the articles, of the faith by opposing errors, or heresies, and through analogies he makes an effort to clarify or make manifest to some degree the truths of the faith. As we have said, numerous difficulties throughout Christian history have demanded diverse responses: 1. terms are not properly understood; 2. arguments opposing Christian belief need to be refuted; 3. believers need examples and analogies to help them better grasp the realities they believe in; 4. in order for faith to be not only an act of the will but also an act of the intellect, arguments are necessary on its behalf. In the statement of his commentary on Boethius's *De Trinitate*, Aquinas already spoke of the need of items 2 and 3. Item 1 can be exemplified in q. 13 of the *Prima pars* of his *Summa*, where Thomas gives an instance where he stresses the importance of understanding terms properly: "When we say 'God is good' the meaning is not 'God is the cause of goodness,' or 'God is not evil.' The meaning is 'Whatever good we attribute to creatures, pre-exists in God, and in a more excellent and higher way.'"[13] This is just one of the innumerable instances throughout his works where Thomas clarifies the meaning of terms—in this case a metaphysical term. Item 4 can be illustrated by the first question of Aquinas's treatment of faith in the *Secunda secundae* of the *Summa theologiae*. There he tells us:

The arguments employed by holy men to prove things that are of faith are not demonstrations, they are either persuasive arguments showing that what is proposed to our faith is not impossible or else they are proofs drawn from the prin-

---

12. Thomas Aquinas, *Expositio super librum Boethii De Trinitate*, ed. Bruno Decker (Leiden: E. J. Brill, 1955), q. 2, a. 2, ad 4. English translation from Thomas Aquinas, *Faith, Reason and Theology: Questions I–IV of his Commentary on the De Trinitate of Boethius*, trans. Armand Maurer (Toronto: Pontifical Institute of Mediaeval Studies, 1987), 43.

13. Thomas Aquinas, *Summa theologiae* (hereafter *ST*) I, q. 13, a. 2 co.: "Cum igitur dicitur *Deus est bonus*, non est sensus, *Deus est causa bonitatis*, vel *Deus non est malus*, sed est sensus, *Id quod bonitatem dicimus in creaturis praeexistit in Deo*, et hoc secundum modum altiorem."

ciples of faith, i.e., from the authority of Scripture, as Dionysius declares. On the basis of such principles some point stands proved for believers in a way similar to that whereby something is proved by principles that are known in the eyes of all. Hence, again, theology is a science, as we stated at the outset of this work.[14]

In question 9 of *Quodlibet IV,* Thomas even goes further: he aims at the heart of what is called declarative theology, especially in regard to item 4. In article 18 of this *Quodlibet,* Aquinas asks whether a master in determining theological questions should more use reason or authority? He answers:

A disputation can be ordered to a twofold end. Some disputations are set up in order to remove doubts about whether something is true [*an ita sit*], and in such disputations authorities are more often used. . . . Other disputations are more characteristic of the way a master teaches in the schools. The end or purpose is not to remove errors but to instruct the listeners so that they may be led to an understanding of the truth on which the master is centering his attention. To achieve this end, it is then necessary to support one's self on reasons that get to the root of the truth and which make one know *how* that which is true is true. Otherwise, if a master determines a question by using pure authorities, then the listener will be guaranteed that something is true [*ita est*], but he will acquire nothing of science or understanding and he will go away with an empty head.[15]

14. Ibid. II-II, q. 1, a. 5 co.: "rationes quae inducuntur a sanctis ad probandum ea quae sunt fidei non sunt demonstrativae, sed persuasiones quaedam manifestantes non esse impossibile quod in fide proponitur. Vel procedunt ex principiis fidei, scilicet ex auctoritatibus sacrae Scripturae, sicut dicit Dionysius. Ex his autem principiis ita probatur aliquid apud fideles sicut etiam ex principiis naturaliter notis probatur aliquid apud omnes. Unde etiam theologia scientia est, ut in principio operis dictum est."

15. Thomas Aquinas, *Quodlibetum IV,* q. 9, a. 3 [18], in *Quaestiones quodlibetales,* ed. Raymundus Spiazzi (Turin: Marietti 1920), 83: "Disputatio autem ad duplicem finem potest ordinari. Quaedam enim disputatio ordinatur ad removendum dubitationem an ita sit; et in tali disputatione theologica maxime utendum est auctoritatibus, quas recipiunt illi cum quibus disputatur; puta, si cum Iudaeis disputatur, oportet inducere auctoritates veteris testamenti; si cum Manichaeis, qui vetus testamentum respuunt, oportet uti solum auctoritatibus novi testamenti; si autem cum schismaticis, qui recipiunt vetus et novum testamentum, non autem doctrinam Sanctorum nostrorum, sicut sunt Graeci, oportet cum eis disputatre ex auctoritatibus novi vel veteris testamenti, et illorum doctorum quod ispi recipiunt. Si autem nullam auctoritatem recipiunt, oportet ad eos convincendos, ad rationes naturales confugere. Quaedam vero disputatio est magistralis in scholis non ad removendum errorem, sed ad instruendum auditores ut inducantur ad intellectum veritatis quam intendit: et tunc rationibus inniti invesrtigantibus veritatis radicem, et facientibus scire quomodo sit verum quod dicitur: alioquin si nudis auctoritatibus magister quaestionem determinet, certificabitur quidem auditor quod ita est, sed nihil scientiae vel intellectus acquiret et vacuus abscedet."

It is within the declarative theology context, exemplified here by Aquinas, that I understand the direction of theology meant by Godfrey's extended meaning of the word *scientia* in *Quodlibet IV,* question 9.

Can theology do anything more? Henry of Ghent would emphatically say, "Yes." It is the consideration of this claim of Henry that fills the pages of Godfrey's *Quodlibet VIII,* question 7 in 1292/1293. The question in *Quodlibet VIII* is "whether in any believer there is some infused light distinct from the light of faith by means of which the believer can acquire beyond the knowledge of faith a knowledge in regard to the objects of belief that truly and properly can be called 'science'?"[16]

Godfrey's response is that if it is a matter of those objects that are properly and unqualifiedly objects of faith, then you cannot at the same time have a habit of faith in regard to them and also a habit that is a properly scientific habit, that is, where you assent because of the evidence that forces it. There is thus no need for a special gift besides the light of faith, a *lumen theologicum,* to explain a situation that is contradictory. Godfrey argues from experience: no matter how developed someone might be in regard to the objects of true faith, he clings to these objects more from the authority of the Revealer or the authority of Scripture than because of any reason that is brought forth to support them.

After providing a few examples, he argues:

Whenever someone assents to something more on account of the authority of the one saying it than because of any reason that is brought forth to support it, so that if the reason were removed, he would still firmly cling to it, whereas if faith were taken away, then no matter what reason still might support it, one could not give unqualified assent to it, because there perhaps might be more probable reasons supporting the opposite or because of the lack of evidence offered by the reasons that were given, such a person would then not be said to have a habit that is properly scientific. The reason for this is that a scientific habit implies that the adherence is principally on account of the evidence of the reason it is based on. Now this is what I suppose and firmly believe to be the case in regard to all who live an ordinary life here on earth, no matter how well-developed their learning might be. Things might be different in cases of those who are rapt to the heavens, or in the cases of those who are in some way elevated in a singular man-

---

16. Godfrey of Fontaines, *Quodlibet VIII,* q. 7 (ed. PB 4.69): "utrum in quolibet fideli sit aliquod lumen infusum aliud a lumine fidei per quod possit acquiri de ipsis credibilibus ultra notitam fidei, notitia quae vere et proprie scientia dici possit?"

ner. Thus, no one having faith concerning the objects of our belief has science in the proper sense of the term. Furthermore, if they did, then they should be able to show it—not this scientific habit as such in their intellects—but through their teaching which would show this evidence which they claim to have, since it is the sign of someone who knows that he is able to teach.[17]

Before he responded to the question, Godfrey said, "if it is a matter of those objects that are properly and unqualifiedly objects of faith," then here is my answer.[18] His conditional clause tells us that the situation could be different if we are dealing with other truths of the faith. Someone, a nonbeliever for example, could assent to some truths of the faith because of evidence. As a metaphysician, he could assent to the existence of God because of evidence. Now if he were later given the gift of faith, what would be his situation? Godfrey says: A philosopher knows in a sure manner that God exists. Now in such a case, he does not just think that God exists, or guess that he exists, or believe that he exists. So, when he converts to the Christian faith, we cannot say, if we speak properly, that God's existence becomes for him an object of belief.[19]

If we would summarize the main points of these two Quodlibetal questions we have examined, we could say that according to Godfrey: 1. We cannot have "science" in the proper sense of the term concerning the truths of the faith that are held by faith and not because of evidence commanding our assent. 2. We can have science of these objects, if we broaden our meaning of "science" so that it embraces knowledge of things that

17. Ibid. (ed. PB 4.70): "quandocumque aliquis assentit alicui magis propter auctoritatem dicentis quam propter quamcumque rationem ad hoc inductam, ita quod ratione cessante nihilominus firmiter assentit; sed si fide cessante, maneret qualiscumque ratio, vel illi non assentiret propter rationes forte probabiliores ad oppositum, vel non firmiter adhaereret propter inevidentiam rationum, talis non dicetur habere habitum proprie scientificum, cum iste habitus importet adhaesionem principaliter propter evidentiam rationis. Sed ita suppono et fimiter credo esse in omnibus quantumcumque perfectis in vita ista vitam communem ducentibus, et non raptis vel aliquo modo singulariter elevatis. Ergo nullus habens fidem de credibilibus habet scientiam proprie dictam. Item, non videmus quod aliquis possit ostendere, non dico lumen intrinsecus informans, sed nec etiam habitum scientiae per illud acquisitum actu exteriori, cum tamen scientis sit posse docere."

18. Ibid.: "circa hoc est intelligendum quod non videtur quod de his, quae proprie et simpliciter sunt credibilia, possit simul cum fide haberi habitus scientificus proprie dictus."

19. Ibid. (ed. PB 4.73–74): "Item, hoc idem sic ostendo (ostendendo ed.): philosophus certitudinaliter scit Deum esse, sed nec hoc opinatur nec aestimat nec credit; ergo cum iste convertetur non efficietur hoc sibi creditum proprie loquendo. . . . Si ergo fidem habens, per studium philosophiae venerit in scientiam huius quod Deus est, quomodo adhuc remanebit sibi de hoc fides?"

bring some understanding to the truths we accept on faith. In Godfrey's technical expression, this is *scientia fidei*. 3. We cannot have "science" in the strict sense regarding the proper objects of the faith, such as the Trinity and the Incarnation, by postulating a special *lumen theologicum*. 4. We can have "science" in the proper sense of the term in regard to certain truths of the faith, such as the existence of God.

This latter claim, along with some other considerations, leads Godfrey to ask in *Quodlibet IX,* question 20 (1293–94), the following question: "Whether among the sciences by which the intellect gains its fulfillment one has to place natural philosophical science ahead of the science of theology?"[20] Even to make a comparison between theology and natural philosophy one has to presume that you cannot even posit such a question unless each can in some way be called "science." The case with natural philosophy is not difficult to establish, since it is generally admitted by everyone that it is "science."[21]

In regard to theology, it must be admitted that it is "science" at least in the sense that beyond the kind of knowledge that is properly considered faith and that is only based on authority, students in the theology faculty acquire some further cognitive habit:

Now this cognitive habit is based not only on authority with its hidden character, but on reason that brings forth some kind of evidence that is gained from what is better known from among <natural> realities themselves. This is clear from the theological questions that are treated with such diligent investigation by the Fathers and the teachers <who have gone before us>. In their treatments they bring forth reasons based on those things that are better known and that have some kind of parallel or likeness to the hidden things presented in the scriptures that we hold because of faith. By means of these examples the objects of faith become somewhat known and evident to the intellect. The result is that the intellect now assents to these objects not only because they have been written down, and because of the authority of the Scriptures and the authority of the one who wrote them down, but also because of the argument that has made these objects of faith in some way evident. Certainly, it would be a tremendous

---

20. Godfrey of Fontaines, *Quodlibet IX,* q. 20 (ed. PB 4.282): "Utrum inter scientias quibus perficitur intellectus magis proprie debet dici scientia ipsa scientia philosophica naturalis quam scientia theologiae?"

21. Ibid.: "Dicendum quod circa comparationem theologiae et naturalis philosophiae est primo intelligendum quod non potest esse comparatio inter illas secundum quod quaerit quaestio, nisi scientia possit dici, et hoc quidem communiter ab omnibus supponitur de scientia naturali."

waste of time to have worked so hard at the study and exposition of Scripture, if those things that are written down and held by obscure faith do not become in some way evident and understood by reason. Now this habit that is developed through study is called "science," in the common meaning of the term, as we realize from the words of St. Augustine in tract 21 of his *Commentary on John's Gospel:* "We should try to come to a knowledge of the words of God. Why were they spoken, except to be heard? Why were they heard, except to be understood?" For the knowledge of something that beforehand was unknown but that becomes known through reasons that employ things that are more evident and better known is commonly called "science."[22]

According to Godfrey, it was on this basis that the Fathers and doctors called a habit "science" when knowledge was to some degree made evident by using reasons in regard to things that were previously held only on the basis of faith. For example, St. Augustine, in his *Letter to Consentius,* noted, "Those things which you already hold by the strength of your faith, may you grasp also by the light of your reason. Do not believe in such a way that you do not also seek a reason."[23] It is to the degree that we pursue such reasons that we attain such evidence as that which brings us beyond the obscurity of faith and leads us into "science," as the Fathers understood that term.

Such is the habit that is acquired in the study of sacred Scripture regarding the things that belong to faith, a habit that goes beyond the habit of faith shared by all believers. For there is not so noticeable a lack of proportion or so remote a

---

22. Ibid. (ed. PB 4.282–83): "Sed circa theologiam est etiam hoc aliqualiter supponendum, scilicet quod ultra notitiam, quae fides proprie dicitur et solum auctoritati innititur, studentes in theologia acquirunt sibi aliquem habitum cognitivum ulteriorem, qui non solum auctoritati in sua obscuritate, sed rationi aliqualem evidentiam facienti ex aliquibus notioribus ex ipsis rebus acceptam innititur. Et hoc patet in quaestionibus theologicis a sanctis et doctoribus diligenti inquisitione tractatis, in quibus ex aliquibus rebus et similitudinibus et proportionibus aliquarum rerum tanquam magis notis sumuntur rationes per quas ea, quae sub obscuritate nudae scripturae sola fide tenentur, aliqualiter nota et evidentia fiunt intellectui; ut iam intellectus talibus assentiat, non solum quia scripta sunt et auctoritate scripturae et ratione auctoritatis scribentis tradita, sed etiam quia per rationem, quae circa talia nota sunt haberi aliquo modo facta evidentia. Frustra enim laboraretur tantum in studio et expositione in sacra scriptura, ut ea quae scripta sunt et fide obscura tenentur aliquo modo evidentia fiant, et ratione intelligantur. Et hic habitus sic per studium acquisitus etiam communi nomine scientia dicitur, prout dicit Augustinus, super Iohannem, vigesimo primo: conari debemus ut sciamus verba Dei; quare enim dicta sunt nisi ut audiantur; quare audita sunt nisi intelligantur; et cetera. Scientia enim dicitur communiter notitia alicuius [pro] prius ignoti, cum per rationes aliquas ex aliquibus evidentiioribus et magis notis innotescit."

23. Augustine, *Epistola CXX,* c. 1, n. 2 (PL 33.453).

link between the things that are held by faith and those that can be known to us naturally by the light of the natural intellect, that some reasons cannot be found among natural things through which with the help of the superior light of faith, we can come to a more evident knowledge. However, due to the excellence of the things to be believed and because of our intellect's imperfection and weakness here in the wayfarer state, we cannot arrive at such great evidence for the objects of faith that the evidence, or the argument producing it, more moves us to assent to the things to be believed as they are in themselves, or according to the knowledge that is acquired from such arguments, than does faith itself, which is founded on the authority of sacred Scripture.[24]

Again, Godfrey directs us to St. Augustine, who says near the beginning of book 9 of the *De Trinitate*,[25] where he begins, using reasons, to investigate the truth of the Trinity of persons: "Concerning the things that we must believe let us question without being unfaithful; concerning the things to be understood, let us affirm them without presumption."[26] The reasons provided by natural realities, however, are weak in relation to the divine realities that they are meant to illustrate in theology. That is why, Godfrey tells us, we call such divine realities supernatural.

The realities of the faith not only exceed the faculty of natural reason according to what they are in themselves, but also exceed the faculty of natural reason insofar as they are considered in their relation to the things that are able to be known naturally and from which we borrow the means to illustrate them. For, although God in himself exceeds the faculty of human reason, and therefore according to his essence itself is not able to be grasped by a human intellect basing itself on its natural ability,

24. Godfrey of Fontaines, *Quodlibet IX*, q. 20 (ed. PB 4.283–84): "Talis autem est habitus qui de his quae fidei sunt in studio sacrae scripturae ultra habitum communem fidei, quem habent communiter fideles, acquiritur; quia non est tanta improportio vel tam remota habitudo inter ea quae fide tenentur et ea quae nobis naturaliter lumine intellectus naturalis nota possunt esse, quin ex istis possunt sumi rationes aliquae, per quas adiutorio luminis superioris fidei possimus ad aliquam evidentiorem notitiam pervenire. Verumtamen, quia propter creditorum excellentiam et intellectus secundum status viae imperfectionem et infirmitatem, non possumus pervenire ad tantam illorum evidentiam quod illa evidentia sive ratio illam faciens moveat magis ad assentiendum creditis secundum se sive secundum quod de talibus rationibus notitia de creditis acquiritur, quam ipsa fides secundum quod auctoritati sacrae scripturae innititur."

25. Augustine, *De Trinitate* IX, c. 1 (PL 42.961).

26. Godfrey of Fontaines, *Quodlibet IX*, q. 20 (ed. PB 4.284): "de credendis nulla infidelitate dubitemus, quia scilicet certi sumus de eorum veritate; de intelligendis nulla temeritate affirmemus."

still God as considered in the relation that he has to created things (that is, as their natural cause) is considered in philosophy. And as the cause of all creatures, he does not exceed the faculty of natural reason.

But God, considered as a Trinity of persons, does exceed the faculty of human reason, and so, even though we are able to borrow from creatures arguments that sufficiently provide evidence concerning God insofar as he is one, because as such created beings have a certain determined relation to him, still in creatures we cannot find the bases capable enough to provide evidence of him insofar as he is triune, since the relation that creatures have to God as triune is not clear and determined. Therefore, Godfrey concludes that it seems that theology is less properly science than natural philosophy is, because even though it has evidence (which is required for science), it has less of it than natural science does. Even more, it does not have the kind of evidence that is required for it to be "science" in the proper sense of the term.

Against Henry in particular, then, Godfrey argues in this way:

I do not see how people cannot say that the natural sciences are properly and perfectly science with the certitude of evidence, since it is necessary that theological truths be made known with the assistance of creatures that are studied in the physical sciences. For, theology does not hand down on its own knowledge about the creatures on whom the arguments of theologians are based, and therefore it is necessary to obtain knowledge of creatures through discovery or from the teaching of those who were the experts in dealing with created things. So, we can take over the things well-said in philosophy and accept them into the science of theology not because the philosophers said it, but because these things are true and the philosophers have brought out the truth that is in them. This is the reason why Augustine, in *De doctrina Christiana,* says: "If there is anything that the philosophers have said that is true, then we must take these things over and put them to our use."[27]

---

27. Ibid. (ed. PB 4.293): "Quomodo ergo dicere possunt aliqui quod theologia est proprie et perfecte scientia per certitudinem evidentia, non sic autem scientiae naturales, non video, cum oporteat theologica notificare per manuductionem creaturarum de quibus consideratur in scientiis physicis; non enim theologia tradit notitiam creaturarum per se, ex quibus sumuntur declarationes theologorum; et ideo oportet illorum notitiam habere per inventionem vel per doctrinam eorum qui praecipui fuerunt in tractando talia. Sic enim bene dicta a philosophia accipere possumus in hac scientia, non quia dixerunt, sed quia vera sunt et veritatem in eis declaraverunt. Unde dicit Auguastinus, De doctrina Christiana: philosophi si quae vera dixerunt, ab illis in usum nostrum accipienda sunt."

Although Godfrey of Fontaines practiced declarative theology, it was, however, in many areas different both from the traditional declarative theology and from that of many of his contemporaries. Basically, declarative theology is a concrete effort to overcome misunderstandings. As we have already indicated, these misunderstandings could come from the unclear use of technical terms, from challenges from heretics and nonbelievers, from inadequate analogies, or from a lack of supporting or confirming arguments. In the era of Thomas Aquinas and Godfrey, these misunderstandings often arose from the encounter between traditional Christian teachings and the philosophical challenges presented by Aristotle and his commentators, especially Avicenna and Averroes. The intelligence required to face these challenges in order to bring understanding often demanded both a technical knowledge of these authors and a critical perspective in judging the truth of their philosophical positions. John F. Wippel's work *The Metaphysical Thought of Godfrey of Fontaines* well illustrates the philosophical strengths of Godfrey as he wrestles with the challenges he faced in his disputations with Thomas Aquinas, Siger of Brabant, Henry of Ghent, Giles of Rome, and James of Viterbo regarding the four basic areas dealing with impediments to understanding mentioned above.[28]

1. *Definition of Terms.* His discussions of essence and existence, of subsistence, nature, and supposit—terms so key to his reflections on our knowledge of God and of the unity of the divine and human natures in Christ—lead us to clearer appreciations of the knowledge and the limitations of our knowledge in regard to God and the mystery of the Incarnation.[29]

2. *Defense of the Faith.* Earlier versions of declarative theology, the type practiced before the arrival of the works of Aristotle and his Arab and Jewish commentators, mostly fulfilled their defensive mission by focusing on heresies. In the era of Godfrey and other late-thirteenth-century Christian authors, their challenges came mainly from these Aristotelian philosophers. Discussions of creation and the composition of creatures show signs of Neoplatonic influence in Godfrey, but these mainly point to his efforts to show the necessary adaptations that need to be made to overcome the

---

28. John F. Wippel, *The Metaphysical Thought of Godfrey of Fontaines* (Washington, D.C.: The Catholic University of America Press, 1981).

29. Ibid., 39–123, 225–57.

inadequacies of Aristotle's portrait of the prime mover, of the makeup of the world, and of God's relation to it. Nonetheless, in dealing with creation there are many points where Godfrey treats conflicts between faith and reason, as when he deals with God's freedom in creating or with the eternity of the world. In such cases, Godfrey is not satisfied simply with "defending the faith." Aquinas, John Peckham, Henry of Ghent, and James of Viterbo also do that. Godfrey tries to defend it through metaphysical arguments that bring forth a better understanding of the nature of the created world.[30]

3. *Use of Analogies.* In consideration of Godfrey's use of analogies, it is ironic to begin with his theoretical discussions of analogy. He opposed any push toward a univocal concept of being. Following Aristotle, in *Metaphysics* III, c. 3 (998b 21–26), he basically argued that this move would make "being" a genus and, as a consequence, *differentiae* would not be beings. "Being," then, must, as Aristotle argues, be analogous. Yet, Godfrey objects to the very analogy that Aristotle uses to establish the analogical character of "being" in *Metaphysics* IV, c. 2 (1003a 32–b 18). Aristotle tied all the realities that are related to health into a unity that would justify one medical science: the formal health of an animal, the diet that was not formally healthy, but that preserved the animal's health, and the urine sample that was not formally healthy but that was indicative of the health of the animal. For Godfrey, this example is not parallel to the case of "being," since all things—God and creatures, substances and accidents—are formally and intrinsically "being."[31]

Still, they are formally and intrinsically "being" in different ways, and thus "being" is predicated of them analogously. Yet, even though God and creatures are "being" in somewhat different senses, and God in such an eminent sense in comparison to creatures, still the concept of "being" predicated of them is not equivocal. As Godfrey stressed in question 20 of *Quodlibet IX*: "There is not so noticeable a lack of proportion or so remote a link between the things that are held by faith and those that can be known to us naturally by the light of the natural intellect, that some grounds (*rationes*) cannot be found among natural things through which, with the help of the superior light of faith, we can come to a more evident knowledge."[32]

30. Ibid., 124–69.   31. Ibid., 19–24.
32. See n. 24 above.

4. *Confirming Arguments.* The *Quodlibet IX* statement just quoted not only indicates the fundamental basis for natural analogies that can be used to illustrate divine and supernatural realities; it also justifies the use of supporting or confirming arguments. In *Quodlibet VIII,* question 7, Godfrey challenges Henry of Ghent's claim to a superior knowledge of the truths of the faith attained by some special light. For Godfrey, we have no special theological light beyond the light of faith, but we do have our intellects, which, guided by faith, can attain some understanding of supernatural truths. Still, Godfrey, in *Quodlibet IX,* question 20, argues against those theologians who allow too little knowledge when they defend the position that theology is only a science of consequences or logical consistencies in drawing conclusions from the articles of the faith:

Certain ones, paying attention to the fact that the arguments given in theology do not bring forth the kind of evidence that we have just spoken of, declare, in a most irreverent way, that theology is in no way science, stating that beyond the knowledge of faith, there is no knowledge that brings any evidence concerning the things themselves that are the objects of faith beyond what faith brings. <According to them,> the only type of evident knowledge that we have <in theology> is the evident knowledge of the consequences that are drawn from the premises that are held because of faith.[33]

Godfrey admits that the knowledge we gain in theology is such that if we were to consider this knowledge just on the basis of the reasons provided, it would only be opinion. However, holding by faith to the truth of the revealed articles, their certitude is anchored in faith, and the arguments brought forth as supporting them confirm our faith. Stronger arguments, like tighter analogies, provide stronger confirmation and support. They reduce intellectual doubts and the confusion caused by opposing arguments. Since in the era of Godfrey many of these opposing arguments are metaphysical, it is important for a theologian to be very adept in metaphysics.

The three *Quodlibeta* that we have here examined show Godfrey's rejection of deductive theology in the case where its practitioners would

33. Godfrey of Fontaines, *Quodlibet IX,* q. 20 (ed. PB 4.285): "Quidam enim attendentes ad hoc quod rationes theologiae non faciunt evidentiam secundum modum nunc ultimo dictum, minus reverenter dicunt eam nullo modo esse scientiam, dicentes quod ultra notitiam fidei non habetur aliqua notitia evidentiam aliquam importans de ipsis creditis, sed solum habetur evidens notitia consequentiarum aliquarum ex aliquibus aliis per fidem suppositis."

claim that it arrives at science in the proper sense of the term. This approach would imply that theological conclusions are accepted because of evidence. Still, Godfrey is a practitioner of deductive theology in the sense of a *scientia fidei*.[34] Theology, as we have seen, is a *scientia fidei* for Godfrey's declarative approach to theology. It is so also in the deductive sense. The immediate direction of deductive theology is to begin with premises that are believed and to deduce further implications. If one were to add beyond the articles of the Creed, which are the first principles of theology, another premise that is certain—such as another article of the Creed or a metaphysical premise—then one would arrive at a necessary truth that makes explicit what was implicit in the starting premise. If, however, one were to add a probable premise, then one would arrive at a theological opinion. It is important to distinguish theological truths from theological opinions, and a scientific approach to deductive theology underscores this difference.

There is, beyond this, another direction that deductive theology may follow. This approach starts with the theological position that one is considering and goes back to look for the character of its guarantee. This is to go from conclusions back to the grounds that support them. This approach may involve a long search, back through present arguments to the earlier discussions of the Fathers of the Church and to the Scriptures on which the truth being considered is ultimately based. If a theologian pursued this effort in regard to all his theological positions, then he would or should arrive at wisdom or a vision of the whole. By means of both the declarative and the deductive methods of disputation, Godfrey aims at this ideal: a vision of the whole.

34. On this point, see Tihon, *Foi et théologie*, 155–78.

John F. Wippel

---

9 ✑ Thomas Aquinas on Philosophy and
the Preambles of Faith

One of Thomas Aquinas's most important explicit discussions of the preambles of faith appears in his Commentary on the *De Trinitate* of Boethius, at q. 2, a. 3. There he asks whether in the science of faith that deals
with God one is permitted to use philosophical arguments and authorities. He responds that the gifts of grace are added to nature in such fashion that they do not destroy nature but perfect it. Therefore, the light of
faith, which is given to us as a grace (*gratis*), does not destroy the natural
light of reason, which is divinely instilled in us. While the natural light
of the human mind is insufficient to manifest those things that are made
known to us by faith, he insists that it is not possible for those things that
are handed down to us by God through faith to be contrary to those that
are instilled in us by nature, that is to say, to be contrary to those things
that we discover by using natural reason. For one or the other would have
to be false and, since both of these ultimately come to us from God, God
himself would then be the author of falsity, something that is impossible. Rather, Thomas continues, because in imperfect things some imitation of perfect things is to be found, among those things known to us by
natural reason are certain likenesses of those things given to us by faith.[1]

An earlier version of this chapter appears under the title "Philosophy and the Preambles
of Faith in Thomas Aquinas" in *Doctor Communis. Nova Series* 12/1–2 (2008): 38–61.

1. Thomas Aquinas, *Super Boetium De Trinitate* (hereafter *In De Trin.*), q. 2, a. 3 co., *Editio Leonina* 50.98:114–99:130: "Respondeo. Dicendum, quod dona gratiarum hoc modo naturae adduntur, quod eam non tollunt sed magis perficiunt; unde et lumen fidei, quod nobis
gratis infunditur, non destruit lumen naturalis rationis divinitus nobis inditum. Et quamvis lu-

Having laid down this fundamental principle for his defense of harmony between faith and reason, Thomas goes on to apply this same general conclusion to the relationship between faith and philosophy. Just as *sacra doctrina* is based on the light of faith, so is philosophy based on the light of natural reason. Hence it is also impossible for those things that pertain to philosophy to be contrary to things that are of faith, even though the former fall short of the latter: "Nonetheless they [the things established by philosophy] contain certain likenesses and certain preambles to them, just as nature is a preamble for grace."[2]

Well aware as he was of conflicts between views contained in the writings of some philosophers and the teachings of Christian faith, Thomas also comments that if something is found in the sayings of the philosophers that is contrary to faith, this is not really philosophy but rather an abuse of philosophy following from a deficiency on the side of reason. Therefore, by using the principles of philosophy it is possible to refute an error of this kind, either by showing that it is completely impossible or else by showing that it is not necessary. Here, of course, he is allowing for the difference between truths contained in revelation that can never be demonstrated by natural reason—revealed mysteries, we may call them—and other truths that, although they too are contained in revelation, can also be established by natural reason. And so he continues, just as those things that are of faith (revealed mysteries) cannot be demonstrated, so too, certain things that are contrary to them cannot be demonstrated to be false. But by using the principles of philosophy one can at least show that positions that contradict matters of faith are not necessary, that is to say, not demonstrated. Unexpressed here is Thomas's recognition that if one could demonstrate the falsity of a denial of a revealed mystery, one would in effect demonstrate the truth of that same mystery.[3]

In applying the above thinking to the main question at issue in ar-

---

men naturale mentis humanae sit insufficiens ad manifestationem eorum quae manifestantur per fidem, tamen impossibile est quod ea quae per fidem traduntur nobis divinitus, sint contraria his quae sunt per naturaam nobis indita: oporteret enim alterum esse falsum, et cum utrumque sit nobis a Deo, Deus nobis esset auctor falsitatis, quod est impossibile; sed magis, cum in imperfectis inveniatur aliqua imitatio perfectorum, in ipsis quae per naturalem rationem cognoscuntur sunt quaedam similitudines eorum quae per fidem sunt tradita."

2. Ibid. (ed. Leon. 50.99:131–37). Note especially: "Continent tamen aliquas eorum similitudines et quaedam ad ea praeambula, sicut natura praeambula est ad gratiam."

3. Ibid. (ed. Leon. 50.99:137–47).

ticle 3—whether it is permissible to use philosophical arguments and authorities in sacred teaching—Thomas concludes that one can do so in three ways. The first of these is of greatest interest to the theme of this chapter since, according to Thomas, one may use philosophy in sacred teaching in order to demonstrate preambles of faith, which, he explains, it is necessary for one to know in one's faith, "such as those things that are proved by natural arguments about God, such as that God exists, that God is one, and other things of this kind concerning God or concerning creatures which are proved in philosophy, and which faith (pre)supposes."[4] Second, one may use philosophy in *sacra doctrina* in order to illustrate (*ad notificandum*) by certain likenesses things that are of faith, as Augustine did in his *De Trinitate.* Thirdly, as he repeats a point he had previously made, one may use philosophical argumentation to resist attacks against the faith, either by showing that those attacks are false or else by showing that they are not necessary.[5]

As regards preambles of faith, here Thomas has indicated that they are certain truths that faith presupposes and that philosophy *demonstrates.* And then, lest the reader remain in doubt about his meaning, he has specified, "such as those that are *proved* about God, such as that God exists, that God is one, and other things of this kind concerning God or concerning creatures which are *proved* in philosophy, and which faith (pre)supposes." I would note Thomas's usage here of two terms—"demonstrate" and "prove"—and that in this context he treats them as equivalent. Hence, there can be no doubt that Thomas Aquinas holds that natural reason can demonstrate such preambles of faith, beginning with the existence of God. As we shall see below, this is a position that he reasserts in other writings. Here, too, in addition to the fact that God exists, he explicitly mentions the conclusion that God is one, and refers to other similar truths as well, but without specifying them. I would also note that here he has referred to other truths of this kind concerning God *or concerning creatures* that are proved in philosophy and that faith presupposes.

---

4. Ibid. (ed. Leon. 50.99:148–54). Note especially: "primo ad demonstrandum ea quae sunt praeambula fidei, quae necesse est in fide scire, ut ea quae naturalibus rationibus de deo probantur, ut deum esse, deum esse unum et alia huiusmodi vel de deo vel de creaturis in philosophia probata, quae fides supponit."
5. Ibid. (ed. Leon. 50.99:154–61).

One challenge in interpreting his thinking on this issue is to determine the number of truths concerning God or concerning creatures that, according to Thomas, may be demonstrated philosophically and are presupposed for faith, in other words, the number of preambles of faith. A second issue has to do with Thomas's reference to these truths—preambles of faith—as (pre)supposed for faith. He cannot mean that every Christian must first have demonstrated one or more of the preambles, such as the existence of God, before making an act of faith. As he himself brings out explicitly in other contexts, for example *Summa contra Gentiles* I, c. 4, to demonstrate or prove that God exists is a very difficult enterprise for human beings, so much so that, in fact, the majority of them will never succeed in doing this. In the first part of this chapter, therefore, I propose to concentrate on Thomas's general thinking on preambles of faith in this and other texts, and in the second part to seek for additional textual evidence to help one determine how many truths he includes or would include under this general heading "preambles of faith."

AQUINAS'S UNDERSTANDING OF A PREAMBLE OF FAITH

The text I have been following, taken from Thomas's Commentary on the *De Trinitate* of Boethius, is usually dated at 1257–58 or perhaps at the beginning of 1259.[6] Very shortly thereafter in this same work, at q. 3, a. 1, Thomas uses the terms "preamble" and "preambulatory" in somewhat different but related senses, that is, to refer to other sciences as preparatory sciences (*in scientiis praeambulis*) for metaphysics, and to refer to the many *praeambula* required to reach knowledge of divine things.[7] But common to all of these usages is the notion that a preamble is something that is in some way presupposed for something else.

As regards his understanding of preambles of faith, one can already

6. See Jean-Pierre Torrell, *Saint Thomas Aquinas*, vol. 1, *The Person and his Work,* trans. Robert Royal, rev. ed. (Washington, D.C.: The Catholic University of America Press, 2005), 68, 345. Here I will follow Torrell's dating for all of Thomas's works.

7. See *In De Trin.*, q. 3, a. 1 co. (ed. Leon. 50.107:117–21): "quia scientia quae est de causis ultimis, scilicet metaphysica, ultimo occurrit homini ad cognoscendum, et tamen in scientiis praeambulis oportet quod supponantur quaedam quae in illa plenius innotescunt": and ibid. (108:145–50): "Tertio propter multa praeambula quae exiguntur ad habendam cognitionem de deo secundum viam rationis: requiritur enim ad hoc fere omnium scientiarum cognitio, cum omnium finis sit cognitio divinorum, quae quidem praeambula paucissimi consequuntur."

find the fundamentals of his thinking concerning this in other texts such as his earlier Commentary on the *Sentences,* book 3, d. 24, a. 2, sol. 2. There he writes that something can belong to faith either *per se* or *per accidens*. What belongs to faith *per se* pertains to it always and everywhere (*semper et ubique*); but what belongs to faith *per accidens* pertains to it only in this or that individual, but not in every human being. Here, then, he is distinguishing between certain truths that can be accepted only on faith—revealed mysteries, we may again call them—and other truths that, while they may be accepted on faith by this or that individual, are capable of being demonstrated philosophically.[8]

In developing his understanding of these truths, Thomas then notes that there are certain things that are prior to faith (*praecedentia ad fidem*), that are matters of faith only *per accidens,* insofar as they surpass the capacities of this or that individual, but that can be demonstrated and known (*possunt demonstrari et sciri*). Here, too, he offers as an example the truth that God exists. This can be demonstrated and known, even though it may only be believed by someone whose intellect has not yet succeeded in demonstrating it. These truths that he here refers to as "prior to faith" (*praecedentia ad fidem*) are his equivalent for what he will later refer to as "preambles of faith."[9]

Shortly thereafter in d. 24 of this same Commentary, at article 3, sol. 1, Thomas returns to this theme. He recalls that it was necessary for faith to be available both regarding truths that are absolutely beyond human reason's ability to discover and regarding other truths that are beyond the capacity of some individuals, but not of all, to discover. As regards this second kind of truth concerning divine things, he now writes that when grace perfects some interior part of the soul (*affectum*), it presupposes nature precisely because it perfects it; so too, in like manner, natural knowledge "stands under" (*substernitur*) faith. He explains

---

8. Thomas Aquinas, *Scriptum super Sententiis* (hereafter *In Sent.*) III, d. 24, q. 1, a. 2, sol. 2, ed. M. F. Moos (Paris: Lethielleux, 1933), 3.769. Note esp.: "Et quod per se pertinet ad fidem, pertinet ad eam semper et ubique; ideo quod pertinet ad fidem ratione huius vel illius, non est fidei per se, sed per accidens. Sic ergo quod simpliciter humanum intellectum excedit ad Deum pertinens, nobis divinitus revelatum ad fidem per se pertinet. . . . Sed quaedam quae sunt praecedentia ad fidem, quorum non est fides nisi per accidens, inquantum scilicet excedunt intellectum huius hominis et non hominis simpliciter, possunt demonstrari et sciri, sicut hoc quod est Deum esse: quod quidem est creditum quantum ad eum cuius intellectus ad demonstrationem non attingit."

9. See the text cited in the previous note.

that faith presupposes such natural knowledge and, thus, that reason can prove that God exists, that God is one, incorporeal, intelligent, and other things of this kind. Thomas comments that faith sufficiently inclines one to an acceptance of such truths so that someone who cannot attain natural proof for them may assent to them by means of faith. In support of the need for faith in (and hence the need for revelation of) such naturally knowable truths about God and divine things, he cites five reasons originally offered by Moses Maimonides in his *Guide of the Perplexed*. He will repeat these five reasons in his Commentary on the *De Trinitate,* and will later reduce them to three major arguments with appropriate supporting arguments in *Summa contra Gentiles* I, c. 4. The third of these five reasons notes that many things are presupposed (*praeexiguntur*) if one is to follow the path of reason in knowing about divine things, since almost the whole of philosophy is ordered to a knowledge of divine things, and only a few could achieve this.[10]

While replying to the first objection in this same text from his Commentary on III *Sentences*, d. 24, Thomas follows up on this point. Since natural knowledge of God will be acquired only late in life, and since our entire lives should be guided throughout by our knowledge of God, it is necessary that those truths that are naturally knowable about God should be held by faith from the beginning of our lives insofar as they are presupposed for faith and are not yet known naturally by us.[11]

---

10. *In Sent.* III, d. 24, q. 1, a. 3, sol. 1 (ed. Moos 3.773–74). Note especially: "Sicut autem est in gratia perficiente affectum quod praesupponit naturam, quia eam perficit; ita et fidei substernitur naturalis cognitio quam fides praesupponit et ratio probare potest; sicut Deum esse et Deum esse unum, incorporeum, intelligentem et alia huiusmodi. Et ad hoc etiam sufficienter fides inclinat, ut qui rationem ad hoc habere non potest, fide eis assentiat. . . . Tertio, quia ad cognitionem divinorum per viam rationis multa praeexiguntur, cum fere tota philosophia ad cognitionem divinorum ordinetur: quae quidem non possunt nisi pauci cognoscere. Et ideo oportuit fidem esse ut omnes aliquam cognitionem de divinis haberent." For the five reasons taken from Maimonides also see *In De Trin.,* q. 3, a. 1 co. (ed. Leon. 50.108:131–63) and n. 7 above for the third reason; Thomas Aquinas, *Quaestiones disputatae de veritate* (hereafter *De ver.*), q. 14, a. 10 co., *Editio Leonina* 22/2.467:184–209. For these as reduced to three major reasons see id., *Summa contra Gentiles* (hereafter *SCG*) I, c. 4 (as already mentioned); id., *Summa theologiae* (hereafter *ST*) I, q. 1, a. 1; ibid., II-II, q. 2, a. 4. For these in Maimonides see his *Dux seu Director dubitantium aut perplexorum* I, c. 33, ed. Augustinus Justinianus (Paris, 1520; reprint, Frankfurt am Main: Minerva, 1964), ff. 12v–13v = *The Guide of the Perplexed* I, c. 34, trans. S. Pines (Chicago: University of Chicago Press, 1964), 72–79.

11. *In Sent.* III, d. 24, a. 3, sol. 1, ad 1 (ed. Moos 3.774): "Alia autem cognitio Dei est commensurata nostrae naturae, scilicet per rationem naturalem. Sed quia haec habetur in ultimo humanae vitae, cum sit finis, et oportet humanam vitam regulari ex cognitione Dei, sicut ea

At approximately the same time when he was writing his Commentary on the *De Trinitate,* in his *De veritate,* q. 14, a. 9, Aquinas distinguishes between two ways in which something can be an object of faith or belief (*credibile*)—either in the absolute sense because it is beyond the capacity of any human intellect, or with respect to only some individuals but not with respect to all. As examples of the latter, he lists truths that can be known demonstratively about God, such as that he exists, or is one, or is incorporeal, and things of this type. And in replying to objection 8 Thomas observes that insofar as it can be demonstrated that God is one, this is not an article of faith but is presupposed for articles of faith; for the knowledge of faith presupposes natural knowledge just as grace presupposes nature.[12]

As one moves forward in time past Thomas's Commentary on the *De Trinitate,* one finds much valuable information concerning preambles of faith in the *Summa contra Gentiles* (1259–64), even though this precise terminology does not appear there. But before examining this work, I will first turn briefly to the *Summa theologiae* I, q. 2, a. 2, ad 1 where this terminology is to be found. There Thomas writes: "To the first therefore it must be said that God exists and other things of this kind which can be known by natural reason about God, as is said in Romans [1:19–20], are not articles of faith but preambles to the articles [of faith]. For faith presupposes natural knowledge, just as grace presupposes nature and perfection presupposes something that can be perfected."[13] And in *ST* II-II, q. 1, a. 5, ad 3, Thomas answers an objection against his view that it

---

quae sunt ad finem ex cognitione finis, ideo etiam per naturam hominis non potuit sufficienter provideri quantum etiam ad hanc cognitionem Dei. Unde oportuit quod per fidem a principio cognita fierent, ad quae ratio nondum poterat pervenire; et hoc quantum ad ea quae ad fidem praeexiguntur."

12. *De ver.,* q. 14, a. 9 co. (ed. Leon. 22/2.463:121–34): "Aliquid vero est credibile non simpliciter sed respectu alicuius, quod quidem non excedit facultatem omnium hominum sed aliquorum tantum, sicut illa quae de Deo demonstrative sciri possunt, ut Deum esse, vel Deum esse unum aut incorporeum, et huiusmodi." Ibid., ad 8 (ed. Leon. 22/2.464:196–200). For discussion of many of these texts and a strong defense of the role of preambles in Thomas's thinking see Ralph McInerny, *Praeambula fidei. Thomism and the God of the Philosophers* (Washington, D.C.: The Catholic University of America Press, 2006), part 1, esp. 26–32.

13. *ST* I, q. 2, a. 2, ad 1, *Editio Leonina* 4.30: "Ad primum ergo dicendum quod Deum esse et alia huiusmodi quae per rationem naturalem nota possunt esse de Deo, ut dicitur Rom. non sunt articuli fidei sed praeambula ad articulos. Sic enim fides praesupponit cognitionem naturalem sicut gratia naturam et ut perfectio perfectibile. Nihil tamen prohibit illud quod per se demonstrabile est et scibile, ab aliquo accipi ut credibile qui demonstrationem non capit."

is impossible for the same thing to be known and believed by the same person at the same time. The third opening argument reasons that those things that have been demonstratively proved are known. But certain things contained in faith have been demonstratively proved by the philosophers, such as that God exists, God is one, and other things of this kind. In response to this Thomas counters:

In reply to the third it must be said that those things that can be demonstratively proved are to be included among those things that are to be believed not because there is faith in the absolute sense concerning them on the part of all, but because they are presupposed [praeexiguntur] for those things that are of faith and it is necessary that they be presupposed at least on faith by those who do not grasp a demonstration of them.[14]

In sum, therefore, although there is some fluctuation in his terminology, Thomas's understanding of preambles of faith is essentially the same in all the texts we have considered.

I noted above that Thomas clearly does not hold that one must have already demonstrated preambles of faith such as the existence of God before making an act of faith. In a number of the texts considered above, he has referred to preambles of faith or to naturally knowable conclusions about God as presupposed for faith. Just what does he mean by this? He seems to mean that certain articles of faith logically presuppose certain preambles of faith, but not chronologically; for instance, for God to be three and one (an article of faith), God must exist. Since God's existence can be demonstrated, this is a preamble of faith. Hence, if someone succeeds in demonstrating this preamble, one will have deepened one's understanding of God and will have advanced in the pursuit of wisdom; but such a person will not in any way have reached scientific knowledge of the article of faith itself.[15]

---

14. *ST* II-II, q. 1, a. 5, ad 3 (ed. Leon. 8.17): "Ad tertium dicendum quod ea quae demonstrative probari possunt inter credenda numerantur, non quia de ipsis sit simpliciter fides apud omnes; sed quia praeexiguntur ad ea quae sunt fidei, et oportet ea saltem per fidem praesupponi ab his qui horum demonstrationem non habent." Also see ibid., q. 2, a. 10, ad 2 (ed. Leon. 8.39): "Sed rationes demonstrativae inductae ad ea quae sunt fidei, praeambula tamen ad articulos, etsi diminuant rationem fidei, quia faciunt esse apparens id quod proponitur; non tamen diminunt rationem caritatis, per quam voluntas est prompta ad ea credendum etiam si non apparerent. Et ideo non diminuitur ratio meriti."

15. Rudi te Velde expresses this point well, in commenting on a remark by Bruce D. Marshall who, te Velde says, "rightly emphasizes that the preambles are not an epistemic war-

At this point I now propose to turn to the *Summa contra Gentiles* both to determine how Thomas proposes to deal there with what he elsewhere refers to as "preambles of faith" and to see how widely he extends the list of truths concerning God and divine things that are capable of being demonstrated philosophically. Regarding the last-mentioned point, so far we have seen him always citing as examples the fact that God exists, usually also that God is one, and occasionally that God is incorporeal, and intelligent, along with the constant indication that there are other preambles.

If, as I mentioned above, in his *Summa contra Gentiles* Thomas does not use the terminology "preambles of faith," the doctrine itself is much in evidence there. Indeed, after his preliminary discussion in the opening chapters of book 1, he spends most if not all of the remaining chapters of that book in arguing for the truth of a whole series of preambles of faith, and he continues with this procedure well into book 2. But the opening chapters of book 1 are also important for our understanding of his general thinking concerning preambles, and so I propose to begin by turning briefly to some of these.

∽

The title *Summa contra Gentiles* was apparently not given to this work by Thomas himself, and there is a long-standing tradition indicating that its correct title is rather *Liber de veritate catholicae fidei contra errores infidelium*. In any event, this second title seems to correspond very well to the contents of the work. There is, of course, a dispute concerning Thomas's purpose in writing this particular book, fueled in large measure by

---

rant for believing the articles, but rather logical presuppositions of the arguments, statements which must be true since the articles are true. I want to go just one step further: the articles are true of God, hence their truth requires the truth that God exists and that He possesses all ontological features a divine being must have in order to be understood to be divine." See te Velde's *Aquinas on God. The "Divine Science" of the Summa Theologiae* (Burlington, Vt.: Ashgate, 2005), 34–35, n. 44. There he is referring to Marshall's "*Quod Scit Una Vetula*. Aquinas on the Nature of Theology," in *The Theology of Thomas Aquinas*, ed. Rik Van Nieuwenhove and Joseph Peter Wawrykow (Notre Dame, Ind.: University of Notre Dame Press, 2005), 35. In this interesting chapter, Marshall is writing as a theologian, not as a philosopher. Unfortunately, however, while rightly rejecting a purely rationalistic or naturalistic interpretation of the act of faith itself and of apologetics, he greatly understates the importance of philosophy, and especially of metaphysics, for Aquinas when considered both in its own right and as he employs it in his theologizing. Something of this dismissive attitude is expressed by Marshall's reference to the "so-called preambles to the articles" (ibid., 22).

the testimony of Peter Marsilio, who, writing in 1313 and reporting about St. Raymond of Pennafort, states that it was at Raymond's request that Thomas composed this work. Moreover, Peter's report has often been interpreted as also indicating that it was written to assist missionaries working for the conversion of Muslims in Moorish Spain.[16] While the historical accuracy of this report, along with this interpretation of its purpose, has been accepted by many, it has also been strongly disputed by others, especially by R.-A. Gauthier, both regarding the claim that Thomas wrote this work at Raymond's request and that he did so in order to assist Christian missionaries in their efforts to convert Moors in Spain. But I will not linger over this dispute here.[17]

In chapter 1 of this work, Thomas borrows heavily from Aristotle in developing his understanding of wisdom. The name of the wise person taken in the absolute sense (*simpliciter*) is reserved for someone whose consideration is directed to the end of the entire universe, an end that is in fact identical with the principle (*principium*) of the universe. And so Aristotle writes in *Metaphysics* I, cc. 1–2, that it pertains to the wise person to consider the highest causes. But the ultimate end of each thing is that which is intended by its first author and mover. And the first author and mover of the universe is an intellect. Therefore "the ultimate end of the universe must be a good of the intellect. But this is truth. Therefore, truth must be the ultimate end of the entire universe." And wisdom must deal primarily with this.[18]

But now, in filling out his understanding of the nature of wisdom and the wise person, Thomas writes that it belongs to one and the same science to pursue one of two contraries and to refute its opposite. And so, if it belongs to the wise person to meditate about the first principle and to speak of it to others, it also belongs to him to reject opposed falsity. And Thomas finds this twofold office of the wise person confirmed by

16. See *Editio Leonina* 13.6 for the Latin text, and for an English translation see Saint Thomas Aquinas, *Summa contra Gentiles. Book One: God,* trans. Anton Pegis (Notre Dame, Ind.: University of Notre Dame Press, 1955; reprint, 2005), 20–21.

17. See Pegis, 21ff., who favors the general reliability of Peter's testimony and, therefore, views this work as having an apologetical mission. For Gauthier, see his *Saint Thomas d'Aquin. Somme contre les Gentils. Introduction* (Paris: Éditions Universitaires, 1993), 165–76.

18. *SCG* I, c. 1, *Editio Leonina manualis* (Rome, 1934), 1: "Oportet igitur ultimum finem universi esse bonum intellectus. Hoc autem est veritas. Oportet igitur veritatem esse ultimum finem totius universi; et circa eius considerationem principaliter sapientiam insistere."

the scriptural text with which he had opened chapter 1: "My mouth shall meditate truth, and my lips shall hate impiety" (Proverbs 8:7).[19]

And so in chapter 2, Thomas writes that having assumed the duty to pursue the office of the wise man—even though this may be beyond his powers—in this work he intends to manifest the truth that the Catholic faith professes, and to eliminate errors that are opposed to this truth. Regarding the second part of this task, he notes that it is difficult to proceed against the opposed errors for two reasons. First of all, in his time the sacrilegious statements of the individuals who are in error (*singulorum errantium dicta sacrilegia*) are not so well known to him as they were in ancient (patristic) times to early Christian writers; for those writers either had been gentiles themselves or at least had been educated in the teachings of the gentiles. Secondly, he notes that among those people currently holding erroneous views, some of them—Mohammedans and pagans, he specifies—do not agree with Christians in accepting any common scripture to which he might appeal in refuting them. In disputing with Jews he can appeal to the Old Testament, and in dealing with Christian heretics he can appeal to the New Testament as well. Therefore, in order to deal with all four types of unbelievers he has just distinguished—Muslims, pagans, Jews, heretics—he writes that he must turn to natural reason, to which all must assent, even though, he immediately adds, natural reason falls short in dealing with divine truths. He concludes therefore that when he is investigating a particular truth concerning divine things, he will also show what errors are excluded by it, and how demonstrated truth is in agreement with the faith of the Christian religion.[20]

As regards his purpose in writing this work, therefore, since in it he intends to pursue wisdom by setting forth the truth of the Catholic faith against unbelievers, he is clearly not restricting it to nor, it seems to me, primarily writing it for, the use of Christian missionaries striving to convert Muslims in Spain. Nonetheless, a broader apologetical perspective is included within his overall purpose of pursuing Christian wisdom, and the book is directed to dealing with all four kinds of unbelievers he has

19. Ibid. Note the scriptural quotation: "veritatem meditabitur guttur meum, et labia mea detestabuntur impium," and see the end of chapter 1 for Thomas's application of this verse to the office of the wise person (ed. Leon. man. 2).

20. Ibid. (ed. Leon. man. 1): "Simul autem veritatem aliqualem investigantes ostendemus qui errores per eam excludantur; et quomodo demonstrativa veritas fidei Christianae religionis concordat."

identified. And he is evidently going to appeal very heavily to natural reason in this effort.

Accordingly, in chapter 3 he immediately recalls the distinction between the two kinds of truth concerning divine matters that are available to human beings, that is, revealed mysteries such as the Trinity and those that natural reason can discover, such as that God exists, that God is one, and other truths of this kind, which the philosophers have also proved demonstratively, guided by the light of natural reason.[21] Here again, then, he introduces what he both previously and subsequently refers to as preambles of faith, and as usual he lists the existence and unity of God, along with other truths of this kind that can be demonstrated philosophically. In order to show why there may also be truths concerning divine things that completely surpass the capacity of natural reason, he explains that this follows from the fact that human beings in this life can never arrive at knowledge of the divine essence, that is to say, at quidditative knowledge of God, and that such knowledge would be required to discover truths of this kind.[22]

In chapter 4 he argues at length to show that it was appropriate for God to reveal those truths concerning divine matters that natural reason can discover, and that this is so for three major reasons that Thomas has now reworked from the five he had originally taken from Maimonides. To summarize briefly, three unhappy consequences (*inconventia*) would follow if God had not revealed such truths—preambles of faith, presumably—to human beings. The first is that then very few human beings would ever arrive at knowledge of God because they would lack the natural ability, or the considerable amount of time, required for this, or because they would be too lazy to master all that is presupposed for one to reach such knowledge. The second consequence is that even those who did succeed in arriving at natural knowledge of God would do so only after much time in their lives had passed. The third is that, even in their case the truths about God that they had demonstrated would sometimes be intermingled with falsity because of the weakness of the human intellect in judging, and because of what Thomas refers to as a mixing of phantasms, that is, of sense im-

---

21. Ibid. (ed. Leon. man. 2). Note in particular: "Quaedam vero sunt ad quae etiam ratio naturalis pertingere potest, sicut est Deum esse, Deum esse unum, et alia huiusmodi; quae etiam philosophi demonstrative de Deo probaverunt, ducti naturalis lumine rationis."
22. Ibid. (ed. Leon. man. 2–3).

ages produced by the imagination. Hence it was beneficial that God in his mercy should reveal even such naturally knowable truths about himself so that, by relying on faith, all human beings could share in a knowledge about divine matters that is free from error and free from doubt.[23]

In chapter 5 he offers a series of arguments to show that it was necessary for God to propose for human belief certain truths that unaided natural reason is incapable of discovering, ultimately because human beings have been ordered by divine providence to a greater good than human weakness can achieve in this life, that is, to a supernatural end.[24]

And in chapter 6 he argues that it is not foolish for human beings to accept such truths on faith even though natural reason cannot demonstrate them. He appeals to various "motives of credibility," as we might name them—in particular to the miracles that were observed by the first followers of Christ, such as cures and raising the dead and, he says, even more wonderful, the inspiration given to the minds of simple and uneducated people that enabled them when filled with the Holy Spirit to possess the greatest wisdom and eloquence. These remarkable signs led many to join the early Church, to accept certain truths that surpass all human understanding, to restrain pleasures of the flesh, and to spurn things of this world, violent persecutions not withstanding. Thomas contrasts the presence of such testimonies supporting the claims of the first Christian preachers with the way the founders of erroneous sects advanced their doctrines. He cites Mohammed as an example, saying that he spread his religion by appealing to promises of carnal pleasures in the next life and by relaxing the reins upon them in this life. Far from supporting the veracity of his claims by appealing to supernatural signs and miracles, he appealed to the force of arms to spread his religion, which signs are not lacking to robbers and tyrants, Thomas comments, and Mohammed used "brutal men and desert wanderers" to do this.[25]

---

23. Ibid., c. 4 (ed. Leon. man. 3–4). Note at the end: "Salubriter ergo divina providit clementia ut ea etiam quae ratio investigare potest, fide tenenda praeciperet: ut sic omnes de facili possent divinae cognitionis participes esse, et absque dubitatione et errore."

24. Ibid. (ed. Leon. man. 4–5). Note especially: "Quia ergo ad altius bonum quam experiri in praesenti vita possit humana fragilitas, homines per divinam providentiam ordinantur, ut in sequentibus investigabitur, oportuit mentem evocari in aliquid altius quam ratio nostra in praesenti possit pertingere, ut sic disceret aliquid desiderare, et studio tendere in aliquid quod totum statum praesentis vitae excedit."

25. Ibid., c. 6 (ed. Leon. man. 6). Note: "sed homines bestiales in desertis morantes, omnis

In chapter 7 Thomas presents a series of arguments to show that the truth that can be discovered by natural reason cannot be opposed to the truth of the Christian faith. According to the first argument, that with which our intellect is naturally endowed is clearly most true and cannot be rejected as false. Nor can that which is divinely revealed be regarded as false, since this has been confirmed in a way that is clearly divine. Therefore it is impossible for revealed truth to be contrary to the principles that reason knows naturally. He supports this defense of harmony with a number of other arguments as well, even though, in my judgment, none of the arguments as presented here is quite as clear and effective as that which he had presented in our opening text in this chapter, that is, in q. 2, a. 3 of his Commentary on the *De Trinitate* of Boethius.

In chapter 8 he develops briefly another of the three ways in which, according to his Commentary on the *De Trinitate* (q. 2, a. 3), philosophy can be of service to sacred science. Sensible objects, from which our intellectual knowledge originates, contain within themselves some trace (*vestigium*) of an imitation of God their cause, since every effect is in some way like its cause. However, in this case the likeness falls far short of its divine cause, and so such likenesses to God that human reason finds in creatures can never lead to knowledge of the essence of God or to a comprehensive or demonstrative knowledge of the mysteries of faith. Nonetheless even this small and weak consideration of the highest things is a source of great joy.[26]

And then in the extremely important chapter 9 Thomas indicates the order and the method that he will follow in the *Summa contra Gentiles*. He recalls that it should be the intention of the wise person to pursue both kinds of truths about divine things that he has distinguished above and to refute errors opposed to them. With respect to the first—preambles of faith—Thomas must proceed by means of demonstrative argu-

---

doctrinae divinae prorsus ignari, per quorum multitudinem alios armorum violentia in suam legem coegit." Also see Gauthier, *Saint Thomas d'Aquin. Somme contre gentiles*, esp. 124–28, who concludes from this that Thomas's presentation of Islam does not reveal much firsthand knowledge of this religion (even though the Koran was available in two Latin translations), and thus indicates that converting Muslims in Spain was not his primary purpose in writing this work.

26. See *SCG* I, c. 8 (ed. Leon. man. 7). Note: "Utile tamen est ut in huiusmodi rationibus, quantumcumque debilibus, se mens humana exerceat, dummodo desit comprehendendi vel demonstrandi praesumptio: quia de rebus altissimis etiam parva et debili consideratione aliquid posse inspicere iucundissimum est, ut ex dictis apparet."

ments by which an adversary can be convinced.[27] Since such rational arguments are not possible regarding the second kind of truths (revealed mysteries), Thomas will instead resolve unbelievers' arguments against them because of his conviction that natural reason cannot be opposed to a truth of faith.

As for a positive approach toward convincing unbelievers of such truths, Thomas writes that one must argue from the authority of Scripture as divinely confirmed through miracles since one can believe truths of revealed mysteries only on the authority of God who reveals them.[28] He adds that one may also appeal to certain likely arguments (*rationes aliquae verisimiles*) to manifest such truths for the practice and consolation of believers, but such arguments should not be used to convince adversaries; for the insufficiency of these arguments would only confirm them in their error since they would think that we Christians accept the truths of faith for such weak reasons (rather than on the authority of God who reveals them).[29]

Given this background, Thomas now sets down the order he intends to follow in the *Summa contra Gentiles*. First he will strive to make manifest those truths that faith professes and that reason can investigate, which he will do by introducing demonstrative arguments and probable arguments. He notes that he has taken some of these arguments from the books of the philosophers and the saints, and that by means of these arguments truth can be confirmed and an adversary may be convinced.[30] Then, by moving from the more evident to the less evident, he will turn to a manifestation of the other kind of truth that faith professes—revealed mysteries—by re-

27. Ibid., c. 9 (ed. Leon. man. 7): "Ad primae igitur veritatis manifestationem per rationes demonstrativas, quibus adversarius convinci possit, procedendum est."

28. Ibid. (ed. Leon. man. 8): "Singularis vero modus convincendi adversarium contra huiusmodi veritatem est ex auctoritate Scripturae divinitus confirmata miraculis: quae enim supra rationem humanam sunt, non credimus nisi Deo revelante." Note his remark in *In Sent.* III, d. 24, a. 2, sol. 2, ad 4 (ed. Moos 3.770:64): "Ad quartum dicendum quod argumenta quae cogunt ad fidem sicut miracula, non probant fidem per se, sed probant veritatem annuntiantis fidem. Et ideo de his quae fidei sunt scientiam non faciunt." In other words, signs such as miracles do not prove the truth of articles of faith themselves, but only attest to the truth of the one who proclaims the faith. Hence they do not result in scientific knowledge of the truths of faith.

29. *SCG* I, c. 9 (ed. Leon. man. 8).

30. Ibid. Note especially: "Modo ergo proposito procedere intendentes, primum nitemur ad manifestationem illius veritatis quam fides profitetur et ratio investigat, inducentes rationes demonstrativas et probabiles, quarum quasdam ex libris philosophorum et Sanctorum collegimus, per quas veritas confirmetur et adversarius convincatur."

solving the arguments offered by adversaries against these truths, and by using probable arguments and authorities, thereby manifesting the truth of faith. He will in fact devote book 4 to this second task and books 1, 2, and 3 to pursuing those kinds of truths that human reason can investigate, beginning in book 1 with those that pertain to God in himself, then in book 2 taking up the procession of creatures from God, and in book 3 the ordering of creatures to God as to their end.[31]

Given this plan, we may expect to find books 1, 2, and, perhaps, 3 of the *Summa contra Gentiles* dealing with what he regards as preambles of faith, to the extent that they include truths that Christians believe and that can be proven about God and about creatures, insofar as they come forth from God and return to him.

Noteworthy is the fact that in chapter 9 of the *Summa contra Gentiles* he has first remarked that, in dealing with those truths concerning divine things that reason can reach, he will use demonstrative arguments. But later in this same chapter he has stated that he will introduce both demonstrative and probable arguments in manifesting those truths that reason can investigate.[32] This remark is somewhat surprising, since it seems to muddy the waters in some way. Why use probable arguments when demonstrative arguments are available? Is this perhaps in order to persuade certain adversaries who cannot grasp the force of the demonstrations? Or is it perhaps to allow for a distinction between preambles of faith, for which demonstrative argumentation is possible, and certain articles of faith which cannot be demonstrated philosophically, but which reason can investigate (*quam fides profitetur et ratio investigat*)—such as the temporal beginning of the universe—and for which only probable or dialectical argumentation is possible?[33] While I will not offer a definitive response to this, the fact that Thomas allows for both demonstrative

31. Ibid.: "Intendentibus igitur nobis per viam rationis prosequi ea quae de Deo ratio humana investigare potest, primo occurrit consideratio de his quae Deo secundum seipsum conveniunt; secundo vero, de processu creaturarum ab ipso; tertio autem, de ordine creaturarum in ipsum sicut in finem."

32. Note the texts quoted above in nn. 27 and 30.

33. For a reading similar to this see Helmut Hoping, *Weisheit als Wissen des Ursprungs. Philosophie und Theologie in der "Summa contra gentiles" des Thomas von Aquin* (Freiburg im Breisgau: Herder, 1997), 117–18. For this solution to succeed, however, one would have to think that Thomas intends to distinguish here between those truths of faith that reason can *demonstrate* (preambles), and those that it can only *investigate* without reaching demonstrative knowledge. For the text see n. 30 above.

and probable argumentation in dealing with naturally knowable truths does help account for the fact that in many chapters of this work he offers a whole battery of arguments to support his position. One need not assume that he regards every individual argument within such a series as demonstrative.

But, be this as it may, it poses a challenge to any reader of the first three books of the *Summa contra Gentiles*. Because Thomas himself frequently does not explicitly tell the reader whether he regards as demonstrative or as probable a particular argument in support of a naturally knowable truth concerning divine matters, his reader must often determine for himself or herself whether a given argument offered by Thomas is in his eyes demonstrative or probable.

In any event, Thomas concludes chapter 9 with a very strong statement regarding his procedure in book 1: "But among those things that are to be considered about God in himself, one must put before everything else as the necessary foundation for the entire work the consideration by which it is demonstrated that God exists. Without this, every consideration about divine things is necessarily undermined."[34] Given this, even though limitations of space will not permit me to dwell on this here, we may be confident that Thomas views as demonstrative the detailed argumentation he offers in chapter 13 and in other writings to prove that God exists.[35] And with this I now turn to the second part of this chapter in an effort to see how extensive Aquinas's list of preambles really is.

THE NUMBER OF PREAMBLES OF FAITH

In *Summa contra Gentiles* I, c. 14, Thomas repeats his well-known view that because we cannot in this life know the substance (essence) of God, quidditative knowledge of him is not available to us. Therefore, he intro-

---

34. *SCG* I, c. 9 (ed. Leon. man. 8): "Inter ea vero quae de Deo secundum seipsum consideranda sunt, praemittendum est, quasi totius operis necessarium fundamentum, consideratio qua demonstratur Deum esse. Quo non habito, omnis consideratio de rebus divinis necessario tollitur."

35. Note how he introduces *SCG* I, c. 13 (ed. Leon. man. 10): "Ostenso igitur quod non est vanum niti ad demonstrandum Deum esse, procedamus ad ponendum rationes quibus tam philosophi tam doctores Catholici Deum esse probaverunt." For my own examination of these arguments see *The Metaphysical Thought of Thomas Aquinas: From Finite Being to Uncreated Being* (Washington, D.C.: The Catholic University of America Press, 2000), 413–34.

duces the way of negation (*remotionis*) whereby in order to advance in one's knowledge of God, one renders one's knowledge of God more precise by systematically eliminating everything that is incompatible with him as the Unmoved Mover and the First Efficient Cause of everything else in the universe, whose existence Thomas had proved in chapter 13. Thus in chapter 15 he proves that God is eternal by showing that because he is immobile, he is not subject to the succession involved in temporal existence. Thomas also introduces there what is in fact still another very interesting argument for God's existence based on the distinction between necessary and possible beings.[36] He uses the way of negation to show in chapter 16 that there is no passive potentiality in God; in chapter 17 that there is no matter in God; in chapter 18 that there is no composition in him or that he is simple; and in chapter 20 that God is not a body. As the reader will recall, the incorporeity of God was one of the preambles of faith he had explicitly identified in his Commentary on III *Sentences*.[37] In chapter 21 he proves that God is identical with his essence by showing that he is not distinct from his essence, and in chapter 22 that he is not distinct from his act of existing (*esse*). And Thomas does so always by using the way of negation.

He continues to use the way of negation until chapter 28, where he argues that no possible kind of perfection can be lacking to God and, therefore, that God is all perfect. This is a very important step because, by negating any lack or negation of perfection to God, Thomas ends up with an affirmation—that God is perfect. This affirmation in turn proves to be pivotal because he can appeal, and subsequently does, to God's perfection in order to assign other names to him, including some that have positive content, although he will apply them to God only analogically rather than univocally or purely equivocally (see chapters 32–34).

Thomas argues for the first of these names with positive content in chapter 37, by showing that God is good. He introduces his argumentation for this point by writing that from the divine perfection one can conclude that God is good, and Thomas immediately presents an argument

---

36. See *SCG* I, c. 15 (ed. Leon. man. 15 ["Amplius"]). On this as a more successful argument than the better known "Third Way" of *Summa theologiae* I, q. 2, a. 3 co., with which it bears similarities in its second part as well as substantial differences in its first part, see my *Metaphysical Thought*, 435–39.

37. See n. 10 above for this text.

based on this. He refines this in chapter 38 by also showing that God is his very goodness itself, and concludes in chapter 39 that there can be no evil in God. After showing in chapter 40 that God is the good of every other good thing, he concludes in chapter 41 that he is the highest good. In light of these chapters, it seems clear enough that Thomas regards the claim that God is good as another preamble of faith.

In chapter 42 he argues at length that God is one, which is another explicitly named preamble of faith as we have seen above in other texts. Most of his argumentation here is intended to show that God is one in the sense of being unique, that is to say, that there is only one God; but near the end of this chapter he reasons that God enjoys unity of being, that is, ontological or transcendental unity, meaning that he is not divided from himself.[38]

In chapter 43 Thomas argues that God is infinite. He begins by distinguishing between infinity taken as the privation of a limit in continuous or numerical quantity and, hence, as an imperfection (which must be denied of God), and infinity taken as a simple negation of any limit or terminus to God's being and, hence, as a perfection that must be affirmed of him. Thomas then offers forceful arguments to demonstrate that God is infinite in the latter sense, and so we may regard this as another preamble.

That this so is confirmed by a helpful summarizing statement Thomas makes in his *Compendium theologiae* I, c. 35. There he refers back to chapters 3–34, where he had presented arguments based on reason to prove in chapter 3 that God exists, and in the subsequent chapters many of the other truths about God concerning the unity of the divine essence that we have been examining in the *Summa contra Gentiles*. In chapter 35 of the *Compendium* he summarizes a number of these to show how they are also included in the brief article of the creed in which we profess that we believe in one omnipotent God, namely, that he is one, simple, perfect, infinite, and intelligent, and that he wills. And in chapter 36 Thomas comments that these truths have been subtly considered by many of the gen-

---

38. *SCG* I, 42 (ed. Leon. man. 40): "Adhuc. Secundum hunc modum res habet esse quo possidet unitatem: unde unumquodque suae divisioni pro posse repugnat, ne per hoc in non esse tendat. Sed divina natura est potissime habens esse. Est igitur in eo maxima unitas. Nullo igitur modo in plura distinguitur." Note that in *ST* I, q. 11, Thomas shows in art. 3 that there is only one God, and in art. 4 that God is one in the ontological sense, that is, undivided from himself, and *maxime unus*.

tile philosophers, although some fell into error concerning them, whereas those philosophers who succeeded were able to reach these truths only after long and laborious investigation.[39] Moreover, if, as I have argued elsewhere in trying to resolve a seeming inconsistency within Thomas's texts on this point, he also maintains that divine omnipotence can be demonstrated philosophically, this too may be regarded as a preamble of faith.[40]

In *Summa contra Gentiles* I, c. 44, Thomas offers a series of arguments to prove that God is intelligent. One is based on his prior proof that God is purely immaterial, and another on the fact that God is all perfect and that intelligence is the most powerful (*potissima*) of perfections to be found among existing entities. As will be recalled, in his Commentary on III *Sentences* Thomas lists God's intelligence as another preamble of faith, and in the *Compendium theologiae* I, c. 35, he includes the fact that God is intelligent among those truths about God that he has there proved by philosophical argumentation in the preceding chapters, specifically in chapter 28.[41] In subsequent chapters of the *Summa contra Gentiles* I, ranging from chapter 45 until chapter 71, Thomas introduces

---

39. For these see Thomas Aquinas, *Compendium theologiae* I, c. 35, *Editio Leonina* 42.92:1–93:18. Note esp. "Ex his autem omnibus quae supra dicta sunt, colligere possumus quod Deus est unus, simplex, perfectus, infinitus, intelligens et volens." On this see Jean-Pierre Torrell, "Philosophie et théologie d'après le Prologue de Thomas d'Aquin au *Super Boetium de Trinitate*. Essai d'une lecture théologique," *Documenti e Studi sulla tradizione filososfica medievale* 10 (1999): 328–29, and n. 102. Note that in the same context (329) Torrell also lists as preambles of faith the reservation of creative power to God alone (*ST* I, q. 45, a. 5), immortality of the soul (*ST* I, q. 75, a. 6), and the impossibility for man to find beatitude in any created good (*ST* I-II, q. 2, a. 8).

40. See my *Metaphysical Themes in Thomas Aquinas II* (Washington, D.C.: The Catholic University of America Press, 2007), c. 8 "Thomas Aquinas on Demonstrating God's Omnipotence." The difficult text is found in *De ver.*, q. 14, a. 9, ad 8 (ed. Leon. 22/2.464:200–204): "sed unitas divinae essentiae talis qualis ponitur a fidelibus, scilicet cum omnipotentia et omnium providentia et aliis huiusmodi quae probari non possunt, articulum constituit." There I cite from many other writings by Thomas where he does maintain that divine omnipotence can be proven philosophically, and at the end I attempt to reconcile them with the text from the *De veritate*. This is also confirmed by a remark he makes in the *Compendium theologiae* I, c. 36 (ed. Leon. 42.93:14–18): "Per hoc autem quod dicimus omnipotentem, ostenditur quod sit infinitae virtutis cui nihil subtrahi possit; in quo etiam includitur quod sit infinitus et perfectus, nam virtus rei perfectionem essentiae eius consequitur." For the argument that moves from the infinity of the divine essence (ibid., c. 18) to the infinity of God's power, also see ibid., c. 19 (ed. Leon. 42.88:1–5).

41. See n. 10 above for the text from his Commentary on *Sentences* III, d. 24, a. 3, sol. 1. For the Latin from *Compendium theologiae* I, c. 35, see n. 39 above. For his explicit argumentation in c. 28 to show that God is intelligent, see ed. Leon. 42.91. There he repeats the two arguments from *SCG* I. c. 44, based on the fact that God is all perfect and that he is completely immaterial.

many precisions into his understanding of intelligence in God, too numerous for me to list here.

Let it suffice to mention that he defends on philosophical grounds God's knowledge of himself (c. 47) and of all other things (cc. 49, 50), and in the case of the latter, his knowledge of singulars (c. 65) including knowledge of future contingents (c. 67). And Thomas defends these points against many objections. In chapter 72 he argues at length to prove that God wills, and maintains that this follows directly from the fact that he has intellect. Hence it follows that Thomas also regards the presence of will in God as a preamble of faith since this is a necessary consequence from the presence of intellect in God. And he has included this in the summarizing passage in *Compendium theologiae* I, c. 35, mentioned above in the preceding paragraph.

In the opening chapters of *Summa contra Gentiles* II Thomas justifies examining creatures as part of his investigation about the truth of the Catholic faith against unbelievers, that is, insofar as creatures are made by and proceed from God himself. And this investigation corresponds to his earlier description of preambles of faith as also applying to certain truths concerning creatures insofar as they are both proved in philosophy and presupposed by faith (*In De Trinitate*, q. 2, a. 3).[42]

In chapter 1 he notes that perfect knowledge of any thing must take into account its operation, since it is through its operations that the power of something is known, and through its power that its nature is manifested. He introduces Aristotle's distinction between two kinds of operations. One kind begins within and remains within an agent and perfects the agent, such as to sense or to understand or to will; another passes outside the agent and is a perfection of what is made or done, such as to cut or to heat or to build. Thomas reasons that both kinds of operations can be attributed to God, the first insofar as he understands, wills, rejoices, and loves, and the second insofar as he brings things into existence, and conserves and governs them. While the first kind is to be viewed as a perfection of the agent, the second kind is a perfection of what is done or made. Hence the first may properly be called "operation" or "action," while the second, since it is a perfection of what is made, may be called a "making," as that is said to be "manufactured" (*manufacta*) which is produced by an artisan.[43]

---

42. See n. 4 above.

43. *SCG* II, 1 (ed. Leon. man. 93).

Thomas recalls that he has already dealt with the first kind of divine operation in book 1 while treating of God's knowledge and will. It remains for him in book 2 to deal with the second kind, whereby things are produced and governed by God. In chapter 2 he presents a series of reasons in support of the need for him to engage in this second kind of consideration in his present task of manifesting the truth that (the Catholic) faith professes. For instance, by considering the things God has made, we are led to ponder and to wonder at the divine wisdom. This also leads us to admire God's power and enkindles in us a reverence for him, and a love for his goodness. And, finally, this consideration forms human beings themselves into a certain likeness of the divine perfection, meaning, perhaps, that by enabling them to consider God in these ways, in some way they imitate him as he knows himself. Moreover, in chapter 3 Thomas notes that a consideration of created things is also necessary in order to remove certain errors concerning creatures that may lead to errors about God himself. And so here again we see the two sides of Thomas's employment of philosophical argumentation in books 1–3—to give positive instruction and to refute erroneous views.[44]

In chapter 4 Thomas draws some interesting contrasts between the ways in which Christian faith and human philosophy consider creatures. Human philosophy studies them precisely insofar as they are creatures, whereas Christian faith considers them not insofar as they are in themselves, for instance, fire insofar as it is fire, but insofar as they represent the divine heights. Hence the philosopher considers those things that belong to creatures in terms of their proper natures, while the Christian believer studies those aspects of creatures that pertain to them insofar as they are related to God, that is, insofar as they are created by him, subject to him, and so on. Given this distinction, Thomas also warns that Christian faith should not be criticized for passing over many properties of created things, for instance, the configuration of the heavens. His remark is important since it indicates that, while Thomas will say a considerable amount about creatures in book 2 (and book 3, for that matter), he does not intend to offer a complete account of them considered simply in themselves. And it suggests that, in accord with his remark in q. 2, a. 3,

---

44. Ibid., cc. 2–3 (ed. Leon. man. 93–95). Also see Norman Kretzmann, *The Metaphysics of Creation: Aquinas's Natural Theology in "Summa contra Gentiles" II* (Oxford: Oxford University Press, 1999), 18–25.

of his Commentary on the *De Trinitate,* insofar as certain truths about creatures are proved in philosophy and presupposed for faith, they, too, may be regarded as preambles of faith.

As regards truths that are considered by both the philosopher and the Christian believer, Thomas now comments that the two proceed by means of different principles. The philosopher takes his arguments from the proper causes of creatures, whereas the believer takes his argumentation from the First Cause because it is in this way that something has been handed down to him by God, or because it leads to the glory of God, or because God's power is infinite. Since the teaching of faith deals with the highest cause, it deserves to be called the highest wisdom, and human philosophy is of service to it. And sometimes divine wisdom proceeds from and uses the principles of human philosophy.[45]

Consequent upon these reflections Thomas also points out that the two kinds of teaching differ in the order in which they proceed. In the teaching of philosophy, which considers creatures in themselves and moves from them to a knowledge of God, one begins with a consideration of creatures and ends with a consideration of God. But in the teaching of faith, which considers creatures only insofar as they are related to God, one begins with a consideration of God, and only subsequently turns to a consideration of creatures. Thomas concludes that in the *Summa contra Gentiles* he is proceeding according to the second order, having first dealt with God in book 1, and now in book 2 turning to a consideration of creatures.[46]

In chapter 6 Thomas begins by offering a series of arguments to prove that it belongs to God to be the principle and cause of existing for other things.[47] It is interesting to note that his first argument recalls the very brief proof he had presented in book 1, chapter 13, to prove that there

---

45. *SCG* II, c. 4 (ed. Leon. man. 95–96).

46. Ibid. (ed. Leon. man. 96). Note: "Unde, secundum hunc ordinem, post ea quae de Deo in se in primo libro sunt dicta, de his quae ab ipso sunt restat prosequendum." The fact that Thomas deliberately follows the second order in *SCG* rather than the first shows that this work cannot be regarded as simply a work of pure philosophy, and not even in its first three books, for it does not follow the philosophical order. On the other hand, the fact that it relies so heavily upon philosophical argumentation throughout the first three books makes of it a rich source for Aquinas's philosophy, especially for his metaphysics, and, in my view, means that it should not be regarded as simply a work of pure theology, as some assert.

47. Ibid., c. 6 (ed. Leon. man. 96): "Supponentes igitur quae in superioribus ostensa sunt, ostendamus nunc quod competit Deo ut sit aliis essendi principium et causa."

is some first efficient cause.[48] Then only in second place does he appeal to the two lengthy arguments from motion he had presented in book 1, chapter 13, for the existence of a first immobile being. He now reasons that since many things are brought into being from the movements of the heavenly bodies, and since God is the first mover in that order, he is the *causa essendi* for many things.[49] Pursuant to this conclusion Thomas reasons that there is active power in God (see c. 7), and in chapter 8 that God's active power is identical with his substance.

In chapter 15 he offers a series of very interesting metaphysical arguments to prove that God is the cause of existence not only for some other things (see c. 6), but for all other things—or as he puts it in this text, that nothing apart from God exists except by reason of God himself. But this is not enough for him to prove that God produces things from no preexisting subject, and so he devotes chapter 16 to prove that God is also a creating cause. His treatment of these issues in separate chapters is significant because it indicates that for Thomas it is not enough to prove that God is the *causa essendi* for all other things to prove that he creates, as some contemporary interpreters fail to see. Hence I conclude that Thomas regards both of these points as preambles of faith.

While I grant that in his explicit listing of preambles of faith Thomas does not include any that do not deal with God himself, I would recall again that in our key text from q. 2, a. 3, of his Commentary on the *De Trinitate* he has referred in general to "other things of this kind concerning God or concerning creatures that are proved in philosophy, and that faith (pre)supposes." It would seem, then, that it is in accord with Thomas's thinking to include under preambles of faith certain truths about creatures that are proved in philosophy and that faith presupposes.

---

48. For this argument for God's existence in *SCG* I, c. 13, see ed. Leon. man. 14: "Et haec via talis est. In omnibus causis efficientibus ordinatis primum est causa medii, et medium est causa ultimi: sive sit unum, sive plura media. Remota autem causa, removetur id cuius est causa. Ergo, remoto primo, medium causa esse non poterit. Sed si procedatur in causis efficientibus in infinitum, nulla causarum erit prima. Ergo omnes aliae tollentur, quae sunt mediae. Hoc autem est manifeste falsum. Ergo oportet ponere primam causam efficientem esse. Quae Deus est." In bk. II, c. 6, Thomas simply recalls this demonstration (which he attributes to Aristotle) that there is a first efficient cause. "Efficiens autem causa suos effectus ad esse conducit. Deus igitur aliis essendi causa existit" (ed. Leon. man. 96).

49. *SCG* II, c. 6 (ed. Leon. man. 96). Note especially: "Cum igitur multa ex motibus caeli producantur in esse, in quorum ordine Deum esse primum movens ostensum est, oportet quod Deus sit multis rebus causa essendi."

For instance, further on in *Summa contra Gentiles* II he argues for the immortality of the human soul by establishing its incorruptibility (see cc. 79–81). This, too, it seems to me, may be regarded as another preamble of faith, this time a truth that is logically required to support Christian belief in life after death.[50]

In sum, therefore, I would suggest that among the preambles of faith, which can be demonstrated and in fact have been demonstrated philosophically, Thomas includes at least the following: (1) that God exists; (2) that God is one; (3) that God is simple; (4) that God is perfect; (5) that God is good; (6) that God is infinite; (7) that God is incorporeal; (8) that God is intelligent and all that follows from this; (9) that God wills; (10) that God is omnipotent; (11) that everything other than God depends upon him for its existence; (12) that God is a creative principle; and (13) that the human soul is immortal. I do not regard my list in any way as exhaustive. And if one extends preambles to truths established in moral philosophy that are presupposed for articles of faith, even though Thomas himself does not explicitly do this, the list will be increased accordingly.[51] And I have omitted discussion of another very important likely preamble—divine providence—because I had intended eventually to devote a separate article to it. But since Brian Shanley addresses this in the following chapter, I gladly leave that to him.

---

50. See n. 39 above for a reference to Torrell, who also lists as preambles the reservation of creative power to God alone (*ST* I, q. 45, a. 5), immortality of the soul (*ST* I, q. 75, a. 6), and the impossibility for man to find beatitude in any created good (*ST* I-II, q. 2, a. 8).

51. Note Torrell's third suggestion as indicated in the previous note; and also Guy de Broglie, "La vraie notion thomiste des 'praeambula fidei,'" *Gregorianum* 34 (1953): 341–89, esp. 375–77, who argues that for Thomas the preambles include all the major theses of natural theology (adding divine omnipresence to those I have mentioned), and other truths concerning creatures, including the spirituality and immortality of the human soul, the reality of free choice, the substantial union of soul and body, and the fundamental theses of moral philosophy.

Brian J. Shanley, O.P.

---

10 ✂ Thomas Aquinas on Demonstrating God's Providence

The inspiration for this chapter, and even its very title, comes from chapter 8 of John F. Wippel's *Metaphysical Themes in Thomas Aquinas II*: "Thomas Aquinas on Demonstrating God's Omnipotence." The occasion for that chapter is a certain *dubium* raised by Aquinas's reply to an objection in *De veritate*, q. 14, a. 9, ad 8, wherein he seems to imply that divine omnipotence is an article of faith rather than a demonstrable truth: "But the unity of the divine essence in the way that it is posited by believers, namely, with omnipotence and providence over all and other features of this kind which cannot be proven, constitutes an article [of faith]."[1] Wippel goes on to show, however, that throughout his writings Aquinas did indeed hold that God's omnipotence was philosophically demonstrable. He concludes by noting that the text from the *De veritate* really implies not that God's omnipotence is not demonstrable by reason, but rather that "when the acceptance of God's unity is taken in the full sense in which believers profess it, i.e., together with omnipotence and providence, and together with other truths of this kind that cannot be proved, including most especially the Trinity of Persons, then it does constitute an article of faith."[2]

---

1. Thomas Aquinas, *Quaestiones disputatae de veritate* (hereafter *De ver.*), q. 14, a. 9, ad 8, *Editio Leonina* 22/2.464:200–204: "sed unitas divinae essentiae talis qualis ponitur a fidelibus, scilicet cum omnipotentia et omnium providentia et aliis hujusmodi quae probari non possunt, articulum constituit." All Latin translations are my own.

2. John F. Wippel, *Metaphysical Themes in Thomas Aquinas II* (Washington, D.C.: The Catholic University of America Press, 2007), 217.

Wippel's focus on God's omnipotence rather than God's providence is related to the contemporary scholarly interest in the thirteenth- and fourteenth-century debates over God's absolute and ordained power. He therefore leaves unexamined the question of whether and how Aquinas thinks that God's providence is demonstrable. Now I happen to have a more than passing interest in providence because my doctoral work was on the foreknowledge problem in Aquinas and because I happen to be the president of a school named Providence College. Hence it is the purpose of this chapter to examine whether and how Aquinas thought that God's providence could be demonstrated rationally. In homage to John F. Wippel, I will carefully examine, in chronological order, Aquinas's major treatments of divine providence. The focus of my concern will be how Aquinas establishes the general thesis that God is provident over all things; I will not examine the special problems related to God's special providence over human beings. After examining six texts, I shall offer some concluding remarks.

IN LIBRUM PRIMUM SENTENTIARUM

Thomas's first systematic discussion of divine providence is in book 1, distinction 39, question 2, of his commentary on the *Sentences* of Peter Lombard.[3] Following his discussion of divine omniscience, Aquinas first examines what divine providence is (*quid sit*) by considering its relationship to other divine attributes. As the objections indicate, the dominant authority on providence is Boethius, and Aquinas begins his reply by parsing the differences in meaning between *providentia* and two other terms that Boethius closely associates with it: *scientia* and *dispositio.*

In his earlier discussion of divine omniscience in distinction 38, Thomas had suggested that God's knowledge of creation should be understood by analogy with the practical knowledge that an artisan has of an artifact, and he continues with that analogy in his discussion of providence.[4] Drawing on house building as an example, Aquinas says that a

---

3. Jean-Pierre Torrell dates this commentary between 1252 and 1256. All references to dates will be to his *Initiation à saint Thomas D'Aquin* (Fribourg: Editions Universitaire, 1993).

4. Thomas Aquinas, *Scriptum super Sententiis* (hereafter *In Sent.*) I, d. 39, q. 2, a. 1 co., ed. Pierre Mandonnet and M. F. Moos (Paris: Lethielleux, 1929–47), 1.928: "Cum enim Deus de rebus creatis scientiam quasi practicam habeat, ad modum scientiae artificis ejus scientia consideranda est."

builder thinks first about the end to be achieved and the order of what he intends to produce to that end. Secondly, he considers the internal relationship of the parts of the house to each other—the walls rest on the foundation and the roof rests on the walls—and how this mutual ordering is related to the end of the house as a whole.[5] Thirdly, the builder considers those things that will help him to achieve the end in order to eliminate the factors that would impede the end; so he thinks about supports, additional rooms, windows, and all the things that make a house more habitable.[6]

This kind of activity could be called *scientia,* but only insofar as it involves thinking and not insofar as it involves doing something; it involves thinking about the end and what is ordered to the end.[7] But when the order is considered with respect to being in the thing to be made, then it is called *dispositio,* because "disposition" refers to the order in the things that are made.[8] Finally, it is called "providence" by virtue of those things that conduce to the end, "for someone is called provident because he conjectures well with respect to what is conducive to the end and to what could impede the end."[9]

Aquinas then goes on to apply this analogy to God. *Scientia* is said of God insofar as God has knowledge of himself and what he makes.[10] *Dispositio* refers to the twofold order that is found in things: (1) the order of one thing to another whereby things help each other achieve the ultimate end and (2) the order of the entire universe to God. Finally, *providentia* is said of God insofar as we attribute to God those things that promote the

5. Ibid.: "Sciendum est ergo, quod artifex praeconcipiendo artificiatum suum considerat finem primo; et deinde considerat ordinem rei quam facere intendit ad finem illum, et ordinem partium ad invicem, sicut quod fundamentum sit sub pariete, et paries sub tecto; et iste ordo partium ad invicem ordinatur ulterius ad finem domus."

6. Ibid.: "Tertio oportet quod consideret ea quibus promoveatur ad consecutionem finis, et ut tolleantur ea quae possunt impedire finem; unde excogitat sustenamenta domus per aliquas appendicias et fenestras, et hujusmodi, quibus domus sit apta ab habitationem."

7. Ibid.: "Ista ergo excogitatio nominatur nomine scientiae, ratione solius cognitionis et non ratione alicujus operationis. Unde est et finis, et eorum quae sunt ad finem."

8. Ibid.: "Sed ratione ordinis excogitati in re operanda, vocatur nomine dispositionis: quia dispositio ordinem quemdam significet; unde dispositio dicitur generationis ordiniatio."

9. Ibid.: "Sed ratione eorum quae promovent in finem, dicitur providentia: providus enim dicitur qui bene conjectat de conferentibus in finem, et de his quae impedere possunt."

10. Ibid.: "Sed dispositio dicitur ratione duplicis ordinis quem ponit in rebus; scilicet rei ad rem, secundum quod jubant se invicem ad consequendum finem ultimum, et iterum totius universi ad ipsum Deum: sicut etiam Philosophus ponit in XI Metaph., text 52, ubi etiam ponit exemplum de ordine partum exercitus ad invicem, et ad bonum ducis."

order to the end and insofar as God wards off all that causes disorder.[11]

Aquinas further clarifies the meaning of these three terms in his reply to the first objection, where he notes that an artisan can have purely speculative knowledge of something to be made without having any intention to make it; this sort of knowledge is purely intellectual *scientia*. But insofar as the artisan further intends to execute the design and bring it into being, the design pertains to intellect and will. Finally, insofar as the artisan actually makes the artifact, the design pertains to intellect, will, and the power by which it is accomplished. Applying this consideration to God, Aquinas notes that God's providential knowledge and will with respect to creation are eternal, whereas the execution of God's plan in time is called governance.[12]

Thomas further clarifies the distinction between providence and governance in the reply to the fifth objection. Aquinas notes that the form of the house as it exists in the mind of the builder, which is called "art," is essentially different from the form of the house as it actually exists in stone or wood, which is called an "artifact." Similarly, the order governing all things as it exists in the mind of God is called providence, whereas the execution of the plan through secondary causes is called divine governance.[13] Providence thus refers to the eternal *ratio* by which God orders all things, and governance refers to the temporal unfolding of the eternal plan through secondary causes.

With these terminological clarifications out of the way, Aquinas goes on in the second article to pose the question of whether everything is subject to providence. He begins his reply by saying that this issue has been debated by almost every thinker, so before he gives his own solu-

11. Ibid.: "Providentia autem dicitur secundum quod rebus ita ordinatis attribuit ea quae ordinem conservant et propellit omnium inordinationem."

12. Ibid., ad 1 (ed. Mandonnet 1.928): "Potest enim aliquis artifex cognitionem habere de artificiatis speculative tantum, since hoc quod operari intendat: et sic providentia et dispositio ejus pertinet ad scientiam. Secundum autem quod ulterius ordinat in opus cum proposito exequendi, pertinet ad scientiam et voluntatem. Secundum autem quod exequitur in opere, sic pertinet ad scientiam, voluntatem et poteniam per quam operatur. Ita etiam in Deo est. Patet etiam quod primis duobus modis accepta sunt in aeterna, sed tertio modo sunt ex tempore. Et ipsa executio providentiae, gubernatio dicitur."

13. Ibid., ad 5 (ed. Mandonnet 1.929): "Sicut enim form domus est aliud per essentiam secundum quod est in mente artificis ubi nomen artis habet, et secundum quod est in lapidus et lignis ubi artificiatum dicitur; ita ratio gubernationis rerum alius esse habet habit in mente divina, ubi providentia dicitur, et aliud in causis secundis, quarum officio gubernatio divina expletur."

tion he rehearses three major historical positions.[14] He begins first with the view that there is no such thing as providence and that everything happens by chance; he ascribes this view to Democritus and other Greek natural philosophers who held the view that the only real cause is matter in motion. He dismisses this view on the grounds that it has already been persuasively refuted, presumably by Aristotle himself.

Aquinas spends much more time in this article examining the views of his Arabic interlocutors who argue for a limited divine providence. He first outlines the view of Averroes, who argued that God's providence extends only to species, such that only necessary beings are individually knowable by God; material contingent singulars, such as human beings, thus remain outside the purview of providence because they lie outside the purview of God's knowledge. Aquinas notes that Averroes erroneously imputes this view to Aristotle in his commentary on the *Metaphysics*. Aquinas then rehearses the view of Moses Maimonides, which extends God's knowledge and, thus, providence to human beings on the ground of the human intellect's capacity to know universals. Thomas criticizes this position because it does not allow for God's providential knowledge of other material individuals.[15]

Finally, he considers and criticizes erroneous formulations of universal providence such as Manichean dualism, divine determinism, and the denial of a special providence for human beings. While there is no time to delve into these various theories, it is worthwhile noting that by ranging his glance over the entire history of Western speculation about order in the cosmos, Thomas would seem to imply that the question of providence is both a perennial philosophical question and a theological problematic.[16]

When Aquinas begins in this article to outline his own account, the key principle that he exploits is that not everything is subject to providence in the same way. Providence presupposes a disposition in things whereby there is a hierarchical order of being in which each kind of thing is guided by providence to its end in accord with the intrinsic principles of its nature. Citing Pseudo-Dionysius, Aquinas says that provi-

---

14. Ibid., a. 2 co. (ed. Mandonnet 1.930): "Respondeo dicendum, quod haec quaestio fere ab omnibus sapientibus ventilata est, et ideo oportet diversorum positiones videre, ut erroribus evitatis, viam veritatis teneamus."

15. Ibid.   16. Ibid.

dence does not destroy the nature of things, but rather preserves their natures.[17] Aquinas goes on to explain that the fundamental distinction in providence is between those things that pursue their ends voluntarily and those that pursue them nonvoluntarily in accord with their natures. Aquinas then goes on to consider the details of how providence works differently in the heavenly bodies, the realm of generation and corruption, and the free choices of human beings.

To sum up, in his commentary on the *Sentences* Aquinas clarifies the meaning of providence and how it works differently in different things, but as yet there is no argument for why we must consider God to be provident or why the order of the world demands a provident cause.

DE VERITATE

Question 5 of the disputed questions *De veritate* is consecrated to the question of providence.[18] The first article parallels the first article in Aquinas's *Sentences* commentary insofar as it seeks to establish the relationship of divine providence to the other divine attributes of intellect and will. Thomas begins by asserting that because of the infirmity of our intellects, whatever we know about God is derived from what is more immediately known by us; thus if we are going to discuss how "providence" is attributed to God, we first have to examine how providence is found in us.[19] He notes that Cicero argues that providence is the critical part of the virtue of prudence because it completes what memory and intelligence supply.

Thomas then turns to Aristotle's discussion of prudence in book 6 of the *Nicomachean Ethics,* where prudence is defined as *recta ratio agibilium.* He recalls the distinction that Aristotle makes between what is to be done (*agibilia*) and what is to be made (*factibilia*): what is to be made by someone proceeds out of the agent and into the matter of the artifact,

---

17. Ibid. (ed. Mandonnet 1.932). "Dictum est enim, quod providentia dispositionem supponit, quae ordinem in rebus determinat in diversarum naturarum gradu salvatum. Cum igitur providentiae non sit destruere ordinem rerum, expletur effectus providentiae in rebus secundum conventiam res prout nata est consequi finem. Sicut enim Dionysius, IV cap. *De div. nom.,* non est providentiae naturas rei destruere, sed salvare."

18. Torrell argues that the *De veritate* was written between 1256 and 1259.

19. *De ver.,* q. 5, a. 1 co. (ed. Leon. 22/1.138:106–139:111): "Dicendum quod ea quae de Deo intelliguntur propter nostri intellectus infirmitatem cognoscere non possumus nisi ex his quae apud nos sunt, et ideo ut sciamus quomodo providentia dicatur de Deo, videndum est quomodo providentia sit in nobis."

and right reason with respect to making is called "art." Moral actions to be done by an agent, however, do not flow into something else, but rather perfect the agent's own moral character if they are done in a virtuous fashion. The capacity to reason rightly about moral action is called "prudence." When it comes to moral action, an agent has to consider both the end and what will conduce to the end. Prudence is especially concerned with reasoning well with respect to the means to the end.[20]

Thomas summarizes Aristotle's teaching about how the end of action is present in us in two ways: first, we have a natural knowledge of our end in our intellect; second, our appetites are inclined to the end by the development of the moral virtues. Aquinas discusses how knowledge is perfected by counsel and the appetites by election, both of which are directed by prudence. Prudence orders actions to their proper end by a reasoning that presupposes those ends as already in place both intellectually and morally. Thomas concludes that "in all the powers and actions of a rightly ordered soul, this is common: that the virtue of what is first is preserved in all that follows, such that prudence includes in some way both will, which is of the end, and knowledge of the end."[21]

Aquinas then applies this analysis to God. God's knowledge involves both the end (himself) and everything else as ordered to the end. Providence properly pertains to God only with respect to the knowledge of what is ordered to the end precisely insofar as it is ordered to the end. So while it presupposes the will to bring about the end, providence is essentially an act of the practical intellect. Aquinas describes providence as an executive power, such that every act of divine power presupposes the direction of providence. Hence, there is no need to bring power into the definition of providence.[22]

---

20. Ibid. (ed. Leon. 22/1.139:112–35).

21. Ibid. (ed. Leon. 22/1.139:166–70): "In omnibus autem viribus et actibus animae ordinatis hoc est commune quod virtus primi salvatur in omnibus sequentibus, et ideo in prudentia quodam modo includitur et voluntas, quae est de fine, et cognitio finis."

22. Ibid. (ed. Leon. 22/1.139:171–85): "Ex dictis patet quomodo providentia se habeat ad alia quae de Deo dicuntur. Scientia enim se habet communiter ad cognitionem finis et eorum quae sunt ad finem; Per scientiam enim Deus scit se et creaturas; sed providentia pertinet tantum ad cognitionem eorum quae sunt ad finem secundum quod ordinatur in finem, et ideo providentia in Deo includit et scientiam et voluntatem, sed tamen essentialiter in cognitione manet, non quidem speculativa sed practica. Potentia autem executiva est providentiae, unde actus potentiae praesupponit actum providentiae sicut dirigentis, unde in providentia non includitur potentia sicut voluntas."

In the reply to the ninth objection, Aquinas returns to the example of the artisan to explain the relationship between disposition and providence. He begins by noting that we can think about things being ordered in two different ways. First, we can think about the order of things as they proceed from their principle. "Disposition" refers to this kind of order: the hierarchical diversity of kinds of beings as related to each other.[23] "Providence" refers to a different kind of order: the order to the end. It is the disposition of things that is properly referred to as the work of the divine artisan because it is immanent in the created things themselves. But the disposition of things in a hierarchical order is subordinate to providence because it is for the sake of the order to the ultimate end that things are disposed as they are; the order to the end determines the order of the parts to each other. Providence is thus the final cause of the disposition of things. Aquinas concludes by stating emphatically that providence is neither the art of the production of things nor their resulting disposition.[24]

Aquinas's description of providence according to the model of prudence rather than art marks a subtle and important shift in his thought. In the parallel passage in his *Sentences* commentary, Aquinas described providence as though it were like the art of an artisan. Now he expressly repudiates that view (without acknowledging that he previously held it!). Divine providence is not something located in created things, but rather is immanent, eternal, and identical with the divine nature precisely as knowing and willing all things to their proper ends and to the end of the universe that is the divine goodness. As Jean-Pierre Torrell has noted in commenting on this shift of perspective, the practical knowledge of

---

23. Ibid., ad 9 (ed. Leon. 141:276–82): "Dispositio ergo pertinet ad illum ordinem quo res progrediuntur a principio: dicuntur enim aliqua disponi secundum quod in diversis gradibus collocantur a Deo sicut artifex diversimode collocat partes sui artificii, unde dispositio ad artem pertinere videtur."

24. Ibid. (ed. Leon. 141:282–98): "Sed providentia importat illum ordinem qui est ad finem, et sic providentia differt ab arte divina et dispositione quia ars divina dicitur respectu productionis rerum, sed dispositio dicit respectu ordinis productorum, providentia autem dicit ordinem in finem. Sed quia ex fine artificiati colligitur quidquid est in artificiato, ordo autem ad finem est fini propinquior quam ordo partium ad invicem et quodam modo causa ei, ideo providentia quodam modo est dispositionis causa, et propter hoc actus dispositionis frequenter providentiae attribuitur. Quamvis ergo providentia nec sit ars, quae respicit productionem rerum, nec dispositio, quae respicit ordinem rerum ad invicem, non tamen sequitur quod non pertineat ad practicam cognitionem."

an artisan is useful for explaining creation. Still, since this analogy connotes a transitive action, it is better to conceive of God's care for creation as analogical to prudence, a comparison that clearly connotes something immanent to God.[25]

One other point of note before moving on to the more important second article of question 5 is the way in which Aquinas primarily identifies providence with the divine intellect, with the will playing a necessary but subordinate note. As we shall see going forward, for Aquinas providence is fundamentally the activity of divine wisdom ordering all things to their ends. He deliberately leaves power out of the definition. The exercise of divine power is not the sheer exercise of will, but is the unfolding of God's benevolent and providential plan to bring all things to their proper good.

In the second article Aquinas finally asks the question: is the world ruled by providence or not? The opening lines of his reply provide the key to Aquinas's philosophical understanding of providence: "Providence concerns the order to the end, and thus whoever denies final causality consequently denies providence."[26] Thomas notes that the denial of final causality in antiquity took two forms: first, as a reductive materialism that denies both agent and final causality in the Aristotelian sense; second, as the view that there is agent causality but no final causality.[27] What these positions have in common is the view that effects follow from the preceding cause by necessity.

Aquinas notes that this position has already been criticized by other philosophers (Aristotle, Averroes, and Avicenna) on the grounds that

25. Jean-Pierre Torrell, "'Dieu conduit toutes choses vers leur fin': Providence et gouvernement divin chez Thomas d'Aquin," in *Ende und Vollendung. Eschatologische Perspektiven im Mittelalter*, ed. Jan A. Aertsen and Martin Pickavé, Miscellanea Mediaevalia 21 (Berlin: Walter de Gruyter, 2001), 566.

26. *De ver.*, q. 5, a. 2 co. (ed. Leon. 22/1.143:120–24): "Dicendum quod providentia respicit ordinem ad finem, et ideo quicumque causam finalem negant oportet quod negent per consequens providentiam."

27. Ibid. (ed. Leon. 22/1.143:124–34): "Negantium autem causam finalem in antiquitus duplex fuit positio: quidam enim antiquissimi philosophi posuerunt tantum causam materialem, unde cum non ponerent causam agentem, nec finem ponere poterant qui non est causa nisi in quantum movet agentem; alii autem posteriores ponebant causam agentum, nihil dicentes de causa finali. Et secundum utrosque omnia procedebant ex necessitate causarum praecedentium vel materiae vel agentis." Following Aristotle's discussion of his predecessors in the opening book of his *Metaphysics*, Aquinas is thinking primarily of Democritus in the first group, while the later group would include Empedocles and Pythagoras.

the material cause and the agent cause together can only explain the be-ing of the effect, but they cannot account for the goodness of the effect, whereby it is apt to maintain itself in being and take its place in an order wherein it is related to the good of other beings.[28] Fire, for example, is by nature a destructive force; if there were no limits or order to its action, it would only destroy. Without an appeal to final causality, there is no way to explain why natural things generally happen in a suitable and be-neficent manner. If there were no final causality, then everything would happen by chance, and chance cannot explain the regularity of nature's workings. What happens by chance happens only rarely and is intelli-gible as chance only against the backdrop of what happens regularly for the good of natural things. Thomas concludes: "We see many useful and felicitous things happen in the works of nature either always or for the most part, which cannot be the result of chance, and thus they must pro-ceed from an intention of the end."[29]

Aquinas goes on to note that whatever lacks intelligence can tend to an end only on the basis of some kind of preexisting knowledge that es-tablishes the end and directs that thing to the end. Thus things that lack knowledge are directed to their ends as arrows are said to be directed to their targets by the archer. Just as the arrow's finding the target is the work of the archer, so every operation of nature is the work of intelli-gence. Thomas concludes: "thus it is necessary that the intellect that pre-scribes the order in nature governs the world by providence."[30] He then likens this divine activity to the domestic foresight by which someone provides for a family, or to the political foresight by which someone pro-vides for a city or a kingdom. What is common to both cases is the act of ordering the actions of others to the end.[31]

28. Ibid. (ed. Leon. 22/1.143:136–41): "Causa enim materialis et agens in quantum huismo-di sunt effectui causa essendi. Non autem sufficiunt ad causandum bonitatem in effectu secun-dum quam sit conveniens et in se ipso ut permanere possit et aliis ut eis opituletur."

29. Ibid. (ed. Leon. 22/1.143:158–144:162): "Videmus autem huiusmodi convenientias et ul-tilitates accidere in operibus naturae aut semper aut in maiori parte, unde non potest esse quod casu accidant, et ita oportet quod procedant ex intentione finis."

30. Ibid. (ed. Leon. 22/1.144:163–74): "Sed id quod intellectu caret vel cognitione, non po-test directe in finem tendere nisi per aliquam cognitionem ei praestituatur finis et dirgatur in ipsum: unde oportet, cum res naturales cognitione careant, quod praeexistat aliquis intellectus qui res naturales in finem ordinet ad modum quo sagittator dat sagittae certum modum ut ten-dat ad determinatum finem; unde sicut percussio quae fit per sagittam non tantum dicitur opus sagittae sed proicientis, ita etiam omne opus naturae dicitur a philosophis opus intelligentiae."

31. Ibid. (ed. Leon. 22/1.144:177–82): "Et similiter providentia ista qua Deus mundum gu-

As Wippel has noted, the argument for providence here presages the argument for the existence of God in the *quinta via*.[32] What emerges in the *De veritate* is a theme that we will discover at the heart of Aquinas's philosophical argument for divine providence: *omne opus naturae dicitur esse opus intelligentiae.* Natural teleology in noncognitive agents provides a posteriori grounds to infer that there must be some divine intelligence ordering and guiding all things to their ends.

SUMMA CONTRA GENTILES

The *Summa contra Gentiles* constitutes Thomas's longest sustained treatment of divine providence.[33] I shall concentrate on chapter 64 of book 3, which is explicitly devoted to arguing that God governs all things by his providence. Before considering that text, however, it is worth noting that there is no formal treatment of divine providence in book 1, which is devoted to God's nature. Unlike the *Summa theologiae,* where Aquinas will take up divine providence in two distinct treatises, here he concentrates his entire discussion in one place. Because so much has already been established about the divine nature in book 1, and because Aquinas has spent the first sixty-three chapters establishing that God is the end of all things, Aquinas has many premises to argue from when he finally turns to divine governance and providence. Given this context and the genre of the book, it is not surprising to find more arguments for divine providence here (ten in all) than anywhere else in his entire work. I shall try to give a sense of them all, but I will consider only a few in any depth.

The first argument is based on the principle that when many things are ordered to the same end, they all fall under the guidance of the one to whom the end belongs principally, as in the case of a general leading an army to victory or a ruler governing a city. Since it has already been established that God is the ultimate good of all things (III, 17), who essentially possesses his own goodness first, it follows that God must govern all things.[34]

---

bernat providentiae oeconomicae qua aliquis gubernat familiam, vel politicae quo aliquis gubernat civitatem aut regnum, per quam aliquis ordinat actus aliorum in finem."

32. See John F. Wippel, *The Metaphysical Thought of Thomas Aquinas* (Washington, D.C.: The Catholic University of America Press, 2000), 410–13.

33. Torrell dates the *Summa contra gentiles* from 1259 to 1265.

34. Thomas Aquinas, *Summa contra Gentiles* (hereafter *SCG*) III, c. 64, *Editio Leonina*

Second, whoever makes something for the sake of an end may employ that thing for that end. Since it has already been established that God is the creative source of the existence of all things (II, 15) and that God creates all things for the sake of the divine goodness (I, 75), it follows that God uses all things by directing them to their end through the governance of providence.[35]

Third, it was previously proven (I, 13) that God is the cause of all motion as first unmoved mover. In book 3, chapter 3, Aquinas had argued that all motion is for the sake of some end, primarily because agency is unintelligible unless it is directed to something definite. So if God is the source of motion, God must move things to their ends. Since God acts by intellect and will, and not by necessity of nature, God must move things to their ends in that manner. Hence to rule and govern through providence is *movere per intellectum aliqua ad finem*. Aquinas notes that God moves some things to their ends physically and some spiritually, as the object of love moves the lover.[36]

The fourth argument is from natural teleology and is close to *De veritate*, q. 5, a. 2. We see natural bodies moving and acting for the sake of their ends and achieving what is best for them for the most part, even though they lack knowledge; indeed it seems that if the actions had been designed by art, they would not be different. But it is impossible for things that do not know their end to achieve it in an orderly fashion unless they are moved by some intelligence, like an arrow directed to a tar-

---

manualis (Rome: Desclée and Herder, 1934), 295–96: "Quandoque enim aliqua ordinantur ad aliquem finem, omnia dispositioni illius subacent ad quem principaliter pertinet ille finis . . . cum igitur omnia ordinentur ad bonitatem divinam sicut in finem, ut ostensum est, oportet quod Deus, ad quem principaliter illa bonitas pertinet, sicut substantialiter habita et intellecta et amata, sit gubernator omnium rerum."

35. Ibid., 296. "Quicumque facit aliquid propter finem, utitur illo ad finem. Ostensum autem est supra quod omnia quae habent esse quocumque modo sunt effectus Dei; et quod Deus omnia facit propter finem qui est ipse. Ipse igitur utitur omnibus diregendo ea in finem. Hoc autem est gubernare. Est igitur Deus per suam providentiam onnium gubernator."

36. Ibid.: "Ostensum est quod Deus est primum movens non motum. Primum autem movens non minus movet quam secunda moventia, sed magis: quia sine eo non movent alia. Omnia autem quae moventur, moventur propter finem, ut supra ostensum est. Movet igitur Deus omnia ad fines suos. Et per intellectum: ostensum enim est supra quod non agit per necessitatem naturae, sed per intellectum et voluntatem. Nihil est autem aliud regere et gubernare per providentiam quam *movere per intellectum aliqua ad finem*. Deus igitur per suam providentiam gubernat et regit omnia quae moventur in finem; sive moveantur corporaliter; sive spiritualiter, sicut desiderans dicitur moveri a desiderato."

get by an archer. Hence we must conclude that all the workings of nature are ordered by intelligence.[37]

The fifth argument introduces an interesting new theme. Things that have distinct natures do not come together in one order unless they are brought together by something ordering them into one. Now in the universe there are found distinct and even contrary natures, yet they all come together in one order such that they make use of each other's actions. Therefore there must be one governor of the whole of things.[38]

The sixth argument is based on the need of an orderer of the various celestial motions.

The seventh argument is based on the principle that the nearer something is to its cause, the more it participates in its influence and manifests its nature. What is closest to God, namely separate substances and celestial bodies, are the most perfectly ordered beings. What is farthest from God, namely material things, are less ordered because they are subject to chance mutations. Therefore we can conclude that God is the ultimate cause of all order and is the providential governor of creation.[39]

The eighth argument begins with the premise that God's free decision to create can be motivated only by God's desire to communicate his own goodness to other beings by drawing them back to himself. Every-

---

37. Ibid.: "Probatum est quod corpora naturalia moventur et operantur propter finem, licet finem non cognoscant, ex hoc quod semper vel frequentius accidit in eis quod melius est; et non aliter fierent si fierent per artem. Impossibile est autem quod aliqua non cognoscentia finem operentur propter finem et orinate perveniant in ipsum nisi sint mota ab aliquo habente cognitionem finis: sicit saggita dirigitur ad signum a sagittante. Opertet ergo quod tota operatione naturae ab aliqua cognitione ordinetur."

38. Ibid.: "Ea quae sunt secundum suam naturam distincta, in unum ordinem non conveniunt nisi ab uno ordinante colligantur in unum. In universitate autem rerum sunt res distinctas et contrarias naturas habentes, quae tamen omnes in unum ordinem conveniunt, dum quaedam operationes quorundam excipiunt, quaedam etiam a quibusdam iuvantur verl imperantur. Oportet igitur quod sit universorum unus ordinator et gubernator."

39. Ibid.: "Quanto aliquid propinquius est causae, tanto plus participat de effectu ipsius. Unde si aliquid tanto participatur perfectius ab aliquibus quanto alicui rei magis appropinquant, signum est quod illa res sit causa illius quod diversimode participatur: sicut, si aliqua magis sunt calida secundum quod est magis appropinquant igni, signum est quod ignis sit causa caloris. Inveniuntur autem tantum aliqua perfectius ordinata esse, quanto magis sunt Deo propinqua: nam in corporibus inferioribus, quae sunt maxime a Deo distantia naturae dissimilitudine, invenitur esse defectus aliquando ab eo quod est secundum cursum naturae, sicut patet in monstruosis et aliis casualibus; quod nunquam accidit in corporibus caelestibus, quae tamen sunt aliquo modo mutabilia; quod non accidit in substantiis intellectualibus separatis. Manifestum est ergo quod Deus est causa totius ordinis rerum. Est igitur ipse per suam providentiam gubernator totius universitatis rerum."

thing that is participates by similitude in the divine goodness. The greatest good in creation is not the particular good of any creature, however, but the good of the universe as a whole. All of the particular ends of creatures come together in a greater good that is the complete ordering of all particular goods into a common good of the universe as a whole. The order of the universe as a whole constitutes an integral common good of all the parts. The good of the universe as a whole is what is principally intended by God in creation. The God who creates this integral order must also direct and guide it to completion through providence.[40]

The ninth argument complements the eighth. Anyone who intends an end cares more about what is closest to it because this will be the end of everything else. What is closest to the divine goodness itself is the good of the order of the universe as a whole. All the particular goods pursued by creatures are ordered to the good of the entire universe as to an end. The good of the universe is the perfect created good toward which all other less perfect created goods are ordered. The good of every part is ordered to the more perfect good of the whole. Hence God cares most for the good of the universe and acts as its provident governor.[41]

The tenth and final argument is likewise based on teleology. Every created thing attains its end through the activities proper to it based on its nature. Since God creates substantial natures with their proper activities ordered to their ends, God therefore providentially governs them.[42]

---

40. Ibid.: "Sicut supra probatum est, Deus res omnes in esse produxit, non ex necessitate naturae, sed per intellectum et voluntatem. Intellectus autem et voluntatits ipsius non potest esse alius finis ultimus nisi bonitas eius, ut scilicet eam rebus communicaret, sicut ex praemissis apparet. Res autem participant divinam bonitatem per modem similitudinis, inquantum ipsae sunt bonae. Id autem quod est maxime bonum in rebus causatis est bonum universi, quod est maxime perfectum ut Philosophus dicit dui etiam consonat Scriptura divina. . . . Bonum igitur ordinis rerum causatarum a Deo est id quod est praecipue volitum et causatum a Deo. Nihil autem aliud est gubernare aliqua quam eis ordinem imponere. Ipse igitur Deus omnia suo intellectu et voluntate gubernat."

41. Ibid.: "Unumquodque intendens aliquem finem, magis curat de eo quod est proprinquius fini ultimo: quia hoc etiam est finis aliorum. Ultimus autem finis divinae voluntatis est bonitas ipsius, cui propinquissimum in rebus creatis est bonum ordinis totius universi: cum ad ipsum ordinetur, sicut ad finem, omne particulare bonum huius vel illius rei, sicut minus perfectum ordinatur ad id quod est perfectius; unde et quaelibet pars invenitur esse propter suum totum. Id igitur quod maxime curat Deus in rebus creatis est ordo universi. Est igitur gubernator ipsius."

42. Ibid.: "Quaelibet res creata consequitur suum ultimam perfectionem per operationem propriam: nam oportet quod ultimus finis et perfectio rei sit vel ipsa operatio, vel operationis terminus aut effectus, formo vero secundum quam res est, est perfectio prima, ut patet in II *De*

Aquinas ends the chapter by citing three scriptural passages—two Psalms and the Book of Job—which reveal God as Ruler and Governor of creation. He ends with the conclusion that he has thus shown that the error of the ancient materialist naturalists—the gentiles with whom he is arguing—is thus refuted. Everything happens not by chance, but by providence. Aquinas clearly thinks that providence is both a revealed doctrine and a philosophical conclusion. He obviously thinks that there are many ways to argue for divine providence, depending upon the starting point.

Before we move to the *Summa theologiae,* however, where it will become clearer which arguments are most important, it is worth noting that Aquinas is generally believed to have been working on another treatise on providence while composing the third book of the *Summa contra Gentiles: Expositio super Job ad litteram.*[43] The reference to Job at the end of chapter 64 is thus no accident. While the lack of a systematic treatment of questions in the *Commentary on Job* makes it unsuitable for extended treatment, it is worth consideration because there Aquinas addresses the deepest problem for divine providence, namely human suffering; and he does so by bringing to bear the themes that we have seen laid out in our texts.

In particular it is worth noting that in commenting on Job 5:8, Aquinas says that "Since Eliphaz had proposed that everything terrestrial has a determinate cause whereby it comes about, and this he had proven by the fact that natural things appear to be disposed to their proper ends, this—namely that natural things exist for the sake of their ends—is *the most powerful argument* to show that the world is subject to divine providence and not everything is subject to chance, and therefore Eliphaz immediately concludes from these premises the rule of divine providence."[44] The next section will confirm this.

---

anima. Ordo autem rerum causatarum secundum distinctionem naturarum et gradum ipsarum, procedit ex divina sapientia, sicut in Secunda [45] est ostensum. Ergo et ordo operationum, per quas res causatae magis appropinquant ad ultimum finem. Ordinare autem actiones aliquarum rerum ad finem, est gubernare ipsa. Deus igitur per suae saptientiae providentiam rebus gubernationem et regimen praestat."

43. Torrell dates this work between 1261 and 1265.

44. Thomas Aquinas, *Expositio super Iob ad litteram,* c. 5, *Editio Leonina* 26.36:127ff.: "Quia Eliphaz proposuerat omnia quae in terris fiunt determinatum causam habere et hoc probaverat per hoc quod res naturales sunt propter finem, *potissimum argumentum* est ad ostendendum mundum regi divina providentia et non omnia agi fortuito, idcirco Eliphaz statim ex praemis-

IV. *SUMMA THEOLOGIAE*

Thomas first considers divine providence in *Prima pars,* question 22.[45] After considering what pertains strictly to the divine will, Aquinas mentions in the prologue that it is now time to consider what belongs to both intellect and will in God. The first article concerns whether it is fitting to ascribe providence to God. Thomas begins by saying that it is *necessary* to ascribe providence to God. He argues on the already established premise that God is the ultimate source of all that is good in creation. But created things are good not only in their substance, but also in their being ordered to the divine goodness as to their end. This ordering to an end is a good in creatures that must therefore have its source in the Creator.[46]

As an intelligent cause, the *ratio* or divine idea of the order of creation exists eternally and first in the divine intellect. Divine providence is nothing other than the "idea of the order of things to their end in the divine mind" (*ratio ordinis rerum in finem in mente divina*). He then goes on to argue that divine providence should be thought of by analogy with human prudence. Not personal prudence, however, since nothing God does is ordered to an end outside himself, but rather the domestic or political prudence whereby one orders others to the end. The final line of the reply notes that when Boethius defines providence as the "divine idea itself established in the highest principle of all things which disposes all things" (*ipsa divina ratio in summo omnium principe constituta quae cuncta disponit*), disposition can be said to apply to both the order of things to their ends and the order of parts to the whole.[47]

---

sis concludit de regimine divinae providentiae." As cited by Denis Chardonnens in *L'Homme sous le regard de la providence* (Paris: Librarie Philosophique J. Vrin 1997), 61 n. 2 (emphasis mine). I have found Chardonnens's study of the theme of providence in the Commentary on Job an invaluable resource, especially chapter 3. On the theme of finality in Aquinas, Chardonnens is much influenced by J. H. Nicolas, "L'univers ordonné à Dieu par Dieu," *Revue Thomiste* 91 (1991): 357–76.

45. According to Torrell, the *Prima pars* was written between 1265 and 1268.

46. Thomas Aquinas, *Summa theologiae* (hereafter *ST*) I, q. 22, a. 1 co., ed. I. T. Eschmann (Ottawa: Institutum Studiorum Medievalium Ottaviensis, 1941–45), 1.153a: 21–31: "Dicendum quod necesse est ponere providentiam in Deo. Omne enim bonum quod est in rebus, a Deo creatum est, ut supra ostensum est [6,4]. In rebus autem invenitur bonum non solum quantum ad substantiam rerum, sed etiam quantum ad ordinem earum in finem, et praecipue in finem ultimmum, qui est bonitatas divina, ut supra habitum est [21,4]. Hoc igitur bonum ordinis in rebus creatis existens, a Deo creatum est."

47. Ibid. (ed. Ottawa 1.153b:11–13): "Dispositio autem potest dici tam ratio ordinis rerum in finem, quam ratio ordinis partium in toto."

In the second article Aquinas asks whether God's providence extends to all things. After rehearsing the usual ancient views to the contrary, he argues that God's providence must extend to all things because God's causality extends to all things: "Since every agent cause acts for the sake of an end, the ordering to the end extends as far as the causality itself extends."[48] Since God's efficient causality extends to every principle of every being, everything that has *esse* from God is thereby ordered by God to an end. Everything that participates in *esse* ipso facto is subject to divine providence.[49] Here is an argument for divine providence based on the nature of efficient causality in general and on the specific nature of God's causation of *esse*.

Aquinas then offers a second argument for divine providence, one based on divine omniscience. Since God's knowledge of creation is like that of an artisan to an artifact, it is necessary that everything is under God's ordering, as every artifact is under the art of the artisan.[50] Here we see Aquinas returning to the analogy of providence with artistic knowledge.

If we turn to the treatise on divine government later in the *Prima pars* in question 103, the first article asks the question whether the world is governed by God. After noting that some ancient philosophers thought the world was subject to chance rather than governance, Thomas says that their position is impossible based on two arguments. The first is a posteriori and based on the teleology of nature. We observe in natural things that what is best eventuates either always or for the most part. This would not happen if natural things were not subject to divine providence directing them to the end or good, which is the meaning of governance. "Hence the certain order of things demonstrates clearly the governance of the world." Quoting Cicero who quotes Aristotle, Thom-

48. Ibid. (ed. Ottawa 1.154b:22–25): "Cum enim omne agens agat propter finem, tantum se extendit ordinatio effectuum in finem, tantum se extendit ordinatio effectuum in finem."

49. Ibid. (ed. Ottawa 1.154b:29–44): "Causalitas autem Dei, qui est primum agens, se extendit usque ad omni entia, non solum quantum ad principia specei, sed etiam quantum ad individualia principia, non solum incorruptibilium, sed etiam corruptibilium, secundum illud Apostoli, Ad Rom. 8:1: "Quae a Deo sunt, ordinata sunt." Cum ergo nihil aliud sit Dei providentia quam ratio ordinis rerum in finem, ut dictum est, necesse est omnia, inquantum participant esse, intantum subdi divinae providentiae."

50. Ibid. (ed. Ottawa 1.154b:44–155a:3): "Similiter etiam supra ostensum est quod Deus omnia cognoscit, et universalia et particularia. Et cum cognitio eius comparetur ad res sicut cognitio artis ad artificiata, ut supra dictum est, necesse est quod omnia supponantur suo ordini, sicut omnia artificiata subduntur ordini artis."

as says that the inference from natural finality to divine providence is like the inference that you would make from a well-designed home to the mind of its architect.[51]

The second argument for divine governance is based on divine goodness. Since it belongs to the best being to produce the best effects, it would be incompatible with God's perfect goodness for God to create things and then not guide them to completion. Now the perfection of anything is that it attain its end. Hence it pertains to the divine goodness that just as God produces the existence of things, he also guides them to the end, which is governance.[52]

In two replies to objections in this article, Thomas stresses the importance of natural finality as the primary premise for providence. In replying to the first objection—that what lacks knowledge of the end cannot be said to be governed—Thomas argues that things can act for an end in two different ways. The first is by actually knowing it, as in the case of rational creatures, who move themselves to their end. The second manner of acting for an end is be directed toward it by another, as an arrow finds its target according to the archer's knowing aim. So just as the flight of an arrow to its intended target demonstrates obviously that it has been directed by one having knowledge, so too does the certain course of natural things lacking knowledge manifestly declare that the world is governed by some rationality.[53]

In reply to the third objection—that what acts by virtue of natural necessity has no need of a ruler—Aquinas argues that the natural necessity inherent in things whereby they are determined to a particular end is a kind of impression of God's directing them to that end, as the determinate flight of an arrow is an impression of the archer's intelligent aim.

---

51. *ST* I, q. 103, a. 1 co. (ed. Ottawa 1.614b:44–48): "Ipse ordo certus rerum manifeste demonstrat gubernationem mundi, sicut si quis intraret domum bene ordinatam, ex ipsa domus ordinatione ordinatoris rationem perpenderet."

52. Ibid. (ed. Ottawa 1.614b:50–615a:8): "Secundo autem apparet ex consideratione divinae bonitatis, per quam res in esse productae sunt, ut ex supra dictis patet. Cum enim optimi sit optima producere, non convenit summae Dei bonitati quod res productas ad perfectum non perducat. Ultima autem perfectio est uniusquisque in consecutione finis. Unde ad divinam bonitatem pertinet, sicut produxit res in esse, ita etiam eas ad finem perducat. Quod est gubernare."

53. Ibid., ad 1 (ed. Ottawa 1.615a:19–25): "Unde sicut motus sagittae ad determinatum finem demonstrat aperte quod sagitta dirigitur ab aliquo cognoscente; ita certus cursus naturalium rerum cognitione carentium, manifeste declaret mundum ratione aliqua gubernari."

What differentiates natural things from an arrow, however, is that their very created natures are the principles whereby they aim at their ends. Hence the necessity found in natural creatures demonstrates governance by divine providence.[54]

DE SUBSTANTIIS SEPARATIS

Aquinas's last consideration of divine providence is found in *De substantiis separatis*.[55] In the context of having defended the view that God and separate substances have a knowledge of particulars, in chapter 14, Aquinas goes on in chapter 15 to argue for divine providence. The first argument begins with the claim that there is an order to be found whereby things subserve each other and are ordered to an end. But just as every existing thing is derived from the First Being who is identical with his existence, so too every good thing is derived from the First Good who is goodness itself. The order of individual things, which is identified as good, must therefore be derived from the first and pure truth. Whatever is derived from the First Being must accord with its own modality, however, which is an intelligible mode. Hence the meaning of providence is that an order be established by an intelligent being in the things that are subject to its providence.[56]

The second argument reasons from the premise that God is the First Unmoved Mover and, thus, the cause of all motion. In an essentially or-

54. Ibid., ad 3 (ed. Ottawa 1.35–50): "Dicendum quod necessitas naturalis inhaerens rebus quae determinatur ad unum, est impressio quaedam Dei diregentis ad finem; sicut necessitas qua sagitta agitur ut ad certum signum tendat, est impressio sagittantis, et non sagittae. Sed in hoc differt, quia id quod creaturae a Deo recipiunt, est earum natura; quod autem ab homine rebus naturalibus imprimitur praeter earum naturam, ad violentiam pertinet. Unde sicut necessitas violentiae in motu sagitae demonstrat sagittantis directionem, ita necessitas naturalis creaturarum demonstrat divinae providentiae gubernationem."

55. Torrell dates this work in early 1271.

56. Thomas Aquinas, *De substantiis separatis*, c. 15, *Editio Leonina* 40.67:3–19: "Sicut autem in divinam cognitionem necesse est secundum praemissa usque ad minima rerum extendere, ita necesse est divinae providentiae curam universa concludere. Invenitur enim in rebus omnibus bonum esse in ordine quodam secundum quod res sibi invicem subserviunt et ordinantur ad finem; necesse est autem sicut omne esse derivatur a primo ente quod est ipsum esse, ita omne bonum derivari a primo quod est ipsa bonitas: oportet igitur singulorum ordinem a prima et pura veritate derivari. A qua quidem aliquid derivatur secundum quod in eo est, per intelligibilem scilicet modum; in hoc autem ratio providentiae consistit quod ab aliquo intelligente statuatur ordo in rebus quae eius providentiae subsunt; necesse est igitur omnia divinae providentiae subiacere."

dered series of causes, the first cause is the cause of all causing in the subordinate causes. Thus God is more strongly the cause of all motion than is any individual cause of motion. Since God's causation must follow the mode of God's being, and since the mode of God's being is identical with *intelligere,* God moves things to their proper ends in an intelligent manner. Aquinas concludes that this is just what it means to provide; hence, all things fall under divine providence.[57]

The third argument is premised on God's goodness. Things must be ordered in the best manner because they are all dependent upon the highest goodness. Now it is better that they be ordered essentially rather than accidentally. Hence the entire universe must be ordered essentially. But if this is true, then the intention of the First Cause must include the very last members of the order of causes. For if the intention of the First Cause includes only the second cause, then the order of causes is no longer essential but rather accidental. Hence God's causal intention must extend to every being and, thus, all things fall under divine providence.[58]

Finally, Aquinas argues that what is common to both cause and effect is found more eminently in the cause from which the effect is derived. So whatever is found to exist in inferior causes must be attributed to the First Cause in a more excellent manner. Therefore God must be provident. The assumed premise here is that we find other causes acting intelligently for the sake of the end. The alternative, that everything happens by chance, is thus ruled out.[59]

---

57. Ibid. (ed. Leon. 40.67:20–34): "Adhuc, primum movens immobile quod Deus est omnium motionum principium est, sicut et primum ens est omnis esse principium; in causis autem per se ordinatis tanto aliquid magis est causa quanto in ordine causarum prior est, cum ipsa aliis conferat quod causae sint: Deus igitur omnium motionum vehementius causa est quam etiam singulares causae moventes. Non est autem alicuius causa Deus sicut intelligens, cum sua substantia sit suum intelligere, ut per supra posita Aristotilis verba patet; unumquodque autem agit per modum suae substantiae; Deus igitur per suum intellectum omnia movet ad proprios fines. Hoc autem est providere: omnia igitur divinae providentiae subsunt."

58. Ibid. (ed. Leon. 40.67:35–50): "Amplius, sic sunt res in universo dispositae sicut optimum est eas esse, eo quod omnia ex summa bonitate dependent; melius est autem aliqua esse ordinata per se quam quod per accidens ordinentur: est igitur totius universi ordo non per accidens sed per se. Hoc autem requiritur ad hoc quod aliqua per se ordinentur, quod primi intentio feratur usque ad ultimum; si enim primum intendat secundum movere et eius intentio ulterius non feratur, secundum vero movet tertium, hoc erit praeter intentionem primi moventis; erit igitur talis ordo per accidens. Oportet igitur quod primi moventis et ordinantis intentio, scilicet Dei, non solum usque ad quaedam entium procedat sed usque ad ultima; omni igitur eius providentiae subsunt."

59. Ibid. (ed. Leon. 40.68:51–58): "Item, quod causae et effectui convenit eminentius in-

CONCLUSION

By now it should be abundantly clear that Aquinas does indeed think that it is possible to demonstrate philosophically that the world is governed by divine providence. In assessing his arguments, I would make the following distinction. It is one thing to argue for the existence of a provident God, and it is another to argue that God must be provident based on the already established existence of God with logically prior attributes.

We have seen Aquinas do both in the course of examining his writings throughout his career. On some occasions he argues a posteriori for divine providence on the basis of natural teleology. In so doing, he is essentially mounting a teleological argument for the existence of God, and we have seen some passages that come very close to the argument of the Fifth Way in the *Summa theologiae*. When we observe noncognitive agents acting in a consistent manner to achieve a perfective state suitable to their species, and in so acting contribute to the good of other natures as part of a larger order, the only reasonable inference is to the existence of an intelligent and provident God. For Aquinas, the only alternative to positing the existence of an overarching intelligence is the appeal to chance, which for him, and for Aristotle, is really no explanation at all. Whether this appeal to finality is still a valid starting point today is, of course, a much-debated question.[60]

That is why it is important to note that Aquinas thinks you can also demonstrate divine providence based on appeals to various divine perfections that can be established on other arguments for the existence of God. We have seen him begin arguments for divine providence based on God as First Mover, First Efficient Cause, Creator, the perfect source of goodness, and omniscient. In the *De substantiis separatis* we see an appeal to two legs of the *triplex via:* whatever is found in an effect must preexist in a more eminent manner in its cause. Once the existence of God is established on grounds other than the finality of nature, Aquinas believes that the logic of divine perfection entails providence. Perfect goodness and perfect wisdom require that once God freely decides to create, it

---

venitur in causa quam in effectu, a causa enim in effectum derivatur; quicquid igitur in inferioribus causis existens primae omnium causae attribuitur excellentissime convenit ei. Opertet autem aliquam providentiam Deo attribuere, alioquin universum casu ageretur; oportet igitur divinam providentiam perfectissumum esse."

60. On the viability of the fifth way, see Wippel, *Metaphysical Thought*, 480–85.

is impossible for him not to take care of his creatures and to order them to their ends.

The kind of providence that philosophers attribute to God is not to be confused with what believers hold about divine providence. In the passages noted by Wippel, where Aquinas appears to be saying that divine providence and divine omnipotence are objects of faith rather than demonstrable philosophical truths, Aquinas is taking those terms to mean what believers mean by those terms. In the *Summa theologiae* Aquinas defines belief in divine providence to include "all those things that God arranges in history for the sake of human salvation that make up our way to beatitude."[61]

So when he goes on in the next article to say that "by faith we hold to many truths about God that philosophers could not investigate through natural reason, such as providence and omnipotence,"[62] he does not mean that philosophers could not know anything about divine providence, but rather that they could not come to know the deepest meaning of divine providence as revealed to faith in the triune God's loving plan of salvation. The philosopher can know that "there is a divinity that shapes our ends, rough hew them how we will." But the deepest hewing of history, the hewing of the Cross, escapes the philosopher's ken. There is nothing in the finality of nature or even in the logic of divine perfection that discloses the breadth and depth of the loving plan of providence for our salvation. That is the object of belief, not proof. What the ancient Greeks were talking about in the debate between teleology and chance was never confused by Aquinas with Jesus's musings over sparrows or with Paul's meditation on providence in Romans 8. And as long as we remember the difference ourselves, we can both *know* that God is provident and *believe* that God is provident. Thus, by the providence of God, we can save Thomas Aquinas from the horror of a contradiction.

---

61. *ST* II-II, q. 1, a. 7 co. (ed. Ottawa 3.1408a:10–13): "In fide autem providentiae includuntur omnia quae temporaliter a Deo dispensantur ad hominem salutem, quae sunt via in beatitudinem."

62. Ibid., a. 8, ad 1 (ed. Ottawa 3.1410a:9–15): "Dicendum quod multa per tenemus de Deo quae naturali ratione investigare philosophi non potuerunt, puta circa providentiam eius et omnipotentiam, et quod ipse solus sit colendus. Quae omnia continentur sub articulo unitatis Dei."

11 ✑ Eternity, Simplicity, and Presence

The doctrine of omnipresence implies that each point of space is equally *here* for God. On the doctrine, God is present to all places and to all persons. But what is it for God to be present? What is it for human persons to have God present to them? What does this presentness consist in?

Biblical stories portray God as personally present to human beings in the way in which one person is present to another, but in an especially powerful way. In Genesis, for example, Abraham hears God calling his name and responds with instant recognition of God. Abraham knows God when God calls, and God is present to Abraham then. When Rebecca is perplexed about what she feels happening in her womb, the text says that Rebecca went to inquire of God. She found God present to her when she turned to him, and that is why she asked him the question troubling her.[1] In these and many other biblical stories, there is a strong connection of some sort between God and a human person who finds God personally present to him or her. The ultimate expression in the Old Testament of a human being's experiencing God as present to him in this way is found in one of Job's last lines to God, when Job tells God: I had heard of you by the hearing of the ear, but now my own eye has seen you.[2] Job not only experiences something he describes as seeing God, but he acknowledges that experience in terms of second-person address to God. God's personal presence to Job is what Job is trying to express.

---

1. For the story of Abraham, see Genesis 12–23. For this episode in Rebecca's life, see Genesis 25:22.

2. Job 42:5.

A similar point about God's presence to human beings can be found also in the New Testament in stories about Jesus. When Philip asks Jesus to show God the Father to the disciples, Jesus tells Philip that in seeing Jesus Philip is seeing God. The personal presence of Jesus to Philip is apparently somehow also the personal presence of God to Philip. That is why Jesus maintains that, in knowing Jesus, his disciples are also knowing God.[3]

Biblical stories in both the Old and the New Testaments, then, portray God as able to be known directly and immediately by human beings and as able to be personally present to them.

This portrayal is in sharp contrast to the theological picture sometimes thought to be entailed by the doctrines of divine eternity and simplicity. In fact, some philosophers and theologians have rejected these doctrines, basic in the medieval Christian tradition, just because they suppose that these doctrines undermine or overturn the biblical portrayal of God's relations with human beings.[4] If God is eternal and so timeless, then in the view of the objectors to the doctrine of God's eternity God cannot be present to human beings, because human beings are in time. And if God is simple, then in the view of the objectors to the doctrine of God's simplicity God is unknowable by human beings; and because God is incomprehensible to human knowledge, God cannot be personally present to human beings either. One major reason for the rejection of the doctrines of eternity and simplicity on the part of some philosophers and theologians is therefore that they take these doctrines to imply a religiously pernicious disconnection between God and human beings.

In this chapter, I will argue that these doctrines have no such implication. I will begin by looking more carefully at what it is for persons to be present to one another. Then I will consider and argue against an attempt to show that the doctrine of divine eternity rules out such personal presence between God and human beings. Next, I will consider the challenge posed by the doctrine of divine simplicity. I will give reasons for thinking that the doctrine of divine simplicity does not in fact entail

---

3. John 14:8–9.

4. For one example of this sort of position, see Howard Wettstein, "Against Theology," in *Philosophers and the Hebrew Bible,* ed. Charles Manekin and Robert Eisen (College Park: University Press of Maryland, 2008), 219–45.

the agnosticism frequently associated with it. I will also argue, however, that there is another kind of knowledge of God, which is compatible with the doctrine of simplicity even if, contrary to my arguments, that doctrine did imply a kind of agnosticism about God's nature. In my view, this alternative kind of knowledge of God is sufficient for God's being personally present to human beings in the way the biblical stories describe. Finally, I will show that Thomas Aquinas, one of the main medieval proponents of the doctrines of divine eternity and divine simplicity, recognizes this alternative kind of knowledge of God and supposes it is available to all Christians in this life.

For all these reasons, I will claim, neither the doctrine of eternity nor the doctrine of simplicity rules out God's being personally present to human beings.

PERSONAL PRESENCE

What is it for one person to be present to another? In an earlier work, Norman Kretzmann and I tried to capture the relation of one person's being personally present to another in terms of one person's having direct and unmediated causal contact with and cognitive access to another.[5] I now think, however, that the attempt to capture personal presence in terms of direct and unmediated cognitive and causal contact misses something in the sense of personal presence even as between human beings. Consider, for example, one person, Paula, who is blind and falls over another person, Jerome, when he is unconscious in her path. Paula may cause Jerome to be moved by falling over him; and she may know by touch that it is a human person she has fallen over. Paula will thus have direct and unmediated causal and cognitive connection with Jerome; but she is not present to Jerome, in any normal sense of personal presence, in consequence of falling over him while he is unconscious.

5. Eleonore Stump and Norman Kretzmann, "Eternity, Awareness, and Action," *Faith and Philosophy* 9 (1992): 463–82. By "direct and unmediated" in this context, I mean only that the cognitive access or the causal connection does not have as an intermediate step the agency of another person; I do not mean that there is no intermediary of any sort. In this sense of "direct and unmediated," if I am wearing my glasses when I see a person, I still have direct and unmediated cognitive access to him; and if I am on the phone with him when I cause him grief by telling him that his mother has died, I am still exercising direct and unmediated causality on him.

What has to be added to the condition of direct and unmediated causal and cognitive contact for personal presence, I now think, is something psychologists call "shared attention." This is a cognitive state hard to define precisely but very familiar to us. Mutual gaze is one means for mediating a primary kind of shared attention; but there are many other kinds as well. Even newborn infants can exercise what seems to be an inborn capacity for shared attention. A newborn infant is capable of discriminating persons as persons, and the infant is also able to be aware of his mother's awareness of the infant. By two months of age, an infant can even exercise some control over shared attention. It can turn its face away, for example, and so avert mutual gaze with another person. The mutual awareness brought about by mutual gaze is a particularly powerful kind of shared attention. Psychologists call this "dyadic shared attention." But it is also possible for shared attention to be triadic. When a baby points out a dog to his mother, gazing alternately at the dog and at his mother, who is looking at the dog with him, then there is what psychologists call "triadic shared attention" between them.

In each of the biblical stories I mentioned at the outset, shared attention between God and a human person is a notable feature of the story. God says to Abraham, "Abraham, Abraham!" and Abraham replies, "Here I am." This conversation does not communicate information between God and Abraham so much as it establishes shared attention between them. When Rebecca turns to God in order to ask God a question, the point of the turning seems just to put her in a position to share attention with God before asking God her question. And when Job says to God, now my own eye sees you, he is using words to enhance what vision itself has somehow established for him: personal presence based on shared attention. This shared attention, mediated by hearing or even by some kind of seeing (as in Job's case), is a critical element in the personal presence of God to a human person in the biblical stories.

By contrast, consider, for example, Homer's depiction of Zeus. Wherever in physical reality he is, Homer's Zeus has direct and unmediated causal connection with the Trojans and also direct and unmediated cognitive access to them. That is, Zeus knows directly and immediately what is happening to the Trojans in the fighting with the Greeks, say, and he can affect the way the fighting goes just by willing it. But Zeus can continue to have such cognitive and causal contact with the Trojans even when he is (as Homer sometimes says) having dinner with the Ethiopians, for instance. While Zeus is among the Ethiopians, however, he is not present at but absent from the scene of the Greek and Trojan war. So although Zeus has direct and unmediated causal and cognitive connection with the Trojans even while he is among the Ethiopians, he is not present to the Trojans then. Although he can affect and know the Trojans when he is in Ethiopia, Zeus cannot share attention with them when he is at that distance from them. While he is in Ethiopia, his power is present to the Trojans, we might say, but Zeus himself is not present to them. For this reason, Zeus is not omnipresent, even if he can know and control things at a distance from himself.

So for personal presence, not only does there have to be direct and unmediated causal and cognitive contact between persons, but there has to be the practical possibility of shared attention as well. Mutatis mutandis, the same point applies also to God. For real omnipresence, as distinct from mere power at a distance such as Homer's Zeus has, it needs to be the case that God is in a position to share attention with any human person able and willing to share attention with God.

In the example in which a blind Paula falls over unconscious Jerome in her path, Jerome is not present to Paula primarily because, in virtue of being unconscious, Jerome is not available to share attention with Paula. But shared attention can be ruled out for other reasons besides unconsciousness. As the example of Zeus among the Ethiopians makes clear, for knowers other than omnipresent God, physical distance can undermine shared attention.[6] There is also psychological distance, and it is at least as important an obstacle to personal presence as physical distance. If Jerome is in the same room as Paula but is totally absorbed in his work, for example, and never looks up at Paula or speaks to her, she will feel rightly that he is not present to her on that occasion. Or if Jerome is habitually secretive and self-absorbed, so that Paula is entirely shut out of his inner life, Jerome will not be present to Paula. The absence of psychological closeness undermines or obviates shared attention, and therefore vitiates or prevents personal presence, too.

---

6. On the other hand, perception is not necessary for shared attention. The Internet, for example, can make shared attention even among people who are at some distance from each other. Two people engaged in animated discussion with each other by means of a computer are sharing attention as much as two people talking together on the telephone.

It is not possible to examine the notions of psychological distance or closeness in detail here;[7] but however exactly we understand these notions, it is clear that there will be psychological distance between persons if the mind of one of the persons in the relationship is hidden from the other. Distance of this sort can be a function of difference of abilities. If Jerome's chief work and chief joy is music, for example, but Paula is tone-deaf and musically illiterate, then Jerome will not be able to share attention with Paula in the part of his life that involves music. The distance resulting from this absence of shared attention between them will keep Jerome from being present to Paula, at least where the part of his life involving music is concerned. As an extreme of this sort of case, imagine that Jerome is incomprehensible to Paula, not just in his music making and music listening but in every way, entirely. In that case, the relationship between Paula and Jerome would be like the relationship between a dolphin and a human being who cross paths. A dolphin and a human being are each members of an intelligent species, but there will typically be little or no shared attention between them when they interact. Insofar as shared attention is necessary for personal presence, then to the extent to which Jerome is unknowable to Paula, to that extent he is not present to Paula either.

These conclusions obviously make a difference to the question of whether an eternal and simple deity can be personally present to human beings. And so, with this much reflection on the idea of personal presence, we can turn to the complaint that the doctrines of eternity and simplicity rule out personal presence between God and human beings.

THE DOCTRINE OF GOD'S ETERNITY

It is easiest to begin with the doctrine of God's eternity.

In *Summa contra Gentiles* I, c. 15, Aquinas describes God's eternity this way: "God is entirely without motion. . . . Therefore, he is not measured by time . . . nor can any succession be found in his being . . . [Rather, he has] his being all at once (*totum simul*)—in which the formula of eternity consists."

---

7. For detailed discussion of these notions, see my "Presence and Omnipresence," in *Liberal Faith: Essays in Honor of Philip Quinn*, ed. Paul Weithman (Notre Dame, Ind.: University of Notre Dame Press, 2008), pp. 59–82.

In *Summa theologiae* (hereafter *ST*) I, q. 10, a.1, Aquinas cites the combination of illimitability and the lack of succession as the heart of the concept of eternity. As he explains there,[8] "Two things make eternity known: first, the fact that what is in eternity is interminable, that is, lacking beginning and end (since 'term' refers to both); second, the fact that eternity lacks succession, since it exists all at once."

In *ST* I, q. 10, a. 2, Aquinas argues that God is his own duration; and in *ST* I, q. 10, a. 2, ad 2, he explains that God endures beyond all ages (*durat ultra quodcumque saeculum*). These passages, combined with the preceding text, make it clear that the interminability of God's existence is to be understood as the interminability of unending duration of some sort, rather than as the interminability of a point or instant.[9] It is evident from these texts and others as well that the concept of eternity as Aquinas accepts it is the concept of a life without succession but with infinite atemporal persistence or atemporal duration, where "duration" is understood analogically with temporal duration.

There has been considerable debate in the secondary literature about the coherence of the doctrine of divine eternity. What is of interest to me here, however, is not the objection that the doctrine is incoherent but rather only the complaint that the doctrine is religiously pernicious because it rules out God's being present to human beings, contrary to the portrayal of God in the biblical stories.

One person who has argued that if God is not temporal but eternal, then God cannot be present to human beings is William Hasker.[10] Hasker's argument for this position depends on a claim that I will call "Hasker's principle":

8. For purposes of this chapter, I have used the Marietti editions. Apart from the specific texts noted explicitly in the footnotes, the translations are my own. In the case of texts in *ST,* my translations are informed by the excellent translation of the Fathers of the English Dominican Province.

9. Cf. also *ST* I, q. 39, a. 8, obj. 1 and co.; *ST* I, q. 46, a. 1, obj. 8 and ad 8. In *ST* I, q. 10, a. 4, the first objection takes as a premise the claim that eternity, like time, is a measure of duration; in the reply to the objection, Aquinas disputes only the assumption that time and eternity are the same kind of measure of duration, not that eternity is a measure of duration. In *ST* I, q. 10, a. 4, ad 3, this point is developed. In that reply, Aquinas maintains that time as a measure of duration is the measure of motion, whereas eternity as a measure of duration is the measure of permanent being.

10. William Hasker, *God, Time, and Knowledge* (Ithaca, N.Y.: Cornell University Press, 1989); cf. especially 169. For more discussion of Hasker's argument and others related to it, see the chapter on eternity in my *Aquinas* (London: Routledge, 2003).

(Hasker's principle): To be present to temporal beings requires being temporal oneself.

Aquinas himself does not accept Hasker's principle. On the contrary, Aquinas tends to emphasize that the temporal things an eternal God knows are present to God in his knowing of them. So, for example, Aquinas claims that God's eternal gaze views future events "present-ly" (*praesentialiter*).[11] On Aquinas's view, God knows future contingent things in the same way he knows everything in time, namely, insofar as future contingent things are present to God.[12]

In addition to the many passages in which Aquinas talks about God's knowledge of temporal things as gaze or sight, or some other divine analogue of a kind of direct awareness, there are also many passages in which Aquinas expresses forcefully his sense that (eternal) God is personally present to (temporal) human beings. For example, in his commentary on Galatians, in discussing the relation of eternal God to human persons, Aquinas says, "the ultimate perfection, by which a person is made perfect inwardly, is joy, which stems from the presence of what is loved. Whoever has the love of God, however, already has what he loves, as is said in 1 John 4:16: 'whoever abides in the love of God abides in God, and God abides in him.' And joy wells up from this."[13]

Aquinas develops the same idea in discussing the mission of an eternal divine person. In that context, Aquinas says:

There is one general way by which God is in all things by essence, power, and presence, [namely,] as a cause in the effects participating in his goodness. But in addition to this way there is a special way [in which God is in a thing by essence, power, and presence] which is appropriate for a rational creature, in whom God is said to be as the thing known is in the knower and the beloved is in the lover. . . . In this special way, God is not only said to be in a rational creature but even to dwell in that creature.[14]

So Aquinas does not suppose that being present to something temporal requires being temporal oneself. On the contrary, on Aquinas's un-

11. *Quaestiones disputatae de veritate*, q. 12, a. 6 co.
12. *ST* I, q. 14, a. 13.
13. *In Gal* 5.6. There is an English translation of this work: *Commentary on Saint Paul's Epistle to the Galatians by St. Thomas Aquinas*, trans. Fabian Larcher and Richard Murphy (Albany, N.Y.: Magi Books, 1966); for this passage, see 179–80. I have used my own translation here.
14. *ST* I. q. 43, a. 3.

derstanding of the nature of divine eternity, an eternal God can be more present to a human person than any temporal being could be. The one, infinitely enduring present of eternity is simultaneous with each moment of time as that time is present. Since that is so, each moment of the life of a human person is always present at once to eternal God. By contrast, when Paula is present to Jerome in her middle age, her childhood is past and gone, and her old age is not yet here. What Jerome has present to him of Paula's life is only the temporally thinnest part, that part which is temporally present *now*; and he has this part available to him only instant by instant. By contrast, God has present to him, all at once, the whole of Paula's life.

Aquinas would therefore reject Hasker's principle. And, in my view, he would be right to do so. Hasker's principle can be generalized in this way:[15]

(General Principle): One person can be present to other things or persons only if he shares their mode of existence with them.

But this general principle is not true. If the general principle were true, it would follow from it that a nonspatial God could not be present to spatial beings. But virtually no serious theologian would accept such a claim; presumably Hasker himself would not be willing to accept it. If the general principle is unacceptable as applied to space, however, why should we suppose that it is acceptable as applied to time? If God can be present to his creatures without sharing their *spatial* mode of existence,[16] why should we not suppose that God can be present to his creatures without sharing their *temporal* mode of existence?

THE DOCTRINE OF GOD'S SIMPLICITY

Even if the complaint as regards the doctrine of divine eternity could be dispatched in this way, however, there is a worse problem raised by the

15. Hasker disputes the claim that his principle can be generalized in this way in "The Absence of a Timeless God," in *God and Time: Essays on the Divine Nature*, ed. Greg Ganssle and David Woodruff (New York: Oxford University Press, 2002), pp. 182–206. But Hasker's argument is effectively refuted by Thomas Senor, "The Real Presence of an Eternal God," in *Metaphysics and God*, ed. Kevin Timpe (New York: Routledge, 2009), 39–59; and so I will not deal with it further here.

16. Consider relationships of direct awareness in which the subject and object are of different orders of dimensionality. A three-dimensional observer can be and very frequently is effortlessly aware of a two-dimensional object as such; an imagined two-dimensional observer could not be aware of a three-dimensional object as three-dimensional.

doctrine of divine simplicity. It seems that an eternal, *simple* God could not be personally present to human beings even if an eternal nonsimple God could be.

The doctrine of divine simplicity is perhaps the most difficult and controversial piece of medieval philosophical theology but also one of the most important.[17] It derives from the conviction that God is a being whose existence is self-explanatory, an absolutely perfect being.[18] Aquinas was among the most influential expositors and defenders of this doctrine. But Aquinas is often enough interpreted as holding the view that, because of the doctrine of simplicity, it is not possible for human beings to have any positive knowledge of God. On this interpretation of Aquinas's views, Aquinas maintains that because God is simple, human beings can know what God is *not*, but they cannot know anything of what God is. This is sometimes thought to be the heart of the *via negativa* in theology.

Aquinas puts a discussion of God's simplicity near the beginning of his treatment of the nature of God in the *Summa theologiae*,[19] and he begins that discussion with a short prologue. In the prologue, he says:

> When we know with regard to something *that* it is, we still need to ask about its mode of being [*quomodo sit*], in order to know with regard to it what it is [*quid sit*]. But because we are not able to know with regard to God what he is, but [rather] what he is not, we cannot consider with regard to God what the mode of being is but rather what the mode of being is not. . . . It can be shown with regard to God what the mode of being is not by removing from him those things not appropriate to him, such as composition and motion and other things of this sort.

This passage and others like it have sometimes been pressed into service as evidence for a thoroughgoing agnosticism on Aquinas's part with

17. This doctrine has also been the subject of a voluminous literature. The most sustained and sophisticated attack on Aquinas's position can be found in Christopher Hughes, *A Complex Theory of a Simple God* (Ithaca, N.Y.: Cornell University Press, 1989). Hughes's attack, however, seems to me based on misunderstandings of crucial elements of Aquinas's metaphysics, as reviewers have pointed out (see, for example, David B. Burrell, *Journal of Religion* 72, no. 1 [Jan. 1992]: 120–21), and so I will not consider it here.

18. The derivation of divine simplicity from such considerations is apparent in Aquinas's *Quaestiones disputatae de potentia*, 7, a. 1, as Mark D. Jordan has recently pointed out in his article "The Names of God and the Being of Names" in *The Existence and Nature of God*, ed. Alfred J. Freddoso (Notre Dame, Ind.: University of Notre Dame Press, 1983), 161–90; see esp. 176–79.

19. *ST* I, q. 3.

regard to knowledge of God. So, for example, Leo Elders says, "The comprehension of God's essence is altogether excluded. This conclusion is presupposed in the Prologue to the Third Question. . . . Even if we say that God is perfect, good or eternal, we must realize that we do not know what these terms mean when predicated of God."[20]

But caution is warranted here. It is true that Aquinas explains divine simplicity only in terms of what God is not—not a body, not composed of matter and form, and so on. On the other hand, however, in the course of showing what God is not, Aquinas relies heavily on positive claims about God. So, for example, Aquinas argues that God is not a body on the basis of these claims among others: God is the first mover; God is pure actuality; God is the first being; God is the most noble of beings. In arguing that God is not composed of matter and form, Aquinas actually makes a huge substantial positive metaphysical claim about the nature of God. He says, "a form which is not able to be received in matter but is subsistent by itself [*per se subsistens*] is individuated in virtue of the fact that it cannot be received in something else. And God is a form of this sort."[21]

In fact, in *ST* I, q. 13, Aquinas repudiates the sort of agnosticism some scholars in effect attribute to him. Aquinas himself associates such a position with Moses Maimonides and rejects it explicitly. Elsewhere Aquinas bluntly denies the view that human beings can have no positive knowledge of God. In *Quaestiones disputatae de potentia*, q. 7, a. 5, for example, he says, "the understanding of a negation is always based on some affirmation. And this is clear from the fact that every negation is proved by an affirmation. For this reason, unless the human intellect knew something affirmatively about God, it would be unable to deny anything of God."

These texts and others like them strongly suggest that it is a mistake to read the prologue to *ST* I, q. 3, as implying agnosticism with regard to the knowledge of God.

How, then, are we to understand that prologue? I am inclined to think that part of the problem in interpreting Aquinas's remarks in the prologue correctly has to do with the expression *quid est* in the text that claims that we do not know of God *quid est* (that is, *what he is*).[22]

The expression *quid est* is a technical term of medieval logic. Peter of

---

20. Leo Elders, *The Philosophical Theology of St. Thomas Aquinas* (Leiden: E. J. Brill, 1990), 143.

21. *ST* I, q. 3, a. 2, ad 3.

22. See, in this connection, particularly *Summa contra Gentiles* I, c. 14.

Spain, for example, gives the standard medieval formula for a genus as "that which is predicated of many things differing in species in respect of what they are (*in eo quod quid est*)." In the terms of this technical understanding of *quid est* in medieval logic, it is certainly possible for someone who does not know the *quid est* of a thing nonetheless to know a great deal even about the essence of that thing. The differentia of a thing is also part of its essence, but the differentia is *not* predicated *in eo quod quid est*. So whatever exactly *quid est* means in Aquinas's thought, in the terms of medieval logic Aquinas's claim that we cannot know with regard to God *quid est* does not *by itself* imply that we can know nothing positive about God. On the contrary, the claim that we cannot know the *quid est* of God is apparently compatible in Aquinas's own mind with the many positive claims he makes about God. In examining Aquinas's understanding of the doctrine of divine simplicity, therefore, we should not simply assume on the basis of the prologue to the question on simplicity in *ST* that Aquinas has adopted a thoroughgoing agnosticism as regards human knowledge of God's nature.

In addition, however, it is also important in this connection to note what a human knower *would* have, on Aquinas's views, if he did indeed grasp the *quid est* of a thing, any thing, including God. To see this, we need to remember something of Aquinas's philosophical psychology.

Aquinas thinks that the proper object of the intellect is the *quid est* or *quiddity* of a thing. Just as the external senses have their proper objects, such as color, for example, so the intellect also has its proper object; the intellect apprehends quiddities as the eyes apprehend colors.[23] Aquinas calls the simple acts of cognition by which the intellect grasps the *quid est* of things "the cognition of non-complexes." This is what he thinks of as "the first operation of the intellect," and it is the foundation for propositional knowledge.[24] The second operation of the intellect is what Aquinas calls "compounding and dividing." Composition or division occurs when the intellect combines its apprehension of quiddities or divides them to form affirmative or negative "complexes" or propositional judgments.[25] These judgments are then available to the knower to use in discursive reasoning, which is the third operation of the intellect.

---

23. *ST* I, q. 85, a. 8.

24. For detailed discussion of this part of Aquinas's thought, see the section on the mechanisms of cognition in my *Aquinas*.

25. See, for example, *Sentencia libri De anima* III, lect. 11, nn. 746–60.

So when a person does have knowledge of the *quid est* of a thing, that knowledge is the first element in propositional knowledge and propositional reasoning.

THE KNOWLEDGE OF PERSONS

It is important to see, however, that propositional knowledge is not the only kind of knowledge possible for human beings. There is a different kind of knowledge available to human beings that is not reducible to knowledge *that* something or other is the case, and it does not depend on the grasp of the quiddity of a thing.

To get some intuitive feel for this nonpropositional knowledge of persons, imagine a woman, Mary, who has been kept in an isolated imprisonment since birth by some mad scientist. Imagine that Mary, in her imprisonment, has had access to any and all information about the world that can be transmitted in terms of propositions.[26] So, for example, Mary has available to her the best science texts for any of the sciences, from physics to sociology. She knows that there are other people in the world, and she knows all that science can teach her about them. But she has never had any personal interactions of a direct and unmediated sort with another person. She has read descriptions of human faces, for example, but she has never been face-to-face with another person.[27] And then suppose that Mary is finally rescued from her imprisonment and united for the first time with her mother, who loves her deeply.

When Mary is first united with her mother, it seems indisputable that Mary will know things she did not know before, even if she knew everything about her mother that could be made available to her in expository prose.[28] Although Mary knew that her mother loved her before she met

26. I am here adapting Frank Jackson's original thought experiment. For this thought experiment and the extensive discussion it has generated, see Peter Ludlow, Yujin Nagasawa, and Daniel Stoljar, eds., *There's Something about Mary. Essays on Phenomenal Consciousness and Frank Jackson's Knowledge Argument* (Cambridge, Mass.: MIT Press, Bradford Book, 2004).

27. More than one person has suggested to me that if Mary had been kept from all second-person experiences, she could not have learned a language, and she would be unable to read. But this objection seems to me insufficiently imaginative. We can suppose that Mary has been raised in a sophisticated environment in which carefully programmed computers taught her to speak and to read.

28. Nicholas Wolterstorff has suggested to me in correspondence that if Mary had had the requisite sort of experience of personal interaction before her period of isolation, then it would have been possible to communicate to her in the expository prose of a third-person ac-

her, when she is united with her mother, Mary will learn what it is like to be loved. And this will be new for her, even if in her isolated state she had as complete a scientific description as possible of what a human being feels like when she senses that she is loved by someone else. Furthermore, it is clear that this is only the beginning. Mary will also come to know what it is like to be touched by someone else, to be surprised by someone else, to ascertain someone else's mood, to detect affect in the melody of someone else's voice, to match thought for thought in conversation, and so on. These will be things she learns, even if before she had access to excellent books on human psychology and communication.

The way in which I have formulated what Mary learns—what it is like to be touched by someone else, and so on—may suggest to someone that Mary learns things just about herself, and that she learns them in virtue of having new first-person experiences. It seems, then, that whatever Mary learns can be explained adequately in terms of a first-person account.[29] But this is clearly wrongheaded. Even if Mary does learn new things about herself, what will come as the major revelation to Mary is *her mother*. Even this way of putting what Mary learns is misleading, because it suggests that Mary's new knowledge can be expressed in a third-person description of her mother. But neither first-person nor third-person accounts will be adequate for Mary to describe what is new for her. What is new for her, what she learns, has to do with her personal interaction with another person. What is new for Mary is a second-person experience.

This thought experiment thus shows that we can come to know a person and that this knowledge is difficult or impossible to formulate in terms of propositional knowledge.[30] The kind of knowledge at issue

---

count what personal interaction with her mother would be like. On this view, the difficulty in communicating to Mary by a third-person account the nature of a second-person experience with her mother is just a function of Mary's innocence of second-person experiences. But I am inclined to think this diagnosis of Mary's difficulty is not correct. In ordinary circumstances involving persons socialized in the usual way, it remains true that when we meet a person for the first time, we learn something important that we did not know before we met that person, even if before the meeting we were given an excellent and detailed third-person account of that person.

29. Although insofar as some of what is at issue for Mary in the relevant first-person experiences has to do with qualia, it may be that what she knows in that first-person experience is *also* not expressible in terms of knowing *that*.

30. In correspondence, Al Plantinga has suggested to me that I am here in fact explaining in expository prose what it is that Mary learns, namely, what it is like to be loved by her moth-

in the thought experiment about Mary is only the beginning of the examples of such nonpropositional knowledge. To take one more example, consider this sentence:

(1) Joseph saw his brothers in the crowd and knew them at once.

What is at issue in this sentence is Joseph's knowledge of the men before him, and so what is known in this case, we might suppose, is paradigmatically expressible in propositional form, in terms of knowledge *that*. This sentence is equivalent, we might think, to

(1′) Joseph knew *that* the men he saw in front of him in the crowd were his brothers.

It is true that in the recognition scene in Genesis Joseph does know *that* the men in front of him are his brothers, but this is not the same as seeing the men in front of him and knowing them as his brothers. Joseph might have known the identity of the men in front of him in any number of ways, but the sense of the first sentence is that Joseph knew their identity in virtue of knowing *them*, by face recognition, among other things.

It is clear that the brain of a normally functioning human being has the capacity to know a face, and it is equally clear that it is extremely difficult, if not impossible, to translate the knowledge conveyed by the sight of a particular face into a description of that face. As far as that goes, it is possible for one person, Paula, to see and describe appropriately the face of another person, Jerome, and yet *not* know Jerome in virtue of knowing his face, even though Jerome is a person otherwise familiar to Paula. In the neurological debility of prosopagnosia, a patient can see a face and describe it adequately, but on the basis of that perception alone the patient is unable to know the person whose face she is perceiving, however well acquainted she is with that person. By contrast, a normally functioning human being has the ability to identify a person on the basis of swift and reliable face recognition.

And so knowledge of a person on the basis of face recognition is an-

---

er, and so on. But that some sort of description of what Mary learns is possible does not mean that we can explain what Mary learns adequately with an expository account. Consider, for example, that while it is possible to describe the experience of seeing red to a person who has been blind from birth by saying that when a sighted person sees a red object, she knows what it is like to see red, this description is not an adequate explanation in expository prose of what the sighted person knows in knowing what it is like to see red.

other example of knowledge that is difficult or impossible to translate into propositional knowledge.

The rapid, perplexing increase in the incidence of autism has led scientists and philosophers to a deeper understanding of the knowledge of persons and a new appreciation for its importance in normal human functioning. Various studies have demonstrated that the knowledge that is impaired for an autistic child cannot be taken as knowledge *that* something or other is the case. An autistic child can know *that* a particular macroscopic object is her mother or *that* the person who is her mother has a certain mental state. But the autistic child can know such things without the knowledge that a normally developing child would have. For example, an autistic child might know that his mother is sad, but in virtue of the impairment of autism he will not be able to know the sadness of his mother. And these are different items of knowledge. An autistic child might know that the person he is looking at is sad because, for example, someone who is a reliable authority for the child has told him so. But this is clearly not the same as the child's knowing the sadness in the face of the person he is looking at.[31]

In these cases, and in many other cases of perfectly ordinary human experience, it is arguable that it is not possible to express adequately what is known in terms of propositional knowing. Rather, it is a knowledge of persons.

Mutatis mutandis, the same distinction applies where God is concerned. Consider, for example, these two claims:

(2) Thomas Aquinas knew that God is really present in the Eucharist.

and

(2′) Thomas Aquinas knew the real presence of God in the Eucharist.

These are clearly not equivalent claims, and the second cannot be reduced to the first. Obviously, the first could be true and the second could be false. Or consider this pair of claims:

(3) Thomas Aquinas knew that God exists.

31. See Derek Moore, Peter Hobson, and Anthony Lee, "Components of Person Perception: An Investigation With Autistic, Non-autistic Retarded and Typically Developing Children and Adolescents," *British Journal of Developmental Psychology* 15 (1997): 401–23.

and

(3′) Thomas Aquinas knew God.

Here, too, the claims are not equivalent, and the second cannot be reduced to the first. In both these cases, what is at issue in the first sentence is propositional knowledge, and what is at issue in the second is the knowledge of persons with regard to God.

KNOWLEDGE AND PRESENCE

No doubt, propositional knowledge of another person can deepen and enrich the knowledge of persons, at least among adult human beings. Nothing in the claims I have made about the importance of the knowledge of persons should be taken to imply a discounting of propositional knowledge of persons. But for shared attention between two persons, and for the personal presence of one of them to the other that shared attention provides, the knowledge of persons is sufficient. That is why, no matter how much propositional knowledge of her mother the Mary of the thought experiment might have in her isolated condition, she cannot share attention with her mother or have her mother present to her without having the knowledge of persons of her mother.

What *undermines* personal presence, therefore, is not missing propositional knowledge. It is rather an absence of the knowledge of persons. As far as I can see, however, there is nothing about the doctrine of simplicity that rules out knowledge of persons with respect to God. Obviously, in the human case, it is possible for one person to have such knowledge of another even if he has little or no propositional knowledge with regard to that other person. Jerome can know Paula with the knowledge of persons without having much if any propositional knowledge about her. What the doctrine of simplicity rules out explicitly, however, is just propositional knowledge of the *quid est* of God.

So even if, contrary to what I have argued, the doctrine of simplicity gave us reason for accepting a general sort of agnosticism about God, that agnosticism would have to do only with propositional knowledge. The knowledge of persons with respect to God would still be available.

AQUINAS'S POSITION

Someone might suppose that whether or not this conclusion, informed by contemporary science and philosophical thought experiments, is right, it is nonetheless thoroughly anti-Thomistic. But this would be a mistaken supposition. In many places, Aquinas shows unequivocally that he recognizes and accepts knowledge of persons and thinks that it is available to human beings in this life as a mode of knowledge where God is concerned.

To begin with, in his commentaries on New Testament texts, Aquinas makes it clear that on his view human beings are in a position to know the incarnate Christ with the knowledge of persons. This is, of course, the case for the disciples living at the time of Christ; but it is also the case, on Aquinas's view, for people born after the earthly life of Christ. In the interest of brevity, I will illustrate these claims by considering just Aquinas's commentary on the Gospel of John.[32]

In that work, Aquinas clearly supposes that Christ can be known with the knowledge of persons even by people living after Christ's earthly ministry. Speaking to his own readers, Aquinas says, "If then, you ask which way to go, accept Christ, for he is the way. . . . If you ask where to go, cling to Christ, for he is the truth, which we desire to reach. . . . If you ask where to remain, remain in Christ because he is the life" (1870).

That these descriptions of connection between human beings and Christ are not meant as metaphors for the acceptance of theological truths but are meant to be taken literally, as descriptions of personal relationship to Christ and personal knowledge of Christ, is attested by myriad texts in this same commentary. Consider, for example, this comment of Aquinas's on Christ's claim that he is the true vine. Aquinas says, "Christ is a true vine producing a wine which interiorly intoxicates us . . . and which strengthens us. . . . [T]hose united to Christ are the branches of this vine" (1979, 1983). Without personal relationship to someone and personal knowledge of him, one could hardly be said to be *united* with that person.

---

32. For purposes of this chapter, I found it convenient to use the translation of this text in James Weisheipl and Fabian Larcher, *Commentary on the Gospel of St. John* (Albany, N.Y.: Magi Books, 1980).

Aquinas also clearly takes the knowledge of persons with respect to Christ to be the knowledge of persons with respect to God as well. For example, in commenting on Christ's rebuke to Philip that anyone who has seen Christ has seen the Father, Aquinas remarks, "[Christ] shows that knowledge of the Son is also knowledge of the Father, [and] he . . . [asserts] the disciples' knowledge of the Father. . . . [T]here is no better way to know something than through its word or image, and the Son is the Word of the Father. . . . Therefore, the Father is known in the Son as in his Word and proper image" (1876, 1878). And Aquinas goes on to say, "[T]he Father was in the incarnate Word because they had one and the same nature, and the Father was seen in the incarnate Christ" (1881).

That is also, on Aquinas's view, the reason why Christ disapproved of Philip's request that Christ show them the Father. Aquinas says, "[Christ] is displeased with . . . [Philip's] request because the Father is seen in the Son" (1890).

In fact, not only is God the Father known in the Son, but, on Aquinas's views, part of the divine purpose in the Incarnation is precisely to make the Father known. God wants human beings in this life to know him, and that is why God provides an incarnation. Aquinas says, "No one can acquire a knowledge of the Father except by his Word, which is his Son. . . . [S]o God, wanting to be known by us, takes his Word, conceived from eternity, and clothes it with flesh in time" (1874).

As far as that goes, this knowledge of God is *necessary* for being in grace, in Aquinas's view. In commenting on the passage in which Christ says that those who persecute his followers will do so because they lack knowledge of God, Aquinas says of such persecutors that they will even kill Christians because, as he says, "they have not known the Father . . . or the Son" (2076). One should notice in this connection that Aquinas does not here ascribe a lack of propositional knowledge about God to these putative persecutors. What Aquinas says about them is that they lack personal knowledge of God: "they have not known the Father."

Furthermore, on Aquinas's account, one of the great benefits of Christ's sending the Holy Spirit, which indwells in every one of those in grace, is that the Holy Spirit enables believers to know Christ—that is, to have the knowledge of persons as regards Christ. So, commenting on Christ's line that the Holy Spirit will glorify him, Aquinas says that for the Holy Spirit to glorify Christ is just for the Holy Spirit to give every believer knowledge of Christ (2106).[33] In fact, the wisdom that is one of the seven gifts of the Holy Spirit is the knowledge of God; that is why Aquinas allies it with *caritas,* the love of God (*ST* II-II, q. 45).

CONCLUSION

It is evident, then, that neither the doctrine of eternity nor the doctrine of simplicity gives a good reason for denying that God can be present to human beings, not only with direct and immediate causal and cognitive connection, but also with the shared attention that is the basis for personal presence. It is not necessary for God to share a temporal mode of existence in order to be present to a person in time, as long as God can be known by that temporal person. And the doctrine of simplicity gives us no reason for supposing that God cannot be known in the way necessary for personal presence.

As I explained in connection with the prologue to Aquinas's discussion of simplicity in *ST,* there are reasons for rejecting the view that, for Aquinas, human beings cannot have any positive propositional knowledge of God in this life even if they cannot apprehend the quiddity of God. But it is also true that human beings are ordinarily capable of a nonpropositional knowledge of persons, which cannot be reduced to propositional knowledge and which does not depend on the apprehension of the quiddity of a thing. And this knowledge of persons is sufficient for personal presence. So, even if the doctrine of simplicity ruled out positive propositional knowledge of God, it would not rule out the knowledge of God necessary for personal presence.

That this is a view Aquinas shares is made clear from his commentary on the Gospel of John. In that commentary, Aquinas undoubtedly supposes that Christ's disciples had personal knowledge of this sort of the incarnate Christ, and he also clearly holds that in having this knowledge of Christ, they had personal knowledge of God the Father as well. As the passages cited above make clear, Aquinas also thinks that such personal knowledge of Christ, and through Christ of God the Father, is

---

33. Aquinas explains that claim in this way: "The Son is the principle of the Holy Spirit. For everything which is from another manifests that from which it is. Thus the Son manifests the Father because he is from the Father. And so because the Holy Spirit is from the Son, it is appropriate that the Spirit glorify [i.e., make manifest] the Son" (2107).

available to all Christians at any time through the operations of the Holy Spirit, without whose indwelling no human being can be saved.

For all these reasons, then, however we are to interpret Aquinas within the tradition of negative theology, it is not the case on his account that the doctrines of God's eternity and simplicity allow only negative knowledge of God or rule out the personal presence of God to human beings.

12 ∽ Why Bodies as Well as Souls in the Life to Come?

Christians believe that despite the fact that we die and our bodies revert to dust, human beings will rise to live embodied forever after in the life to come. It seems reasonable that *we* could not exist without our souls. They are our personal centers of thought and choice without which we would not be ourselves. But why bodies? In Aristotelian nature as in art, "form follows function." Medieval accounts of the life to come do not seem to give bodies anything to do. The elect will be principally occupied with the beatific vision and enjoyment of God; surely these are activities of the intellectual soul that the body does not share! Even if bodies have been functional partners in our antemortem careers, why resurrect them if they play no essential role in what we do after death?

For dogmatic theology, the answer is straightforward. The New Testament proclaims, the Nicene and Apostles' creeds declare, both Jesus's resurrection and the promised general resurrection. What the primary authorities lay down, the faithful must confess! But philosophical theology seeks understanding in the form of theoretical coherence. Prior to proof are philosophical formulation and explanation that show how the data of revelation fit with or follow from other core philosophical and theological commitments. Two integrative strategies suggest themselves. (1) "Form follows function" invites arguments that—despite appearances—soul-body reunion will be required for optimal functioning in the life to come. (2) The neo-Thomist tag "grace builds on nature" forwards the normative hypothesis that supranatural ends and what orders us to them do not take anything away from nature, but rather add something to nature over and above what nature could provide. Since rational animals are what we *are*, reunited soul-body composites will be presupposed for whatever grace adds.

In what follows, I call three witnesses—Bonaventure (in the first section), Aquinas (in the second), and Scotus (in the third)—and cross-examine each with respect to his views on human soul-body relations, in the hope of uncovering clues. All three agree that there will be bodies as well as souls in the life to come, because embodied intelligence is what we are metaphysically. Bonaventure and Aquinas do mount arguments from optimal functioning. For Aquinas, it is what we are as knowers; for both Bonaventure and Aquinas, it is what we are as subjects of appetite that demands the resurrection of the body. All three authors concur: embodied intelligence is what we are as agents whose merits and demerits will be weighed before the judgment seat of Christ. Nevertheless, Scotus's treatment casts doubt on both integrative strategies, and his analysis challenges the notion that the tag "grace builds on nature" accurately captures medieval accounts of the life to come. Finally (in the fourth section), I look in another direction for an explanation of why our authors would be so committed to bodily survival, when their accounts of the life to come give the body so little to do.

BONAVENTURE ON BODIES IN THE LIFE TO COME

Bonaventure is clear. Faith testifies to the future resurrection of our bodies. The Church is the Body of Christ. The apostles bear witness to Christ's resurrection, and it would be silly to raise a bodiless head! Bonaventure insists that these dogmatic convictions can be defended by rational persuasion. They find their systematic explanation in what we human beings *are:* in what we are *metaphysically,* in what we are *as lovers,* and in what we are *as agents.*[1]

The Metaphysical-Completeness Argument

As to what we are metaphysically, Bonaventure holds that—by contrast with angels but like other animals—human being is composite. We are— as Augustine had taught—souls using bodies as instruments.[2] But our

---

1. Bonaventure, *Commentarius in librum Sententiarum* (hereafter *In Sent.*) IV, d. 43, a. 1, q. 1, *Editio Quaracchi* 4.883–84.

2. *In Sent.* IV, d. 43, a. 1, q. 1, 4.884.

bodies are not used as external instruments—human souls do not use human bodies the way carpenters use hammers; rather our bodies are used as *internal* instruments—the way a carpenter uses her or his hand. The human soul is related to its body, not only as a mover the way the angel moved a human body in the story of Tobit. The human soul is also related to its body as a perfecter of substance.[3] The human soul has a *natural inclination* to be joined to its body.[4] Indeed, after death, the soul retains a natural inclination to be joined to *numerically* the same human body it had before.[5] The human soul shares its functions (*operationes*) with its body, and the sensory powers are subordinate to and minister to the intellectual powers as instruments.[6] Like the angels, the rational soul is immortal by nature.[7] Like other heterogeneous or mixed bodies, the human body is corruptible by nature.[8] Like other animals, human beings were created with a natural aptitude for death. Unlike other animals, human death means that the human soul does not itself perish but does separate from and cease to animate the human body.[9]

For Bonaventure as for other medieval philosophical theologians, human being has not only a nature but a history, which is marked by distinct states. Adam and Eve in Eden were mortal in the sense that they were the kind of things that could die, but—had they never sinned—God would have prevented their deaths, with the result that in Eden they could not-die. After the fall, Adam and Eve and their descendants (apart from Christ), in this present "state of misery," have the necessity of dying. In the meantime, soul-body conjunction means that the soul suffers when the body is wounded.[10] By contrast, in the life to come, divine power and infused supranatural dispositions will resurrect Adam's race in such a condition that human beings will be unable to die again.[11] For

3. *In Sent.* IV, d. 44, p. 1, a. 2, q. 2, 4.914.

4. *In Sent.* IV, d. 43, a. 1, q. 1, 4.884.

5. *In Sent.* IV, d. 43, a. 1, q. 4, 4.888.

6. *In Sent.* II, d. 19, a. 1, q. 1, 2.461.

7. *In Sent.* II, d. 19, a. 1, q. 1, 2.460; *In Sent.* IV, d. 43, a. 1, q. 2, 4.885.

8. *In Sent.* IV, d. 43, a. 1, q. 2, 4.886.

9. *In Sent.* II, d. 19, a. 1, q. 1, 2.461; *In Sent.* II, d. 19, a. 1, q. 2 2.463; *In Sent.* IV, d. 43, a. 1, q. 4 4.889–90.

10. *In Sent.* IV, d. 19, a. 1, q. 1, 2.461. Bonaventure also emphasizes this point in his Christology. See *In Sent.* III, d. 16, a. 1, q. 1 co. and ad 5, 3.340.

11. *In Sent.* II, d. 17, a. 2, q. 3, 2.425; *In Sent.* II, d. 19, a. 2, q. 2, 2.467; *In Sent.* II, d. 19, a. 3, q. 2, 2.472; *In Sent.* IV, d. 43, a. 1, q. 4, 4.889–90; *In Sent.* IV, d. 44, p. 2, a. 2, q. 1, 4.925; *In Sent.* IV, p. 2, a. 3, q. 1, 4.93.

damned as well as for elect souls, God will reform numerically the same bodies that the souls had before and will permanently reunite the souls with their bodies.[12] The Recreator is power and wisdom, able to raise all human beings in a perfect and complete state with respect to their metaphysical essentials. What we metaphysically *are* furnishes a reason (as it were, makes it a point of honor) for God to do exactly that![13]

The Appetite-Satisfaction Argument

Bonaventure declares that "the consummation of glory" "fulfills and satisfies the soul's every appetite."[14] The fourth pro argument observes that the soul's natural appetite for the body is so strong that the soul does not want to be separated from the body, even when the body is miserable.[15] Bonaventure also quotes Bernard of Clairvaux (in *On the Love of God*, ch. 11), who maintains that the soul has such an affection for its body that it cannot be consummately happy when separated from it. Bonaventure himself concludes that the unsatisfied natural appetite of the separate soul for its body would hold the soul back from rejoicing as intensely as possible.[16]

Not only does Bonaventure doubt whether the same soul metaphysically could perfect a numerically distinct hunk of matter,[17] Bonaventure explains that the soul will want numerically the same body as before, for old time's sake! He imagines a man choosing which of two equally beautiful and virtuous virgins to marry. Other things being equal, he should be indifferent. But once he has joined to one in love, he would not find consolation in having the other, or even in having another who is still more beautiful and more virtuous. So, Bonaventure imagines, the soul has such an affection for the substance of the flesh to which it was united and which it animated earlier, that this affection would not be completely satisfied until the same one it lost is restored.[18]

Reforming the disintegrated body, however, is *contrary to nature*: it belongs to natural powers to build up animal bodies in the first place, but

---

12. *In Sent.* IV, d. 43, a. 1, q. 4, 4.889.

13. *In Sent.* IV, d. 43, a. 1, q. 1, 4.883; *In Sent.* IV, d. 44, p. 1, a. 1, q. 2, 4.909–10; *In Sent.* IV, d. 44, p. 1, a. 3, qq. 1–2, 4.915–16.

14. *In Sent.* IV, d. 43, a. 1, q. 1, 4.884.

15. *In Sent.* IV, d. 43, a. 1, q. 1, 4.883.

16. *In Sent.* IV, d. 49, p. 2, a. 1, q. 1, 4.1012. See also *In Sent.* IV, d. 44, p. 2, a. 3, q. 2, 4.934.

17. *In Sent.* IV, d. 43, a. 1, q. 4, 4.888.

18. *In Sent.* IV, d. 43, a. 1, q. 5, 4.894; *In Sent.* IV, d. 44, p. 1, a. 2, q. 1, 4.910.

goes against natural powers to return them the numerically same again once destroyed. Permanent conjunction is, rather, *supranatural,* going beyond what any natural power could achieve. Still, Bonaventure thinks it is *according to nature* that the soul be united to the optimally organized body, to which it desires to be united.[19] But who we are *as lovers,* what we *love by nature,* means that we cannot be maximally happy when our souls are separated from our bodies, when they are not united to the very ones we have (or had) in our *ante-mortem* careers.[20]

The Divine-Retribution Argument

Theologically decisive for Christian insistence on individual immortality was the conviction that we must all stand before the great judgment seat of Christ, where the plusses and minuses of our earthly careers will be exposed and the verdict rendered, sentencing each human being to the eternal destiny she or he deserves. For Bonaventure, this consideration takes us further. Justice demands that rewards and punishments go to *the very same agent* who acted or refrained from acting. But what we are *ante mortem* is *embodied* agents. Soul and body are partners—the body, a *united* instrument of the soul—in action and omission. Therefore, they should be partners in rewards or punishments deserved thereby.[21]

For Adam's fallen race, both body and soul already participate together in *ante-mortem* punishments. Original guilt is the reason why the soul suffers separation from its body at death, and why the body first disintegrates, dust to dust,[22] and then gets reduced to elements in the great end-time conflagration.[23] Just as the body gets destroyed without the soul being destroyed (since the latter is metaphysically impossible), so the soul suffers purgatorial punishments,[24] the damned suffer mental anguish, and the elect experience "a resurrection" or glorification of the soul in advance of bodily resurrection.[25] But justice will not allow soul and body to remain separated where the eternal rewards of heaven and the eternal punishments of hell are concerned.

19. *In Sent.* IV, d. 43, a. 1, q. 5, 4.892.
20. *In Sent.* IV, d. 49, p. 2, a. 1, q. 1, 4.1012.
21. *In Sent.* IV, d. 43, a. 1, q. 1, 4.883–84.
22. *In Sent.* IV, d. 43, a. 1, q. 2, 4.885–87.
23. *In Sent.* IV, d. 48, a. 2, qq. 2–4, 4.991–94.
24. *In Sent.* IV, d. 43, a. 1, q. 2, 4.885–86.
25. *In Sent.* IV, d. 43, a. 1, q. 3, 4.887.

Soul-satisfying heavenly happiness has God as the object of beatific vision and enjoyment, and the soul is the first subject of these acts and of the deiformity that is God's influence on the soul. Beatific vision and enjoyment are the elect soul's dowry and unite it to God as spouse to spouse.[26] Bonaventure admits that even separate from the body, the soul could be (indeed before the resurrection, the souls of the elect are) thereby happy.[27] Nevertheless, the soul's beatific enjoyment will be the more intense because of reunion with its body, and the soul will be happy over more (though not better) things than it would be had it remained separate.[28] When the reformed body is united with the happy soul, joy-related well-being redounds onto the body (the reverse of fall-induced weakness and vulnerability).[29] The body's dowry consists both in the dispositions endowed by God at its reformation and in the perfections flooded into it when it is perfected by the happy soul. Impassibility disposes it to immortality and clarity beautifies it, while agility and subtlety make it apt for ease of motion.[30]

Biblical identification of fire as God's instrument in the torments of the damned is multiply problematic. For fire does have natural power to act on bodies to destroy them and—in the case of plants and animals—to kill by causing bodily damage and soul-body separation. But fire cannot harm the damned that way, because the damned as much as the elect are raised to permanent metaphysical completeness. And fire has no natural power to damage or destroy incorporeal things at all. Bonaventure replies that God will allow the fire power to inflame but not to consume, while the bodies of the damned will have passive power to suffer in the flames but not to lose parts. Immortal and passible bodies can be afflicted without ceasing to exist, and so the composite can be afflicted without dying.[31]

Bonaventure admits that mental anguish requires only perception in the cognitive power and hate of what is perceived in the affective power. But the soul's torment will not involve mere imagination, but real fire.

---

26. *In Sent.* IV, d. 49, p. 1, a.u, q. 5, 4.1009.
27. *In Sent.* IV, d. 49, p. 1, a.u. 3, 4.1005–6.
28. *In Sent.* IV, d. 49, p. 2, a. 1, q. 1, 4.1012–13.
29. *In Sent.* IV, d. 49, p. 1, u. 3, 4.1005–6.
30. *In Sent.* IV, d. 49, p. 2, a. 1, q. 2, 4.1014, 1016; *In Sent.* IV, d. 49, p. 2, a. 2, q. 1, 4.1022–25.
31. *In Sent.* IV, d. 44, p. 2, a. 3, q. 1, 4.929–30.

Just as *ante mortem* the soul is joined to a body for the purpose of giving it life and comes to love that body in the process, so *post mortem* the souls of the damned are inescapably joined to real fire, which God makes sure they necessarily hate. Bonaventure does not elaborate on the metaphysics of the latter conjunction. It need not be more than definitive location of the soul in a place close enough to the fire for the flames continually to affect the soul's perception. After the resurrection, this is achieved by the soul's existing definitively in its inflamed body, where both suffer together in perpetuity.[32]

Stripped-Down Cosmos

Bonaventure does not super-spiritualize the life to come by turning it into a scene of love and hate relationships between divine and created spirits. But this is not because bodies are necessarily required for supranatural degrees of spiritual happiness or everlasting torment. Bonaventure makes it absolutely clear that bodies figure in the remodeled cosmos just as they figured in the original cosmos, principally because of what human beings essentially are. According to Bonaventure, the material world exists for the sake of human beings. All generation and corruption is ordered to the (re)production of human beings for the heavenly city. That purpose having been accomplished, in the world to come, generation and corruption will cease.[33] Likewise, plants and other animals do not exist for the praise of God or for the perfection of the universe, but to serve human beings and to ornament the universe with variety. In the world to come, human bodies will be impassible and not need plants or animals for food. Likewise, the universe will instead be ornamented by uniformity (Bauhaus in place of baroque).[34] So in the world to come, the material universe will be stripped down to human bodies and to what Bonaventure regards as incorruptible bodies[35]—the supercelestial bodies, which are rewarded with increased brightness for the sake of their usefulness to humans as light givers,[36] and the elements, which are all "weapons in the hand of the Creator" for the punishment of the damned.[37]

32. *In Sent.* IV, d. 44, p. 2, a. 3, q. 2, 4.934.
33. *In Sent.* IV, d. 48, a. 2, q. 2, 4.991.
34. *In Sent.* IV, d. 48, a. 2, q. 4, 4.994.
35. *In Sent.* IV, d. 48, a. 2, q. 4, 4.994.
36. *In Sent.* IV, d. 48, a. 2, q. 1, 4.990.
37. *In Sent.* IV, d. 44, p. 2, a. 2, q. 2, 4.938.

AQUINAS ON BODILY RESURRECTION

Appetite, Deliberative or Natural?

Aquinas agrees with Bonaventure that the human soul has an appetite for its body—indeed, after death, an appetite for numerically the same body it had before.[38] But Aquinas clarifies by distinguishing *natural* will, which he identifies with natural appetite or natural inclination, from *deliberative* will, which is the choice that issues out of rational deliberation. Bonaventure's analogy of the man choosing between two equally beautiful and virtuous virgins suggests that the human soul's appetite for its body is deliberative. Aquinas thinks, on the contrary, that the human soul's appetite for its body is not deliberative but fundamentally and primarily natural: namely, that of a substantial form for the subject with which it combines to make an individual substance that is one *per se*.[39] Nor is Aquinas content with mere assertion. Aristotelian nature follows function. For Aquinas, the primary human function is cognitive. Human cognitive psychology spawns philosophical consequences about *what we are as knowers*. In particular and famously, Aquinas's psychology underwrites the conclusions that the human soul is both incorporeal and subsisting[40] and related to its human body as substantial form.[41]

What We Are as Knowers

The human soul is incorporeal and subsisting, because it has an activity that the body cannot share. Logically, Aquinas begins with the *contents* of understanding. As Aristotle has taught us, understanding is of universals; as philosophically tutored experience shows, the natural function of human beings is to understand the quiddities of material things.[42] Broadly Aristotelian cognitive psychology lays it down that "knowledge is by assimilation," namely that "knowledge involves the knower's receiving the form of the thing known." Whether this form is taken to be the same species of form, or merely any form that has the capacity to rep-

---

38. Thomas Aquinas, *Scriptum super Sententiis* (hereafter *In Sent.*) IV, d. 43, q.u, a. 2, *Editio Parma* 22.417; id., *Summa contra Gentiles* (hereafter *SCG*) IV, c. 84.

39. *In Sent.* IV, d. 49, q. u, a. 4, 22.433; *SCG*, II, c. 83; *SCG.* IV, c. 79; Thomas Aquinas, *Summa theologiae* (hereafter *ST*) I, q. 76, a. 1.

40. *In Sent.* IV, d. 44, a. 2, aa. 1–2, 22.421; *ST* I, q. 75, a. 2.

41. *ST* I, q. 76, a. 1 co.

42. *ST* I, q. 12, a. 4, ad 4; *ST* I, q. 84, a. 8 co.; *ST* I, q. 85, a. 1 co.

resent the form that is in the known object,[43] Aquinas reasons that the receiving subject has to be immaterial. For "what is received is received after the manner of the receiver." If the subject of understanding were a composite of matter and form, the forms would be received materially and so would not be actually intelligible. Forms in matter are individuated, not universal. The form of stone in matter constitutes a stone, not a thought of a stone. So understanding is an activity of the soul that the body cannot share.

Finally, Aquinas contends, "what functions *per se*, exists *per se* or subsists."[44] Not only is the intellectual soul the sole formal active principle, it is also the lone subject of acts of understanding. By contrast, the soul of Beulah the cow and all substantial forms in nonhuman hylomorphic composites are "immersed" in matter, in that all of the natural functions of which such substantial forms are the formal principle are functions of the composite; there is none of which the form alone is the subject.[45] Since nothing subsistent can remain inert, these latter forms cannot exist alone. From the fact that the intellectual soul "exceeds" matter in having an activity that it does not share with matter or the composite, Aquinas draws the strong conclusion that the human intellectual soul, as much as the other intelligences, exists *per se* or subsists, in the sense that it does not depend for its existence on existing in anything else as in a subject.[46] Because only hylomorphic composites are corruptible properly speaking, and because the intellectual soul is simple and immaterial, it follows that the intellectual soul is incorruptible.[47]

Notwithstanding, Aquinas argues from the essentials of human cognitive psychology that the intellectual soul is the form of the body. For it is essential and natural that the human intellect begin as a *tabula rasa* and acquire mental representations only by abstraction from sense images. Moreover, its range is restricted to the quiddities of material things. These features make humans distinct in species from the angels. Aquinas then reasons that since understanding is an essential function of human beings it pertains to human beings either as a whole or as a part. But we experience in ourselves that the same human being senses as understands.[48]

---

43. *ST* I, q. 88, a. 1 ad 2; *ST* I, q. 78, a. 3 co. & ad 2–3.
44. *ST* I, q. 75, a. 2 co.   45. *ST* I, a. 3 co.
46. *ST* I, q. 75, a. 2 co.
47. *ST* I, q. 75, a. 6 co.; *SCG* II, c. 55. See *In Sent.* IV, d. 44, q. 2, a. 1.
48. *ST* I, q. 76, a. 1 co.

Aquinas relies on several other implicit assumptions. First, not only is it true that the same human in fact both senses and understands. It follows from distinctively human cognitive psychology that sensation is also an essential function of human beings. Second, there is the Aristotelian principle that where *F* is a natural function of a species *S*, and *x* is a nondefective member of *S*, then *x* has built into it whatever is necessary to give it first actuality with respect to *F*-ing.[49] Third, Aquinas's human cognitive psychology involves the still stronger assumption that the human intellect by nature depends on the exercise of the senses for its own functioning.[50] Given these claims, Aquinas infers that since sensation cannot occur without body, body must somehow be part of a human being, and hence the intellect is only a part that is somehow united to the body to constitute one human being. After presenting arguments to eliminate Averroes's understanding of conjunction, and soul-as-mover hypotheses, Aquinas concludes that the intellectual soul is related to the body as its substantial form.[51]

Not only is it natural for the human intellect to abstract its intelligible contents from sense images, but it is also natural for it in actually understanding anything to "turn to the sense images" from which the content was abstracted. When death separates the human soul from its body, the soul loses its access to sense images; instead, it understands through intelligible species directly infused into it by God. In itself, this mode of understanding is more perfect than the mode that depends on abstracting from and turning to sense images. It is a mode essential to angels but—Aquinas insists—less suitable to humans, with the result that the human soul cannot think as clearly when separated from the body. What we are as knowers is embodied intellectual souls![52]

The Argument from Aristotelian Optimism

For Aristotle, all animals are hylomorphic composites. All animal souls are substantial forms of animal bodies and as such have a natural appetite to be united with them. This claim does not, by itself, constitute philosophical grounds for belief in bodily resurrection. For animals are by nature generable and corruptible. Their soul-forms are "immersed in

49. *ST* I, q. 76,a. 1 co
50. *ST* I, q. 84, a. 7 co.; *ST* I, q. 89, a. 1 co.
51. *ST* I, q. 76, a. 1 co.
52. *ST* I, q. 89, a. 1 co. & ad 3; *ST* I, a. 2 co. & ad 2; *ST* I, q. 89, a. 3 co.

matter" in that they are not the root organizing principle of any activities that the body does not share. When nonhuman animals die, the soul-forms simply cease to be, while their matter becomes a constituent of something else.[53] What is different about human animals is that the intellectual soul is incorruptible. When separated, it persists, along with its frustrated natural appetite for its body. It is the intellectual soul's incorruptibility and persistent natural appetite that combine with Aristotelian optimism—the thesis that nothing contrary to nature is perpetual—to furnish a philosophical argument for eventual resurrection.[54]

Moreover, if it is contrary to the nature of the human intellectual soul to exist without its body, because it is naturally united to its body, it is likewise contrary to the nature of the body to lack a natural part, insofar as one part depends on another. The soul itself is naturally apt to be the act of the whole body. Incorruptibility plus natural appetite argue—via Aristotelian optimism—for the resurrection of the perfect and complete whole.[55] Thus, for Aquinas, human cognitive psychology plus Aristotelian optimism give us bodies as well as souls in the life to come![56]

Embodiment and Perfect Happiness

Nevertheless, this long argument from cognitive psychology to the soul's natural appetite for embodiment does not entirely put our opening question to rest. For Aquinas agrees that the principal activity of the blessed will be beatific vision and enjoyment of God. But beatific vision is supranatural, something for which natural human cognitive equipment cannot deliver even the passive capacity. Natural human cognitive psychology equips humans to understand the quiddities of material things by abstracting from and then turning to sense images. It does not enable us to conceive of immaterial beings except by analogy with material things. Even supernaturally infused intelligible species of spiritual things would be of no use for beatific vision. For, on Aquinas's analysis, vision requires a *perfect* likeness of the object seen. No finite created likeness can medi-

---

53. *ST* I, q. 75, a. 3 co.

54. *In Sent.* IV, d. 43, q.u, a. 1; *In Sent.* d. 44, q. 1, a. 1; *SCG* IV, c. 79.

55. *In Sent.* IV, d. 44, q. 1, a. 1.

56. Viewed as a proof, this argument has a serious gap. Aristotelian optimism is about the reliability of natural processes. But if the soul does have a natural inclination to unite with its body, or with prime matter, to make something one *per se*, still—as noted above—no natural agent has power to return numerically the same body again.

ate a *vision* of the infinite being![57] If any created intellect is to see God, the divine essence itself must be united to the cognitive power.[58] The fact that humans need their bodies for natural-mode cognition of the quiddities of material things has no bearing on whether or not God could join the divine essence to human souls just as well when they are separate as when they are conjoined.

Aquinas tries to meet this worry by arguing that perfect human happiness does require soul-body reunion. He gives two characterizations of happiness, on the one hand as "the perfect human good"[59] and on the other as union with God, which is essentially vision perfected by love.[60] Aquinas understands the first to build into happiness, not only the intellectual acts identified by the second, but also the metaphysical perfection of the human being.

The perfect human good would involve perfect functioning, and perfect functioning requires everything that pertains to the perfection of the functioner.[61] Although the body does not contribute to the act of happiness directly, Aquinas insists, it does so indirectly, insofar as the nature of the soul and its intellectual powers are more perfect by virtue of the soul's union with its body. This is not because the intellectual cognitive or appetitive powers become stronger or more intensified, but for the general metaphysical reason that the part existing in the whole has a certain natural perfection that it lacks when it is separate from the whole. The frustrated natural appetite of the separate soul for its body does not diminish the soul's happiness by distracting its conscious attention the way a deliberate appetite would (as Bonaventure seems to suggest in agreement with Bernard of Clairvaux). Nor does frustrated natural appetite diminish infused habits of love or the light of glory. Rather frustrated natural appetite diminishes the soul's happiness simply by being concomitant with (a side effect of) an imperfection of the nature.[62]

---

57. *In Sent.* III, d. 14, q. 1, a. 1, ql. 3 co, 7.1.150AB; *In Sent.* III, d. 14, q. 1, a. 2, ql. 1 co, 7.1.152G; *In Sent.* III. d. 14, q. 1, a. 3, ql. 1, 7.1.156A.

58. *In Sent.* III, d. 14, q. 1, a. 1, ql. 3, ad 1, 7.1.150B; *In Sent.* IV, d. 49, q. a. 2, ql. 1 co. & ad 2, 7.1.152B–153A.

59. *In Sent.* IV, d. 49, q. u, 3, 22.432.

60. *In Sent.* IV, d. 49, q. u, 2, 22.432.

61. *In Sent.* IV, d. 49, q. u, 2; cf. *SCG* IV, c. 79.

62. *In Sent.* IV, d. 49, q. u, a. 4, 22.433; *SCG* IV, c. 79.

Bodily Participation in Divine Retribution

Two theological arguments come closer to telling us what bodies are doing in the life to come. For Aristotle, human beings—like all other animals—are mortal by nature. However that may be, Western medieval
theologians agree that actual death is a punishment for sin. According
to the soteriological plot, God's original intention for human beings
was *permanent* metaphysical perfection. Soul-body separation is a punishment for Adam's fall. Christ's passion merits a return to God's initial policy: the final and complete repair, the permanent restoration to
metaphysical perfection of the whole human race. In the resurrection,
damned as well as elect souls will rise, their souls united to whole and
complete bodies of perfect age and stature.[63] God is the author of nature,
and God will restore to every human being the whole of human nature,
free from essential defects.[64]

Moreover, divine retributive justice requires the very same agents to
be judged, rewarded or punished, as merited or demerited in this life. For
Aristotelian reasons, Aquinas insists that hylomorphic composites are
what we are as agents. Although distinctively *human* action essentially involves acts of reasoning and willing in the intellectual soul,[65] human action is properly speaking the action of the whole composite. Since human
agents merit or demerit in soul and body together, they will be eternally
rewarded or punished in both when they stand before the great judgment
seat of Christ.[66] Human bodies are there to secure agent-identity and to
share in the punishments and rewards.

Following theological convention, Aquinas declares that glory redounds to the human body insofar as it is completely subject to the happy soul. Since it will be perfectly subject to the soul as mover, the glorified body will be agile, ready, and yielding to any motion that the soul
might command it. Insofar as the happy soul perfects the body as its
form, the body receives subtlety, impassibility, and clarity.[67] Interesting-

---

63. *In Sent.* IV, d. 44, q. 1, a. 1, 22.418; *In Sent.* IV, d. 49, q. 1, a. 2, 22.419.

64. *In Sent.* IV, d. 44, q. 1, a. 4, 22.420.

65. *ST* I-II, q. 1, a. 1 co.

66. *In Sent.* IV, d. 43, q. u, a. 1; *In Sent.* IV, q.u, a. 2, 22.417; *In Sent.* IV, d. 44, q. 1, a. 1, 22.419;
SCG IV, c. 79, cc. 88–89.

67. *In Sent.* IV, d. 44, q. 1, a. 3, 22.420; *SCG* IV, c. 86.

ly, Aquinas holds on to his philosophical conviction that the quantitative dimensions of bodies are by nature mutually incompatible with one another, and therefore refuses to identify subtlety with the ability to exist in the same place at the same time as another body. Rather, he maintains, subtlety consists in perfect subsistence in the nature of the species.[68] Likewise, he seems to attribute the body's impassibility to the soul's augmented power, not only to give, but to conserve the body in existence.[69]

Turning to the fiery torments of the damned, Aquinas explains how for intelligent beings fire is not a suitable object of prolonged attention. Likewise, even separate intelligences can be located (even if they cannot be extended) in place. God so binds fallen angels and the souls of the damned to fire that they cannot go anywhere else, and so God torments them by taking away their freedom of movement. Fire is thus an instrument used by divine power to afflict separate intelligences, not by altering their real qualities but by detaining them.[70] To explain how fire afflicts the bodies of the damned, Aquinas appeals to his distinction between forms existing in a body according to natural *esse* (e.g., heat in the fire, whiteness in the sugar) and according to intentional *esse* (e.g., sensible species in the medium or sense organ, the species of whiteness in the air or the aqueous humor of the eye). Fire acts on the bodies of the damned only to change their sensible species and not their natural properties, and so it does not corrupt the human body itself.[71]

To Bonaventure's account of the stripped-down material universe, Aquinas adds the observation that post-resurrection bodies will generally enjoy a greater participation in divine goodness, so that in looking at them the bodily eye can see God somehow by seeing God in them![72]

SCOTUS ON *POST-MORTEM* EMBODIMENT

Hylomorphic Composition

Scotus takes for granted that hylomorphic composites are *what we are metaphysically.* After all, we are rational animals, and it is the nature of

---

68. *In Sent.* IV, d. 44, q. 1, a. 3, 22.420.
69. *In Sent.* IV, d. 44, q. 1, a. 3, 22.240.
70. *In Sent.* IV, d. 44, q. 2, a. 3, 22.422; *SCG* IV, c. 90.
71. *In Sent.* IV, d. 44, q. 2, a. 4, 22.422.
72. *In Sent.* IV, d. 48, q. 2, a. 2, 22.430.

animals generally to come into being and pass away.[73] Scotus accepts Aristotle's theoretical analysis of generation and corruption in terms of matter that persists through the change, matter's potency to be subject to any substantial forms that it lacks but can receive, and substantial forms, which are lost and gained, respectively. Scotus's leading question is, what is the dominant substantial form of human beings? He admits that we have no immediate cognitive access to substantial forms themselves. Methodologically, Aristotelian research programs have to begin with our knowledge of *actions* (*passions*) and infer from actions (passions) to *powers* to act (be acted upon), and further from powers to *natures*. Accordingly, Scotus reasons from the fact that we sometimes do and other times do not experience acts of understanding immaterial contents, to the conclusion that the acts are in us, produced by an intellectual power rooted in an inorganic substantial form or intellectual soul.[74] By the time Scotus wrote *Quodlibeta*, q. 9, he was convinced that he could prove that the intellectual soul, left to its own nature, can exist without matter.[75] Thus, he agrees with Aquinas that the intellectual soul is an incorruptible substantial form that is also the form of the body.

Scotus also concurs that the intellectual soul's independence in being able to exist without matter does not keep it from being able to be the form of the human body, indeed from having a natural aptitude to share its perfection by being such a form.[76] Because human being is a substance species, the human soul and the human body have matching aptitudes to unite with one another to form one substance *per se*.[77] For Scotus, plant and animal substances are composed of many really distinct things (*res*)—prime matter, a substantial form of corporeity, and a substantial soul form—each of which is apt to combine with the others to make one substance *per se*. Composites of prime matter and the form of corporeity alone are incomplete beings and inherently unstable because they lack their dominant substantial form. Whether or not soul-body reunion would in itself make *the parts* more perfect, it would perfect *the composite* by rendering it a complete being.[78]

---

73. Scotus, *Opus Oxoniense* (hereafter *Op. Ox.*) II, d. 29, q. u, nn. 3–6 (ed. Wadding 6.921).

74. *Op. Ox.* IV, d. 43, q. 2, nn. 9, 11, 12, 10.24–26.

75. *Quodlibeta*, q. 9, n. 6, 12.228.

76. *Quodlibeta*, n. 12, 12.230.

77. *Op. Ox.* IV, d. 43, q. 4, n. 5.

78. *Op. Ox.* IV, d. 11, q. 3, nn. 46, 54, 8.649, 653; *Op. Ox.* IV, d. 45, q. 2, n. 14, 10.182.

Challenging the Cognitive Psychology

Nevertheless, Scotus queries his predecessors' functional arguments. Scotus disputes the cognitive psychology underlying Aquinas's argument that *who we are as knowers* will require soul-body reunion. Aquinas is wrong to identify material quiddities as the proper object of the human intellect and wrong to make abstraction from and turning toward sense images *essential* to human understanding. Aquinas is accordingly mistaken in his conclusion that the separate human soul, cut off from its supply of sense images, will not be able to think clearly by means of the divinely infused species.

Scotus has no trouble joining Aristotle and Aquinas in the inference from acts that are immaterial in content to an inorganic soul-power, and from an inorganic soul-power to the intellectual soul as the dominant substantial form of human being. Scotus thinks that Aristotle and Aquinas merely apply this methodology again when they reason from what they represent as universal (at least, always or for the most part) human experience in this life—where our cognitive processes begin with sense experience and our intellectualizing depends on abstraction from and turning toward sense images—to the conclusion that this process is *essential* to human cognitive psychology.[79]

Scotus's reply rests on two points. First, if Aristotle and the philosophers restrict themselves to data available to experience and natural reason, Christian philosophical theologians must add to this the data of revelation. Looming large among these is the claim that our supranatural end is intellectual vision and enjoyment of God, Who is most definitely not a material thing!

Second, Scotus explains that what distinguishes the different states of human history—in Eden before the fall, after the fall, and in the life to come—are contrasting always-or-for-the-most-part regularities. Since human nature (what-it-is-to-be human, with its defining genus and differentia and essential powers) remains the same in the different states by metaphysical necessity, it follows that human nature underdetermines state-regularities. Differences among the states are a function of divine

---

79. *Quodlibeta*, q. 14, n. 12, 12.373. These texts and issues were brought to the fore decades ago (in 1949) by Allan B. Wolter in his article, "Duns Scotus on the Natural Desire for the Supernatural," reprinted in *The Philosophical Theology of John Duns Scotus*, ed. Marilyn McCord Adams (Ithaca, N.Y.: Cornell University Press, 1990), 125–47.

governance, of freely and contingently established divine laws, which lay down contrasting patterns of divine concurrence with and/or obstruction of natural causes as well as different policies of divine donation (of supranaturally infused qualities, such as the theological virtues and spiritual gifts in this life). Hence any attempted inference from always-or-for-the-most-part experience to essential powers or nature has to take into account another factor: God's freely chosen state-policies or laws. Aristotle and the philosophers were not in a position to do this because God's free and contingent choices are not accessible to natural reason. But Christian philosophical theologians must draw on revelation to bring these into play.[80]

Developing the first point, Scotus reasons that the proper object of the human intellect—what it is essentially power to cognize—must be estimated not only from the acts possible for us in our present state (after the fall and before death), but also from the acts that revelation tells of our having in the other states.[81] The proper object of a power is characterized by a universal that subsumes all of its particular objects. Thus, if elect humans will see and enjoy God in the life to come, then our cognitive power must be essentially receptive of (by nature, the kind of thing that has the passive power to receive) such acts.[82] So the proper object of the human intellect cannot be the quiddity of material things, because God is not an material thing. Rather, Scotus infers, the proper object of the human intellect must be being in general.[83]

Scotus rejects as unintelligible Aquinas's idea that although the proper object of the human intellect is material quiddities, God will infuse the cognitive power of the elect with a special disposition that will enable it to see God. Scotus insists that powers are *essentially* defined by their proper objects (e.g., vision by color, hearing by sound). It is unintelligible to suppose that any added disposition could turn the power to understand material quiddities into a power for seeing God any more than added dispositions could turn vision into a power to perceive sounds as well as colors. If restriction to material quiddities were what makes human intellects specifically different from angelic ones (as Aquinas claims), then the

---

80. *Ordinatio* I, d. 3, p. 1, q. 3, nn. 186–87, *Editio Vaticana* 3.112–14; *Ordinatio* I, d. 44, q. u, 7–12, 6.365–69; *Quodlibeta*, q. 14, n. 2, 12.348–49.

81. *Ordinatio*, Prologus I, q. u, nn. 33, 38, *Editio Vaticana* 1.19–20, 22.

82. Scotus, *Lectura* I, d. 3, p. 1, qq. 1–2, nn. 92–110, *Editio Vaticana* 16.259–65.

83. *Quodlibeta*, q. 14, nn. 10–12, 12.373.

power to understand immaterial substances would be specifically distinct from that cognitive power with which humans are naturally endowed. Besides, if human cognitive power is essentially power to understand by abstracting and turning to sense images, the power to understand without species such as Aquinas posits for seeing God would have to be a specifically distinct power!

If, however, the proper object of the human intellect were being in general, Scotus would need to explain why immaterial things do not act on our cognitive faculties to cause cognitions already in this life. Whatever sort of awareness of our own mental acts we may have or lack, why do we have no experience of angels? Here Scotus applies his second methodological point. If our regular range of experience is narrower than the proper object of the power would permit, that must be because of freely and contingently established divine laws governing this state, to the effect that only material things are allowed to exercise their power to move human cognitive faculties.[84] As to God's reasons for this, Scotus thinks revelation affords us two speculations: positively, it may be that God wanted to harmonize human sensory and intellectual functions in this present state; negatively, the restriction of cognitive access to angels might be part of divine punishment for Adam's fall.[85]

Consideration of the separate human soul between death and resurrection gives Scotus the opportunity to split out what is *essential* to human intellectual functioning from what is merely characteristic of it in this present state. Scotus's considered opinion is that while angels and humans are distinct in species relative to Porphyry's tree, human souls have the same passive/receptive capacities as angels but weaker active powers, with the result that human acts of understanding have less perfect intensity.[86] This means that—unless God obstructs the natural process—objects that can act on angelic cognitive powers can act on the human intellect as well.[87] Scotus speculates that nearby particulars—both sensible and immaterial—can act on angelic intellects to cause intellectual intuitive cognitions; likewise, he infers, they can act on the

---

84. *Ordinatio*, Prologus I, q. u, nn. 29, 61–62, 1.17–18, 37–38.

85. *Ordinatio*, Prologus I, q. u, n. 37; *Ordinatio* I, d. 3, p. 1, q. 3, n. 187, 3.113–14; *Op. Ox.* IV, d. 45, q. 1, n. 7, 10.163.

86. *Op. Ox.* III, d. 13, q. 3, nn. 1, 18, 7.1.260, 275; *Op. Ox.* III, d. 14, q. 2, n. 17, 7.1.297; *Op. Ox.* III, d. 14, q. 4, n. 1, 7.1.309.

87. *Op. Ox.* IV, d. 45, q. 2, n. 12, 10.182.

separate soul.[88] Moreover, Scotus maintains that angels would be able to understand the quiddities of material things even though angels lack sensory imagination, but not because of divinely infused species. Rather, Scotus reasons, if a sense image of an object could carry the intelligible content to be abstracted, a fortiori the object itself could. The angels abstract intelligible species of the quiddities of material things from the objects themselves. Scotus reckons that the separate soul would be able to do the same.[89]

The upshot is that—for Scotus—soul-body reunion wins no advantage for human intellectual functioning. The divine policy of coordination for sensory and intellectual functioning will not be in force *post mortem*. Once we are out from under it, our intellectual souls' cognitive opportunities (but not their essential capacities) will be expanded. Scotus's estimate of who we are as knowers affords no explanation of why there must be bodies as well as minds in the life to come.

The Nature of Human Happiness

For the elect, the life to come will be the scene of ultimate happiness. Here Scotus makes himself unmistakably clear: the soul is the beatifiable part of human beings and is the immediate subject of happiness, whereas the whole nature is the mediate and not the immediate subject. To explain *what happiness is,* Scotus distinguishes between the first *esse* or perfection of a thing and its second *esse* or perfection. First *esse* has to do with the essence of a thing; first perfection is had when nothing is lacking to the essential being of a thing.[90] Second *esse* or perfection has to do with the functional activity (*operatio*) that perfects a power.[91]

Scotus has in mind functional activities that have intentionality, specifically, cognitive and appetitive acts that unite their subject X to something external Y by having the external thing Y as their intentional object. The power is perfected by the cognitive or appetitive act, while—where Y is nobler than X—the subject X may be said to be perfected by the external thing Y, without X really being Y (*pace* ancient tags, the knower does not have literally to *become* the thing known) and without

88. *Op. Ox.* IV, d. 45, q. 2, n. 16, 10.183.
89. *Op. Ox.* IV, d. 45, q. 2, n. 12, 10.182.
90. *Op. Ox.* IV, d. 49, q. 2, n. 13, 10.338; *Op. Ox.* IV, d. 49, q. 2, n. 22, 10.349.
91. *Op. Ox.* IV, d. 49, q. 2, n. 15, 10.339.

Y informing *X* (the thing known or loved does not thereby inhere in or denominate the knowing or loving subject).[92] Scotus makes it explicit: if the power could exist *per se,* it could be perfected by the functional activity (*operatio*) without the essence, but the essence as remote subject could not receive second *esse* without the power.[93]

Strictly speaking, mere bodies that lack cognition do not have second *esse* or perfection.[94] Second *esse* involves the internal act of the cognitive or appetitive power, the external object, and a relation of union founded on the internal act and having the external object as its term. For animals, sensory cognition unites them with external objects less perfect than they are (with sensible qualities); and sensory appetite cannot aim beyond individual or species perfection.[95] But created intellectual cognition can conceive of something more perfect than its subject (such as God and nobler created intellectual natures), and created intellectual appetite can will and love something better than the subject itself. Thus, created intellectual cognition and will can unite their subject to something external that is nobler than the subject itself.[96] Drawing on his arguments that there is an eminence hierarchy in natures and that it is bounded by an infinite being—a nature that is not the sort to be loved for the sake of another but only for its own sake[97]—Scotus concludes that the infinite being is supremely appetible by intellectual natures. Cognitive and appetitive union with the infinite being would constitute the ultimate second perfection of such intellectual natures.[98]

With this distinction in hand, Scotus proceeds to identify happiness not with first perfection, but with second perfection—that is to say, not with *esse* but with *bene esse.*[99] Metaphysically, happiness is an accident: either the functional activity (*operatio*) that unites its subject with the infinite being, or the relation of union that it founds.[100] Scotus distinguishes the happiness of the power (of the intellect or the will) from the

92. *Op. Ox.* IV, d. 49, q. 2, nn. 22–23, 10.349; *Op. Ox.* IV, d. 49, q. 2, n. 27, 10.355.
93. *Op. Ox.* IV, d. 49, q. 2, nn. 15, 18, 10.339.
94. *Op. Ox.* IV, d. 49, q. 8, n. 6, 10.503.
95. *Op. Ox.* IV, d. 49, q. 8, n. 6, 10.502–3.
96. *Op. Ox.* IV, d. 49, q. 2, n. 22, 10.349; *Op. Ox.* IV, q. 4, n. 2, 10.380.
97. *Op. Ox.* IV, d. 49, q. 2, nn. 19–21, 10.344–45.
98. *Op. Ox.* IV, d. 49, q. 2, nn. 22–23, 10.349.
99. *Op. Ox.* IV, d. 49, q. 2, n. 26, 10.354; *Op. Ox.* IV, d. 49, q. 2, n. 32, 10.357.
100. *Op. Ox.* IV, d. 49, q. 2, nn. 26–27, 32, 10.354–55, et7.

happiness of the intellectual nature. The happiness of a *power* consists in any functional activity (*operatio*) that unites its subject with the infinite being. This way, an intellectual vision of God beatifies the intellect, while friendship love of God beatifies the will.[101] The happiness of the intellectual *nature,* however, consists not in the aggregate of such acts, but in the one act by which it is most immediately united to the infinite being:[102] according to Scotus, this is fruition, the will's act of friendship love for God.[103] Either way, as above, the proximate subject of happiness is the power or the soul whose power it is.[104] Nonintellectual animals and their powers can be beatified *secundum quid,* insofar as they can be joined to their best objects.[105] Mere bodies cannot be beatified either way because they cannot be subjects of such intentional acts. Scotus quips that a heavy body moves toward the center of the earth, but it has only an *action* of moving toward the center, not a functional activity (*operatio*)![106]

Happiness and Appetite-Satisfaction

These reflections do not settle the question of whether soul-body reunion is required for perfect human happiness, if "perfect happiness puts every desire to rest." Even if the separate soul and its formally distinct but really identical soul-powers of intellect and will can be subjects of functional activities that unite it to God, would that be enough to satisfy all of the soul's desires? How would intellectual vision and enjoyment of God fulfill my desire to taste chocolate or to feel the summer breeze in my face or to solve a philosophical problem? What about the soul's natural inclination to perfect its body and to unite with it to make something one *per se*? Can the soul be perfectly happy when these appetites are left unsatisfied?

In effect, Scotus offers two responses. The first is that while my desires to taste chocolate and feel the breeze and solve philosophical problems are distinct from one another and from my desire for God, nevertheless, God as the infinite being contains "unitively and eminently" whatever one can rightly will. It is a medieval commonplace that the di-

---

101. *Op. Ox.* IV, d. 49, q. 3, 10.371–72.

102. *Op. Ox.* IV, d. 49, q. 3, n. 6, 10.37–72; *Op. Ox.* IV, d. 49, q. 3, n. 5, 10.3510; *Op. Ox.* IV, n. 8, 10.376.

103. *Op. Ox.* IV, d. 49, q. 5, n. 3, 10.423–25.

104. *Op. Ox.* IV, d. 49, q. 8, n. 7, 10.503.

105. *Op. Ox.* IV, d. 49, q. 8, n. 6, 10.502.

106. *Op. Ox.* IV, d. 49, q. 8, n. 6, 10.503.

vine essence contains created perfections in a more eminent way. Scotus may mean that though seeing God will not literally satisfy these desires, I will be more than glad to give up on them and accept the substitution, so that it is not the case that happiness involves the satisfaction of all desires. Alternatively, Scotus may intend that since God is loved above all and for God's own sake, everything and anything else will be loved for God's sake, so that God unites the other desires as their end. When the end is reached, I will not care about the subordinate desires any more.[107] If so, then surely union with God could get me to give up on any conscious deliberative desire my soul had for my body as well.

Scotus's second approach takes up Bonaventure's distinction between intensive and extensive perfection. Beatific enjoyment of God would constitute intensive perfection in an intellectual nature. But where the "extensional totality" of the nature is concerned, the nature will not be at rest unless whatever is capable of being at rest is in fact at rest. The extensional totality of human nature includes both body and soul, each of which has a natural appetite for the other. He concludes that so far as extensive perfection is concerned, human happiness could not exist without the soul's reunion with its body.[108]

Scotus is clear (as above) that soul-body reunion perfects the composite whole, which is principally intended by human nature.[109] But he does not grant the general truth of Aquinas's and Henry of Ghent's assumption that a part receives its perfection in the whole. On the contrary, Scotus finds it defensible to maintain that the soul remains equally perfect in itself, whether or not it shares its perfection with the body, whether it is separate or whether it is joined to the body. Reaching back to his distinction between first and second esse/act/perfection, Scotus declares that natural inclinations to first act are of the imperfect to the perfect and are concomitant with essential potency. But natural inclinations to second act are of the essentially perfect to the perfection to be shared and are concomitant with accidental potency. Scotus says that the soul's inclination for the body is of the second sort, evidently implying that the soul is essentially perfect in itself (is in first act), and that it is accidental to the soul whether or not it shares its perfection with its body—this

---

107. *Op. Ox.* IV, d. 49, q. 2, n. 27; *Op. Ox.* IV, q. 6, n. 1, 10.475.
108. *Op. Ox.* IV, d. 49, q. 3, n. 9, 10.377.
109. *Op. Ox.* IV, d. 45, q. 2, n. 14, 10.182.

even though, when it does, they unite to form a composite that is one *per se*! This means that no violence would be done to the separate soul if it were never reunited; for the perpetual separation would frustrate not an essential but only an accidental potency.[110] This also suggests that the *esse* that the *bene esse* of beatific enjoyment presupposes is the first *esse* of *the soul,* not that of *the whole human being;* likewise, it suggests that the soul's functional activities that unite it with God are unaffected by whether the soul is separate or united.

Even if the soul did receive perfection from the body *ante mortem,* it would not follow that it needed to continue to do so *post mortem.* Scotus reads Avicenna as maintaining that the soul's appetite for the body is satisfied by perfecting the body and acquiring perfections through the conjunction before death. Scotus's Avicenna does not think that the separate soul would need to reunite to do so again.[111]

The Contingencies of Divine Justice

If Scotus's estimates of who we are as subjects of knowledge and appetites do not require *post-mortem* resurrection and reunion, his reflections on divine justice recontextualize the argument from who we are as agents standing before the great judgment seat of Christ. Scotus contrasts *commutative* justice, which has to do with rewards and punishments, with *distributive* justice, which has to do with natures and what is proportioned to perfect them.[112] Likewise, if justice is uprightness of will, Scotus recognizes two measures: what befits the divine will and what befits the needs of creatures. Scotus declares that God cannot will or do anything outside the first, but God can will or do some things that lie outside the second.[113]

Distributive Justice?   Scotus's view is that when it comes to natures, only infinite being is compelling. Divine justice inclines the divine will to render divine goodness its due: namely, to be loved above all and for its own sake. Creatable natures are finite goods: their natural goodness constitutes some reason to love them. But because each may be incompatible

110. *Op. Ox.* IV, d. 43, q. 2, n. 24, 10.33–34.
111. *Op. Ox.* IV, d. 43, q. 2, n. 25, 10.34.
112. *Op. Ox.* IV, d. 46, q. 1, n. 4, 10.240–41*.
113. *Op. Ox.* IV, d. 46, q. 1, nn. 5–6, 10.241.

with other finite goods, this reason is always defeasible. Therefore, divine justice does not incline the divine will determinately one way or the other where creatures are concerned. Whatever it wills, it could, absolutely speaking, will the opposite justly. Thus, it pertains to the nature of fire to be hot, but to the nature of water to be cold; to the nature of fire to be up high, but to the nature of earth to be down low. Nevertheless, God would violate no obligation to creatures if God made fire without heat and water without coldness, fire down low and earth up high.[114]

In general, whether or not God gives to creatures those things that perfect their natures is not a matter of divine obligation *to them,* but rather is one of free and contingent divine choice. To be sure, God owes it to Godself to be of consistent purpose. In this present state, God does have a general policy of always-or-for-the-most-part concurrence with natural regularities. Thus, free and contingent divine policy is what underwrites Aristotelian optimism for this present state. Always-or-for-the-most-part divine distributive justice is a fact of our *ante-mortem* lives. Three-legged or blind sheep occur in particular cases, but defective specimens are rare. But what makes the world to come a different *state* is that divine policies regarding supranatural donations, concurrence, and obstruction will be different. What they will be, once again, is a function of free and contingent divine choice. For God to be true to Godself, God must stick with divine plans for the different states. But whether or not that means resurrecting human beings into metaphysical perfection depends on what divine plans for the world to come are.

Commutative Justice? The argument for resurrection from divine retribution depends upon the premise that acts of the composite are what God targets for evaluation. Within medieval philosophical theology, this would not have been an uncontroversial assumption. Both Abelard[115] and Ockham[116] contend, on the contrary, that the proper loci of moral evaluation are acts of the soul that are within the soul's power to con-

---

114. *Op. Ox.* IV, d. 46, q. 1, nn. 8–9, 10.252.

115. See Peter Abelard, *Ethics,* ed. and trans. D. E. Luscombe (Oxford: Oxford University Press, 1971). See also Calvin Normore, "Goodness and Rational Choice in the Early Middle Ages," in *Emotions and Choice from Boethius to Descartes,* ed. Henrik Lagerlund and Mikko Yrjonsouri (Dordrecht: Kluwer, 2002), 29–47.

116. Ockham, *Quaest. in III Sent.,* q. 11 (OTh 6.351–90); *Quodlibeta* III, q. 14 (OTh 9.253–57). For a fuller discussion of this issue in Scotus, Ockham, and Wodeham, see Rega Wood and Marilyn McCord Adams, "Is to Will It as Bad as to Do It?" *Franciscan Studies* 41 (1981): 5–60.

trol—acts of consent or free volitions. Outward acts caused by such inner acts might be called morally good or bad in some derivative sense. But—Abelard and Ockham contend—even voluntary outward acts are not proper subjects of moral evaluation themselves.

In fact, Scotus sides with Aquinas in maintaining that outward acts have their own distinct suitability-conditions, and hence that acts of the composite are proper subjects of moral evaluation.[117] But the relevance of this fact is not direct, because Scotus denies that careers of moral virtue are intrinsically worthy of any eternal destiny (after all, humans are by nature mortal), much less of beatific vision and enjoyment of God. What is at stake on Judgment Day is merit and demerit, divine acceptance and divine reproval. The criteria that divide the sheep from the goats and the fact that there are any such criteria are both products of free and contingent divine volition. In fact, Scotus does think that divine statutes make merit and demerit a function of moral performance and sacramental participation, so that body and soul earn merit and demerit together. That it is so is an expression not of divine debts and creaturely entitlements but of divine liberality. Evaluating composite agents is what God wants to do.[118]

Charting Divine Purposes in Creation

Scotus characterizes God as a maximally well-organized lover. Scotus explains that rational agents begin by willing the end, then what are proximately, next what are remotely ordered to attain it. In several texts, Scotus makes bold to analyze the means-end structure of divine purposes in creation, to identify the explanatory or natural priorities and posteriorities among divine will-objects. Surely these would be the passages to clarify God's reasons for freely and contingently purposing permanent soul-body reunion! Unfortunately, Scotus's focus on other issues means that the material cosmos does not always loom large.

In some places, Scotus is commending the idea that predestination and hypostatic union are naturally prior to divine consideration of sin and evil. Distinguishing instants of nature analogous to instants of time, Scotus charts divine intentions as follows:

117. *Quodlibeta*, q. 18, 12.474–91.
118. *Quodlibeta*, q. 17, 12.459–66.

n1: God loves Godself and the infinite goodness of divinity.

n2: God loves Godself and the infinite goodness of divinity in others [i.e., other persons of the Trinity].

n3: God wills—i.e., all three divine persons will—to widen the Trinitarian friendship circle, to be loved by a creature in the highest degree possible for something created.

n4: God intends the union of that created nature which ought to love God in the highest degree even if no one fell.[119]

Scotus's further comments fill out his picture of what God intends for rational creatures. At *n3* God wills created persons to share with the Trinity in the intimate friendship-love and enjoyment of God above all. The primary finite object of divine love is the rational soul of Christ, with whom God wanted to share love whether or not any other creatures existed. Secondarily, God wills that Christ be the head of many co-lovers, some angels and others human souls. At *n4* God wills as the *proximate means* to that end conditions that fit rational creatures for such intimacy with the eternal Trinity. The soul of Christ is infused with fullness of grace, maximal human knowledge, and impeccability of will, and it is hypostatically united to the divine Word. Angels and other human souls are fitted for sharing the divine love life by infused grace. God freely and contingently legislates a system of merit that creates *conventional and statutory* connections between the finite and temporal acts and states of created persons and divine acceptance, infused grace, and eternal glory on the other, thereby giving finite and temporal created acts and states eternal significance. On this scheme, God does not purpose predestination or hypostatic union to solve "the sin problem." It would be foolish for the best thing God does in creation to be motivated by the worst thing rational creatures do!

In *Ordinatio* I, d. 41, Scotus develops this analysis further to make explicit how the division between the predestinate and reprobate arises.

n3: Peter and Judas are represented to God as alike in natural features; God wills glory for Peter, and elicits no positive act regarding Judas.

---

119. *Op. Ox.* III, d. 4, q. 4; in *Ioannis Duns Scoti Doctoris Mariani Theologiae Marianae Elementa*, ed. Carolo Balić OFM (Sibenik, Jugoslavia, 1933), 14–15. Cf. *Op. Par.* III, d. 7, q. 4 (Balić, 14–15); *Rep. Barcin.* III, d. 2, q. 3 (Balić, 182–84).

n4: God wills grace—faith, merits, and a good use of free will for Peter, and elicits no positive act regarding Judas.

n5: God wills to permit Peter and Judas to sin (and therefore wills not to obstruct their exercise of free choice so as to eliminate the possibility of sin).

n6: Judas is presented to God as one who will commit the sin of final impenitence, while Peter is presented as dying in a state of grace.

n7: God justly punishes or reprobates Judas.[120]

Here Scotus is keen to stress the asymmetry between predestination and reprobation. Because God is not a punisher before humans are debtors, divine reprobation is naturally posterior to God's eternal knowledge of human free choice. God takes the initiative in predestining to glory (at *n3*) and ordering to grace (at *n4*). But sinning to the end is something God merely permits (at *n5*); Judas has the initiative (at *n6*) in his own reprobation (divinely willed at *n7*).

Striking for present purposes is that these maps tell us nothing about how a material creation fits in—about "when" in the natural sequence God opts to embody human souls and place them in a material cosmos. Likewise, in *Ordinatio* I, d. 41, the features of created agency that make the eternal difference are acts of free choice—perseverance to the end versus final impenitence. Unless it is built into Scotus's use of the proper names "Peter" and "Judas," Scotus says nothing to indicate that these are acts of a composite human being rather than of the intellectual soul alone. By themselves, the charts offer a "spiritualized" picture of divine purposes for human beings.

Only in Scotus's replies to objections does it become clear that this was not Scotus's intention. In two texts, Scotus halfway meets traditional views—that Incarnation would not have happened apart from sin. Even if God would have purposed hypostatic union for the soul of Christ no matter what, there remains something that would not have happened apart from sin: Christ would not have assumed passible and mortal flesh. Scotus explains that apart from sin, the glory of Christ's happy soul would have redounded to his flesh immediately. God sees Christ's role as mediator in the flesh naturally posterior to divine vision of human sin.[121]

120. *Ordinatio* I, d. 41, q. u, nn. 45–46, 6.332–33; *Op. Ox.* III, d. 7, q. 3 (Balić, 5); *Rep. Barcin.* III, d. 2, q. 3 (Balić, 183).

121. *Op.Par.* III, d. 7, q. 4 (Balić, 15); *Rep. Barcin.* III, d. 2, q. 3 (Balić, 184).

Yet, if glorified souls would flood human bodies with perfection "immediately"—namely, as soon as they were united with their bodies or, if already united, as soon as the souls were glorified—the question arises just "when" that would be relative to the above charts.

Of all of the maps, only that found in a passage quoted by Allan Wolter from *Ordinatio* III (suppl.), d. 32 (Assisi com.137, fol. 174ra–va) tries to answer the question. On its simple scheme,

> *n1:* God loves Godself ordinately and so not in an envious or jealous manner.
>
> *n2:* God wills those things that are immediately ordered to God: namely, to have co-lovers.
>
> *n3:* God wills what is necessary for this end: namely, grace.
>
> *n4:* God wills for the sake of the co-lovers other things such as the material world to serve the human co-lovers.

Expanding on God's willing of the material world, Scotus cites Aristotle's comment in *Physics* II: that human being is somehow the end of all sensible things. Scotus says first that God wills the material world at *n4* because God wills human co-lovers at *n2*, and wills the former for the sake of the latter. Scotus adds, "That which is closer to the ultimate end is customarily said to be the end of the sensible world, whether because God wills the sensible world to be ordered to predestined human beings, or because God's more immediate concern is not that the sensible world exist, but rather that human beings should love God."[122]

On this analysis, God's primary purpose in creating human souls is that they should love God above all and for God's own sake. This much could be secured spirit-to-spirit. But literally as an afterthought so far as the explanatory priorities are concerned, God wills the material cosmos for our sake, evidently not—according to Scotus—so that we might think clearly, not so that we might enjoy a more intense degree of happiness, but so that we might be metaphysically complete. Scotus does not say, but perhaps he is thinking, that God wills soul-body (re)union because it enhances our natural goodness. Apart from sin, human souls would have been created unified, graced, and glorified, and the glory of

---

122. *Ordinatio* III (suppl.), d. 32 (Assisi com.137, fol. 174ra–va), ed. and trans. Allan B. Wolter, in *Franciscan Christology*, ed. Damian McElrath (St. Bonaventure, N.Y.: Franciscan Institute Publications, 1980), 154–57.

the soul would have redounded onto its body "immediately." Despite the fall, Christ's soul was glorified immediately upon its creation. Because of the fall, the soul's glory did not redound onto Christ's body immediately so that he could redeem Adam's race through the passion of his mortal and passible flesh. Because of the fall, Adam's race was given over to its natural mortality, and glory for elect souls was postponed until after death. Resurrection restores us to that metaphysical perfection that divine liberality originally intended.

Grace Builds on Nature?

Bonaventure, Aquinas, and Scotus all agree: beatific vision and enjoyment of God is the supranatural end of human being. The neo-Thomist tag invites us to imagine God starting with metaphysically complete human being and then supranaturally infusing it with qualities that furnish it with active and passive powers beyond what nature could provide. Is this not what God did when God created Adam and Eve with original justice? Is it not what God does now with Adam's fallen race when God infuses grace in the soul, as well as the theological virtues—faith, hope, and charity—in the soul's powers? Bonaventure and Aquinas expect God to restore, augment, and infuse new powers to give the soul complete control over its body. All three use hydraulic imagery, when they speak of the risen body's dowry of perfections redounding from the happy soul. Likewise, some medievals tried to explain the end of generation and corruption by the elements in terms of their receiving supranatural qualities instead of the contraries Aristotelian physics takes them to have now.

Scotus does not entirely reject this "infused quality" strategy for explaining differences between this present state and the life to come. Scotus seems to think clarity (which he understands as apt coloration) involves infused qualities.[123] Likewise, agility is to be explained partly in terms of the intensification of the soul's natural power to move its body, and partly in terms of accidental changes that remove impediments in the body (e.g., replacing some heavy humors with lighter ones).[124]

Nevertheless, Scotus thinks that nature itself sets boundaries on what

---

123. *Op. Ox.* IV, d. 49, q. 15, nn. 2, 5, 10.545–46.
124. *Op. Ox.* IV, d. 49, q. 14, nn. 6–7, 10.543; *Op. Ox.* IV, d. 49, q. 14, n. 9, 10.543; *Op. Ox.* IV, d. 49, q. 14, n. 11, 10.544.

can inhere in and what can be the subject of what: more precisely, a subject S cannot receive a form F if there is a natural repugnance or formal incompatibility between S and F. In consequence, nothing can receive a quality that is formally incompatible with its necessary accidents. The intellectual soul cannot be a subject of the accidental form of whiteness, nor a body be the subject of an act of understanding. The human soul by nature can perfect only bodies of a certain density and complexion. Thus, it is no good assuming that an infused quality could make an adult human body light as a feather, because a certain degree of heaviness is essential to a body's being of the right type. Nor would it work to explain subtlety (or the body's ability to be in the same place at the same time as another body) in terms of the body's becoming porous, because human souls are metaphysically incapable of perfecting such lightweight rarefied bodies.[125] Scotus also thinks it metaphysically impossible for human souls to acquire omnipotent power to control and subdue their own bodies. *Post-mortem* subordination of human bodies to what their souls will, will be the result of divine policy for that state; its efficient cause can be none other than the divine will itself.[126]

Significantly, Scotus thinks that the future impassibility of human bodies and incorruptibility of the elements cannot be explained by appeal to supranaturally infused qualities. Human bodies are composites of prime matter and the substantial form of corporeity. Prime matter is by nature in potency with respect to any form it lacks but could receive. Its being subject to one—no matter which one—does not take away its potency to receive the others and, hence, does not remove the composite's susceptibility to corruption. Moreover, like all living bodies, human bodies are by nature heterogeneous. The elements by nature have contrary qualities, and the qualities that they have are by nature contrary. The natures of these things do not change from one state to the next. Scotus concludes that there will be no *internal* cause of impassibility in human bodies or the elements. Rather, its explanation will be *external*: the divine will's general policy for that state of withholding divine concurrence with corruptive agents.[127]

Where subtlety is concerned, Scotus maintains—against Aquinas—

---

125. *Op. Ox.* IV, d. 49, q. 14, n. 11, 10.544.
126. *Op. Ox.* IV, d. 49, q. 13, n. 11, 10.540.
127. *Op. Ox.* IV, d. 49, q. 13, nn. 2–3, 10.538; *Op. Ox.* IV, n. 9, 10.539–40.

that the quantitative dimensions of one body are not *formally* incompatible with those of another. Rather they are *virtually* incompatible, in that the quantity of one causes the space to be filled by the first body, and this effect is incompatible with the same space simultaneously being occupied by something else as well. For Christ to exit the virgin's womb or pass through a closed door, the divine will has to obstruct the natural efficient causal connection between quantity and space-filling. Divine policy in the life to come is to obstruct quantity from producing the space-filling effect, whenever a glorified soul wants its body to be in the same place as something else.[128] Because God has a general policy of concurrence for this present state, God cannot obstruct the production of the space-filling effect in this present state nonmiraculously.[129]

What these reflections of Scotus bring forcibly to our attention is how divine policies for the life to come involve not only metaphysically complete humans and supranaturally infused qualities, but also the systematic obstruction of natural causes, more exactly, divine policies of nonconcurrence with such causes in producing their natural effects.

Consider the fundamental contention by all three authors: God wills all human beings to be permanently metaphysically complete in the life to come. Permanence for human composites requires the systematic and permanent obstruction of natural corrupting causes, within the human body as well as without. Grace does not simply add what is *beyond* nature (what is, literally, *supra*natural). Grace traffics in what is *contrary* to nature, not only to the nature of the elements, but to the nature of the human body itself. Grace obstructs all human vegetative functions. Grace obstructs some sensory functions—notably taste and smell, which involve natural changes in the sense organ, and perhaps indirectly hearing, if there is no sound in the life to come. Grace also obstructs the wills of the damned and of the elect from changing their fundamental orientations. Evidently, from Scotus's point of view, "grace builds on nature" can no more integrate the data of Christian eschatology than functional arguments can.

---

128. *Op. Ox.* IV, d. 49, q. 16, n. 19, 10.551.
129. *Op. Ox.* IV, d. 49, q. 12, n. 6, 10.574.

BODIES IN THE LIFE TO COME: WHAT GOOD ARE THEY?

Why will there be bodies as well as souls in the life to come? The source of the problem also sponsors a distinctive solution. The end-time picture inherited and embraced by our authors does not give the body much to do because it is rooted in the contemplative ideal.[130] In *Summa theologiae* II-II, qq. 179–82, Aquinas reshapes Aristotle's distinction between the contemplative life that aims at contemplation of the truth and as much as possible withdraws from outward distractions, and the active life that focuses on outward actions and social institutions and is enabled by moral virtues. Aristotle declares that the contemplative life is "godlike" and so "too high for us," but urges those who can to seek it all the same.[131] Aquinas recognizes that simple intuitive apprehension of the truth is natural to God and the angels, whereas the human way of knowing is naturally discursive.[132]

Nevertheless, for Aquinas, contemplation of divine truth is the *supra*natural end of every human being.[133] Not everyone can be a full-time contemplative in this present state; someone has to organize society and provide the necessities of life.[134] Those who can, prepare for beatific vision and enjoyment through a life-long process of "alienating" the soul from dependence on sensory functions.[135] Such alienation is not metaphysical—human beings are not to hope with Socrates that death will bring permanent separation of the soul from the body—but functional. Contemplative perfection for human beings will mean the complete *subordination* of body to soul, which resolves into the soul's utter *independence* from the body so far as its contemplative activities are concerned, and the soul's complete *control* of the body's movements. In short, the contemplative ideal hopes that death will usher the elect into a state in which their bodies are no longer useful, and in which their bodies no longer get in the way!

---

130. Thanks to Stephen Brown, whose remarks in another connection at the Scotus conference in Bonn, November 7, 2008, brought the salience of the contemplative versus active distinction to mind. Thanks to him also for so much helpful work!

131. Aristotle, *Nicomachean Ethics* X, 7, 1177b30–1178a1; X, 8, 1178b9–23.

132. *ST* II-II, q. 180, a. 3, c. and ad 1; *ST* II-II, a. 6 ad 2.

133. *ST* II-II, q. 180, a. 4, c.; *ST* II-II, q. 181, a. 1, c.

134. *ST* II-II, q. 179, a. 2, c. & ad 3; *ST* II-II, q. 181, a. 1, c.

135. *ST* II-II, q. 180, a. 5, c.

The systematic reasons furnished by the contemplative ideal for including bodies in the life to come have to do not with functional utility—that is why our authors have difficulty in producing plausible functional arguments—but with metaphysical dignity (with *bona honesta*), with symbolic function, and with ornamentation. Because soul-body composites are what we *are* metaphysically, the intellectual soul is only a metaphysical fragment of a human being. Resurrection and reunion make the human individual a better being because metaphysically perfect and complete. Likewise, resurrection and reunion are a more impressive manifestation of how much there is to God. Divine power is able not only to create things *ex nihilo* and conserve separate souls in existence; divine power can also return numerically the same body after it has been reduced to the elements and reunite it to numerically the same soul that animated it before!

Back in the twelfth century, Hugh of St. Victor explains that soul-body union can contribute to human dignity another way, namely by furnishing the opportunity for greater Godlikeness. To be sure, Godhead itself is simple and incorporeal. But God exercises providence over creation. In the beginning, God creates human souls embodied and places them in a material world, to give them something to govern, so that they can imitate God in exercising dominion and providential control. Good government required appropriate hierarchy: human souls, subordinate to God; human bodies and the material world generally, subordinate to human reason. This order was disrupted by the fall, but will be secured for the elect in heaven.[136] In effect, three of the body's heavenly endowments are given to enhance the contemplative soul's dominion. Impassibility means an end to death and to life-preserving vegetative functions, and so serves the soul's independence by freeing it from worries about food and health and from the distractions of child-rearing. Subtlety and agility make bodily movements easier and are there to augment the soul's control. By contrast, clarity (which Bonaventure and Aquinas understand as brightness) is *symbolic*: the bodies of the righteous, shining like the sun (Mt 13:43), will be outward and visible signs of glorified happy souls within. Supranatural brightness will also make both heavenly and human bodies more *ornamental*.

---

136. Hugh of St. Victor, *De sacramentis,* trans. Roy Deferrari (Cambridge, Mass.: Medieval Academy of America, 1951), I, 1.19.23; I, 1.25.25; I, 2.1.28–29; I, 6.1.94.

Where the damned are concerned, the picture is more mixed. God bestows the dignity of metaphysical completeness on the damned as much as on the elect. But separate souls already suffer the indignity of being unable to control their thoughts or their location. Their eternal lack of control is a symbol of their own failed providence, that is, of their refusal to govern themselves according to right reason and divine commands. The bodies of the damned are raised to take their punishment, insofar as they have distracted the soul from higher things. Human bodies and the elements remain useful insofar as they serve as God's instruments in augmenting the torment.

Bibliography

Aertsen, Jan A. "Aquinas and the Human Desire for Knowledge." *American Catholic Philosophical Quarterly* 79 (2005): 411–30.

————. "Thomas von Aquin: Alle Menschen verlangen von Natur nach Wissen." In *Philosophen des Mittelalters: eine Einführung,* edited by Theo Kobusch, 186–201. Darmstadt: Primus, 2000.

————. "Was heißt Metaphysik bei Thomas von Aquin?" In *"Scientia" und "ars" im Hoch- und Spätmittelalter,* edited by Ingrid Craemer-Ruegenberg and Andreas Speer, 217–39. Miscellanea Mediaevalia 22. Berlin: Walter de Gruyter, 1994.

————. "What Is First and Most Fundamental? The Beginnings of Transcendental Philosophy." In *Was ist Philosophie im Mittelalter?* edited by Jan A. Aertsen and Andreas Speer, 305–21. Berlin: Walter De Gruyter, 1998.

Albert the Great. *De causis et processu universitatis a prima causa.* Edited by Winfried Fauser. *Editio Coloniensis,* 17/2. Münster: Aschendorff, 1993.

————. *Metaphysica.* Edited by Bernhard Geyer. *Editio Coloniensis,* 16/1. Münster: Aschendorff, 1960.

Alexander of Aphrodisias. *Commentarius Alexandri Aphrodisiensis in libros metaphysicos Aristotelis.* Edited by Hermann Bonitz. Berlin: George Reimer, 1847.

————. *Commentary on Aristotle's Metaphysics 1.* Translated by William Dooley. London: Duckworth, 1989.

————. *Commentary on Aristotle's Metaphysics 2 and 3.* Translated by William Dooley and Arthur Madigan. London: Duckworth, 1992.

————. *Commentary on Aristotle's Metaphysics 4.* Translated by Arthur Madigan. London: Duckworth, 1993.

————. *De anima.* Edited by Ivo Bruns. Berlin: George Reimer, 1887.

————. *In Aristotelis metaphysica commentaria.* Edited by Michael Hayduck. Berlin: George Reimer, 1881.

————. *On Aristotle's Metaphysics 1.* Translated by W. E. Dooley. Ithaca, N.Y.: Cornell University Press, 1989.

Anonymous. *Commentarium in Platonis "Parmenidem."* Edited by Alessandro Linguiti. Florence: Olschki, 1995.

Aris, Marc-Aeilko. "'Praegnans affirmatio.' Gotteserkenntnis als Ästhetik des Nichtsichtbaren bei Nikolaus von Kues." *Theologische Quartalsschrift* 181 (2001): 97–111.

Aristotle. *Categories*. Translated by E. M. Edghill. In *The Works of Aristotle*. Vol. 1. Edited by W. D. Ross. Oxford: Clarendon Press, 1928.

————. *De Anima*. Edited by Sir David Ross. Oxford: Clarendon, 1961.

————. *Metaphysica. Lib. I–XIV. Recensio et Translatio Guillelmi de Moerbeka*. In *Aristoteles latinus*. 2 vols. Edited by Gudrun Vuillemin-Diem. Aristoteles Latinus XXV 3. Leiden: Brill, 1995.

————. *Metaphysics*. Edited by W. Jaeger. Oxford: n.p., 1957.

————. *Metaphysics*. Edited by W. D. Ross. Oxford: Clarendon, 1958.

————. *Nicomachean Ethics*. Edited by I. Bywater. Oxford: n.p., 1894.

————. *Posterior Analytics*. Edited by J. Barnes. 2nd ed. Oxford: Oxford University Press, 1994.

Aubenque, Pierre. "Aristoteles und das Problem der Metaphysik." *Zeitschrift für Philosophische Forschung* 15 (1961): 321–33.

————. *Le problème de l'être chez Aristote*. 2nd ed. Paris: Presses universitaires de France, 1994.

Augustine. *Confessionum Libri XIII*. Edited by Lucas Verheijen, O.S.A. Corpus Christianorum Series Latina 27. Turnhout: Brepols, 1986.

————. *Confessions*. Edited with commentary by James J. O'Donnell. Oxford: Clarendon Press, 1992.

————. *De ordine*. Edited by W. M. Green. Corpus Christianorum Series Latina 29. Turnhout: Brepols, 1970.

————. *De Trinitate*. Edited by J.-P. Migne. Patrologia Latina 42. Paris: Migne, 1845.

————. *Epistolarum Classes Quatuor*. Edited by J.-P. Migne. Patrologia Latina 33. Paris: Migne, 1845.

Averroes. *Aristotelis opera cum Averrois commentariis*. Venice: Juntas, 1562–74. Reprint, Frankfurt: Minerva, 1962.

————. *In II Metaph*. Ed. Ven. 1562–1574. Reprint, Frankfurt a. M. 1962.

Avicenna. *Liber de philosophia prima sive scientia divina*. In *Avicenna Latinus: Liber de philosophia prima sive scientia divina I–IV*. Edited by Simone Van Riet. Leuven: Peeters and Leiden: E. J. Brill, 1977.

Barber, Kenneth, and Jorge J. E. Gracia, eds. *Individuation and Identity in Early Modern Philosophy*. Albany: State University of New York Press, 1994.

Bergmann, Gustav. "Individuals." *Philosophical Studies* 9 (1958): 78–85.

Bertolacci, Amos. *The Reception of Aristotle's* Metaphysics *in Avicenna's* Kitāb al-Sifā': *A Milestone of Western Metaphysical Thought*. Islamic Philosophy, Theology and Science. Texts and Studies 63. Leiden: E. J. Brill, 2006.

Black, Max. "The Identity of Indiscernibles." In *Universals and Particulars: Readings in Ontology*, edited by Michael Loux, 250–62. Notre Dame, Ind.: University of Notre Dame Press, 1976.

Boethius. *De Trinitate*. In *The Theological Tractates*. Edited by H. F. Stewart and E. K. Rand. Cambridge, Mass.: Harvard University Press, 1918; reprint, 1968.

Bonaventure. *Commentarius in librum Sentiarum*. In *Opera Omnia*. Vols. 1–4. Edited by Collegii S. Bonaventura. Florence: Quaracchi, 1882.

Bonelli, Maddalena. *Alessandro di Afrodisia e la metafisica come scienza dimostrativa*. Naples: Bibliopolis, 2001.

Braine, David. *The Reality of Time and the Existence of God.* Oxford: Clarendon Press, 1988.

Brower, Jeffrey. "Medieval Theories of Relation." In *The Stanford Encyclopedia of Philosophy.* http://plato.stanford.edu/entries/relation-medieval/.

Brown, Stephen F. "*Duo Candelabra Parisiensia:* Prosper of Reggio in Emilia's Portrait of the Enduring Presence of Henry of Ghent and Godfrey of Fontaines Regarding the Nature of Theological Study." In *Nach der Verurteilung von 1277: Philosophie und Theologie an der Universität von Paris im letzten Viertel des 13. Jahrhunderts. Studien und Texte,* edited by Jan A. Aertsen, Kent Emery Jr., and Andreas Speer, 320–56. Miscellanea Mediaevalia 28. Berlin: Walter de Gruyter, 2000.

Burkert, Walter. *Weisheit und Wissenschaft: Studien zu Pythagoras, Philolaos und Platon.* Nürnberg: H. Carl, 1962.

Burrell, David B. "Review of Christopher Hughes, *A Complex Theory of a Simple God.*" *Journal of Religion* 72, no. 1 (1992): 120–21.

Chalmers, David. "Does Conceivability Entail Possibility?" In *Conceivability and Possibility,* edited by Tamar Szabó Gendler and John Hawthorne, 145–200. Oxford: Oxford University Press, 2002.

Chardonnens, Denis. *L'Homme sous le regard de la providence.* Paris: Librarie Philosophique J. Vrin, 1997.

Collingwood, R. G. *An Autobiography.* London: Oxford University Press, 1939.

Damascius. *Commentaire du Parménide de Platon.* Edited and translated by Leendert Gerrit Westerink. Introduction, translation, and commentary by Joseph Combès. Paris: Les Belles Lettres, 1997–2003.

———. *Traité des premiers principes.* Edited and translated by Leendert Gerrit Westerink and Joseph Combès. Paris: Les Belles Lettres, 1986–91.

Davies, Stephen. *Philosophical Perspectives on Art.* Oxford: Oxford University Press, 2007.

———. *The Philosophy of Art.* Malden, Mass.: Blackwell, 2006.

De Broglie, Guy. "La vraie notion thomiste des 'praeambula fidei.'" *Gregorianum* 34 (1953): 341–89.

De Couesnongle, Vincent. "La causalité du maximum. Porquoi Saint Thomas a-t-il cité Aristote?" *Revue des sciences philosophique et théologiques* 38 (1954): 658–80.

———. "La causalité du maximum: L'utilisation par S. Thomas d'un passage d'Aristote." *Revue des sciences philosophiques et théologiques* 38 (1954): 433–44.

Dewan, Lawrence. "Importance of Substance." In *Form and Being: Studies in Thomistic Metaphysics.* Washington, D.C.: The Catholic University of America Press, 2006.

———. "'Obiectum.' Notes on the Invention of a Word." *Archives d'Histoire Doctrinale et Littéraires du Moyen Âge* 48 (1981): 37–96.

———. "What Does It Mean to Study Being 'as Being'?" In *Form and Being: Studies in Thomistic Metaphysics.* Washington, D.C.: The Catholic University of America Press, 2006.

Doolan, Gregory. *Aquinas on the Divine Ideas as Exemplar Causes.* Washington, D.C.: The Catholic University of America Press, 2008.

Dreyer, Mechthild. "Regularmethode und Axiomatik. Wissenschaftliche Methodik im Horizont der *artes*-Tradition des 12. Jahrhunderts." In *"Scientia" und "ars" im Hoch- und Spätmittelalter,* edited by Ingrid Craemer-Ruegenberg and Andreas Speer, 147–55. Miscellanea Mediaevalia 22. Berlin: Walter de Gruyter, 1994.

Duns Scotus. *Ioannis Duns Scoti Doctoris Mariani Theologiae Marianae Elementa.* Edited by Carolo Balić. Sibenik, Jugoslavia: Ex Typographia Kacic, 1933.

———. *Lectura in librum primum sententiarum.* In *Opera omnia.* Vol. 16. Edited by Carolo Balić et al. Vatican City: Typis Polyglottis Vaticanis, 1960.

———. *Opera Philosophica.* Vol. 3, *Quaestiones super libros metaphysicorum Aristotelis. Libri I–V.* Edited by Girard J. Etzkorn et al. St. Bonaventure, N.Y.: Franciscan Institute, 1997.

———. *Opus oxoniense.* In *Opera omnia.* Vol. 17. Edited by Carolo Balić et al. Vatican City: Typis Polyglottis Vaticanis, 1966.

———. *Opus oxoniense.* In *Opera Omnia.* Vols. 5–10. Edited by Lucas Wadding. Lyon: Lawrence Durand, 1639. Reprint: Hildesheim: Georg Olms Verlag, 1968–69.

———. *Ordinatio.* In *Opera omnia.* Vol. 3. Edited by Carolo Balić et al. Vatican City: Typis Polyglottis Vaticanis, 1954.

———. *Ordinatio.* In *Opera omnia.* Vol. 6. Edited by Carolo Balić et al. Vatican City: Typis Polyglottis Vaticanis, 1963.

———. *Ordinatio III.* Edited and translated by Allan B. Wolter. In *Franciscan Christology.* Edited by Damian McElrath, 139–82. St. Bonaventure, N.Y.: Franciscan Institute, 1980.

———. *Prologus.* In *Opera omnia.* Vol. 1. Edited by Carolo Balić et al. Vatican City: Typis Polyglottis Vaticanis, 1950.

———. *Quodlibeta.* In *Opera Omnia.* Vol. 12. Edited by Lucas Wadding. Lyon: Lawrence Durand, 1639. Reprint: Hildesheim: Georg Olms Verlag, 1968–69.

Elders, Leo. *The Philosophical Theology of St. Thomas Aquinas.* Leiden: E. J. Brill, 1990.

Eliot, T. S. *The Complete Poems and Plays: 1909–1950.* New York: Harcourt, 1952.

Esposito, Costantino, and Pasquale Porro, eds. *Quaestio 1: Heidegger e i medievali.* Turnhout: Brepols, 2001.

Fabro, Cornelio. *Participation et Causalité selon S. Thomas d'Aquin.* Paris: Publications Universitaires, 1961.

Fine, Kit. "The Varieties of Necessity." In *Conceivability and Possibility,* edited by Tamar Szabó Gendler and John Hawthorne, 253–82. Oxford: Oxford University Press, 2002.

Folger-Fonfara, Sabine. *Das "Super"-Transzendentale und die Spaltung der Metaphysik: Der Entwurf des Franziskus von Marchia.* Studien und Texte zur Geistesgeschichte des Mittelalters 96. Leiden: Brill, 2008.

Francis of Marchia. *In libros Metaphysicorum, Prooemium.* Edited by Russell L. Friedman. *Documenti e Studi sulla tradizione filosofica medievale* 16 (2005): 502–13.

————. *Quaestiones in Metaphysicam*. Edited by Albert Zimmermann. In *Ontologie oder Metaphysik? Die Diskussion über den Gegenstand der Metaphysik im 13. und 14. Jahrhundert, Texte und Untersuchungen*, 84–98. Leuven: Peeters, 1998.

————. *Quodlibet cum quaestionibus selectis ex commentario in librum Sententiarum*. Edited by Nazzareno Mariani. Spicilegium Bonaventurianum 29. Grottaferrata: Collegium S. Bonaventura, 1997.

Frede, Michael. "Aristotle's Account of the Origins of Philosophy." *Rhizai: Journal for Ancient Philosophy and Science* 1 (2004): 9–44.

Garson, James. "Modal Logic." In *The Stanford Encyclopedia of Philosophy*. http://plato.stanford.edu/entries/logic-modal/.

Gauthier, René-Antoine. *Saint Thomas d'Aquin. Somme contre les Gentils. Introduction*. Paris: Éditions Universitaires, 1993.

Gendler, Tamar Szabó, and John Hawthorne, eds. *Conceivability and Possibility*. Oxford: Clarendon Press, 2002.

Gilson, Étienne. "Quasi Definitio Substantiae." In *St. Thomas Aquinas 1274–1974: Commemorative Studies*, edited by Armand Maurer, 1:111–29. Toronto: Pontifical Institute of Mediaeval Studies, 1974.

Godfrey of Fontaines. *Le huitième Quodlibet de Godefroid de Fontaines*. Edited by Jean Hoffmans. Les Philosophes Belges 4. Leuven: Institut supérieur de philosophie de l'Université, 1924.

————. *Le neuvième Quodlibet de Godefroid de Fontaines*. Edited by Jean Hoffmans. Les Philosophes Belges 4. Leuven: Institut supérieur de philosophie de l'Université, 1928.

————. *Les quatre premiers Quodlibets de Godefroid de Fontaines*. Edited by Maurice De Wulf and Auguste Pelzer. Les Philosophes Belges 2. Leuven: Institut supérieur de philosophie de l'Université, 1904.

Goris, Wouter. *Absolute Beginners: Der mittelalterliche Beitrag zu einem Ausgang vom Unbedingten*. Leiden: Brill, 2007.

————. *The Scattered Field: History of Metaphysics in the Postmetaphysical Era*. Leuven: Peeters, 2004.

Grabmann, Martin. *Die theologische Erkenntnis- und Einleitungslehre des hl. Thomas von Aquin auf Grund seiner Schrift "In Boethium de trinitate": im Zusammenhang der Scholastik des 13. und beginnenden 14. Jahrhunderts dargestellt*. Freiburg/Schweiz: Paulusverlag, 1948.

Gracia, Jorge J. E. *Individuality: An Essay on the Foundations of Metaphysics*. Albany: State University of New York Press, 1988.

————. *Introduction to the Problem of Individuation in the Early Middle Ages*. 2nd rev. ed. Munich: Philosophia Verlag, 1988.

————. "Metaphysical, Epistemological, and Linguistic Approaches to Universals: Porphyry, Boethius, and Abailard." In *Medieval Masters: Essays in Memory of Msgr. E. A. Synan*, edited by R. E. Houser. Thomistic Papers 7. Houston: University of St. Thomas, 1999.

————. *Suarez on Individuation*. Milwaukee, Wisc.: Marquette University Press, 1982 and 2000.

————. "Suarez's Criticism of the Thomistic Principle of Individuation." *Atti del Congresso di S. Tommaso d'Aquino nel suo VII Centenario* (1977): 563–68.

————. *Surviving Race, Ethnicity, and Nationality: A Challenge for the Twentieth Century.* Landham, Md.: Rowman and Littlefield, 2005.

————, ed. *Individuation in Scholasticism: The Later Middle Ages and the Counter-Reformation, 1150–1650.* Albany: State University of New York Press, 1994.

Guldentops, Guy, Andreas Speer, Michele Trizio, and David Wirmer. "Philosophische Kommentare im Mittelalter." *Allgemeine Zeitschrift für Philosophie.* First Part: I. Einführung—II. Sprachkreise, 32, no. 2 (2007): 157–77. Second Part: III. Platonica—IV, 1–2—Aristotelica arabica et byzantina, 32, no. 3 (2007): 259–90. Third Part: IV, 3 Aristotelica latina—V Hebraica—VI Ausblick, *Allgemeine Zeitschrift für Philosophie,* 33, no. 1 (2008): 31–57.

Hasker, William. "The Absence of a Timeless God." In *God and Time: Essays on the Divine Nature,* edited by Greg Ganassle and David Woodruff, 182–206. New York: Oxford University Press, 2002.

————. *God, Time, and Knowledge.* Ithaca, N.Y.: Cornell University Press, 1989.

Heidegger, Martin. *Die Grundbegriffe der Metaphysi: Welt, Endlichkeit, Einsamkeit.* Edited by F.-W. von Herrmann. Gesamtausgabe 29/30. 2nd ed. Frankfurt am Main: V. Klostermann, 1992.

————. *Nietzsche II.* 6th rev. ed. Stuttgart: Günther Neske, 1998.

————. "Zeit und Sein." In *Zur Sache des Denkens.* Gesamtausgabe, Abteilung I, Band 14. Frankfurt am Main: Klostermann, 2007.

Henry of Ghent. *Summa quaestionum ordinarium.* Edited by Jodocuss Badius Ascensius. Paris, 1520.

————. *Summa (Quaestiones ordinariae), art. XXXI–XXXIV. Opera omnia.* Vol. 27. Edited by R. Macken. Leuven: University Press, 1991.

Hoenen, Maarten J. F. M. "Being and Thinking in the 'Correctorium fratris Thomae' and the 'Correctorium corruptorii Quare.' Schools of Thought and Philosophical Methodology." In *Nach der Verurteilung von 1277: Philosophie und Theologie an der Universität von Paris im letzten Viertel des 13. Jahrhunderts. Studien und Texte,* edited by Jan A. Aertsen, Kent Emery Jr., and Andreas Speer, 417–35. Miscellanea Mediaevalia 28. Berlin: Walter de Gruyter, 2000.

Homer. *Ilias.* Edited by Thomas W. Allen. Oxford: n.p., 1902.

Hoping, Helmut. *Weisheit als Wissen des Ursprungs. Philosophie und Theologie in der "Summa contra gentiles" des Thomas von Aquin.* Freiburg im Breisgau: Herder, 1997.

Hoyle, Fred. *Frontiers of Astronomy.* New York: Harper and Row, 1954.

Hugh of St. Victor. *De sacramentis.* Translated by Roy Deferrari. Cambridge, Mass.: Medieval Academy of America, 1951.

Hughes, Christopher. *A Complex Theory of a Simple God.* Ithaca, N.Y.: Cornell University Press, 1989.

Isidor of Seville. *Etymologiarum siue Originum libri XX.* 2 vols. Edited by W. M. Lindsay. Oxford: n.p.,1911.

Jordan, Mark D. "The Names of God and the Being of Names." In *The Existence and Nature of God,* edited by Alfred J. Freddoso, 161–90. Notre Dame, Ind.: University of Notre Dame Press, 1983.

Kant, Immanuel. *Immanuel Kant: Kritik der reinen Vernunft.* Edited by Georg Mohr and Marcus Willaschek. Klassiker Auslegen 17/18. Berlin: Akademie Verlag, 1998.

Klima, Gyula. "Buridan's Logic and the Ontology of Modes." http://www .fordham.edu/gsas/phil/klima/MODI.HTM.

Knuuttila, Simo. "Medieval Theories of Modality." In *The Stanford Encyclopedia of Philosophy.* http://plato.stanford.edu/entries/modality-medieval/.

Kobusch, Theo. "Objekt." In *Historisches Wörterbuch der Philosophie,* edited by Johann Ritter and Karlfried Gründer, 6:1026–1052. Basel: Schwabe, 1984.

Koch, Josef. *Durandus de S. Porciano O.P. Forschungen zum Streit um Thomas von Aquin zu Beginn des 14. Jahrhunderts.* Beiträge zur Geschichte der Philosophie des Mittelalters 26. Münster: Aschendorff, 1927.

———. *Kleine Schriften.* 2 vols. Storia e Letteratura 128. Rome: Edizioni di storia e letteratura, 1973.

Krebs, Engelbert. *Theologie und Wissenschaft nach der Lehre der Hochscholastik an der Hand der bisher ungedruckten "Defensa doctrinae D. Thomae" des Hervaeus Natalis.* Beiträge zur Geschichte der Philosophie des Mittelalters 11.3–4. Münster: Aschendorff, 1912.

Kremer, Klaus. *Der Metaphysikbegriff in den Aristoteles-Kommentaren der Ammonius-Schule.* Beiträge zur Geschichte der Philosophie und Theologie des Mittelalters, Band 39, Heft 1. Münster: Aschendorff, 1961.

Kretzmann, Norman. *The Metaphysics of Creation: Aquinas's Natural Theology in "Summa contra Gentiles" II.* Oxford: Oxford University Press, 1999.

Kripke, Saul. *Wittgenstein on Rules and Private Language.* Cambridge, Mass.: Harvard University Press, 1982.

Ladyman, James, and Don Ross, et al. *Every Thing Must Go: Metaphysics Naturalized.* Oxford: Oxford University Press, 2007.

Leisegang, Hans. "Sophia." In *Realencyclopädie der Classischen Altertumswissenschaft* 2/5. Coll. 1010–1039. Stuttgart: Metzler, 1927.

Lewis, David. *On the Plurality of Worlds.* Oxford: Blackwell, 1986.

Linguiti, Alessandro. *L'Ultimo Platonism greco. Principi e conoscenza.* Florence: Olschki, 1990.

Lizzini, Olga. "Utility and Gratuitousness of Metaphysics: Avicenna, *Ilāhiyyāt* I, 3." *Quaestio* 5 (2005): 307–44.

Long, R. James. "The Moral and Spiritual Theology of Richard Fishacre; Edition of Trinity Coll. MS O.1.30." *Archivum Fratrum Praedicatorum* 40 (1990): 5–143.

———. "The Science of Theology according to Richard Fishacre: Edition of the Prologue to his *Commentary on the Sentences.*" *Mediaeval Studies* 34 (1972): 71–98.

Long, R. James, and Maura O'Carroll. *The Life and Works of Richard Fishacre OP.* Veröffenlichungen der Kommission für die Herausgabe ungedruckter

Texte aux der mittelalterlichen Geisteswelt 21. München: Verlag der Bayer-ischen Akademie der Wissenschaften, 1999.

Loux, Michael J. "Introduction." In *The Possible and the Actual: Readings in the Metaphysics of Modality,* edited by Michael J. Loux. Ithaca, N.Y.: Cornell University Press, 1979.

Ludlow, Peter, Yukin Nagasawa, and Daniel Stoljar, eds. *There's Something about Mary: Essays on Phenomenal Consciousness and Frank Jackson's Knowledge Argument.* Cambridge, Mass.: MIT Press, Bradford Book, 2004.

Luna, Concetta. *Trois études sur la tradition des commentaires anciens à la Métaphysique d'Aristote.* Leiden: Brill, 2001.

Magrini, Aegidius. *Ioannis Duns Scoti Doctrina de scientifica theologiae natura.* Rome: Pontificium Athenaeum Antonianum, 1952.

Mansion, Augustin. "Philosophie première, philosophie seconde et métaphysique chez Aristote." *Revue philosophique de Louvain* 56 (1958): 165–221.

Margolis, Joseph. "The Ontological Peculiarity of Works of Art." *Journal of Aesthetics and Art Criticism* 36 (1977): 45–50.

Marinus. *Vita Procli.* Edited and translated by Henri Dominique Saffrey and Alain-Philippe Segonds, Marinus. Proclus ou sur le Bonheur. Paris: Les Belles Lettres, 2001.

Marshall, Bruce D. "*Quod Scit Una Vetula.* Aquinas on the Nature of Theology." In *The Theology of Thomas Aquinas,* edited by Rik Van Nieuwenhove and Joseph Peter Wawrykow. Notre Dame, Ind.: University of Notre Dame Press, 2005.

Marvell, Andrew. *The Poems and Letters of Andrew Marvell.* 3rd ed. Edited by H. M. Margoliouth. Vol. 1, *Poems.* Revised by Pierre Legouis with E. E. Duncan-Jones. Oxford: Clarendon Press, 1971.

McDermott, Charlene Senape. "Notes on the Assertoric and Modal Propositional Logic of the Pseudo-Scotus." *Journal of the History of Philosophy* 10 (1963): 273–306.

McEvoy, James. *Robert Grosseteste.* New York: Oxford University Press, 2000.

McInerny, Ralph. *Aquinas and Analogy.* Washington, D.C.: The Catholic University of America Press, 1996.

———. *The Logic of Analogy: An Interpretation of St. Thomas.* The Hague: Nijhoff, 1961.

———. *Praeambula Fidei: Thomism and the God of the Philosophers.* Washington, D.C.: The Catholic University of America Press, 2006.

Menzel, Christopher. "Actualism." In *The Stanford Encyclopedia of Philosophy.* http://plato.stanford.edu/entries/actualism/.

Montangnes, Bernard. *The Doctrine of the Analogy of Being according to Thomas Aquinas.* Translated by Edward M. Macierwoski. Milwaukee, Wisc.: Marquette University Press, 2004.

Moore, Derek, Peter Hobson, and Anthony Lee. "Components of Person Perception: An Investigation with Autistic, Non-autistic Retarded and Typically Developing Children and Adolescents." *British Journal of Developmental Psychology* 15 (1997): 401–23.

Moses Maimonides. *Dux seu Director dubitantium aut perplexorum.* Edited by Augustinus Justinianus. Paris, 1520. Reprint, Frankfurt am Main: Minerva, 1964.

———. *The Guide of the Perplexed.* Translated by S. Pines. Chicago: University of Chicago Press, 1964.

Napoli, Valerio. *Epekeina tou henos. Il principio totalmente ineffabille tra dialettica ed esegesi in Damascio.* Catania, Italy: CUECM, 2008.

Newman, John Henry Cardinal. *An Essay in Aid of a Grammar of Assent.* Notre Dame, Ind.: University of Notre Dame Press, 1979.

Nicholas of Cusa. *De apice theoriae. Opera omnia iussu et auctoritate Academiae litterarum heidelbergensis ad codicum fidem edita.* Vol. 12. Hamburg: F. Meiner, 1981.

———. *De coniecturis. Opera omnia iussu et auctoritate Academiae litterarum heidelbergensis ad codicum fidem edita.* Vol. 3. Hamburg: F. Meiner, 1972.

———. *De docta ignorantia. Opera omnia iussu et auctoritate Academiae litterarum heidelbergensis ad codicum fidem edita.* Vol. 15a. Hamburg: F. Meiner, 1977.

———. *De venatione sapientiae. Opera omnia iussu et auctoritate Academiae litterarum heidelbergensis ad codicum fidem edita.* Vol. 12. Hamburg: F. Meiner, 1981.

———. *Idiota de sapientia. Opera omnia iussu et auctoritate Academiae litterarum heidelbergensis ad codicum fidem edita.* Vol. 5. Hamburg: F. Meiner, 1983.

Nicolas, J. H. "L'univers ordonné à Dieu par Dieu." *Revue Thomiste* 91 (1991): 357–76.

Nolan, Daniel. "Modal Fictionalism." In *The Stanford Encyclopedia of Philosophy.* http://plato.stanford.edu/entries/fictionalism-modal/.

Normore, Calvin. "Goodness and Rational Choice in the Early Middle Ages." In *Emotions and Choice from Boethius to Descartes,* edited by Henrik Lagerlund and Mikko Yrjonsouri, 29–47. Dordrecht: Kluwer, 2002.

———. "Scotus' Modal Theory." In *The Cambridge Companion to Duns Scotus,* edited by Thomas Williams. Cambridge: Cambridge University Press, 2003.

O'Meara, Dominic. "Intentional Objects in Later Neoplatonism." In *Ancient and Medieval Theories of Intentionality,* edited by Dominik Perler, 115–25. Leiden: Brill, 2001.

———. "La Science métaphysique (ou théologie) de Proclus comme exercice spirituel." In *Proclus et la Théologie Platonicienne,* edited by Alain-Philippe Segonds and Carlos Steel, 279–90. Paris: Les Belles Lettres, 2000.

———. "Le Fondement du principe de non-contradiction chez Syrianus." In *Syrianus et la métaphysique de l'Antiquité tardive,* edited by Angela Longo. Naples: Bibliopolis, 2009.

———. "Le problème de la métaphysique dans l'Antiquité tardive." *Freiburger Zeitschrift für Philosophie und Theologie* 23 (1986): 3–22.

———. *Pythagoras Revived: Mathematics and Philosophy in Late Antiquity.* Oxford: Clarendon Press, 1989.

O'Rourke, Fran. *Pseudo-Dionysius and the Metaphysics of Aquinas.* New York: E. J. Brill, 1992.

Owens, Joseph. "Aristotle on Categories." *Review of Metaphysics* 14 (1960): 73–90.

———. *The Doctrine of Being in Aristotelian Metaphysics.* 3rd ed. Toronto: Pontifical Institute of Mediaeval Studies, 1978.

———. "Thomas Aquinas." In *Individuation in Scholasticism: The Later Middle Ages and the Counter-Reformation, 1150–1650,* edited by Jorge J. E. Gracia, 173–94. Albany: State University of New York Press, 1994.

Patzig, Günther. *Ethik ohne Metaphysik.* Göttingen: Vandenhoeck & Ruprecht, 1971.

Peter Abelard. *Ethics.* Edited and translated by D. E. Luscombe. Oxford: Oxford University Press, 1971.

———. *Glossae secundum magistrum Petrum Abaelardum super Porphyrium.* Edited by B. Geyer. *Beiträge zur Geschichte der Philosophie des Mittelalters,* Band XXI, Heft 1–3. Münster: Aschendorff, 1919–27.

Peter Aureoli. *Scriptum super Primum Sententiarum.* Edited by Eligius M. Buytaert. St. Bonaventure, N.Y.: Franciscan Institute, 1952.

Pickavé, Martin: "Heinrich von Gent über das Subjekt der Metaphysik als Ersterkanntes." *Documenti e Studi sulla tradizione filosofica medievale* 12 (2001): 493–522.

Pindar. *Nemean Odes.* In *Pindari carmina cum fragmentis.* Edited by Cecil M. Bowra. Oxford: Clarendon Press, 1935.

Porphyry. *Vita Plotini.* In *Plotinus,* vol. 1. Edited and translated by Arthur Hilary Armstrong. Cambridge, Mass.: Harvard University Press, 1966.

Proclus. *Elements of Theology.* Edited with an English translation by E. R. Dodds. Oxford: Clarendon Press, 1963.

———. *Procli in Platonis Parmenidem commentaria.* Edited by Carlos Steel. Oxford: Oxford University Press, 2007–9.

———. *Proclus' Commentary on Plato's "Parmenides."* Translated by Glenn R. Morrow and John M. Dillon. Princeton, N.J.: Princeton University Press, 1987.

———. *Théologie platonicienne.* 6 vols. Edited and translated by Henri Dominique Saffrey and Leendert Gerrit Westerink. Paris: Les Belles Lettres, 1968–97.

Prufer, Thomas. "A Protreptic: What Is Philosophy?" In *Studies in Philosophy and the History of Philosophy,* edited by John K. Ryan, 2:1–19. Washington, D.C.: The Catholic University of America Press, 1963.

———. *Recapitulations: Essays in Philosophy.* Washington, D.C.: The Catholic University of America Press, 1993.

Putnam, Hilary. *Realism and Reason: Philosophical Papers.* Vol. 3. Cambridge: Cambridge University Press, 1983.

Raedts, Peter. *Richard Rufus of Cornwall and the Tradition of Oxford Theology.* New York: Oxford University Press, 1987.

Rappe, Sara. *Reading Neoplatonism: Non-discursive Thinking in the Texts of Plotinus, Proclus and Damascius.* Cambridge: Cambridge University Press, 2000.

Reiner, Hans. "Die Entstehung der Lehre vom bibliothekarischen Ursprung des Namens Metaphysik." *Zeitschrift für philosophische Forschung* 8 (1954): 77–99.

———. "Die Entstehung und ursprüngliche Bedeutung des Namens Metaphysik." *Zeitschrift für philosophische Forschung* 8 (1954): 210–37.

Richard Rufus of Cornwall. *Commentarium in libros Sententiarum.* Codex Oxoniensis, Balliol 62.

Rocca, Gregory P. *Speaking the Incomprehensible God.* Washington, D.C.: The Catholic University of America Press, 2004.

Rompe, Elisabeth. "Die Trennung von Ontologie und Metaphysik. Der Ablösungsprozeß und seine Motivierung bei Benedictus Pererius und anderen Denkern des 16. und 17. Jahrhunderts." PhD diss., University of Bonn, 1968.

Ross, James. "Aquinas' Exemplarism, Aquinas' Voluntarism." *American Catholic Philosophical Quarterly* 64 (1990): 171–98.

———. "Contextual Adaptation." *American Philosophical Quarterly* 46 (2009): 19–30.

———. "The Crash of Modal Metaphysics." *Review of Metaphysics* 43 (1989): 251–79.

———. "God: Creator of Kinds and Possibilities." In *Rationality, Religious Belief, and Moral Commitment,* edited by Robert Audi and William J. Wainwright, 351–84. Ithaca, N.Y.: Cornell University Press, 1986.

———. *Philosophical Theology.* Indianapolis: Bobbs-Merrill, 1968.

———. *Thought and World.* Notre Dame, Ind.: University of Notre Dame Press, 2008.

Senger, Hans Gerhard. "Die Sprache der Metaphysik." In *Ludus sapientiae: Studien zum Werk und zur Wirkungsgeschichte des Nikolaus Cusanus,* 63–87. Leiden: Brill, 2002.

Senor, Thomas. "The Real Presence of an Eternal God." In *Metaphysics and God,* edited by Kevin Timpe, 39–59. New York: Routledge, 2009.

Sheppard, Anne. "*Phantasia* and Mathematical Projection in Iamblichus." *Syllecta Classica* 8 (1997): 113–20.

Sokolowski, Robert. *The Phenomenology of the Human Person.* New York: Cambridge University Press, 2008.

Speer, Andreas. "Das 'Erwachen der Metaphysik.' Anmerkungen zu einem Paradigma für das Verständnis des 12. Jahrhunderts." In *Metaphysics in the Twelfth Century: On the Relationship among Philosophy, Science and Theology,* edited by Matthias Lutz-Bachmann, Alexander Fidora, and Andreas Niederberger, 17–40. Textes et Études du Moyen Âge 19. Turnhout: Brepols, 2004.

———. "Das Glück des Menschen." In *Thomas von Aquin: Die Summa theologiae—Werkinterpretationen,* edited by Andreas Speer, 141–67. Berlin: Walter de Gruyter, 2005.

———. "Endliche Weisheit. Eine Annäherung an die Philosophie." *Recherches de Théologie et Philosophie médiévales* 49, no. 1 (2002): 3–32.

———. "The Epistemic Circle: Thomas Aquinas on the Foundation of Knowledge." In *Platonic Ideas and Concept Formation in Ancient and Medieval*

Thought, edited by Gerd van Riel and Caroline Macé, 119–32. Ancient and Medieval Philosophy, series 1, vol. 32. Leuven: Leuven University Press, 2004.

———. "*Sapientia nostra.* Zum Verhältnis von phlosophischer und theologischer Weisheit in den Pariser Debatten am Ende des 13. Jahrhunderts." In *Nach der Verurteilung von 1277: Philosophie und Theologie an der Universität von Paris im letzten Viertel des 13. Jahrhunderts. Studien und Texte,* edited by Jan A. Aertsen, Kent Emery Jr., and Andreas Speer, 248–75. Miscellanea Mediaevalia 28. Berlin: Walter de Gruyter, 2000.

———. "Verstandesmetaphysik. Bonaventura und Nicolaus Cusanus über die (Un-) Möglichkeit des Wissens des Unendlichen." In *Die Logik des Transzendentalen. Festschrift für Jan A. Aertsen zum 65. Geburtstag,* edited by Jan A. Aertsen and Martin Pickavé, 525–53. Miscellanea Mediaevalia 30. Berlin: Walter de Gruyter, 2003.

———. "Weisheit." In *Historisches Wörterbuch der Philosophie.* Vol. 12. Coll. 371–97. Basel: Schwabe, 2004.

Steel, Carlos. *Der Adler und die Nachteule, Thomas und Albert über die Möglichkeit der Metaphysik.* Lectio Albertina 4. Münster: Aschendorff, 2001.

———. "Theology as First Philosophy. The Neoplatonic Concept of Metaphysics." *Quaestio* 5 (2005): 3–21.

Stevens, Wallace. *The Collected Poems of Wallace Stevens.* New York: Knopf, 2008.

———. *The Necessary Angel: Essays on Reality and the Imagination.* New York: Vintage Books, 1965.

Strawson, P. F. *Individuals.* London: Methuen, 1959.

Studtmann, Paul. *The Foundations of Aristotle's Categorial Scheme.* Milwaukee, Wisc.: Marquette University Press, 2008.

Stump, Eleonore. *Aquinas.* London: Routledge, 2003.

———. "Presence and Omnipresence." In *Liberal Faith: Essays in Honor of Philip Quinn,* edited by Paul Weithman, 59–82. Notre Dame, Ind.: University of Notre Dame Press, 2008.

Stump, Eleonore, and Norman Kretzmann. "Eternity, Awareness, and Action." *Faith and Philosophy* 9 (1992): 463–82.

Suárez. *Disputationes metaphysicae V: De unitate individuali ejusque principio.* In *Opera omnia.* Vol. 25. Edited by Charles Berton. Paris: Vivès, 1866.

Syrianus. *In metaphysica commentaria.* Edited by Wilhelm Kroll. Berlin: George Reimer, 1902.

———. *On Aristotle's "Metaphysics 3–4."* Translated by John Dillon and Dominic O'Meara. London: Gerald Duckworth, 2008.

———. *On Aristotle's "Metaphysics 13–14."* Translated by John Dillon and Dominic O'Meara. London: Gerald Duckworth, 2006.

Te Velde, Rudi. *Aquinas on God. The "Divine Science" of the Summa Theologiae.* Burlington, Vt.: Ashgate, 2005.

———. *Participation and Substantiality in Thomas Aquinas.* New York: E. J. Brill, 1995.

Theophrastus. *Métaphysique.* Edited and translated by André Laks and Glenn Most. Paris: Les Belles Lettres, 2002.

Thom, Paul. *Medieval Modal Systems: Problems and Concepts.* Ashgate Studies in Medieval Philosophy. Aldershot, UK: Ashgate, 2003.

Thomas Aquinas. *Commentary on the Gospel of St. John.* Translated by James Weisheipl and Fabian Larcher. Albany, N.Y.: Magi Books, 1980.

———. *Commentary on Saint Paul's Epistle to the Galatians by Saint Thomas Aquinas.* Translated by Fabian Larcher and Richard Murphy. Albany, N.Y.: Magi Books, 1966.

———. *Commentum in quatuor libros sententiarum magistri petri lombardi.* In *Opera Omnia.* Vol. 7. Parma: Petrus Fiacciadori, 1868. Reprint, New York: Musugia, 1948.

———. *Compendium theologiae. Opera omnia,* iussu Leonis XIII edita cura et studio Fratrum Praedicatorum 42. Rome, 1979.

———. *De ente et essentia. Opera omnia,* iussu Leonis XIII edita cura et studio Fratrum Praedicatorum 43. Rome, 1976.

———. *De principiis naturae. Opera omnia,* iussu Leonis XIII edita cura et studio Fratrum Praedicatorum 43. Rome, 1976.

———. *De substantiis separatis. Opera omnia,* iussu Leonis XIII edita cura et studio Fratrum Praedicatorum 40. Rome, 1968.

———. *Expositio libri Peryermenias.* Editio altera retractata. *Opera omnia,* iussu Leonis XIII edita cura et studio Fratrum Praedicatorum 1. Rome, 1989.

———. *Expositio super Iob ad litteram. Opera omnia,* iussu Leonis XIII edita cura et studio Fratrum Praedicatorum 26. Rome, 1965.

———. *Expositio super librum Boethii De Trinitate.* Edited by Bruno Decker. Leiden: E. J. Brill, 1955.

———. *Expositio super librum Boethii De Trinitate.* 2nd ed. Edited by B. Decker. Leiden: Brill, 1959.

———. *Faith, Reason and Theology: Questions I–IV of His Commentary on the De Trinitate of Boethius.* Translated by Armand Maurer. Toronto: Pontifical Institute of Mediaeval Studies, 1987.

———. *In Aristotelis libros de caelo. Opera omnia,* iussu Leonis XIII edita cura et studio Fratrum Praedicatorum 3. Rome, 1886.

———. *In Aristotelis libros Physicorum. Opera omnia,* iussu Leonis XIII edita cura et studio Fratrum Praedicatorum 2. Rome, 1884.

———. *In duodecim libros Metaphysicorum Aristotelis expositio.* Edited by M.-R. Cathala and R. M. Spiazzi. Turin: Marietti, 1950.

———. *In librum beati Dionysii De divinis nominibus exposition.* Edited by Ceslaus Pera. Turin: Marietti, 1950.

———. *Quaestiones disputatae de anima. Opera omnia,* iussu Leonis XIII edita cura et studio Fratrum Praedicatorum 24, 1. Rome, 1996.

———. *Quaestiones disputatae de malo. Opera omnia,* iussu Leonis XIII edita cura et studio Fratrum Praedicatorum 23. Rome, 1982.

———. *Quaestiones disputatae de potentia.* In *Quaestiones disputatae,* edited by P. Bazzi, M. Calcaterra, T. S. Centi, E. Odetto, P. M. Pession. Vol. 2. Turin: Marietti, 1965.

———. *Quaestiones disputatae de veritate. Opera omnia,* iussu Leonis XIII edita cura et studio Fratrum Praedicatorum 22. Rome, 1970–76.

————. *Quaestiones quodlibetales.* Edited by Raymundus Spiazzi. Turin: Marietti, 1920.

————. *Questio disputata de spiritualibus creatures. Opera omnia,* iussu Leonis XIII edita cura et studio Fratrum Praedicatorum 24, 2. Rome, 2000.

————. *Scriptum super libris magistri sententiarum.* In *Opera Omnia.* Vol. 22. Parma: Petrus Fiacciadori, 1868. Reprint, New York: Musurgia, 1950.

————. *Scriptum super libros Sententiarum magistri Petri Lombardi Episcopi Parisiensis.* Edited by Pierre Mandonnet (vols. 1–2) and M. F. Moos (vols. 3–4). Paris: Lethielleux, 1929–47.

————. *Sentencia libri de anima. Opera omnia,* iussu Leonis XIII edita cura et studio Fratrum Praedicatorum 45. Rome, 1984.

————. *Summa contra Gentiles. Opera omnia,* iussu Leonis XIII edita cura et studio Fratrum Praedicatorum 13–15. Rome, 1918–30.

————. *Summa contra Gentiles. Editio Leonina manualis.* Apud sedem Commissionis Leoninae et apud Librariam Vaticanam. Rome: Desclée and Herder, 1934.

————. *Summa contra Gentiles.* 2 vols. Edited by Laureano Robles Carcedo, O.P., and Adolfo Robles Sierra, O.P. Madrid: Biblioteca de Autores Cristianos, 1967–68.

————. *Summa contra Gentiles. Book One: God.* Translated by Anton Pegis. Notre Dame, Ind.: University of Notre Dame Press, 1955; reprint, 2005.

————. *Summa theologiae. Opera omnia,* iussu Leonis XIII edita cura et studio Fratrum Praedicatorum 4–11. Rome, 1888–1903.

————. *Summa theologiae.* Edited by I. T. Eschmann. Vols. 1–5. Ottawa: Institutum Studiorum Medievalium Ottaviensis, 1941–45.

————. *Summa theologiae.* Edited by Petrus Caramello. 3 vols. Turin: Marietti, 1952–56.

————. *Super Boetium De Trinitate. Opera omnia,* iussu Leonis XIII edita cura et studio Fratrum Praedicatorum 50. Rome, 1992.Tihon, Paul. *Foi et théologie selon Godefroid de Fontaines.* Paris-Bruges: Desclée–De Brouwer, 1966.

Tomarchio, John. "Aquinas's Concept of Infinity." *Journal of the History of Philosophy* 40 (2002): 163–87.

Torrell, Jean-Pierre. "'Dieu conduit toutes choses vers leur fin': Providence et gouvernement divin chez Thomas d'Aquin." In *Ende und Vollendung. Eschatologische Perspektiven im Mittelalter,* edited by Jan A. Aertsen and Martin Pickavé, 561–94. Miscellanea Mediaevalia 21. Berlin: Walter de Gruyter, 2001.

————. *Initiation à saint Thomas D'Aquin.* Fribourg: Editions Universitaire, 1993.

————. "Philosophie et théologie d'après le Prologue de Thomas d'Aquin au *Super Boetium de Trinitate.* Essai d'une lecture théologique." *Documenti e Studi sulla tradizione filososfica medievale* 10 (1999): 328–29.

————. *Saint Thomas Aquinas.* Vol. 1, *The Person and His Works.* Translated by Robert Royal. Rev. ed. Washington, D.C.: The Catholic University of America Press, 2005.

Tresson, Carole. "L'Aporie ou l'expérience métaphysique de la dualité dans le Peri Archôn de Damascius." PhD diss., University of Fribourg, 2009.

Tresson, Carole, and Alain Metry. "Damaskios' New Conception of Metaphysics." In *History of Platonism: Plato Redivivus,* edited by Robert Berchman and John Finamore, 222–26. New Orleans: University Press of the South, 2005.

Veatch, Henry. *Intentional Logic.* New Haven, Conn.: Yale University Press, 1952.

Verbeke, Gérard. "Aristotle's Metaphysics Viewed by the Ancient Greek Commentators." In *Studies in Aristotle,* edited by Dominic O'Meara, 107–27. Washington, D.C.: The Catholic University of America Press, 1981.

Vollrath, Ernst. "Die Gliederung der Metaphysik in eine Metaphysica generalis und eine Metaphysica specialis." *Zeitschrift für philosophische Forschung* 16 (1962): 258–83.

Westerink, Leendert Gerrit, Jean Trouillard, and Alain-Phillippe Segonds. *Prolégomènes à la philosophie de Platon.* Paris: Les Belles Lettres, 1990.

Wettstein, Howard. "Against Theology." In *Philosophers and the Hebrew Bible,* edited by Charles Manekin and Robert Eisen, 219–45. College Park: University Press of Maryland, 2008.

William of Ockham. *Quaestiones in librum tertium sententiarium.* In *Opus Theologica.* Vol. 6. Edited by Francis E. Kelley and Girard I. Etzkorn. St. Bonaventure, N.Y.: Franciscan Institute Publications, 1982.

———. *Quodlibeta.* In *Opus Theologica.* Vol. 9. Edited by Joseph C. Wey, C.S.B. St. Bonaventure, N.Y.: Franciscan Institute Publications, 1980.

Williamson, Timothy. "Laudatio: Professor Ruth Barcan Marcus." In *Themes from Barcan Marcus,* edited by M. Frauchiger and W. K. Essler. Lauener Library of Analytical Philosophy 3. Frankfurt: Ebikon, forthcoming.

Wilson, Alistair. "Modal Metaphysics and the Everett Interpretation." *Pittsburgh Philosophy of Science Archive* (2006). http://philsci-archive.pitt.edu/archive/00002635/.

Wippel, John F. "Godfrey of Fontaines, Peter of Auvergne, and John Baconthorpe." In *Individuation in Scholasticism: The Later Middle Ages and the Counter-Reformation, 1150–1650,* edited by Jorge J. E. Gracia, 221–56. Albany: State University of New York Press, 1994.

———. *Metaphysical Themes in Thomas Aquinas.* Washington, D.C.: The Catholic University of America Press, 1984.

———. *Metaphysical Themes in Thomas Aquinas II.* Washington, D.C.: The Catholic University of America Press, 2007.

———. *The Metaphysical Thought of Godfrey of Fontaines.* Washington, D.C.: The Catholic University of America Press, 1981.

———. *The Metaphysical Thought of Thomas Aquinas: From Finite to Uncreated Being.* Washington, D.C.: The Catholic University of America Press, 2000.

———. "The Reality of Non-existing Possibles according to Thomas Aquinas, Henry of Ghent and Godfrey of Fontaines." *Review of Metaphysics* 34 (1981): 729–59.

Wolff, Christian. *Philosophia prima sive Ontologia. Gesammelte Werke.* Vol. 2. Edited by Jean Ecole. Lateinische Schriften 3. Hildesheim: Georg Olms, 1962.

Wolter, Allan B. "Duns Scotus on the Natural Desire for the Supernatural." In *The Philosophical Theology of John Duns Scotus,* edited by Marilyn McCord Adams, 125–47. Ithaca, N.Y.: Cornell University Press, 1990.

————. *The Transcendentals and Their Function in the Metaphysics of Duns Scotus*. St. Bonaventure, N.Y.: Franciscan Institute, 1946.

Wolterstorff, Nicholas. "Toward an Ontology of Art Works." *Nous* 9 (1975): 115–42.

Wood, Rega, and Marilyn McCord Adams. "Is To Will It as Bad as To Do It?" *Franciscan Studies* 41 (1981): 5–60.

Zimmermann, Albert. *Ontologie oder Metaphysik? Die Diskussion über den Gegenstand der Metaphysik im 13. und 14. Jahrhundert. Texte und Untersuchungen*. 2nd rev. ed. Leuven: Peeters, 1998.

Contributors

MARILYN MCCORD ADAMS is Distinguished Research Professor of Philosophy at UNC Chapel Hill. Previously she taught at UCLA, at Yale Divinity School, and most recently at Oxford University, where she was Regius Professor of Divinity. Her books include *William Ockham* (1987, 2 vols.), *Horrendous Evils and the Goodness of God* (1999), *Christ and Horrors: The Coherence of Christology* (2006), and *Some Later Medieval Theories of the Eucharist: Thomas Aquinas, Giles of Rome, Duns Scotus, and William Ockham* (2010).

JAN A. AERTSEN was appointed professor at the Free University of Amsterdam in 1984. He became professor of philosophy and director of the Thomas Institute at the University of Cologne in 1994. Since 2003 he has been professor emeritus. His extensive research and writing in medieval philosophy include his seminal work on the doctrine of the transcendentals, most notably *Medieval Philosophy and the Transcendentals: The Case of Thomas Aquinas*.

STEPHEN F. BROWN received his PhD in philosophy at the University of Louvain, where he began his longtime friendship with John F. Wippel and worked under the direction of Professor Fernand Van Steenberghen. His early scholarly life was dedicated to the edition of the works of William of Ockham. He taught at St. Bonaventure University and the University of the South and is presently in the Department of Theology at Boston College. He is the director of the Institute of Medieval Philosophy and Theology there and has written on various medieval authors of the thirteenth and fourteenth centuries.

GREGORY T. DOOLAN received his PhD in philosophy from the Catholic University of America, where he wrote his dissertation under the direction of John F. Wippel. After teaching philosophy for a short time at the

Dominican House of Studies in Washington, D.C., Doolan returned to the Catholic University of America to join the faculty of the School of Philosophy in 2005. He has published articles in the areas of medieval philosophy and Thomistic metaphysics, and he is the author of the book *Aquinas on the Divine Ideas as Exemplar Causes.*

JORGE J. E. GRACIA holds the Samuel P. Capen Chair in Philosophy at the University at Buffalo and is State University of New York Distinguished Professor. Gracia is the author of sixteen books, including *Surviving Race, Ethnicity, and Nationality: A Challenge for the Twenty-First Century* (2005), *Old Wine in New Skins: The Role of Tradition in Communication, Knowledge, and Group Identity* (2003), *Metaphysics and Its Task: The Search for the Categorial Foundations of Knowledge* (1999), *Individuality: An Essay on the Foundations of Metaphysics* (1988), *Introduction to the Problem of Individuation in the Early Middle Ages* (1984, 1986), and *Suarez on Individuation* (1982). He has also edited numerous volumes and authored over two hundred articles published internationally. Gracia has been president of the Metaphysical Society of America, Society for Medieval and Renaissance Philosophy, Society for Iberian and Latin American Thought, International Federation of Latin American and Caribbean Studies, and American Catholic Philosophical Association.

DOMINIC O'MEARA was born in Ireland and studied at Cambridge University (BA, MA) and in Paris, where he wrote his doctoral thesis on Plotinus, with Pierre Hadot. A fellow of the Dumbarton Oaks Center for Byzantine Studies and of the Humboldt-Stiftung, he was assistant and associate professor of philosophy at the Catholic University of America (1974–1984), and Professeur ordinaire, Chair of Metaphysics and Ancient Philosophy, at the University of Fribourg (Switzerland) (1984–2009). His main publications are *Pythagoras Revived: Mathematics and Philosophy in Late Antiquity* (1989), *Plotinus. An Introduction to the Enneads* (1993), *The Structure of Being and the Search for the Good: Essays on Ancient and Early Medieval Platonism* (1999), and *Platonopolis: Platonic Political Philosophy in Late Antiquity* (2003). He has also edited and translated texts of Plotinus, Syrianus, and Michael Psellos.

JAMES ROSS received both his BA and his MA in philosophy at the Catholic University of America, where he became friends with fellow classmate John F. Wippel. Ross received his PhD in philosophy from Brown University in 1958, as well as a law degree from the University of Pennsylvania in 1974. Beginning in 1962, he taught at the University of Pennsylvania both in philosophy and eventually in law. His research interests were in the areas of medieval philosophy, philosophy of religion, contemporary metaphysics, and philosophy of mind. His list of publications is extensive, including numerous articles, and he authored several books, including *Philosophical Theology; Introduction to the Philosophy of Religion* and *Portraying Analogy.* His most recent book is *Thought and World: The Hidden Necessities,* published in 2008. Ross passed away in 2010 during the editing of this volume.

BRIAN J. SHANLEY, O.P., received a licentiate in philosophy from the Catholic University of America in 1984, where he studied with John F. Wippel, and his doctorate in philosophy from the University of Toronto in 1994. He has also received two degrees in theology from the Dominican House of Studies—a masters of divinity and a licentiate in sacred theology. From 1994 to 2005 Shanley taught in the School of Philosophy at the Catholic University of America. Since 2005, he has served as the president of Providence College. He has also served as the editor of the journal *The Thomist.* His research interests include Thomas Aquinas, philosophy of religion, metaphysics, medieval philosophy, and ethics. In addition to his articles published in these areas, he is the editor of the book *One Hundred Years of Philosophy,* published by the Catholic University of America Press in 2001, and the author of the book *The Thomist Tradition* published in 2002. His most recent book, published in 2006, is entitled *The Treatise on the Divine Nature: Summa Theologiae I 1–13.*

ROBERT SOKOLOWSKI is the Elizabeth Breckenridge Caldwell Professor of Philosophy at the Catholic University of America. Both Msgr. Sokolowski and Msgr. Wippel obtained their doctorates at the Catholic University of Louvain in 1963 and have taught as colleagues at Catholic University since then. Msgr. Sokolowski teaches and writes primarily in phenomenology and Aristotle, and on the relation between Christian faith and human reason. His most recent book is *Phenomenology of the Human Person.* In 2010 he was president of the Academy of Catholic Theology.

ANDREAS SPEER studied philosophy, theology, classical philology, and art history at the University of Bonn, where he received his doctorate in 1986. From 1988 he served as a researcher at the Thomas-Institut of the University of Cologne, where he received his venia legendi (Habilitation) in 1994.

From 1995 to2000 he was Heisenberg Research Fellow and visiting professor at the University of Notre Dame (1996), the University of Leuven (1999),
and the University of St. Louis (2006). In 2000 he became ordinary professor of philosophy at the University of Würzburg and in 2004 ordinary
professor for philosophy at the University of Cologne and director of the
Thomas-Institut. His main publications are in the field of the history of
medieval philosophy and medieval sciences, the history of epistemology,
and medieval aesthetics. He also edited numerous volumes of the Miscellanea Mediaevalia, of which he is general editor as well as of the STGM
(Studien und Texte zur Geistesgeschichte des Mittelalters).

ELEONORE STUMP is the Robert J. Henle Professor of Philosophy at Saint
Louis University, where she has taught since 1992. She has published extensively in philosophy of religion, contemporary metaphysics, and medieval
philosophy. Her books include her major study *Aquinas* (2003) and her extensive treatment of the problem of evil, *Wandering in Darkness: Narra-
tive and the Problem of Suffering* (2010). She has given the Gifford Lectures
(Aberdeen, 2003), the Wilde Lectures (Oxford, 2006), and the Stewart Lectures (Princeton, 2009). She is past president of the Society of Christian
Philosophers, the American Catholic Philosophical Association, and the
American Philosophical Association, Central Division.

JOHN F. WIPPEL is the Theodore Basselin Professor of Philosophy at the
Catholic University of America. He is the author of *The Metaphysical
Thought of Godfrey of Fontaines* (1981); *Metaphysical Themes in Thomas
Aquinas* (1984); *Boethius of Dacia: "On the Supreme Good," On the Eternity of the World, On Dreams* (1987); *Mediaeval Reactions to the Encounter between Faith and Reason* (1995); *The Metaphysical Thought of Thomas
Aquinas* (2000); *Metaphysical Themes in Thomas Aquinas* (2007); coauthor
and coeditor (with Allan B. Wolter) of *Medieval Philosophy: From St. Augustine to Nicholas of Cusa* (1969); coauthor (with B. C. Bazán, G. Fransen,
and D. Jacquart) of *Les questions disputées et les questions quodlibétiques
dans les facultés de théologie, de droit et de medicine* (1985); editor of *Studies
in Medieval Philosophy* (1987); and author of many articles and book chapters dealing with the thought of Thomas Aquinas, radical Arts Masters at
Paris in the 1260s and 1270s, Henry of Ghent, Giles of Rome, and Godfrey
of Fontaines.

Index of Names

Index of Terms

angels, 11, 21–23, 25–30, 32, 105, 113n41, 114, 118n56, 119n61, 265–66, 272–73, 277, 280–82, 289, 295. *See also* immaterial substances; separate substances

art, 24, 73–74, 136, 137, 224, 227, 228, 232, 237, 264

being: as being, 2, 4, 9–23, 25, 27, 33–35, 38–40, 43, 55, 59, 61–62; cause of 219, 219n49, 230n28; chain of, 47; Divine, 43–45, 49, 55, 94, 169, 204n15; finite, 11, 22, 25, 125, 127–28; material, 22, 24, 27, 56, 145n22; premetaphysical notion, 18; primitive notion, 18. *See ens*

categories, 39, 40, 58, 106, 107, 109n29, 112, 118, 127, 134

causality, 82n41, 122, 237, 245n5

cause : 1, 4, 12, 19–22, 32–33, 38, 40, 43, 47–48, 50–51, 53, 60–62, 73, 75–77, 80–81, 82n42, 84, 88, 92–94, 116–17, 119–23, 126, 146, 168, 184, 191, 205, 209, 218–19, 224–25, 229, 232–33, 235, 239–41, 245, 250, 280–81, 293–94; agent, 229–30, 237; of being (*causa essendi*), 219, 219n49, 230n28; Divine, 32, 209; efficient, 159n21, 213, 219, 219n48, 237, 241, 293; first, 47, 62, 218, 229–30 240; final, 32, 228; formal, 34; intelligent, 236; material, 230; provident, 226,

cognition, 19, 74–75, 80–81, 84–85, 87, 88, 91, 92, 93n76, 94, 254, 275, 283

common sense, 18

composition, 124–26, 160n22, 192, 213, 252, 277

composition and division, 17, 254. *See also* judgment; judgments

conceivability, 3, 154, 157, 159, 162–64, 174

convergence, 74

creation, 62, 170n51, 172, 192–93, 222, 224, 229, 233–34, 236, 288–90, 292, 296;

Creator, 3, 29, 33, 45, 63, 156–57, 163, 173, 236, 241, 270

differentiae, 90n69, 116n50, 193

discernibility, 130, 133, 140, 145, 146, 147, 149, 150, 153

disposition (*dispositio*), 222–23, 224n12, 228n23, 228n24, 236n47

Divine: 54, 70, 79–80, 99n1, 171–72, 196, 209, 270, 288, 290; activity, 230; attributes, 222, 226; being, 43–45, 49, 55, 94, 169, 204n15; determinism, 225; election, 166; essence, 207, 214, 215n40, 221, 275; eternity, 5, 244–45, 249–50; existence, 30; goodness, 31, 122, 214, 217, 228, 231–33, 234, 236, 238, 240, 277, 286, 289; governance, 224, 231, 237–38, 279–80; ideas, 170n51, 236; intellect, 43–45, 48, 226, 229, 231, 236; knowledge, 78; law, 280–81; nature, 192, 228, 231; omniscience, 222, 237; omnipotence, 215, 221, 242; omnipresence, 220n51; operation, 217; perfection, 123, 213, 217, 241–42; person, 250, 289; power, 156n11, 158n17, 227, 229, 266, 277, 296; providence, 4, 208, 220, 222, 225–26, 228, 231, 235–242; punishment, 281; realities, 47, 190, 194; retribution, 268, 276, 287, 290; science, 184; simplicity, 5, 244–45, 252–54; substance, 38, 40, 43–44, 46, 54; things, 21, 60–62, 79, 199–201, 204, 206–7, 209, 211–12; truths, 206, 295; understanding, 170n51; will, 170n51, 214, 216–17, 220, 226, 228–29, 232, 236, 286–90, 293–94; wisdom, 217–18, 229

The Science of Being as Being: Metaphysical Investigations was designed and typeset in Minion by Kachergis Book Design of Pittsboro, North Carolina. It was printed on 55-pound Natures Recycled and bound by Sheridan Books of Ann Arbor, Michigan.

LIBERAL
EDUCATION
AND THE
PUBLIC
INTEREST

LIBERAL EDUCATION AND THE PUBLIC INTEREST

JAMES O. FREEDMAN

UNIVERSITY OF IOWA PRESS 𝚿 IOWA CITY

University of Iowa Press, Iowa City 52242
Copyright © 2003 by James O. Freedman
All rights reserved
Printed in the United States of America
Design by Richard Hendel
http://www.uiowa.edu/uiowapress

The publication of this book was generously supported
by the University of Iowa Foundation.

Printed on acid-free paper

Library of Congress
Cataloging-in-Publication Data
Freedman, James O.
Liberal education and the public interest / by James O. Freedman.
p.   cm.
Includes bibliographical references and index.
ISBN 0-87745-825-1 (cloth)
1. Education, Humanistic—United States.   2. Education, Higher—Aims and
objectives—United States.   3. College presidents—United States.   I. Title.
LC1011.F724 2003
370.11′2—dc21   2002066491

03   04   05   06   07   C   5   4   3   2

❧ CONTENTS ❧

❧ PREFACE ❦

This book is about the possibilities of presidential leadership in higher education. More specifically it is about the opportunities for college presidents to make the case for liberal education. It reflects my experience as president of the University of Iowa, from 1982 to 1987, and as president of Dartmouth College, from 1987 to 1998. During those sixteen years, I became a devout advocate of the power of liberal education. These essays seek to enlarge upon and advance the arguments I made in an earlier book, *Idealism and Liberal Education* (1996).

One of the principal obligations of a college president is to ask: What is expected of those who have been privileged to acquire a liberal education and the renewing capacities that it instills? Many things, of course, but two especially: the obligation, as John F. Kennedy once said, to make the world safe for personal distinction, and the obligation to be an effective citizen of a democracy.

It is personal distinction that represents the fullest flowering of individual talents. It offers one of the earth's most sublime sources of human satisfaction, sets standards of achievement for others to emulate, and gives our society its heroes. By striving to create a world that honors personal distinction — a world in which talent tells and merit matters — we reinforce the aspirations that a liberal education nurtures, and we advance the human condition.

John Adams, the nation's second president, once wrote in a letter to his wife, Abigail, "I must study politics and war that my sons may have liberty to study mathematics and philosophy. My sons ought to study mathematics and philosophy, geography, natural history, naval architecture, navigation, commerce, and agriculture, in order to give their children a right to study painting, music, architecture, statuary, tapestry, and porcelain."

Adams thus recognized that education promised progress and

greater privilege from generation to generation. As the members of one generation pursued the more practical sides of higher learning, they created opportunities for the children of the next generation to devote their time to the classical pursuits of a cultured mind.

But what kind of obligations, a college president should ask, does a liberal education impose upon successive generations of children? Among the highest obligations of an educated person in a democracy is to be a citizen, a person devoted to the ideals of the nation and to the well-being of the entire commonwealth, rather than to only a narrow segment of it. And yet the achievement of that obligation is increasingly rare.

More than two hundred years ago, Jean-Jacques Rousseau wrote, "We have physicists, geometers, chemists, astronomers, poets, musicians, painters." But, he added, "we no longer have citizens." What Rousseau said about eighteenth-century France is ominously accurate about the United States today.

One of the principal venues for exhorting students to public service is commencement. In one of the finest commencement speeches I know, William Faulkner told the graduation class of Pine Manor Junior College in 1953: "What's wrong with this world is, it's not finished yet. It is not completed to that point where man can put his final signature to the job and say, 'It is finished. We made it, and it works.'"

Faulkner, of course, was right. The world is not yet "finished," and it presents a daunting agenda of work to be done. Who can view the international scene and not find challenges in the elimination of nuclear weapons, the resettlement of international refugees, and the development of a foreign policy that at once protects our national interests and reflects our devotion to principles of human rights? Who can witness events in the nations of Africa and not be concerned with ethnic conflict and the problems of genocide, hunger, malnutrition, population control, and disease that afflict a great portion of the planet?

Who can look at the Third World and not be shaken by the relentless force of globalization — by a distribution of resources that thwarts the aspirations of millions of persons, that stunts the health of innocent children, and that threatens a global confrontation between the haves and the have-nots? Who can survey the nation's landscape and not be troubled by looming issues of sustainability — by the pollution of our rivers, the poisoning of our air, the erosion of our soil, and the unremitting encroachments upon our wilderness and wildlife? Who can participate in American society and not appreciate that our nation faces enduring questions of bringing minorities into the mainstream of educational and occupational opportunity?

A liberal education seeks to strengthen students' capacities to deal with the world's and the nation's agendas, to expand their horizons, enrich their intellect, and deepen their spirit. It asks them to accept responsibility for their actions and for the welfare of others.

I nurture the ardent hope that a liberal education will encourage students to dedicate their talents, energy, and idealism to the task of what Faulkner called "finishing" the world. And even if, as Faulkner understood, the intractable reality of the human condition means that men and women will never be able to put their final signatures to the job and say, "It is finished. We made it, and it works," the effort of seeking to bring the world nearer to completion is an undertaking worthy of the most devout dedication.

This college generation has been widely criticized. Sociologists have suggested that it lacks an interior landscape, is preoccupied with career ambitions and financial security, and consists of yuppies without a cause. Psychologists have asserted that it has succumbed to the moral hazards of affluence and adopted the selfish credo "more for me."

These characterizations are profoundly disconcerting. My own experience has given me a quite different perspective. In a time of civic atrophy, this is a generation of ambition and of energy. Its altruism is reflected in the record numbers who volunteer for public interest causes while in college, as well as for the Peace Corps and AmeriCorps upon graduation. Its members want to be part of something larger than themselves, but have not quite figured out how. Few, I believe, are likely to lament in retrospect, with J. Alfred Prufrock, "I have measured out my life with coffee spoons."

The critics are watching to learn where this generation puts its ambition, energy, and education. They are looking to learn whether it chooses, in the poet Philip Larkin's words, merely to "listen to money singing." Larkin wrote:

> I listen to money singing. It's like looking down
> From long french windows at a provincial town,
> The slums, the canals, the churches ornate and mad
> In the evening sun. It is intensely sad.

Few of us who know this generation well believe that it will, in fact, claim its adulthood by the intensely sad and profoundly banal act of choosing to "listen to money singing." It has the opportunity to confound its critics by making choices worthy of its talents and idealism, choices that will make the common good its own.

I have tried in these pages to emphasize some of the many opportunities available to college and university presidents for celebrating liberal education, from preaching from the bully pulpit to taking note of inspiring lives to judiciously selecting honorary degree recipients.

I am grateful to Chancellor Robert M. Berdahl of the University of California at Berkeley for inviting me to deliver the Jefferson Memorial Lectures for the 2000–2001 academic year, upon which some of this book is based.

Delivery or publication of earlier versions of chapters of this book have been as follows. Chapter 1 was originally delivered as the Howard R. Bowen Memorial Lecture at Claremont Graduate University and appeared in *Harvard Magazine*, January–February 1999. Chapter 3 was originally delivered as the Simon H. Rifkind Memorial Lecture at the City College of New York. Chapter 4 was originally delivered as a speech to the National Press Club, October 16, 1997. Chapter 5 was originally delivered as the Francis Greenwood Peabody Lecture at the Memorial Church, Harvard University, and as the Bishop John P. Boles Lecture at the Catholic Chaplaincy, Harvard University, and appeared in *Harvard Magazine*, November–December 2000. Chapter 6 was originally delivered as the Henry N. Rapaport Memorial Lecture at the Jewish Theological Seminary and appeared in the *Chronicle of Higher Education*, December 1, 2000. Chapter 7 appeared in the *Chronicle of Higher Education*, May 24, 2002.

I am indebted to three friends and colleagues, Steven Biel, Peter A. Gilbert, and Edward Connery Lathem, for their editorial assistance, and to Kimberly Watson for her conscientious preparation of the manuscript.

Three books — *He Walked Alone* by Bernard Bellush, *Dorothy Day: A Radical Devotion* by Robert Coles, and *By Little and By Little: The Selected Writings of Dorothy Day*, edited by Robert Ellsberg — were especially useful in the preparation of chapter 5. Edward Tenner's article "Honorary Degrees Are Worth Receiving, but They're Not Worth Envying," in the *Chronicle of Higher Education*, was helpful in the preparation of chapter 7.

❋ 1 ❋
MOUNTING
THE PUBLIC
STAGE

Collegeand university presidents occupy prominent, even prestigious, positions in their communities and in society at large. Yet to many citizens they are strangely invisible and oddly silent on many important public issues. They are not often counted among society's public intellectuals. This has not always been the case, and it is worth asking why the change has occurred.

Having served for sixteen years as the president of two institutions — one a public university, the other a private college — I have perforce had many opportunities to think about the role of college presidents in the public life of the nation.

In earlier periods, college presidents regularly served for two or three decades. Today the average tenure is thought to be six or seven years, although some presidents now serve second or even third presidencies. Two-thirds of the presidents of the thirty-one private institutions that constitute the Consortium on the Financing of Higher Education (COFHE) typically have taken office within the last five years.

Although it is hazardous to generalize about presidents as a class if only because they serve at more than three thousand very different institutions, it can safely be said that for many presidents today the jobs are simply too demanding to sustain for an extended period of years. These presidents determine after a few years of service that their constituencies are routinely mutinous, their hold on office insufficiently secure, and their daily satisfactions depressingly few to justify the burdens and frustrations of office. They conclude, as A. Bartlett Giamatti ruefully introduced his book *A Free and Ordered Space* (1988), "Being president of a university is no way for an adult to make a living."

It has not always been so. When Charles W. Eliot announced his retirement as president of Harvard in 1909, he said, "The occupation which has been mine for a lifetime has been a most pleasant one, and I regret that it is about to terminate. Forty years of service has been given me in the pursuance of a profession that has no equal in the world." My speculation is that few college presidents would leave office today in such a generous frame of mind. We need to ask why college presidencies are not more stable and more satisfying, and what consequence this circumstance may have for the leadership of our colleges and universities, as well as for the public life of the nation.

The expectations of the office, to begin with, are so inflated as to be virtually impossible to meet. Humorous descriptions, barely concealing the truth, abound. Henry Wriston, who served as president of Brown University for many years, once noted that a university president should "speak continuously in words that charm and never offend, take bold positions with which no one will disagree, consult everyone and follow all proffered advice, and do everything through committees, but with great speed and without error."

In the days before many women had become chief executives, Clark Kerr, the former president of the University of California, added that a university president was expected to be, among other things, "a friend of the students, a colleague of the faculty, a good fellow with the alumni, a sound administrator with the trustees, a good speaker with the public, an astute bargainer with the state legislature, a friend of industry, labor, and agriculture, a persuasive diplomat with donors, a champion of education, a supporter of the professions (particularly law and medicine), a spokesman to the press, a scholar in his own right, a public servant at the state and national levels, a devotee of opera and football equally, a decent human being, a good husband and father, an active member of a church, and a person who enjoys traveling in airplanes and eating his meals in public."

Finally, the search committee that ultimately selected A. Whitney

Griswold as president of Yale University agreed that it was looking for "a leader, a magnificent speaker and great writer, a good public relations man and fund raiser, a man of iron health and stamina, married to a paragon — a combination of Queen Victoria, Florence Nightingale, and best dressed woman of the year — a man of the world but with great spiritual qualities, an experienced administrator who can delegate authority, a great scholar, and a Yale man." The committee recognized that "there is only One who has most of these qualifications." But then it asked itself, "Is God a Yale man?"

These high expectations are mocked by reality. They inevitably encourage the steady round of criticism that may be foremost among the possible explanations for the brief tenure of presidents. President Eliot surely must have experienced occasional moments of darkness during his forty years in office — moments of conflict, disappointment, and failure — but one can be confident that he did *not* experience the constancy or intensity of criticism that his present-day successors typically undergo.

The available grounds for criticizing college presidents are many: leadership style, educational philosophy, financial competence, public-speaking skills, fund-raising effectiveness, relationships with alumni, availability to students. In an era in which many constituencies believe that they have a significant stake in the fortunes of a college, a president is exposed on virtually every side. In my experience, the complaints, if not quite criticisms, are so constant and diverse that at times of exasperation I wished I had had the courage to follow Edmund Wilson's truculent example of printing postcards that read "Dear Sir: You may well be right. Sincerely."

There is, of course, a relationship between the relatively short average tenure of college presidents and the breadth of the constituencies whose members believe they have the right to criticize presidents. The greater the sources and volume of criticism, the more painful the stress that presidents (and their family members) suffer and the briefer their tenure is likely to be. Perhaps this has ever been so. When Daniel Dana resigned as president of Dartmouth College in 1822 after only eleven months in office, he told the board of trustees, "This College, Gentlemen, needs a president not only of powerful talents, but of strong nerves." But it is more acutely so today than it was a half century ago.

In the face of recurring criticism from manifold sources, upon whom can a president reliably count for support? Two immediate possibilities are her faculty and her board of trustees.

Faculty members always have ambivalent feelings toward their president. They look to him for leadership at the same time that they resent his efforts to disturb them professionally. They jealously guard their own institutional prerogatives, and praise collegial governance for its tendency toward a horizontal hierarchy of power. To many faculty members, the president represents a contending professional class; to others, he seems largely irrelevant, needed primarily for ceremonial and fund-raising purposes. Often faculty members joke about the president's constant absence from campus and highlight the rare occasions upon which he is sighted. Yet in auspicious circumstances, presidents of unusual character, vision, and eloquence can appeal successfully to the most independent of faculties. John Kenneth Galbraith captured the balance well when he wrote, "A college president can lead a faculty but he cannot defeat it." However, the task is difficult.

In order to lead a faculty, a president must establish herself as a colleague. She must be able to engage with its members intellectually and to devote a part of her month to attending faculty seminars and colloquia. She must take the initiative in learning of individual faculty members' academic interests, reading the books they have written as well as the serious books of the moment that they are reading. In short, she must establish that she appreciates the dignity of the academic life and is worthy of respect on the academy's terms. These efforts take time — uncluttered, untroubled, unhurried time — and that is precisely what the complexity of her position often denies a president.

A board of trustees of constancy and fortitude can support a president in ways that nourish his efforts and prolong his tenure. The most important function of a board is to work collaboratively with the president to examine the strength and long-range opportunities of the college and to develop a clear vision, always subject to midcourse modification, of the goals that the college seeks to achieve. In the end, it is the board that has the best opportunity to see the future of the college as a whole, unlike other groups, such as alumni and students, that see it only from afar and sporadically or from too near and constantly. The board must then have sufficient confidence in its goals to preserve that larger perspective during the periodic storms of criticism that a college may face. Unfortunately, some boards grow weary of conflict among the college's constituencies and, rather than staying the course, seek the relief of resolution by abandoning the president prematurely.

I want to address a particular form of criticism that is increasingly directed against even those college presidents who serve for relatively substantial lengths of time: that they do not use their positions as bully pulpits to speak out on important issues of the day. I choose this particular criticism because most college presidents enter upon their service with the expectation that participation in public discussion will provide them with a wider audience for their views and be one of the most rewarding aspects of their tenure.

College presidents of the present generation are frequently compared unfavorably to presidents of bygone eras — eras in which, it is said, giants walked the land. "A generation ago . . . college and university presidents cut striking figures on the public stage," a journalist for the *New York Times* has lamented. "They called for the reform of American education, proposed safeguards for democracy, sought to defuse the cold war, urged moral standards for scientific research, and addressed other important issues of the time. Today, almost no college or university president has spoken out significantly . . . about dozens of . . . issues high on the national agenda."

Criticisms of this nature are easily lodged and may even be true, but there is much more to be said if the reasons underlying the truth are to be understood. College presidents of a prior era were, indeed, prominent figures in the public life of the nation and of their communities. These titans — or at least some of them — wrote shelves of books, published articles in the *Atlantic Monthly* and *Scribner's Magazine*, advised presidents of the United States, and chaired national commissions. In the nineteenth century, some took an active part in politics;

Charles W. Eliot of Harvard, Mark Hopkins of Williams, Andrew D. White of Cornell, and Theodore Dwight Woolsey of Yale were conspicuous participants in Republican party activities. Those who served at the most prestigious institutions were members of the country's unofficial House of Lords: of eminent dignity and beyond popular election.

Nicholas Murray Butler, the legendary president of Columbia University, is a good example. Even H. L. Mencken, who did not hold college presidents in high esteem, gave grudging praise to Butler. "As a class," Mencken wrote of college presidents, "they are platitudinous and nonsensical enough, God knows. But there is at least one among them, Dr. Nicholas Murray Butler of Columbia, who actually says something when he speaks."

Not least among Butler's remarkable accomplishments was his longevity in office. He became president of Columbia in 1902 when he was forty; he retired in 1945 when he was eighty-three. Although often derided for his authoritarian style, Butler was praised by many intellectuals — including Henri Bergson, H. G. Wells, and Benjamin N. Cardozo—for his powerful qualities of mind. In his two-volume autobiography, appropriately entitled *Across the Busy Years* (1939–40), Butler described how he managed, for more than four decades, to combine his responsibilities as president of Columbia with a vast range of public activities.

Throughout his career at Columbia, Butler spoke out on domestic issues and played a significant role in national Republican politics. He was an adviser to Presidents Roosevelt, Taft, and Harding, and campaigned vigorously for the repeal of Prohibition. In 1912 he was William Howard Taft's vice-presidential candidate on the Republican ticket. And in 1920 he was considered a serious contender for the Republican presidential nomination; the *New York Times* endorsed his candidacy, calling him "undoubtedly the best fitted of all candidates."

Butler's role in the public discussion of foreign affairs was even more prominent. For the last twenty years of his presidency of Columbia, he served simultaneously as president of the Carnegie Endowment for International Peace. Before the onset of World War I, he called for the use of military force and economic sanctions against nations that invoked military power. After the war, he spoke out against United States participation in the League of Nations on the terms negotiated by Woodrow Wilson. In 1927, he became perhaps the most influential public advocate of the Kellogg-Briand pact, which renounced war as an instrument of international diplomacy. For his efforts on behalf of disarmament and world peace, he was awarded the Nobel Prize for Peace in 1931.

The career of A. Lawrence Lowell, president of Harvard University from 1909 to 1933, is equally revealing. Throughout the twenty-four years of his tenure, Lowell often mounted the public stage. He took strong stands on public issues. He favored American participation in the League of Nations, which he regarded as essential to world peace, and was an outspoken critic of the New Deal, which he feared would undermine individual responsibility and initiative, and of labor unions, which he believed promoted organized selfishness. Having been trained as a lawyer, Lowell spoke out against President Wilson's appointment of Louis D. Brandeis to the United States Supreme Court, ostensibly because he thought Brandeis did not enjoy the confidence of the bar. However, many thought he objected to the appointment because he rejected Brandeis's progressive political and social views and because Brandeis was a Jew.

On some occasions, Lowell entered public controversy even though he clouded Harvard's reputation by doing so. In 1927 he served, by appointment of the governor of Massachusetts, as the chairman of a three-man committee to review the convictions of Nicola Sacco and Bartolomeo Vanzetti, who had been sentenced to death for the murder of two men during a payroll robbery. Having reviewed the transcript of the trial and the evidence presented, and being aware of the fact that the presiding judge had publicly boasted of having convicted "those anarchist bastards," the committee concluded that both men had received a fair trial. Sacco and Vanzetti were executed. Controversy about the Sacco-Vanzetti case (memorialized in a series of powerful gouache paintings by Ben Shahn) followed Lowell for the rest of his life. The historian Ernst Earnest concluded that "Lowell will go down in history" not as an educator "but as the man who sent Sacco and Vanzetti to death." The episode serves as a cautionary reminder that when a president mounts the public stage, he runs risks, both for himself and his institution.

The assurance that Lowell felt in inviting notoriety by his outspoken participation in public affairs doubtless derived in part from the self-confidence he enjoyed as a member of Boston's Brahmin elite; he did not, as one historian has written, shy away from the personal pronoun. But that assurance also derived from the public expectation that college presidents, especially the presidents of leading colleges, would address vital issues of the day — would act in their capacities as citizens quite apart from their capacities as educators.

A third educational leader of an earlier generation who played a prominent role on the public stage was Robert Maynard Hutchins, who served as president of the University of Chicago from 1929 to 1945 and as chancellor from 1945 to 1951. A part of Hutchins's celebrity stemmed from the stunning fact that he had been appointed president of the university at the age of thirty, after having served already for two years as dean of the Yale Law School. But his celebrity also rested upon his extensive participation in public affairs. He testified before Congress against universal military service and in favor of loosening security restrictions on atomic research. He spoke out against the cold war policies of the Truman administration and served as president of the Committee to Frame a World Constitution. Indeed, Hutchins became such a well-known public figure that newspapers regularly speculated that he would be appointed to high political office, perhaps even to a seat on the U.S. Supreme Court, by Franklin D. Roosevelt. In 1940, Sinclair Lewis, addressing a large audience at Constitution Hall in Washington, recommended that Hutchins be elected president of the United States.

Hutchins was a serious, if iconoclastic, thinker about the nature of an ideal university. To a greater degree than Butler or Lowell, he attracted public attention because of his views as an educator, which he expressed passionately and disseminated widely. During his tenure at the University of Chicago, he radically transformed the complexion of the institution, emphasizing undergraduate education as the central mission of the university. In league with the philosopher Mortimer Adler, he envisioned a bold and controversial alternative to the elective system: a required interdisciplinary curriculum that would offer undergraduates a liberal education organized around the "Great Books." "An Aristotelian and a Thomist," as Saul Bellow would later describe him, "he saw to it that the huge fortunes amassed in slaughterhouses and steel mills were spent teaching generations of students the main achievements of Western culture."

Describing himself proudly as the "worst kind of troublemaker" and "the man who insists upon asking about first principles," Hutchins was not diffident in criticizing American higher education, which he regarded as not only "unintellectual but anti-intellectual as well." Having once declared that there were only two ways for a university to be great — "It must either have a great football team or a great president" — he took the daring step of abolishing the University of Chicago's intercollegiate football program.

From 1944 to 1947, Hutchins headed the Commission on Freedom of the Press, which issued a scathing report that criticized the journalistic enterprise. As one historian has described the commission's conclusions, the press had failed "miserably to discharge its moral obligation to the community, more often than not reflecting the views of its owners and advertisers in the treatment of news, and pandering to the lowest tastes of the readers who had to depend on it for the understanding of the great issues that confronted them in a democratic society." Yet, for all his contempt for the professional standards of the press, Hutchins did not hesitate to use the press as a bully pulpit, publishing articles in popular magazines, cultivating newspaper coverage of his activities, and regularly addressing national radio audiences. During his tenure as president, he wrote three books and constantly delivered public addresses, occupying the public stage as few other college presidents have before or since.

College presidents like Butler, Lowell, and Hutchins were significant public figures even if they did not always speak wisely or temperately, and they made their voices heard. They were muscular intellectuals, in the mold of Theodore Roosevelt or Woodrow Wilson, the latter himself a former college president. The fact that they occupied prominent academic positions lent weight to their mandarin views. Respect for their office made their public roles seem a part of the natural order of things.

Not every college president, of course, was as gifted, as bold, or as effective as these three were. The contemporary writer Sinclair Lewis joined Mencken in his general disdain for the occupational class. In his 1925 novel *Arrowsmith*, Lewis recounts the terms in which the young scientist Martin Arrowsmith was berated by his revered mentor Max Gottlieb for cutting scientific corners in a way that might bring him celebrity: "You want fake reports of cures to get into the newspapers, to be telegraphed about places, and have everybody in the world that has a pimple come tumbling in to be cured. . . . You want to be a miracle man, and not a scientist?" And in his final words of fury, reaching for the most apt term of derogation he could find, Gottlieb says, "Get out of my office! You are a — a — a college president!"

Men like Butler, Lowell, and Hutchins — and the college presidents of their era were, indeed, almost exclusively men — surely did, in the words of the *New York Times*, "cut striking figures on the public stage." When my colleagues and I encounter unfavorable comparisons to these presidents — comparisons virtually in the nature of indictments — that suggest we lack the aura or genius of greatness that they possessed, our first reaction is to protest that we hold more difficult jobs than they did, that we serve in a period in which campus availability, consultation, and visibility have become more demanding measures of our performance, that we preside over institutions that are larger, more complex, and more publicly accountable than theirs, and that we are obliged to pay considerably more attention to a wider set of constituencies — faculty, students, staff, alumni, federal, state, and local governments, the media, and foundations. We add that we must spend significantly more time raising money — most presidents estimate that they spend at least one-third of their time on fund-raising, conducting themselves, as one wag has said, as "members of the mendicant class."

Moreover, to a much greater extent than was the case a generation ago, the institutions over which we preside are democratic microcosms of the larger society and they reflect the ideological tensions of that more diverse and ethnically fragmented society. These are the tensions that have given rise to the alleged phenomenon of political correctness. These are the tensions that often cause presidents to find themselves hemmed in by spoken and unspoken pressures from numerous and multifaceted constituencies, especially on such sensitive and polarizing issues as racial diversity, ethnic separatism, sexual harassment, multiculturalism, campus speech codes, defense and weapons research, intercollegiate athletics, investment policy, fraternities and sororities, and core curricula.

"Presidents (and, to a degree, provosts, and deans) hold what have become political offices," as Donald Kennedy, former president of Stanford University, has written. "It is difficult to occupy one of these positions without some sense that you are running for it every day." Moreover, the conflict among a president's many constituencies often induces decisions that sap his morale and compromise his sense of idealism. As Kennedy continued, "There is a powerful temptation to engage in the politics of self-preservation, which most often turn out to be the politics of caution. In hard times, this is likely to encourage pseudoequitable budget reductions across-the-board, rather than bold assaults on weak programs; in good times, it yields a form of bland opportunism, in which almost any plausible plan for growth is rewarded if it is offered under the right credentials."

Maintaining the fragile equilibrium among the many constituencies of a university is no small challenge. The president's job, as the *New York Times* has written editorially, "requires the management skills of a corporate CEO and the political skill to mediate between vastly disparate, and often stubborn, constituencies — a school's faculty members, students, administrators and alumni."

No president wants to make new enemies for her college, especially in a period of what seem to be perpetual capital campaigns seeking the support of alumni and friends. Many presidents believe that they must be especially careful not to alienate the college's most important constituencies because the price to be paid by their institutions, for what sometimes seems to be the indulgence of stating their personal convictions, is simply too high. "Every idea," Justice Holmes once said, "is an incitement." And for every controversial idea that a college president espouses, there is a constituency she may incite and whose goodwill she may jeopardize. A president who speaks out on public issues may be respected for her courage by those who agree with her, but her college may lose the support of those who do not.

There are issues of professional protocol as well. One of the nation's most respected students of higher education, Martin Trow, has suggested that it is not appropriate for college presidents to advocate publicly academic policies that their Boards of Regents formally oppose. He had in mind statements that the chancellors of the University of California campuses made in 1997 in support of affirmative action after the state's Board of Regents had prohibited the practice. "Like civil servants everywhere," Trow wrote, "university administrators have the right, and indeed the obligation, to present their views on any issues to their superiors . . . in private, and even to press their opinions vigorously. But when they announce their views publicly, they enter a political realm in which they have no special authority or standing."

Despite Trow's injunction, presidents from time to time do speak publicly on important national issues. Yet many of the presidents I know best quietly bemoan the moral hypocrisy that governs their professional lives. Few college presidents, for example, have played a more honorable or vigorous role on the public stage than Vartan Gregorian. Yet when Gregorian retired as president of Brown University, he said, "I can't express my opinion on important issues without fear of alienating segments of the faculty, students, and alumni. It burns me up, because I am highly political."

College presidents like Butler, Lowell, and Hutchins served at a time when the "public" was synonymous with college-educated white men.

They could speak on a national stage as if they were addressing an especially large alumni reception, rather than the heterogeneous publics — plural — that college presidents are obliged to engage today.

Those who held positions of authority in an earlier generation were also accorded far more respect by virtue of these positions than their successors are today. The attention that American society pays to persons holding positions of leadership has steadily eroded since the 1960s, ushering in a period that the sociologist Robert Nisbet has called the "twilight of authority." In 1992, a Louis Harris poll reported that only 25 percent of Americans responded that they had "a great deal of confidence" in academic administrators, down from 61 percent in 1966.

College presidents, like leaders in many other professions, have suffered from a loss of stature and voice because of today's prevailing skepticism — perhaps a product of the war in Vietnam and of Watergate — toward figures of authority. Sometimes they have lost authority as the result of self-inflicted wounds. The rise of intercollegiate athletics, with its relentless emphasis upon winning, has proven a significant source of embarrassment and sometimes humiliation for some college presidents. Dependence upon athletic revenues, especially from television contracts, and the support of sports-crazy taxpayers and alumni has reduced the authority of presidents over one of their institutions' most visible activities.

When an investigation in 2000 into the behavior of Bob Knight, the notorious basketball coach at Indiana University, revealed a pattern of unacceptable and often abusive conduct, most observers expected the school to fire him. Instead, the university's president announced that, with minor chastisements, Knight would remain at Indiana despite his "pattern of inappropriate behavior." To many the president appeared to have succumbed to external forces he could not control by placing athletics and revenue streams ahead of moral and ethical standards of behavior. The *Chronicle of Higher Education* reported that "many agree that the Knight saga has wounded the university and has detracted from its attempts to rise in the ranks of the nation's public institutions." (Four months later, after still other incidents of self-destructive behavior, the university finally fired Knight.)

Finally, there is almost certainly a relationship between the relatively brief average tenure of college presidents and the extent of their participation in national policy discussions. When a person accepts the presidency of an institution not his own, he is likely to arrive as a virtual stranger, knowing few members of the faculty or administration, lacking local guides against the pitfalls that the personnel and culture of the institution will inevitably throw in his path. The adjustment to the position can easily occupy most of his energies for several years. By the time he has made the adjustment, the end of his tenure may be in sight.

Moreover, for many presidents, the fit with the new institution may not be a comfortable one. Every college is a kingdom unto itself, with its own distinctive history and traditions; many institutions are resistant to presidents who are outsiders, fearing they have been brought in to carry out a specific agenda of the Board of Trustees. Many local communities, beyond the immediate campus, often view a new president with a show-me skepticism and are slow to grant her legitimacy. Some new presidents are fortunate in receiving a public endorsement from a respected predecessor, although others must abide the dismissive dinner-party small talk of their predecessor.

Few leaders of American higher education have made a more important contribution than Henry Rosovsky, who was dean of the faculty of Arts and Sciences at Harvard for thirteen years. Yet when Rosovsky was offered the presidency of Yale in 1977, he had serious doubts about the circumstances he would face as an outsider. As Dean A. Oren has written in *Joining the Club: A History of Jews and Yale* (1985), Rosovsky believed that "the best academic administrators were those who had developed a strong sense of loyalty to their particular institutions." Rosovsky declined Yale's offer.

In judging the participation of college presidents in public life, we need to recognize that they will not feel confident in taking a role in public debate beyond their institutions until they first feel confident of their standing within those institutions. Too often, their tenure in office concludes just at the point when they might be expected to have gained such confidence.

Given all of these occupational circumstances, is it any wonder that college presidents wince when critics assert that they do not exercise leadership on public issues as readily as their predecessors did? The fact is that today's college presidents hold jobs that are simply different than they once were. The social context in which presidents function is also unlike that of their celebrated predecessors. The facts that universities are larger today and the pace of events more accelerated condition the ways in which college presidents perform their responsibilities.

Still, presidential self-pity is not an attractive trait. It may be salutary to recall that it is not a new one, either. One of Lowell's early predecessors, Edward Holyoke, who was president of Harvard College for thirty-two years, from 1737 to 1769, is supposed to have said on his deathbed, "If a man wishes to be humbled and mortified, let him first become President of Harvard College." (The Harvard College that so traumatically tested President Holyoke's soul had 15 faculty members and 180 students.)

However, even in the terms invoked by the critics, the unfavorable assessment of today's presidents, especially with respect to the contributions they make to public discussion, are overstated. Even though they are confined more tightly to campus governance than their predecessors, many college presidents have chosen to speak out. I think specifically of Presidents Hesburgh of Notre Dame, Brewster and Giamatti of Yale, Bok of Harvard, and Kemeny of Dartmouth, to mention only five not now serving.

Of these five, I know my predecessor John G. Kemeny the best. He was one of the most important figures in Dartmouth's modern history — a brilliant scholar, a born teacher, a humane man, and an epoch-making president. He was, for me, nothing less than a hero.

John Kemeny came to the United States from Budapest in 1940 as a boy of fourteen, part of an intellectual migration that brought to this nation inestimable human resources of talent and creative energy. Once he reached these shores, John Kemeny's achievements were the stuff of which legends are made. He entered George Washington High School in New York knowing virtually no English, and graduated first in a class of 2,300 students. At twenty-two, he became research assistant to two preeminent members of that intellectual migration, Albert Einstein and John von Neumann. At twenty-three, he received his Ph.D. in mathematics from Princeton. At twenty-seven, he was appointed professor of mathematics at Dartmouth. He became a citizen in 1945. And in 1970, at forty-three, he was named president of the college.

As a member of the Dartmouth faculty, John Kemeny earned a position of eminence by the power of his mind and the vitality of his nature. He advanced the fields of mathematics and computer science and pioneered the use of computers in higher education. He wrote several books, including *A Philosopher Looks at Science* (1972). As Dartmouth's thirteenth president (1970–81), he led the college with wisdom and skill during a decade of social tumult and institutional change. Intellectual and introspective, John Kemeny was by temperament a private person whose destiny it was to lead a public life. He knew Dartmouth intimately and guided it through an important period of redefinition, enhancing its academic status and enriching the experience of its students.

Kemeny well understood the political nature of his responsibilities. "The Presidency of Dartmouth," he wrote in an annual report, "is the only job I know where you are elected first and then spend your remaining years as if you are running for office." But through it all, he remained a man of principle. His greatest achievements as president of Dartmouth stemmed from his courage in acting decisively on his most deeply held beliefs. Without wide consultation, he audaciously announced in his inaugural address that Dartmouth would rededicate itself to its original mission of educating Native Americans. He championed the admission of minority students and what later became known as affirmative action. In the wake of the invasion of Cambodia and the shooting of four student protesters at Kent State, he canceled classes for a day of reflection and discussion — the action of a wise and pragmatic educator.

In the face of intransigent opposition from many tradition-bound alumni, John Kemeny grasped a historical moment and presided over Dartmouth's transformation into a coeducational institution. He was, of course, the first president to address the student body with the words, "Men and Women of Dartmouth." In convocation exercises in the fall of 1972, when he first enunciated that simple salutation in the gentle accent of his Hungarian youth, he received a resounding ovation. Several months before his death in 1992, when he and I were discussing those early years of coeducation, he told me, with characteristic wit, how he used to concede that there was, indeed, a place for an all-male college — and that that place was Williams! (Subsequently, Williams became coeducational, too.)

Appointed by President Jimmy Carter in 1979 to chair the commission to investigate the nuclear accident at Three Mile Island, he performed a significant public service, submitting a report sharply critical of the nuclear power industry and its federal regulators.

Finally, with eloquence as well as action, John Kemeny spoke out against bigotry. With words that are as powerful today as they were when he spoke them in his final commencement address in 1981, he urged the graduating class to reject "a voice heard in many guises throughout history — which is the most dangerous voice you will ever hear. It appeals to the basest instincts in all of us — it appeals to human prejudice. It tries to divide us by setting whites against blacks, by setting Christians against Jews, by setting men against women. And if it succeeds in dividing us from our fellow human beings, it will impose its evil will upon a fragmented society." Instead, he exhorted the graduates to listen "to the voice that is within yourself — the voice that tells you that mankind can live in peace, that mankind can live in harmony, that mankind can live with respect for the rights and dignity of all human beings." And then he closed with the valedictory words that he invoked at every commencement ceremony, "All mankind is your brother and you are your brother's keeper." The Dartmouth of today is in significant part the result of John Kemeny standing where he did for what he did: coeducation, racial diversity, academic excellence, and generosity of spirit. By the force of his character, he moved Dartmouth forward.

Of course, the pattern among presidents is necessarily uneven. Presidents of distinguished private institutions have the greatest security in speaking out; those who hold these positions appreciate that they have a special responsibility to be among the moral leaders of the profession. Presidents of public institutions, beholden to legislative bodies, and of small private institutions, often struggling for students and resources, are in a more precarious position and understandably find it more difficult to speak out.

How, then, ought we evaluate the portrayal of college presidents as less engaged in the nation's public policy debates than once was the case? In part, the portrayal reflects the fact that in an age of celebrity, college presidents must compete with many other public figures for the limited space available on the op-ed pages of the nation's newspapers and for the limited airtime assignable in the crowded and cacophonous spectrum of the electronic media; in that competition, mean-spirited and adversarial voices are typically more likely to prevail. In part, the portrayal reflects the fact that college presidents today face a proliferation of administrative responsibilities and internal pressures created by the ethic of constituency participation and consultation.

Presidents Butler, Lowell, and Hutchins were, no doubt, men of extraordinary brilliance and energy. But they also served at a time when the circumstances of American academic life were more relaxed and the strictly professional demands upon a college president less taxing than they are today. Butler, for example, could sail to England on Memorial Day to spend a summer full of reading and reflection — dining with the rich and conversing with the wise, as the witticism of the time put it — before returning to New York on Labor Day. Of course he had time to reflect extensively upon public affairs, to maneuver through the thickets of domestic and international politics, and to write more than a dozen books and three thousand articles. Similarly, according to one historian, when A. Whitney Griswold served as president of Yale from 1950 to 1963, "his schedule customarily consisted of one appointment every morning and one appointment every afternoon. (If he had an evening appointment, he would cancel the afternoon appointment.)"

Although college presidents are ostensibly chosen for their academic leadership capacities, their intellectual achievements, and their educational vision — indeed, many Boards of Trustees may hope that, in appointing a president, they have found another John Dewey or Alfred North Whitehead — the responsibilities that consume their days, evenings, and weekends in today's campus cultures give them, ironically, too few opportunities to display these credentials. Even as productive and obsessive a scholar as Woodrow Wilson saw his scholarly career end when he became president of Princeton.

Once they take office, many college presidents soon find that they are spending far more time on the grueling responsibilities of fund-raising, alumni relations, and ceremonial activities than they had anticipated or would like. New presidents soon learn, as they make their incessant fund-raising rounds, that the most likely places to renew acquaintances with other presidents are the airline lounges at LaGuardia, Reagan National, and O'Hare airports. Many despise the need to cut a figure as "a song-and-dance man, stepping brightly through the paces of beggar's pantomime," in A. Bartlett Giamatti's phrase. There must be college presidents who enjoy shuttling between God and mammon, but I have rarely met one. Of course there is the rising exhilaration of the chase, and there is the gamesman's thrill of bagging the big one. But that occasional thrill comes at the expense of time lost to academic pursuits and of the constant anxiety that capital campaigns are, inevitably, a referendum on the president's performance as leader of his institution.

Many college presidents would see themselves in Lytton Strachey's description, in *Eminent Victorians* (1918), of John Henry Newman's efforts to establish an Irish university:

> For the next five years Newman, unaided and ignored, struggled desperately, like a man in a bog, with the over-mastering difficulties of his task. His mind, whose native haunt was among the far aerial boundaries of fancy and philosophy, was now clamped down under the fetters of petty detail and fed upon the mean diet of compromise and routine. He had to force himself to scrape together money, to write articles for the students' Gazette, to make plans for medical laboratories, to be ingratiating with the City Council; he was obliged

to spend months travelling through the remote regions of Ireland in the company of extraordinary ecclesiastics and barbarous squireens. He was a thoroughbred harnessed to a four-wheeled cab; and he knew it.

From my own experience, the pace of a president's daily life is stimulating but often frenetic, his schedule of events diverse but disconcertingly kaleidoscopic. Dozens of groups and individuals clamor for his daily attention. One president of my acquaintance told me that he had enjoyed his first year in office except for the fact that the incessant interruptions made it difficult for him to do his job effectively. It was only in his second year that he grasped that those interruptions *were* the job!

Still, for all of the campus demands they face, most college presidents appreciate that the privilege of holding a position of leadership in higher education imposes the responsibility of speaking out on public issues, especially those affecting higher education. They want to be seen as educators, not merely fund-raisers or publicity persons. Despite the risk of offending one or another of their many constituencies, many presidents dearly want to seize opportunities to venture onto the public stage and conscientiously advance their views for public consideration.

But they also appreciate the virtual impossibility of doing so wisely and deliberatively so long as they must routinely respond to the tyranny of the urgent and the transient. The time available to them for reflection and reading is demonstrably inadequate to the responsibility. They recognize that they are academic leaders, and therefore men and women from whom meticulous standards of argument are expected; they are not elected officials who may be excused for substituting righteous indignation and superficial generalizations for reason and measured analysis.

Is it possible that presidents are reluctant to mount the public stage because they fear that they have nothing to say? The depletion of a president's own intellectual substance is one of the debilitating aspects of many presidencies. Frank H. T. Rhodes, the former president of Cornell University, has described this poignant circumstance: "because most college presidents are drawn from the faculty ranks, intellectual starvation is a particularly threatening disease. Busy with this, preoccupied by that, distracted by a dozen pressing issues, presidents develop an inner emptiness and personal hollowness; they are starved of the intellectual and spiritual nourishment which is the sustenance of the campus."

Moreover, the less confident a president feels, the more likely she is to have her speeches written by others. Yet when a president has not prepared a speech herself, her presentation may become artificial and self-conscious, and her capacity to expound credibly about the issue she is discussing may suffer further.

In a culture already too greatly dominated by a rhetoric of slogans and sound bites, college presidents ought to represent different values. They ought to express the essential nature of idealism. They ought to stand firm against the corrosive forces of a market culture. They ought to use their professional stature to bring fresh and independent insights to the unhurried consideration of large questions of public policy.

If college presidents are to take a larger role in making thoughtful contributions to that discourse, what they will need most is time — time to read, time to reflect, time to ruminate, time to test their thoughts by the discipline of writing. These activities cannot be crammed into odd moments between attendance at fund-raising dinners in distant cities, cultivation calls upon affluent alumni, athletic contests, festival rites, ceremonial duties, and other nonacademic activities that disproportionately command a president's calendar and conduce to a short attention span.

A case can be made that a president's attendance at such events carries an essential symbolic significance, and so it does. But for most presidents, the demands of travel and fund-raising, of pomp and ceremony, are simply incompatible with serious intellectual work. Those who press these institutional demands on their present scale fail to appreciate sufficiently that the quality of presidential leadership and the power of presidential pronouncements may carry even greater potential significance, and that these would be strengthened if presidents

21

were able to arrange their schedules to claim fuller, more extended opportunities to simply think and write about significant subjects.

Most presidents estimate that they devote more than a third of their time to alumni, development, and ceremonial activities. If those relentless activities could be reduced to perhaps 10 percent of a president's schedule, the gain would be meaningful: presidents could reclaim a significant portion of their time and privacy for intellectual pursuits that would enhance their contributions to public discourse. (Contemporaries have reported that Robert Maynard Hutchins found time to accept one hundred speaking engagements a year by never attending athletic events and never entertaining or attending social functions in the evening.)

My training as a lawyer inevitably leads me to draw a comparison to Supreme Court justices, who are often criticized for the intellectual deficiencies of their written opinions. In a famous law review article published in 1959, Professor Henry L. Hart of the Harvard Law School argued that the cause of those deficiencies was that the justices did not have sufficient time for the "maturing of collective thought." Professor Hart encouraged the justices to reduce their workload so that they could devote more time to developing and articulating the rationale for their decisions. What goes for Supreme Court justices goes for college presidents as well. (It is interesting to note, more than forty years later, that the Court has reduced the number of cases it accepts for decision each year from approximately 150 in the recent past to approximately 75.)

It is, of course, more difficult for presidents than it is for Supreme Court justices unilaterally to reduce the range of their activities. But it is well to ask whether structural solutions are possible. British universities have separated the ceremonial role of head of state, who is the chancellor, from that of the chief educational officer, who is the vice-chancellor; typically, the chancellor is a public figure — like Charles, Prince of Wales at Cambridge University or Lord Jenkins at Oxford — while the vice-chancellor is chosen from the university's academic ranks. An increasing number of museums of art have devised dual systems of leadership in which the president is, in effect, the chief administrator and fund-raiser, while the director is the chief connoisseur and curator. Whether such an arrangement would work in a university is an interesting and at least problematic question. In his book *Higher Learning* (1986), Derek Bok reflected upon dividing the academic and managerial responsibilities of the university: "In practice . . . it is difficult to separate these functions, since intellectual aims condition the choice of management policies while administrative decisions impinge upon the intellectual life of the institution. Hence, a dual system can work only so long as the two leaders have the patience and understanding to work in harmony together. Such a relationship certainly cannot be counted upon indefinitely."

In a world addicted to sound bites, instant analyses, and fast-paced rhetorical responses, the disciplined insights and deliberative approaches that college presidents might bring to public discussion are hardly democratic luxuries. If college presidents are to be effective intellectuals, participating in national policy debates in a visible way, they must be permitted to carve out more time to read and think and reflect. They must be permitted to liberate themselves from a multitude of tasks only tangentially related to the central goals of higher education.

Indeed, the participation of college presidents in public life would serve to underscore that society means the positions they hold to be ones of intellectual leadership. Unless we enable such participation, we could well end up selecting presidents from a class distinguished more by its managerial competence and fund-raising skills than by its academic and intellectual distinction. As Lord Jenkins has written from his experience at Oxford, "It is not desirable that fund-raising ability, which while highly useful is not the highest of intellectual arts, should become the major qualification of high academic office."

In speaking out on public issues, presidents must, of course, be careful to avoid speaking on behalf of their institutions, given the central academic value of promoting vigorous debates within their faculties. The danger is a real one. Some observers believe that many universities, in an attempt at self-protection, have honored an unspoken compact with public officials: we will not enter the political arena in the hope that you will not drag us into it.

Would the American public listen to college presidents if they entered the lists of public debate? Those in journalism and elsewhere who criticize college presidents for not cutting "striking figures on the public stage" must think so. To bemoan the erosion of authority and the loss of public voice by college presidents without attempting to respond to the challenge that those conditions represent is to fall into cynicism. Unless college presidents regularly occupy the public stage, we will not know whether anyone will listen.

Would the quality of democratic discourse be enriched by an enlarged participation of college presidents? Although the contributions of college presidents might not be notably wiser than those of other public figures, they are hardly likely to be less wise, and they would be made from a perspective — higher education — that goes to the heart of the nation's future. Moreover, a greater freedom to address the American public just might make college presidencies more satisfying and attractive, and therefore more stable.

❋ 2 ❋
DEFENDING
HIGHER
EDUCATION

Once a college president mounts the public stage, one of her chief obligations is to explain and defend the contributions that higher education, and especially liberal education, makes to the larger society. This is not always an easy task, as I found in regular appearances before legislative committees, civic groups, service clubs, and alumni associations.

Many members of such audiences will not themselves have attended college, and many others will not have found their college years stimulating or exceptionally valuable. The author of *The Education of Henry Adams* (1918), for example, described his undergraduate years at Harvard as "negative and in some ways mischievous." The entire four years, he wrote, "were, for his purposes, wasted." The stage may seem to be a bully pulpit, but a president will often apprehend early in his remarks that he is not preaching to the choir. But the effort must go forward.

In my experience, audiences invariably want to know what the future of higher education may hold. Although predicting the future has ancient antecedents, we are properly skeptical when anyone asserts that he or she can do so. From Nostradamus to Jules Verne, from Edward Bellamy to George Orwell, prophets have had a mixed, if not dubious, record. Many, of course, have been famously wrong, in seeking to divine what lies, in Learned Hand's phrase, in "the womb of time" — notably Lincoln Steffens, who returned from revolutionary Russia in 1919 and remarked, "I have seen the future, and it works."

Nevertheless, many people believe, as the legend inscribed on the facade of the National Archives states, that the past is prologue, and that one can foresee the future by an act of sociological extrapolation. Indeed, for much of our history, an observer might have captured a small bit of truth by saying, "I have seen the future of higher education and it looks very much like the past." Had one made such a prediction in 1950, there would be grounds for concluding in 2000 that in some respects he or she was not too far from the mark.

Consider, for example, the state of these four characteristics of higher education during the last half century:

First, college in 2000 remains primarily a four-year undergraduate experience, just as it was in 1950. Even though more of today's students arrive at college better prepared than students were in 1950 — indeed, many are intellectually ready for advanced placement directly into the sophomore year — the possibility of organizing undergraduate education as a three-year experience has not been seriously entertained.

The fact that the universe of knowledge has expanded so dramatically during these last fifty years has prompted many to contend that the undergraduate experience, if altered at all, ought to be extended to five years, not reduced to three. But this has not been a serious debate, and the consequence has been the retention of the status quo.

Much the same is true for doctoral education. For all of the concern that the time (typically six to eight years) required to attain the Ph.D. is too protracted, universities have done little to shorten it. Too many graduate students feel lonely, neglected, and exploited, in thrall to the requirement of an exhaustive dissertation and, in a tight job market, dependent for economic sustenance upon annual renewals of their teaching fellowships. Too many choose not to complete their degree programs. In this regard, the experience of graduate students today is very similar to that of their predecessors fifty years ago.

Second, the traditional disciplines continue to control the ways we organize universities into academic departments and fit new areas of knowledge onto their procrustean beds, very much as they did fifty years ago. At the most fundamental level, the disciplines control the ways in which we shape our curricula and fields of concentration and how we make decisions on academic qualifications for appointment, promotion, and tenure. Indeed, even the architecture of most campuses, with buildings widely separated from one another, works to reinforce the academic Maginot lines that separate the disciplines.

To be sure, there has been a considerable increase in the extent to which interdisciplinary work has been introduced into universities. Familiar examples include African American Studies, Asian American Studies, Native American Studies, Women's Studies, Latin American and Caribbean Studies, and Asian and Pacific Studies.

By and large, however, universities have not significantly altered their organizational arrangements better to reflect these new disciplinary and interdisciplinary concerns. Most faculty members who teach interdisciplinary courses continue to have their primary appointments in an established department and, as a consequence, serve that master first.

Third, lectures and seminars remain the dominant vehicles for conveying knowledge to students, just as they were in 1950. Despite dramatic advances in instructional technology, President Garfield's statement that the best educational experience is Mark Hopkins on one end of a simple bench and a student on the other is still widely admired. It remains the basic model by which faculty members teach students.

Ever since Thomas Edison predicted in 1913 that the movie projector would replace books, social scientists have asserted that the delivery of education was on the threshold of revolutionary changes. Yet learning technologies have produced only modest changes in the ways universities teach. Even television, the technological development that reaches back the nearest to 1950, has had only a minor impact upon educational practice.

Many other new technological inventions have, of course, aided the work, especially the research and writing, of teachers. Faculty members today could not get along, as they did in 1950, without computers, photocopiers, fax machines, CD-ROMs, VCRs, and tape recorders. And yet for all their wondrous versatility, these advances in technology have not yet proven to be adequate substitutes for a master teacher.

Fourth, there has been little change since 1950 in the basic ways in which universities are governed. On academic issues, presidents and faculties continue to collaborate in evolving forms of collegial governance. On large matters of policy, boards of trustees or regents remain the ultimate legal authority, appointing presidents, protecting institutions and especially their academic freedom from the political forces of the outside world, and superintending the expenditure of the money of taxpayers, donors, and students. Although the social activism of the sixties resulted in the appointment of a few faculty members and students to governing boards at some institutions, the basic models of university governance remain essentially as they were fifty years ago.

From these four examples, one might conclude that the future that is 2000 does not look very different from the past that was 1950. The existence of these continuities ought not be surprising, however. Universities are in many respects conservative institutions, as Henry Adams recognized in lamenting at the outset of the twentieth century that he had received an eighteenth-century education at a nineteenth-century institution. Universities change slowly. They embody the truth that Thomas Wolfe expressed in *Look Homeward, Angel* (1929): "Every moment is the fruit of forty thousand years." For many students of higher education, that is one of the secrets of a university's strength.

But does the experience of the past fifty years mean that we can expect universities fifty years from now to look very much like they do today? None of us can know the answer to that question. Thomas J. Watson, the IBM executive, is said to have predicted in 1943 that there was a world market for perhaps five computers. Rarely is the future merely a linear extension of the past; as J. Robert Oppenheimer once said, "When the time is run and the future become history, it will be clear how little of it we today foresaw or could foresee."

The apparent stability of universities with respect to the four areas just cited surely tells only a very small part of the story, and that part may be misleading. The larger part is the powerful and dynamic portents of change currently at work, many tracing their origins to the watershed year of 1968, that suggest that the future of higher education is not likely to look very much like the past.

As virtually every student of society now argues, we are in the midst of a vast Information Revolution driven by the explosive emergence of computers, data processing, artificial intelligence, the Internet, e-commerce, and other new technologies — a transformation that is moving society swiftly from an industrial to an information basis. This transformation is likely to be as profound as the Industrial Revolution — with the telegraph, the railroad, and the mass-production factory — was in moving society from an agricultural to an industrial basis. Peter F. Drucker wrote in 1999: "The Information Revolution is now at the point at which the Industrial Revolution was in the 1820s, about forty years after James Watt's improved steam engine (first installed in 1776) was first applied, in 1785, to an industrial operation — the spinning of cotton. And the steam engine was to the first Industrial Revolution what the computer has been to the Information Revolution — its trigger, but above all its symbol."

Given the acceleration of the Information Revolution, we can confidently predict that it will simply not be good enough for universities in 2050 to look like universities in 2000. Universities that ignore the Information Revolution will, like Rip Van Winkle, wake up in 2050 to a brave new world they do not recognize. As Woodrow Wilson wrote in 1909, "New inventions, fresh discoveries, alterations in the markets of the world throw accustomed methods and the men who are accustomed to them out of date and use without pause or pity."

Significant changes are occurring on virtually every side. Today's curriculum is vastly more comprehensive than the curriculum of fifty years ago — it looks considerably more like a newspaper than a catechism — and fifty years from now the curriculum will undoubtedly be more extensive still. Dramatic advances in the sciences have enlarged knowledge at an exponential rate. The half-life of scientific knowledge is shorter today than it has ever been. Indeed, the major new departments established most widely at universities during the last fifty years have been primarily in the sciences, like computer science, cognitive neuroscience, environmental studies, genetics, and cell biology.

These developments have been paralleled by the establishment of interdisciplinary departments that stand astride the places where the former boundaries met. These new departments seek to dissolve the disciplinary segmentation of the past and to create integrated new fields of study. The fact that they have been accepted not simply as academic ornaments but as enterprises justified on their own intellectual merits speaks to their theoretical and unifying power.

Many changes in the curriculum have been brought about by a profound desire to understand cultures beyond those of North America and western Europe. This inexorable interest in achieving a more comprehensive perspective on the cultures of Africa, Latin America, South America, and Asia will assuredly have worked powerful and disruptive changes in the curriculum by the year 2050, just as other changes in the curriculum have been wrought by historical events of the last fifty years — by intellectual and political trends like McCarthyism, the Cold War, the civil rights movement, the women's movement, the environmental movement, human rights initiatives, and the concern with the impact of race, class, and gender on the ways in which we organize ourselves socially and economically.

The advent of multiculturalism has reinforced the international nature of universities and the professoriate. Many universities have now become international institutions in such a full sense that the loyalty of faculty members to their institutions is at risk of erosion. "The academic profession," as Burton R. Clark has written, has come to consist of "a multitude of academic tribes and territories." Many members of the faculty are more likely to regard themselves primarily as members of the international community and scholarly societies of their disciplines than as members of the universities at which they teach — a trend that will surely grow apace.

But what of the vaunted possibilities of lifelong learning, distance education, and the Internet? We do know that the digital revolution will emancipate many activities from the constraints of place. But we do not yet know how significantly these concepts will transform liberal education into what one commentator has called "learning bit by byte." The abstract promise may turn out to be greater than the actual performance.

The Internet is undoubtedly creating a global information marketplace that is distinctly more porous than a campus, providing the means for offering online college courses taught by the same gifted professors who are present in the classroom and the laboratory. Some envision online universities earning $1 billion in annual tuition and claiming 100,000 students worldwide taught by charismatic, entrepreneurial professors earning $500,000 a year.

Questions abound. Professors and residential colleges alike are hardly what some economists call "efficient asset allocations," but is the Internet likely to render traditional campus-based higher education obsolete? Will faculty members agree to participate in the production of knowledge as a commercial commodity? Can virtual knowledge-providers hope to duplicate the rewarding personal richness of a residential college experience? Who will accredit Internet courses? Will the introduction of a profit motive make colleges vulnerable to new waves of public criticism? How significant will be the cost savings brought about by distance learning? The online revolution — with its emphasis upon connectedness and instantaneousness — seems invincible. It has the potential to transform the nature of the university, but the ways in which it will do so are not clear.

Public interest in higher education has rarely been more intense than it is today. Yet to many members of the public, the changes that have occurred during the last fifty years have proven disconcerting, especially to those who view their own college years from the nostalgic distance of a generation or more. The universities they see today are often strikingly different from the ones they attended. I once remarked to an alumnus attending his fiftieth reunion, "There have been a lot of changes since your day." "Yes," he replied, "all for the worse." The promise of even greater changes in the future can only increase that sense of bewildering unease. (Change is always disturbing. Many scholars ascribe the surge in religious fundamentalism that occurred worldwide in the second half of the twentieth century — in Christianity, Judaism, and Islam — to the scope of the secular changes introduced into society by modernity and technology.)

The imperative of change is a part of the paradox of universities. In order to preserve the best qualities of a university in a period of technological revolution and globalization, a university must find new ways of expressing its mission that preserve the essence of its character.

As I look toward the future, I fear that we may not be doing enough to acknowledge genuine public concerns about the purpose of these changes and to explain how they support the mission of universities. One only has to look at the cynical titles of a number of recent books about higher education, including *The Closing of the American Mind* (1987), *Tenured Radicals* (1990), *Killers of the Spirit* (1990), *Illiberal Education* (1991), and *Imposters in the Temple* (1993), to appreciate the character of *Paradise Lost* animating the concerns.

Attacks on higher education remain frequent. Allan Bloom's laments about "the closing of the American mind" and the decline and fall of the Great Books seem tame by comparison to the ferocity of much of today's criticism. For example, the former Speaker of the House of Representatives, Newt Gingrich, once an assistant professor of history at West Georgia College, has argued that colleges are "out of control" because of rising costs and the attitudes of faculty members who are bent on "rejecting the culture of the people who pay their salaries." Gingrich adds: "Most successful people get an annual letter saying, in effect, 'Please give us money so we can hire someone who despises your occupation and will teach your children to have contempt for you.'"

Another, more sympathetic, observer, Andrew Delbanco, has made much the same point. We are experiencing, he wrote, a threat to

> the unstated compact between universities and the middle class. . . . Under this compact, the middle class consented to pay a lot, and especially since the nineteen-sixties, to pay even more in order to subsidize those who could not pay; in return, the university agreed to inoculate habits of intellectual discipline in their children, and to justify their faith that America remains a society where what you know and what you can do are more important than who, in some genealogical sense, you are.
>
> This bargain is beginning to come apart. Given the post-Cold War contraction of government support for defense-related research, the exploding cost of fringe benefits for students, faculty, and staff, and

the rise of tuition to insupportable levels, universities have never been more vulnerable than they are today.

Public concerns, I believe, have been growing faster than the ability, or the willingness, of universities to respond. I do not mean to suggest that the state of higher education is uniquely dispiriting today. At least since the presidency of Charles W. Eliot of Harvard from 1869 to 1909, critics have lamented higher education's various failings of the moment. Despite these laments, universities have flourished. But if we do not address today's concerns honestly, clearly, and persuasively, universities face the possibility that public anxiety and skepticism will result in the imposition of uncongenial consequences.

In a provocative article written several years ago, Dr. Thomas W. Langfitt, president of the Pew Charitable Trusts, argued that higher education stands in the same position today as medical care did ten or fifteen years ago. He noted that there was then a growing public frustration over the cost of medical care and a rising unrest that too many members of the public, especially the elderly and the uninsured, were not receiving adequate care. He noted, too, that the profession seemed indifferent to responding to those gathering concerns. The consequence was that managed care and governmental regulation were introduced. The health care professions, against their will, found themselves subject to administrative regimes that second-guessed their treatment decisions and changed the very nature of the practice. For many members of the profession, these changes reduced their professional satisfaction as physicians, nurses, and caregivers. In short, Dr. Langfitt argued that universities today are inviting similar sorts of public regulation because they were seen as too expensive, primarily interested in research and scholarship, and insufficiently devoted to undergraduate teaching — self-serving when they ought to be altruistic, self-indulgent when they ought to be self-disciplined, self-absorbed when they ought to be socially committed.

Many of us who have spent our professional lives within universities regard them — at least most of the time — as shining cities upon a hill. We are saddened that others view them as self-centered, cynical, and complacent. Yet it is difficult to deny completely the force of Dr. Langfitt's argument. If his predictions have not yet proven true, it may only be because society's continuing absorption with the state of health care has delayed the redirection of public focus to higher education.

Perhaps it is in the nature of large institutions to be misunderstood. Perhaps it is in the nature of society to resent institutions that occupy such powerful positions in American life. The public appreciates that higher education has now become as essential to success and well-being in our society as medical care. It will not nurse its grievances passively. It will demand change in those practices it does not understand. The issue is whether change will come voluntarily or involuntarily. That outcome may turn upon how well universities respond to public concerns about their social accountability.

What, then, are these concerns? I don't suggest that these concerns are held by every member of the public, or even by a majority of the public. They don't need to be that widely held to constitute a political threat to universities. They need be held only by an influential minority of dedicated and distressed citizens capable of making their views known through the political process.

Perhaps the principal public concern about higher education is its total cost, now reaching (counting tuition, room, board, and books) toward $35,000 a year at many private institutions. No concern is voiced more frequently than that tuition, now approaching $30,000 at many private institutions, is beyond the capacity of middle-class families, and that universities, even those with endowments nearing or exceeding $1 billion, are not sufficiently concerned with keeping it down.

The absolute numbers are intimidatingly high. Yet few students at private colleges pay the so-called sticker price because of the provision of financial aid. Moreover, even at the more expensive institutions, tuition for "full pay" students covers only about 50 to 60 percent of the actual cost of educating a student. By the homely yardstick used for a generation, tuition levels at private colleges remain about the equivalent of the cost of a midsized Chevrolet.

Nevertheless, the rate of tuition increases has been dizzying. Between 1980 and 1999, the average price of attending college — tuition, room, and board — rose by more than 300 percent. In 2000–01, the most recent year for which statistics are available, the average cost of attending college rose 5.2 percent at private four-year institutions and 4.4 percent at public four-year colleges. Those were among the smallest tuition increases in more than a decade — clearly colleges and universities have heard a message in recent years — but the increases still exceeded the Consumer Price Index, which was 3.1 percent for the prior twelve months. Many families feel that they are on a treadmill. The tenor of concern can be heard in the statement of Senator Joseph Lieberman: "If college becomes a luxury that an increasing percent of our population cannot afford, the economic divide between higher education 'haves' and 'have nots' will widen to the point where it undercuts the American dream and stunts our economic growth."

On top of all this, universities seem to be perpetually engaged in mammoth fund-raising campaigns. There are currently under way more than two dozen campaigns, half by public institutions, that seek to raise $1 billion or more; several seek to raise $2 billion. These ambitious, unending efforts have bred a skepticism that the very rich, greedy and arrogant, are seeking to become even richer.

This skepticism is enhanced by the fact that most universities, seeking to provide future generations with a purchasing power equal to or greater than today's, typically limit the rate of spending from endowment income to no higher than a conservative 5 percent. Many critics regard this practice as excessively prudent, emphasizing deferred gratification at the expense of present consumption. They do not understand why so many well-endowed universities believe they need so much more money or why they will not spend a part of their endowments to reduce tuition. Why, some ask, does Harvard, with an endowment in 2000 of $19 billion, charge tuition at all?

Universities need to disclose to the public more detailed financial information. They need to explain that higher education is expensive because it is a labor-intensive activity in which the common devices for increasing productivity — larger class sizes, reductions in faculty, increases in faculty teaching loads, delayed replacement of laboratory equipment, diminished purchasing of library books, deferred maintenance of facilities — compromise an institution's quality. They need to outline the significant part of educational costs that are devoted to providing financial aid and health care, installing new technology and cutting-edge laboratory equipment, maintaining library strength, improving computer access and capacity, and complying with a multitude of federal regulations. They need to demonstrate that the items supported by tuition increases translate into a richer educational experience for students.

Private colleges are undeniably expensive. And yet even at a cost of $35,000 a year, students who attend for approximately nine months a year pay approximately $125 a day — about what they would pay, as more than one wag has mischievously noted, for a day's stay at a typical Marriott. For that $125, universities not only provide students with a room, as a Marriott would, but also with three meals, health care, counseling, private security services, tutoring, career guidance, foreign study programs, libraries, computer networks, Internet access, exercise and fitness facilities, museums, movies, cultural programming, athletic opportunities as both participant and spectator, and a large set of interesting companions. Universities also throw in the opportunity to attend classes and to conduct experiments in laboratories.

The criticism of the costs of higher education and the skepticism over fund-raising campaigns are amplified by the fact that many people believe that universities are mismanaged and administratively inflexible, slow to react to market pressures, and unable, in a cliché of the moment, to reinvent themselves as new circumstances require. As the chair of a major state's board of higher education said recently, "There isn't an institution in America less open to new ideas than colleges and universities." Critics also point to congressional hearings into indirect cost-recovery practices at a number of prominent universities several years ago — hearings that some regarded as having exposed the hollowness of protestations that universities are well managed.

These critics demand the introduction of corporate-style management techniques to achieve greater "productivity." The difficulty with these demands is that they do not take account of the fact that the work of universities is inherently labor-intensive, and therefore not readily susceptible to cost savings through conventional efficiency initiatives. A *New York Times* reporter explained that fact well: "When Mozart was alive, it took two to three months for a craftsman to make a watch and about 18 minutes for an ensemble to perform 'Eine Kleine Nachtmusik.' Today, it takes two minutes for a machine to make a watch. But a performance of Mozart's familiar composition still takes musicians more than a quarter-hour."

On several occasions in recent years, I have participated in conversations with public officials about cutting college costs. These officials proposed the "no-frills" university as a marketing model in which universities would regard students as "customers." A no-frills university would be a less expensive university than those we know today because it would eliminate many of the so-called superfluous items that allegedly drive up costs. What are those frills?

A no-frills university, adopting a cost-benefit mentality, would eliminate classes with fewer than, say, ten students. One could expect that the future of advanced classes in important areas of learning — such as classics, linguistics, philosophy, and the less popular foreign languages — would be jeopardized by such a cost-conscious rule. It would also limit library holdings in these and other areas of learning. A no-frills university would not compete with other institutions, or at least not so comprehensively, on the basis of what the critics scornfully denominate as amenities — facilities and services that critics believe are not part of the central educational mission of a university.

Students would be charged full price, for example, for the use of recreational facilities, such as gyms, squash courts, swimming pools, and fitness centers, just as they would be if they used such facilities in their home communities. Similarly, student attendance at cultural events would not be subsidized; if students wished to attend public lectures, plays, ballets, or concerts, they would pay whatever the market required the university to charge in order to bring such events to campus. A no-frills university would compel its museum — if it had one — to be self-supporting through admissions charges and outside grants. If the prices charged for the use of recreational facilities or attendance at cultural events and museums proved too high for students to pay, that would simply be a consequence of cost-efficient fiscal administration.

A no-frills university would carry the concept of abolishing amenities into the provision of certain health services. It would not offer counseling services for students who are depressed or suffer other kinds of psychological or emotional problems, even though suicide is the third leading cause of death among fifteen- to twenty-four-year-olds and even though 8.5 percent of college students reported in 1994 that they had considered committing suicide. It would not offer nutritional counseling for students who are struggling with anorexia or bulimia. It would not offer support for students with learning disabilities. These services are not directly related to a university's central mission of education, or so the argument for the elimination of frills goes, and are readily available on the private market for those who want or need them.

By comparison to the universities we know today, a no-frills university would indeed be an impoverished institution. If universities do not want to be coerced, not merely by the marketplace but also by policymakers, into becoming such institutions, they need to find effective ways of persuading the public that what others regard as frills are in fact an essential part of a stimulating and responsive residential college environment. Unless higher education makes a plausible case for its fiscal arrangements and its cost-cutting efforts, those who control public resources or who are concerned about the academy's claims upon private resources may well act to reduce the costs of higher education, even though they appreciate, as Benjamin Franklin observed, that "an investment in knowledge pays the best interest."

Public concerns about access to higher education implicate not only the high cost of attendance but also the criteria for admission, especially the use of standardized tests. For several decades, these concerns have been expressed primarily by minority communities that believe that standardized tests are biased against them. The point has been clearly made by William Julius Wilson, the eminent Harvard sociologist: "If we rely solely on the standard criteria for college admission like SAT scores, even many children from black middle class families would be denied admission in favor of middle class whites who are not weighted down from the accumulation of disadvantages." As a result of such views, efforts to eliminate any possible racial bias have been a high priority for the College Board.

In recent years, however, in what Robert B. Reich calls "the headlong rush toward greater selectivity," concerns about standardized tests have begun to be heard from other quarters as well. Among the most vocal have been affluent families deeply involved in conspicuous consumption — second homes in the Hamptons or Aspen, a Mercedes Benz or a Lexus in the garage, and deluxe international travel. For them, admission of their children to prestigious colleges has become a final cachet of social achievement. Used to having access and influence, accustomed to relying upon their wealth and social connections to advance the prospects of their children, many of these families resent the extent to which standardized tests disadvantage the admissions prospects of their sons and daughters, even though the SAT is often regarded as more of a measure of family resources than of reasoning.

Other criticisms come from still other quarters. In 2001, the president of the University of California, Richard C. Atkinson, proposed dropping the SAT exams as a criterion for all applicants and substituting a more holistic measure. Nicholas Lemann's recent book, *The Big Test: The Secret History of the American Meritocracy* (1999), argues that these examinations, which ostensibly seek only to assess educational attainment and intellectual potential, in fact also determine "the structure of success in America" by allocating society's most prized opportunities for upward mobility and privilege to those who score well on them. These students, in his view, constitute an elite new class of "Mandarins," selected on the dubious basis of performance on an imperfect test rather than on their potential to provide leadership for the public good.

It is easy to find fault with the SATs. These tests, as Lemann writes, "don't find wisdom, or originality, or humor, or toughness, or empathy, or common sense, or independence, or determination — let alone moral worth." Moreover, scores can be improved by expensive coaching courses, and even then are best only at predicting first-year college

39

grades. Thus, while universities see admissions examinations as impartial instruments of meritocratic destiny, their critics see them as flawed, ill-conceived, and discriminatory devices of exclusion, too often lazily relied upon as surrogates of innate worth.

And yet, standardized tests remain better predictors of academic success than high school grades or class rank. Moreover, the critics fail to acknowledge that selective colleges have always given weight to many other criteria — athletic ability, musical talent, rural roots, legacy status, unusual life experience — in composing their classes. This tendency has been sharpened by the desire of colleges to compose racially diverse, socially heterogeneous student bodies. Indeed, Harvard College announced in 1940 that it intended to create a plan to admit students "whose likelihood to succeed can be measured not so much by a scholastic aptitude test . . . as by steady work habits, good judgment, and an interest in studies." Few have suggested alternatives to the SATs that are not themselves limited in significant ways.

Still another public concern is the institution of tenure, which seeks to guarantee academic freedom by granting a professor, following successful completion of a probationary period, employment from which he or she cannot be dismissed without adequate cause. William Van Alstyne has stated the rationale eloquently: "The function of tenure is not only to encourage the development of specialized learning and professional expertise by providing a reasonable assurance against the dispiriting risk of summary termination; it is to maximize the freedom of the professional scholar and teacher to benefit society through the innovation and dissemination of perspectives to the conventional wisdom. The point is as old as Galileo."

One of the wisest students of higher education, Henry Rosovsky, in *The University: An Owner's Manual* (1990), has advanced the argument for tenure with a forceful clarity born of experience and conviction. He defends tenure as the principal guarantor of academic freedom, especially for the unconventional and the nonconformist; as a source of internal discipline in the selection of faculty; and as a social contract essential to maintaining the quality of the faculty. A related argument was made by Howard R. Bowen and Jack H. Schuster in *American Profes-*

sors: A National Resource Imperiled (1986). They write: "a college or university to be maximally effective must be a community to which people belong and which they care about, not merely an entity for which they work and from which they receive paychecks." They go on to argue, "Institutions of higher education require the sharing of common ideals, people of ability to work together toward distant goals, their capacity to weave ideals and goals into the fabric of the institution and thus to convey to students what the institution is and stands for, not merely what it teaches. Such collegiality is not created instantly or spontaneously. It is developed over time through the presence of committed faculties. Tenure is a powerful tool for enlisting that commitment."

Although tenure has been an established feature of higher education for almost a century, having been formulated by the American Association of University Professors in 1915, it is now under a considerable assault. Many regard tenure as a sinecure that entrenches so-called "deadwood," impedes the replacement of incompetent faculty members, prevents the appointment of younger, more intellectually committed and vigorous faculty members, stifles institutional reform, and devalues the art and craft of teaching. In fact, it does none of these things.

Even within the academy, the institution of traditional tenure is undergoing change and examination, prompted in part by the elimination in 1994 of a mandatory retirement age and the desire for a more flexible workforce. More than one-third of those now teaching are on short-term contracts rather than tenure tracks, raising the question in the minds of some of whether tenure is essential to preserving academic freedom. Prominent educators are exploring contractual alternatives to tenure in an effort to devise a more flexible employment relationship. Many believe that tenure may be slowly dying of natural causes. But in the absence of constructive alternatives, we need to emphasize that tenure or some functionally similar arrangement is crucial for the protection of academic freedom and the vitality of open intellectual inquiry.

For me, the question of tenure is framed most usefully in this way: To what extent is it appropriate for a society to enable its so-called

41

theory class to devote a professional lifetime to exploring the largest problems of being human and of conducting a humane society? Assume for a moment that there are 100 research universities in the United States, although that number is high. Assume also that there are 100 research colleges, although that number, too, is high. Assume further that each of those institutions has 1,000 faculty members, a high number for most of the universities and all of the colleges. If we make all three of these generous assumptions, we are describing at most 200,000 faculty members. They constitute the core of subsidized intellectuals in a country of more than 280 million people. They make up less than .0001 percent of the nation's population.

What is principally at stake in tenure, then, is whether we are prepared as a nation, with the unprecedented resources we possess, to provide a form of professional security to .0001 percent of the population — some of our most supremely talented and promising citizens — so that they may pursue careers of creative discovery. Thus, our society will say to them, "We have such high faith in the quality of your mind and the promise of your intellect that we are prepared to permit you thirty or forty unhurried years to think about the problems that consume you most. We are not going to demand production on an artificial schedule. Rather, we are prepared to permit you a lifetime of speculative thinking, to let your mind roam and your ideas gestate, because we believe that the long-term results will benefit humankind and amply justify the commitment." Tenure thus sustains the very specialization that is often at the heart of new discoveries.

The most reliable index of the quality of a faculty member's thought is the strength of her published work, judged by peers in the world of scholarship. For the job of a tenured professor is to extend the understanding of her discipline beyond the point where she found it, and to communicate her understanding to colleagues and students. Professors therefore have a fundamental obligation to engage in the dialectic of their profession, by which questions beget answers, and answers beget further questions. An authentic commitment to scholarship is the best assurance of a lifetime of contagious intellectual vitality and engagement in one's field.

42

Scholarship, of course, is intimately related to teaching and the classroom experience of students. A professor's tale of original, cutting-edge research has an unsurpassed capacity to strike a spark of curiosity and enthusiasm in students, to inspire as well as to illuminate. Few classroom moments are more thrilling — or more effective — than those in which a professor professes his own original ideas.

Conversely, classroom teaching enhances scholarship because it affords experts the opportunity — indeed, the necessity — of clarifying the issues involved in their research. T. H. Huxley, the eminent British biologist, once observed, "Some experience of popular lecturing had convinced me that the necessity of making things plain to uninstructed people was one of the very best means of clearing up the obscure corners in one's own mind." One need only consider the large number of seminal books that began as lectures or a series of lectures. The spoken lecture affords both the occasion and the vehicle by which a scholar sets down in a coherent and compelling fashion the fruit of her scholarship and thinking. Teaching and scholarship are thus two facets of the same activity — the creation and conveying of new understanding.

I do appreciate the fact that at some institutions, dedicated and able teachers, whose truest calling is the effective conveying of the thoughts of others, regard publication as, at best, a distraction, and at worst an inefficient use of their talents. There are those, too, who argue that effective teaching alone justifies a place on a college faculty. That may be true of some teaching colleges, but it cannot be true of great research universities. In the end, the commitment of tenure is justified by the results it produces.

Having argued for that commitment, I would not want to extol every piece of scholarship that the academy produces. Few defenders of tenure would. In an elegantly introspective passage, Lord Annan, in *The Dons* (1999), draws upon the experience of a distinguished career:

> Is scholarship worth it? . . . Scholarship resembles reproduction. Millions of spermatozoa are needed before an egg is fertilized, and hundreds of articles have to be written by different hands before a major

work on a topic that revolutionizes our understanding of that topic can be written. It would be comforting to picture all the articles published in learned journals piling up and contributing to truth at compound interest: but it is not so. . . .

It is these articles that provide the stones used by the great synthesizers and innovators to build their castles. Yet how many scholars, as the day of their retirement comes round, and the speeches and presentations are made . . . wonder whether the contributions they have made to learning will still be used by scholars fifty years hence?

Another public concern, and one that is deeply troubling to college presidents as well, is intercollegiate athletics. Although we are a nation of sports fans, more than 70 percent of those questioned in public opinion polls regularly indicate their belief that intercollegiate athletics have become commercialized, out of control, and often corrupt, past any point of likely reform or redemption in their present form.

As long ago as 1929, the Carnegie Foundation Report on College Athletics stated: "Commercialism motivates the recruiting and subsidizing of players and the commercial attitude has enabled many young men to acquire college educations at the cost of honesty and sincerity. More than any other force, it has tended to distort the values of college life and to increase its emphasis upon the material and the monetary." In 1935, President James Rowland Angell of Yale asserted that "in college football it is the crowd, the winners, the receipts, that count above everything else." This is especially so when millions of television dollars and bowl game receipts ride on whether a sophomore converts a last-second field goal or free throw. (When a Notre Dame placekicker missed an extra point in a football game against the University of Southern California in 1996, Notre Dame lost a bowl game opportunity worth $8 million.)

With the stakes that high, the traditional celebration of the "amateur ideal" has too often become, in the minds of many, an exercise in camouflage and hypocrisy. Rarely are athletes in the major sports representative of the student body as a whole. In many instances the players are better described as mercenaries than students, acting out a pageant that the Roman poet Juvenal described as *panem et circenses* (bread and circuses). Imagine the tittering that broke out when the president of one of the nation's leading universities proposed, at a meeting of his Ivy League colleagues, that football coaches be prohibited from sending in plays to the quarterbacks! Commercialism has come to infuse every aspect of many intercollegiate sports. As Andrew Zimbalist writes in his book *Unpaid Professionals* (1999): "With big bucks dangling before their eyes, many NCAA schools find the temptations of success too alluring to worry about the rules. Schools cheat. They cheat by arranging to help their prospective athletes pass standardized tests. They cheat by providing illegal payments to their recruits. They cheat by setting up special rinky-dink curricula so their athletes can stay qualified. And when one school cheats, others feel compelled to do the same."

With each year, the moral and financial costs of intercollegiate athletics grow greater. The contract between the NCAA (National Collegiate Athletic Association) and the CBS network for television rights to the national college basketball tournament, played each March, provides payments in the staggering amount of $6 billion over eleven years, beginning in 2003. Universities routinely admit athletes who would be inadmissible on the basis of their academic records, allow them to become isolated from the rest of campus life by the intense demands of practice, travel, and competition, permit them to bunch together in relatively undemanding "jock" majors, and then tolerate their low graduation rates. They also allocate scarce resources to athletics that could otherwise be directed to the academic classroom.

Colleges that belong to major athletic conferences typically pay their football coaches many times what they pay their presidents, to whom the coaches nominally report; salaries and other arranged income totaling $1 million a year are not uncommon. In so doing, such colleges corrupt their academic values. Bob Blackman, who coached football at Dartmouth for sixteen seasons, once said, "I like the Ivy League — the only conference where the coaches are paid more than the players." All of the pressures — from coaches, alumni, boosters, and the media — are in the direction of expansion, of longer seasons,

45

extended postseason competition, enlarged schedules for off-season practice. The result has been a masquerade that compromises educational standards as well as the interests of so-called student-athletes.

In a period in which Title IX has prompted the wholesome effort to achieve gender equity in intercollegiate athletic programs, universities that care about public esteem would also do well to seek a better balance between their athletic and their academic programs. As James L. Shulman and William G. Bowen have carefully concluded in *The Game of Life: College Sports and Educational Values* (2001), "Intercollegiate athletics has come to have too pronounced an effect on colleges and universities — and on society — to be treated with benign neglect. Failure to see where the intensification of athletics programs is taking us, and to adjust expectations, could have the unintended consequence of allowing intercollegiate athletics to become less and less relevant to the educational experiences of most students, and more and more at odds with the core missions of the institutions themselves."

Another concern that roils many members of the public is affirmative action — one of the most daunting issues of public policy in American life at least since the Civil Rights Act of 1964. Much of the antipathy toward affirmative action derives from the dubious assumption that diversity is the enemy of merit. Indeed, considerable evidence points to public disenchantment with any system of student admissions or faculty appointments that is based on rigid quotas or is not color-blind.

No college with which I am familiar uses quotas in its admissions process. Colleges do, however, aggressively seek out and admit outstanding students from a broad range of backgrounds, including racial. These efforts of affirmative action, arising out of this country's tragic history on the question of race, extend back to Lyndon B. Johnson's famous commencement address at Howard University in 1965, in which he said that "ability is not just the product of birth. Ability is stretched or stunted by the family you live with, and the neighborhood you live in, by the school you go to and the poverty or richness of your surroundings. It is the product of a hundred unseen forces playing upon the infant, the child, and the man."

However, in 1975, about a decade after the advent of affirmative action, Alexander M. Bickel, perhaps the leading constitutional scholar of the time, came close to stating that race-conscious distinctions, no matter how attractive the consequences, are always wrong: "The lesson of the great decisions of the Supreme Court and the lesson of contemporary history have been the same for at least a generation: discrimination on the basis of race is illegal, immoral, unconstitutional, inherently wrong, and destructive of democratic society." To this pronouncement Bickel ruefully added, "Now this is to be unlearned, and we are told that this is not a matter of fundamental principle but only a matter of whose ox is gored."

A serious debate over affirmative action has continued ever since over whether a nation that has harmed a group in one generation has an obligation to make it whole in another. The debate has become more heated and partisan in recent years, threatening to reject Martin Luther King, Jr.'s fundamental assertion that "it is impossible to create a formula for the future which does not take into account that our society has been doing something special *against* the Negro for hundreds of years."

Justice Harry A. Blackmun, in his opinion in *Regents of the University of California v. Bakke* (1978), echoed Dr. King's view, commenting, "It would be impossible to arrange an affirmative-action program in a racially neutral way and have it successful. To ask that this be so is to demand the impossible. In order to get beyond racism, we must first take account of race. There is no other way. And in order to treat some persons equally, we must treat them differently." It would be ironic indeed, as Justice Blackmun further observed, to interpret the equal protection clause of the Fourteenth Amendment, which was adopted immediately after the Civil War in order to achieve equality for emancipated Negroes, in a manner that would "perpetuate racial supremacy."

The national debate having been joined, it provoked a comprehensive review of affirmative action by President Clinton, who concluded that the United States ought to "mend it, not end it." Christopher Edley, Jr., the Harvard Law School professor who headed the White House review of affirmative action, has demonstrated in his book *Not*

All Black and White (1996) that the question of affirmative action — of awarding racial preferences in college and university admissions in the belief that they will enhance the educational experience of *all* students — is socially complex and philosophically subtle, full of nuance and hard choices among legitimate competing interests, not readily susceptible of absolutist embrace or categorical denunciation. Edley appreciates that affirmative action imposes a cost upon some persons, especially white men, even as it gives a preference to others. It is a social folly, he argues, to ignore the cost. "The kernel of truth is that there is indeed a moral cost to race-based decision making," he writes, "and this moral cost stands independent of any utilitarian calculations of the effectiveness of anti-discrimination laws."

Another prominent scholar, Amy Gutmann of Princeton, defends affirmative action in *Color Conscious* (1996) by arguing compellingly that government must be color conscious because society is not color-blind. For Gutmann, the strongest argument for preferential treatment is that "it paves the way for a society in which fair equality of opportunity is a reality rather than merely an abstract promise." Preferential hiring, for example, will serve to break down racial stereotypes, create identity role models for minority children, and establish diversity role models for all citizens. She urges that affirmative action be seen as an effort to "help create the background conditions for fair equality of opportunity," and that an individualized calculus be applied to such differentiated situations as college admissions, employment practices, and political representation.

The efforts made by higher education in the last generation to open its doors to minorities and to achieve racial and ethnic diversity, both in the student body and on faculties, have been noble. The passage in 1996 of Proposition 209, the constitutional amendment prohibiting affirmative action by state agencies in California, and the federal court decision that same year banning affirmative action in academic admissions programs in Texas are discouraging steps backward. We already know the alarming results at the law school of the University of California at Berkeley, where no black students were enrolled in the next year's entering class of 270, and at the University of Texas Law School, where only three black students were enrolled in an entering class of 500. It would be devastating if other states and other courts were to follow suit.

Affirmative action has been an essential response to the nation's historical legacy of official discrimination. It has enhanced the value of exposing all students to differing perspectives and values, enriching the age-old associative process by which students educate other students. As Ralph Waldo Emerson wrote in his journal, "I pay the schoolmaster, but 'tis the schoolboys that educate my son." Colleges and universities have put their faith in the proposition that students learn more on an integrated campus than on a segregated one.

When Kingman Brewster was criticized by many alumni in the 1960s for moving Yale toward a more meritocratic and diverse institution, he replied, "An excessively homogeneous class will not learn anywhere near as much from each other as a class whose backgrounds and interests and values have something new to contribute to the common experience." Familiarity with variety and diversity was a necessary qualification, Brewster argued, for those who would be called upon to exercise leadership in "mold[ing] disparate interests and ambitions into group effort." His views anticipated Justice Lewis F. Powell's assertion in *Bakke* that "people do not learn very much when they are surrounded only by the likes of themselves."

Some academics, like John H. McWhorter of the University of California at Berkeley, have argued that affirmative action creates divisiveness on campus, breeds cynicism in the student body, and actually hurts blacks. In his book *Losing the Race: Self-Sabotage in Black America* (2000), McWhorter contends that affirmative action contributes to a spirit of "anti-intellectualism" among blacks and to a "deep-reaching inferiority complex" that encourages blacks to portray themselves as victims of society.

This conclusion is sharply at odds with the views of William G. Bowen and Derek Bok in *The Shape of the River* (1998) that "racially-sensitive" admissions policies at the selective institutions they studied have conferred benefits on all students, members of majority and minority groups alike, and have enabled minority students to make

49

successful contributions to their professions and communities. Affirmative action, the authors conclude, has had "many of the attributes of long-term investment decisions involving the creation of human and social capital." Seen in the light of this evidence, affirmative action need not be time-limited, as it must be when it is justified merely as righting past wrongs.

Indeed, except for the military and professional athletics, universities have probably done more than any other institution to bring minorities into full membership in American life. More than insurance companies, more than law firms, more than hospitals, more than investment banks, more than newspapers, magazines, and the electronic media, American higher education has made an extraordinary commitment to encouraging participation by persons of color. These efforts have served to unite our shared destinies and burnish the legitimacy of democratic ideals.

Few endeavors serve this country better than the provision of educational opportunity. It is education that has marked this country's progress, however uneven, toward the achievement of equality; that has permitted young men and women, who were once confined to the margins of society by poverty and discrimination, to aspire to full participation in the promise of American life; and that holds the greatest promise of defusing the time bomb of inequality that might still ignite the fire next time.

We still have far to go. In 1995, when African American, Hispanic, and Native American students constituted more than a quarter of the student population, they earned only 13 percent of the nation's bachelor's degrees, 11 percent of the professional degrees, and 6 percent of the doctoral degrees. This is not a problem to be treated, as some once argued, with benign neglect. The effort is under way, and in time it will make a material difference in the social and economic life of this country.

Public opinion polls indicate that while a majority of Americans oppose preferences based on race, most Americans support measures that guarantee fairness or seek to compensate for social and economic disadvantage. These data suggest that there may, in fact, be a receptive audience for the defense of affirmative action if higher education can do a better job of making the case.

In his novel *Sybil* (1846), Benjamin Disraeli warned that wide discrepancies in opportunity could result in two nations "as ignorant of each other's habits, thoughts, and feelings as if they were inhabitants of different planets." If we in this country are to avert that disastrous fate, we must explain to the public why policies seeking the full participation of minorities in American higher education are essential to binding together the *pluribus* that form our *unum*.

I have discussed five concerns: the cost of higher education, admissions criteria, tenure, intercollegiate athletics, and affirmative action. If the federal government were to become aroused by public concerns such as these, it might well address them in ways that would significantly intrude upon university flexibility and impose new administrative costs. Let me suggest some of the possible forms that further public regulation might take.

The power of the federal government to award grants to universities is also the power to attach conditions to those grants. Universities live with a web of such conditions now — conditions relating to compliance with such federal policies as pursuing affirmative action, providing access for the disabled, distributing financial aid, maintaining laboratory safety, protecting occupational health, and safeguarding the disposal of hazardous waste. These federal policies are often unduly burdensome and sometimes impose an unwise uniformity on diverse institutions. But they serve important public goals, and universities can hardly protest when they are asked, often in common with the rest of society, to work toward achieving these goals. Indeed, these federal requirements are healthy for our institutions.

And yet one could imagine the federal government, in a political mood of frustration, conditioning the grant of federal funds to universities upon any number of less congenial factors. It might, for example, declare the following:

- No federal funds shall go to a university unless it requires faculty members to teach a certain minimum number of hours a week.

- No federal funds shall go to a university unless it requires every faculty member, or a specified percentage of faculty members, to teach courses for undergraduates.
- No federal funds shall go to a university unless it caps the number of foreign students at a certain number.
- No federal funds shall go to a university unless it holds down tuition increases by reference to a particular formula, perhaps the rate of growth of the consumer price index.
- No federal funds shall go to a university unless it limits the percentage of undergraduate teaching done by graduate students.
- No federal funds shall go to a university unless it enrolls at least 1 percent of its student body from each of at least forty states.

These would be blunderbuss, blunt-edged approaches — approaches that would diminish the flexibility of universities and constrain their capacity to take advantage of new opportunities — taken in the name of a public frustration that our institutions have not been sufficiently accountable to the concerns of the public.

As the result of thousands of decentralized decisions, as well as the democratic extension of higher education wrought by the Morrill Act in 1862 and the GI Bill after World War II, the United States has created the strongest, most versatile system of higher education in the world. It is a system whose origins predate the American Revolution; it now comprises more than 3,900 institutions — research universities, undergraduate colleges, historically black institutions, women's colleges, junior colleges, community colleges, and technical schools, all with their own individual characters, emphases, and goals. Some of these institutions are public, some private, some sectarian, some nonsectarian. Together, they are fitted to a wide variety of human needs and aspirations.

It is a system that attracts students, as a magnet, from all over the world. If one examines where the greatest number of students from foreign countries choose to go for their higher education, the answer is no longer England, France, or Germany, as it was seventy-five years ago. It is surely not Russia, China, or Japan. When students vote with their feet and their tuition dollars today, by predominant numbers they choose the United States for their higher education. The number of foreign students enrolled in United States universities has risen for fifteen consecutive years, to a record high of 490,000 in 1998–99.

It would be a shame to permit that system to be jeopardized by blunt-edged federal regulation because of our failure to be responsive to legitimate criticism and to explain what the values of academe are and why they are important.

The future may, indeed, look less like the past than we are accustomed to experiencing, but in a world of change the prospects are exciting. The obligation of college presidents is to nurture the opportunities for constructive and creative change by responding to higher education's critics. To fail to respond, or to respond defensively or patronizingly, could well be to invite public regulation.

The responding voices from the academy will doubtless be various, emphasizing different, perhaps contradictory, explanations. How could it be otherwise, given the different perspectives of so many variegated institutions? Nevertheless, these voices will more finely delineate the issues and thereby enrich the public debate. The existence of public concerns on a range of subjects provides an opportunity for college presidents to state the case for the nobility of higher education — for the thrilling contribution it makes to individual lives, for the essential role it plays in sustaining American democracy.

❊ 3 ❊
PRESERVING
LIBERAL
EDUCATION

Although liberal education may strike some as a well-worn and cliché-ridden subject, there are many reasons to believe that this country needs advocates for liberal education more urgently today than it has for some time. For a college president, few opportunities are more rewarding than to be such an advocate.

Although the proportion of high school graduates who now go on to some kind of postsecondary school education has increased dramatically in recent decades, the percentage of those students who pursue a liberal education has actually diminished, from 50 percent in 1970 to 40 percent in 1995, according to the Carnegie Corporation of New York. In fact, the greatest number of today's undergraduates major in programs other than the liberal arts. They study resolutely practical subjects like marketing and retailing, finance and real estate, journalism and social work, pharmacy and nursing — and the list could go on.

Subjects like these have, of course, always been a part of the mission of public universities, but that part is now growing at the expense of the liberal arts. When higher education is taken as a whole, more than half of the course offerings and the largest number of bachelor's degrees are earned in some aspect of business. Moreover, many private institutions that formerly devoted themselves wholly to the liberal arts have now adulterated their curricula with vocational offerings in a reactive effort to attract and retain greater numbers of tuition-paying students.

Vocational and preprofessional subjects undeniably have their value, especially when they are the alternative to full-time employment directly after high school. In those circumstances, they are a concession to economic reality, a melancholy measure of the economic — and increasingly social — pressures of premature vocationalism. It was against these pressures that Robert Maynard Hutchins railed when he declared that education "is the singled-minded pursuit of the intellectual virtue." Vocational education, he said, leads to "triviality and isolation."

More than three-quarters of a century ago, in his volume of philosophical lectures entitled *Science and the Modern World* (1925), Alfred North Whitehead pointed out that the rate at which the world was changing was accelerating ever more rapidly — so much so, he predicted, that in the course of a lifetime a professional person would be called upon to face novel situations for which neither prior training nor previous experience could provide a parallel. Whitehead observed, "The fixed person for the fixed duties, who in older societies was such a godsend, in the future will be a public danger." He also noted that the expansion of professional knowledge had been accompanied by a contraction of general knowledge — a contraction that produced "minds in a groove." As he put it, "Each professional makes progress, but it is progress in its own groove." As a result, Whitehead feared the loss of a directive force in democratic society. "The leading intellects lack balance," he warned. "They see this set of circumstances, or that set; but not both sets together." The melancholy consequence, he declared, is that "the task of coordination is left to those who lack either the force or the character to succeed in some definite career."

Many families view a liberal education as a luxury appropriate primarily for the affluent few, an entitlement for the fortunate minority who can afford to delay the necessity of earning a living. If this view were to become widely accepted, it would stand as a terrible indictment of our failure to achieve the noble aspirations of Jeffersonian democracy.

It is well to recall that John Dewey, in so many respects Hutchins's philosophical adversary, insisted that education is not a preparation for life, but life itself. Writing in 1897, at a time of widespread industrial change, Dewey observed: "With the advent of democracy and modern industrial conditions, it is impossible to foretell definitely just what civilization will be twenty years from now. Hence it is impossible to prepare the child for any precise set of conditions. To prepare him for the future life means to give him command of himself." It is a liberal education that, of course, instills precisely that sense of command. Those of us who believe in liberal education — who believe, in Alan Ryan's phrase, "that what makes higher education higher is its adherence to the verities according to [Matthew] Arnold" — must continue to resist the current momentum toward premature vocationalism. Indeed, we must also persuade mainstream America that liberal education is of intrinsic, not simply economic, value.

Someone once asked Woodrow Wilson, when he was president of Princeton, what the function of a liberal education ought to be. Wilson replied, "To make a person as unlike one's father as possible." What he meant, I think, was that liberal education ought to make a person independent of mind, skeptical of authority and received views, prepared to forge an identity for himself or herself, and capable of becoming an individual not bent upon copying other persons (even persons as persuasive as one's father).

The kind of liberal education to which Wilson referred is more necessary today than ever before because the qualities it nurtures are more imperiled than ever before. We are immersed in a dot-com digital culture — a social environment of constant and hyperkinetic stimulation, significantly influenced by the mass media and other unrelenting prescribers of opinion and feelings. But it is not the media alone that are to blame for the accelerated tenor of our daily lives. Telephones, television, VCRs, compact disks, fax machines, computers, the Internet, e-mail, cellular phones, beepers, and other forms of instant communication too often create a distracting barrage of noise and frenetic movement. It is almost as if we have surrounded ourselves with such technology in order to avoid suspended moments of silence and contemplation.

If we are to succeed in preserving our individuality against such technological tyranny, we need to slow the tempo of our lives and extend the span of our attention. We need to emphasize a form of humane education that helps students to establish a rich interior life and an enduring openness of mind. We need to enable students to maintain a sturdy private self where moral self-examination can occur, so that they can find sustenance in what Hawthorne called "the communications of a solitary mind with itself."

But it is not just the baleful omnipresence of the media and the compulsive urgency of the contemporary world that warps public discourse and makes the reflective temper of liberal education more essential than ever before. Our society has descended into polarities of thought that do not serve us well — polarities in political views, religious tenets, and cultural attitudes. These polarities make social discourse and companionable community more awkward to sustain. They make consensus and compromise more difficult to achieve. They make us worse listeners than we ought to be.

The steady trend toward the fragmentation of American life risks isolating each of us, causing us to speed past one another and turning us into special pleaders for our own preserves of privilege and economic interest. The problem is not that the voices are too numerous, but that they are too demanding, parochial, self-serving, and unforgiving. They are too loud and yet too small. Too few of these voices are directed to the common good or focused upon the largest aims of the nation. Too few are devoted to creating that sense of community that enables a pluralistic nation to celebrate a common destiny. Too much of our current political discourse is rancid and mean-spirited, displaying a common denominator of division — division between races and nationalities, between young and old, between immigrant and native-born, between the affluent and the poor, between those who serve government and those who assert that they are oppressed by it. When divisions such as these are exploited for their short-term political potential, the ideals of citizenship are defamed.

Liberal education urges upon us a reflectiveness, a tentativeness, a humility, a hospitality to other points of view, a carefulness to be open to correction and new insight, that can mitigate these tendencies toward polarity, rigidity, and intolerance. There are few more powerful examples on this point than Abraham Lincoln. In his second inaugural address, Lincoln observed that both parties to the Civil War "read the same Bible and pray to the same God, and each invokes His aid against the other. It may seem strange that any men should dare to ask a just God's assistance in wringing their bread from the sweat of other men's faces, but let us judge not, that we be not judged. . . . The Almighty has His own purposes." It is remarkable that, even after four years of military bloodshed, Lincoln could still speak about the withering war effort with such a profound moral diffidence. Despite his heart-and-soul commitment to the Union's cause, he could not discern, or claim he knew, the Almighty's purposes. Surely we ought to be able to emulate Lincoln's example by entertaining the possibility in our own political and cultural lives that sometimes we may be wrong and our adversary may be right.

That is why a liberal education seeks to impress upon students that one of the most important words in the English language is "perhaps," and that we would all do better if we prefaced our most emphatic statements with that modest qualifier. Liberal education teaches the importance of tempering profound convictions with a measure of tolerance and a judicious sense of humility. That is what Socrates, in searching for the eternal truth and decrying the unexamined life, illustrated by his utter lack of dogmatism. That is what Oliver Cromwell intended when he declared, "I beseech thee in the bowels of Christ, think that ye may be mistaken." That is what the great judge Learned Hand meant when he said that the spirit of liberty is "the spirit which is not too sure that it is right." (Judge Hand sometimes quoted Bernard Berenson as saying, "In the beginning was the Guess." And he would add, "In the beginning and at the ending let us be content with the 'Guess.'" His secret moments were never free from the knowledge that the infinite mystery of life makes guessers of us all.) That is what Justice Oliver Wendell Holmes underscored when he declined to elevate personal beliefs to the level of universal truths. "Certitude is not certainty," he said. "We have been cock-sure of many things that were not so." In an essay published in 1915, Holmes wrote: "When I say that a thing is true, I mean that I cannot help believing it. I am stating an experience as to which there is no choice. But as there are many things that I cannot help doing that the universe can, I do not venture to assume that my inabilities in the way of thought are inabilities of the universe. I therefore define the truth as the system of my limitations, and leave absolute truth for those who are better equipped." As the examples of these thinkers indicate, the notion of tentativeness — of skepticism about certainty and conventional wisdom, of recognition that truth is fragile and elusive — is an important characteristic of a refined mind and of a good citizen.

Lest anyone think that liberal education is for college students only, let me tell you about my friend Chris Hedges. Chris has been a reporter for the *New York Times* since 1990. He specializes in covering insurgencies and wars. He covered the Gulf War for the *Times* from Saudi Arabia, Kuwait, and Iraq (Chris writes and speaks Arabic) and, operating out of Sarajevo, the war in Bosnia and later the war in Kosovo. He is, in short, no sheltered intellectual but a thoroughgoing and courageous man of the world.

Early in his career, Chris realized that he was destined to spend years of lonely nights in foreign hotel rooms. He resolved to spend those nights reading great literature. When he was captured and held prisoner by the Iraqi Republican Guard in Basra during the Gulf War in 1991, he had three books with him: *Anthony and Cleopatra*, Joseph Conrad's *An Outcast of the Islands*, and the *Iliad*. During the Gulf War, Chris read the *Iliad*, as he later did when he was covering the war in Bosnia, because, as he wrote, "it was, at its core, a book about Bosnia, about force, about total war, about how egos, specifically the ego of Achilles, can drive leaders to stand by as their compatriots and followers die over issues as slight as personal vanity, ambition, and pride. One can understand much about the Serbs and Slobodan Milosevic, or about Saddam Hussein and the Iraqis, from Homer."

In the autumn of 1998, Chris went to Harvard to spend an academic year as a Nieman Fellow, a rare opportunity for a journalist to draw upon the resources of a great university to enrich his professional competence. Most of Chris's Nieman classmates chose to take courses and gain expertise in the areas they expected to cover in the years ahead: economics, health care, international affairs, constitutional law, China. Chris chose to take an entire year of classics.

"The beauty of the classics," he wrote in assessing his year at Harvard, "is that it is too old for any one group to own, although some have tried. The ancient world, with its institutions of slavery, its attitudes towards women and work, belief in magic, barbarity in the amphitheater, and acceptance of customs as diverse as infanticide to sacrifice, is vastly different from our own, although many of the emotions ancient writers struggled with are the same. This at once makes it immediate . . . but in the end remote and difficult to grasp."

He lamented the loss of a classical education in America's secondary schools — a loss which he had personally experienced. "By the time I was in high school," he wrote, "Latin was optional and Greek nonexistent. Homer, Aeschylus, Plato, Sophocles, Thucydides, Ovid, Cicero, and Virgil were no longer the authors who, along with the writers of the King James version of the Bible, formed our intellectual framework, taught us how to express ourselves, and helped us dissect the world. The teaching of rhetoric, passed down to us from the Sophists of fifth-century Greece, had been replaced by audio-visual presentations. Myth and ritual, once kept alive by weekly attendance at church or synagogue, had nearly vanished." And he added ironically, "We could all have the things we desired."

What is the consequence of losing this heritage of classical learning? It is, of course, an indifference to language and to the life that has gone before. For Chris Hedges, it is "the loss of a perspective, one that once informed how we viewed ourselves and our society, as well as our place in the vast sweep of human history. By losing that grounding, by creating a world where the past has less and less relevance, we are forming societies that, as T. S. Eliot warned in his 1944 essay 'What Is a Classic?', foster a kind of global provincialism." Hedges then quotes a powerful paragraph from Eliot's essay:

In our age, when men seem more than ever prone to confuse wisdom with knowledge, and knowledge with information, and to try and solve problems of life in terms of engineering, there is coming into existence a new kind of provincialism which perhaps deserves a new name. It is a provincialism, not of space, but of time; one for which history is merely the chronicle of human devices which have served their turn and been scrapped, one for which the world is the property solely of the living, a property in which the dead hold no shares. The menace of this kind of provincialism is, that we can all, all the peoples on the globe, be provincials together; and those who are not content to be provincials, can only become hermits.

Few writers knew better than Eliot those occasions of despair when we perceive our lives to be reduced to "fear in a handful of dust." A liberal education ought to equip students to deal with those moments of existential weariness that test our souls and challenge our moral foundations — those moments, as F. Scott Fitzgerald described them in *Tender Is the Night* (1934), when "in a real dark night of the soul it is always three o'clock in the morning."

Life is inevitably checkered with disappointments — for example, in the raising of children, the breakup of marriages, the death of loved ones, the reluctant acceptance of personal limitations, the enduring of illness, the failure to grasp opportunities, the premature shortening of careers, the bankruptcy of businesses, the disintegration of friendships — and some of these disappointments are bitter to abide. They constitute what Wordsworth in "Tintern Abbey" called "the still, sad music of humanity."

Because we are human, profound perplexities haunt our anguished souls, especially when we fear "Time's winged chariot hurrying near." What is the meaning of life? Why does God permit the innocent to suffer? Why are we such mysteries to ourselves and each other? Why is the self we present to the world sometimes so different from the self we know in our private hearts? Why, as Oscar Wilde once asked, do we kill the things we love?

Few efforts are more treacherous than those that seek to understand ourselves and others. When Nathan Zuckerman, the narrator of Philip Roth's novel *The Human Stain* (2000), ponders the smug assertion that "everyone knows" the truth about another character's behavior, he explodes in anger:

Because we don't know, do we? *Everyone knows* . . . How what happens the way it does? What underlies the anarchy of the train of events, the uncertainties, the mishaps, the disunity, the shocking irregularities that define human affairs? *Nobody* knows. . . . "Everyone knows" is the invocation of the cliché and the beginning of the banalization of experience, and it's the solemnity and the sense of authority that people have in voicing the cliché that's so insufferable. What we know is that, in an unclichéd way, nobody knows anything. You *can't* know anything. The things you *know* you don't know. Intention? Motive? Consequence? Meaning? All that we don't know is astonishing. Even more astonishing is what passes for knowing.

When the ground seems to shake and shift beneath us, when life seems to be poignantly painful and perversely unfair, liberal education provides perspective, enabling us, as Matthew Arnold counseled, to see life steadily and see it whole. By providing us with perspective, it nourishes courage and inner strength. It helps in the most human of desires — that yearning to make sense out of the painful perplexities and confusing ironies of experience. It responds to what Saul Bellow's character Abe Ravelstein calls "the purpose of our existence: say, the correct ordering of the human soul."

Liberal education urges us to be not only tentative in our opinions, but also skeptical of the dominant modes of thought. My own undergraduate years (1953–57) were dominated intellectually by a number of doctrines: Marxism, Freudianism, Keynesianism, existentialism. The courses we took in the humanities and the social sciences routinely celebrated the explanatory power of Marx and Freud and Keynes and Sartre. Indeed, the fact that the work of these thinkers appeared on the reading lists of more than one course served to emphasize their intellectual significance.

None of us today would accept so uncritically the broad-gauged, all-encompassing explanations that my professors in the fifties attributed to these intellectual icons. We know too much about the shortcomings of their theories now. Marx's prophecy that "capitalist production begets, with the inexorability of a law of nature, its own negation" proved decisively wrong, and now is a dead letter. In an age of psychotherapeutic drugs, Freud's conviction that psychoanalysis could discover buried motives in the unconscious and exorcise one's inner demons carries more literary than scientific authority. Even Keynes's unorthodox view that government deficits could be powerful tools of fiscal management seems less relevant in an era that venerates balanced budgets and holds free markets in high esteem.

Looking back, I can't help but believe that even at that time my professors should have been more skeptical. Something has gone wrong with liberal education when it does not rigorously question the prevailing paradigms of the moment. And that experience from my undergraduate days makes me wonder: What are the prevailing paradigms today, and are we questioning them sufficiently? Are we saying "perhaps" even as we necessarily rely upon convenient paradigms to order our intellectual universe?

But despite the power of liberal education, it is not a surefire preventative against the rule of foolish emotions. There are few better examples than the lifelong relationship between Martin Heidegger and Hannah Arendt. Heidegger was a professor at the University of Marburg and the leading German philosopher of his time; he was also a member of the Nazi party from 1933 to 1945. At age thirty-five, despite having a wife and two children, he started a clandestine affair with Arendt, his student, who was eighteen years old and Jewish. Arendt admired him beyond all of her other teachers.

Their affair went on for four years. When Heidegger was inaugurated as the rector of the University of Freiburg in 1933, he infamously offered to enlist the university in the cause of the German Reich. He was an unapologetic Nazi who complained of the "Judaization" of German intellectual life, who used his position as rector to block the promotions and obstruct the careers of many worthy Jewish colleagues, who tried in vain to ignore the reality of the Holocaust, and who gave propaganda lectures across Germany, always concluding with the valediction, "The Führer himself and alone is the present and future German reality and its law. Learn ever deeper to know: that from now on each and everything demands decision, and every action, responsibility. Heil Hitler!"

Even after Arendt moved to the United States, where she became the embodiment of the public intellectual, she could not bring herself to break off her relationship with Heidegger. She spent a lifetime pursuing her former lover, sustaining an emotional attachment for more than fifty years. She traveled annually to Germany to visit him and his wife, worked to rehabilitate his philosophy to a skeptical public in the United States, and sought until the day of her death to be his friend and colleague. In an article published in *Partisan Review* in 1946, she attributed Heidegger's Nazism not to a malign character but to "a spiritual playfulness that stems in part from delusions of grandeur and in part from despair," in short, to a *déformation professionelle*.

How could an intellectual of Arendt's brilliance and moral seriousness, a woman who devoted much of her scholarly career to exploring the origins of totalitarianism, be so emotionally dependent upon Heidegger? How could she, for the rest of her life, ignore his anti-Semitism, excuse his fateful embrace of National Socialism, and permit him to use her to restore his disfigured reputation? How could a woman of conscience, which Arendt surely was, permit her emotions to compromise her intellectual integrity and overlook the moral contradictions implicit in Heidegger's noxious career? Was she a victim, perhaps motivated, as one scholar has suggested, "out of a deep psychological need for affection from a father figure, out of Jewish self-hatred, or out of a foolish wish to ingratiate herself with a charlatan she mistook for a genius"? We shall never know; such questions simply present an enigma.

The deeply paradoxical relationship between Arendt and Heidegger prompts us to ask further: What is it about human beings that sometimes permits even the most brilliant and morally uncompromising to deceive themselves, unable to see evil that is all too visible to others, unable to accept in their hearts what they must know by their intellects?

Beyond its concerns for understanding ourselves and the meaning of life, liberal education in America is also about understanding the foundations of a democratic society and appreciating the responsibilities of citizenship. It is about settling upon the delicate accommodations of federalism — the achievement of a more perfect union — and attaining equality for all of our citizens. It is about striking a proper balance between the opportunities for individualism and the demands of community and the common good. It is about crafting what Harvard Law School's degree citations have long called those wise restraints that make men and women free. It is about ascertaining where the moral limits of political and social action lie.

A useful example of the challenge that political and social issues present for liberal education is the role and condition of cities, where the greatest number of Americans live. Many historians argue that cities are among the principal vehicles of culture. They are where some of the finest fruits of civilization — architecture, art, dance, literature, learned societies, museums, opera, symphony orchestras, and theater — have always thrived. As Jane Jacobs wrote in a 1993 foreword to her classic work *The Death and Life of Great American Cities* (1961), "Whenever and wherever societies have flourished and prospered rather than stagnated and decayed, creative and workable cities have been at the core of the phenomenon; they have pulled their weight and more. It is the same still. Decaying cities, declining economies, and mounting social troubles travel together. The combination is not coincidental."

Many of our cities today, especially our megacities, are in a state of decay and decline. They are no longer places of welcome. They have lost the inviting scale of human communities and are cut off from the natural world of fresh air and water, of forests and green havens. They have lost many of the amenities and conveniences, from quality public schools and safe parks to efficient services and easy access to jobs, that give cities their vital center. Often they seem to have lost their soul. The future of cities, as the novelist Don DeLillo has observed, may well belong not to individuals but to crowds.

Moreover, much of the social life of urban centers is pathological — in terms of crime, drug addiction, homelessness, hunger, overcrowding, teenage pregnancy, and the persisting problem of poverty. And the shameful gap between our cities' rich and poor grows wider by the year, forming economic and social fault lines that threaten to break apart even the semblance of a civic culture.

In significant ways the wealthy virtually have withdrawn from the common life and public spaces of cities, minimizing their involvement with civic groups and secluding themselves in exclusive suburbs and within gated compounds. They have essentially isolated themselves in private enclaves. By 1997, there were more than 20,000 gated communities consisting of more than 3 million housing units — all inaccessible to poor inner-city residents. All too often, the wealthy are devoting their discretionary resources to conspicuous private consumption — what one economist calls "competitive consumption" — rather than to the public weal, purchasing an exemption from the travails of urban life. In a period of unusual affluence, they have been reluctant to share their good fortune with those less economically blessed. Their example poses the question: What are the spiritual costs of pursuing material wealth?

All across the country, the rich have created their own forms of security so that they don't have to rely upon municipal police; for the first time in our history, more Americans are now employed as private security officers than as public police officers. The rich travel by private limousines so that they don't have to rely upon public transportation. They have established their own places of recreation — private country clubs, parks, and fitness centers — so they don't have to use community facilities. They send their children to private and for-profit schools so they don't have to rely upon public schools.

It is important to pause on the subject of public schools. Nothing is more essential to the quality of a city than its public schools. American cities have little reason to take pride in their systems of public education. Mayors, city councils, and ruling majorities have simply not been prepared to make the investments in schools that are necessary for the attainment of high quality. Indeed, it is striking that virtually no major city in the United States has a public university of world class.

Urban leaders, both public officials and business executives, often insist that no city can claim to be world class without one or more financially viable professional athletic franchises. When a professional baseball or football team threatens to move elsewhere because of an inadequate ballpark, more often than not the city in question will find millions of dollars to invest in construction of a new park, citing the promised, often phantom, economic returns to the community. If it doesn't do so, another city will hasten to supply the subsidy, and the team will be lured away. Can anyone remember a political leader arguing that no city can claim to be world class without an outstanding public university or public school system?

These contemporary developments are ominous. They signal a growing physical isolation of the poor from the rest of society and a retreat from a healthy regime of civic virtue. They erode support for public institutions that serve all social classes in common. They are a far cry from the reliance upon private initiatives for the betterment of the entire community that Tocqueville, almost two centuries ago, noted as one of the distinguishing features of democracy in America.

The premise of Pericles's funeral oration was the expectation that every Athenian citizen would participate in the political life of the city. There was no place for saying "I don't have time for politics" or "politics does not interest me." As Thucydides reported, Pericles told his fellow citizens, "We do not allow absorption in our own affairs to interfere with participation in the city's. We differ from other states in regarding the man who holds aloof from public life as useless."

Not since the corrupt excesses of the Gilded Age has the United States experienced such a rapid accumulation of wealth and individual fortunes. But the materialistic excesses of that period eventually gave rise to an era of progressive reform — Theodore Roosevelt's New Nationalism, the Sherman Antitrust Act, the income tax, minimum wage and maximum hour laws — that sought to ameliorate the effects of economic inequality by strengthening public institutions. Such an era does not seem to be dawning in our country today. As a consequence, the growing gap between rich and poor in the cities damages the life chances of those at the bottom of the economic order and threatens the prospect of a shared civic life. As Michael J. Sandel has noted, baseball fans, rich and poor alike, used to mingle in the grandstands and bleachers. Now the rich watch the game from premium seats in private luxury boxes. "When we all drank the same stale beer and ate the same cold hot dogs, it was possible to believe that we were all equal," he said.

A liberal education ought to make us search for the relationship between cities and culture, and between cities and democracy. It ought to give students the historical and cultural breadth to consider why cities don't flourish today in the fabled way that Periclean Athens and Renaissance Florence and Elizabethan London once did. It ought to make them ask why American democracy has done so little to improve the condition of the poor in the cities and why it tolerates such an enduring and massive chasm between the wealthy and the poor.

Finally, a liberal education ought to introduce students to the mysteries of the universe, the workings of the natural world, and the fundamental laws of science. The great English physician William Harvey described science as "a department of the republic of letters." Yet, for all its prestige, science remains a forbidding mystery to most Americans — a powerful magician capable at once of wondrous feats and destructive outcomes. A liberal education ought to emphasize the methods of reasoning by which scientists test hypotheses in order to figure out why things are the way they are. It ought to impart the skills necessary, as one scholar has written, "to distinguish . . . probability from certainty, rational beliefs from superstitions, data from assertions . . . theory from dogma." It ought to develop in students an appreciation of the imaginative achievements — the poetry, the drama, the startling serendipity — of scientific inquiry.

Indeed, it is one of the obligations of a liberal education to teach the vivid ways in which science serves the powerful human aspiration for an ordered understanding of the universe. For without such an understanding, citizens of a democracy can hardly make wise decisions about the social, political, and moral consequences of scientific achievement and technological development. In a time of projects seeking to decode the human genome, perform in vitro fertilization, fashion antidotes to bioterrorism, and conduct stem-cell research, liberal education ought, in short, to plumb the meaning of being human and seek to bridge the "gulf of mutual incomprehension" between the two cultures of scientists and literary intellectuals that C. P. Snow lamented in his celebrated Rede Lecture more than forty years ago.

Having celebrated the value of a liberal education, I do not mean to suggest that it is a panacea for all of our personal or social dilemmas. It does not answer all of our questions or solve all of our problems. It is no guarantor of character, as the occurrence of the Holocaust in one of the most cultivated nations in Europe — the nation of Goethe and Schiller and Mann — reminds us; it does not protect us from our worst selves, as the baffling compulsion that governed Hannah Arendt's lifelong relationship with Martin Heidegger mordantly illustrates. What lessons, then, does a liberal education ultimately teach? What do those demanding and expensive years finally mean?

We are, I take it, clear that a college must be more than merely a dispenser of occupational and social credentials, more than simply a provider of a passport to privilege or of the necessary currency for attaining a secure job and a proper marriage. If college is to be worth the effort, the time, and the financial cost, it must lay open the minds and souls of its students to the wondrous possibilities of growth. It must till the soil of being, so that the lessons of a lifetime fall not on barren rock but on places where they may take root and thrive. College must prepare students to continue to learn for the rest of their lives, and most especially at those unguarded and surprising times when they may not be aware that they are learning at all.

In a poem called "Graduates," published in the *American Scholar* in the Spring 1989 issue, E. B. de Vito writes:

Knowledge comes, in a way, unsought,
as in the Chinese tale
of the youth who came for daily lessons
in what there was to learn of jade.
And each day, for a single hour,
while he and the master talked together,
always of unrelated matters,
jade pieces were slipped into his hand,

till one day, when a month had passed,
the young man paused and with a frown,
said suddenly, "That is not jade."

As Life is something, we are told,
that happens while you make other plans,
learning slips in and comes to stay
while you are faced the other way.

The poem suggests two points. The first is that a true education prepares men and women to grow morally and intellectually — to bond into their being those epiphanies of experience that confront us, sometimes quietly, often subversively, while we are "faced the other way." The second is that a true education enables men and women to discriminate — to distinguish the genuineness of jade from the falsity of imitations. These are essential capacities — the abilities to grow and to judge — that define the joy of being human and contribute to the formation of character and of conscience, of public lives and private selves.

And so, although liberal education is not perfect, it does have the redemptive potential to heighten the glories and exhilarations of life, as well as to prepare us for its trials and anxieties. It has the capacity to enable us, as I have argued, to see the world clearly and steadily, to be conscious of the desirability of qualifying what we say with the word "perhaps," to think deeply about the large questions of organizing our communal life, to understand the implications of scientific achievement, and to be whole and humane human beings.

And so, I hope that those who have experienced the emancipating joy of a liberal education will want to become its advocates. In the end, the cause of liberal education — the cause of well-educated men and women — is one of America's best hopes for establishing a more humane democracy.

CELEBRATING INTELLECTUALS

I begin with a paradox. Although Americans talk endlessly about the importance of higher education, in fact we undervalue the role of intellectuals, including those who make higher education such a valuable resource for the nation. When we focus only on issues such as which books should be taught in the curriculum or what forms of language should be avoided in the classroom, we fail to address the most basic and vital purposes of higher education in a democracy: to foster the life of the mind, to help us understand ourselves and to form our moral identities, to establish equal opportunity, and to prepare young men and women for the responsibilities of citizenship. We need especially to acknowledge and celebrate the contributions that intellectuals make to achieving these purposes and to improving the human condition through their scholarship.

The word "intellectual" has, of course, many meanings. A definition that I particularly like is that of Václav Havel. An intellectual, he writes, "is a person who has devoted his or her life to thinking in general terms about the affairs of this world and the broader context of things."

We have long admired intellectuals who work in the natural sciences for their instrumental achievements in eliminating disease, perfecting new surgeries, inventing computers, launching satellites, exploring the universe, and mastering the atom. But we have been less than hospitable to — even skeptical of — intellectuals of other kinds. In looking for immediate and specific results, we often ignore the less readily quantifiable but critical contributions of social scientists and humanists. Yet with respect to virtually every pressing social issue of our own time — race, poverty, immigration, individualism, and civic life, for example — books by intellectuals have served to put the issue involved on the national agenda and to shape our thoughts about it.

Intellectuals (sometimes derided as "pseudo" or "self-styled") have rarely enjoyed high favor. Perhaps the best exploration of the subject is *Anti-intellectualism in American Life* (1963) by Richard Hofstadter. Hofstadter was most immediately concerned with the pervasive disdain toward intellectuals that characterized the 1950s, made manifest by Senator Joseph R. McCarthy and his followers, when intellectuals were mocked as "eggheads." But Hofstadter also wanted to understand and explain why Americans historically had persistently been so suspicious and resentful of the life of the mind. His answer was both complex and fascinating.

As long ago as 1642, the Puritan John Cotton wrote, "The more learned and witty you bee, the more fit to act for Satan will you bee." The connotation of the word "academic" as "impractical" or "useless" has its origins in the nineteenth century, when, as Hofstadter observed, "business criteria dominated American culture almost without challenge, and when most business and professional men attained eminence without much formal schooling." In that era, the purpose of education was "not to cultivate certain distinctive qualities of mind but to make personal advancement possible." As Hofstadter wrote, "an immediate engagement with the practical tasks of life was held to be more usefully educative, whereas intellectual and cultural pursuits were called unworldly, unmasculine, and impractical."

But if one American tradition — the hardheaded tradition of American business success — located the life of the mind in a distant ivory tower, another tradition saw it as nearby and dangerous. Religious evangelicalism and political populism joined in contributing to a very different view of intellectuals: far from being impractical and useless, intellectuals were potentially *too* influential and *too* powerful. For those of an evangelical cast of mind, the rational pursuit of truth seemed to threaten religious dogma; they believed that professors who taught the superiority of reason to faith were corrupting America's youth. And for those of a populist cast of mind, intellectuals represented the authority of experts rather than the sovereignty of the people. They feared that power was slipping away from the "common man" into the hands of an educated elite — discrete, insular, and self-appointed — endangering democratic values and challenging egalitarian ideals.

Today, a generation after the publication of *Anti-intellectualism in American Life*, suspicion of intellectuals reveals itself still: in widespread attacks on higher education, and on the professoriate in particular, in renewed calls for a narrow vocationalism and practicality in college curricula, and in perennial efforts to abolish the National Endowments of the Humanities and the Arts, both of which are vital sources of support for intellectuals.

I came of age and attended college in the 1950s — the Eisenhower era, ostensibly a stodgy period of piety and patriotism, of complacency and conformity, of "the organization man" and "the man in the gray flannel suit." And yet, at a lengthening distance, I am astonished by the boldness and enduring authority of many books of social criticism published by intellectuals during that decade. Those intellectuals grappled with contemporary reality, even as they stood back and viewed it from the broader perspective that a contemplative life invites. I want to discuss four books of that era — each written for a general rather than an exclusively scholarly audience — because they reveal, with striking clarity, the power of intellectuals to open our minds to some of the most important issues facing society and to deepen our understanding of them.

The first is *An American Dilemma* by Gunnar Myrdal, the Swedish economist whom the Carnegie Corporation of New York enlisted to direct "a comprehensive study of the Negro in the United States, to be undertaken in a wholly objective and dispassionate way as a social phenomenon." Although published in 1944, this book changed our understanding of race relations and profoundly influenced the civil rights revolution of the 1950s and 1960s; it remains a seminal treatise on issues of race in the United States.

Myrdal's argument was fundamentally moral. His term "American dilemma" referred to the conflict he perceived between the "American Creed of liberty, equality, justice, and fair opportunity for everybody" and the less lofty attitudes that Americans brought to their daily activities, especially conformity, selfishness, and racial prejudice. Myrdal's analysis of economic inequality emphasized the nation's failure to include African Americans in the American creed's promise of equal opportunity. African American poverty, he explained, was the result of a "vicious circle of cumulative causation" — a circle in which white prejudice and discrimination kept black standards of living low, and those low living standards seemed, in turn, to justify white prejudice and discrimination.

Myrdal knew that it was impossible to create a color-blind society — transforming two hundred years of discrimination into genuine equal opportunity — simply by proclamation. But while his research made him keenly aware of the problem, it also caused him to have an extraordinary confidence in the power of education and scholarship to produce beneficial changes. A decade before *Brown v. Board of Education* (1954) and the Montgomery bus boycott (1955–56), Myrdal believed that "there should be the possibility to build a nation and a world where people's great propensities for sympathy and cooperation would not be so thwarted." He concluded his great work with the sentence, "we have today in social science a greater trust in the improvability of man and society than we have ever had since the Enlightenment." (Ten years later, the Supreme Court's decision in *Brown* illustrated the role of intellectuals in policymaking by relying upon Myrdal's book as authority.)

Myrdal's words warrant attention at a time when the impulses that animated the civil rights movement have weakened and this country is considering whether to diminish its commitment to the American creed of equality by dismantling affirmative action. His exhaustive analysis provides an enduring exhortation that the United States must commit itself to full equality for African Americans. The civil rights issues of today may seem more textured, complicated, and ambiguous than those of three decades ago, but affirmative action remains an important part of our commitment to a multiracial society, not only as a matter of social justice but also as a recognition of our common humanity.

The second book is *The Affluent Society* by John Kenneth Galbraith, published in 1958. In his opening chapter, Galbraith made an eloquent statement of the intellectual's role as critic of the conventional wisdom. He declared that these are days "when men of all social disciplines and all political faiths seek the comfortable and the accepted; when the man of controversy is looked upon as a disturbing influence; when originality is taken to be the mark of instability; and when, in minor modification of the scriptural parable, the bland lead the bland."

Galbraith was anything but bland. In witty and ironic prose, he argued that extensive poverty persisted within our affluent society, even though it had virtually disappeared as a subject of public discussion. He pointed out that "the concern for inequality had vitality only so long as the many suffered privation while a few had much. It did not survive as a burning issue in a time when the many had much even though others had much more." Poverty was no longer seen as "a massive affliction [but] more nearly an afterthought."

The Affluent Society defied the conventional wisdom of both liberals and conservatives by arguing that limitless growth and increasing productivity, rather than solving poverty and unemployment, had created new problems — such as inflation and the expansion of consumer debt — that endangered the very economic stability that growth and productivity were supposed to secure. Most of all, the "implacable tendency" toward corporate growth and private profits threatened, Galbraith declared, to despoil the environment and impoverish public services by artificially generating even more consumer wants, thereby steering resources away from education, health care, social services, the alleviation of poverty, transportation, the urban infrastructure, and other important components of the quality of life.

Galbraith summed up the nation's distorted priorities in a scathing, if hyperbolic, image:

The family which takes its mauve and cerise, air-conditioned, power-steered, and power-braked automobile out for a tour passes through cities that are badly paved, made hideous by litter, blighted buildings, billboards, and posts for wires that should long since have been put underground. They pass on into a countryside that has been rendered largely invisible by commercial art. . . . They picnic on exquisitely packaged food from a portable icebox by a polluted stream and go on to spend the night at a park which is a menace to public health and morals. Just before dozing off on an air mattress, beneath a nylon tent, amid the stench of decaying refuse, they may reflect vaguely on the curious unevenness of their blessings. Is this, indeed, the American genius?

Writing at the height of the Cold War, amid the consensus that the United States had solved most of its serious domestic problems, Galbraith set out to demonstrate the "uncorrected obsolescence" of orthodox economic thinking. He contended that an economy directed so extensively toward defense and the production of consumer goods was diminishing the quality of the nation's public services in a manner not conducive to a humane society. The "central goal" of the affluent society, Galbraith concluded, should be a "social balance" that secures "to all who need it the minimum income essential for decency and comfort" and "education or, more broadly, investment in human as distinct from material capital." His book helped shape public policy by laying the intellectual foundation for the efforts of the Kennedy and Johnson administrations to eradicate poverty in America.

The issues that Galbraith addressed are with us still. The conventional wisdom that he challenged so powerfully continues to invoke economic growth as a universal remedy, even as the disparities in the distribution of wealth grow wider and the services provided by the public sector fail to meet our social needs.

The third book that supports my argument is *The Uprooted* by Oscar Handlin, published in 1951. Handlin made an original contribution in conferring upon immigrants and the immigrant experience a prominent place in American history. "Once I thought to write a history of the immigrants in America," he recalled in the very first line of the book, "then I discovered that the immigrants *were* American history."

Before *The Uprooted* was published, the prevailing folklore was that many generations of immigrants had been absorbed — perhaps the better word is "homogenized" — into an already-existing American culture. As Handlin put it, "to be Americanized, the immigrants must conform to the American way of life completely defined in advance of their landing." If they were successful, they became assimilated; if they were not, they became a "problem" to be dealt with by more concerted efforts at Americanization or by restrictive legislation.

Handlin described the wrenching adjustments required of immigrants. He noted how immigrants, in seeking opportunity, had contributed to the creation of American culture by virtue of their very uprootedness: "A society already fluid, the immigrants made more fluid still; an economy already growing, they stimulated to yet more rapid growth; into a culture never uniform they introduced a multitude of diversities. The newcomers were on their way toward being Americans almost before they stepped off the boat, because their own experience of displacement had already introduced them to what was essential in the situation of Americans."

But *The Uprooted* was not a celebratory book. It recognized that the metaphor of the melting pot was clumsy. It was candid in depicting the psychological and social costs of immigration: alienation, depression, loneliness, loss of identity and status, poverty, prejudice, and strains on public resources. It was also candid in reminding us that each new generation of immigrants has typically been branded as worse and more problematic than earlier generations — slower to learn English, more insular in its consciousness of group identity, lazier or less ambitious, more likely to become public charges.

In recent years, the political rhetoric concerning immigrants has again turned nativist and intolerant. Legislation reducing the eligibility of certain immigrants for welfare benefits has demonstrated an alarming measure of unfounded suspicion. The harsh tone of the rhetoric and the punitive character of the legislation have suggested a lack of generosity and hospitality — indeed, a scapegoating — that threatens to undermine a historic national interest.

When we declare that we are a nation of immigrants, we properly speak in the present tense — as President Franklin D. Roosevelt did in

1938 when, tongue in cheek, he addressed the Daughters of the American Revolution as his fellow immigrants. Immigration has been a rich, even miraculous, source of American pluralism and renewal, bringing to our shores ambitious and creative men and women from more than one hundred and seventy countries. Its numbers have included such indispensable citizens as Hannah Arendt, Mikhail Baryshnikov, Joseph Brodsky, Albert Einstein, Erik Erikson, Walter Gropius, I. M. Pei, Itzhak Perlman, Isaac Bashevis Singer, and Elie Wiesel — to mention only intellectuals and artists.

As Handlin's book reminds us, ethnic and national diversity have been central to a cosmopolitan vision of our national identity, as well as a source of strength for our democracy. We need to continue to welcome new generations of immigrants to our society and to ensure that we nurture their talents to the fullest.

My final exemplar is *The Lonely Crowd* by David Riesman, with Reuel Denny and Nathan Glazer, published in 1950. This was perhaps the most searching exploration since Tocqueville of the competing claims in America of self and society, of the tension between individualism and community, of the link between a retreat into privatism and the fragmentation of social life and civic engagement. (Glazer has pointed out that *The Lonely Crowd* "is in large part a conversation with *Democracy in America*" and in some instances "an argument with it.") Riesman's title captured a disturbing paradox of modern American life. As the nation gradually evolved into a mass society dominated by large bureaucratic organizations, the sense of belonging to a cohesive community became attenuated. Americans increasingly felt isolated and alone in their atomistic individualism.

The Lonely Crowd described an important aspect of this historical transformation: a shift in American character from "inner-direction" to "other-direction." Inner-directed individuals, in Riesman's view, developed out of an emerging nineteenth-century capitalist economy. They were self-reliant or reliant on firm principles inculcated by an older generation and internalized at a young age. The thrift, diligence, and self-discipline of inner-directed individuals were well suited to a competitive, entrepreneurial economy in which production was valued over consumption. Inner-direction, in Riesman's view, gave individuals a clear-cut but flexible moral code, freeing them of constant concerns about other people's approval.

As the United States changed from a production-oriented to a consumption-driven economy, however, a new form of character — the other-directed type — began to emerge. For the middle class, work no longer engaged what Riesman called "the hardness of the material" but rather the "softness of men." An increasingly impersonal, bureaucratic workplace brought with it a new premium on making good impressions on others instead of leaving a distinctive mark on the affairs of the world.

Americans had become more restrained by their characters than by their circumstances. As David Halberstam, in his book *The Fifties* (1993), described Riesman's other-directed types, "These people wanted to be a part of the larger community so much they would adjust their morality and ethics to those of the community almost unconsciously; in the end, they seemed to take on the coloration of their institutions and neighborhoods with frightening ease." Parents obsessed with other-direction now raised their children to be professionals equipped by personality to win friends and influence people — in Willy Loman's desperate phrase, to be well-liked. The inculcation of the older values of autonomy, hard work, self-confidence, steadfastness, and self-denial no longer seemed socially appropriate. Parents who tried, "in inner-directed fashion, to compel the internalization of disciplined pursuit of clear goals" ran the risk, Riesman said, "of having their children styled clear out of the personality market" where popularity, not principle, determined success.

The Lonely Crowd brought home the dangers to the social contract of other-directed character: a lack of meaningful attachments and public involvements, as well as a diminution of personal autonomy and the capacity for self-government. Genuine individuality was buffeted by conformity: by the expectations of the white-collar workplace; by the imperatives of advertisers; and by coercive peer groups that took the place of vibrant democratic communities. "The other-directed person," Riesman wrote, "is in a sense at home everywhere and nowhere, capable of a tepid if sometimes superficial intimacy with and response to everyone."

For all that has changed since the 1950s, we still face many of the troubling issues that Riesman addressed in *The Lonely Crowd*. We still are threatened by social and economic forces that erode the status of individuals from active citizens, working within a web of public and communal associations, to passive consumers, detached from one another and inundated by commercials, sitcoms, and headline news. As Riesman wrote in his book's closing lines, "The idea that men are created free and equal is both true and misleading; men are created different: they lose their social freedom and their individual autonomy in seeking to become like each other."

These four books — *An American Dilemma, The Affluent Society, The Uprooted,* and *The Lonely Crowd* — were all widely read in their day, and they are today more familiar and relevant than ever. They have changed our lives by influencing and shaping how we think about ourselves and our society. They have given us memorable phrases that have passed into the common language because of their accuracy of analysis and their explanatory power. And they are all the works of intellectuals, supported by the colleges and universities at which they taught, nurtured by their engagement with students, enriched by the healthy criticism of their academic colleagues, tempered by public reactions to their work.

In a society excessively devoted to the bottom line — what the philosopher William James called the "cash value" of ideas — intellectuals play a vital role in offering a more elevated approach to democratic debate. Through their teaching and writing, they free us from the tyranny of short-sightedness by enlarging our understanding of historical and social context. They provide us with an alternative to a culture of celebrity and sound bites.

And so I speak not merely in defense of intellectuals but in celebration of them. We need to appreciate that intellectuals are gifted individuals with unconventional angles of vision, often endowed with an exceptional capacity to advance the common good. We need to acknowledge that intellectuals make significant and enduring contributions to our lives and to helping Americans exercise the responsibilities of democratic citizenship. We need, in short, to affirm that supporting the mission of intellectuals as critics, scholars, teachers, thinkers, and writers is one of the wisest investments we can make as a people.

✷ 5 ✷
APPRAISING
SIGNIFICANT
LIVES

One of a college president's greatest opportunities is to elevate the sights of undergraduates. In talking to a group of students I often begin with a plaintive query by the eighteenth-century poet Edward Young: "Born Originals," Young asks, "how comes it to pass that we die Copies?" I have always found it helpful to approach that subject by reflecting upon those whose lives and careers may serve as inspirations and guides. The idea is hardly a new one. Plutarch, in his *Parallel Lives*, emphasized the educational benefits of studying the lives of significant individuals in order to ascertain how we might "adjust and adorn" our own lives.

A significant individual about whom a modern-day Plutarch might write is John Gilbert Winant — born in 1889, died in 1947, a child of the first half of the twentieth century. Winant was an idealist. His life of public service embodied the highest purposes of a liberal education, and it was rooted in New Hampshire, the state in which I grew up. In the end, Winant's story is a poignant and tragic one. I want to share his story for two reasons: because it exemplifies an inspiring idealism and because it teaches an important lesson in humility, reminding us of the limits on our capacity to understand the interior lives of others.

One could not grow up in New Hampshire without realizing that John Winant was an extraordinary human being, a man set apart by character and by a singular devotion to the common weal — a man who was one of New Hampshire's contributions to national greatness, much as Jefferson was one of Virginia's. Our teachers in elementary school said that he was New Hampshire's most notable citizen since

Daniel Webster. But now the name of John Gilbert Winant is almost forgotten; it rarely appears in histories of his time. The only biography of him, *He Walked Alone* (1968) by Bernard Bellush, has, oddly, not been published in this country. Yet Winant was widely admired during his lifetime, regularly receiving respectful, even adulatory, attention in the national press, especially for his exemplary service as governor of New Hampshire. Comparisons of his character and personal appearance to that of Lincoln were frequent and sincere; both men were tall, somewhat stooped, hesitant as public speakers, and serene in adversity. The historian Allan Nevins described Winant as "one of the best idealists and most truly humane men" of the age.

In 1936 Winant was prominently mentioned as a candidate for president of the United States. During World War II, he served with distinction as ambassador to the Court of St. James. In 1946 he returned to his home in Concord, a glowing toast from his wartime friend and admirer Winston Churchill still ringing in his memory. He had earned the respect of the world for his quiet, selfless contributions to winning the war. At age fifty-eight, he seemed to have many years of public service still before him. But that was not to be.

A descendant of an old Dutch family, Winant was raised in New York City and educated at St. Paul's School in Concord, New Hampshire. He attended Princeton with the class of 1913, majoring in politics and government, but he did not graduate. Instead, he returned to teach history at St. Paul's, where the rector recognized in him "a great and rare gift of influencing boys along the very highest paths."

His political career began with his election to the state legislature in 1916. After serving in the American Air Service during World War I, he became assistant rector at St. Paul's. But public life again beckoned, and Winant went on to serve three terms as governor of New Hampshire — from 1925 to 1927 (when he was the youngest governor in the nation) and from 1931 to 1935, the worst years of the Great Depression. His aim, he said, was "to be as progressive as science [and] as conservative as the multiplication table."

Winant was a liberal Republican — he supported the Bull Moose effort of Theodore Roosevelt in 1912 — whose humanitarian principles transcended party lines. Influenced by the writings of Charles Dickens and John Ruskin and inspired by the examples of Lincoln and Theodore Roosevelt, as governor he was an advocate of progressive reform initiatives, including a forty-eight-hour workweek for women and children, a minimum wage, and the abolition of capital punishment. His speeches as governor reflect a quiet New England simplicity and courage.

In 1935 Franklin D. Roosevelt, seeking a liberal Republican to guide the newly established Social Security Board during its formative years, appointed Winant as its first chairman. It is a mark of Winant's thoughtfulness that he arranged for his secretary as governor to receive the first Social Security card to be issued, bearing the number 001-01-0001.

When Social Security became a major issue during the 1936 presidential campaign, Winant resigned his position so he could better defend the new program, alongside President Roosevelt, from criticisms by the Republican candidate Alfred M. Landon and his party. His reforming spirit crossed party lines. Many of his friends considered him, as they did Roosevelt, a "traitor to his class." Winant's decision to resign in order to support a program in which he believed unreservedly — even though it meant repudiating his own political party and jeopardizing his own political future — offers a model of principled action that is, alas, rare in contemporary politics.

From 1939 to 1941, Winant served, by appointment of President Roosevelt, as director of the International Labor Organization in Geneva. He was now an impartial international civil servant, working for social and economic reform, even as the world collapsed into war. He had found still another suitable outlet for his idealism.

In February 1941, President Roosevelt appointed Winant ambassador to Great Britain. The *New York Times* praised his appointment, saying that Winant "will understand thoroughly the cause for which all the people of Britain are fighting." Committed — body and soul — to defeating totalitarianism, Winant was responsible for implementing Roosevelt's energetic policy of aiding Britain's war efforts.

He drove himself relentlessly, day and night, without a break; his devotion was all-consuming. He never lost sight of the fact that the pain of the great international depression and the suffering brought on by war had a human face — indeed, individual human faces. "You could not live in London in those early years," he wrote, "and not realize how narrow was the margin of survival." During the long trial of the Blitz, Winant walked the streets of London, ablaze from the aerial bombardments, offering assistance to the injured amidst the rubble of their homes and stores, sharing their hardships and dangers. His shy sincerity and quiet fearlessness endeared him to the British and helped buoy the nation. As Prime Minister Clement R. Attlee said many years later, he "brought a feeling of warmth, confidence and courage to the British people in their time of greatest need."

Winant was rare among public men in being a private man as well. The temper of the private man, in his case, created and influenced the actions of the public man. Usually we have distrusted such men in our politics (they have too much of Cassius, if not Hamlet, about them) and have made them figures of our literature instead. Winant's career is a reassuring illustration that a person with a thoughtful private life can be an effective public figure.

To read Winant's speeches is to sense the same greatness of soul, the same magnanimity of purpose, the same simplicity of language that appears in Lincoln's speeches. Consider, for example, the words of farewell that Winant spoke to the New Hampshire legislature when he was named ambassador to the Court of St. James: "We are today the 'arsenal of democracy,' the service of supply against aggressor nations. Great Britain has asked that we give them the tools that they may 'finish the job.' We can stand with them as free men in the comradeship of hard work, not asking but giving, with unity of purpose in defense of liberty under law, of government answerable to the people. In a just cause, and with God's goodwill, we can do no less."

Winant's commitment to social justice was well known on both sides of the Atlantic. He was confident, as he told striking coal miners in Durham, England, in June of 1942, that "our supply of courage will never fail. We have the courage to defeat poverty as we are defeating

Fascism; and we must translate it into action with the same urgency and unity of purpose that we have won from our comradeship in this war." With a simple eloquence, Winant told the striking miners:

This is the people's democracy. We must keep it wide and vigorous, alive to need, of whatever kind, and ready to meet it, whether it be danger from without or well-being from within, always remembering that it is the things of the spirit that in the end prevail — that caring counts, that where there is no vision people perish, that hope and faith count and that without charity there can be nothing good, that daring to live dangerously we are learning to live generously, and believing in the inherent goodness of man we may meet the call of your great Prime Minister and "stride forward into the unknown with growing confidence."

His speech was a resounding success: he had not mentioned the work stoppage, but, rather, had praised the miners' role in the long and hard war effort. The Manchester *Guardian* called it "one of the great speeches of the war." Winant's words, it said, had invested the phrase "a people's war" with new meaning. By joining the life-or-death struggle to preserve democracy with the concrete social purpose of improving the economic circumstances of working people, Winant had deepened the war's meaning for the common man. The miners went back to their crucial work.

Throughout the war, Winant traveled with Winston Churchill to many parts of England, and he was a frequent weekend guest at the prime minister's country home, where their work together continued. His warm sympathy made him beloved by the British people. Both Oxford and Cambridge Universities awarded him honorary degrees. While his diplomatic efforts were often eclipsed by the unusually close relationship between Roosevelt and Churchill, Winant nevertheless deserves much credit for coordinating the Lend-Lease program and managing the crucial relations between this country and Great Britain during those perilous times.

President Roosevelt died on April 12, 1945. For Winant, the death of his close friend and mentor was devastating. He keenly felt the loss of a man he admired so greatly, and the loss came when Winant himself was utterly exhausted. He must have felt isolated and abandoned — that his career had been cut short. By supporting Roosevelt in the 1936 election, Winant had alienated himself from his fellow Republicans. With Roosevelt gone, he now reported to Harry S. Truman, a president who neither knew him well nor appreciated the extent of his wartime efforts. Then, but three months later, a landslide victory by the Labour Party swept Churchill out of office. Clement Attlee was now prime minister. Everywhere Winant turned, he saw the drama in which he had participated so significantly drawing to a close.

From the outset of the war in Europe, Winant had dreamed of the peace that would follow victory. He had told President Roosevelt that he hoped to be made secretary-general of the newly formed United Nations. In the end, however, international politics and the choice of New York as the site of the UN would preclude the appointment of an American. Increasingly, too, the new president turned to others to form and effectuate policy pertaining to relations with Great Britain. Finally, in March of 1946, President Truman appointed W. Averell Harriman to be Winant's successor as ambassador to London. It was time for Winant to return home to New Hampshire.

In a farewell tribute, Churchill said that Winant had "been with us always, ready to smooth away difficulties and put the American point of view with force and clarity and argue the case with the utmost vigor, and always giving us that feeling, impossible to resist, how gladly he would give his life to see the good cause triumph. He is a friend of Britain, but he is more than a friend of Britain — he is a friend of justice, freedom, and truth."

When, more than a year after President Roosevelt's death, Congress met in joint session to pay homage to the president who had led the nation in meeting the two most formidable challenges of the century — the Great Depression and World War II — it was Winant who was chosen to give the memorial address. He said: "The things a man has lived by take their place beside his actions in the true perspective of time, and the inner pattern of his life becomes apparent. In the long range, it is the things by which we live that are important, although the timing and circumstance play their part."

At home in New Hampshire, Winant's frustrations grew. Local newspaper accounts reported that he was under consideration for appointment as president of the University of New Hampshire, but the outcome was hardly certain. After three decades of public service, he confronted the necessity of accommodating himself to the quieter, more solitary life of a private citizen. The loneliness that had shadowed his introverted life may have become more painful. He was in debt, under pressure to complete a series of books on his experiences, and troubled by a darkening personal depression.

On November 3, 1947, fifteen days before his only book, *Letter from Grosvenor Square*, was published, John Gilbert Winant committed suicide at his home in Concord. His publisher had rushed an advanced copy of the book to him, but he never saw it. In chronicling his ambassadorial years, Winant decried "the growing disillusionment of today; which not only dims and obscures the present, but is trying to cloud the past."

Winant had reportedly been despondent for some time. His diplomatic stature, his public achievements, and his great capacities for service gave no protection against the brooding depths of melancholia and hopelessness that ultimately overwhelmed him. His friends and admirers inevitably searched, in their infinite sadness, for the reasons that a man of such gifts and distinction would take his own life. Was it, they wondered, because he suffered throughout his life — from his early, frustrated days at Princeton — from a persistent and painful self-doubt? Was it because he was exhausted from years of selfless overwork and was sick from fatigue? Was it because he felt unworthy of the professional success he had achieved?

Was it because he thought his career was over and that, as a man without a political party, he was permanently cut off from power, influence, and prospects, unable to secure a constructive position from which to continue his labors for world peace? Was it because, with the emergence of the Cold War, he believed, like Hamlet, that the times were out of joint, and despaired of the achievement of a more generous nation at home and a more peaceful international community abroad? Or was it because of the deterioration of his marriage to Constance Rivington Russell, his wife of twenty-seven years, who was said to have been more interested in foreign travel, haute couture, and high society throughout their years together than in her husband's ambitions and work?

We shall never know whether any of these explanations is correct. As Reinhold Niebuhr has written, those who commit suicide make their decisions alone. We know only that his private life must have been tormented, for many years, by demons that went unaddressed; and that depression, as Dante said of hell, is an endless, hopeless conversation with oneself, and that its outcome is sometimes self-destruction.

A liberal education is one of the means by which we prepare ourselves to understand the nature of being human. It enlarges our understanding of men and women and deepens our insight into the most intimate reaches of the human heart. But a liberal education, for all of its illuminating power, ultimately casts only a partial light on the moral tensions and anguished emotions of others.

Standing mute before the numbing fact of Winant's death, I think inevitably of Edwin Arlington Robinson's poem "Richard Cory":

Whenever Richard Cory went down town,
We people on the pavement looked at him:
He was a gentleman from sole to crown,
Clean favored, and imperially slim.

And he was always quietly arrayed,
And he was always human when he talked;
But still he fluttered pulses when he said,
"Good-morning," and he glittered when he walked.

And he was rich — yes, richer than a king —
And admirably schooled in every grace;
In fine, we thought that he was everything
To make us wish that we were in his place.

So on we worked, and waited for the light,
And went without the meat, and cursed the bread;
And Richard Cory, one calm summer night,
Went home and put a bullet through his head.

John Winant's death reminds us that we can never fully know how other persons experience their lives. We can never assume that those who are more eminent than we must therefore be more happy. When we compare ourselves unfavorably to others, when we envy those who seem more fortunate than we, it is wise to remember that what we see from the outside may not be what those persons experience from the inside.

In assessing the life of John Gilbert Winant, few observations are more apt than the words he spoke in his tribute to President Roosevelt: "But greatness does not lie in the association — even the dominating association — with great events. . . . Greatness lies in the man and not the times; the times reflect it only. Greatness lies in the proportion." John Winant's death was a grievous public tragedy as well as an excruciating personal loss, for we will never know the further contributions he might have made, the future roles he might have played. That is especially true because his life, like Roosevelt's, had a proportion between action and idealism that truly bespeaks greatness.

John Winant was a quiet man from a small state — a school teacher without a college degree — who was imbued with an innate sense of destiny. By drawing upon an elevated spirit and an unswerving idealism, he exemplified values worthy of emulation and contributed honorably to the nation's coral reef of character. He was, in Edward Young's phrase, truly an "Original," but it never came to pass that he died a "Copy."

A second person about whom I have spoken to students is Dorothy Day. Although she never graduated from college, she spent her remarkably rich eighty-three years struggling to answer questions that lie at the heart of a liberal education: How should I live my life? What kind of work should I do? For what purpose am I on Earth? What are my responsibilities to myself and to others?

Dorothy Day chose to live a life of faith and of service to the poor.

For forty-seven years, from 1933 until her death in 1980, she led the Catholic Worker movement — a movement dedicated to bearing living witness to the teachings of Jesus Christ by fighting for peace and social justice. As the editor of the *Catholic Worker* newspaper, which she founded, Day consistently articulated a vision of cooperative labor, racial and economic equality, decentralized power, and a militant form of pacifism. She advocated reliance on "the weapons of the spirit," but she refused to dwell only in the realm of theory. For Dorothy Day, the question of "How should I live my life?" was neither abstract nor (if you will pardon the expression) academic. It was a matter of determining how to translate her Catholicism into her daily existence — a matter finally of practicing, as well as preaching, in a realm of faith. Committing herself to living with the poor, she resided in the first of many Catholic Worker "hospitality houses" — St. Joseph's House on New York's Lower East Side — where she and her fellow Catholic Workers offered food, shelter, conversation, and empathy to society's outcasts.

Dorothy Day was born on November 8, 1897, in Brooklyn and was raised in Oakland and Chicago. Her parents were conventional, conservative, and nominally Episcopalian, although actually agnostic. After only two years at the University of Illinois, Day put her formal education behind her and returned to her parents' home in New York, inspired to become a writer by the class-conscious writings of Jack London and Upton Sinclair. Because her father, a sportswriter, believed that women should not be journalists, she soon moved out of the house to become a reporter for a Socialist daily newspaper, *The Call*.

When she was twenty, Day went to jail for participating in a protest for women's suffrage. She was jailed again in the "Red Scare" of the early 1920s — this time as a member of the radical International Workers of the World (the "Wobblies"). Day's political activism, writes her friend Robert Coles, was based "less on theory and ideology than on observation of the world around her. . . . Her writings were those of a pamphleteer aroused by the poverty and suffering that persisted during America's post–World War I 'return to normalcy.'"

She joined the bohemian world of Greenwich Village, coming to know Max Eastman, Michael Gold, John Reed, Emma Goldman, Margaret Sanger, John Dos Passos, Eugene O'Neill, and Hart Crane — individuals with whom she debated art and literature, philosophy, politics, and sexual morality. She participated in the Village's rebellion against Victorian gentility and its experiments in free love and hard drinking — and had a series of unhappy love affairs and an abortion.

In March of 1927, at the age of thirty, she and her common-law husband, an anarchist and atheist, had a daughter. It was a sense of overwhelming joy and gratitude at the birth of her daughter that caused Dorothy Day to join the Catholic Church. Her decision was a conscious, affirmative commitment. And it was then, she insisted, that her life truly began. If she meant that her conversion to Catholicism was the moment when her spiritual life began in earnest, perhaps she was right. But her idealism and selflessness, her concern for the powerless and love for the poor, had been just as important to Day before she converted to Catholicism as it would be for the rest of her life. Her conversion did not make Day an activist, but it rooted her activism in Christian teachings and gave it a sharper focus.

The question remained: How was she to live a Christian life in twentieth-century America? How was she to transform her Catholicism from ritual and faith into acts that were practical and relevant to the poor? No one was more influential in helping Day discover her calling than Peter Maurin, a Frenchman who knocked on her door one day in 1932. Like Day, Maurin was an idealistic social activist, a journalist, and a devout Catholic. It was Maurin who persuaded Day to start the *Catholic Worker*. Funded with $57 scrounged from friends, the monthly tabloid's first edition of 2,500 copies was published on May Day 1933 in Day's tiny tenement apartment, and then hawked for a penny a copy amid the soapbox speakers and heckling factions of Union Square. Within several months, circulation had increased to 25,000, by the end of the year to 100,000, and by 1936 to 150,000.

For more than forty years, Day wrote a column in the newspaper, driven by the belief that "in the long run all man's problems are the same, his human needs of sustenance and love." The *Catholic Worker* is still published seven times a year, the price is still a penny a copy, and the editorial policy remains the same as it was when it was founded:

grassroots Christianity, pacifism, and social justice.

Since its founding, the *Catholic Worker* has had considerable influence in alerting the nation to poverty and injustice. In the early 1960s, the socialist Michael Harrington worked as an editor of the *Catholic Worker*, and his experiences formed the basis of his seminal book *The Other America* (1963), which shocked President Kennedy with its description of the plight of the nation's poor and which helped inspire President Johnson to declare a "war on poverty."

In 1933, at the beginning of their relationship, Day and Maurin conceived the houses of hospitality that Robert Coles has described as "a twentieth-century version of the ancient notion of a hospice," and opened St. Joseph's House in a rented store. Its purpose was to serve the destitute, the hungry, the homeless, and the unemployed. During the Great Depression, their fellow workers — including many non-Catholics, agnostics, and atheists — founded thirty more such houses across the country. Today, more than a hundred and seventy-five such communities across the country still provide food and shelter.

Serving the poor at St. Joseph's House and the other houses of hospitality fulfilled Dorothy Day's deep yearning to lead an active Christian life, rather than a life simply of contemplation. She "wanted to be an anarchist," one of her colleagues is supposed to have remarked, "but only if she got to be the anarch." She was always suspicious of "telescopic philanthropists" who, like Mrs. Jellyby in Dickens's *Bleak House*, forever sermonize about distant wrongs while ignoring injustice and suffering in their own communities. She was equally suspicious of paternalistic reformers who, like George Bernard Shaw's character Major Barbara, moralized about the poor, condescended to their circumstances, and sought to change their behavior. Genuine Christian charity, she believed, came with no strings attached. "Who are we to change anyone," she asked, "and why cannot we leave them to themselves and God?"

Because of these beliefs, Day was opposed to the welfare bureaucracy, which she saw as impersonal, unsympathetic, and degrading. She was suspicious of social workers who spoke professional jargon and measured success in bureaucratic ways, who mistakenly viewed the houses of hospitality as conventional shelters and soup kitchens that just happened to indulge in quaint rituals, like prayer. "We are here to bear witness to our Lord," Day said. "We are here to follow His lead. We are here to celebrate Him through these works of mercy. . . . We are *not* here to prove that our technique of working with the poor is useful, or to prove that we are able to be effective humanitarians."

From our largely secular perspective, it is difficult to grasp the depth and political significance of Dorothy Day's faith. In the public square of today, the religious foreground has largely been claimed by the political right. Day claimed Christianity for the religious left, for a radical politics of localism, communitarianism, pacifism, and participatory democracy. She was drawn to the Catholic Church because she saw it as "the Church of the poor." It belonged, she said, "to all its people, and especially its most humble men and women and children."

Day was convinced that Catholic worship, prayer, and faith illuminated contemporary society and gave direction to how it might be changed. Whether feeding striking longshoremen on the New York waterfront, joining the young men and women of the Student Nonviolent Coordinating Committee in the fight for voting rights in Mississippi, or standing on picket lines in California with Cesar Chávez and the United Farm Workers, Day believed that she was supporting the central tenets of Catholicism: radical love, a losing of the self for others, the dignity of labor, voluntary poverty, a shared responsibility for the common good, and a rejection of violence.

Day's example of how to live the Catholic faith reminds us that it is possible to be conscious of sin and to struggle against evil without succumbing to self-righteousness or becoming judgmental. As Day once said, "A person can be self-righteous about his own righteousness; a person can use the Bible to bring more fear and hate in the world." She was catholic in the largest and broadest sense of that word: inclusive, sympathetic, understanding, welcoming.

If Dorothy Day was an idealist and an activist before her conversion to Catholicism, she remained a rebel and an iconoclast afterwards. Her conversion itself was a rebellion against the secular modernism of her Bohemian friends. Her choice of celibacy, after the sexual freedom of her early life, was a rejection of her own generation's revolt against Victorian repression. Her embrace of voluntary poverty was a rejection of the century's gathering consumer ethos. Michael Harrington recalled in his autobiography that when the Ford Foundation wanted to give the *Catholic Worker* a large grant in the 1950s, "Dorothy Day turned it down on the grounds that the followers of St. Francis of Assisi could not have a balance in a bank account."

Dorothy Day defied easy categorization. Although she was among the most theologically conservative of believers, one who accepted unconditionally the Church's authority on religious doctrine, she did not hesitate to take the Church to task for what she saw as its hypocrisies, its political obtuseness, and its moral failings. Her consistent criticism of the Church for its complacency, its arrogance, its lavish displays of luxury and wealth, came out of her love for a flawed institution. "There are days," she once remarked, "when I want to stop all those poor people, giving their coins to the church, and tell them to march on the offices of the archdiocese — tell all the people inside those offices to move out of their plush rooms and share the lives of the hungry and the hurt. Would Jesus . . . let Himself be driven in big black limousines, while thousands and thousands of people who believe in Him and His church are at the edge of starvation, . . . while people come to church barefooted and ragged and hungry and sick?"

In her political vision, Day was complex and iconoclastic, even paradoxical. Her radicalism had a traditionalist cast — looking to the past, away from modern continental-size bureaucracies, toward egalitarian and cooperative communities and small-scale local institutions. Like other compelling intellectuals and activists of the twentieth century — John Dewey, Hannah Arendt, Lewis Mumford, Randolph Bourne — Day cannot be pigeonholed. She was as skeptical of the liberal welfare state as she was of the conservative industrial complex.

Day bridged worlds and time: She was an admirer of Saints Thérèse de Lisieux and Catherine of Siena, as well as of immigrant women raising families in the difficult circumstances of urban America. She was a living link between the Bohemian radicals of pre–World War I Greenwich Village, the Old Left of the Great Depression, and the New Left of the 1960s. Idealistic college students born when she was well past middle age looked to her as an inspiration in their own struggle to bear nonviolent witness against racism, poverty, the nuclear arms race, and the war in Vietnam.

Dorothy Day was an idealist but never a romantic. Her love for vulnerable people allowed her to see the despair, filth, illness, indignities, and sorrow that they endured. She welcomed every derelict and drifter — unkempt, beaten down, emotionally ill, even at times menacing — who appeared at her door. She was able to do so, she said, because as each new person approached, she reminded herself that "he may be Christ returned to earth."

As I consider how Dorothy Day chose to live her life, I am struck by the firmness of her convictions as well as by the depth of her faith, by the extent of her self-understanding as well as by her fearlessness and the nature of her compassion for others. "The biggest mistake, sometimes," she once said, "is to play things very safe in this life and end up being moral failures." Dorothy Day never played things safe. She searched out the intellectual and spiritual values that a liberal education ideally imparts. In answering the question, "How should I live my life?" Dorothy Day marched to a different drummer — seeking sanctity rather than celebrity, enlarging the boundaries of human love, choosing to do good rather than to live well.

She would have been the first to confess that she had not attained moral perfection — she knew that no human being could do that — but she did achieve what Willa Cather defined as happiness: "to be dissolved into something complete and great." She was one of those rare people who, in the words of the English poet Stephen Spender, are "truly great . . . those who in their lives fought for life, / Who wore at their hearts the fire's centre." Dorothy Day chose not to live a life of fame. But in bearing witness to how a life of idealism and character can be lived, she may possibly have become a saint.

As the lives of John Gilbert Winant and Dorothy Day suggest, one of the important issues that a liberal education can help students to address is: What are our goals in life and how do we best go about achieving them?

The task of identifying and then pursuing one's aspiration is made more difficult by the tangled skeins of effort and coincidence, design and chance, that govern the ways in which each of us works out our destiny. The role of uncertainty in life is one of the themes of Ann Beattie's novel *Picturing Will* (1989). The novel is about the vulnerabilities of children and the attendant anxieties of parents who raise them. It is an extended meditation on the ways in which individual lives are shaped by the random accidents of experience and the puzzling vagaries of fate.

In the novel, a stepfather muses in his journal about what life may have in store for his young son:

> Do everything right, all the time, and the child will prosper. It's as simple as that, except for fate, luck, heredity, chance, the astrological sign under which the child was born, his order of birth, his first encounter with evil, the girl who jilts him in spite of his excellent qualities, the war that is being fought when he is a young man, the drugs he may try once or too many times, the friends he makes, how he scores on tests, how well he endures kidding about his shortcomings, how ambitious he becomes, how far he falls behind, circumstantial evidence, ironic perspective, danger when it is least expected, difficulty in triumphing over circumstance, people with hidden agendas, and animals with rabies.

Life, the stepfather seems to be saying, is shaped by contingencies we cannot predict. They simply happen, sometimes providing us serendipitously with sublime satisfaction, sometimes condemning us indiscriminately to awful pain. All of the contingencies that Beattie's character records in his journal — and many more that one can easily imagine — can govern our opportunities for success and our susceptibility to failure.

We cannot know what boon or bane the future holds. Yet each of us, wary of fate, wants to believe that we can set a reliable course for the future. We want to deny that the stepfather in Beattie's novel is correct. We yearn for — we dearly need — a sense of control over our own destinies. We strive to reduce the likelihood of uncertainty by leading our lives in ways that seem most likely to assure the outcomes we want. We cling to the strict belief that hard work will be rewarded and that the universe is indeed just.

And when we begin to fear that even our most committed efforts may not be wholly successful, when we begin to sense that even our most modest and halting hopes will not all be realized, we dream romantically that the same laws of coincidence that have dashed our brightest possibilities might also lift us out of the realm of the ordinary and elevate us, worthy or not, onto a higher plane of status or wealth or satisfaction.

Take, for example, the protagonist of another novel, and one of my favorites, *Saint Jack* (1973) by Paul Theroux. Jack Flowers is a middle-aged American expatriate who languishes as a pimp in Singapore, longing for an affirmation of his moral innocence and for the achievement of goals he cannot summon the self-discipline to pursue. "For as long as I could remember," he writes, "I had wanted to be rich, and famous if possible."

Unable to achieve wealth or fame by his own efforts, he lived, as Theroux writes, "in expectation of an angel." He daydreams about receiving letters that bestow great wealth upon him and confirm the esteem in which he wishes he were held. One such letter begins: "Dear Jack, I am asking my lawyer to read you this letter after my death. You have been an excellent and loyal friend, the very best one could hope for. I have noted you in my will for a substantial portion of my estate as a token thanks for your good humor, charity, and humanity. You will never again have to think of. . . ." Another letter states: "Dear Sir, Every year one person is singled out by our Foundation to be the recipient of a large cash disbursement. You will see from the enclosed form that no strings whatever are attached . . ." And still another: "Dear Mr. Flowers, The Academy has entrusted to me the joyful task of informing you of your election. This carries with it as you know the annual stipend of. . . ."

The letters are self-indulgent fantasies, as Jack Flowers, in his heart of hearts, acknowledges. But the impulse behind the burlesque is real. "I wasn't kidding," Flowers says, "even the most rational soul has at least one moment of pleasurable reflection when he hears a small voice addressing him as *Your Radiance*. I had a litany which began *Sir Jack, President Flowers, King John*, and so forth. And why stop at king? *Saint Jack!*"

Such, then, are the very human yearnings for protection against the contingencies of life and the indifference of the universe, for achievement of success and riches and recognition — all made more clear and dramatic by artistic hyperbole.

The fantasies that men and women nourish to give them such vicarious protection are harmless when we experience them as daydreams. They may even be a useful counterpoint — or so the psychologists might tell us — to the inexplicable harshness of so much of life and to the random unfairness that so often frustrates our most deserving efforts. But such fantasies are not the stuff of which full and satisfying lives are created. Waiting passively "in expectation of an angel" is no substitute for grappling with the dilemmas of being human.

In a world in which luck or fate or providence or chance plays such a large part (as the stepfather in Ann Beattie's novel instructs us), in a world in which elaborate fantasies are evanescent substitutes for unattained satisfactions (as Jack Flowers in Paul Theroux's story suggests), how ought one to lead a life? That is one of the great questions that a liberal education addresses. The most effective protection against the contingencies of experience are values that appeal to our very best natures and anchor us most securely in the churning ocean of fate. Foremost among those values is idealism.

In talking with students over the years, I have been struck by how many desire to identify with role models by whom they might be guided and inspired — men and women whose conduct of their lives is commensurate, morally and intellectually, with their own most selfless aspirations. I tell students that if their life's goal is to make a buck, or to accumulate trinkets and stock certificates, or to peddle advertisements for themselves, then role models abound. But the grey and uninspired existence that these models propose, the meretricious goals that they propose, cannot be what the glory of a liberal education is about. Surely life and liberal learning mean more than that.

As students seek appropriate role models, they cannot do better than to emulate men and women who are idealists. Who are idealists? They are people who are inspired by an idea greater than themselves, who are driven by a moral imperative to imagine a world better than the one they found. They are people animated by principle, who dedicate their lives to fortifying the spirit and improving the lot of those on the brink of hopelessness. They are people who sail against the wind and persevere despite setbacks or ambiguous success.

Idealists are informed on political matters and involved in the civic life of their communities. They devote their energies to the debates that make wise and humane public policy, as all Athens did in the age of Pericles. Idealists care about those who need help and commit themselves to national service and to a lifetime of civic engagement. They care about the health and well-being of neighbors and strangers alike. They care about the legal rights of all, especially those without advocates. They care about the working poor who struggle to make their way and to preserve their families in a global economy of bewildering technological change. They care about children, who need the full support of society in order to achieve their potential.

Idealists remind us, by the way in which they advance the lives of others, that, as Matthew Arnold said, "Life is not a having and a getting, but a being and a becoming." And they invite us, through their generosity, to be open to the possibility that what they have been for us, we might be for others. Idealists are not mere dreamers. They are known by their deeds and by the pride and purpose that animate their altruism. They instruct us, by their example, in the best meaning of character. Idealists are not rare. But there are not enough of them, in this society or any other.

The idealist who most shaped my own life was Thurgood Marshall, civil rights lawyer and Supreme Court justice. His lifelong struggle to end racial discrimination and to achieve equal rights for all Americans was a remarkable example of pragmatic idealism at its most steadfast. Contingency influenced Justice Marshall's successes and failures. His life was filled with wrenching defeats and tragic unfairness. But he was sustained during a career of more than fifty years by his magnificent adherence to idealism.

Near the end of his life, he told a reunion of his law clerks, in a moment I will remember for the rest of my life: "The goal of a true democracy such as ours, explained simply, is that any baby born in these United States, even if he is born to the blackest, most illiterate, most unprivileged Negro in Mississippi, is merely by being born and drawing his first breath in this democracy, endowed with the exact same rights as a child born to a Rockefeller. Of course it's not true. Of course it never will be true. But I challenge anybody to tell me that it isn't the type of goal we should try to get to as fast as we can." When Justice Marshall stopped speaking, the room was absolutely still. The nobility of his idealism had transfixed us all.

I have the feeling that many of us regard life as beginning, in an important sense, only after we pass some future milestone — after we have been graduated from college, or after we have settled into a prestigious job or a comfortable home or a proper marriage, or after we have achieved a measure of professional success or personal security. It is only then — several decades into middle age — that many people finally give themselves permission to live generously.

But life, of course, is not what happens after we pass some future milestone. Life is what we are doing now. And so the necessity of leading a life guided by ideals, a life that each of us is proud to lead, is present from the start and is always there. My message to students is that a life motivated by idealism promises the deepest kind of personal satisfaction.

❋ 6 ❋
ADDRESSING
MORAL
QUESTIONS

However reluctant many college presidents may be to mount the public stage, however sensitive they may be to the political and social limitations of their office, moments do arise when candor or conscience requires that they speak out, especially to vindicate an important principle or teach a relevant moral. It is at such moments that many presidents attain heightened stature in their communities.

In November 1997, at the start of my eleventh year as president of Dartmouth, I confronted a moment when I felt compelled to discard the conventional constraints and to speak out. The occasion was the dedication of a handsome new campus facility, the Roth Center for Jewish Life. The subject was Dartmouth's anti-Semitism of almost a half century earlier.

Until I became president of Dartmouth in 1987, anti-Semitism had never been a significant concern in my life. Although I now believe that my undergraduate class of 1957 at Harvard was chosen at a time when an admissions quota still existed, I did not realize that until many years later. (At the same period of time, Wellesley College not only enforced quotas against Jews, it also routinely assigned rooms strictly on the basis of religion. Thus, my contemporary Madeleine Albright, a member of the class of 1959 and a Catholic, found herself rooming with another Catholic.)

My subsequent experience as a student at Yale Law School (1959–62) was buoyant. The law school was an authentic meritocracy; Jews were a significant proportion of the student body, even though admissions quotas were still enforced at the undergraduate college. My classmate Alan M. Dershowitz expressed it well in his book *Chutzpah* (1991) when he wrote, "Though my fellow classmates numbered among them children of presidents, Supreme Court Justices, and multimillionaire industrialists, the only hierarchy I ever saw at Yale Law School was based on grades, *Law Journal* writing, moot court competition, and classroom performance." In short, to my knowledge I had never been disadvantaged as a student by anti-Semitism.

My interest in the subject of anti-Semitism in academe was first piqued in 1994 when I published an essay, written for the American Jewish Committee, in the *New York Times* entitled, "What Being Jewish Means to Me." In that essay, I noted that the faculty at Harvard College during my undergraduate years (1953–57) "provided but a handful of Jewish academic role models." One of the first responses came from McGeorge Bundy, who had been dean of the faculty of arts and sciences during my undergraduate years. He found himself "astonished" by my remarks. "I began by wondering if it was right," he wrote, "to say that there were only a handful of Jews on that faculty when my feeble memory could recall such names as Fainsod, Levin, Bruner, Handlin, Hartz, Harris, Wolff, Riesman, Kaysen, Schwinger, and perhaps most notable of all the great Harry Wolfson." Bundy's list, at first reading, was formidable. After some investigation, I replied: "Although I recognize that the faculty list you set forth was intended to be illustrative and not inclusive, a number of professors on that list had not yet been appointed to the Harvard faculty while I was an undergraduate. That to the side, I do believe that even a list perhaps twice as long would still properly be characterized as a "handful" among a faculty of approximately four-hundred and fifty persons."

By this time, I was more than curious to learn about the admissions and appointment practices of colleges such as Harvard, Yale, and Columbia. I wanted to know what the historical record held. I knew, of course, that anti-Semitism and the *numerus clausus* had been facts of life in the United States during the first half of the twentieth century. Indeed, when my father was graduated from Lynn (Massachusetts) English High School in 1916, he applied to Harvard. The admissions exam was scheduled on Rosh Hashanah. Leaders of the Jewish community asked A. Lawrence Lowell, the president of Harvard, to reschedule the exams a day earlier or a day later so that Jewish students might take them without compromising their religious convictions. President Lowell refused. (An official of Columbia rejected a similar request in 1909, arguing, "If they wish to attend a Christian college, let them submit to its requirements or *stay away*.")

As a result of Lowell's decision, dozens, perhaps hundreds, of young men like my father declined to take the examination and therefore could not qualify for admission to Harvard. I dearly wish that my father, who had also encountered anti-Semitism in finding his early high school teaching positions, had lived long enough to see the installation of Jewish presidents at numerous Ivy League universities.

Sometimes the anti-Semitism of the 1920s and 1930s was enforced quietly, and sometimes it was accompanied by an air of condescension. When Percy W. Bridgman, a Nobel laureate in physics, wrote to Ernest Rutherford in 1925 recommending his Harvard student J. Robert Oppenheimer, he described him as "a Jew, but entirely without the usual qualifications of his race. He is a tall, well set-up young man, with a rather engaging diffidence of manner, and I think you need have no hesitation whatever for any reason of this sort in considering his application." (Rutherford declined to take Oppenheimer into his laboratory.)

In expressing such views, Bridgman was echoing prejudices held by many Americans. Charles A. Lindbergh, while sailing across the Atlantic in 1939, confided to his journal: "The steward tells me that most of the Jewish passengers are sick. Imagine taking these Jews in addition to those we already have. There are too many in places like New York already. A few Jews add strength and character to a country, but too many create chaos. And we are getting too many. This present immigration will have its reaction."

Many years later, at her confirmation hearing to be an associate justice of the U.S. Supreme Court, Ruth Bader Ginsburg recalled as a child being in a car with her parents and passing a resort in Pennsylvania with a sign in front that read: "No Dogs or Jews allowed."

Among intellectuals, T. S. Eliot was open in his denunciation of

Jews, as such poems as "Gerontion," "Sweeney among the Nightingales," and "Burbank with a Baedeker: Bleistein with a Cigar" make explicit. For Eliot, Judaism was "a mild and colourless form of Unitarianism." In *After Strange Gods* (1934), Eliot assailed Jews in the course of ceremoniously emphasizing the necessity of tradition in a stable society: "The population should be homogeneous. . . . What is still more important is unity of religious background; and reasons of race and religion combine to make any large number of free-thinking Jews undesirable. . . . A spirit of excessive tolerance is to be deprecated." The critic Christopher Ricks, in his book *T. S. Eliot and Prejudice* (1988) is compelled to describe Eliot's perverse attitude toward Jews as "instinct with animus."

Anti-Semitism flourished at many Ivy League colleges, beginning in the 1920s. This was especially true at Harvard. President Lowell, who served from 1909 to 1933, was an outspoken public figure. He often mounted the public stage. Having been trained as a lawyer, he opposed President Wilson's appointment of Louis D. Brandeis to the U.S. Supreme Court, ostensibly because he believed that Brandeis did not enjoy the confidence of the bar. Many thought that he objected to the appointment because he rejected Brandeis's progressive political and social views and because Brandeis was a Jew. More to the present point, Lowell became immersed in 1922 in an ugly public controversy because of his attempt to institute quotas for Jewish students at Harvard. At the time, Jews constituted 21 percent of the student body. The waves of immigration during the prior three decades, especially from eastern Europe, had increased the size and shaped the character of the Jewish applicant pool. Lowell believed, as his biographer Henry Aaron Yeomans has written, that the presence of too many Jewish students would erode Harvard's "character as a democratic, national university, drawing from all classes of the community and promoting a sympathetic understanding among them." The presence of too many Jews — whom Lowell, a former vice president of the Immigration Restriction League, linked with African Americans, Asian Americans, French Canadians, and others "if they did not speak English and kept themselves apart" —

would invite separatism rather than assimilation, Lowell argued, and could therefore "not only be bad for the Gentiles . . . but disastrous for the Jews themselves."

After Jewish enrollment at Harvard rose from 7 percent in 1900 to 21 percent in 1922, Lowell took steps to impose a quota, noting that if "every college in the country would take a limited proportion of Jews, I suspect we should go a long way toward eliminating race feeling among the students." He believed, in short, that a limitation upon the number of Jews would serve to reduce anti-Semitism. Lowell began by suggesting that Harvard should limit the percentage of total scholarship aid that could be awarded to Jewish students to the percentage of such students in the class. He then advised the committee on admissions, in a manner typical of the fashionable anti-Semitism of the period, that "all doubtful . . . cases shall be investigated with the nicest care, and that such of this number as belong to the Hebrew race shall be rejected except in unusual and special cases."

When Lowell's proposals were reported on the front page of the *New York Times*, an outcry ensued, and he was forced to retract his plan. Several years later, however, Lowell informally directed the admissions committee to require a photograph of applicants and to place greater emphasis upon qualities of geographic distribution and personal fitness. He wrote, "To prevent a dangerous increase in the proportion of Jews, I know at present only one way which is, at the same time, straight forward and effective, and that is selection by a personal estimate of character." He did not want any Jews, he said, who were unwilling to modify their "peculiar practices." In due course, Jewish enrollment was cut to 10 percent.

A dissenting voice came in a letter from one of Harvard's most distinguished graduates, Judge Learned Hand:

> I cannot agree that a limitation based upon race will in the end work out any good purpose. If the Jew does not mix well with the Christian, it is no answer to segregate him. Most of these qualities which the Christian dislikes in him are, I believe, the direct result of that very policy in the past. . . .

If anyone could devise an honest test for character, perhaps it would serve well. I doubt its feasibility except to detect formal and obvious delinquencies. Short of it, it seems to me that students can only be chosen by tests of scholarship, unsatisfactory as those no doubt are. . . .

A college may gather together men of a common tradition, or it may put its faith in learning. If so, it will I suppose take its chance that in learning lies the best hope, and that a company of scholars will prove better than any other company.

The policy implications of adopting religious quotas for admission to the nation's most respected university radiated well beyond Harvard. Events similar to those at Harvard occurred at Yale, where the proportion of Jewish students rose from 2 percent in 1901 to 13 percent in 1925. When a member of the Yale Corporation saw a list of the university's entering class in 1929, he commented, "The list as published reads like some of the 'begat' portions of the Old Testament and might easily be mistaken for a recent roll call at the Wailing Wall." Yale became alarmed, as one dean reported, that "every single scholarship of any value is won by a Jew." The dean noted that although Jewish students often led the class in terms of scholarship and intelligence, "their personal characteristics make them markedly inferior." By 1924, Yale had instituted an admissions policy that placed enhanced emphasis upon "character" and more detailed personal information about each applicant. That policy remained in place for the next four decades. In his book *The Big Test* (1999), Nicholas Lemann quotes Yale's Catholic chaplain as telling William F. Buckley, Jr., when he was an undergraduate in the late 1940s, that "Yale maintained a [combined] ceiling of 13 percent on Catholics and on Jews."

The consequences of Yale's anti-Semitic actions were to reverberate many decades later. When Henry Rosovsky, who was dean of the faculty of Arts and Sciences at Harvard for thirteen years, was offered the presidency of Yale in 1977, he had serious doubts about the circumstances he would face as an outsider. He believed, as Dan A. Oren quoted him in his book *Joining the Club: A History of Jews and Yale* (1985), that "I represented bitter medicine to them. They made the choice, but I felt I didn't fit their image. I wasn't a graduate. I was a Jew. In style and appearance I wasn't their kind of guy." Rosovsky declined Yale's offer. (The amber glow of nostalgia may cause many to forget that until recently, Yale and most other universities would not have considered a Jew for their presidencies.)

Finally, Columbia had been every bit as anti-Semitic as Harvard and Yale. Concerned that the presence of Jews was causing the loss of students from what a dean called "homes of refinement," Columbia adopted admissions quotas in 1914. By emphasizing such nonacademic factors as geographic balance and personal character, and by asking for a photograph of the applicant, for the maiden name of the applicant's mother, and for the parents' place of birth, Columbia reduced the proportion of Jewish students enrolled from about 40 percent in 1914 to 21 percent in 1918, and eventually to 15 percent during the 1920s, despite the size of the Jewish population in the city around it.

Like Harvard and Yale, Columbia also discriminated in the appointment of Jews to its faculty. The most celebrated incident involved Lionel Trilling, who was to become one of the nation's most distinguished literary critics. Trilling was appointed as an instructor in the English Department in 1932. The appointment was "pretty openly regarded as an experiment," as Trilling later wrote, "and for some time my career in the College was complicated by my being Jewish." The department apparently believed that a Jew could not properly appreciate Anglo-Saxon literature. When Trilling's appointment came up for renewal in 1936, he was told that the department believed that "as a Freudian, a Marxist, and [a] Jew," he would be more comfortable elsewhere. Only the intervention of Nicholas Murray Butler, the university's formidable president, who was deeply impressed by his book on Matthew Arnold, preserved Trilling's place at Columbia. Clifton Fadiman, a contemporary, was told that he had no hope of securing a position at Columbia because "we can take only one Jew, and it's Lionel." (Prejudices die hard, however. Trilling's widow Diana recounted in her memoirs that after her husband's appointment became official, a senior member of the department told him "now that Lionel was a member of the department, he hoped he would not use it as a wedge to open the English department to more Jews.")

Having made inquiry into the admissions practices at Harvard, Yale, and Columbia, I could hardly fail to do so at Dartmouth. In that endeavor I was greatly assisted by an honors thesis written by Alexandra Shepard of the class of 1992. Entitled "Seeking a Sense of Place: Jewish Students in the Dartmouth Community, 1920–1940," the thesis collects a wealth of material. It confirms that Dartmouth's practices were as noxious as those at Harvard, Yale, and Columbia. The actions at all four institutions illustrated the lesson that Karl Shapiro drew in his poem "University": "To hurt the Negro and avoid the Jew / Is the curriculum."

The foremost defender of the religious quotas that defaced Dartmouth's admissions policy was Ernest Martin Hopkins, a revered educator who served as president from 1916 to 1945. When the dean of admissions reported in 1933 that Dartmouth faced a shortage of students as a result of the depression, he recommended raising the Jewish quota by 1 percent rather than lowering academic standards. President Hopkins replied, "Life is so much pleasanter in Hanover, the physical appearance of the place is so greatly benefited, and friends of the college visiting us are so much happier with the decreased quota of the Hebraic element, that I am not enthusiastic at all about your suggestion." In a letter to an alumnus written a few months later, Hopkins declared that "it would be quixotic to allow ourselves to be overrun racially." Hopkins speaks of Jewish students as if they were poison ivy or unsightly weeds.

By requiring applicants to provide photographs of themselves, Dartmouth was able to eliminate those who appeared to be "too Jewish" because of their "strongly demonstrated Hebrew physiognomy." By the end of the 1930s, Dartmouth accepted only one out of ten Jewish applicants, compared to three out of four non-Jewish applicants.

In June 1934, a Dartmouth alumnus wrote to the dean of admissions, "I believe that your five percent or six percent" — meaning the quota for Jewish students — "is OK, but not eight percent or nine percent, which I'm afraid this fall's class will turn out to be. It certainly is a very serious problem. The campus seems more Jewish each time I arrive in Hanover. And unfortunately many of them (on quick judgment) seem to be the 'kike' type. I will be glad to help you in any way I can as long as the problem lasts." The dean of admissions replied, "I am glad to have your comments on the Jewish problem, and I shall appreciate your help along this line in the future. If we go beyond five percent or six percent in the Class of 1938 I shall be grieved beyond words, for at the present time the group is only five percent of the total that has been selected. It may well be that all of the Jewish boys will come, in which case we may get up to six percent, but I do not see it can climb as high as eight percent or nine percent." The archives are filled with similar correspondence.

One of the concerns at Dartmouth, as much of the correspondence indicates, matched that at Yale: that Jewish students dominated campus life, occupying the leading positions in student organizations, from class president to editor in chief of the newspaper. They also dominated the awarding of academic honors; one dean complained that the Phi Beta Kappa society was getting "too swarthy."

Among the most poignant folders of correspondence in the entire Dartmouth archives involves the plea of a Jewish father to President Hopkins in 1935. The father writes that his son, graduating that year from Dartmouth, has been denied admission to every medical school to which he applied, including Dartmouth, despite being an excellent student, an athlete, and "a fine honest upright boy who has won the respect of all who have known him." The father expresses the hope that "your experience will place you in a position to advise me." President Hopkins first sought an explanation from his own medical school, which reported lamely that it had found the applicant unacceptable "on the basis of those intangible qualities, which I will not attempt to define." President Hopkins then replied to the father that "there is no medical school in the country of which I know . . . that does not labor under the difficulty that the overwhelming majority of applications are from the racial group of Jewish blood." In responding so candidly and in such odious language, President Hopkins confirmed the existence of a Jewish quota. In fact, for more than two decades the quota at Dartmouth Medical School was exactly two Jews per class.

There was not a year as president of Dartmouth that I did not receive a letter from an alumnus of that era, recalling his own experience as a Jewish undergraduate. Many quoted the well-known interview with President Hopkins that appeared in the New York *Post* and was reported in *Time* and *Newsweek* magazines in 1945, even as World War II was coming to a conclusion. In that interview President Hopkins acknowledged, "We cut the quotas more on our Jewish applicants than we do the basis for applications from Anglo-Saxons. I think if you were to let Dartmouth become predominantly Jewish, it would lose its attraction for Jews." In pressing for the removal of quotas, he said, "those with Jewish blood are their own worse enemies." And then he added, "Dartmouth is a Christian college founded for the Christianization of its students."

As the date for the dedicatory ceremony approached, I reflected upon what a significant milestone the opening of the Roth Center was for the realization of the promise of American life at Dartmouth — an institution that, in common with its sister institutions, had erased every vestige of anti-Semitism. I also considered what a decade's experiences at Dartmouth had done to challenge my sense of Jewish identity. The question I faced was this: What ought a college to do, what ought I as a Jew to do, on such a triumphant occasion when the institution had such a morally troubling past?

I concluded that it was important for any institution to acknowledge — to name — what I called "the ghosts of the past," to undertake a process of moral reckoning and accountability. That is why, after all, the United States continues to press Russia for information about the mysterious disappearance of Raoul Wallenberg, the Swedish diplomat who saved tens of thousands of Hungarian Jews from Nazi death camps in the final months of World War II. That is why Switzerland, however reluctantly, is investigating the role of its banks in concealing Nazi money during the Holocaust. That is why South Africa conducted lengthy hearings, through its Truth and Reconciliation Commission, to fix personal responsibility for the horrors of apartheid. In the body politic, as in the process of psychotherapy, health is restored by acknowledging the character of the past.

The most recent relevant example was the decision of the government of France to hold a trial, in 1997, to respond to the collaboration of the Vichy regime with the Nazis during World War II, more than fifty years earlier. It charged Maurice Papon, an eighty-seven-year-old former high-ranking civil servant, with crimes against humanity; specifically, with helping, as a collaborationist and member of the Gestapo, to organize the arrest and deportation of Jewish men, women, and children from Bordeaux to Auschwitz from 1942 to 1944. After the longest and most expensive trial in modern French history, Papon was convicted and, despite his advanced age, sentenced in 1998 to ten years of criminal detention. The trial forced the French to confront a part of their past that many had tried to forget. It taught the French to ask how the moral atrocities of the Vichy government could be fitted into their idealized view of the grandeur of French history.

The instinct that animated the French government to confront its past was a sound one for France, it seemed to me, and a sound one for Dartmouth as well. Indeed, the quality and strength of an institution might well be measured by its willingness to explore the past.

On a personal level, I recalled a whole series of troubling incidents: my frequent embarrassment when Jewish parents of prospective college students told me they would not consider sending a son or daughter to Dartmouth; my chagrin when friends told me how surprised they were to learn that a Jew would choose to be president of Dartmouth; my anger when a fund-raising consultant warned me that a Jewish president should expect to face difficulty in raising money from Dartmouth alumni; my exasperation when the tirades of the *Dartmouth Review*, an off-campus conservative newspaper, were often characterized by the national press as anti-Semitic and erroneously attributed to the college; and my impatience when the press found it relevant to continually refer to me, alone among Jewish college presidents, as Jewish. These humiliating suggestions of a persisting anti-Semitism at Dartmouth hurt me to the quick. They challenged my identity as a Jew.

Because I had already announced that I would step down as president at the end of the academic year, I knew that this ceremony would probably be my last chance to address the question publicly. What was the value of having a public platform if I was not prepared to mount it? Having come to believe that acknowledging the past would work a redemption both institutionally and personally, I resolved to take the occasion of the Roth Center dedication to recite the ignoble history of discrimination against Jewish students by Dartmouth and by other Ivy League institutions. Contrary to my usual practice, I alerted none of my colleagues to what I planned to say; I wanted my remarks to have the maximum possible impact.

I emphasized in my speech that the dedication of the Roth Center was a joyous and important event, symbolic of a gratifying stride forward. Jewish students at Dartmouth now had a place at which to come together — to conduct Friday evening and Saturday morning services, maintain a kosher kitchen, to hold Sabbath dinners, to invite speakers, to organize social events, to make their presence known. The ugly days of official anti-Semitism, in which colleges caused so much sadness and pain, were many decades in the past. Dartmouth now embraced religious tolerance in the fullest sense and enabled Jewish students to feel a complete and significant part of its community.

One of the lessons of this history, I concluded, was that colleges and society must exercise a continuing vigilance toward discrimination against those who are different — whether they be Jews, Irish Americans, Italian Americans, Native Americans, African Americans, Asian Americans, or Hispanic Americans. So long as it does so, our educational institutions will be meritocracies in which the primary criteria for admission are talent, idealism, ambition, and the promise of making a contribution to American life. By accepting the historical legacy, we have accepted the responsibility of keeping things right.

As I spoke, I was increasingly aware of a heightened sense of electricity, even danger, in the air. When I concluded, the applause from the startled audience, almost all of whom were significant donors to

the Roth Center, was immensely reassuring. I felt cleansed and unbur-
dened, as if a psychological boil had been lanced. I felt, too, that I had
honored my father's thwarted ambition.

Several days later, the *New York Times* covered my speech in an article
that spread across the top of the entire page. The article began, "The
president of Dartmouth College has confronted the anti-Semitism in its
past, giving one of the most vivid illustrations ever of an attitude that
was prevalent for years at elite private colleges and universities." The article went on to reproduce several of the anti-Semitic letters from which
I had read, and noted that many members of the audience "were
stunned by the language in some of the documents read by Mr. Freedman." In addition, the *Times* included a photograph of my wife and me,
with two rabbis, reading from the Torah in the Roth Center's sanctu-
ary — the first time, I suspect, that a college president ever appeared in
the pages of that newspaper wearing a yarmulke and a tallith! Friends
sent me clippings from the Jewish press nationally — including papers
from San Francisco, Chicago, Cleveland, Philadelphia, Denver, and
Minneapolis — which carried accounts of my speech.

More than two dozen Jewish alumni wrote to share their experiences as undergraduates. One wrote, "The embarrassment I felt for
my alma mater when reading of your speech at the Roth Center was
eclipsed by my pride in a school whose president has the courage and
sensibility to make these matters public." Another wrote, "Just as we
long have had some among our *landsman* who would not 'rock the
boat' and sought only what was allowed of them, so today I speculate
that you may have made some Jews uncomfortable. So be it." Still another expressed the hope that "your example will inspire the presidents
of other leading schools, including all of the Ivy League schools, to do
the same." Several suggested that Dartmouth's actions were the result
of ignorance rather than anti-Semitism.

A few alumni were critical of my remarks. One wrote, "It is the duty
of a college president to point out the positive aspects of his school, not
tarnish it. What good did it do?" Some granted that racial quotas existed at the time they were admitted, but insisted that their experience
as Jewish undergraduates had been positive, almost entirely free of

anti-Semitism. One reported his impression that "the Jewish quota in the 1950s was filled with mediocre students because Dartmouth did not want a disproportionate number of the graduation awards to be given to Jews." Many described President Hopkins as an "honest conservative" who was simply a product or prisoner of his time, and they expressed admiration for his leadership of the college.

Predictably, William F. Buckley, Jr., devoted an op-ed page essay in the *New York Times* to the subject. (Buckley sometimes seemed mildly obsessed with Dartmouth. He invariably wrote at least one column a year about events at the college; his book *In Search of Anti-Semitism* [1992] includes an entire chapter on my confrontation with the *Dartmouth Review* in 1990–91.) Usually the provocateur, his tone in fact was pensive. Writing under the editor's resonant title of "God and Man at Dartmouth," Buckley praised the abolition of religious discrimination, but asked, "is it meant, in welcoming students of other creeds, that a college must foreswear its own traditional creed?" Why, he wondered, must Dartmouth abandon "the ideal of Christianizing those students susceptible to Christian mores"?

Religious quotas are now a thing of the past. Jews have long since succeeded in making their mark on American life, and primarily by means of education. As two distinguished social scientists, Seymour Martin Lipset and Earl Raab, noted in their book *Jews and the New American Scene* (1995), while Jews constitute less than 3 percent of the American population, they make up "50 percent of the top two hundred intellectuals, 40 percent of American Nobel Prize winners in science and economics, 20 percent of professors at the leading universities, 21 percent of high level civil servants, 40 percent of partners in the leading law firms in New York and Washington."

Jews now attend Ivy League colleges at twelve times their presence in the general population. They constitute approximately one-third of the students at those eight institutions. Although the percentage of Jewish students at Dartmouth remains to this day considerably lower than that of the other Ivy League institutions (about 10 to 12 percent), the explanations for this circumstance do not include anti-Semitism but, rather, factors like Dartmouth's rural location.

Jews are now among the leaders of the mainstream rather than its victims. They serve as presidents of many of the same institutions that once had scorned their fathers and grandfathers. No longer the "fragile remnant" that Benjamin Disraeli pointed to in the nineteenth century, no longer the "despised minority" that Justice Brandeis described in the twentieth century, they have made good on what Herbert Croly called "the promise of American life."

❊ 7 ❊
CONFERRING
HONORARY
DEGREES

C eremonial occasions provide college presidents with an opportunity to emphasize an institution's values, and no occasion is more potent in its illustrative capacity than the conferral of honorary degrees at commencement ceremonies. There were few perquisites of office that I treasured more than working with the board of trustees and a faculty committee in selecting honorary degree recipients. In bestowing an honorary degree, a university makes an explicit statement to its students and the world about the qualities of character and attainment it admires most. It is a practice rich in opportunity as well as ripe for abuse.

Honorary degrees have been awarded in America from an early date. Some place that date at 1692, when Harvard University conferred the degree of Doctor of Sacred Theology upon its own president, Increase Mather. Others place it at 1753, when that institution awarded an honorary master's degree to Benjamin Franklin for "his great improvements in Philosophic Learning, particularly with Respect to Electricity." (Harvard later awarded honorary doctorates to both George Washington and Thomas Jefferson.)

Although few American institutions awarded honorary degrees before the Revolution, by 1800 many had adopted the practice. In any event, purely honorary awards have long had an imaginative appeal, going back perhaps to the crowns of laurel, myrtle, and oak bestowed in ancient times and to the patents of nobility and orders of knighthood celebrated in the chivalric legends of the Middle Ages. Montaigne regarded it as "a very good and profitable custom to find a means of recognizing the worth of rare and excellent men, and of contenting and satisfying them by payments which are no load on the public and cost the prince [who confers them] nothing." Those who receive such honors, Montaigne wrote, are "more jealous of such rewards than of those in which there was gain or profit."

Although no reliable count exists, in the aggregate several thousand honorary degrees are conferred every year by the nation's more than three thousand colleges and universities. In eleven years as president of Dartmouth, I had the opportunity to hold up to the graduating students and our commencement guests the lives of more than ninety men and women worthy of emulation, a living tableau of persons from different walks of life, different areas of genius and accomplishment.

In choosing honorands, I emphasized intellectual distinction and public service. If Dartmouth was to confer honorary degrees at all, I believed, the reason had to be to celebrate distinguished and sublime achievement. In most years at least one of the eight or nine recipients was a Nobel laureate, and in many years one was an "unsung hero or heroine" — for example, someone had founded a statewide day-care program for children in poverty or had rescued from bankruptcy a college for Native American students. Among those Dartmouth honored were Marian Wright Edelman, Joseph Brodsky, Oscar Arias Sanchez, Claire Bloom, Robert Coles, Rita Dove, John K. Fairbank, Helen Frankenthaler, Carlos Fuentes, Seamus Heaney, A. Leon Higginbotham, Jr., David Mamet, Wilma Mankiller, V. S. Naipaul, Jessye Norman, I. M. Pei, Robert M. Solow, Aleksandr Solzhenitsyn, Derek Walcott, C. Vann Woodward, and August Wilson. (Three recipients received a standing ovation from the graduating students: C. Everett Koop, Jonas Salk, and Maurice Sendak.)

Reaction among prospective honorary degree recipients is usually enthusiastic. When Booker T. Washington, the principal of the Tuskegee Institute, received word from President Charles W. Eliot in 1896 that Harvard wished to confer an honorary degree upon him, he was swept by emotion. Recalling the moment in his autobiography, *Up from Slavery* (1901), Washington wrote:

This was a recognition that had never in the slightest manner entered into my mind, and it was hard for me to realize that I was to be honoured by a degree from the oldest and most renowned university in America. As I sat upon my veranda, with this letter in my hand, tears came into my eyes. My whole former life — my life as a slave on the plantation, my work in the coal-mine, the times when I was without food and clothing, when I made my bed under a sidewalk, my struggles for an education, the trying days I had had at Tuskegee, days when I did not know where to turn for a dollar to continue the work there, the ostracism and sometimes oppression of my race — all this passed before me and nearly overcame me.

A courtly reaction was registered by Oliver Wendell Holmes, Jr., when he was awarded an honorary degree by Yale in 1886. Responding to the reading of the citation, Justice Holmes said:

I know of no mark of honor which this country has to offer that I should value so highly as this which you have conferred upon me. I accept it proudly as an accolade, like the little blow upon the shoulder from the sword of a master of war which in ancient days adjudged that a soldier had won his spurs and pledged his life to decline no combat in the future. . . . I shall try to maintain the honor you have bestowed.

For some, the joy of the honor has come at particularly opportune moments. Kenneth Roberts, the author of such popular historical novels as *Arundel* (1930), *Rabble in Arms* (1933), and *Northwest Passage* (1937), reported that he was despondent and "at the nadir of my discouragement" in 1934 when he received word that Dartmouth wished to bestow upon him an honorary degree. That news, he wrote, offered "literary re-birth, resuscitation, and rehabilitation." When Mark Twain received an honorary degree from Oxford University in 1907, he happily exclaimed that an Oxford degree was "worth twenty-five of any other, whether foreign or domestic."

Few would deny that at some universities political considerations sometimes influence the selection (or nonselection) of honorary degree recipients. In November 1959, President Nathan M. Pusey of Harvard received a letter from two eminent members of his faculty, Arthur M. Schlesinger, Jr., and John Kenneth Galbraith:

> We should like, with all respect and good will, to draw your attention to present practice in awarding honorary degrees at Harvard for public service. We feel that this practice reflects on the fairness, liberalism, and, indeed on the good judgment of the University. And we feel that, given the facts, you will wish to agree. We refer to the continuing preference for members of the Republican Party and the near exclusion from such honors of liberal Democrats. We note with equal concern the virtually total exclusion of labor leaders. Without attributing undue importance to these awards, we would like to urge an end to the present practice as something which can only be explained as a vestigial remnant of emotions and attitudes now happily far behind us.

As Schlesinger and Galbraith suggest, the conferring of honorary degrees has always been one of the ways in which the establishment honors its own. It often seems to follow party lines. Brandeis University, for example, has awarded an honorary degree to virtually every prime minister of Israel who was a member of the Labor Party; it has yet to honor a prime minister who was a member of the Likud.

There are, as one might expect, conspicuous instances of omission quite aside from political considerations. A few years before William Faulkner received the Nobel Prize for Literature, the University of Mississippi voted against awarding him an honorary degree. Even after Faulkner received the Nobel Prize, the university never corrected the rejection. (The Reverend Sun Myung Moon took steps to make certain that he would not experience the pain of omission. He bought the University of Bridgeport, and two years later the institution conferred its doctorate upon him.)

Until recent decades, men were the overwhelming, if not exclusive, choices for honorary degrees. Only in 1922 did Dartmouth award its first honorary degree to a woman, the novelist Dorothy Canfield Fisher. It did not award its second until 1938, when it honored the journalist Dorothy Thompson. Harvard was even slower in recognizing women; the first woman to receive its honorary degree was Helen Keller in 1955. However, three institutions — the University of Nebraska, Columbia University, and Smith College — honored Willa Cather in the early decades of the twentieth century. Other women honored by various colleges and universities in those decades included the writer Julia Ward Howe, the social reformer Jane Addams, the novelist Edith Wharton, and the scientist Marie Curie.

During the nineteenth century, most honorary degree recipients were Protestant, including many clergymen. The first Jew to receive an honorary degree in the United States was probably Judah Monis, an instructor in Hebrew at Harvard, in 1720. Religious restrictions have long since disappeared. (But the median age of honorary degree recipients remains high, probably more than sixty years.)

Some institutions, on occasion, have engaged in the mass awarding of honorary degrees as a means of celebrating an anniversary and augmenting its pomp and ceremony. Harvard seems to have been the grand master of this practice. In 1886, on the 250th anniversary of its founding, it conferred forty-two honorary degrees. In 1909, at the inauguration of A. Lawrence Lowell as its president, it granted thirty. Then, in 1936, on the 300th anniversary of its founding, it bestowed eighty-six. And Princeton, in celebrating its 150th anniversary in 1896, conferred seventy-nine honorary degrees. But Columbia surpassed both Harvard and Princeton in the scope of its generosity. In 1929, while commemorating the 175th anniversary of the granting of the original charter to King's College, it conferred 134 honorary degrees. James Bryce may have had such ceremonies in mind when he tartly observed, in *The American Commonwealth* (1888), that honorary degrees are sometimes awarded "with a profuseness which seems to argue an exaggerated appreciation of inconspicuous merit."

But not every potential recipient is interested in receiving an honorary degree. George Bernard Shaw, perhaps the foremost playwright of the English-speaking world at the time, made it amply clear that he did not wish to be honored at Harvard University's 300th anniversary celebration in 1936. When an alumnus asked Shaw if he might suggest him for a Tercentenary honor, Shaw replied: "I cannot pretend that it would be fair for me to accept university degrees when every public reference of mine to our educational system, and especially to the influence of the universities on it, is fiercely hostile. If Harvard would celebrate its 300th anniversary by burning itself to the ground and sowing its site with salt, the ceremony would give me the greatest satisfaction as an example to all the other famous old corrupters of youth, including Yale, Oxford, Cambridge, the Sorbonne, etc. etc. etc."

Modesty, or perhaps an egalitarian aversion to titles, may occasionally impel an individual to decline an honorary degree. The clergyman Henry Ward Beecher turned down an invitation from Amherst College because he "preferred to continue to bear the name that had been given [me] when [I] was baptized in [my] mother's arms." William Faulkner, always an original, declined an honorary degree from Harvard in 1952 on the ground that honoring someone of such limited formal education "would violate and outrage the entire establishment of education, of which degrees are the symbol and the accolade. That is, I would defend the chastity of Harvard, the mother of American education, even if Harvard herself would not."

Thomas Jefferson wrote to his son-in-law that one should accept "only those public testimonials which are earned by merit." He prohibited the University of Virginia from awarding honorary degrees, but himself gathered several from leading universities of his day, including Harvard, Yale, and Brown. Similar stances, taken for whatever reasons, led President Millard Fillmore to decline an honorary degree from Oxford and President Grover Cleveland one from Harvard.

Their actions are a reminder that presidents of the United States constitute a special category. No other individual brings such prestige to a commencement ceremony — and, on occasion, few others are as likely to arouse such controversy. When Harvard awarded an honorary degree to Andrew Jackson in 1833, his predecessor, John Quincy Adams, recorded in his diary that his alma mater had bestowed its "highest literary honors upon a barbarian who could scarcely spell his own name." And historians have recorded the clash between college president and trustees that denied Dartmouth the opportunity of honoring Abraham Lincoln. Although the president of the college, Nathan Lord, a Congregational minister, had been an abolitionist when he took office in 1825, he gradually came to give the Bible a literal interpretation and to believe that slavery was a divine institution condoned by God's law. He wrote a pamphlet to that effect — one so popular that it went into four editions. In 1863 the trustees adopted a resolution against the institution of slavery and voted, over Lord's objection, to confer an honorary degree upon President Lincoln. When Lord refused to issue the invitation, the trustees asked for and received his resignation. The trustees themselves forwarded to Lincoln the invitation to receive his degree at the commencement of 1865. But by that time Lincoln was dead.

In May 2001, more than two hundred faculty members at Yale signed a letter protesting the prospective award of an honorary degree to George W. Bush. The letter pointed out that although four of the six most recent presidents held Yale degrees, Yale had not honored one of those presidents at all (Clinton), had honored another only after he left office (Ford), and had honored still a third only after he had served for three years (G. H. W. Bush). Because this pattern indicated that the university's practice had been to honor individuals, not the office, the letter said, Yale's decision to honor Bush after only four months in office was at least premature. Despite the letter, Yale went ahead and awarded the degree.

Over the years, certain individuals have not been shy about suggesting themselves for honorary degrees. In 1773, when Dartmouth was four years old, one Oliver Whipple of Portsmouth, New Hampshire, wrote to the college's founder and first president, Eleazar Wheelock, requesting "the favor" of an honorary degree, noting that he already held a master's degree from the University of Cambridge "and would gladly become an adopted Son of Yours." He added that he would "always wish to give some mark of my Affection to your Seminary." No record of the president's response exists. In the course of my presidential years in Hanover, I heard periodically from several such persons, including one alumnus who had written several books and served as the president of three universities. Year after year, he brazenly approached me with renewed requests for a degree, always supplying an exhaustive resumé and fistfuls of adulatory articles. He never was honored. Celebrities, too, have been known to volunteer themselves for such honors, the twins of egotism and insecurity being as insatiable as they are.

Tales persist of persons who never entirely recovered from the failure of a particular institution, usually their alma mater, to award them an honorary degree. John O'Hara, the novelist who wrote *Appointment in Samarra* (1934) and who regretted the fact that he had not attended Yale, complained to the Yale alumni magazine about the university's refusal to honor him. When Kingman Brewster, the president of Yale, was asked why the university had never given O'Hara an honorary degree, he is supposed to have replied, "Because he asked for it." And Huey Long, for all his flamboyant exercise of power and capacity for intrigue, was never able to induce Tulane University, a private institution in New Orleans, to award him an honorary degree. In retaliation, Long colorfully vowed that Louisiana State University would make Tulane look like "a hole in the ground."

Occasionally, honorary degrees can be the subject of ironic humor. In 1953, James Thurber received a letter, ostensibly from the president of Eureka College in Eureka, Illinois, offering him an honorary degree. Before Thurber could respond, however, the president of that institution wrote to Thurber, reporting that the first letter was a student hoax and expressing the hope that Thurber would take the incident as a sign of "appreciation" on the student's part. Thurber was not amused:

> I don't really know the etiquette that should be followed in such a predicament as mine, but I feel that I owe you and Eureka College my sincere apologies. In my college days we played pranks too, but not on aging blind humorists. We selected stuffed shirts. If I had been able to read the letterhead I received and to examine the typing and the signature, I don't think I would have been taken in. I was on the point of having my secretary reply signing her name Virginia Creeper, but I do not regard honor or honors as a fitting subject for kidding around....
>
> I am afraid I do not regard this hoax as a sign of "appreciation" by

a student. If writers my age depended on appreciation from the modern college student, we would probably languish of some kind of malnutrition. . . .

Honorary degrees are, of course, one of the ways in which universities advertise themselves. Most announce the names of their honorands well in advance of commencement, and thereby often generate favorable publicity. But the practice can backfire. Not all proposals for honorary degrees are well received. From time to time, controversies have erupted among faculty or students (sometimes both) on college campuses when the names of prospective honorary degree recipients have been made or become public before the ceremony. A celebrated example involved Oxford University's proposal in 1985 to award an honorary degree to its alumna Prime Minister Margaret Thatcher. After much contention centering upon her government's parsimony in the funding of higher education and scientific research, the university faculty turned down the proposal by a vote of 738 to 319.

Similarly, when Cambridge University announced in 1992 that it was conferring an honorary degree upon the literary critic Jacques Derrida, members of the philosophy faculty circulated a statement deriding Derrida's work for "denying the distinctions between fact and fiction, observation and imagination, evidence and prejudice." In a letter to the *Times* (London), a reader commented, "Many French philosophers see in Mr. Derrida only cause for silent embarrassment, his antics having contributed to the widespread impression that contemporary French philosophy is little more than an object of ridicule." Nonetheless, the degree was awarded.

Sometimes campus controversy leads a prospective honorand to withdraw. When Macalester College announced in 1998 that it would award an honorary degree to the media magnate Ted Turner, students occupied a campus building to protest Turner's continued use of an Indian nickname, the Braves, for his Atlanta baseball team. The protest prompted Turner to decline the degree. A similar result occurred when faculty members and students protested Vassar College's intention to offer an honorary degree to William F. Buckley, Jr. (When Buckley's alma mater, Yale, conferred a doctorate of humane letters upon him in 2000, an alumnus complained to the *Yale Alumni Magazine* that the degree was a "total oxymoron" and the laudatory citation "an enormous stretch.")

So, too, the novelist Anna Quindlen withdrew from a commitment to a prominent Catholic university after she foresaw that the church hierarchy, when it realized that she held a pro-choice position on abortion, would eventually cancel the invitation. Indeed, in 1990 the Vatican blocked the University of Fribourg in Switzerland from honoring Archbishop Rembert Weakland of Milwaukee because it believed that his statements on abortion had caused "a great deal of confusion among the faithful."

In 1986, Drew Lewis, the former secretary of transportation, stunned the commencement audience at Haverford College, a Quaker institution, by ripping off his ceremonial hood and declining the honorary degree that had just been bestowed upon him. He acted upon learning that there was substantial faculty and student opposition to the award because of his role in responding to a controversial strike by air traffic controllers during his government tenure. He told the audience that he came from a Quaker background and shared the denomination's strong belief in the principle of consensus. "There is no consensus on this degree when one-third of your faculty object," he told the audience.

The original purpose of honoring distinguished personal achievement has widely been modified — some would say blighted — by institutional desires to flatter generous donors and prospective benefactors to whom more relaxed standards (typically pecuniary) are typically applied. (Indeed, some wags have argued that this degeneration into a quid pro quo style enables a college "to get rich by degrees.")

Similarly, any aspiration to populate an American peerage is surely trivialized by decisions to garner a fleeting moment of public attention by awarding an institution's ultimate accolade to mere celebrities — who are often famous principally for being famous. Purists have criticized Yale for lowering the bar in honoring actresses Jodie Foster, an alumna, and Julie Andrews; the University of Pennsylvania for honoring Candice Bergen, a dropout; and Princeton for honoring Bob Dylan — although all were accomplished members of their professions. In similar bows to celebrity culture, institutions have honored such performers as Barbra Streisand, Captain Kangaroo, Robert Redford, Jerry Seinfield, Chevy Chase, and Neil Diamond. In recent years, athletes have come into favor; Columbia and Holy Cross honored Joe DiMaggio and Dartmouth honored Hank Aaron. Reacting against awards such as these, John R. Tunis wrote, in 1935, "When will these institutions realize that by giving degrees to the majority of those chosen they repudiate the ideals for which they are supposed to stand?" He added, "If men like Shakespeare, Voltaire, and Victor Hugo were alive in this country today they would have to wait a long while to get a Litt.D. from any American university."

Among any institution's list of honorary degree recipients, there are bound to be curiosities. For reasons now obscure, Dartmouth has conferred honorary doctorates twice upon two of its alumni: Robert Frost (in 1933 and 1955) and Nelson Rockefeller (in 1957 and 1969). Many institutions have realized that husbands and wives make a fetching combination for degree-granting occasions. Among the most popular in this category have been Alfred Lunt and Lynn Fontanne, Hume Cronyn and Jessica Tandy, and Melvyn Douglas and Helen Gahagan Douglas.

Public officials who have a moral dimension to their character are especially prized because they are thought likely to use the occasion of being a commencement speaker to make an important public pronouncement. The model most cited is George C. Marshall, who as secretary of state proclaimed the Marshall Plan at Harvard's commencement in 1947. High on such lists in recent years have been Mikhail Gorbachev, Nelson Mandela, Archbishop Desmond Tutu, and Václav Havel. (In an interview, Havel once said, "I was awarded honorary degrees at universities around the world and at every one of those ceremonies I had to listen to the story of my life. And those biographies were always the same fairy tale.") In recent years, African American artists and scholars, especially Maya Angelou, Toni Morrison, Alice Walker, Spike Lee, Cornel West, John Hope Franklin, and Henry Louis Gates, Jr., have also been popular.

Every president is conscious, at honorary degree time, of being caught up in a prestige race with other colleges and universities. This is an age, as one observer has written, "of fevered competition between colleges to secure the hottest speakers of the moment"— meaning figures of commodified fame. Students want to be able to boast to their friends that their college had a more fashionable commencement speaker, or more widely known honorary degree recipients, than other colleges. Marquee value matters. During my tenure, Dartmouth's moment of fleeting glory in this contrived competition was enlisting President Clinton to be the commencement speaker in 1995.

So intense is the competition for great names that many colleges now pay honorary degree recipients, at rates that commonly exceed $10,000, in order to lure them to deliver the commencement address. Dartmouth never did so. In paying an honorary degree recipient to speak, a college seems to be acknowledging that it desires having the speaker's services more than the speaker values having the college's degree.

When student newspapers suggest names for honorands and speakers, the lists tend to be dominated by celebrities who may well prove to be, in Mark Twain's words, "of small and temporary notoriety": for example, Michael Jordan, Bill Cosby, Garry Trudeau, Madonna, Jay Leno, and Tom Hanks. Newspapers occasionally keep track of the personal record holders. Nicholas Murray Butler, the longtime president of Columbia University, John H. Finley, the editor of the *New York Times*, and the industrialist Owen D. Young were once among the leaders. Herbert Hoover, during his lifetime, held more honorary degrees than any other American. The reigning champion is Father Theodore M. Hesburgh of the University of Notre Dame; he holds more than one hundred and fifty honorary degrees.

Some have proposed that one honorary degree per person ought to be enough. Stephen Edward Epler, in *Honorary Degrees: A Survey of Their Use and Abuse* (1943), argued that if honorary degrees are a measure of merit, "there is little point in having the merit rediscovered several times by several colleges. . . . After all, what can an individual do with several honorary degrees that he cannot do with one?" I was personally disappointed when I received responses to this effect from two Nobel laureates in literature. The German writer Günter Grass replied to my invitation by writing, "During the sixties and early seventies I received honorary degrees from Kenyon College and Harvard University. Further offers followed from other institutions, all of which I felt compelled to refuse as I would not wish to contribute to inflationary values concerning honorary degrees; I recently sent a corresponding reply to the University of Liège." Similarly, the South African novelist Nadine Gordimer wrote me, "I regret to have to tell you that I feel I have my full share of honorary degrees by now, and I have decided I shall not accept any more. I hope this does not sound arrogant; the fact is, I believe one devalues the whole process if one allows vanity to pile them up. This response to Dartmouth is, I assure you, no reflection on the standing of the College, which I know to be very high." When I tried Gordimer two years later, she continued to hold to her conviction. "I remain adamant in my decision not to receive any more such honors in the United States," she wrote.

The recipient whose presence gave me the greatest sense of triumphant satisfaction was Aleksandr Solzhenitsyn, who had ceased accepting honorary degrees after the furor that followed his commencement address at Harvard in 1978. Solzhenitsyn regularly commuted from his home in Cavendish, Vermont, to use Dartmouth's library and most especially its borrowing privileges from archives in the Soviet Union. In accepting Dartmouth's invitation, he told me, he made an exception to his usual practice out of gratitude to the college.

The person I was most disappointed in not securing as an honorand was the writer J. D. Salinger, whose work was familiar to every student. Although he lived no more than twenty miles from Dartmouth, in Cornish, New Hampshire, and had been, like Solzhenitsyn, a longtime user of the college library, Salinger did not respond to several letters of invitation.

Despite all the effort that is devoted to selecting and then attracting honorary degree recipients, there is little evidence that commencement speakers have more than a fleeting impact on their audience. Most adults, in my experience, cannot recall the speaker or the honorary recipients at their own commencement, probably because in the excitement of the day their thoughts were elsewhere.

The role of institutional prestige is accentuated in instances where rules require that the identity of honorands be kept secret until the moment of commencement and that intended honorands appear in person to accept the degree. Such rules are intended to add an element of surprise to the ceremonies and to ensure the presence of the honorands. When the sculptor Louise Bourgeois, who was eighty-seven, became ill the day before she was to receive an honorary degree from Harvard in 1999, she was denied the honor. Her name became public, however, when it was leaked to the *Harvard Crimson* along with the names of the other honorands. Her son, a Harvard graduate, protested the decision, arguing that the degree was principally for his mother's benefit, not Harvard's. "Is an honorary an award for outstanding achievement," he asked, "or is the Commencement ceremony merely a show?"

Honorary degrees serve at least one important purpose beyond suggesting role models to students and enhancing institutional prestige. They often forge enduring bonds of friendship and mutual regard between the college and the recipient. In the years that follow, honorands often are amenable to visits from students, becoming sources of summer jobs and career counseling, opening doors to professional opportunities, and providing personal encouragement. Often they return to the college to deliver speeches, appear at symposia, or meet with classes. As David Halberstam, a Harvard graduate, told Dartmouth's graduating class in 1996, "I look forward to seeing you, my classmates, on *our* side—the Dartmouth side—at Harvard-Dartmouth football games!"

There are of course risks to colleges in the granting of honorary degrees. Perhaps the greatest risk is that a recipient will turn out, in retrospect, to have been ill-chosen. Ten universities — including Princeton, the University of Chicago, and Brown — conferred honorary degrees upon Count Johann Heinrich von Bernstorff, the German ambassador to the United States before World War I; many withdrew them after the war began, on the ground that, as one said, "he was guilty of conduct dishonorable alike in a gentleman and a diplomat." Northwestern University and other institutions that awarded honorary degrees to Samuel Insull, the Chicago industrialist, who later fled to Greece in order to avoid criminal prosecution after the collapse of his utility empire, must, in later years, have had second thoughts. And, surely, more than one university came to regret awarding an honorary degree to the Shah of Iran and to Benazir Bhutto. Few writers have supplied a more graphic illustration than Will Cuppy, who described how Peter the Great, after receiving an honorary degree from Oxford University, returned home to reform the National Guard "by beheading some, hanging some, roasting others over slow fires, and burying the rest alive." Risks, indeed!

Finally, a few words about honorary degree citations. Such efforts are something of an art form unto themselves. Unfortunately, the crafting of elegant citations has fallen into considerable disuse. Too often presidents read citations that have been written by others — that is why they sometimes seem unfamiliar with the text — and are prolix, clichéd, and embarrassingly fulsome. In 1922, for example, Princeton saluted President Warren G. Harding for "his capable handling of complicated difficulties" as well as for his "self-effacing modesty" and went on to proclaim grandiosely that he "stands in the tradition of Lincoln."

Although I always wrote my own citations, I now see that I, too, may sometimes have been guilty of lapsing into excessive adulation. For example, I saluted Maurice Sendak, who wrote such classic children's books as *Chicken Soup with Rice*, *Where the Wild Things Are*, *In the Night Kitchen*, and *Outside Over There*, as one whose "claim upon a generation of readers has been so great that, among members of this graduating class, you may well be the single most widely read author." Although the graduates applauded in a shock of recognition, I promptly heard from indignant friends and admirers of Theodor S. Geisel — a Dartmouth graduate, no less! — who as Dr. Seuss was the author of more than a few books widely popular with the graduating generation.

Harvard has always been a notable exception to these tendencies toward excess, tempered by its self-imposed constraint of capturing in a single sentence the essence of each recipient's distinction. Thus, it celebrated the essayist E. B. White with the elegant words, "Sidewalk superintendent of our times, voice of our conscience, literate exponent of the belief that humor ought to speak the truth," and the dancer Martha Graham with the exquisite description, "She speaks to us of grandeur, tragedy, and beauty through transient movements of the human form."

Not constrained by Harvard's single-sentence regimen, I always searched for the precise words that would deftly illuminate, with concision, the achievements of a lifetime. I looked for vivid verbs, striking adjectives, and suggestive metaphors that might capture some of the elusive qualities of truth. I expressed my admiration for Solzhenitsyn with these words: "With exemplary courage and unrivaled conviction, you have taught us anew the meaning of suffering and reminded us, in the noble words of one of your fictional characters, that 'a great writer is, so to speak, a second government of his country.'"

In conferring honorary degrees, I hoped to persuade our students and commencement guests that each honorand's character and attainment were worthy of emulation and admiration. So long as every recipient meets that mark, a college is entitled to believe that the public ritual of awarding honorary degrees addresses sacred matters and illuminates the relevance of a liberal education to the lives of men and women.

❁ SELECTED BIBLIOGRAPHY ❁

Annan, Noel, *The Dons*. Chicago: University of Chicago Press, 1999.

Appiah, Anthony, and Amy Gutmann. *Color Conscious: The Political Morality of Race*. Princeton, N.J.: Princeton University Press, 1996.

Ashmore, Harry S. *Unseasonable Truths: The Life of Robert Maynard Hutchins*. Boston: Little, Brown, 1989.

Atlas, James. *Bellow: A Biography*. New York: Random House, 2000.

Bate, Walter Jackson. "As Rich and Varied as Life Itself. . . ." *Harvard Magazine*, November–December 1991.

———. "The Crisis in English Studies." *Harvard Magazine*, October 1982.

Beattie, Ann. *Picturing Will*. New York: Random House, 1989.

Bellush, Bernard. *He Walked Alone*. The Hague: Mouton, 1968.

Bok, Derek. *Beyond the Ivory Tower*. Cambridge: Harvard University Press, 1982.

———. *Higher Learning*. Cambridge: Harvard University Press, 1986.

Bowen, Howard, and Jack Schuster. *American Professors: A National Resource Imperiled*. New York: Oxford University Press, 1986.

Bowen, William G., and Derek Bok. *The Shape of the River: Long-Term Consequences of Considering Race in College and University Admissions*. Princeton, N.J.: Princeton University Press, 1998.

Bowen, William G., and Neil Rudenstine. *In Pursuit of the Ph.D.* Princeton, N.J.: Princeton University Press, 1992.

Bowen, William G., and Harold T. Shapiro, eds. *Universities and Their Leadership*. Princeton, N.J.: Princeton University Press, 1998.

Bowen, William G., and Julie Ann Sosa. *Prospects for Faculty in the Arts and Sciences*. Princeton, N.J.: Princeton University Press, 1989.

Bryce, James. *The American Commonwealth*. 3d ed. New York: Macmillan, 1900.

Buckley, William F., Jr. *In Search of Anti-Semitism*. New York: Continuum, 1992.

Butler, Nicholas Murray. *Across the Busy Years: Recollections and Reflections*. New York: Scribner, 1940.

Coles, Robert. *Dorothy Day: A Radical Devotion*. Reading, Mass.: Addison-Wesley, 1987.

Conant, James Bryant. *The Citadel of Learning*. New Haven, Conn.: Yale University Press, 1956.

Day, Dorothy. *By Little and By Little*. New York: Knopf, 1983.

Dershowitz, Alan. *Chutzpah*. Boston: Little, Brown, 1991.

Drucker, Peter. "Beyond the Information Revolution." *Atlantic Monthly*, October 1999.

Edley, Christopher. *Not All Black and White: Affirmative Action, Race, and American Values*. New York: Hill & Wang, 1996.

Ehrenberg, Ronald G. *Tuition Rising: Why College Costs So Much*. Cambridge: Harvard University Press, 2000.

Eliot, T. S. *After Strange Gods: A Primer of Modern Heresy*. New York: Harcourt, Brace, 1934.

Epler, Stephen Edward. *Honorary Degrees: A Survey of Their Use and Abuse*. Washington, D.C.: American Council on Public Affairs, 1943.

Finkin, Matthew E. *The Case for Tenure*. Ithaca, N.Y.: Cornell University Press, 1966.

Freedman, James O. *Idealism and Liberal Education*. Ann Arbor, Mich.: University of Michigan Press, 1996.

Galbraith, John K. *The Affluent Society*. Boston: Houghton Mifflin, 1958.

Giamatti, A. Bartlett. *A Free and Ordered Space: The Real World of the University*. New York: Norton, 1988.

Halberstam, David. *The Fifties*. New York: Random House, 1993.

Handlin, Oscar. *The Uprooted*. Boston: Little, Brown, 1951.

Harvard Committee on the Objectives of a General Education in Free Society. *General Education in a Free Society*. Cambridge: Harvard University Press, 1945.

Hofstadter, Richard. *Anti-intellectualism in American Life*. New York: Knopf, 1963.

Hollinger, David A. *Science, Jews, and Secular Culture*. Princeton, N.J.: Princeton University Press, 1996.

Holmes, Oliver Wendell. "Ideals and Doubts." In *Collected Legal Papers*. New York: Harcourt, Brace, 1921.

Hutchins, Robert M. *Education and Democracy*. Chicago: University of Chicago Press, 1948.

———. *Education for Freedom*. Baton Rouge: Louisiana State University Press, 1943.

————. *The Higher Learning in America.* New Haven, Conn.: Yale University Press, 1936.

————. *The Learning Society.* New York: Praeger, 1968.

————. *Morals, Religion, and Higher Education.* Chicago: University of Chicago Press, 1950.

Jacobs, Jane. *The Death and Life of Great American Cities.* New York: Random House, 1961.

Keller, Morton and Phyllis. *Making Harvard Modern: The Rise of America's University.* New York: Oxford University Press, 2001.

Keller, Phyllis. *Getting at the Core: Curricular Reform at Harvard.* Cambridge: Harvard University Press, 1982.

Kerr, Clark. *The Uses of the University.* Cambridge: Harvard University Press, 1963.

Kimball, Bruce A. *The Condition of American Liberal Education.* New York: College Entrance Examination Board, 1995.

————. *Orators and Philosophers: A History of the Idea of Liberal Education.* New York: College Entrance Examination Board, 1986.

Lemann, Nicholas. *The Big Test: The Secret History of American Meritocracy.* New York: Farrar, Straus & Giroux, 1999.

Levine, Arthur, ed. *Higher Learning in America, 1980–2000.* Baltimore, Md.: Johns Hopkins University Press, 1993.

Lipset, Seymour Martin, and Earl Raab. *Jews and the New American Scene.* Cambridge: Harvard University Press, 1995.

McLaughlin, Judith Block, and David Riesman. *Choosing a College President.* Princeton, N.J.: Carnegie Foundation for the Advancement of Teaching, 1990.

McWhorter, John H. *Losing the Race: Self-Sabotage in Black America.* New York: Free Press, 2000.

Myrdal, Gunnar. *An American Dilemma.* New York: Harper & Bros., 1944.

Oakley, Francis. *Community of Learning: The American College and the Liberal Arts Tradition.* New York: Oxford University Press, 1992.

Oren, Dan A. *Joining the Club: A History of Jews and Yale.* New Haven, Conn.: Yale University Press, 1985.

Pelikan, Jaroslav. *The Idea of the University.* New Haven, Conn.: Yale University Press, 1992.

Ravitch, Diane. *The Troubled Crusade.* New York: Basic Books, 1983.

Ricks, Christopher. *T. S. Eliot and Prejudice.* Berkeley: University of California Press, 1988.

Riesman, David. *The Lonely Crowd.* Glencoe, Ill.: Free Press, 1950.

Rosovsky, Henry. *The University: An Owner's Manual.* New York: Norton, 1990.

Roth, Philip. *The Human Stain.* Boston: Houghton Mifflin, 2000.

Ryan, Alan. *Liberal Anxieties and Liberal Education.* New York: Hill & Wang, 1998.

Shepard, Alexandra. "Seeking a Sense of Place: Jewish Students in the Dartmouth Community, 1920–1940." Honor's thesis, Dartmouth College, 1992.

Shulman, James L., and William G. Bowen. *The Game of Life.* Princeton, N.J.: Princeton University Press, 2001.

Strachey, Lytton. *Eminent Victorians.* New York: Modern Library, 1933.

Tenner, Edward. "Honorary Degrees Are Worth Receiving, but They're Not Worth Envying." *Chronicle of Higher Education,* 8 June 1988.

Theroux, Paul. *Saint Jack.* Boston: Houghton Mifflin, 1973.

Washington, Booker T. *Up from Slavery: An Autobiography.* Garden City, N.Y.: Doubleday, 1901.

Whitehead, Alfred North. *The Aims of Education.* New York: Macmillan, 1925.

———. *Science and the Modern World.* New York: 1948.

Winant, John Gilbert. *Letter from Grosvenor Square.* Boston: Houghton Mifflin, 1947.

Yeomans, Henry A. *Abbott Lawrence Lowell.* Cambridge: Harvard University Press, 1948.

Zimbalist, Andrew. *Unpaid Professionals.* Princeton, N.J.: Princeton University Press, 1999.

❖ INDEX ❖